Essential Mac OS X Panther Server Administration

Other resources from O'Reilly

Related titles

Apache: The Definitive Guide

DNS & BIND

IPv6 Network Administration

Kerberos: The Definitive Guide

Mac OS X Tiger for Unix Geeks

Mac OS X Tiger in a Nutshell

Managing IMAP

Network Security with OpenSSL

Perl for System Administration

Postfix: The Definitive Guide

SSH, the Secure Shell: The Definitive Guide

Using Samba

Macintosh Books Resource Center

mac.oreilly.com is a complete catalog of O'Reilly's books on the Apple Macintosh and related technologies, including sample chapters and code examples.

oreillynet.com is the essential portal for developers interested in open and emerging technologies, including new platforms, programming languages, and operating systems.

Conferences

O'Reilly brings diverse innovators together to nurture the ideas that spark revolutionary industries. We specialize in documenting the latest tools and systems, translating the innovator's knowledge into useful skills for those in the trenches. Visit *conferences.oreilly.com* for our upcoming events.

Safari Bookshelf (*safari.oreilly.com*) is the premier online reference library for programmers and IT professionals. Conduct searches across more than 1,000 books. Subscribers can zero in on answers to time-critical questions in a matter of seconds. Read the books on your Bookshelf from cover to cover or simply flip to the page you need. Try it today with a free trial.

Essential Mac OS X Panther Server Administration

Michael Bartosh and Ryan Faas

O'REILLY®

Beijing · Cambridge · Farnham · Köln · Paris · Sebastopol · Taipei · Tokyo

Essential Mac OS X Panther Server Administration
by Michael Bartosh and Ryan Faas

Published by O'Reilly Media, Inc., 1005 Gravenstein Highway North, Sebastopol, CA 95472.

O'Reilly books may be purchased for educational, business, or sales promotional use. Online editions are also available for most titles (*safari.oreilly.com*). For more information, contact our corporate/institutional sales department: (800) 998-9938 or *corporate@oreilly.com*.

Editor:	Chuck Toporek
Production Editor:	Adam Witwer
Cover Designer:	Emma Colby
Interior Designer:	David Futato

Printing History:

May 2005:	First Edition.

 This book uses RepKover,™ a durable and flexible lay-flat binding.

ISBN: 0-596-00635-7

[M]

Table of Contents

Part II.   Directory Services

Part III.   IP Services

Part IV.   File Services

Part VII. Client Management

Preface

As Apple's place in institutional and enterprise marketplaces has grown, so has Mac OS X Server, Apple's server software product. Mac OS X Server seeks to provide centralized services to a variety of cross-platform clients, and has only grown in scope since its introduction in 2000. That tremendously expanding scope gave birth to this book.

Little or no in-depth documentation exists for Mac OS X Server. Sure, Apple provides about 1,200 pages worth of PDF documentation, but you have to wade through fields of Apple marketing jargon to get to the tasty bits, and even then, you're left holding crumbs and scratching your head. A lot. *Essential Mac OS X Panther Server Administration* seeks to fill that void, approaching Apple's server systems in a thorough and fundamental way, from the command line to Apple's graphical tools.

Essential Mac OS X Panther Server Administration is for the IT professional who wants to push Mac OS X Server to its limits. Server administration all too typically is a complex task, requiring integration with not one but several disparate systems, often run by different administrators, and this book is written with that in mind. If you've ever wondered how to safely manipulate Mac OS X Server's many underlying configuration files or needed to explain AFP permission mapping—this book's for you.

Audience for This Book

This book is written for Macintosh system administrators responsible for running Mac OS X Server. While the focus is oriented towards IT professionals, this book should also be of interest to anyone pursuing an accumulated knowledge of server products and their evolution. Whether you're a seasoned Unix or Windows administrator or a long-time Mac professional, *Essential Mac OS X Panther Server Administration* provides you with the depth you're seeking to maximize the potential of your Mac OS X Server deployment.

This is not a book for beginners. If you are a graphic artist looking to install a web server, you should probably look for another book, such as *Foundation Mac OS X Web Development* by Phil Sherry (Apress, 2004). Schoun Regan's *Mac OS X Server 10.3 Panther: Visual Quick-Pro Guide* (Peachpit, 2005) provides a basic introduction to Mac OS X Server.

This book is also an analysis of Mac OS X Server including the infrastructures and tools used to manage Apple's Server services. As mentioned earlier, Mac OS X Server is an extremely broad product providing a variety of services. This book is not meant as a complete, protocol-level discussion of HTTP, DNS, or any other of the well-documented technologies implemented in Mac OS X Server. It is instead concerned primarily with Apple-specific changes, management techniques and configuration architectures.

How This Book Is Organized

This book is organized into eight parts, each of which deals with a generally related set of Mac OS X Server Services. Each part is made up of several chapters, that examine a specific service in greater depth. Each part also has an introduction of varying length, used to introduce its component services or document some feature that is relevant through all its chapters. The actual layout of the book looks something like this:

Part I, *Server Installation and Management*
> This first part of the book provides you with the prerequisites for Mac OS X Server Administration. A variety of tasks not specific to the management of any one service are documented here. The chapters in this part include:

Chapter 1, *Designing Your Server Environment*
> This chapter acquaints you with the basic concerns of deployment planning. Hardware and infrastructure challenges are covered in depth with special consideration given to Apple's Server products and common networking and storage issues.

Chapter 2, *Installing and Configuring Mac OS X Server*
> The beginning of a server's life is critical. Careful planning can alleviate later issues and lessen ongoing headaches as the size and scope of server services are forced to scale with organizational growth. Apple has given special attention to Server installation, and a large body of knowledge has developed around technologies that complement Apple's efforts. The most thorough documentation of its type available, this chapter provides an analysis of the Mac OS X Server installation process through several variations: graphical, command-line, remote, and local.

Chapter 3, *Server Management Tools*
> The centerpiece of Mac OS X Server is its management tool suite. With an eye towards remote management, these tools tie the user experience together and provide cohesiveness among the product's many services and options. This chapter examines both those tools and the underlying infrastructures that support their functionality.

Chapter 4, *System Administration*
> In the past 20 or 30 years, a number of trends have developed in the field generally known as system administration. This chapter examines those trends and techniques in the context of how they specifically apply to Mac OS X Server. Specific topics such as backup and software updates are also included in this chapter.

Chapter 5, *Troubleshooting*
> When things break, they need to be fixed. This chapter consists of a rich set of tools and heuristics that may be leveraged towards those ends.

Part II, *Directory Services*
Traditional system administration titles have not had to focus much on user management. As centralized systems have developed, though, and as directory services have risen in visibility in core Apple markets, it has become necessary to devote increasingly large amounts of documentation to these increasingly complex systems. Part III documents the server side of Apple's directory services infrastructure.

Chapter 6, *Open Directory Server*
> Open Directory Server is Apple's Directory Service—like Microsoft's Active Directory, it is used to store administrative data (such as user and group accounts and security policies) centrally on the network. The biggest strength of this architecture is perhaps its standardized configuration mechanism. This chapter concerns the configuration and management and coordination of the underlying services that make up Open Directory Server.

Chapter 7, *Identification and Authorization in Open Directory Server*
> Identity management is central to any directory service. This chapter discusses Apple's use of OpenLDAP in identification and authorization.

Chapter 8, *Authentication in Open Directory Server*
> Mac OS X Server maintains a robust authentication platform suited to the wide variety of services it must support. This chapter discusses those authentication technologies and their place in the larger world of directory services.

Chapter 9, *Replication in Open Directory Server*
> Replication adds a high availability aspect to Open Directory Server. This chapter takes a look at each component of that architecture and the

processes and protocols used to keep user account and authentication data synchronized.

Part III, *IP Services*

Network services can be described generally as services on which other services depend. They provide the basic functionality that makes networks useful and more friendly.

Chapter 10, *xinetd*

xinetd (which replaces the traditional Unix *inetd*) is a critical underlying process that starts certain system services on demand. Due to its central nature, I've devoted a chapter to it, even though it cannot be configured graphically.

Chapter 11, *DNS*

This chapter looks at Mac OS X DNS Services—from Apple's graphical tools to the configuration infrastructure put into place to help manage BIND, the underlying open source DNS server. Also included are a variety of advanced configuration techniques often useful in moderately sophisticated infrastructures.

Chapter 12, *DHCP*

DHCP can provide a variety of configuration data to Mac OS, Windows and Unix clients. This chapter goes beyond the basics and examines Apple's homegrown DHCP server.

Chapter 13, *NAT*

Network Address Translation, or NAT, has come to be a fundamental building block in network services everywhere. This chapter shows you how to use the Server Admin tool, as well as the command line, to set up and configure NAT services.

Part IV, *File Services*

File and print services have long been a vital aspect of Apple Server products. This section of the book takes a close look at those services, with an emphasis on their commonalities and advanced configurations.

Chapter 14, *File Services Overview*

One of Mac OS X Server's strong points is its ability to make share points available via a variety of file-sharing protocols. This chapter concerns the cross-protocol management systems put in place to set up shares and customize their behavior.

Chapter 15, *Apple Filing Protocol*

The Apple Filing Protocol is Apple's homegrown file service, and is also the filesystem most commonly used for high-demand roles like network home directories.

Chapter 16, *Windows File Services*

Apple does not exist in a vacuum, and a flexible and robust Windows Services implementation is vital to the success of Mac OS X Server in nearly any market.

Chapter 17, *FTP*

As ubiquitous as it is insecure, FTP unfortunately cannot be ignored. Users both inside and outside of your server framework will most likely need FTP services for transferring files back and forth. This chapter shows you how to set up and configure FTP services, and discusses use of Kerberos authentication and SSH's *sftp* utility for secure FTP.

Chapter 18, *Network File System*

NFS is a useful remnant of Mac OS X Server's Unix legacy and heritage. Used mostly in heterogeneous Unix environments and Mac OS X's NetBoot service, it is documented extensively in Chapter 18.

Chapter 19, *Print Services*

Server-side print management has not proven to be Mac OS X Server's forte. This chapter provides an analysis of Apple's print service infrastructure and its Common Unix Printing System (CUPS) backend.

Part V, *Security Services*

Central to any modern IT component is the question of security. Although good security principles are illustrated throughout the book, this part covers Mac OS X Server services specifically geared toward security.

Chapter 20, *The Mac OS X Server Firewall*

Oversold perhaps as often as they are correctly deployed, firewalls (or packet filters) are a vital part of any security strategy. This chapter, written by Andre LeBranche, shows you how to set up and configure firewall services on your Server installation.

Chapter 21, *Virtual Private Networks*

Virtual Private Networks have arrived only recently as an easily deployable technology. This chapter, written by Joel Rennich (of *afp548* fame), attempts to decipher VPN services on Mac OS X Server.

Part VI, *Internet Services*

Internet services is a convenient category created for portions of Mac OS X Server that are most commonly provided over the Internet (rather than to a local LAN).

Chapter 22, *Mail Services*

Panther represents a huge step for Apple's mail services, moving from a Workgroup-centric legacy mail server to a more modern and modular mail system built on powerful software. Completely open source, Mail is the canonical example of Apple's "Open source made easy" moniker.

Chapter 23, *Web Services*

This chapter, written by James Duncan Davidson, details the inner workings of Apache on Mac OS X Server, along with Apple's graphical management toolkit and its underlying configuration infrastructure.

Chapter 24, *Application Servers*

Most modern web content is dynamic, with information drawn from databases, user input, or a combination of the two. This chapter, written by Wil Iverson, discusses the Java-based software packages that Mac OS X Server uses to provide these dynamic web services.

Part VII, *Client Management*

High on the list of features important to many administrators is client management. This broad term applies to a variety of Server and OS features, but generally refers to the ability to impose user experience restrictions on users, such as which applications they are permitted to run and what their dock looks like. These capabilities are detailed in this part, which was written by Ryan Faas.

Chapter 25, *Managing Preferences for Mac OS X Clients*

Managed preferences allow you to preconfigure many of the settings users would typically configure on a standalone Mac OS X workstation. This chapter shows you how to use Workgroup Manager to manage the user environment for individual users, groups, workstations, or a combination of all three.

Chapter 26, *Managing Classic Mac OS Workstations Using Mac Manager*

This chapter shows you how to use the Mac Manager to tap into Mac OS 9's multiple users feature for managing Classic Mac OS workstations. You'll learn about Mac OS 9's multiple users feature and how to create limited-access users, and also learn about Mac Manager's server component, installed with Mac OS X Server.

Chapter 27, *Managing Windows Clients Using Mac OS X Server*

Windows services under Mac OS Server include the ability to share files and printers using the SMB protocol, which is the default file and print protocol for Windows, and Windows name resolution services, as well as the ability to function as a Windows *Primary Domain Controller* (PDC) and host a Windows domain. This chapter discusses how to support and manage Windows computers from Mac OS X Server.

Chapter 28, *Workstation Deployment and Maintenance*

This chapter covers the various ways in which you can deploy Mac OS 9 and Mac OS X client machines. It shows you how to image a system, and describes NetBoot and NetInstall—not only what they do and how to use them, but also how they differ. You'll also learn how to use Apple Software Restore (ASR) to apply Mac OS 9 and Mac OS X client images.

Chapter 29, *Apple Remote Desktop*

Although not included with Mac OS X Server, Apple Remote Desktop (also called simply Remote Desktop, or ARD) is an incredibly robust and useful tool that can make several of the tasks of deploying and managing a Mac network much easier for administrators and technical support staff alike. This chapter discusses the administrative and reporting functions of Apple Remote Desktop 2.1 (the current version as of this writing) and how they can be of use to system administrators and other IT staff.

There is also one appendix to this book:

Appendix, *Introduction to Directory Services*

This appendix delves into some client-side aspects of Mac OS X's Open Directory Architecture.

The chapters in this book provide you with a complete overview of Mac OS X Server's services and software. This in-depth architectural knowledge will guide you through a variety of deployment scenarios.

Conventions Used in This Book

The following typographical conventions are used in this book:

Italic

Used to indicate new terms, URLs, filenames, file extensions, directories, commands and options, program names, and to highlight comments in examples. For example, a path in the filesystem will appear as */Applications/Utilities*.

`Constant width`

Used to show the contents of files or the output from commands.

`Constant width bold`

Used in examples and tables to show commands or other text that should be typed literally by the user.

`Constant width italic`

Used in examples and tables to show text that should be replaced with user-supplied values.

Menus/Navigation

Menus and their options are referred to in the text as File → Open, Edit → Copy, and so on. Arrows are also used to signify a navigation path when using window options; for example, System Preferences → Desktop & Screen Saver → Screen Saver means that you would launch System Preferences, click on the icon for the Desktop & Screen Saver preferences panel, and select the Screen Saver pane within that panel.

Pathnames

Pathnames are used to show the location of a file or application in the filesystem. Directories (or folders, for Mac and Windows users) are separated by a forward slash. For example, if you see something like, "launch the Terminal application (*/Applications/Utilities*)" in the text, that means the Terminal application can be found in the Utilities subfolder of the Applications folder.

The tilde character (~) refers to the current user's Home folder, so *~/Library* refers to the Library folder within your own Home folder.

↵

A carriage return (↵) at the end of a line of code is used to denote an unnatural line break; that is, you should not enter these as two lines of code, but as one continuous line. Multiple lines are used in these cases due to printing constraints.

$, #

The dollar sign ($) is used in some examples to show the user prompt for the *bash* shell; the hash mark (#) is the prompt for the root user.

Menu symbols

When looking at the menus for any application, you will see some symbols associated with keyboard shortcuts for a particular command. For example, to open a document in Microsoft Word, you could go to the File menu and select Open (File → Open), or you could issue the keyboard shortcut ⌘-O.

Figure P-1 shows the symbols used in the various menus to denote a shortcut.

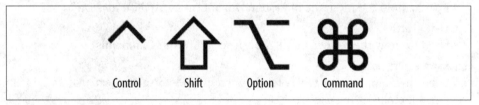

Figure P-1. Keyboard accelerators for issuing commands.

Rarely will you see the Control symbol used as a menu command option; it's more often used in association with mouse clicks or for working with the *tcsh* shell.

 Indicates a tip, suggestion, or general note.

 Indicates a warning or caution.

Using Code Examples

This book is here to help you get your job done. In general, you may use the code in this book in your programs and documentation. You do not need to contact us for permission unless you're reproducing a significant portion of the code. For example, writing a program that uses several chunks of code from this book does not require permission. Selling or distributing a CD-ROM of examples from O'Reilly books *does* require permission. Answering a question by citing this book and quoting example code does not require permission. Incorporating a significant amount of example code from this book into your product's documentation *does* require permission.

We appreciate, but do not require, attribution. An attribution usually includes the title, author, publisher, and ISBN. For example: "*Essential Mac OS X Panther Server Administration,* by Michael Bartosh and Ryan Faas. Copyright 2005 O'Reilly Media, Inc., 0-596-00635-7."

If you feel that your use of code examples falls outside fair use or the permission given here, feel free to contact us at *permissions@oreilly.com*.

Safari® Enabled

 When you see a Safari® Enabled icon on the cover of your favorite technology book, it means the book is available online through the O'Reilly Network Safari Bookshelf.

Safari offers a solution that's better than e-books. It's a virtual library that lets you easily search thousands of top technology books, cut and paste code samples, download chapters, and find quick answers when you need the most accurate, current information. Try it for free at *http://safari.oreilly.com*.

We'd Like to Hear from You

Please address comments and questions concerning this book to the publisher:

O'Reilly Media, Inc.
1005 Gravenstein Highway North
Sebastopol, CA 95472
(800) 998-9938 (in the United States or Canada)
(707) 829-0515 (international or local)
(707) 829-0104 (fax)

We have a web page for this book, where we list errata, examples, and any additional information. You can access this page at:

http://www.oreilly.com/catalog/macxserver/

The author additionally maintains a site for further reading and discussion of book content:

> *http://www.pantherserver.org*

To comment or ask technical questions about this book, send email to:

> *bookquestions@oreilly.com*

For more information about our books, conferences, Resource Centers, and the O'Reilly Network, see our web site at:

> *http://www.oreilly.com*

You can also visit the author's companion web site at:

> *http://www.pantherserver.org*

Acknowledgments

This book wouldn't have been feasible without the help, tolerance, and support of many people, chief among them my wife Amber, who has not yet had the good sense to leave me.

Thanks also to the following contributors:

- Andre LeBranche, for contributing Chapter 20, *The Mac OS X Server Firewall*.
- Joel Rennich of *afp54.com* (and now at Apple) has been a friend, a sounding board, and finally a contributor when the first edition of this book came close to the wire. Joel contributed Chapter 21, *Virtual Private Networks*.
- James Duncan Davidson, for contributing Chapter 23, *Web Services*.
- Wil Iverson, for contributing Chapter 24, *Application Servers*.
- Ryan Faas, for contributing all of the chapters in Part VII, *Client Management* after O'Reilly decided to fold our two books together.

When every screen shot in the book had to be re-done at the last minute, a nmber of folks pitched in.

- Josh Wisenbaker
- Michael Dhaliwal
- Justin Krisko (thanks to Justin also for showing me London)
- Timothy Wilkinson
- Michael Dinsmore
- Christopher Mackay
- Craig Kabis
- Jon L. Gardner (thanks also to Jon for showing me around Doha, Qatar)

- John Gonder
- Jason Deraleau

And here's a long list of thanks to all the people who supported me throughout the year or so it took me to write this book; it's been a long haul, but I couldn't have done it without you all:

- My editor, Chuck Toporek, had way more faith in the whole thing than I did (he says he never doubted me, and since you now hold this book, it must be true).
- Kurt Ackman was always there to grab a drink and simmer down a little whenever I was in Denver. He was the best AE Apple ever had.
- Michelle, Jeff, and Gary at CU Boulder have been supportive since I was their SE, and Scott Brekken convinced me I wanted to work with Apple.
- Greg Hydle. Rock on!
- No one really knows what to say about Bodhi, least of all me, but he's an alright guy, and he provided some keen feedback.
- Schoun Regan is a good guy who's put all sorts of opportunities in front of me, most of which I haven't blown.
- Iris Burdett is a hell of a lot of fun.
- Daveo, Jason, Eric, and Simon have never really steered me wrong and have put up with a bunch of my not-so-positive all-the-time feedback.
- Eric, Scott, Leland, Robert, and countless others at Apple have paved the way to make this thing happen, and if they all quit I wouldn't have anything much to write about.
- Brad Suinn has been particularly instructive over the years.
- Material support was provided by Juan, the folks at Brocade, and several who wish to remain nameless.
- Mike Bombich is an all-around great guy and thinks about IT in a way that should be embraced more thoroughly throughout Apple.
- Many Education SEs and CEs have been very supportive, and to you guys, thanks.
- All the folks at *macosxlabs*. I mean *enterprise*. Whatever. Thanks for all your input and inclusion.
- Todd Snider and Robert Earl Keen provided the soundtrack for the development of this book, although I'd have been done sooner if I went to fewer concerts.
- My mom has no clue what this book is about, but, you know, thanks.
- James Rabe first interested me in the Mac way back. I'm grateful even if the world is still slightly pissed.

- Mark McCann introduced me to the real heuristics of Unix system administration.
- Thanks to everyone who has shared with me a good time at some point somewhere in the bars, beaches, venues, pastures, and clubs that keep me juiced for all this computer stuff. Thanking all of you would be a book in itself, but probably a good one.

Don't read any order into this other than having Amber first. Put a fork in me. I think I'm done.

PART I

Server Installation and Management

Beginnings can be very delicate times, particularly where servers are concerned. By its very nature, a server affects more users than a workstation would; ensuring a proper initial configuration thus becomes doubly important. This section of the book concerns beginnings—both the beginning of a particular server's lifetime (planning and installation) and the beginning of an administrator's experience with Mac OS X Server, from its basic graphical tools to more advanced system administration and troubleshooting techniques. In every case, care is taken to undertake a thorough analysis, highlighting the configuration infrastructures Apple has placed around various open source tools as well as the fundamental operating principals of the underlying daemons and services themselves.

Chapters in this part include:

Chapter 1, *Designing Your Server Environment*

Chapter 2, *Installing and Configuring Mac OS X Server*

Chapter 3, *Server Management Tools*

Chapter 4, *System Administration*

Chapter 5, *Troubleshooting*

Designing Your Server Environment

Installation seems like such a benign thing, and traditionally, in the Mac OS world, it has been: sit down in front of the server, insert the install CD, format the drive, install, and repeat. Largely unchanged since the word *CD* replaced *floppy*, server installation is a process most administrators and technical staff are familiar with, and if nothing else it seems like a logical—if also a very boring—way to begin a book. Unix administrators, however, have long had a number of other options: possibly still boring, but in any case much more powerful and flexible from a systems management standpoint. With Mac OS X, and especially with Mac OS X Server, many of these options make their way to the Mac world, often with Apple's characteristic ease of use.

A second and very important aspect of this process is planning. Technology vendors—particularly Apple—endeavor to remove complexity from the computing experience, in many cases very successfully. Integration into heterogeneous environments, though, is still a complex issue with a number of facets. Good planning can go a long way towards reducing the number of headaches and unexpected speed bumps that administrators experience. Unfortunately, planning is a little-documented and often-neglected part of deployment. This chapter examines that pre-installation process, starting with purchasing and policy decisions and traveling down several feasible installation and configuration routes.

 Covering installation planning in the first chapter might seem a little awkward. You'll be asked to take a lot of things into consideration, many of which you may not have any experience with yet, but most of which will be covered later in the book. With that in mind, this first chapter contains a lot of forward pointers to other material. Feel free to use it as a jumping-off point in order to explore concepts that are new to you.

Planning

The installation process actually begins well before a machine is booted for the first time. It can and *should* begin even before the machine arrives on site. Planning is an often-neglected aspect of server management, and probably the single most important factor in reducing support costs. This is especially true for a server product, since a server installation by its very nature affects more end users than a workstation install. While it's important to keep from getting stuck in the quagmire of chronic bureaucratic deliberation and massive committee decision making, rushing into a server install is the last thing you want to do. Specific areas of planning focus should include the hardware platform, storage platform, volume architecture and management, and networking.

Hardware

Apple's Xserve, a 1U (single standard rack–size) server product, has effectively ended most conversations about hardware choices. When the numbers are run, the Xserve, with its included unlimited client license version of Mac OS X Server, is almost always a better value than a Power Mac G5 with a separate Server license tacked on. The only real exceptions are very small deployments—particularly in education environments,[*] environments with existing hardware that can be put to work as a server, or when the purchase of new hardware can't be justified.

That said, Mac OS X Server can run on virtually any hardware platform that Mac OS X can. In fact, much of the testing that went into this book was carried out on a set of iBooks I carry around while traveling. This isn't to imply that Apple supports such a configuration; in fact, portables are specifically *not* supported by Mac OS X Server. Real deployments should always conform to Apple's list of supported hardware, if for no reason other than that getting support for an unsupported hardware platform can be quite difficult.

> According to Apple's web site, Mac OS X Server requires an Xserve, Power Mac G5, G4, or G3, iMac, or eMac computer; a minimum of 128 MB RAM or at least 256 MB RAM for high-demand servers running multiple services; built-in USB; and 4 GB of available disk space. These specifications are probably underestimated for most server roles.

The choice of a supported platform, though, is really only the beginning of a good planning process. Hardware configuration is an entirely different matter. Mac OS X Server is a general-purpose server product with literally hundreds of features. This

---

[*] In the education market, Mac OS X is sold for approximately half of its retail price.

means that it's very difficult to draw conclusions about hardware requirements without defining what the server will be used for. For instance, an iMac with 128 MB RAM could easily support thousands of static-content HTTP queries a day, while an Apple Filing Protocol (AFP) server supporting the same number of connections would need to be significantly more capable. The point is that different services—even at the same scale—can have very different requirements, and those requirements play an important role in your choice of hardware. Going into great depth regarding the performance bottlenecks of various services is well beyond the scope of this chapter, but is covered in some depth in chapters specific to each service. From this chapter you should take a framework for this planning; the actual details will come later.

One very important concept relates to system architecture: determining where bottlenecks actually exist in a system (be it a single machine or a very large network) in order to either work around those bottlenecks or more effectively optimize performance. A good example of this is the SCSI 320 standard (discussed later in this chapter). A SCSI 320 bus is theoretically capable of 320 megabytes per second (MBS) of data throughput. However, when installed in Macs prior to the G5, a SCSI 320 disk's throughput would max out at a speed very similar to the much more affordable SCSI 160, mainly due to the constraints of the G4's PCI bus. Luckily, Apple publishes fairly detailed hardware schematics in its hardware developer tech notes. See *http:// developer.apple.com/documentation/Hardware/Hardware.html* for details.

Storage

Storage is one of the biggest variables in a server install, probably because the price of hard disk space has dropped enough for a wide variety of solutions to develop. The gauntlet of choices has only increased with Apple's entry into the storage market. First, the Xserve was designed specifically to accommodate a large internal storage. Later, Apple released the Xserve RAID, an IDE-based Fibre Channel storage array. More recently, the introduction of Xsan, Apple's Storage Area Network (SAN) product, has added another piece to the puzzle.

 Two trends should be noted. First, in both the Xserve and Xserve RAID, Apple has chosen the economy of various IDE flavors—specifically—ATA 100 and Serial ATA—over the well-established nature of SCSI connectivity. Time will tell whether or not this choice—of size and redundancy over performance and reliability—was a good one. In the meantime, it is yet another area in which Apple has taken a strong stand in defense of some technology in a new role. Second, on a related note, the choice of fiber and the adoption of SAN technology illustrates a common trend seen in Apple products: bringing enterprise technology into the workgroup and driving down the price of previously very expensive products. Xsan is not covered in this book.

Confusion regarding storage really arises on two different levels: choice of storage technology and storage configuration. We'll look at both of these issues as they relate to the planning process, as well as examine some specific products and the architectural decisions that went into them. Our discussion focuses on the Xserve, since it is the most common Mac OS X Server platform. This focus doesn't really narrow our conversation much, since the Xserve is mostly a Mac in a server enclosure. It does, though, give us some focus.

Storage technologies

At one time in the not-so-distant past, discussions of server storage technologies (outside of very massive high-end hardware) tended to be fairly simple. Server platforms have traditionally supported SCSI disks—that was that—and then you could move into discussions of volume management. Apple was the first vendor to change that, by using ATA disks in the Xserve in such a way that they became viable for server products. This feature has spurred considerable debate and (toward the overall good of the server industry) made our discussion more complex. This section examines various storage technologies and highlights their strengths, weaknesses, and relative cost. Discussion of generic storage technologies might seem to be beyond the scope of this book, given its stated goal of refraining from rehashing material that's widely available elsewhere. However, the topic of storage technologies is particularly germane to Mac OS X Server system administration for a number of reasons:

- As mentioned, Apple has really pioneered use of IDE/ATA drives in server products in both the Xserve and Xserve RAID. This design necessitates a number of discussions that previous system administration titles have had the luxury of glossing over.

- The introduction of the Xserve RAID brings Fibre Channel to the Mac in a big way. Fibre is an exciting technology and, as something new to a large portion of this book's audience, something worth talking about.

- Most Unix or Windows administrators wouldn't consider FireWire to be a viable storage platform—but due to its popularity in the Mac world, we must cover it.

- The recent rise of serial ATA is a huge development in storage technologies in general, much less the Mac platform alone, and is therefore something that warrants coverage.

What it really boils down to is this: we can no longer say, "Real servers use SCSI." It oversimplifies the issue, and it's just not the case. If you're already familiar with these technologies (ATA, SATA, Fibre Channel, SCSI, and RAID), you might want to skip the remainder of this section. Then again, maybe you want to revisit some of them and possibly gain a new perspective.

AT Attachment (ATA) and Integrated Drive Electronics (IDE)

ATA and IDE are generic terms for a set of technologies and standards that grew out of the Wintel architecture. Long considered a PC-class technology (rather than being applicable to the workstation or server markets), ATA and IDE have come a long way in recent years, enough that under the right circumstances, they can be considered appropriate for server deployments. Specific improvements include:

Vastly improved throughput

Theoretical maximum throughput for IDE drives has risen steadily throughout the evolution of the protocol. Today's IDE drives have a theoretical maximum throughput of 133 MBS. While far less than SCSI's current 320 MB maximum, this performance is sufficient for most applications, especially in the context of a well-engineered storage architecture, and especially given the far larger capacities and far lower prices of IDE drives.

Onboard cache also aids performance significantly. Current high-end IDE drives support up to 8 MB of onboard cache, vastly increasing read performance. Note, though, that theoretical throughput does not always equate with real-world performance, and more often than not, it's IDE that benefits from this phenomenon (*http://www.csl.cornell.edu/~bwhite/papers/ide_scsi.pdf*).

Advanced features

A long-held (and long-correct) assertion regarding IDE drives was that they lacked certain advanced features that SCSI supported; namely, tagged command queuing, scatter-gather I/O, and Direct Memory Access (DMA). The tremendous saturation of the low-end storage market, however, has forced vendors to innovate at a tremendous pace (in fact, all of these features are standard among recent high-end ATA-100 and -133 offerings). It would be presumptuous to assume that these features—in many cases first-generation capabilities—were as mature or stable as their SCSI counterparts; however, initial results have been very promising, and there's no reason to assume that IDE won't continue to evolve at a rapid pace.

Quality and reliability

It is important to realize that there's actually little difference among drive mechanisms inherent the fact that the drive is SCSI or IDE. These terms refer to the protocol and hardware standards used to communicate with the host CPU, which therefore implies that one way or another the drive controller electronics will have certain characteristics. More often than not, actual quality differences are simply reflections of SCSI's higher price and more selective target market. Vendors, using the SCSI to differentiate their product lines, add larger caches and faster drive mechanisms to SCSI products. Faster mechanisms (SCSI drives regularly spin at 10,000–15,000 RPM, whereas even high-end mechanisms used in the IDE space spin at 7,200 RPM) place greater stress on mechanical systems in general and therefore require a higher standard of engineering. They are also primarily responsible for SCSI's superior seek times. There is no technical reason why a drive vendor couldn't drop an ATA-133 controller onto a 15,000 RPM mechanism—and indeed, as illustrated earlier, several vendors are moving to larger and on-disk caches for IDE drives. This trend towards better-engineered, higher-quality ATA features, has resulted in IDE drives that are more appropriate for server roles than ever before.

The SCSI protocol itself does maintain several architectural advantages, although they are not necessarily reflected by performance differences. SCSI is a general-purpose communications protocol, designed to be extensible to talk to a number of systems and devices. ATA is a disk communication protocol that has been extended in a sometimes ad hoc way to include other types of deices. SCSI also wins when it comes to physical interconnect (hardware) features. In any incarnation, but especially more recent ones, it supports much longer cable lengths and many more devices than ATA. In fact, ATA is still limited to two devices per bus, and an IDE device can sometimes monopolize the IDE bus in such a way that the other device on the bus has limited access to system resources. Thus, despite ATA's growth, it should be deployed only very carefully in most servers. There is often a significant cost premium between the low end of ATA and the high end, where greater reliability and more advanced features are showing up. Drives destined for server deployment should, at a minimum, support tagged command queuing and scatter and gather I/O. Large caches—at least 8 MB—are also a must. Additionally, device management and conflict remain big issues in the IDE world, so in a server environment, each drive should have its own dedicated bus. Finally, due to decreased quality assurance and shorter warranties associated with IDE product lines, ATA drives should, whenever possible, be deployed redundantly.

Luckily, Apple has taken care of most of these requirements in its server products, showing that good overall system architecture can overcome many of IDE's shortcomings. The bottom line is that IDE might go a long way towards meeting your storage needs, especially when managed appropriately. While SCSI might be architecturally superior and ostensibly a better performer, its performance and feature-to-price ratio is typically much lower than IDE's, and IDE's vastly lower cost makes for easy redundancy and affordable expansion.

 As of this writing, current Xserves (which use the G5 processor) utilize serial ATA and support three (rather than four) drives. The Xserve RAID, however, still uses ATA 100.

Serial ATA (SATA)

Serial ATA, or SATA (first included by Apple in the PowerMac G5), is a backwards-compatible evolution of the ATA protocol. The fundamental architectural difference between the two is that Serial ATA is, as the name implies, a serial rather than a parallel technology. This might at first seem counter-intuitive; after all, sending a bunch of data in parallel seems faster than sending the same data serially. However, serial technologies have proven their viability in recent years, notably in the form of USB, FireWire, and Fibre Channel. In general, serial technologies require fewer wires—instead of multiple parallel channels, they operate on the concept of having one channel each way, to and from the host to the device. This reduction in the number of wires in the cable means that the electronic noise associated with them is reduced, allowing for much longer wires and (theoretically) much faster operation.

SATA has all the benefits of ATA, along with several added bonuses:

- Because it's a Point-to-Point, rather than a multidevice bus, there are no device conflicts or master-slave issues.
- SATA is also hot-pluggable (similar to FireWire), and requires a much thinner cable than the IDE ribbon.
- It promises more widespread support for advanced drive features that are otherwise just making their way into the ATA space, like tagged command queuing and overlapping commands.

Right now SATA doesn't really offer a significant performance increase over ATA, but as system bus performance improves, that difference will become more and more pronounced. While SATA isn't revolutionary in any sense of the word, it is a very complete evolution of the ATA standard and it does go a long way towards legitimizing ATA in the server space. Nonetheless, the requirements placed on IDE should also be enforced before deploying SATA drives in a server role.

Fibre Channel

Fibre Channel is a serial storage protocol that is common in data center and enterprise environments. It is a high-performance flexible technology that is especially notable due to Apple's move towards it with the Xserve RAID and Xsan products. Fibre Channel was designed to meet several of SCSI's limitations; specifically, those related to architecture, cable length and device support.

An easy way to understand this is to look at the name SCSI. It's an acronym for *Small Computer Systems Interface*, and although it has turned out to be extremely extensible, its evolution from a system designed for small-scale computer systems is undeniable. SCSI is a single-master technology. Generally, a single CPU (by way of a SCSI adaptor) has sole control over multiple SCSI devices. This is a difficult architecture to maintain in today's world of centralized Storage Area Networks (SANs). Similarly, even in its most capable iteration, SCSI is limited to a cable length of 25 meters, and cannot deal with more than 16 devices. Although this is a vast simplification, the primary advantages of Fibre Channel are as follows.

Architecture

Fibre Channel supports three topologies: Point-to-Point, Arbitrated Loop, and Switched Fabric. The simplest is Point-to-Point, which connects a single host to a single device; for instance, an Xserve RAID to an Xserve. Point-to-point connections resemble SCSI or FireWire connections from a conceptual standpoint, and are usually not difficult to grasp. The next topology is a Fibre Channel Arbitrated Loop, or FC-AL. In this architecture, all nodes are connected in a loop. A device wishing to establish communications takes control of the loop, essentially establishing a Point-to-Point connection with its target using other hosts on the loop as repeaters. A Fabric, or *switched topology*, is a Switched Fibre Channel network (relying on one or more Fibre Channel switches). Like any switched network, any node is able to communicate directly with any other. Each topology has its own strengths and weaknesses. Apple's products specifically tend towards Point-to-Point and Switched Fabric topologies, although any host should be able to participate in an Arbitrated Loop. It's worth pointing out that a Switched Fabric topology, while the most flexible and efficient choice, is also the most costly, due to the high cost of Fibre Channel switches. Like any high-end technology, this is likely to change sooner than later, especially with Apple's entry into the fibre market. Apple's Xsan product requires a Switched Fabric topology.

Length

A single channel (using optical interconnects) may be up to 10 kilometers (KM) long. This feature poses a huge benefit to enterprise-wide SAN architectures, allowing for widely distributed systems. It does, though, prompt the question: "What is an optical interconnect?" Fibre Channel supports two kinds of media: copper and fiber optic. Copper media is used for shorter distances (up to 30 meters) and is relatively more affordable. Optical media is relatively more expensive, but can span up to 10 KM.

Devices

A single FC-AL loop supports up to 127 devices. A Switched Fabric may have as many as 15,663,104.

It's important to note that Fibre Channel storage is still limited by the underlying drive technology. A single ATA-backed fibre array typically is able to supply approximately 200 MBS. The real strength of fibre is that a single 2 GB channel could theoretically support several arrays being accessed at their full capacity (possibly a switched network with multiple hosts). This ability poses a huge benefit in even medium-sized enterprises by allowing IT architects to consolidate storage into a central array or group of arrays, allocating space on an as-needed basis to any number of hosts. Fibre is a high-bandwidth, high-performance standard, and there is no doubt that it makes a strong case for being the best storage choice in medium to large multiserver environments. The only real question is one of cost. Fibre, especially in a switched environment, is expensive, and the administrator will be forced to carefully weigh its benefits against its cost.

SCSI

Nobody ever got fired for deploying SCSI on a server (unless, of course, they exceeded their budget). SCSI is the stable, mature storage protocol against which all others are measured, and on which many server deployments are designed. Even referring to SCSI as a single standard, though, is a misstatement—SCSI is a continually evolving set of technologies loosely wrapped into three specifications: SCSI 1, SCSI 2, and SCSI 3. The biggest drawback to SCSI is its cost-per-density—storage vendors typically demand a 30% to 60% premium per megabyte for the privilege of running SCSI. It's also been said that SCSI is unfriendly, although, like Unix in general, it's actually just picky about who it makes friends with—so much that those high priests are said to be versed in SCSI voodoo. Cross-talk issues due to its parallel nature, termination, and cable length make it somewhat complex to deploy in larger environments. Other drawbacks include a complete lack of HVD SCSI adaptors on the Mac platform, keeping SCSI's very high-end hardware away from Mac OS X. When all is said and done, though, SCSI makes a lot of sense in a number of environments, especially high-performance, cost-insensitive ones. SCSI's high cost-per-density should scare anyone else away.

SCSI still stays a half-step ahead of ATA in terms of performance, but only a half step. So, if you deploy SCSI, be sure to choose the fastest hardware that can be considered stable. Also be sure to deploy SCSI sparingly, applying your high-performance SCSI toward high-demand applications (such as QuickTime Streaming or AFP-based Home directories). Even in these environments, though, fibre solutions might be applicable.

FireWire and FireWire 800

FireWire is the brand name for Apple's implementation of the IEEE 1394 specification (*http://developer.apple.com/firewire/ieee1394.html*). Jointly developed by Apple and Sony, FireWire was designed specifically as a serial bus to support high-speed peripherals like digital video cameras and hard drives.

Each FireWire bus is capable of a theoretical throughput of 400 Mbps (100 MBS). FireWire 800—the standard's second and newest version—doubles those capabilities. It is important once again to realize that those are performance numbers for the FireWire bus. When using FireWire as a storage mechanism, you are limited to the speed of the underlying drive (which is more often than not an ATA drive with a FireWire adaptor) and, to a lesser extent, the speed of the system bus. This means that testing, benchmarks, and public review are important components of the decision-making process when considering FireWire solutions.

Performance tends to vary widely. Even at its best, FireWire is not suited to heavy file serving duty. This tendency is due to the nature of FireWire, which was designed toward streaming data rather than random reads and writes (think digital video: both in terms of getting it off the DV camera and storing it on a filesystem). This is not to say that FireWire has no place in the system administrator's toolkit; it's simply that there are better solutions for file serving. Notably, FireWire is a particularly good backup medium. Tape backups, which have never been tremendously fast, are today are having trouble keeping up with current, high-volume, high-density storage solutions. FireWire drives—high-volume and relatively cheap—can play a surprisingly important role in a good backup solution. Similarly, FireWire excels at being sort of an advanced sneaker-net, with the capacity to hold a complete bootable Mac OS X system in addition to several system utilities.

Redundant Array of Inexpensive Disks (RAID)

If you're reading this, you probably already have a good idea of what RAID is, at least in its simplest terms. RAID is a method of combining several disks and making them look like one volume to the operating system. There are a number of reasons for pursuing this strategy; as the name implies, redundancy is a common one. Having data in more than one place is important, especially with the rise of (theoretically) less reliable IDE drives in server roles. Contrary to its naming, though, RAID doesn't always imply redundancy. It's just as common, actually, to use RAID to increase throughput and decrease latency for read and write operations; the theory being that two disks working at once will be able to write or read twice as much data as one. The goal in many cases, of course, is to maximize both factors—redundancy and performance—in a particular RAID installation. Toward those ends, RAID has several configurations, or levels, the most common of which are:

RAID 0

Also known as *striping*, reads and writes data to all drives in the array simultaneously, so that each bit is written to only one drive. (The total size of a RAID 0 volume is equal to the combined sizes of its member disks.) This design is expected to increase filesystem performance, since instead of waiting for one drive to fulfill I/O requests, they can simply be sent to the next drive in the array.

While RAID 0 does not result in truly incremental increases in performance, it does have a substantial impact on the overall performance of read and write operations. The downside, of course, is that RAID 0 provides no redundancy. Since each bit (including the data that keeps track of the filesystem structure) is written to only one drive, the loss of any one drive means the loss of the entire RAID array. Effectively, RAID 0 introduces another point of failure with each new disk added into the array.

RAID 1

Mirroring can be considered the opposite of RAID 0. In a RAID 1 array, each piece of data is written to at least two drives, meaning that all data is fully redundant. (The total size of a RAID 1 volume is generally equal to that of its smallest member disk.) If one drive fails, all data is still preserved; the RAID is simply marked for repair. When a new disk is added, the array can be resynchronized, so that the mirror is once again functioning properly. RAID 1, however, does nothing to aid performance. Depending on the implementation, RAID 1 can impose a slight penalty for write operations.

RAID 0+1

This is a combination of RAID 0 and 1, wherein two striped arrays are set up to mirror each other, resulting in faster performance while maintaining redundancy. If a disk in either stripe is lost, that stripe must be rebuilt and the mirror is marked as degraded. However, since all data is mirrored to the second stripe, the OS will know how to rebuild the stripe, because it's a component in the mirrored array. While this initially sounds like a very good idea, keep in mind that it's not a very efficient use of disk space, and that a loss of a drive in each array, however unlikely that seems, would result in complete data loss.

 Because disks employed in arrays are often identical and purchased in batches, they are somewhat vulnerable to a common trend in storage products—clustered failures. Disk reliability is typically measured in the average period between failures (MTBF, or mean time between failures). Averages, however, give no statistical indication of distribution.

RAID 3

This is often referred to as $n+1$. It is similar to RAID 0, in that data is striped across n drives (where n is the number of drives in the stripe). It gains some amount of redundancy, though, from an additional disk—a parity disk—so that the total number of disks is $n+1$. The RAID controller uses the parity disk to keep track of which data is stored on which disk in the stripe, so that in the case of disk failure, the data can be regenerated. If the parity disk is lost, its data can be regenerated from the remaining stripe. RAID 3 is most effective when dealing with large files, since its high throughput is somewhat offset by the latency associated with each transaction.

RAID 5

This is very similar to RAID 3, except that parity data, instead of being written to a single parity disk, is distributed among every disk in the array. RAID 5 is usually best deployed in environments where reads and writes are random and small. Due to the maintenance of parity data, write performance for both RAID 5 and RAID 3 tends to suffer. One method for overcoming this deficit is to create two RAID 5 or RAID 3 arrays, treating each like a member of a RAID 0 stripe. The result, known as RAID 50 or RAID 30, respectively, is a very high performance array.

It is important to understand what RAID is and also what it isn't. First and foremost, RAID is not backup. Backups preserve a history so that if you delete or otherwise lose a file, it can be recovered. RAID won't do that for you. All RAID provides is redundancy and (in some cases) increased performance. Backup provides long-term protection against a variety of data-loss scenarios. RAID, in a redundant configuration, protects almost solely against hardware failure. Both are important components of a redundancy strategy, but it's very important to not operate under the mistaken assumption that RAID frees you from thinking about backups.

Apple storage products

Current Xserve models support three internal drive bay modules. Each module has its own dedicated SATA controller, resulting (as Apple is fond of pointing out) in nearly 300 MB of total theoretical throughput. Although these results are theoretical, they do result in a very good deal, especially considering the total capacity of all three drive bays. The biggest drawback to these mammoth, yet fairly quick, storage capabilities is a lack of flexibility. The Xserve itself, without the Xserve RAID, until recently, had no hardware RAID options for its built-in drive bays. Instead, Apple's recommended solution is the software RAID capabilities of Mac OS X Server. While the recent (and long delayed) availability of a hardware RAID solution proposes to change this fact of deployment, it is too new, as of this writing, to discuss definitively. Software RAID in Mac OS X comes with a choice—RAID 0 or RAID 1; performance or redundancy— but not both. Mac OS X (and Mac OS X Server) support neither RAID 5 nor RAID 0+1. Apple has clearly put itself in the school of thought holding that software RAID 5, due to its processor-intensive nature, is not a viable solution. While this may be the case, it should be noted that several other operating systems, including most Linux distributions and FreeBSD, *do* support software RAID 5.

 Since Apple's kernel driver abstraction layer (IOKit) bears no relation to FreeBSD, its capabilities here don't really affect Mac OS X.

Be smart about your data. If it is very static, and very well backed up, or if it's just not important in the long term, RAID 0 is a real option. In most circumstances this will not be the case. Perhaps your system files, which are easily replaced, do not need to be protected by redundancy, but in cases where data is sensitive or where a lot of downtime is unacceptable, important data (like user home directories or web server files) should be stored on an array that offers some kind of redundancy. When feasible, consider evaluating Apple's hardware RAID card. What's important here is understanding the capabilities of the storage platform and how those capabilities coincide with your data needs.

Apple's next tier of storage support is the Xserve RAID, a 3U, 14-drive, 3.5 TB (3,520 GB) Fibre Channel storage array. It is a very capable product, supporting RAID 0, 1, 3, and 5 on each of two independent controllers (there are two banks of 7 drives each; each bank connects to a single controller). Both banks may also be striped together, resulting in RAID 0+1, 10, 30, or 50. A drive in each bank may also be configured as a hot spare, so that if some other drive in that bank fails, the RAID may be transparently repaired and brought back to a fully redundant state without any action on the part of the system administrator.

A major component of the Xserve RAID's architecture is its use of Fibre Channel—as touched on earlier, this feature adds a lot of depth and flexibility to Apple's server product line, mostly by adding support for a Switched Fabric network. Beyond the strengths of fibre, though, the Xserve RAID gains a lot of value due to its tremendous density and flexibility. Frankly, it's not like no one has ever thought of these things before—they've just never been common in the Mac space. What Apple has done has been to take a number of very desirable features and combine them into a product with a lot of finish. Successfully managing the Xserve RAID still requires forethought and knowledge of storage needs. It doesn't, though, require a degree in computer science, and thus can be considered a step forward in the storage industry.

 The one real drawback of the Xserve RAID is that its controllers, as of this writing, are truly independent, and are not redundant. If one controller fails, the second will not take over its arrays.

Obviously, Apple doesn't have the RAID market—or especially the fibre market—cornered. There are other solutions from a variety of vendors. We're focusing on the Xserve RAID as a specific option, however, for two reasons. First of all, it's a very common storage product, having a lot of exposure in the Mac market. Pre-existing Mac-compatible Fibre products were largely niche items, generally very expensive and not widely deployed. Secondly, from a support perspective, it is a best practice to choose storage products either from or certified by your server vendor. This reduces the vendor blame-game when you need support.

Although much more affordable per density, the Xserve RAID, like a SCSI drive, is premium storage space next to the Xserve's built-in drives, and should be deployed in conjunction with applications that place a premium on performance and data integrity. This is particularly relevant in a multiple-server environment. Server-attached storage (that is, storage attached directly to the server, rather than being available through a SAN) is fairly inflexible: the storage is where it is, and other servers aren't going to have access to it unless it's shared out over a network protocol of some sort—defeating the benefit of fibre's throughput. A fibre SAN, however, allows for much more efficient allocation of storage resources, since specific portions of the array can be reserved or shared among specific hosts.

Volume management and partitioning

An important factor in storage planning is determining where in the filesystem various storage resources will be mounted. At a basic level, this discussion is much simpler on Mac OS X than it is on other Unix platforms, since non-root volumes are typically mounted in */Volumes* at a mount point based on their name, or volume label, as shown in Example 1-1.

Example 1-1. Using the df command to examine the volumes mounted throughout the filesystem. df's –h flag indicates that the results should be displayed in human-readable format (using megabytes, gigabytes, and kilobytes as units rather than 512 byte blocks).

```
[home:~] admin% df
Filesystem              512-blocks     Used      Avail    Capacity   Mounted on
/dev/disk0s9            117219168    3578448   113128720      3%     /
devfs                         210        210          0    100%      /dev
fdesc                           2          2          0    100%      /dev
<volfs>                      1024       1024          0    100%      /.vol
/dev/disk2s9           2147483647    2009392 2147483647       0%     /Volumes/RAID
/dev/disk1s9            117219168    3322776   113896392      2%     /Volumes/Backup HD
automount -fstab [417]          0          0          0    100%      /Network/Servers
automount -static [417]         0          0          0    100%      /automount
```

What Is a Volume?

Throughout this book we constantly refer to a "volume." This terminology, in large part, is a strategy of ambiguity in order to avoid a lot of explanation. Specifically, a volume is the logical unit that holds the filesystem. Thus it is a superset of (at a minimum) of what would seem to be partitions and drives. This conveniently ignores the fact that in the vast majority of circumstances, almost all drives actually *are* partitioned—even if they appear to have only one usable volume. So we can further clarify that what we're really talking about is the difference between single and multiple partition drives.

There are times when simply having a separate filesystem—even if it's on the same disk—is appropriate. For those circumstances we use the word "partition." There are also circumstances where data really should be on its own physical disk or even its own controller. In those circumstances, the word "disk" is used.

Finally, there is information that applies to both single and multiple partition disks; for instance, generalized information about mounting. In these instances, you'll read "volume."

The *df* command shows you, among other things, where devices are currently mounted. The *mount* command has similar functionality:

```
[home:~] admin% mount
/dev/disk0s9 on / (local)
devfs on /dev (local)
fdesc on /dev (union)
<volfs> on /.vol (read-only)
/dev/disk2s9 on /Volumes/RAID (local, with quotas)
/dev/disk1s9 on /Volumes/Backup HD (local)
automount -fstab [417] on /Network/Servers (automounted)
automount -static [417] on /automount (automounted)
```

However, this approach is inflexible in more sophisticated environments. The first thing to stress is a concept that we've touched on several times already—reserve your high-bandwidth storage for high-bandwidth applications. There is no need for most of the OS or an archival share for older, static data to be stored on an external RAID. Performance and redundancy needs vary widely by application, and it would be quite a headache to reconfigure every such application to find its data files somewhere in */Volumes*. This is especially the case with built-in services like Cyrus (the open source IMAP and POP server used by Mac OS X Server).

Traditionally, Unix OS's have devoted volumes (either partitions or disks) to specific portions of the OS. Note the output of the *df* command on a Solaris installation:

```
(sol:mb) 14:32:04  % df -k
Filesystem              1k-blocks       Used Available Use% Mounted on
/dev/dsk/c0t0d0s0          492422      51257    391923  12% /
/dev/dsk/c0t0d0s6         1190430     797638    333271  71% /usr
/dev/dsk/c0t0d0s4          492422     231346    211834  52% /var
swap                      1051928         24   1051904   0% /var/run
swap                      1055280       3376   1051904   0% /tmp
/dev/dsk/c0t0d0s3         4837350    3754361   1034616  78% /mdx
/dev/dsk/c0t0d0s5         1190430     324556    806353  29% /usr/local
/vol/dev/dsk/c0t1d0/s1-5500
```

There are other, non-performance-related reasons for managing disks in this manner. For instance, it's feasible under a number of circumstances for processes to write lots of data to the filesystem, due to misconfiguration, bugs, or normal, day-to-day operation.

Some good examples include systems where quotas are not in use or were misestimated (iLife applications commonly add a tremendous amount of data to a user's home directory), large amounts of swap files or server logs—which, on a busy server (Apache and Apple-FileServer are common culprits) may grow very large.

Since on an out-of-box install that filesystem is likely to also be the root filesystem, denial-of service-opportunities could be presented for local or remote users once the hard drive's capacity is exceeded. Some administrators also maintain a hot spare boot volume that's instantly available should the root partition experience filesystem corruption or some other malady. This approach is feasible, because the bits that actually boot the machine don't change much and actually make up a small percentage of the disk space used in the filesystem. Obviously, though, it's usually not feasible to maintain a hot-everything spare system—hence the need to keep the root filesystem separate from larger, more mutable data volumes. And finally, in very security sensitive circumstances (commonly high-volume public servers), it's sometimes desirable to have a read-only boot partition. This technique makes several general types of malicious compromises more difficult to execute. Obviously, though, some of the filesystem needs to have write capability enabled—again underlining the need to configure system partitions in very flexible ways.

Note that not all of these scenarios are possible on Mac OS X. Our point is simply to illustrate several common disk management schemes.

What it really comes down to is that there are several valid reasons, established in the Unix community over the course of years, for keeping different portions of your filesystem on different volumes. We'll look at the actual mechanics of configuring Mac OS X a little bit later in this chapter—for now, the point is to think about the deployment planning process, and to consider critically your volume and storage resource options in the context of your application and security needs.

One final point of discussion when considering volume planning and management is *swap space*. Swap space, a component of the kernel's virtual memory system, is stored on its own partition in most Unix-like operating systems. In Mac OS X, however, swap space is managed in a series of files that are by default installed in */var/vm*. A common first impulse among seasoned system administrators is to configure Mac OS X to store its swap files on their own partition. The simple answer to this is that there's really no good way to do it, and even if there were, it wouldn't affect performance much in most circumstances.

Most methods for moving swap space involve manually mounting volumes early in the */etc/rc* script by adding their device files (for instance, */dev/disk5s0*) to the */etc/fstab* file. Unfortunately, as we'll see later, device files are nondeterministic, meaning that *disk2s2* might be *disk3s2* the next time you boot your machine. Mac OS X uses a disk arbitration subsystem to mount disks other than the root volume, and it does not start up early enough to have those disks mounted before dynamic_pager (the process that manages swap files) starts.

More importantly, beyond being maintained on a filesystem that's less fragmented, storing swap files on a dedicated partition doesn't gain you much performance improvement. The server is still writing files to an HFS+ volume—not to a specialized swap filesystem. Those writes are typically competing with other disk operations, at a minimum, and usually with operations from other disks that happen to be on the same I/O channel.

Even if swap space is being written to its own disk on its own I/O channel, it doesn't change the fact that hard disk—even the fastest hard disk—is thousands of times slower than RAM. There's just no reason to spend a lot of time configuring swap in some unsupported configuration when current Macs are capable of using 4–16 GB of tremendously cheap RAM.

Network Infrastructure

By their nature, servers tax networks, both in the physical sense of bandwidth constraints and in the organizational sense of managing heterogeneous systems of hosts.

Every operating system exacts different tolls on the administrator. In this section, I'll highlight some issues that are worth avoiding.

Performance

A number of Mac OS X Server features are undeniably high-bandwidth. Unlike simpler, more traditional services, whose bandwidth tends to be quite manageable at a small scale, these applications are bandwidth-intensive at any volume. NetBoot and QuickTime Streaming Server come immediately to mind. Fortunately, these newer services have prompted the Mac community to think a little more about bandwidth and other networking issues prior to deployment. This is a huge change for the better, because these issues are traditionally neglected in any environment. Unfortunately, networking is made a more complex topic due to its political implications. Typically in all but the smallest environments, the organization managing the network (wires, routers, and access points) is not the same organization managing the servers, and one has little reason to placate the other. This book isn't meant to be a fundamental examination of networking, so we'll limit our discussion to three basic topics: performance, infrastructure, and services.

 The phrase "political implications," in one form or the other, is repeated throughout this book over and over and over again. Unfortunately, this behavior is typical of IT organizations. They are territorial, bureaucratic, and sometimes top-heavy. The right hand rarely knows what the left hand is doing. This is certainly a vast generalization, but it's a common enough one that we feel comfortable illustrating the trend.

Network performance is one of those things that isn't a problem until it is visible. Users rarely approach you with compliments on the server's speed. As an administrator, more often than not, your primary goal, is to hope that your users don't think to complain about it. Fortunately, good planning, and accompanying good budgeting, can help you stay under the radar.

Network performance seems fairly simple—after all, performance everywhere else tends to be straightforward. Big engines mean fast cars. Faster processors really seem to add zip to desktop computers. Professional athletes tend to run fast. Unfortunately, as we've mentioned earlier, in many cases, performance is much more about perception than quantitative analysis, and network performance doesn't always mean buying a bigger switch or faster network interface. For our purposes here, we'll examine two metrics to help you measure performance: latency and throughput. These are very common guidelines and they apply to more than just networking—so we will see them again later.

Latency is the delay in a network transmission. Latency is independent of bandwidth. The classic example is a semi truck full of dlt tapes (or hard drives or DVDs or any other high-capacity media). This is a very high-bandwidth link—but it could have a latency of hours. Lots of things cause latency—from data loss (TCP is an error-correcting protocol, so lost data is retransmitted transparently) to bad routing to outdated Ethernet protocols. What is important is recognizing the situation and recognizing latency-sensitive applications. You might be glad to wait all day for hundreds of terabytes to be delivered by a semi. Waiting for hundreds of very small graphics to load from a web page, or trying to watch streaming video, is a different story.

Throughput is the total amount of data (usually measured per second) that can flow between two given network nodes. Although high latency can contribute to reduced throughput, it is just one of the factors in a very complex ecosystem.

Infrastructure

Certain infrastructure issues are particularly troublesome for the Mac administrator, especially a factor in environments that are mostly homogeneous; introduction of a new platform can negatively affect systems that were built on assumptions about other OSes. Since networks are rather ubiquitous—it's hard to imagine participating in an enterprise without being exposed to them—they are a common forum for this kind of interaction. The overall pain and headache can be reduced, however, if these are accounted for in the planning process leading up to deployment.

One of the most common manifestations of this sort of platform-specific infrastructure is the duplex setting on an organization's network links. Ethernet interfaces for Apple hardware have always been of a fairly high quality, and have always been set to auto-negotiate. Unfortunately, in the commoditized market of *x*86 hardware, low-quality NICs are all too common. Windows administrators are commonly forced to turn off auto-negotiation on their network switches in order to compensate for these poorly implemented NICs. Matters are made worse by the fact that in Jaguar there's no way to manually affect the duplex settings of an Ethernet interface through the included graphical management tools. Instead, the administrator must use the *ifconfig* command, which should otherwise be avoided when making destructive changes. If your network hardware is not set to auto-negotiate, you should be aware that you will most likely have to set the duplex manually on your Mac hardware. Since *ifconfig*'s modifications do not live through reboot, you'll have to do this every time the machine restarts. Apple has a Knowledge Base article detailing this process. Fortunately, Panther presents a much deeper set of graphical configuration options, making speed and duplex options easily configurable in the Network pane of the System Preferences application (Figure 1-1).

In general, most networking settings in Mac OS X are managed by the System Configuration Framework. *configd*, the daemon that does the framework's work, is not notified of changes made manually with *ifconfig*. Since *configd* also manages routing tables, DNS resolver settings, and several facets of directory service configuration, this setup can have unforeseen circumstances. A good rule of thumb is that you should not use *ifconfig* to affect any settings that *configd* is responsible for unless you have a very thorough understanding of the implications. Since *configd* in Mac OS X 10.2 doesn't have an interface for managing duplex settings, they are safe for management with *ifconfig*.

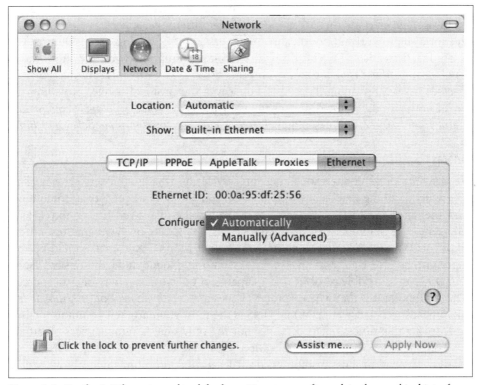

Figure 1-1. Panther's Ethernet speed and duplex settings are configured in the graphical interface.

Several other common Mac OS issues relate mostly to AppleTalk. Let's get this straight up front: you should turn AppleTalk off. There's no reason to rely on it. Previous to Mac OS X, this issue might have been debatable—the "network browser" application on Mac OS 8 and 9 insured that non-AppleTalk service discovery (at that time mostly limited to the Service Location Protocol, or SLP) would be a horrible user experience, banishing most users to the comfortable chooser to locate network resources. That was then, this is now. On a small network, AppleTalk is rather easy to support and fairly innocuous. Scaling up to large, subnetted infrastructures, though, can be extremely painful and difficult, especially now that network vendors, realizing that Apple is moving away from AppleTalk, have vastly reduced their support for it. It's just not worth the pain, and it is totally contrary to our philosophy of reducing impact on existing infrastructures.

That said, it is common for AppleTalk to conflict with Spanning Tree, a common network protocol used to check for loops in Ethernet topologies. The issue is that Spanning Tree in essence forces a port on a switch or router to sit idle for 30 seconds while the hardware itself checks for loops. This is enough time for several legacy protocols including AppleTalk and NetBIOS to time out. TCP/IP tends to do fine, since most IP configuration mechanisms continue to send out DHCP broadcasts regularly if they fail to get a DHCP address on boot. In reality, there is very little reason to run Spanning Tree on ports that are connected to workstations, since it is almost impossible for a single workstation to cause a network loop.* Spanning Tree is quite popular among network engineers, though, so if it's running at your site, it's best to ensure that PortFast is also running on ports associated with workstations. PortFast bypasses several Spanning Tree tests but leaves the protocol active, providing the best of both worlds. Apple discusses the issue here: *http://docs.info.apple.com/article. html?artnum=30922,* and Cisco here: *http:// www.cisco.com/warp/public/473/12.html.*

Services

We now introduce an interesting concept: services on which other services rely. This isn't really anything new—networks are built on a variety of protocols, some more fundamental than others. However, we'd like to take that a bit further and specifically state that a number of subsystems in Mac OS X rely on hostname resolution. All of your Mac OS X servers (and preferably your Mac OS X clients) should be able to perform both forward and reverse host resolution. Note that we didn't say DNS—Mac OS X has a flexible resolver that's capable of querying a variety of data sources. What is important is that when a process issues a *gethostbyname()* or *gethostbyaddr()* call, it needs to be answered. While DNS is the most standard and common method for ensuring this process, it is certainly not the only one. Several services—particularly, directory service–related applications and Mac OS X's graphical management utilities—depend on host resolution, or at least function more smoothly when it is available.

This reliance isn't specific to Mac OS X. In particular, Microsoft Active Directory (AD) depends on DNS—especially forward DNS, dynamic DNS, and DNS service discovery. Since integrating Active Directory's DNS requirements into existing infrastructures can be quite difficult, many organizations—usually on Microsoft's recommendation—have opted to allow Active Directory's DNS to be authoritative for

---

* An exception is an environment where users might plug their own hubs or switches into multiple switches. This is an issue of policy, rather than a technical one.

the *.local* namespace. In other words, all AD hosts live in the *.local* search domain, and all of AD's services (LDAP, Kerberos, and so on) are registered and queried there. There's really nothing wrong with that: no one owns the *.local* namespace, a number of legitimate sources in the DNS world advocate its use, and this practice extends well beyond the Microsoft world.

 These sources include D.J. Bernstein, author of the *djbdns* daemon (*http://cr.yp.to/djbdns/dot-local.html*) and the *comp.protocols.tcp-ip. domains FAQ* (*http://www.intac.com/~cdp/cptd-faq/section5.html#split_ DNS*). Neither of these entities are at all authoritative for the top-level namespace, but both are well-respected in the world of network architects.

However, Apple has also chosen to use the *.local* namespace for its implementation of the multicast DNS portion of Rendezvous, Apple's version of the proposed Zeroconf standard. What this means is that in Mac OS X, all queries for the *.local* namespace will be passed off to *mDNSResponder*, the Multicast DNS responder that ships as a part of Rendezvous, rather than being sent out to the DNS hierarchy. In enterprises that have standardized on the *.local* namespace for local DNS services, this approach is quite problematic, since their DNS servers will never be queried (mDNS is a peer-to-peer technology that allows for name service lookups without the use of a DNS server).

There is much discussion in several communities relating to Apple's use of *.local*. To be fair, Apple has submitted an IETF draft proposing that the *.local* namespace be reserved for multicast DNS (mDNS).* In Rendezvous, they implemented that draft—primarily because waiting for the IETF to actually decide anything can be a very long process. Apple had originally planned on *local.arpa*, but for user experience and marketing reasons settled on *.local*. One has to wonder if the benefits (because most end users have absolutely no understanding of this issue, and becuase the *.local* TLD is mostly hidden in the graphical interface) were really worth the issues this choice has caused in enterprises already using the *.local* namespace. That discussion is mostly irrelevant, though, because a number of vendors aside from Apple—HP, Tivo, and several others—have implemented solutions based on Apple's mDNS specification. The only relevant question now for those enterprises already utilizing the *.local* namespace is how to turn off mDNS resolution in Mac OS X.

If you want to disable mDNS entirely, you have two options. Most simply, you can remove the mDNS startup item: */System/Library/StartupItems/mDNSResponder*. As a matter of consistency, you should also probably disable the Rendezvous service

---

* The draft is available at *http://www.ietf.org/internet-drafts/draft-cheshire-dnsext-multicastdns-02.txt*. As the draft progresses, though, the name will change by iteration of the *02.txt*. For instance, *www.ietf.org/internet-drafts/draft-cheshire-dnsext-multicastdns-01.txt* is no longer available at the above URL.

location—although all this accomplishes is to hide any Rendezvous-enabled services from applications that specifically use the Directory Service API for service location. In order to do this, uncheck the Rendezvous Plug-In in the Service pane of the Directory Access application.

Another option is to reconfigure *.local* queries to be forwarded your local nameserver, rather than allowing them to be forwarded to multicast DNS. To do this, edit the */etc/resolver/local* file, whose contents should look something like this out of the box:

```
nameserver 224.0.0.251
port 5353
timeout 1
```

Edit the nameserver and port entries to reflect your organization. For instance:

```
nameserver 192.168.2.5
port 53
timeout 1
```

After you restart the *lookupd* daemon (which, among other things, is responsible for host resolution), all queries for the *.local* namespace should be sent to the server you've specified.

In Panther, you have another option—the Mac OS X resolver libraries have been updated to reflect the feasibility that more than one DNS system might be responsible for the same namespace (we'll ignore for a second the implications of that when one looks outside of the *.local* domain). Accordingly, you might have multiple entries in the */etc/resolver* directory. Building on the previous case:

```
fury:~ mab9718$ ls -la /etc/resolver
total 32
drwxr-xr-x   6 root  wheel    204 17 Aug 06:02 .
drwxr-xr-x  92 root  wheel   3128 31 Dec  1969 ..
lrwxr-xr-x   1 root  wheel      5 28 Aug 17:13 0.8.e.f.ip6.arpa -> local
lrwxr-xr-x   1 root  wheel      5 28 Aug 17:13 0.8.e.f.ip6.int -> local
lrwxr-xr-x   1 root  wheel      5 28 Aug 17:13 254.169.in-addr.arpa -> local
-rw-r--r--   1 root  wheel     43 17 Aug 06:02 local
```

There are four entries in the default install, three of which are symbolic links to */etc/resolver/local*. These files are concerned with the default resolution of the *.local* domain, including the reverse resolution of the link-local IPv4 and IPv6 address spaces. In Panther, Mac OS X's resolver is extensible, so specific domains might have different DNS configurations (confusingly enough, called clients). *local* is the only client installed by default, but others may be added. For instance, if I wanted to ensure all queries to the *4am-media.com* domain were processed by my own nameserver, I could create a file in */etc/resolver* called *4am-media*. Its content would be similar to the modified */etc/resolver/local* file mentioned earlier.

Generally, the system's resolver determines which domain each configuration file is responsible based on that file's name—for instance *local* is responsible for the *.local* namespace in the previous example. How, then, would you have more than one configuration per namespace? It's actually as simple as adding a domain directive to the file in question. So if I wanted to specify a traditional name server in addition to using mDNS in the *.local* domain (in order to both make use of Rendezvous and meet my organization's business goals), I could append a file called *4amlocal* to */etc/resolver*, as follows:

```
nameserver 192.168.2.5
port 53
timeout 1
domain local
search-order 1
```

In this case, for all queries regarding the .local namespace, my server will be queried initially, before mDNS. This approach, or something like it, is endorsed by Apple's kbase 107800. I'd also have to add the following to adjust */etc/resolver/local*:

```
nameserver 224.0.0.251
port 5353
timeout 1
search-order 2
```

Changing the search order for Apple's mDNS resolver ensures that your organization's .local DNS namespace will be queried before Rendezvous.

Finally, a more granular (and my preferred) approach is to specify a particular domain in your *.local* override, so that rather than query your organization's DNS for the entire *.local* TLD (top-level domain), you query only for your particular local domain (for instance, *4am.local*). This approach, although effective in most circumstances, has not always been compatible with Apple's Active Directory Plug-In, so as always, testing should be undertaken carefully. Example 1-2 shows what my *.local* resolver configuration looks like:

Example 1-2. Since it is specifically for the 4am.local domain, it does not affect the Rendezvous queries. Consequently, I do not have to modify the search order setting in the etc/resolver/local file.

```
nameserver 192.168.1.1
port 53
timeout 1
domain 4am.local
search-order 1
```

Since it is specifically for the 4am.local domain, it does not affect Rendezvous queries. Consequently, I do not have to modify the search-order setting in the */etc/resolver/local* file.

Whatever your approach, the point is to fit it most efficiently within your organization's existing infrastructures. Asking your DNS administrator to change company-wide naming policy simply to use Mac OS X effectively is not a productive way of driving adoption of Apple technologies.

## CHAPTER 2

Installing and Configuring Mac OS X Server

After the planning process is complete and your server hardware is onsite, you can proceed with installation. The exact methodology used will vary tremendously from organization to organization and from site to site.

Jaguar Server marked a fairly substantial departure from previous Apple software installation processes. From a fairly mechanical or procedural standpoint, this difference was not very obvious—sitting down in front of the server console, inserting a CD, and pressing some buttons still yielded a complete install. However, much of Jaguar Server was designed in order to support the Xserve, a design goal of which was complete remote operation—including installation. These remote installation options bring a whole new set of possibilities to deployment planning. In a nutshell, the server install—whether booting from CD or via NetBoot into a network install—sets up a TCP/IP stack, starts an *ssh* daemon, and advertises itself using a multicast response similar to Rendezvous. Mac OS X's Unix heritage allows for a wide range of features, which Apple had essentially finally chosen to leverage. Panther Server builds on that basic architecture, specifically extending its post-install configuration options in order to better suit large-scale deployments. We'll examine that evolution in some depth in this chapter, including even a number of strategies outside of traditional installation.

Mac OS X Server Installation Architecture

In order to best understand installation options, it is important to have a thorough knowledge of the installation architecture. How is the installation environment prepared? What happens during system startup, and what services are available to the OS? Apple has actually developed a very modular boot process, flexible enough that the same sequence is used regardless of whether the machine is booting from CD, off of the network or from the local hard disk. We'll be looking specifically at an OS install in this case, but some of this material is general enough to apply to other types of booting as well.

Power On

When the machine is booted, it is initially controlled by its built-in boot ROM, consisting of a minimal Power On Self Test (POST) and Apple's Open Firmware environment (OF). Unless otherwise configured, OF, after building a device tree, executes BootX, the system's booter. In most cases, BootX is executed from the device specified in OF's boot-device variable, which looks something like Example 2-1 when booting from an internal IDE drive:.

Example 2-1. Here I've used the nvram command's –p flag to print the contents of Open Firmware. This output is filtered using the grep command so that only the boot-device setting is shown.

```
Big15:~ mab9718$ nvram -p | grep boot-device
boot-device     pci2/ata-6@D/@0:9,\\:tbxi
```

However, when installing an OS, it's common to choose a startup volume manually. There are several ways to accomplish this. By far the most common is to hold down the C key at startup, overriding the boot-device variable and booting from CDs. Other options include holding down the N key (boot off the network) and Option, which provides a list of local volumes to boot from.* It's unlikely in many cases that you'll have easy keyboard or monitor access to a server in a rack. With this in mind, Apple has built a completely headless boot menu into the Xserve. Find out more about it here: *http://docs.info.apple.com/article.html?artnum=106482*.

> Of course, the boot-device setting may be set manually using either the Graphical Interface (specifically, the Startup Disk pane of the System Preferences application) or number of commands—among them *bless* and *systemsetup*; consult their manpages for details.

From there startup proceeds normally, as it would when booting from a hard drive, which is explained very well by Apple at *http://developer.apple.com/documentation/ MacOSX/Conceptual/SystemOverview/BootingLogin/index.html*. The first difference between a normal boot and installation comes in */etc/rc.boot*, the script that brings the machine up enough to boot into single-user mode (see Example 2-2). Specifically, if */System/Installation* and */private/etc/rc.cdrom* both exist, the system assumes it is booting from CD.†

---

* If a NetBoot server is available, a NetBoot icon appears on screen with local volumes. However, you won't be able to choose a specific boot image if more than one is available.

† Incidentally, if you've built a custom boot CD, and you're booting from CD for some reason other than an install, you might need to modify this script, since it assumes a CD boot is related to the installation architecture.

Example 2-2. The scripting within /etc/rc.boot that determines whether a machine is being booted from CD.

```
if [ -d /System/Installation ] && [ -f /private/etc/rc.cdrom ]; then
    ConsoleMessage "Root device is mounted read-only"
    ConsoleMessage "Filesystem checks skipped"
    iscdrom=1
else
    iscdrom=0
fi
```

This assumption is used only to determine whether *fsck* should run. The real work comes with the */etc/rc* and */etc/rc.cdrom* commands. The former (based on logic similar, but not identical to, */etc/rc.boot*) executes the latter if the system is booted from an install CD. The *rc.cdrom* script does several things:

- Sets the date to April 1, 1976 if the system clock is set earlier.
- Changes the maximum vnodes, or file structures, that the kernel may cache. In effect, this changes the amount of RAM that may be used as a filesystem cache.
- Disables prebinding (a performance-increasing technology that requires a read-write filesystem.
- If one exists, runs a preheat script that speeds CD booting.
- Loads *kextd*, the daemon responsible for managing the loading and unloading of kernel extensions. *kextd* is run with the J option, which speeds the boot process by loading native drivers (NDRVs), which are minimal and generic.
- Uses the *ifconfig* command to set up the local interface (*configd* hasn't yet started, so it is OK to use *ifconfig*).
- Mounts */.volfs*, a special filesystem used to enable Carbon applications to access files by their file ID, which is an HFS-specific convention.
- Mounts the *synthfs*, a filesystem used solely to create mountpoints for other volumes (usually when the root is read-only) in */Volumes*. This is done so that volumes discovered by disk arbitration can be mounted when booted from CD.
- Registers several processes with *mach_init* using the *register_mach_bootstrap_servers* command. *mach_init*, among other things, is capable of starting certain services on demand.
- Starts a daemon specifically responsible for logging installer processes (*/System/Installation/CDIS/instlogd*).
- Checks for the existence of the GUI Crash Catcher.
- Creates a RAM disk for *syslog*.
- Logs the boot date and time.
- Creates a RAM disk for and then starts *crashreporter*.

28 | Chapter 2: Installing and Configuring Mac OS X Server

- Checks for */etc/rc.cdrom.local*, and runs it if it exists. If you have localized scripts that need to be run, you can add them to this file on an image of the boot CD and re-burn it. This file does not exist on a default install.

- Checks for */etc/rc.cdrom.preWS*, and runs it if it exists. This file is for scripts that should run before WindowServer runs. This file does not exist on a default install.

- Starts AppleTypeServices (ATSServer), which helps the system display fonts. ATSServer requires WindowServer, which is started on demand by *mach_init*.

- Starts the PasteBoard server (*pbs*), used to support end-user cut/copy/paste operations.

- Checks for */etc/rc.cdrom.postWS*, and runs it if it exists. This file is for scripts that should be run after the WindowServer is run. This script exists on the Mac OS X Server install CD. In fact, many of the server-specific startup options live there.

- *rc.cdrom.postWS* runs while *rc.cdrom* waits in the background. *rc.cdrom.postWS* does the following:

  — Creates a RAM disk for *configd*'s data store, mounts it at */private/var/run*, and runs *configd*.

  — Mounts */tmp* as a RAM disk.

  — Creates a RAM disk to support NetInfo (*/var/db/netinfo*) and starts NetInfo.

  — Runs */sbin/SystemStarter*, which is responsible for starting most system services. SystemStarter reads */etc/hostconfig*, where the configuration for several startup items are stored. SystemStarter has a great manpage, so we won't go into a detailed analysis of its architecture.

We will, however, discuss startup items with a specific bearing on installation:

Network
> Brings up all nonloopback interfaces with the *ipconfig*[*] command. The machine attempts to get an address via DHCP on every interface. If this fails, the machine falls back to a link-local (169.254) address, allowing it to be located and configured remotely on the local subnet. Also enables IPv6 and IP forwarding (both using *sysctl* command) if specified in */etc/hostconfig*.

HeadlessStartup
> *HeadlessStartup* should probably be called *HeadlessInstall*, because it does almost nothing to support normal, noninstallation headless booting—the exception being ntpd (the network time server), which is started if the TIMESERV entry is set to -YES- in */etc/hostconfig*). It additionally checks for NetBoot, Hard

---

[*] *ipconfig* is a command-line utility used to access the System Configuration database. Specifically, the *waitall* flag brings up every configured interface.

Drive Boot, or CD Boot, and sets options appropriate for each. For CD and Net-Boot, this includes setting a temporary root password, setting up SSH key-pairs, and starting *sa_responder* (in */System/Library/ServerSetup*), the process responsible for advertising the server via multicast.

The hard drive boot additionally assumes that the server has been installed and is ready for configuration. This requires a number of other operations, including gathering certain data, setting power manager options with the *pmset* command, and setting the *srv variable* in Open Firmware to 1. Naturally, if the server is already configured (based on the presence of the empty file */var/db/.AppleSetupDone*), nothing is done to set it up for install or configuration. HeadlessStartup is also responsible for managing Mac OS X's automatic configuration process, discussed later in this chapter.

 HeadlessStartup is really the heart of Mac OS X Server's remote installation and configuration architecture. It works closely with a number of utilities in */System/Library/ServerSetup*.

SerialTerminalSupport

Quite possibly the finest startup item authored by Apple to date, this script consists of 379 lines, 168 of which are comments. Unfortunately, though, rather than being set in */etc/hostconfig*, its variables are set in the script itself. SerialTerminalSupport, among other things (as the name implies) manages the OS's ability to use the serial port on Apple hardware platforms. It has three variables:

```
ENABLE_SERIAL_TERMINAL=$TRUE
ENABLE_AUTOMOUNT_DISKS_WITHOUT_USER_LOGIN=$TRUE
ENABLE_SERIAL_SYSLOG=$FALSE
```

Respectively, when set they enable serial support, by changing:

```
tty.serial     "/usr/libexec/getty serial.9600"      vt100   off secure
```

to:

```
tty.serial     "/usr/libexec/getty serial.9600"      vt100   on secure
```

in */etc/ttys*, configure external disks to mount when no one is logged into the console by changing the AutomountDisksWithoutUserLogin key from false to true in */Library/Preferences/diskarbitrationd.xml* and turn on syslog output to the serial port[*] by uncommenting the following item in */etc/syslog.conf*:

```
#*.err;kern.*;auth.notice;authpriv,remoteauth.none;mail.crit
/dev/tty.serial
```

---

[*] This is done so that logging is sent to the serial port, which is common in the Unix world.

ENABLE_SERIAL_SYSLOG is the only option that is set to FALSE on an out-of-box installation. The *SerialTerminalSupport* startup item works only on Apple Server hardware; it checks for the RackMac1 tag in the output of the *sysctl hw.model* command.

 At some point during the Panther timeline, the ENABLE_AUTOMOUNT_ DISKS_WITHOUT_USER_LOGIN option was removed from the *Serial-TerminalSupport* startup item, because it is now a default behavior on Mac OS X Server.

After SystemStarter has completed its tasks, *rc.cdrom.postWS* completes, handing control back over to *rc.cdrom*, which starts the graphical installer. In addition to waiting for user input, the server has obtained an IP address, either from a DHCP server or self-assigned, and SSH (started by the *xinetd* process) is enabled, allowing for remote installation. Additionally, the *sa_responder* process is advertising that the machine is booted from CD and ready for installation.

In a noninstallation startup, *loginwindow* is started. However, if *loginwindow* doesn't detect */var/db/.AppleSetupDone* or does detect */var/db/.AppleMultiCDInstall*, it starts the Server Assistant or the Installer, respectively.

Graphical Installation and Configuration

The simplest, most common form of installation is a local, graphical install. We'll start there in order to get a basic understanding of the install process and Apple's goals for it.

Local Installation

A local installation—booting from CD, sitting in front of the server console—is pretty straightforward. By this point in the installation process you should have both a sane plan for deployment and a good understanding of the CD boot environment. When booted from the Panther Server CD, you have easy access to Terminal, Disk Utility, a Reset Password utility (to reset the password for users on an already-installed system) and a utility to change the current startup disk, all under the Installer menu (the Jaguar Server installation process has no Startup Disk utility). The initial installation screen, listed in Figure 2-1, allows for the choice of an installation language.

Your first stop will typically be Disk Utility. In Panther, Disk Copy's functionality has been rolled into a new, single-window disk utility interface, seen in Figure 2-2. Its functionality is very contextual, with the right pane of the application changing to reflect the functions supported on the selected object (disk, partition, or image).

Entire disks may be repaired, erased, partitioned, added to a RAID or restored (the last is a new option in Panther that we'll discuss later in this chapter). It is an

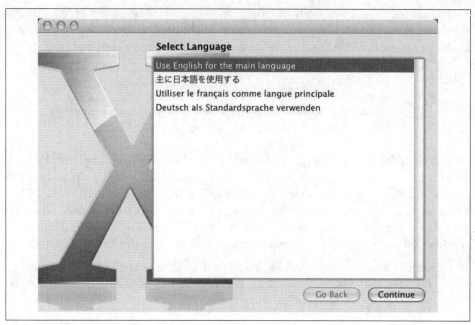

Figure 2-1. *The initial installation screen when booted from the Mac OS X Server install disk.*

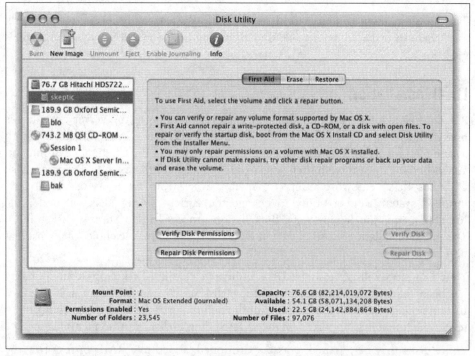

Figure 2-2. *Panther's Disk Utility when booted from the Mac OS X Server install CD.*

intuitive interface. In addition to options similar to Jaguar's, the Erase function in Panther optionally supports two advanced security options:

- Zeroing all data, which writes zeros to the volume in addition to marking all of the space as free.
- 8 Way Random Write Format, which overwrites all data eight times.

The Partitioning, RAID, and First Aid interfaces, aside from fitting into Disk Utility's new look, are very similar to their Jaguar counterparts.

When Disk Utility or any other application bundled with the install CD is quit, you will be taken back to the installer application. The process is designed to be extremely simple—and Mac OS X Server does, in fact, maintain a simpler installation than most other server products, even its far less capable cousin, AppleShare IP. Because of this, we'll stick to the highlights, rather than examine each step (such as agreeing to licensing details) in depth.

After choosing a language and agreeing to the software's license, you're presented with your first real decision—which volume to install the software onto (as shown in Figure 2-3).Be aware that if you are using Apple's hardware RAID card, Panther's disk selection interface will probably not accurately reflect the volumes available for installation, and you should probably proceede to the command line installation instructions later in this chapter.

Once you've selected a volume, the Options button (in the lower lefthand corner of the Installer window) becomes available. This is worth pointing out only because the Options button in Mac OS X Server has fewer options behind it than in Mac OS X. Specifically, there is no Archive and Install feature in Mac OS X Server, making in-place updates a little more difficult than they are for Mac OS X.

The next (and final) screen before the install begins allows you to customize which software packages will be installed. Clicking the Customize button reveals the dialog seen in Figure 2-4.

There's really no hard and fast rule regarding precisely which software you should choose, but you should always make sure to install the BSD Subsystem package (which is marked as optional, probably for licensing reasons). Common targets for exclusion include localizations for languages that you will not use (this speeds installation dramatically on slower hardware) and the additional Printer Drivers package. If you'd like to select manually which packages are listed as required, you can create an image of the server install CD using the Disk Utility application and modify the *OSInstall.mpkg* before burning the image back to CD. Finally, click the Install button and wait while the files are written to disk.

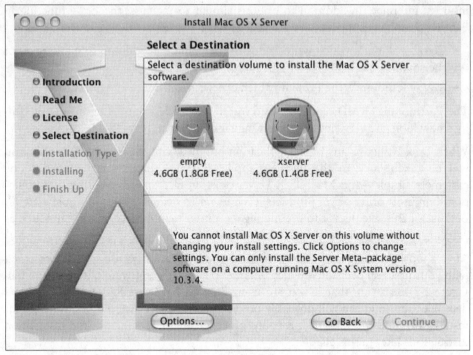

Figure 2-3. Choosing a volume for installation. If you've neglected to configure your filesystems for some reason, it's not too late: you can still choose Disk Utility from the Installer menu and proceed with your formatting, partitioning, and RAID development.

Panther Server is a two-disk install, so the server reboots and asks for a second CD before it's ready to be configured. Once the files from the second CD are installed, the machine will reboot once more and wait for further configuration.

Configuration

Once the software is installed, the server should boot into the Server Assistant, its first screen being a generic Welcome message, seen in Figure 2-5. Most of Server Assistant is very straightforward, but we'll walk though it in order to get a good understanding of the data required for a fully configured server.

An important aspect of Server Assistant is that the configuration you enter is not actually applied until you've finished the configuration process. Instead, data is simply stored until you specifically commit it. This approach provides a lot of flexibility, as it means that you'll be able to move back and forth through the various panes of Server Assistant, going back to change certain details if you choose to do so.

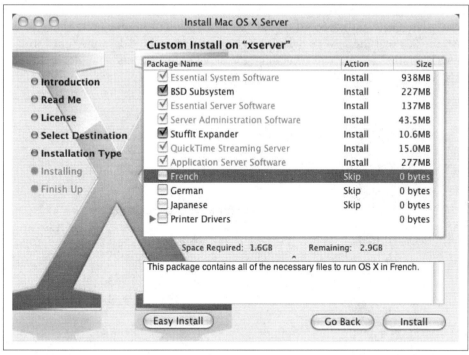

Figure 2-4. Choosing among optional packages during the Mac OS X Server installation process.

Figure 2-5. Mac OS X Server's Welcome screen.

Server Assistant's next two screens (Figures 2-6 and 2-7) prompt you to choose a default language and keyboard layout. There's nothing too unexpected here, other than the fact that the server's default language also affects the date and time formats, as well as the default text encoding for servers and clients that don't support Unicode.

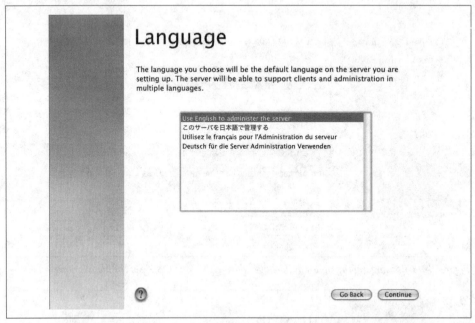

Figure 2-6. Choosing an adminstration language.

You're next prompted to enter a server serial number, as illustrated in Figure 2-8. Naturally, this is an important part of the installation process, since none of Apple's management tools will work on a server without one (nor will the graphical configuration proceed). It's worth mentioning here that the serial number generally relates to file-sharing services—specifically AFP (AppleShare) and Windows (SMB) services. So (although Apple does reserve the right to limit other services in the future) o a 10-user license won't limit you to 10 simultaneous http or lmap connections.

The Administrator Account pane, seen in Figure 2-9, is used to enter account information for the first administrative user on your server. There are a couple of things worth noting about this user. Most importantly, in a default configuration, this user's password is also assigned to the root user.

In a default configuration, Mac OS X Server (unlike Mac OS X) features an enabled root user. The root user is given a password, enabling root logins, both graphically and via SSH. An enabled root user is required for a few Mac OS X Server configuration changes, such as creation of an Open Directory Replica, described in more depth in Chapter 9.

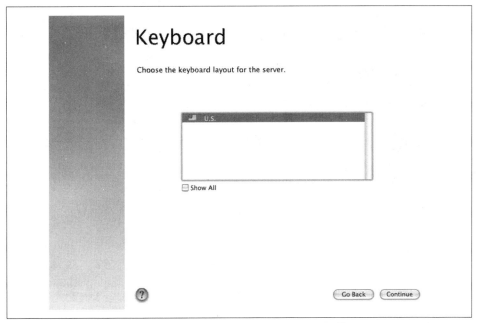

Figure 2-7. Choosing a keyboard layout during Mac OS X Server installation.

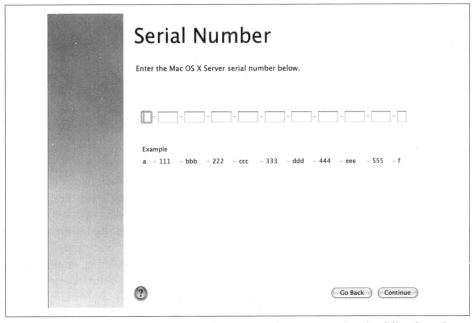

Figure 2-8. Specifying a software serial number. It is worth mentioning that this differs from the hardware serial number of your server.

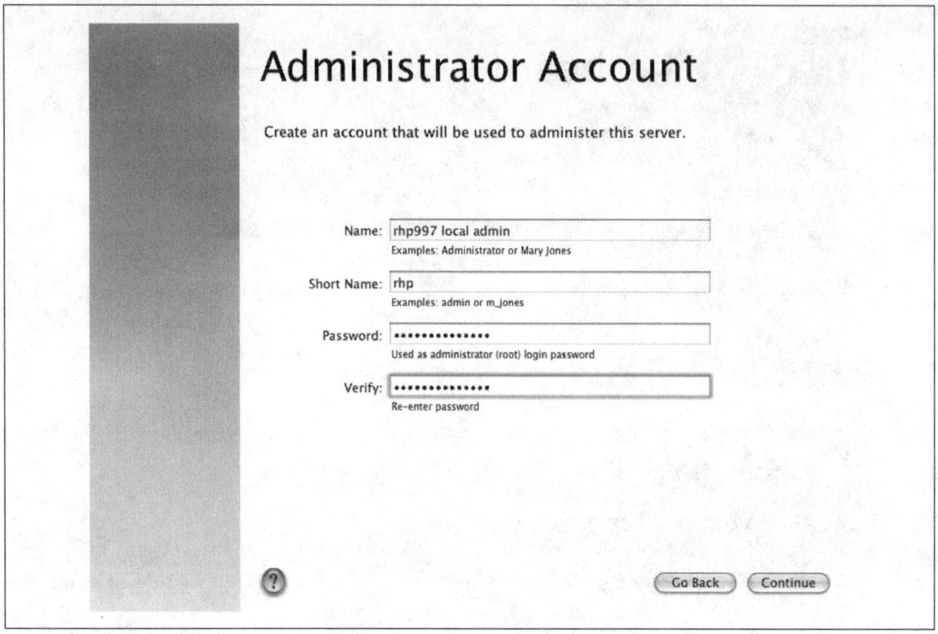

Administrator Account

Create an account that will be used to administer this server.

Name: | rhp997 local admin
Examples: Administrator or Mary Jones

Short Name: | rhp
Examples: admin or m_jones

Password: | ●●●●●●●●●●●●●
Used as administrator (root) login password

Verify: | ●●●●●●●●●●●●●
Re-enter password

(Go Back) (Continue)

Figure 2-9. Creating Mac OS X Server's initial Administrator Account. The password assigned to this administrative user is also assigned to root.

In Jaguar, this root user can be considered a significant security risk, since root's password hash (a 56-bit DES, or crypt, version of the password) is stored in world-readable NetInfo. Panther improves on this deficiency quite a bit, instead storing root's password in a root-only readable shadow file using both SHA-1 and NTLMv1 hashes. (In Mac OS X Server, the administrator, along with most other users, typically has a Password Server password, described in more depth in Chapter 8.) Even so, it is generally my policy to disable root entirely (after installation) much along the lines of a Mac OS X client install. It can be easily enabled on an as-needed basis using the *dsenableroot* command.

Notice that in the earlier example, I've specified what appears to be a generic Local Administrator. Presumably, authorized personnel are able to log in as this administrator to manage the server. While this is a valid and common configuration, it should also be noted that it's not very secure, and lacks accountability enforcement. Since this is a server used in a testing environment for demonstration purposes on a totally isolated network, the issue is less relevant. In a deployed environment, though, it's best to have a specific account for each person with administrative responsibilities, so that way access controls can be made more granular, and a better audit trail is established.

Be aware of the temptation to name your Administrative user "admin" or "Administrator." While this might be acceptable in very small environments, it presents a significant headache when working with Open Directory (or any other directory system). I usually use a host-specific local administrator. For instance the host *rhp997.pantherserver.org* has an administrator called *rhp*. For more details, see Chapter 6.

After the administrator's account data is entered (Figure 2-9), Server Assistant asks for the server's Host, Computer, and Rendezvous Names, as seen in Figure 2-10. These might all seem like the same thing, and in reality, they might actually be related. They all have very different purposes, though, and one big difference between Mac OS X and Mac OS X Server is that Mac OS X Server allows you to specify all of these values separately during the configuration process.

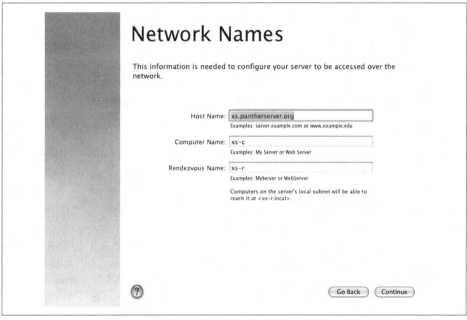

Figure 2-10. Assigning Host, Computer, and Rendezvous Names for your server. The Rendezvous and Computer Names, which are stored in /Library/Preferences/SystemConfiguration/preferences.plist, are managed by the System Configuration framework and its daemon, configd. The Host Name is stored in /etc/hostconfig.

The Host Name is the server's fully qualified domain, or DNS name (for instance *rhp997.pantherserver.org*). Your DNS server (to be specified later) should be able to resolve both forward and reverse queries for this name and your IP address. A Computer Name, on the other hand, is generally used as a label for service discovery queries. For instance, even if your server's Host Name is something fairly obscure,* its Computer Name could be *Home Directory Server*. The Computer Name differs from the Host and Rendezvous Names largely in that it can contain spaces and Unicode characters. This is perceived as more user-friendly than Rendezvous and Host Names, which are limited to the DNS character space.

 Confusion may arise from the many uses of the Computer Name. It can be seen in the context of AppleTalk, SLP (the Service Location Protocol), and even as a more user-friendly label on most Rendezvous services.

The server's Rendezvous Name is a name that's resolvable via mDNS. It's automatically in the *.local* namespace (for instance, *rhp997.local*), and is used strictly for resolution on the local subnet, usually in conjunction with Rendezvous service location.

The Network Interfaces pane, seen in Figure 2-11, allows you to specify which network interfaces you'd like to configure. You'll be prompted separately to configure each interface that is chosen. AppleTalk may also be enabled on a per-interface basis, if that's appropriate at your location. Keep in mind that AppleTalk may be enabled on only one interface at a time. So if you need AppleTalk (generally the only reason for this is to support AppleTalk print services), manage it carefully.

The next series of panes, generally similar to what is seen in Figure 2-12, allows you to enter TCP/IP configurations for the interfaces you chose to enable in the Network Interfaces pane. For each interface, you'll be allowed to select a configuration method and to specify an IP address, subnet mask, DNS servers, and search domains—very similar to the configuration interface available in the Network pane of the System Preferences application.

As illustrated in Figure 2-13, Panther allows you to immediately, from Server Assistant, configure Open Directory, Mac OS X's directory services architecture. Jaguar, on the other hand, starts a second application—Open Directory Assistant (ODA), after Server Assistant has completed its configuration. Rather than examine either of these mechanisms in depth now, we'll defer that topic to Chapter 6. This delay isn't merely in the interest of brevity. Open Directory configuration is rather complex, and I find it more stable from an administrative standpoint to isolate its configuration until after the server is otherwise stable. So for now (in Panther) under Set Directory Usage set your choice to Standalone Server and in Jaguar's ODA Temporary IP Address. Both options allow you to revisit their configuration at a later date.

Something else new in Panther is the importance of Password Server (PWS), Mac OS X's secure, standards-based network authentication mechanism. It is on by default in Panther—there's no easy way to disable it entirely. Jaguar's Open Directory Access

---

* Most IT organizations adopt a consistent naming convention for servers; usually a code that has some meaning. *00-MAC92c.pantherserver.org* might be the third Apple server that department 92 procured in 2000.

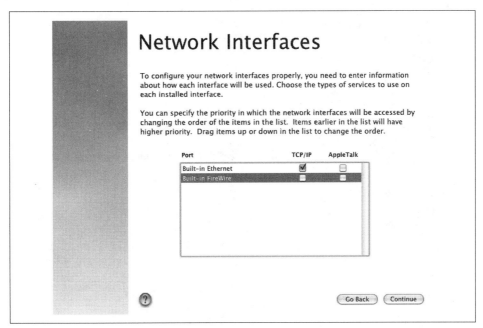

Figure 2-11. Configuration of the Network Interfaces pane is used to drive subsequent per-interface configuration.

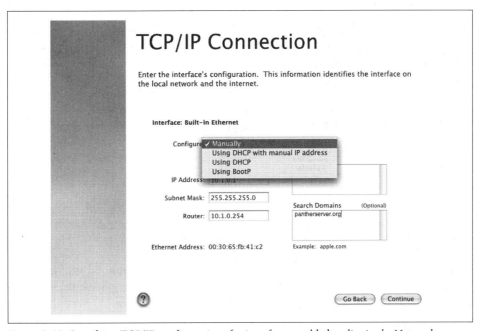

Figure 2-12. Specifying TCP/IP configurations for interfaces enabled earlier in the Network Interfaces pane.

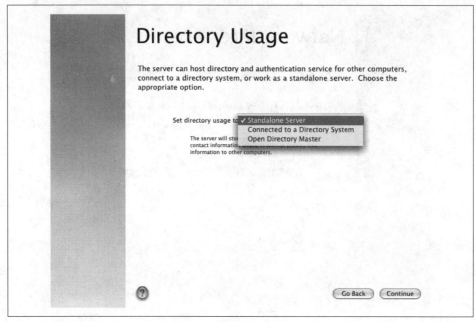

Figure 2-13. Choosing an Open Directory configuration. Because the latest software and security updates have generally not yet been applied at installation time, most servers should initially be left in a standalone configuration.

application allowed the administrator to disable PWS. While the *NeST* command could be used to turn PWS off manually (see Example 2-3), this approach does add to the complexity of management, since most support channels are going to assume that Password Server is in use.

Example 2-3. Using NeST to disable Password Server. In order to successfully support this configuration, the local administrator will have to be manually changed to a ;ShadowHash; password type. Also keep in mind that several server services depend on Password Server (VPN and Windows PDC, to name two) and will be unavailable without it.

```
g5:~ ladmin$ sudo NeST -NOpasswordserver
```

The Services pane, illustrated in Figure 2-14, allows you to enable certain services. The only choice you get, though, is an on or off switch, which isn't very flexible from a management standpoint. Additionally note that this early in the system's configuration, it is unlikely that any recent security updates have been applied, and that it is feasible that some services are in a state vulnerable to compromise. So, similar to the choices available in the Directory Usage pane, unless you have a specific reason to do otherwise, you should usually leave everything disabled.

Oddly enough, the lack of any selected services does not imply that all services are disabled. In an out-of-box configuration, DirectoryService, PasswordService, *servermgrd*, and *sshd* are all enabled and listening on their respective ports (625, 106, 365, 311, 687, and 22) on every active network interface. This feature is intended to facilitate easier remote management. I generally recommend that access to these ports (which are troublesome to disable) be limited to trusted networks, usually by isolating them behind a VPN gateway.

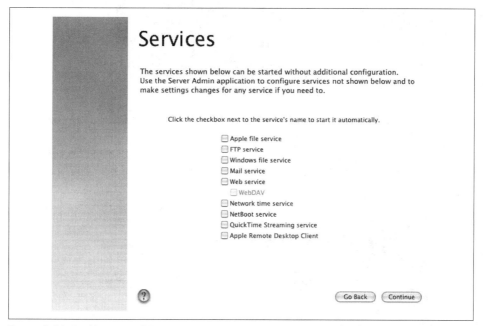

Figure 2-14. Enabling Mac OS X Server Services. Because Security and Software updates have not yet been applied, most of these optional services should be disabled.

The Time Zone, Network Time, and Date & Time panes (Figures 2-15, 2-16, and 2-17, respectively) allow you to choose a time zone, network time protocol (NTP) server, and date and time for your server. These choices are more pressing in Panther than Jaguar due to Panther's use of Kerberos, discussed in Chapter 8. Nonetheless, the configuration probably doesn't require a lot of explanation, since it is virtually identical to the configuration in Mac OS X's System Preferences application.

Finally, the Confirm Settings pane (Figure 2-18) allows you to review and back up your settings. In addition to saving the settings as plain text, Panther gives you the option of saving this data into two reusable formats that allow you to use it later for automatic server configuration—either as a configuration file or saved into the directory service. This development is so significant that it has its own section later in this chapter ("Automatic Server Configuration").

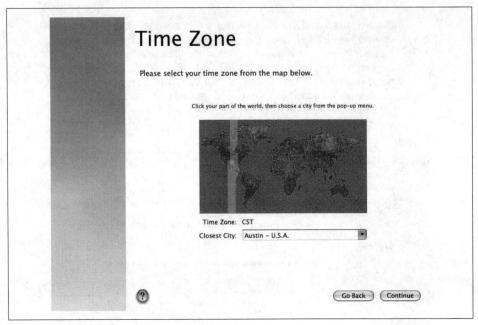

Figure 2-15. Choosing a time zone.

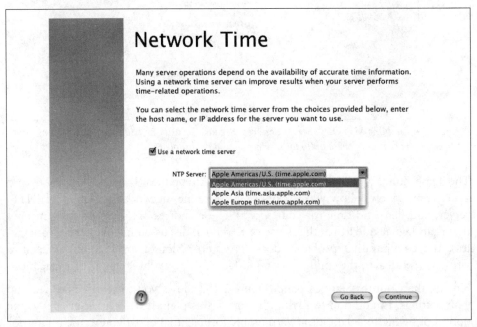

Figure 2-16. Specifying a Network Time Protocol (NTP) Server.

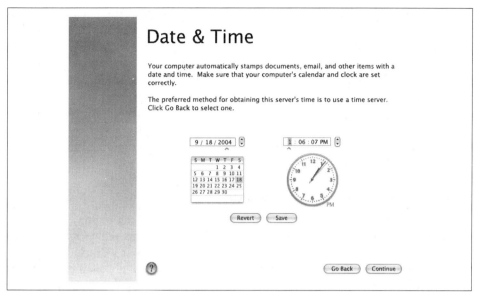

Figure 2-17. Setting the date and time. This interface is nearly identical to that in the Date & Time pane of the System Preferences application.

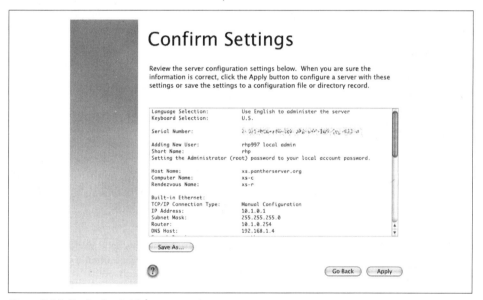

Figure 2-18. Reviewing initial server settings.

When you've reviewed all of your configuration choices you can feel free to click the Apply button. A dialog will appear letting you know your server is being configured. This might take some time, but when it's completed your server reboots to the *loginwindow*, configured and ready to manage.

This is installation and configuration in its simplest form. Those same graphical tools, however, can (with the exception of Disk Utility) also be run remotely, rather than by sitting at the server's console. For this purpose, Apple provides an Admin Tools install CD with each server. It installs several administrative tools, most of which we'll deal with in Chapter 3. The exception is Server Assistant, which is used to both install and initially configure the server.

The Admin Tools package also installs the */System/Library/ServerSetup* directory onto the client. From this directory, we'll use a number of utilities that aid us in the installation process.

Remote graphical installation and configuration

Server Assistant can be run from any Mac OS X workstation running system software that corresponds to the major OS version it is designed to work with. (This means that you cannot run Panther Server Setup from a Jaguar workstation.) Server Assistant's interface for installing Mac OS X Server is actually very similar to the user experience of local server installation at the console, the only real difference being that, since you're not at the console, you have to locate and log into the server you want to manage.

When run remotely, Server Assistant's initial pane (illustrated in Figure 2-19) presents the user with three choices:

- Install software on a remote server.
- Set up a remote server.
- Save setup information in a file or directory record.*

We'll address the latter two choices later in this chapter, since for now we're concerned with server installation, rather than configuration.

The Destination pane (Figure 2-20) allows you to specify a remote server for installation. Servers booted from CD on the local subnet will show up in the provided list, which is populated by a Rendezvous-like multicast DNS query (using the 224.0.0.1 Multicast Address rather than Rendezvous' 224.0.0.251).

The underlying command-line tool used to populate this pane (*/System/Library/ServerSetup/sa_srchr*) is installed with the Server Admin Tools package, and is documented in more depth later in this chapter.

Additionally, Panther's Server Assistant allows you to specify a server manually by entering its IP address (using the Server at IP Address radio button). Remember,

---

* Saving setup information to a file or directory record is a new option in Panther, and does not exist in the Jaguar version of Server Assistant.

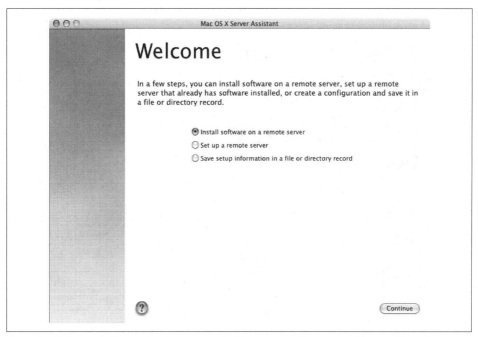

Figure 2-19. Running Server Assistant remotely. You are initially prompted to install, configure, or create a configuration record for Mac OS X Server.

when booted from CD, the server attempts to get an IP address via DHCP. If it cannot, it will assign itself an open IP out of the link-local range.* If a DHCP server is available, however, the server will obtain a lease. This could very well be a lease for a real-world, routable IP address, allowing for remote installation management between distant networks.

Taking things a step further: many DHCP servers are also capable of assigning addresses statically, based on the Mac address of the client. Taking advantage of this capability means that the server could always have a consistent IP address, both during and after installation—*rhp997.pantherserver.org* can always be reached at *rhp997.pantherserver.org*, even before its software is installed. This feature is particularly useful when managing a large number of servers (where re-installs are presumably more common than in smaller environments).

 Panther reduces this functionality somewhat, as its install typically requires multiple CDs. Unless you're using some kind of network install, someone usually has to visit the data center to feed the second CD to the server. Several methods for addressing this limitation are discussed later in this chapter.

---

* The 169.254 Class B subnet. This is standard behavior across Windows and versions of the Mac OS since 8.1.

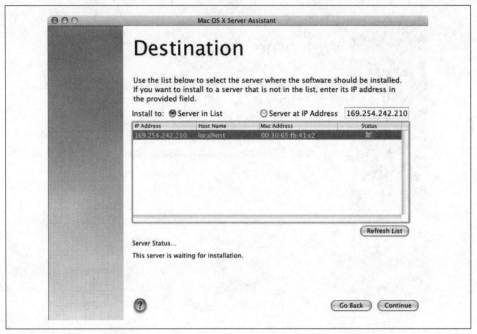

Figure 2-20. Choosing a target host for remote Server installation. Multiple hosts may be differentiated by their MAC address.

Once you've selected a host, you'll need to authenticate before you can manage its installation (making the server installation available anonymously would probably be considered a really bad idea) as shown in Figure 2-21. On all server hardware and most newer desktop models, the password will be the first eight characters of the serial number. In Panther, this is derived by the HeadlessStartup startup item using */System/Library/ServerSetup/SerialNumber*. In Jaguar, it uses a Perl script (*/System/Library/ServerSetup/SerialNumber.pl*) that uniquely illustrates harvesting data from the *ioreg* command. Older hardware will default to a password of *12345678*.

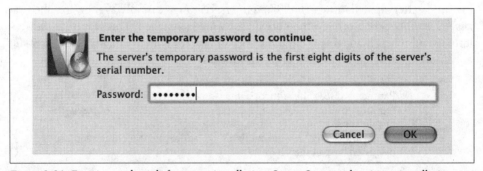

Figure 2-21. Entering credentials for server installation. Server Setup authenticates installation using an SSH connection. If the motherboard of your server has been replaced, the password might also be "Unknown" (that is, the word Unknown, followed by a space).

From this point on, a remote install is very similar to a local one, with choice of the install language, READMEs, licenses to agree to, disk choice, and install customizations. The user interface is somewhat different on a cosmetic level, but other than that it's similar enough that it doesn't warrant separate coverage. For details, refer to the "Local Installation" section earlier in this chapter.

> After the initial installation process has completed, the server will reboot off the hard drive. Due to the existence of */var/db/. AppleMultiCDInstall*, *loginwindow* launches the installer, which prompts you for Install CD 2. Assuming you're attempting a graphical install, there's really no way to avoid this. SSH isn't enabled until the *ServerEssentials.pkg* is installed, and it's on CD 2.

Once CD 2 has completed its install, the server will boot once more off its hard drive. This time, again due to decisions made by the *HeadlessStartup* startup item, it's ready for configuration. Installation is complete, but the server software doesn't have a serial number and any number of other things, from the server's network settings to service configurations, are also missing. Like remote installation, remote configuration is very similar to its local counterpart. Also like remote installation, the only real difference is the need to locate and log into the booted server. On starting Server Assistant, you should specifically choose "Set up a remote server" rather than "Install software on a remote server," as seen in Figure 2-22.

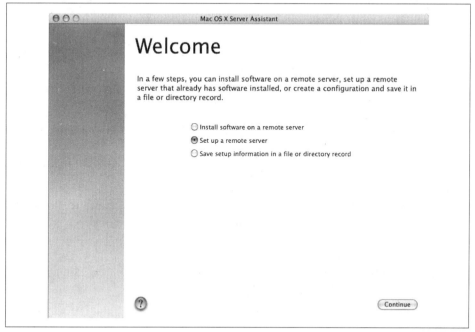

Figure 2-22. Choosing remote configuration using Server Assistant.

The resulting Destination pane (Figure 2-23) allows you to specify which server you want to configure. This data is, once again, populated by execution of the */System/ Library/ServerSetup/sa_srchr* command. For each server, you should populate the Password field by clicking once and entering the appropriate password.* It briefly echoes the clear text password as you type. This reveal is by design, in order to high-light the fact that the temporary passwords used for booting are only as secure as the purchase order for the server, the box it came in, or any other source of data that might have hardware serial numbers on it.

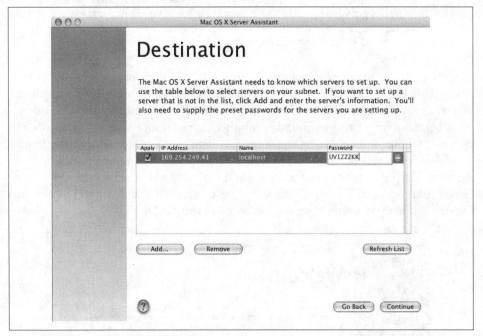

Figure 2-23. Choosing a server for configuration. The Server's password is the same one that was used during remote installation—the first eight characters of the Server's serial nuber, the string 12345678, or in rarer cases "Unknown".

After you've selected a server to configure, and after you've authenticated to it, the configuration procedure plays out exactly like it would locally, without even the cos-metic differences seen between local and remote installation. Refer to the earlier "Remote graphical installation and configuration" section for step-by-step guidance.

 Actual remote configuration is issued over an SSH connection to the remote server, typically executing the */System/Library/ServerSetup/ serversetup* utility, documented later in this chapter.

---

* Server setup uses the same password that software installation did—either the first eight characters of the serial number or the string "12345678", depending on how old your hardware is.

Command-Line Installation and Configuration

You might have already realized that there are some real limitations to the remote graphical installation. It's not currently possible to do any advanced disk management, such as RAID creation or repartitioning, using Server Assistant. Similarly, advanced partitioning schemes—mounting nonroot volumes in places other than */Volumes*—isn't supported in any graphical interface, much less by Server Assistant. Finally, note that Panther Server seems to have trouble installing graphically onto XServe Hardware RAID volumes.

 In Jaguar, the client managing the remote install must typically be on the same subnet as the server (since servers are discovered solely via multicast queries). In most environments, clients may not freely access the data center subnet, although widespread use of VLANS and multicast routing is making it more feasible.

The good news is that, since Server Assistant (both in the case of Server Installation and Configuration) simply uses SSH to log into the server and issue installation commands, a full, flexible, and very powerful installation environment is available to those who would choose to log into the server from an SSH client. This approach has the additional advantage of allowing for administration from non-Apple hosts.

Installation

The first task is locating the server. Once again, given some infrastructure work, this could be very trivial, since a DHCP server could be supplying the server a consistent address when booted from CD. If this isn't the case, however, you can still locate the server with the *sa_srchr* command (like several other utilities we've discussed, *sa_srchr* is in */System/Library/ServerSetup*). Its default usage is to search the multicast address 224.0.0.1:

```
ladmins-Computer:~ ladmin$ /System/Library/ServerSetup/sa_srchr 224.0.0.1
localhost#unknown#169.254.182.38#00:30:65:fb:41:c2#Mac OS X Server 10.
3#RDY4PkgInstall#2.0#512
```

Notice that the *sa_srchr* response contains a number of pieces of data, including a version number, the server's MAC address, and the fact that the machine is waiting for a package install (RDY4PkgInstall, rather than waiting to be configured). This is the exact method that Server Assistant uses to locate data for itself.

If you don't receive a response to you *sa_srchr* query, the corresponding server-side process, *sa_rspndr*, might not have started yet, so wait a couple of minutess and try again. Sometimes, *sa_rspndr* is running but just doesn't respond often or fast enough. If you feel this is the case, try a couple times in rapid succession.

In most shells, hitting the up arrow key allows you to see a history of the commands you've entered. Entering Return executes the command again, so Up Arrow → Return → Up Arrow → Return runs the command twice.

Once the server is located, you can log in as *root* via SSH. Root's password is the same one used to log into Server Assistant (the first eight characters of the serial number on newer hardware, the string *12345678* on older hardware).

In general, I avoid logging in as root, preferring instead use of *sudo* to facilitate root-privileged operations. It doesn't make sense, however, when booted from an installation CD, to include a special admin user whose only purpose is to run *sudo*. So the installation model Apple has pursued involves logging in as root, either transparently, using Server Assistant, or directly (as illustrated next), using an SSH client:

```
ladmins-Computer:~ ladmin$ ssh root@169.254.182.38
The authenticity of host '169.254.182.38 (169.254.182.38)' can't be established.
RSA key fingerprint is c4:ba:d1:39:e4:91:fa:38:83:c4:21:3f:ee:57:73:fa.
Are you sure you want to continue connecting (yes/no)? yes
Warning: Permanently added '169.254.182.38' (RSA) to the list of known hosts.
root@169.254.182.38's password:
-sh-2.05b#
```

Notice that I had to accept the public key generated by the CD-booted server before I could authenticate. Realize that a new SSH key-pair must be generated each time the server boots from CD, so your SSH client might warn you that the server's public key has changed. This change would normally be a security risk, but should be expected in the context of server installation.

Once logged in, you have access to a number of utilities to aid you with the install process. Instead of examining each one from a conceptual standpoint, we'll walk through a sample install to illustrate their uses. It's a good idea to first get an idea of the existing disk layout, using the *df* or *mount* command:

```
-sh-2.05b# df
Filesystem     512-blocks      Used    Avail Capacity  Mounted on
/dev/disk1s1s9    1323216   1242520    67464     95%    /
devfs                 203       203        0    100%    /dev
<volfs>              1024      1024        0    100%    /.vol
<synthfs>            1024      1024        0    100%    /Volumes
/dev/disk2            190        12      170      7%    /private/var/run
/dev/disk3           1926        42     1788      2%    /Library
/dev/disk4            190        34      148     19%    /private/tmp
/dev/disk5            190        54      128     30%    /private/var/db/netinfo
/dev/disk0s10     6284352   3855328  2429024     61%    /Volumes/pserver
/dev/disk0s12     6284352   2444816  3839536     39%    /Volumes/Untitled 2
/dev/disk0s14     6282336     37512  6244824      1%    /Volumes/Untitled 3
```

In Panther (and most other current Unix OSes), *df* has an –*h* flag that makes its output more palatable, showing the disk statistics in human-readable terms, rather than in 512- or 1,024-byte blocks. Also useful in this case is *diskutil*, which, among other things, has some great data-gathering capabilities, as shown in Example 2-4.

Example 2-4. Using diskutil to examine some characteristics of disk0. Notice that it was not necessary to specify the full path to the device file (/dev/disk0). In this case, diskutil's info command was run against a entire disk device. The disk's location (in this case, Bay 3 of an XServe G5) is also specified.

```
sh-2.05b# diskutil info disk0
Device Node:        /dev/disk0
  Device Identifier: disk0
  Mount Point:
  Volume Name:
Device Location: Bay 3
  Partition Type:   Apple_partition_scheme
  Bootable:         Not bootable
  Media Type:       Generic
  Protocol:         ATA
  SMART Status:     Verified

  Total Size:       76.7 GB
  Free Space:       0.0 B

  Read Only:        No
  Ejectable:        No
  OS 9 Drivers:     No
  Low Level Format: Not Supported
```

diskutil can also be run on specific partitions, or slices, as shown in Example 2-5.

Example 2-5. When run against a partition, diskutil's info command yields volume-specific data, such as filesystem type, mountpoint, and volume name.

```
xsg5:~ tadmin$ diskutil info disk0s3
    Device Node:        /dev/disk0s3
    Device Identifier: disk0s3
    Mount Point:        /
    Volume Name:        skeptic
    File System:        Journaled HFS+
    Journal size 8192 k at offset 0x267000
    Permissions:        Enabled
    Partition Type:     Apple_HFS
    Bootable:           Is bootable
    Media Type:         Generic
    Protocol:           ATA
    Total Size:         76.6 GB
    Free Space:         73.6 GB
    Read Only:          No
    Ejectable:          No
```

diskutil is a very important tool to learn. It vastly simplifies the work accomplished by much less sophisticated commands; literally, in the case of volume partitioning reducing a 30-step process to 1 command. Some folks would love to point out that *diskutil* doesn't run in single-user mode, and they are correct. *diskutil* depends on the Mac OS X's disk arbitration capabilities, provided by *autodiskmount* and *diskarbitrationd*, in Jaguar and Panther, respectively. To get *diskutil* to run in single-user mode in Jaguar, all we have to do is start *autodiskmount*:

```
/sbin/autodiskmount -va
```

Panther is a slightly different story. *diskarbitrationd*, which replaces *autodiskmount*, is not designed to be run on its own. Instead, it's started when needed by the *mach_init* process. Although *mach_init* is running in single-user mode, no services have been registered with it yet. This is normally done in */etc/rc*, which hasn't yet run (*/etc/rc. boot* is run in order to bring Mac OS X into single-user mode). During a normal boot, registration is accomplished with this command, which registers every service specified in the */etc/mach_init.d* directory; see Example 2-6.

Example 2-6. Enabling mach_init so that diskarbitrationd can be started on demand.

```
/usr/libexec/register_mach_bootstrap_servers /etc/mach_init.d
```

diskarbitrationd may then be started using SystemStarter's Disks startup item (*/System/ Library/StartupItems/Disks*); see Example 2-7.

Example 2-7. Using the SystemStarter command to start the Disks startup item. Using SystemStarter ensures that diskarbitrationd's prerequisites (namely, SecurityServer) are available.

```
SystemStarter start Disks
```

diskutil will then be available for use in single-user mode.

We're going to support a separate */Users* volume, so we'll use *diskutil* to partition the *root* volume (see Example 2-8). Right now it's not safe to mount filesystems required early at boot time in */etc/fstab*. *mach_init.d* does not start *diskarbitrationd* fast enough to guarantee that required filesystems will be mounted by the time they're needed, and the mount command (called in */etc/rc* in order to mount filesystems that are needed early in the boot process) doesn't have support for mounting volumes by their UUID.

A good example of this is */var*. *netinfod* is started in */etc/rc* shortly after *register_mach_bootstrap_servers* is run. *diskarbitrationd* hasn't yet had time to get */var* mounted, and as a consequence, *netinfod* can't find its data store(s) in */var/db/netinfo*. It is feasible to add a sleep statement to */etc/rc*, or a loop to sleep if */var/db/netinfo* is not available. However, this is far enough outside the realm of Apple's supported configuration that we'll stop short of advocating it. Additionally, note that other portions of */var* (such as */var/logs*) can be stored on nonroot partitions, as long as critical file shares are available early in the boot process. The result can be messy, so right now it's best to avoid storage of filesystem directories required during the boot process on nonroot partitions.

Example 2-8. Using diskutil to repartition disk0. Two volumes will be created, both HFS+. Diskutil knows how to unmount and properly manage disk0, so no additional work is needed.

```
-sh-2.05b# diskutil partitionDisk /dev/disk0 2 HFS+ xserver 3G HFS+ Users 6.1G
Started partitioning on disk disk0
Creating Partition Map                              5% ..
Formatting Disk                                     40% ..
Formatting Disk                                     100% ..

Finished partitioning on disk disk0
/dev/disk0
   #:               type name         size        identifier
   0:    Apple_partition_scheme      *9.4 GB      disk0
   1:    Apple_partition_map         31.5 KB      disk0s1
   2:    Apple_HFS xserver           2.9 GB       disk0s3
   3:    Apple_HFS Users             6.2 GB       disk0s5
```

diskutil's *partitionDrive* flag uses the following syntax:

```
diskutil partitionDrive <disk> <number of partitions> <1stpart-format label size>
<2nd-format label size> ...
```

We're installing onto the *xserver* volume, so we'll mount our *Users* volume below that. First we must unmount the Users volume from its current mountpoint (*/Volumes/Users*). See Example 2-9.

Example 2-9. Creating a mountpoint for the Users volume in preparation for installation. Usually in Mac OS X, we try to avoid using the mount command, since it doesn't notify the disk arbitration framework about what it's doing. In this case that's desirable, because, in the absence of an fstab file, all devices are mounted in /Volumes, which would defeat the purpose of our multivolume install.

```
-sh-2.05b# diskutil unmount /Volumes/Users
-sh-2.05b# mkdir /Volumes/xserver/User
-sh-2.05b# mount -t hfs /dev/disk0s5 /Volumes/xserver/Users
```

Because during installation /etc is on a read-only CD, it would be a lot of work to create a proper *fstab* file, and every *fstab* file would have to be specific to a particular machine and would have to incorporate data available only after the volumes on that machine had been created.

We'd like to have our external Xserve RAID in a RAID 50 configuration; that is, both banks striped together. *diskutil* comes through for us again, as shown in Example 2-10.

Example 2-10. Using diskutil to create a RAID 0 (stripe) array. The df command is then used to check the resulting mountpoint. Notice that when the diskutil command is run improperly, it provides a very detailed usage statement.

```
xsg5:/System/Library/StartupItems tadmin$ diskutil createRAID
Disk Utility Tool       ?2002-2003, Apple Computer, Inc.
Usage:  diskutil createRAID [mirror|stripe] setName
        filesystemName [disk Identifiers|device Nodes]
Create a RAID set.  Ownership of the affected disks is required.
Example: diskutil createRAID mirror MirrorDisk HFS+ disk disk2
Valid filesystems: "Journaled HFS+" "HFS+" "Case-sensitive HFS+" "HFS" "MS-DOS" "UFS"
xsg5:~ tadmin$ diskutil createRAID stripe raid00 "Case-sensitive HFS+" disk3 disk1

The RAID has been created successfully
xsg5:~ tadmin$ df -h /Volumes/raid00
Filesystem   Size   Used  Avail Capacity  Mounted on
/dev/disk4   701G   145M   701G    0%     /Volumes/raid00
```

With my disks prepared, I can run the install. In Jaguar, some installer packages required that the *installer* command be run from the root (/) directory. Although this detail is not required in Panther, I usually execute every install from the root of the file system in order to be safe:

```
cd /
```

We can then run the *installer* command, as shown in Example 2-11.

Example 2-11. Using the installer command to install Mac OS X Server. The package specified is OSInstall.mpkg, a metapackage that actually refers to several component packages.

```
/usr/sbin/installer –verbose –pkg /System/Installation/Packages/OSInstall.mpkg –target
/Volumes/xserver
```

The output is quite verbose, and the process should take about 30 minutes. Don't think that the first # you see in the output means that you've returned to the command prompt—the *installer* command uses the # character as a progress marker.

After the installation has completed, you'll need to create your own *fstab* file, so that our volumes are mounted in the right places on reboot. The first requirement is finding the volume's UUID (Universal Unique IDentifiers), so that it can create the *fstab* file. Remember, in Mac OS X, it's not guaranteed that *disk0* will always be *disk0*—it might be *disk1* on reboot. For this reason, I use volume UUIDs that are consistent between boots and even among different hosts where they happen to be mounted. See Example 2-12.

Example 2-12. Using hfs.util to locate the UUID of disk0s6 (the Users Volume). The UUID is everything starting with the 6 and ending with the 9. You can tell that everything after that is part of the shell prompt by examining the shell prompt on the next line and seeing that it starts with a dash. Once we're aware of the UUID, we can create the fstab file itself.

```
sh-2.05b# /System/Library/Filesystems/hfs.fs/hfs.util -k disk0s6
6CD2B2772B11ABC9-sh-2.05b#
-sh-2.05b#
```

The *fstab* file must then be created. Since it consists of a single line, the easiest method is to use the *echo* command, redirected to a file (see Example 2-13). Note that *vi* has trouble running when booted from CD—it likes to save to the wrong directory—so unless you're highly proficient with it, be very careful.

Example 2-13. Using the echo command to create an fstab file on the target volume.

```
-sh-2.05b# echo "UUID=4E0AF0BA61CBDB67    /Users  hfs     rw " >> /Volumes/xserver/private/
etc/fstab
```

Under most circumstances (including graphical installation), the Startup Disk would be changed and the server would be rebooted. When the machine comes up again, you probably will not be able to log in to it using SSH; as mentioned earlier, this is due to the fact that SSH is not enabled until after CD 2 has been installed. In order to avoid this dead end, we can complete the installation by copying the packages from CD 2 to the server before rebooting it. Because *ssh* is still enabled as long as we've booted from CD1, we can use the *scp* command to securely copy the installer files from our workstation to the server, as shown in Example 2-14.

Example 2-14. The scp command (executed from the client) can be used to securely copy the contents of install CD 2 to any server volume with enough space. Only a portion of the output (which is quite verbose) is shown here. Note the –r (recursive) flag, which enables the directory to be recursively copied.

```
ladmins-Computer:~ ladmin$ scp -r /Volumes/Mac\ OS\ X\ Server\ Install\ Disc\ 2
root@169.254.54.192:/Volumes/xserver/Users/Shared/disk2
root@169.254.54.192's password:
.DS_Store                                  100% 6148     2.2MB/s   00:00
Desktop DB                                 100% 2048     0.9KB/s   00:02
Desktop DF                                 100%    2     0.0KB/s   00:00
```

Once the copy is complete, we can use our SSH session to the server to run through the rest of the install process (Example 2-15). Be sure to first remove the *VolumeCheck* script from *MacOSXserverInstall.mpkg*; otherwise, the installer (designed to run when booted from the hard drive) will be unaware that it's on Panther and will exit.

Example 2-15. Using the installer command (on the server) to install the software from CD 2. Notice the workaround of deleting the VolumeCheck script from the installer's metapackage (.mpkg).

```
-sh-2.05b# cd /Volumes/xserver/Users/Shared/disk2/MacOSXserverInstall.mpkg
-sh-2.05b# rm Contents/Resources/VolumeCheck
-sh-2.05b# cd /
-sh-2.05b# /usr/sbin/installer -verbose -pkg /Volumes/xserver/Users/disk2/
MacOSXserverInstall.mpkg -target /Volumes/xserver
```

After the install has completed, you need to clear the *.AppleMultiCDInstall* cookie, so that *loginwindow* doesn't try to launch the Installer on reboot:

```
-sh-2.05b# cd /Volumes/xserver/var/db/
-sh-2.05b# mv .AppleMultiCDInstall bak-.AppleMultiCDInstall
```

Finally, after setting the server to boot from the hard drive, we're able to reboot and configure the fully installed server:

```
-sh-2.05b# /usr/sbin/bless -folder /Volumes/xserver/System/Library/CoreServices -
setOF
-sh-2.05b# reboot
Connection to 169.254.254.234 closed by remote host.
Connection to 169.254.254.234 closed.
ladmins-Computer:~ ladmin$
```

Server software is now installed, for all intents and purposes. Just as when working with the graphical installer, the server is in an unconfigured state. You'll need to configure it. And for reasons very similar to our study of the command-line install process, we'll be looking now at the command-line configuration process, noting especially the differences between Jaguar and Panther.

Command-line configuration

Command-line install-time configuration for Mac OS X Server has come a long way in Panther, especially as it essentially was not supported in Jaguar. Mostly, this process revolves around the *serversetup* and *systemsetup* commands, and the former wasn't documented in Jaguar, leaving a lot of guesswork to the administrator.

The first necessity is locating the server. Again, *sa_srchr* is the appropriate tool—see Example 2-16.

Example 2-16. Using sa_srchr, this time to locate servers that are ready for installation. Notice that the status of the server is RDY4Setup. This status alerts you that the software installation process has completed.

```
Big15:~ mab9718$ /System/Library/ServerSetup/sa_srchr 224.0.0.1
localhost#unknown#192.168.1.101#00:0a:95:90:5f:2c#Mac OS X Server 10.3#RDY4Setup#2.0#0
```

One of the things Apple has done in order to reduce Panther boot times is make SystemStarter much more asynchronous. So *loginwindow* is started as soon as all of its dependencies are met. In the meantime—especially during a server install—other startup Items are still churning away in the background. In fact, if you happen to be watching the server, it could take up to three or four minutes after Server Assistant's Welcome pane appears before *sa_responder* starts answering queries and *sshd* is ready to handle incoming requests. Be patient.

We can still *ssh* in with the same predefined password we used for the install phase (see Example 2-17).

Example 2-17. Using ssh to access the server located with the sa_srchr utility. Because the server is still unconfigured, the password is the same one used to pursue the installation process—generally either the first eight characters of the server's hardware serial number or the string 12345678.

```
crap:~ mab9718$ ssh root@192.168.1.101
root@192.168.1.101's password:
Last login: Mon Sep 27 11:38:39 2004 from 192.168.1.100
Welcome to Darwin!
```

And, if we're in Panther, we can pretty much immediately get to work. During a graphical configuration (regardless of whether it is locally or remotely controlled) after Server Assistant is finished querying the user for data, it doesn't actually configure the machine itself. Instead, it calls several command-line tools specifically engineered to set up the server for the first time. In Jaguar, these tools were largely undocumented, and the only way to use them was to watch in the server's process listing or examine them forensically. Luckily, in Panther they're better documented and, more importantly, supported.

The following procedure was developed by examining those tools as they did their work. Its example can be used as a recipe for configuration or as the basis for a trivial script that prompts the user for proper values and then invokes the proper commands and options to set the configuration. The listed tools are used in this section to complete a command-line configuration.

We've spoken about *process listings* a couple of times now without any real explanation. Basically, the names and a lot of data about all currently running processes are available to every user logged into a particular machine. You can see the process listing with the *ps* command. Some flags make the *ps* command a little more verbose, such as *ps axwww*, shows a wide-format listing of all running processes. For more information on using process listings to determine what's occurring on your machine, see Chapter 5.

1. Disable access to the restart and shutdown buttons from *loginwindow*, since this isn't appropriate on a server:

   ```
   localhost:~ root# /System/Library/ServerSetup/serversetup -
   setDisableRestartShutdown 1
   1
   ```

2. *SecureSSHD.sh* is a script that disables *ssh* version 1, leaving only version 2 enabled:

   ```
   localhost:~ root# sh /System/Library/ServerSetup/SecureSSHD.sh
   ```

3. Set the default language to English:

   ```
   localhost:~ root# /System/Library/ServerSetup/serversetup -setInstallLanguage
   English
   English
   ```

4. Set the keyboard mappings to U.S.:

   ```
   localhost:~ root# /System/Library/ServerSetup/serversetup -setKeyboardSelection 0
   0 U.S.
   0
   ```

5. Install the server serial number:

   ```
   localhost:~ root# /System/Library/ServerSetup/serversetup -setSerialNumber x-123-
   asd-456-fgh-789-jkl-101-zxc-112-v
   0
   ```

6. If desired, create the default FTP share points. This does not turn FTP on; it just creates the share point:

   ```
   localhost:~ root# /System/Library/ServerSetup/serversetup -createSharePointFTP
   0
   ```

7. Create an initial user; this will be the *admin* user:

   ```
   localhost:~ root# /System/Library/ServerSetup/serversetup -createUserWithIDIP
   "Local Admin" ladmin "apple" 501 169.254.236.249
   0
   ```

8. *AddDockForUID* creates the standard Mac OS X Server Dock for the user in question:

   ```
   localhost:~ root# perl /System/Library/ServerSetup/AddDockForUID.pl 501
   ```

9. Make sure that the user you created has the right keyboard preferences:

   ```
   localhost:~ root# /System/Library/ServerSetup/serversetup -copyKeyboardPref
   ladmin 003065fb41c2
   0
   ```

10. Set the administrator's primary language:

    ```
    localhost:~ root# /System/Library/ServerSetup/serversetup -setNewPrimaryLanguage
    ladmin English English
    0
    ```

11. This NetInfo directory needs to exist for the DHCP or NetBoot server:

    ```
    localhost:~ root# /System/Library/ServerSetup/serversetup -createNetInfoDir /
    config/dhcp/subnets
    0
    ```

12. We're not using a network time server, so the following line disables the NTP service option:

```
localhost:~ root# /System/Library/ServerSetup/serversetup -setNTPService 0 0
Local
0
```

13. Set the time zone to Mountain Time or the time zone where your server is located:

```
localhost:~ root# /usr/sbin/systemsetup -settimezone MST
Set TimeZone: MST
```

14. We want to wait to turn on any services (here we turn on, respectively, file services, print services, Apache, Samba, QuickTime Streaming Server, and the FTP server):

```
localhost:~ root# /System/Library/ServerSetup/serversetup -setAutoStartFile 0
0
localhost:~ root# /System/Library/ServerSetup/serversetup -setAutoStartPrint 0
Server Autostart Disable; status = 0
0
localhost:~ root# /System/Library/ServerSetup/serversetup -setAutoStartApache 0
0
localhost:~ root# /System/Library/ServerSetup/serversetup -setAutoStartSMB 0
0
localhost:~ root# /System/Library/ServerSetup/serversetup -setAutoStartQTSS 0
0
localhost:~ root# /System/Library/ServerSetup/serversetup -setAutoStartFTP 0
0
```

15. Server Assistant runs this command to stop FTP if it's already running for some reason. We've never seen FTP running at this point in the server's life, but since Apple does it, so do we:

```
localhost:~ root# /sbin/service FTP stop
```

16. Enable WatchDog:

```
localhost:~ root# /System/Library/ServerSetup/serversetup -setWatchDog 1
0
```

17. Set the Host, Computer, and Rendezvous names:

```
localhost:~ root# /System/Library/ServerSetup/serversetup -setHostName xserver
0
localhost:~ root# /System/Library/ServerSetup/serversetup -setComputerName
cxserver
0
localhost:~ root# /System/Library/ServerSetup/serversetup -setRendezvousName
rxserver
0
```

18. If you have created any share points with an earlier version of Mac OS X, you should migrate them:

```
localhost:~ root# /System/Library/ServerSetup/serversetup -migratesharepoint
0
```

19. We need to set the IP address manually before we can go any further:

```
localhost:~ root# /usr/sbin/networksetup -setmanual "Built-in Ethernet" 10.1.0.2
255.255.255.0 10.1.0.254
```

20. At this point, the IP address of the server changes, killing the login session, so you'll need to log in again. This time, however, you won't need *sa_rspndr* to log into the server, because you've just set the IP address:

```
Big15:~ mab9718$ ssh root@10.1.0.2
root@10.1.0.2's password:
Last login: Mon Sep 27 11:48:39 2004 from 192.168.1.100
Welcome to Darwin!
xserver:~ root#
```

21. Run the following command to set up *PasswordServer*; this is the same command used by the Server Assistant:

```
/usr/sbin/NeST -hostpasswordserver ladmin "apple" 10.10.0.3 > /dev/null
```

22. In this case we're not planning to enable Open Directory Server until later, so we choose a standalone install:

```
/usr/sbin/slapconfig -setstandalone
```

23. Turn off auto-login:

```
/System/Library/ServerSetup/serversetup -clearAutoLoginUser
```

24. This command sets up, but does not enable, the Cyrus mail delivery agent:

```
/usr/bin/su -m cyrus -c "/usr/bin/cyrus/tools/mkimap"
```

25. If you want to use MailMan, the mailing list manager, use the following command to enable it:

```
sh /System/Library/ServerSetup/SetupExtras/Mailman
```

26. Run a couple of scripts that bring firewall and web Mac OS X Server services into their default states:

```
/System/Library/ServerSetup/MigrationExtras/49_webconfigmigrator
/System/Library/ServerSetup/MigrationExtras/50_ipfwconfigmigrator
```

27. Next, create the token that lets *loginwindow* know that the server is configured:

```
touch /var/db/.AppleSetupDone
```

28. Currently, the *root* user has the default password assigned to it during installation boot. It's a very good idea to change root's password to something secure, or to disable *root* entirely. *root* can be disabled in NetInfo Manager, or by running the following commands:

```
sudo nicl / -create /users/root passwd "*"
sudo nicl / -destroy /users/root authentication_authority
```

As long as *.AppleSetupDone* exists, the server is ready to reboot and manage.

Server Scripts and Utilities

As you've seen, several portions of the installer architecture depend on the tools in the /System/Library/ServerSetup directory. A number of its tools are particularly useful outside the context of server installation, both for system administration and as an example of how to gather various system data using Perl and shell scripts. Here are several we haven't worked with yet:

Encoding
> A shell script that sets the code pages (encoding) for Mac OS X's Samba.

FixPostfix.pl
> A Perl script that configures Postfix to use the proper path to the deliver utility.

InstallEther.pl
> A Perl script that reports the IP address of the *en0* interface.

NetBoot
> A shell script used to set up the share points needed for NetBoot. In Jaguar, the *nbuitil* utility fulfilled this function. It's particularly useful for analysis of the *netboot* process.

Profile.pl
> A shell script that reads a number of system preferences and saves them to an output file. This too is very useful for examining real-world usages of useful system utilities like *serversetup*, *systemsetup*, *networksetup*, *slapconfig*, *dontHaveATool*, *NeST*, and *postconf*.

SetFile
> A command-line utility that sets the HFS attributes on a file, including creator, type, and invisibility.

UsersList
> A command-line utility used that lists all local users on a system.

VolumeInfo
> A command-line utility used to obtain various types of information about packages that are going to be installed and the volumes they might or might not be installed on.

GetServiceState
> A Perl script to retrieve the enabled/disabled state of *xinetd* managed services.

PushKey
> A shell script that runs *sa_srchr* to search for hosts, lets the user choose a host, and then sends a passphrase to that host to be stored at /System/Library/ServerSetup/Configured/POR.pass.

Automatic Server Configuration

We briefly mentioned earlier that Server Assistant—whether run locally or remotely—was able to create persistent configuration records that could be subsequently used to automatically configure other servers. In fact, you don't even have to be logged into a particular machine to do this. Server Assistant can be run from any supported platform, and one of its initial choices on startup is "Save setup information in a file or directory record," illustrated in Figure 2-24 .

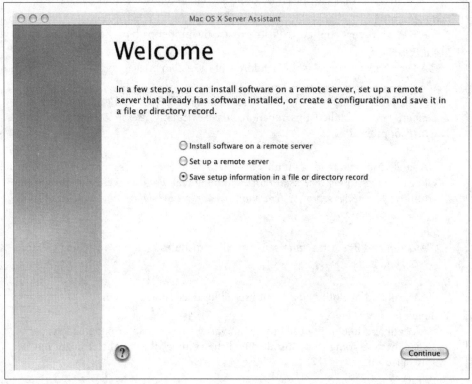

Figure 2-24. Using Server Assistant to save setup information into a file or directory record.

The process to gather the data for this record is identical to any graphical configuration using Server Assistant, so we won't cover it again; you're just running through the configuration options as if you were actually configuring a server. The real differences in the process show up after configuration is finished. When saving the output file, you have several choices. The first, seen in Figure 2-25, is to save to a text file. The result is basically just a record of your configuration choices, and has been around since 10.0. Its output looks something like this:

```
Language Selection:        Use English to administer the server
Keyboard Selection:        U.S.
```

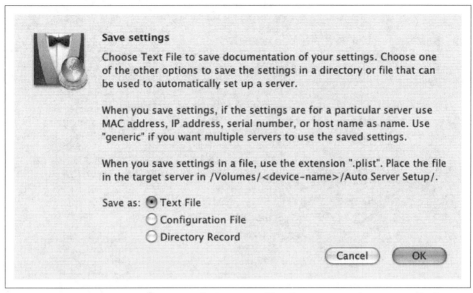

Figure 2-25. Saving server configuration data to a text file. This option produces a record of configuration choices, but does not allow for easy reuse of configuration data.

```
Adding New User:              admin
Short Name:                   admin
Setting the Administrator (root) password to your local account password.

Host Name:                    xserver
Computer Name:                cxserver
Rendezvous Name:              rxserver
```

The second, though, (seen in Figure 2-26) is new with Panther, allowing us to save the configuration for re-use with another host.

You'll next specify a name and save the file, as seen in Figure 2-27. You can then place it on any volume attached to the server—be it a USB keychain drive, an iPod, or some other device—in a top-level directory called "Auto Server Setup." When the server comes up for the first time after having been installed, the configuration file is automatically discovered and applied.

A third option allows for the configured record to be saved into a directory node, illustrated in Figure 2-28. This option does require that you have administrator privileges on that particular node, as indicated in Figure 2-29.

Using network-based Server Auto Configuration requires that the server being configured has access to the Directory Domain in which the configuration record is stored. This requirement presents a logistical difficulty, as the server is, at that point, unconfigured (the whole point of auto-configuration is to remedy this state). This chicken-and-egg problem can be addressed using Apple's DHCP-based LDAP configuration mechanism. When the server boots after its initial installation, it attempts to

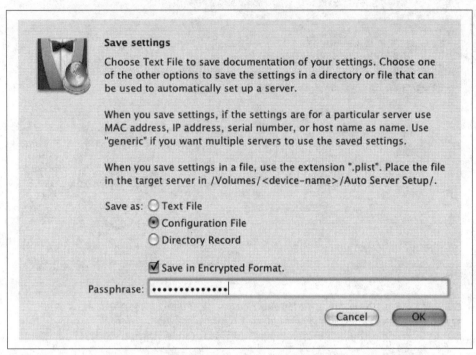

Figure 2-26. Saving configuration data from the Server Assistant to a configuration file. The data may optionally be encrypted, since it might be considered sensitive.

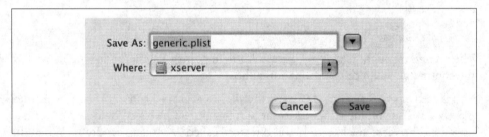

Figure 2-27. Saving a server configuration file.

retrieve a DHCP lease. If an LDAP URL is included in that DHCP reply, it will also attempt to use the specified directory domain, where presumably its Auto Configuration data is stored. For a more in-depth analysis, see Chapters 6 and 11.

In either case (saving the record to a file or to the directory), the actual record is a standard Apple *plist* file, made up of fairly human-readable XML that amounts to something similar to Example 2-18.

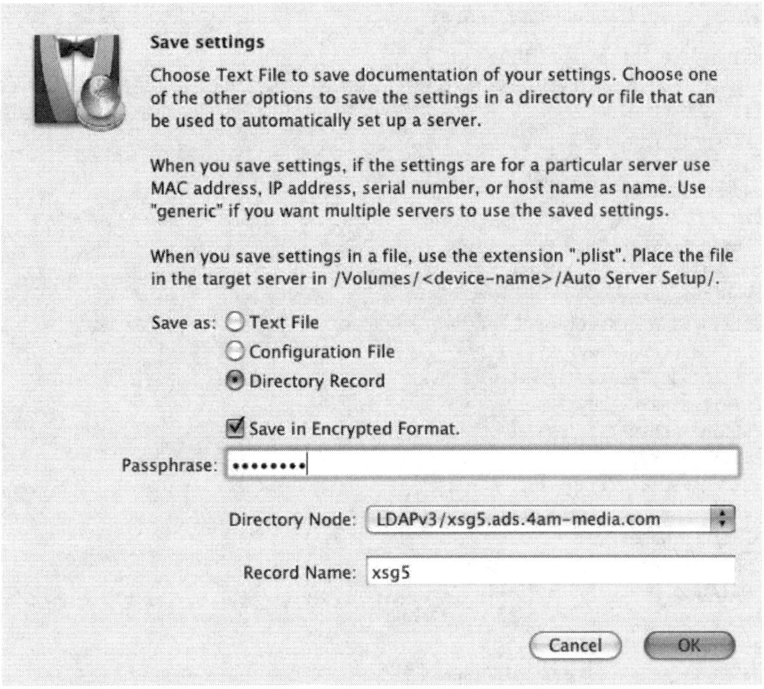

Save settings

Choose Text File to save documentation of your settings. Choose one of the other options to save the settings in a directory or file that can be used to automatically set up a server.

When you save settings, if the settings are for a particular server use MAC address, IP address, serial number, or host name as name. Use "generic" if you want multiple servers to use the saved settings.

When you save settings in a file, use the extension ".plist". Place the file in the target server in /Volumes/<device-name>/Auto Server Setup/.

Save as: ○ Text File
　　　　 ○ Configuration File
　　　　 ⦿ Directory Record

　　　　 ☑ Save in Encrypted Format.

Passphrase: ••••••••

Directory Node: LDAPv3/xsg5.ads.4am-media.com

Record Name: xsg5

Cancel　　OK

Figure 2-28. Saving Server Auto Configuration to a directory node. This save makes it available to every other computer accessing that directory domain.

Authentication

You need to log in as an adminisrator of the domain to save the server settings.

Domain: LDAPv3/xsg5.ads.4am-media.com

Name: nadmin

Password ••••

Cancel　　OK

Figure 2-29. In order to save a configuration to a directory domain, you must first authenticate as a user capable of writing to that domain.

Example 2-18. The first portion of an Auto Server Setup record. Only the first few lines are shown, since the entire record is somewhat lengthy.

```
<?xml version="1.0" encoding="UTF-8"?>
<!DOCTYPE plist PUBLIC "-//Apple Computer//DTD PLIST 1.0//EN" "http://www.apple.com/DTDs/
PropertyList-1.0.dtd">
<plist version="1.0">
<dict>
    <key>AdminUser</key>
    <dict>
        <key>exists</key>
        <false/>
        <key>name</key>
        <string>admin</string>
        <key>password</key>
        <string>apple</string>
        <key>realname</key>
        <string>admin</string>
        <key>uid</key>
        <string>501</string>
    </dict>
    <key>ComputerName</key>
    <string></string>
    <key>DS</key>
    <dict>
        <key>DSType</key>
        <string>3 - standalone</string>
    </dict>
    <key>HostName</key>
    <string></string>
    <key>InstallLanguage</key>
    <string>English</string>
    <key>Keyboard</key>
    <dict>
...
```

Remember that the data stored in this configuration record might be sensitive—especially since the administrator password for the server may be automatically configured. Both the configuration file and the directory record optionally allow for the actual configuration data to be encrypted. When the "Save in Encrypted Format" option is selected, the *openssl* utility encrypts the data with the cast5-cbc algorithm using the command shown in Example 2-19.

Example 2-19. Using the openssl command to encrypt a server Auto Configuration record.

```
openssl cast5-cbc –in /generic.plist -out  /generic.plist.encrypt –k apple
```

Server Assistant uses this syntax when the Save in Encrypted format box is chosen. In this example, the password supplied to encrypt the file was "apple". The command above was simply harvested out of the server's process listing (using the *ps* command) while the file was being exported. This means that the process of creating a secure configuration record should never be undertaken while anyone else has ssh access to the machine where that configuration is taking place—passwords are too easy to obtain.

Also realize the chicken-and-egg problem with encrypting anything. By definition, here, we're trying to automate the install process. Yet if the record is encrypted, either someone has to stand by to decrypt it, or the password for decryption has to be stored in plain text accessible to the server during the auto-configuration process. In this particular case, that file should also be (for file-based configuration) in the same "Auto Server Setup" directory, named similarly to the configuration in question, but with a suffix of *.pass*. So, if the configuration file were *xserver.encrypted*, its *.pass* file would be *xserve.pass*.

Of course, you could encrypt the password file, but then you're faced with the same dilemma: how do you automatically decrypt the password file so that you can use the password to decrypt the record? This is a common question in the realm of security and one we will return to several times in this book. For now, the best answer is to choose a happy medium. There's no question that records saved to a directory domain absolutely must be encrypted (or must be incomplete, not containing sensitive data). Open Directory is world-readable. Storing default usernames and passwords there would not be a good idea. File-based auto-configuration is less open to malicious intrusion, more flexible from a security standpoint, and far less scalable and convenient.

Behind the Scenes

In order for a server that's starting up for the first time to make use of an Automatic Setup configuration file, it has to first be able to find it. Responsible for that step in the installation process are the *HeadlessStartup* startup item and another utility in */System/Library/ServerSetup*, *sa_setup*, which is a shell script that does the following:

- Looks for files in the Auto Server Setup directory based on that server's MAC address, IP Address, unqualified (short) hostname, hardware serial number, fully qualified (long) hostname, or partial IP address—falling back to a *generic.plist* file if it exists.
- Uses the *dscl* tool to search Open Directory for a configuration record, based on the same naming mechanisms used to locate files (MAC address, IP address, etc.).
- Validates any records it finds.
- Decrypts records, if necessary.
- Runs setup based on the records its discovers.
- Runs some of the same post-install clean-up scripts.

The real crux of automatic configuration is that not all data can be both generalized and automatic. Two servers will usually not be exactly the same (with the same hostname, the same IP, and so on). There are several approaches to this issue, regardless of where you're storing the configuration data.

The first is simply to have a file or directory entry for each server. This option is quite flexible, since entries can be differentiated on the basis of MAC address, IP, or hostname. The downside is, of course, that you've got to manage multiple server configurations. In some cases, this management would be automated. The XML of the configuration entries is straightforward, and it would be easy, given a pre-existing tab-delineated file, to write a script that produced a standard server configuration, customized for each entry in the input file.

A second option for dealing with the differences in configuration options inherent to having multiple servers is to minimize them. There's nothing wrong with configuring a server to use DHCP, as long as it always gets the same address and hostname. In fact, this is the normal configuration for both Mac OS X Server and Windows 2003 server if you accept installation defaults, and as noted earlier, this trick can be especially useful during the installation and configuration process. Of course, this option does require some infrastructure work. A datafile corresponding MAC addresses to IP addresses still has to be maintained, regardless of whether your DHCP server is Mac OS X Server or is run on another platform.

A third and final option is to combine automated server setup with another, customized configuration script. Partial hostname or partial IP matches may be used to apply a single configuration to a number of servers, which can then each be customized using some other kind of logic, like a query against an SQL server. Mike Bombich has done a lot of similar work in the infrastructure of his NetRestore product, which can locate its configuration in Apple Remote Desktop 2's SQL database. See *http://www.bombich.com/software/wwdc_04.html* for more details.

Other Installation and Configuration Options

Server installation and configuration should not necessarily be limited solely to Apple's included installation tools. As flexible as they are, no vendor can feasibly meet the needs of every environment within which its products might be deployed. In practice, alternate tools from both Apple and third parties can be used to supplement or replace the standardized install process (this statement is well illustrated by the NetInstall example earlier in this chapter). In the interest of time and space, I cannot cover every aspect of every tool. Instead, the goal of this section is to provide the high points, information from which sane architectures may be customized for your environment and thoroughly tested.

Network Install

The simplest of these installation options eliminates the CD and runs the installation while booted from the network, using Apple's NetBoot technology. The installation process—other than booting the server from a NetBoot server—doesn't differ much from a CD-based install. The obvious benefit is being able to run an install without having to tote around a bunch of CDs. This benefit is counterbalanced by the necessity and added overhead of maintaining a NetBoot server and Network Installation Images.

 NetBoot as a component of Mac OS X Server is covered in Chapter 28.

Network Install is configured using Apple's Network Image Utility, pictured in Figure 2-30. Its use is straightforward, but it is not on the whole a friendly application, being subject occasionally to odd timeouts and unexpected and frustrating pauses. Nonetheless it has progressed remarkably since its introduction, and is now capable of exporting disks to and importing them from remote NetBoot servers (using *sftp*,which is enabled as a part of Mac OS X Server's default OpenSSH configuration).

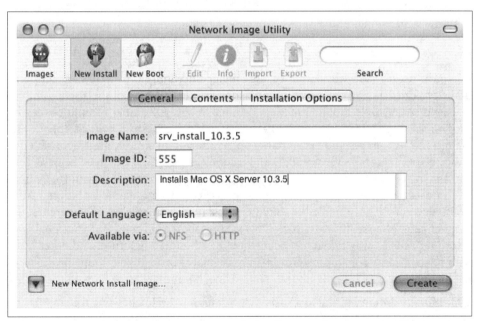

Figure 2-30. Creating a Mac OS X Server Network Install Image. If a CD is inserted, it is automatically listed under the Contents tab. ASR installs, described later, accept either a disk image or nonboot partitions as a source.

Network Install (as of 10.3.3) essentially supports two installation methods—a traditional, CD-like package install and a much faster (but less granular) Apple Software Restore (ASR)–based process. ASR has implications beyond Apple's Network Instalation infrastructure, and is covered in more depth next. Keep in mind that the primary difference in configuring the two methods is their source media. Since the package-based installation closely resembles a CD install, its source is typically a Mac OS X Server Install CD or DVD. ASR is more of a restoration process, and typically uses a fully installed OS as its source.

I use an automated, ASR-based Network Install in my office (coupled with Server Auto Configuration) to manage my testing environment.

Apple Software Restore

Apple Software Restore (or ASR) is a time-tested imaging technology first developed by Apple in the pre–Mac OS X days as a part of the manufacturing process. The thousands of machines leaving Apple's production lines all needed a specific, identical out-of-box experience. Enter Apple Software Restore, which takes a template disk image and applies it to a partition or disk. ASR-based products come in a number of flavors: graphical and command-line, Apple, and third-party. In every case, though, the ASR process largely consists of two distinct tasks—image creation and restoration.

Image creation

In typical usage, ASR utilities take a disk image and apply it to a destination partition—typically erasing that partition's existing contents. Much of the science of ASR management revolves around creating a source image. A number of utilities may be used—Disk Copy, diskutil, and Mike Bombich's NetRestore among them. The premise is both simple and powerful—you, as the administrator, are responsible for creating your perfect server installation. Its configuration can be as specific or as general as you want, ready for deployment as soon as it is restored or requiring extensive post-restoration processing (for instance using Apple's Server Auto Configuration). The point is to build an installation that precisely matches the requirements of your infrastructure. This is your source volume, and your goal is to record it in such a way that it can be restored to a hundred or a thousand other hosts with relative ease. This means creating a disk image, probably with one of the tools mentioned earlier.

Disk Image creation is located in Disk Utility under the Images menu item, via the New option, usually Image From a Folder or From a Device, the difference being primarily that choosing Image From a Folder allows you to image the running OS, whereas imaging from a device requires you to boot from something other than the source.

Before creating an image, you should consider deleting several volatile files from the source. Since these files are usually not preserved through boots, there's no reason to preserve them as a part of an image. Because many of them (for instance, swap files) are required for booting, though, this is not something you can pursue if your source is a running operating system, and hence isn't feasible unless you're imaging from a device.

- */var/vm/swapfile**: The operating system's swap (virtual memory) files are boot-specific and can be large. There's no reason to preserve them.
- */var/run*: This directory is purged on reboot, so it doesn't make sense to add bloat to a source image by preserving it.
- */Library/Caches*: Various applications cache data here, and it can become quite large.

The imaging process is illustrated in Figure 2-31. In this case, you are booting from something other than the source and saving the resulting *.dmg* file to a third volume.

Once your image is perfected, however, it must be processed (enabled for use with ASR) using Disk Utility's Scan Image for Restore option (seen in Figure 2-32) or the *asr* utility's *–imagescan* flag.

Image restoration

Once an image is created and scanned, it is ready for restoration. This image was created using the Image From Device option available from the New selection under the Images menu. It is being saved to a different partition (HFS-CS_Vol). The Images menu is not available when booted from CD. Notice that the read / write Image Format is chosen; choosing Compressed will result in a much smaller disk image (very helpful when installing over a network) but will take a lot longer. Disk Utility's Restore tab (illustrated in Figure 2-33) is by far the simplest interface for this task (although the *asr* utility can be easily leveraged, and is optimal for scripting).

You'll need to boot from something other than the target disk (restoring over the OS that you are running is probably a bad idea) but other than that, the process is very simple.

radmind

radmind, which stands for remote administration daemon, is a suite of Unix command-line tools designed to remotely administer the filesystems of multiple Unix machines. It was developed at the University of Michigan by the Research Systems Unix Group (RSUG, *http://rsug.itd.umich.edu*). Its Unix roots are extremely administration-friendly, and it is much more appropriate for architecturally large-scale management than Apple's built-in tools (which tend to be focused on smaller, less

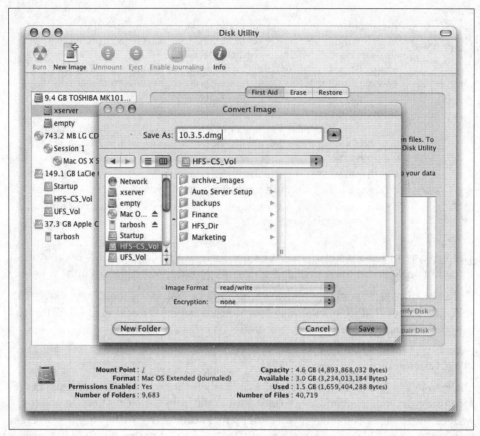

Figure 2-31. Disk Utility is an easy (and convenient) option for creation of disk images for use with ASR.

Figure 2-32. Disk Utility's Scan Image for Restore dialog is accessed using the Images menu. The scan process adds checksumming data to the source image, allowing it to be reliable restored.

managed environments). These same roots for a long time made *radmind* less than palatable for command line–averse administrators. More recently, the graphical *radmind* Assistant has introduced this powerful utility to a much wider audience.

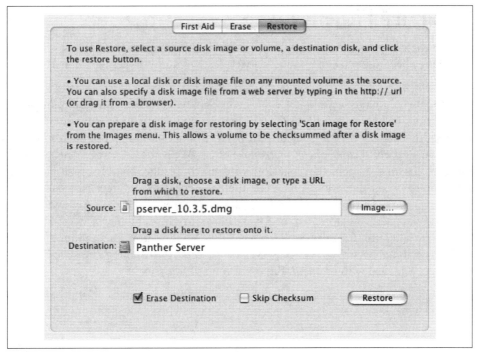

Figure 2-33. Disk Utility's Restore tab is straightforward. It expects a source (image), a destination volume, and options regarding erasure and checksumming. In this case the pserver_10.3.5 image is being restored to the Panther Server Volume.

radmind's strength is its granularity. It supports a file-level checksum that allows you to ensure that the right version of every file is installed at the right time. *radmind* essentially allows for complete control over the filesystem—especially useful in the context of large-scale server management, such as with computational clusters. This control is accomplished using a "Transcript," which is, at a basic level, simply a list of those files. Multiple Transcripts may be applied on top of one another, so that (for instance) a GraphicsApps Transcript could be applied on top of a BaseLab Transcript—resulting in a functionally changed lab.

 A second type of file (called a *Command* file) is typically used to describe a single loadset, which might be made up of a number of Transcripts.

radmind changes may also be rolled back—a comforting thought when applying the newest Software Update to a large group of critical servers. An added bonus is its cross-platform nature. *radmind* is just as capable of managing Linux and Solaris hosts as it is managing Mac OS X. It also supports SSL (for both encryption and client-server verification) and user-level authentication using PAM

Putting It All Together

Most of these tools conform to a common principal—the more granular they are, the slower they become, since that granularity typically requires a file-by-file analysis. So, in most cases several solutions work best together.

When managing large-scale Mac OS X Server deployments, I like to use *radmind* in conjunction with some sort of ASR-based process and Server Auto Configuration. In the past, this usually meant using a third-party product like Mike Bombich's NetRestore (*www.bombich.com/sofware/netrestore.html*). With the advent of ASR-enabled Network Installs, though, that has slowly begun to change. NetRestore is probably still a more powerful option, but given the time constraints often associated with consulting work, I prefer to use built-in tools whenever feasible. At my last cluster installation, I used an automated, ASR-based Network Install to lay down the bulk of the system software. Coupled with Server Auto Configuration, this produced working and well-managed Mac OS X Servers. Fine-tuning (installing site-specific software) was achieved with *radmind*. I'm really fond of this trio.

## CHAPTER 3

Server Management Tools

Management tools can make or break an integrated server product, especially one from Apple. From user creation to the management of share points and services, the maintenance of a server can be quite onerous. Add to that the complexity and breadth of a product like Mac OS X Server—plus its wide feature set and audience, and the diversity of its deployment scenarios—and the outlook only becomes more daunting.

To help surmount this challenge, Apple provides a variety of graphical and command-line tools designed to simplify the deployment and management of Mac OS X Server. This chapter introduces and dissects those tools along with the underlying protocols and technologies that make them possible. Along the way, I'll discuss best practices, security, logistical approaches appropriate for various deployed environments, and practical tips for day-to-day server management.

 A warning about nearly all of Apple's graphical management tools: most allow users to save the administrator's password to the Keychain. This is surely convenient, but beware: it also makes the administrator's machine a valuable target for malicious parties, particularly if that machine happens to be a laptop and if the administrator manages multiple servers. Even though Keychain itself is very secure, adding another link in the security chain necessarily also adds another feasible point of failure. If you do choose to make use of this feature, be sure to protect your Keychain and login passwords accordingly.

Graphical Tools

The user experience is Apple's temple. For a good portion of the company's history, it was (justifiably) the biggest reason behind their existence, and Apple has in many ways continued to revolutionize the user experience with each OS release. Server management, though, has its own set of requirements that are wholly different from those of home users wishing to better organize their digital life. Although Apple's server tools have generally been very simple and easy to use, they have not always scaled up to complex or large deployments as well as the underlying OS has. Toward these ends, Panther Server is a solid step in the right direction, and although it isn't perfect, it provides by far the most scalable management interface Apple has ever presented.

We'll start by analyzing Panther's simplified, reduced toolset. Rather than examining each option of each tool in great depth, we'll instead focus on the tool's high-level functions, revisiting its specific capabilities later, when our focus is the protocols and technologies those tools manage.

One very important aspect of all of these tools is their ability to be run remotely. Mac OS X Server is, by design, a remotely managed platform; every tool we'll look at (even when run locally) connects over TCP/IP to one of several backend daemons running on the server. Given the proper network access, this means that Mac OS X Server can be managed graphically from anywhere, as long as you have access to another Mac. Remote management is so important to Apple that, beginning with the Xserve G5, Apple's servers no longer shipped with a video card as a standard option.

Panther moves a step further, with command-line equivalents to many of these functions. This design takes remote management to another level, since the server can now, given proper network access, be managed remotely from any platform using an *ssh* client. The next logical step is a web interface to these functions, allowing for platform agnosticism in graphical management as well. Apple has not, as of yet, indicated that such a feature is forthcoming, although many server management tools do use HTTP as an underlying protocol.

Workgroup Manager

Workgroup Manager made its first appearance in Jaguar, when the addition of Managed Client settings made account management a task too complex for the minimal 10.0–10.1-era Server Admin application. Its tasks, at a general level, include:

Account management
   The creation and management of user, group, and machine accounts

Preference management (Managed Client settings)
   User experience restrictions and standardized behaviors enforced on user, group, and machine accounts

Share point management
   Server shares (portions of the filesystem made available over server protocols like SMB and AFP), including protocol-specific settings for those shares

Musical Chairs

Mac OS X Server's management applications have had a little bit of an identity crisis over the years. Mac OS X 10.0 and 10.1 featured a fairly consistent tool called Server Admin, which had obvious roots in AppleShare IP's Mac OS Server Admin. Jaguar Server, however, divided Server Admin's features into three applications:

- Workgroup Manager, which also featured Mac OS X managed-client settings (think Macintosh Manager)
- Server Settings, which closely resembled 10.0's and 10.1's Server Admin
- Server Status, which focused on the monitoring of server services and server logs

Mac OS X Server 10.2 also brought Server Monitor, the Xserve-specific hardware monitoring client.

Panther Server (10.3) sports consolidation and much-welcomed simplification. Workgroup Manager is still around, primarily for account and share-point management, and Server Admin has made a return, at least in name. Instead of its minimal, AppleShare-IP-inspired former self, however, it's a full-screen application that encompasses all of Server Status's monitoring features as well.

You might have noticed that both accounts and preferences can actually be managed for three different kinds of objects: users, groups, and groups of computers. Tuck this in the back of your mind; it becomes important later.

Account management

When you initially authenticate as a member of the server's admin group, Workgroup Manager opens in its Account Management mode, seen in Figure 3-1. Its overall function isn't overly complex: it allows you to create and manage users, groups, and computer accounts, each according to the tab that's selected in the Accounts pane.

Data entry fields on the right side of Workgroup Manager's Account Entry interface adjust contextually to the type of account (User, Group, or Computer List) being managed, allowing the administrator to modify the specific settings of the account in question. Accounts of any type may be searched using a variety of metrics in the Filter field (identified by its magnifying glass icon) above the list of accounts in the left pane of the interface. Specific options are documented in Figure 3-2.

In any case, keep in mind that manual addition of any sort of account doesn't really scale. Importing Users, Groups, and Computer Lists is covered in more depth in Chapter 4.

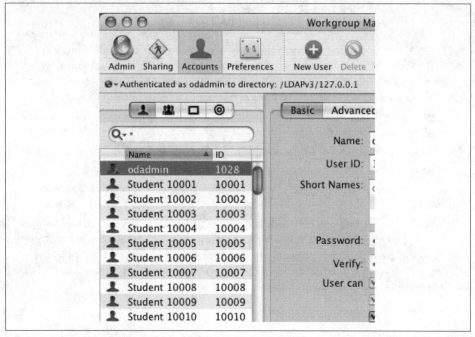

Figure 3-1. When the Accounts button is active, administrators are given a choice of User, Group, or Computer List management.

Creating Users

On a small scale, user creation is relatively simple. From Workgroup Manager's User account management interface, simply click on the New User button in the Tool Bar. The resulting interface (the Basic tab of the new user record) allows for the entry of minimal user data: Name, numerical User ID, Short Name, Password, and administrative rights. If these fields are populated, a user record—albeit a minimal one—will be saved into the current working directory domain.

Also of interest, though, are the Advanced, Groups, and Home tabbed sections of the new user record (Mail, Print, and Windows options are discussed in their respective chapters).

The Advanced tab, seen in Figure 3-3, allows access to a set of largely unrelated options: simultaneous login, login shell, Password Type, and policies along with Comments and Keywords.

The simultaneous login checkbox toggles a true or false value on a key in the user record's MCXFlags attribute that is literally called *simultaneous_login_enabled*. The value of MCXFlags can be viewed using the *dscl* command, as in Example 3-1.

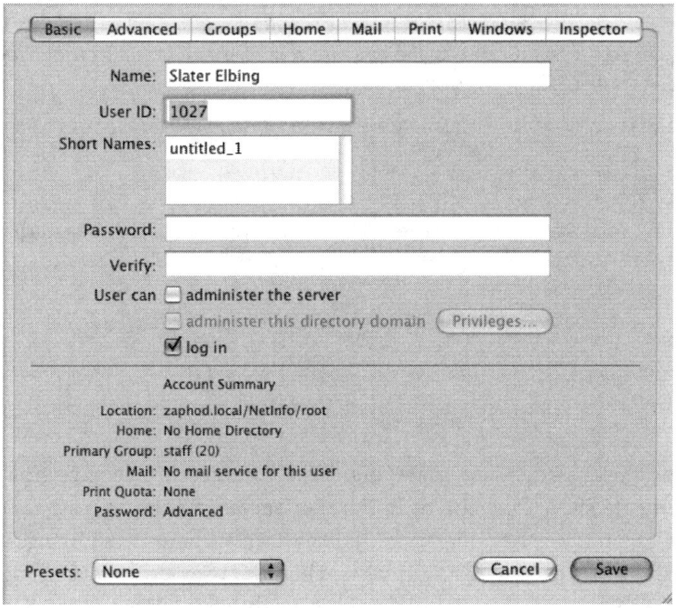

Figure 3-2. Workgroup Manager's interface for adding basic user data. Notice that multiple short names may be added to a single account. This capability is mostly applicable to Mail services, and is discussed in more depth in Chapter 22.

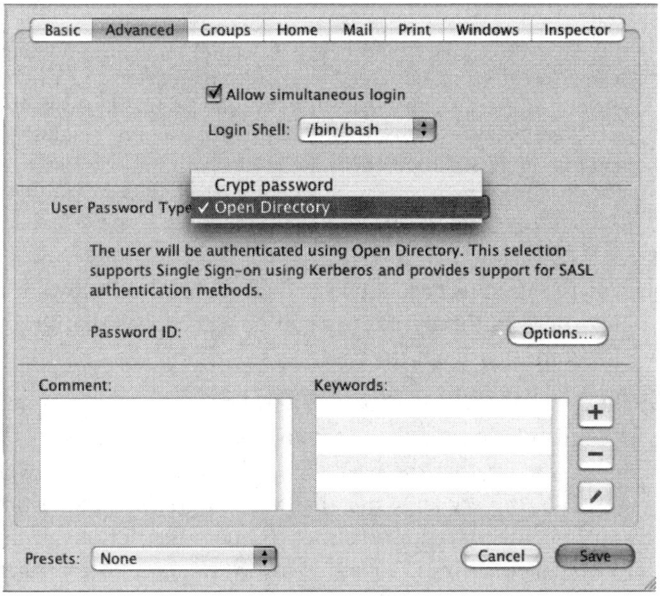

Figure 3-3. The Advanced pane of Workgroup Manager's user management interface. In general, "Advanced" in Mac OS X Server means "stuff that doesn't belong in other categories."

Example 3-1. Using the dscl command to remotely view the user Dolt's MCXFlags. Be aware that MCXFlags may contain other data in addition to the simultaneous login flag, and that this is a fairly simple example. In 10.3.5, simultaneous_login_enabled applies to desktop (console) logins and not to log-ins via services like SSH, FTP, AFP, or SMB.

```
big15:~ mab9718$ dscl -u odadm -p g5.4am-media.com -read /LDAPv3/127.0.0.1/Users/dolt
MCXFlags
Password:
MCXFlags: <?xml version="1.0" encoding="UTF-8"?>
<!DOCTYPE plist PUBLIC "-//Apple Computer//DTD PLIST 1.0//EN" "http://www.apple.com/DTDs/
PropertyList-1.0.dtd">
<plist version="1.0">
<dict>
        <key>simultaneous_login_enabled</key>
        <false/>
</dict>
</plist>
```

Password type, discussed in far more depth in Chapter 8, specifies how the User's authentication data should be stored. In Panther Server, most users should have a Password Type of Open Directory, meaning that they are authenticated using Apple's Password Server and in some cases (specifically, when the user exists in an Open Directory shared domain), Kerberos. The one exception to this tendency is the root user in the local domain, who has a password type of Shadow Hash. Users with Open Directory passwords will also have an additional options button in the Advanced pane of their user record. This button, used to enforce per-user password policies (such as length restriction), is also also discussed in more depth in Chapter 8.

Crypt refers to a legacy (and largely insecure) method of authentication that involved storage of a weakly encrypted form of the user's password in the directory (generally NetInfo or LDAP) itself. Workgroup Manager won't create an encrypted password. Shadow Hash refers to a more secure method that stores both NTLMv1 and SHA1 hashes of the user's password in a root-readable location on the filesystem (*/var/db/shadow/hash*).

The Groups tab of the user record, illustrated in Figure 3-4, allows the user to be added to multiple groups; although the user interface implies that groups are being added to the user record, this is not the case.

By clicking on the + icon next to the Other Groups pane, you can access a list of groups from any of the directory nodes that your server has access to. These groups can then be added to the list that the user should belong to. This drawer interface is illustrated in Figure 3-5. In very large installations, all groups in a particular domain might not necessarily be displayed, due either to query restrictions in the domain or your Workgroup Manager settings. To allow for more granular management, Apple has provided a filter interface identical to the one in the Account List pane, described earlier.

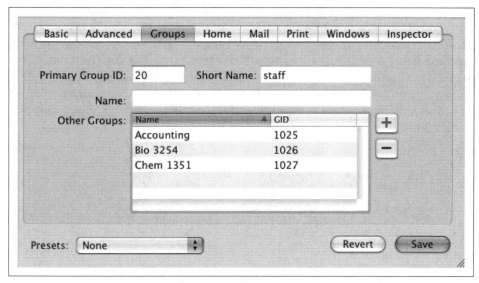

Figure 3-4. The Groups pane in Workgroup Manager's user management interface.

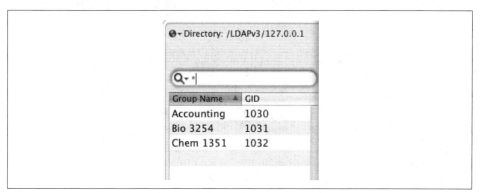

Figure 3-5. Workgroup Manager's group selection drawer. Note the Filter field, identical in functionality to the one in the Account List interface (discussed earlier in this chapter).

Keep in mind that in Mac OS X, users can belong to up to 16 groups (generally their primary group and 15 others) and even though Workgroup Manager will allow you to access more, Mac OS X will not recognize them all.

The Home tab, illustrated in Figure 3-6, allows the location of users' home directories to be specified. While not strictly required for all server services (mail services, for example, do not require the user to have his own home directory), home directories are generally a good idea, offering both a private area for file storage and support for more advanced features, like network accounts.

In their most basic incarnation—supporting a local, rather than a shared domain—management of home directories is fairly straightforward. The administrator merely specifies a Share Point (as defined in Workgroup Manager's Sharing section, described later in this chapter) under which the user's home directory should be located. Once saved, this data is stored as a file system path (such as */Users/jdoe*) in the user record's *NFSHomeDirectory* attribute, and the home directory is created upon first AFP logon. More complex scenarios, involving Network Home Directories and user quotas, are discussed in Chapter 14.

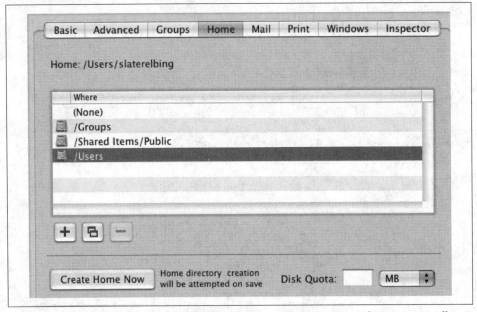

Figure 3-6. The Home pane of a user record in Workgroup Manager. Home directories, usually created on first AFP login, may optionally be created immediately—if the Server that Workgroup Manager is managing is also the server on which the user's home directory exists—by clicking the Create Home Now button.

Once again, note that this treatment of user creation is designed to be rather general, and that service-specific (Mail, Print, and Windows) aspects of the user record are discussed in their respective Chapters. In any case, nearly without exception, the function of the user creation interface is conceptually very simple; it adds and manages attributes to the user's account.

Creating Groups

Group creation, like user creation, is simple on a small scale, and easily managed in Workgroup Manager's interface. It is accomplished by accessing the Groups tab in Workgroup Manager's Accounts section. The initial interface can be seen in Figure 3-7.

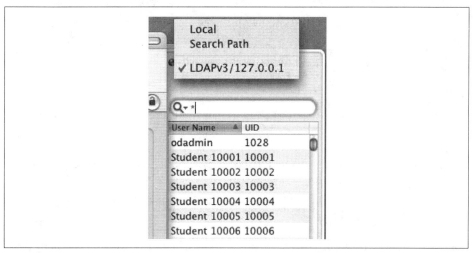

Figure 3-7. Workgroup Manager's interface for managing group membership.

This interface, of course, allows users to be added to the group account being managed. When clicked, the + icon (to the right of the Members: pane) reveals a drawer (pictured in Figure 3-8) from which any user in any available domain can be picked.

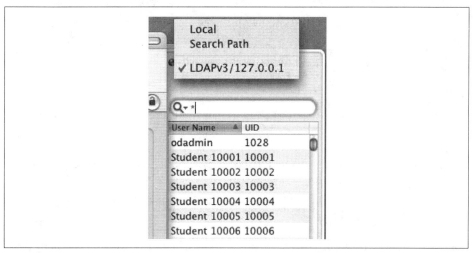

Figure 3-8. The User selection drawer in Workgroup Manager's Group Management interface. Once again, since all users might not be visible, Apple has provided a search field, allowing certain users to be filtered and more granularly managed.

Also available in Workgroup Manager's Group management interface is an option (pictured in Figure 3-9) for specification of a Group Folder, a shared file storage area for that group. The location of the Group Folder may either be chosen from available automounted share points or specified manually by clicking on the + button at the lower lefthand corner of the share selection window.

 For a more thorough analysis of automatically mounted sharepoints (or automounts) see Chapter 14.

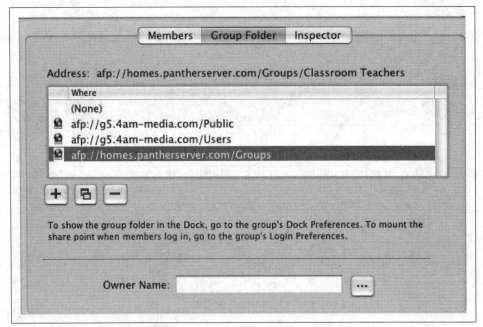

Figure 3-9. Choosing a Group Folder for a group. This data is added to the Group record, and is stored in its HomeDirectory attribute.

Group Folders are usually employed in concert with shared directory domains and Managed Client settings, discussed briefly in Chapter 6.

Creating Computer Lists

Computer Lists, which are mostly used to support Mac OS X managed client policies, can also be managed in the Accounts section of Workgroup Manager. Computer Lists are functionally a lot like groups, except that rather than maintaining a list of user accounts, they maintain a list of computers. They have little application outside of a shared Open Directory domain.

Client Management is covered in more depth in Part VII.

Ironically though, there is no separate interface for creating Computer Accounts—they are added as a part of the Computer List creation interface seen in Figure 3-10. Whenever a computer is added to a Computer List, an account is automatically created for it.

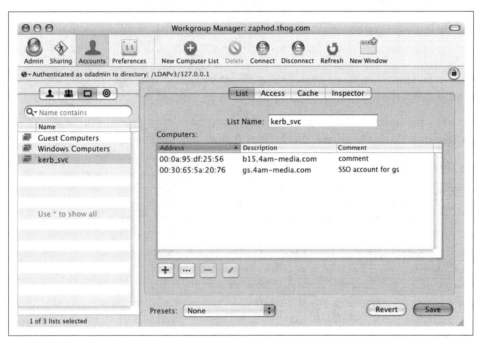

Figure 3-10. *Workgroup Manager's interface for managing Computer Lists. The Lists themselves, somewhat like Groups, appear in the left pane.*

New lists are created using the New Computer List button. This results in an empty, untitled Computer List. Once it is named and saved, computers may be added using either the + (add) or ... (browse) buttons located under the Computers pane. The former triggers the manual entry dialog illustrated in Figure 3-11. This somewhat cumbersome interface requires the MAC address of the machine in question to be typed or pasted into the Address field. This process obviously does not scale—its unlikely that entering 1000 MAC addresses manually would ever be considered a good idea—so Apple provides the browse interface, shown in Figure 3-12.

Initiation of a browse request initiates a Rendezvous (or Zeroconf) query for *_workstation._tcp.local* entities. From this interface, machines on the network

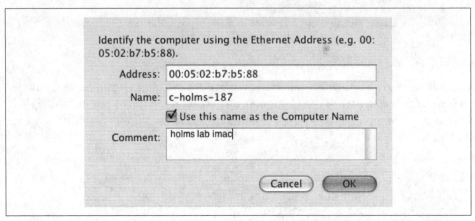

Figure 3-11. Manually adding a computer to a Computer List. Restrictions on the Address field ensure a properly formatted MAC Address.

local to the administrative computer (the host on which Workgroup Manager is being executed) can be added, one by one, to a particular Computer List.

 Multiple selection of computer accounts did not come about until 10.3.5. Although multiple computers could previously be selected in the browse interface, only one could be added at a time. This behavior (a bug) resurfaces periodically in minor releases of Panther.

Both of these methods are rather limited—manual input because it is extremely slow, and browsing because it is mostly local in scope and does not allow access to hosts that are not accessible via Rendezvous (generally because they are not on the same network segment) from the administrative workstation. Because of this, and since even rather small organizations often support hundreds of clients, it is generally best to add this data in a systematic way, using some kind of bulk import. One such method, using the *dsimport* (formerly *dsimportexport*) command-line tool, is demonstrated in Chapter 4.

Managing Users: Comments and Keywords

Organization is one of the foremost goals of IT infrastructures, and little proves as difficult to manage as user accounts. Once they're added, they sometimes need to be managed in bulk, if for no other reason than to delete them or assign them home directories—all students in a particular graduating class, for instance, might need to have their home directory assigned to a particular server or share point. Especially as the number of accounts increases, this is easier said than done. Supporting this goal are two user attributes specifically implemented to facilitate more granular management of user accounts: Comments and Keywords. Both may be set graphically in the Advanced pane of any user record in Workgroup Manager, as pictured in Figure 3-13.

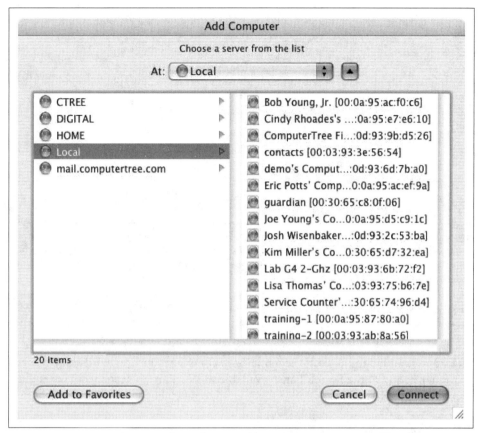

Figure 3-12. *Using Rendezvous to locate hosts to add to a Computer List. A computer account is created for each machine added to a list.*

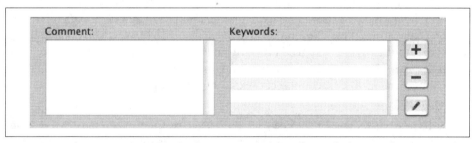

Figure 3-13. *The Comment and Keyword components of the Advanced tab in Workgroup Manager's User management interface.*

Comments are simply entered into the user's Comment field. Keywords, on the other hand, must be created (using the pencil button seen in the lower righthand corner of Figure 3-13) before they may be applied to a user. This process can be seen in Figure 3-14.

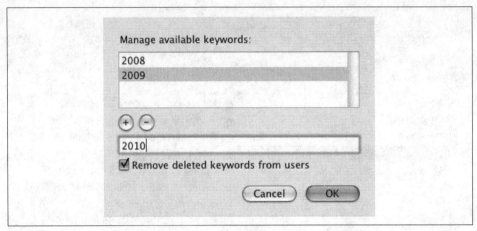

Figure 3-14. Adding keywords to a domain. Ironically enough, even though these comments are global in nature and may be subsequently assigned to any user, they are managed in a user-specific tab in Workgroup Manager's user management interface. Keywords are stored at /Config/User\ Keywords in whatever domain they are added to.

Once keywords are added to the domain in question, they may be assigned to a user back in the Advanced pane, using the + button seen in the upper right-hand corner of Figure 3-13. Clicking this button results in the selection dialog seen in Figure 3-15.

After they're added to the user's account, both comments and keywords may be used as a Filter in any of the Search Panes available in Workgroup Manager. This is illustrated in Figure 3-16.

Preference management

In addition to managing account data (in the form of Users, Groups, and Computer Lists), Workgroup Manager is also capable of administering Managed Client data, called Preferences in the user interface. This capability is managed in the Preferences section of the application, the icon for which (a double light switch) is located in the Menu Bar, to the right of the Accounts button. By accessing it you can gain access to its Preferences Management functions, as shown in Figure 3-17. Notice that Preference Management, like Accounts, can exist on three separate levels: the User, the Group, and the Computer List.

This interface allows you to enforce user experience restrictions on users logged into machines in the directory domain in question. Depending on the tab selected, these restrictions can be based on either their own account, the groups they belong to, or the machine they've logged into.

 Managed Client data (often called MCX, for Managed Client, Mac OS X) is stored as an XML *.plist* file in the User, Group, or computer List object that it is assigned to, in both the *MCXFlags* and *MCXSettings* attributes.

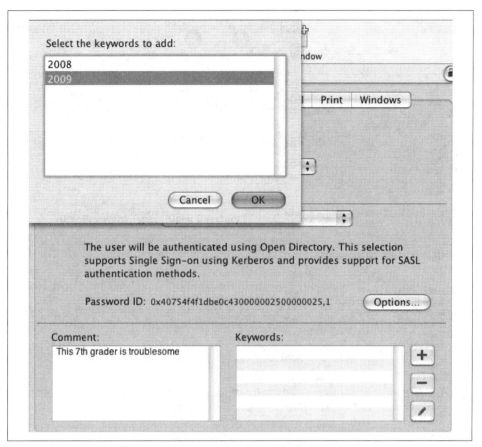

Figure 3-15. Assigning Keywords to a user in the Advanced tab of Workgroup Manager's user management interface.

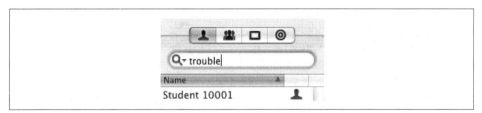

Figure 3-16. Both comments and keywords can be used in the Filter interface available in Workgroup Manager.

For instance, an organization's sales force could be limited to the use of certain applications, while a set of public web kiosks might have very limited access to the Finder's features. These are simplistic examples, but they do serve a point. Apple's client management capabilities are quite rich, and in fact, as a complete topic unto themselves, are discussed in Chapter 25. For further information, see John DeTroye's Tips & Tricks documents at *http://homepage.mac.com/johnd*.

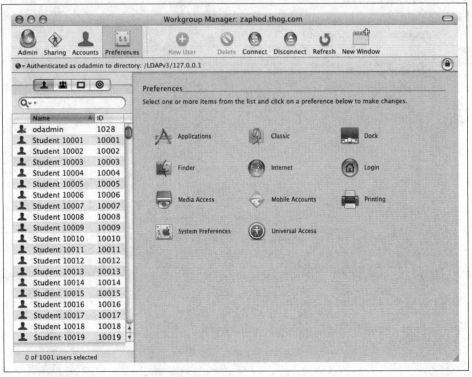

Figure 3-17. Workgroup Manager's interface for managing preferences or managed client data. Preferences, like accounts, can be managed for Users, Groups or Computer Lists.

The back end

Both account and preferences management (as opposed to share point management, discussed later in this chapter) occur over port 625; Workgroup Manager communicates in both cases with the DirectoryService daemon, documented both later in this chapter and in much more depth in the Appendix. This traffic is protected by a 512-bit Diffe-Hellman key exchange. It's important to think of the DirectoryService daemon as a sort of proxy. Account and preferences data, given the proper credentials, may be written to any directory domain that the server has access to. For instance, if a child server has been bound to an Active Directory domain, Workgroup Manager could be used to manage Mac-specific data for users in that domain. Even though you're connecting to your server, the changes you make might very well be sent to another directory.

> While it is feasible to use WGM to write data to non-Apple directories, this is not something I'd recommend without a lot of testing, and few Windows administrators are likely to want to use a Mac tool to manage their Active Directory.

Share Point Management

In addition to accounts and Managed Client data, Workgroup Manager is also used to set up share points and manage their protocol-specific options. For instance, a share's name can be overridden so that clients connecting over SMB see a different name than those connecting via AFP. Unlike user and preference management, though, this management occurs over port 311 (registered by Apple as *asip-webadmin*) and is implemented on the server side using the *servermgrd* process, discussed in more depth later in this chapter.

This dual-daemon model means that each time you use Workgroup Manager to manage your server, it is actually authenticating twice, both to the DirectoryService daemon over port 625 and to the *servermgrd* process, over port 311. Due to a bug, use of the Administrator's RealName (for instance *John Doe*) rather than Record-Name (*jdoe*) can result in an authentication failure to *servermgrd*, rendering Workgroup Manager's Sharing section inaccessible. Because of this, the RecordName should generally be used to log in. This is somewhat counterintuitive, since Workgroup Manager auto-populates the User Name field in its login dialog with the long form of the user's long name (RealName).

Share point data is in most cases stored on a per-share basis in the server's local *netinfo* directory, with each share having a subdirectory of *netinfo://config/ SharePoints*. Unlike account and preference data, share point data is always written locally, to the server you're connected to, rather than to some other directory domain the server has access to. Share point management is discussed in more depth in Chapter 14.

Inspector

New in Panther is Workgroup Manager's interface for management of raw directory data—the Inspector. This allows access to a variety of user attributes that are otherwise not available in the graphical user interface. Enabled in the application's preferences pane, Inspector provides the administrator with a precise view of the data that the DirectoryService daemon is aware of. Once enabled, the Inspector is accessed either using the target (All Records) icons available in the Accounts section or via the Inspector tab added to each user record. The Inspector can be seen in Figure 3-18.

Clicking the Options button (seen in Figure 3-18 below the Attribute window) allows for a certain amount of customization in the Inspector interface. The resulting dialog (pictured in Figure 3-19) exposes four specific options:

Show Standard Prefix

Show Native Prefix

> Of more use to developers examining the Open Directory API, attribute prefixes are generally used to more explicitly identify object (user, group, computer) attributes. Both of these options are deselected out of the box.

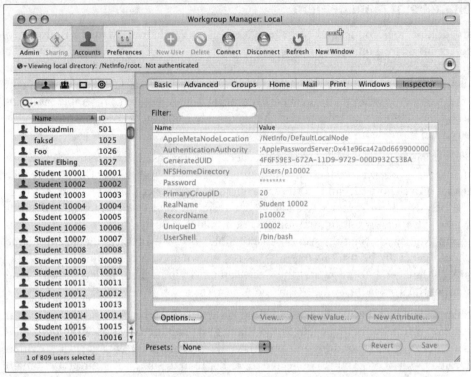

Figure 3-18. Workgroup Manager after enabling the Inspector. Notice the new target icon in the account selection interface as well as the Inspector tab added to the right side of the user management interface.

Show Standard Attributes

"Standard" describes the normalized, Open Directory names for the attributes of a directory object (RecordName, for instance, is used to specify the user's short name, and UniqueID refers to the user's unique integer identifier, regardless of the nature of the directory domain the user record is located in). This option, which is selected by default, controls the display of Standard attributes.

Show Native Attributes

"Native," in this case, describes the directory-specific names for object attributes. A user's short name, for instance, is called *name* in NetInfo, *uid* in most LDAP environments, and *sAMAccountName* in Active Directory. Similarly, a user's unique integer identifier is called *uid* in NetInfo and *uidNumber* in most LDAP environments. This option, which is enabled by default, toggles the Inspector's display of Native attributes.

Because both Show Standard Attributes and Show Native Attributes are selected in a default Workgroup Manager configuration, each attribute is generally displayed twice: once in its Native, directory-specific form, and once in its normalized, Open

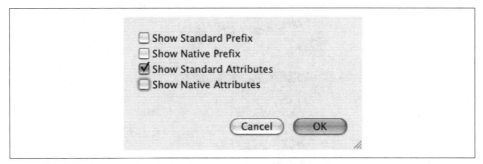

Figure 3-19. Options associated with the presentation of Inspector data.

Directory (Standard) form. This behavior can be seen in Figure 3-20. Because of this, and in order to avoid confusion and visual clutter, I generally disable Show Native Attributes unless I specifically need to know what the DirectoryService daemon thinks a native attribute is called. This generally means that the Native attribute has no standard equivalent, as is the case with a number of Active Directory user attributes.

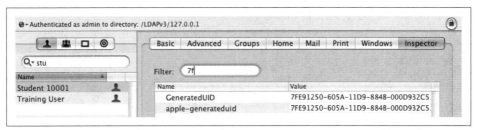

Figure 3-20. When both Standard and Native attributes are shown in the Inspector, two versions of each attribute will be displayed: one using the native directory terminology and one using standard, normalized Open Directory names. In this case, a rather extensive user record is filtered down to the GeneratedUID attribute, which is called apple-generateduid in its native LDAP environment.

Of considerable importance in the context of the Inspector is the All Records tab, accessed (once enabled in Workgroup Manager's preferences pane) via the target icon in the Account selection pane. Its selection reveals a pop-up menu (pictured in Figure 3-21) that allows for an analysis of a complete array of Open Directory objects. In addition to the User, Group, and Computer List records generally available throughout Workgroup Manager, this feature means that nearly any type of Open Directory object can be graphically managed (albeit in the Inspector's raw data mode), as shown in Figure 3-22.

This is the only relatively simple graphical method for directly managing several types of data, including domain-wide LDAP and Kerberos configurations and automount records (discussed in more depth in Chapters 7, 8, and 14, respectively).

If the administrator is authenticated to the directory domain in question, the Inspector can be used to edit existing record attributes or, if allowed by the underlying

Figure 3-21. Using the All Records (Target) tab to view specific Open Directory data types. Standard (normalized Open Directory) names may be chosen from the pictured pull-down menu, while native attribute names can also be specified using the native selection at the top of the menu.

directory store, to add new ones. (It is difficult to draw conclusions, since the configuration of non-Apple directory domains varies substantially, both by vendor and deployed configuration.) In any case, such management should be undertaken with great care, because the directory data itself is being manipulated without the benefit of its typical management tools, which generally make some attempt to ensure that entered data is valid.

View Directories

When initially opened, Workgroup Manager immediately prompts for the address of a server to log in to. Hasty entry, though, ignores a valuable feature that is specifically very useful in the context of local and cross-platform management: the View Directories option. Chosen from the Server menu (as pictured in Figure 3-23), View Directories, rather than establishing a TCP connection, allows Workgroup Manager to view and administer any directory domains that the administrative workstation is a member of.

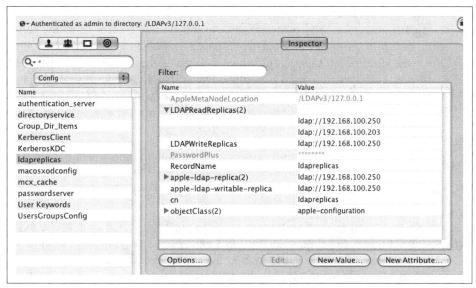

Figure 3-22. Using Workgroup Manager's All Records tab to examine the LDAP Replica data on an Open Directory Master. The Inspector provides the only graphical method for managing this and several other types of directory data.

Figure 3-23. Using Workgroup Manager's View Directories option.

The View Directories feature has two very important repercussions:

- As of 10.3.4, Apple began providing a Server Admin Tools installer as a publicly available free download to help Server Administrators keep their remote administration software up-to-date. Workgroup Manager, installed with this package, can be use to facilitate local management in a much more granular fashion than any of Apple's included client-management tools.

- During the course of directory integration with Active Directory or any other third-party directory service, it is often desirable to add users from the third-party directory to groups hosted in a shared Open Directory domain. Open Directory Masters, though, should not (In Panther) be members of any other, non-Apple directory domain. Using View Directories from a workstation that is connected to both domains eases this headache, allowing users from the third-party domain to be easily dropped into the membership list of any Open Directory group.

Preferences

Workgroup Manager's preferences yield several interesting options:

Resolve DNS names when possible
> If DNS resolution is slow or inconsistent in your infrastructure, it's probably a good idea to fix it, since much of Mac OS X Server requires a proper DNS environment. However, deselecting this option alleviates several issues that can result from Workgroup Manager injecting hostnames into the data that writes out.

Use secure transactions (SSL) for sharing
> Deselecting this option forces Workgroup Manager's sharing capabilities to communicate over port 687 (*asip-registry*). Traffic over 687 isn't encrypted, so this option isn't useful in most circumstances. It does, though, help to expose the HTTP-based communication used by the *servermgrd* daemon, and due to the overhead associated with SSL, might be marginally faster.

Show system users and groups
> Selection of this option shows the built-in users and groups that Mac OS X Server uses to provide certain system-wide services. In general, these users are configured correctly and do not need to be modified.

Show "All Records" tab and Inspector
> This option enables the Inspector, discussed earlier in this chapter.

Limit search results to requested records
> Workgroup Manager features a filter field (discussed earlier) that allows an administrator to focus in a fairly granular fashion on a subset of user records. Rather than showing all available records (Workgroup Manager's default behavior), this option limits displayed records to those that were specifically requested. This option is particularly useful with servers that manage a large number of accounts.

List a maximum of X records
> Limits the number of records that can be displayed. Workgroup Manager tends to become sluggish as greater and greater numbers accounts are displayed. Although this behavior has improved somewhat in Panther, it is still a good idea to make use of this feature when working with very large directories.

Auto-refresh sharing every X seconds

> *servermgrd*, the process responsible for management of Workgroup Manager's "Sharing" data, communicates via HTTP, which is a stateless protocol. This means that in order to refresh sharing data, a new HTTP query must be made. This setting allows you to specify the time interval between those queries.

Reset "Don't show again" messages

> Several Workgroup Manager alerts have a checkbox that allows the user to specify that they should not be shown again. This option resets those dialogs so that they are shown again.

Server Admin

Focused mostly on service monitoring and configuration, Panther's Server Admin is (for Apple) a leap forward in server management. It is a wholly new application, with very little in common with its 10.0/10.1 namesake. It combines service management and monitoring capabilities into a new, scalable interface with some impressive features.

Like other server management applications, Server Admin first forces the user to authenticate as a member of the admin group in a directory domain hosted on the server in question. At that point, Server Admin defaults to its standard management and monitoring view, seen in Figure 3-24. Note that Server Admin sheds the idea of single server management, and instead lends itself to management of multiple servers. Each server, found in the Server and Services pane, can be maximized in order to get a quick overview of every service it hosts. Selection of any one of these services really gets into the meat of Server Admin's purpose, contextually changing the right pane of the application to offer several service-specific options. While we'll examine each later on, it's important now to examine some common themes.

At a minimum, each service offers two options:

Overview

> A generalized view of the service, often including the number of connections and/or current throughput.

Settings

> Most service configuration takes place with the selection of the Settings button. In many cases, a service's settings will actually expose a number of other, service-specific options in Server Admin's main configuration interface. In every case, the Settings button also exposes a small, barely noticeable proxy icon in the bottom righthand corner.

Most, though, offer several other views:

Logs

> One of the great tendencies of Unix operating systems is the use of logging. Processes tend to be very good about letting you know what's going on. The logging

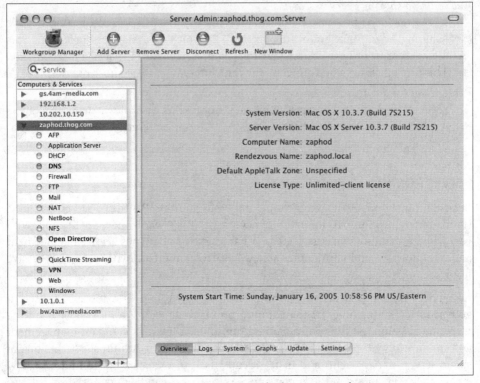

Figure 3-24. Server Admin's default, service-centric multiple-server interface.

selection frames those logs in a graphical interface. The upside is that this tendency makes logs much more approachable to the average administrator. The downside is that, since Server Admin communicates via HTTP, monitoring is not as immediate as it would be when logging into the server via *ssh* and using the *tail* or *less* commands.

Graphs

An even more graphical and easy-to-digest representation of various services, Server Admin graphs everything from per-service throughput and connections to CPU usage and network traffic. Most graphs are even adjustable in scale, so that you can narrow your analysis to anything from an hour to a week.

Connections

Connections usually display the user or hostname associated with a particular service's connections. AFP and SMB additionally allow the administrator to disconnect particular users.

All of these options are well represented in the Server's Info module, which provides access to a number of global options that are not specific to any other Mac OS X Server service. It is reached by selecting the Server's hostname or IP address in the lefthand service selection pane (as seen in Figure 3-24). This action, in turn, exposes a number of more detailed selections: Overview, Logs, System, Graphs, Updates, and Settings.

The Overview section of Server Admin's info module (seen earlier in Figure 3-24) presents a variety of basic information that Server administrators are generally interested in: system start time, OS version, license type, among others.

The *serveradmin* command, examined in more depth later in this chapter, can be used to gather the same data. For more information, see the examples presented with it, which follow these graphical processes.

Choosing the Logs section of Server Admin's Info module (seen in Figure 3-25) reveals three logs: System, Watchdog Events, and Software Updates (*/var/log/system. log*, */Library/Logs/watchdog.event.log*, and */Library/Logs/Software\ Update.log*, respectively). If you are logged into a 10.2 server, the logs for the *serversettingsd* daemon are also available.

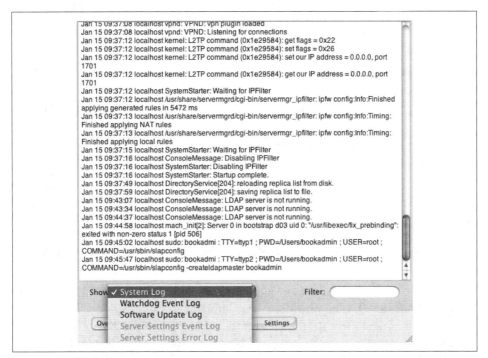

Figure 3-25. The Info Module's Logs interface reveals several commonly accessed system-wide logs. Unlike other log analysis interfaces in Server Admin, this one features a Filter option, allowing for a more granular treatment of the logs in question.

Selection of the System portion of the Info module reveals two specific monitoring interfaces: Hardware and Quotas. The former, pictured in Figure 3-26, packs a variety of data (most of which is self-explanatory) into a surprisingly uncluttered user interface. This same data can be gathered with the *serveradmin* command, using its *getHardwareInfo* flag:

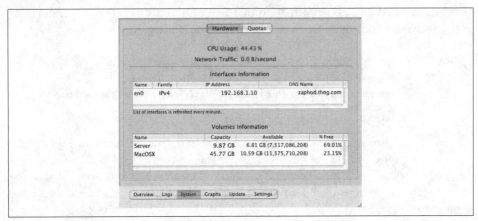

Figure 3-26. The Info Modules Hardware section, which includes data about local disks, networking, and CPU load.

```
serveradmin command info:command = "getHardwareInfo"
```

The Quota interface, seen in Figure 3-27, is also fairly straightforward. Quotas are generally set using Workgroup Manager, and are described in more depth in Chapter 14.

The Graphs section of the module provides an adjustable-scale historical analysis of CPU Usage and Network Traffic (Figure 3-28). While not really suitable for a scientific analysis, this screen is extremely useful for an at-a-glance overview of system load.

Monitoring and installing appropriate software updates is a challenge on any platform, and one of the many tools Apple has provided to help administrators successfully deal with the associated complexity is the Update function of *servermgrd*'s Info module, pictured in Figure 3-29. Although it provides a limited subset of the functionality available in either System Preferences or the command-line *softwareupdate* tool, this interface does allow for granular selection of updates to install.

The Settings section includes four subsequent tabs (General, Date & Time, Time Zone, and Advanced), each providing some kind of generalized, global settings management. The initial view (of the General tab) is illustrated in Figure 3-30. In this interface, the serial number, Computer Name or Rendezvous Name may be set. These settings may also be set with the *serversetup* (Example 3-2) and *sereradmin* command-line tools. Panther Server's serial number is stored in the local NetInfo Domain in the */Config/SerialNumber* object. The Computer and Rendezvous Names are managed by the configd daemon, and are stored in its configuration database at (in 10.3) */Library/Preferences/SystemConfiguration/preferences.xml*.

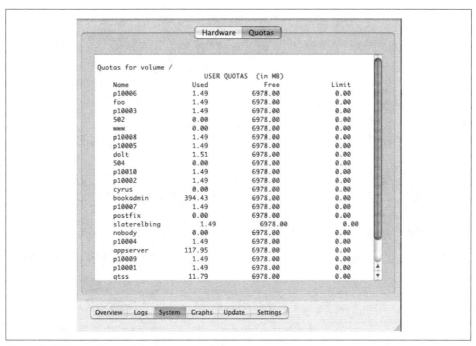

Figure 3-27. Using Server Admin to monitor system quotas.

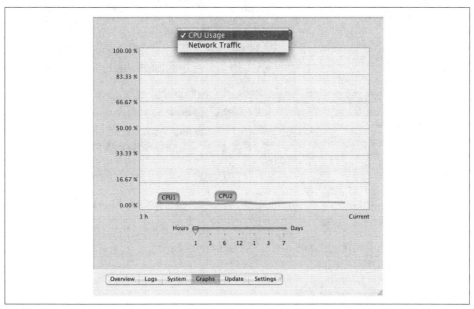

Figure 3-28. The CPU Usage graph (with a scale that is adjustable from 1 to 7 days) displays multiple CPUs independently.

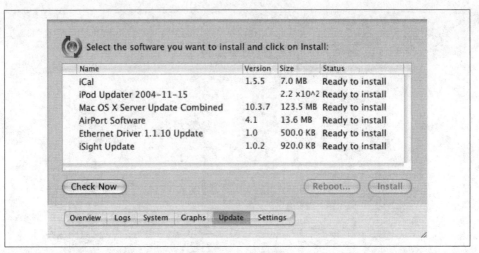

Figure 3-29. Server Admin's Software Update function. For more information regarding software updates and their impact on Server deployment, see Chapter 4.

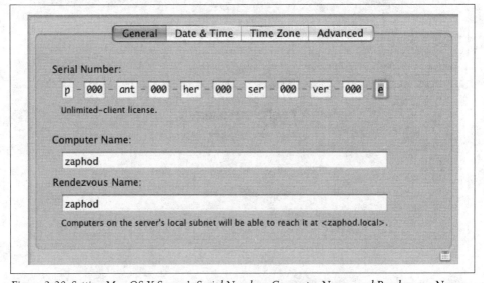

Figure 3-30. Setting Mac OS X Server's Serial Number, Computer Name, and Rendezvous Name using Server Admin.

Example 3-2. Using the serversetup utility to set various settings.

```
serversetup -verifySerialNumber
serversetup -setSerialNumber
serversetup -setComputername computername
```

Date & Time (Figure 3-31) and Time Zone (Figure 3-32), like their System Preferences equivalents, require little explanation. Once again, a variety of tools may be used to set this data from the command line.

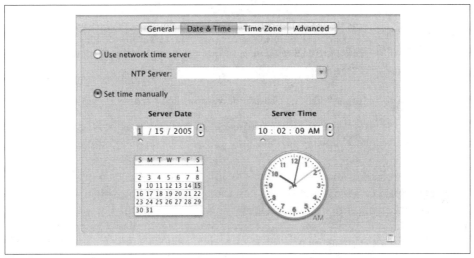

Figure 3-31. Setting the date and time. This interface is very similar to both the local System Preferences method and Mac OS X Server's initial configuration using Server Assistant. The same can be accomplished with a variety of command-line tools including systemsetup, date, and ntpdate.

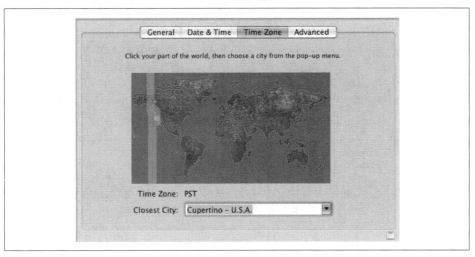

Figure 3-32. Server Admin's graphical interface for setting the time zone.

```
serversetup -setTimeZone timezonedescription
serversetup -setDate date
serversetup -setTime 12:34:56
date
```

The *ntpdate* command can set the date using network time without actually committing to using a network time server for the long term. The syntax is trivial: *ntpdate hostname*, where *hostname* is the name or IP address of an NTP server. For example:

```
318116:~ mab9718$ sudo ntpdate time.apple.com
Password:
 2 Sep 00:29:29 ntpdate[1064]: step time server 17.254.0.31
offset -62.945196 sec
```

The Info modules Advanced Settings tab establishes one of the less-appealing aspects of Apple's graphical server management tools: the grouping of several (generally unrelated) more obscure options under an Advanced heading. There's nothing particularly advanced about any of the three options pictured in Figure 3-33. SNMP (Simple Network Management Protocol) and NTP (Network Time Protocol) are well-established in the server world, and Macintosh Manager has been around since AppleShare IP. Nonetheless, all are enabled in this interface.

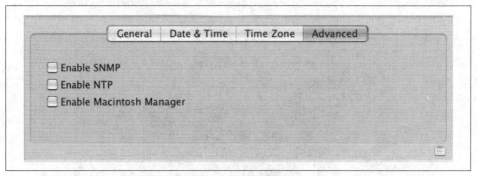

Figure 3-33. The Advanced tab of Server Admin's Info module.

Apple ships a virtually unmodified Net-SNMP distribution, with no Mac OS X or Xserve-specific NIBs. For more documentation, see *http://net-snmp.sourceforge.net*.

Enabling SNMP actually sets the `SNMPSERVER` variable to `-YES-` in */etc/hostconfig*, so that it can be started by the SNMP Startup Item. Similarly, the `HeadlessStartup` item checks for */etc/hostconfig*'s `TIMESERV` variable, starting *ntpd* if it is set to `-YES-`. See Example 3-3.

Example 3-3. The shell scripting in the HeadlessStartup startup item that starts ntpd.

```
if [ "${TIMESERV:=-YES-}" = "-YES-" ] && ! GetPID ntpd > /dev/null; then

        CheckForNetwork
        if [ "${NETWORKUP}" = "-NO-" ]; then
```

Example 3-3. The shell scripting in the HeadlessStartup startup item that starts ntpd. (continued)

```
        exit
    fi
    ConsoleMessage "Starting network time server"
    ntpd -f /var/run/ntp.drift -p /var/run/ntpd.pid
fi
```

Macintosh Manager (which is actually implemented by MacintoshManagement-Server in */usr/sbin*), unlike its peers in the Advanced tab, is started by the watchdog daemon (described in more depth in Chapter 4). Enabling Macintosh Manager graphically simply changes the *mm* entry in */etc/watchdog.conf* from off to respawn. See Example 3-4.

Example 3-4. Using cat and grep to view Macintosh Manager's entry in /etc/watchdog.conf.

```
[ace2:~] mbartosh% cat /etc/watchdog.conf | grep ^mm
mm:off:/usr/sbin/MacintoshManagementServer -x   # Macintosh Manager service
```

Once again, note that this general layout—Overview, Logs and Graphs, with more extensive selections of tabs available in the Settings section—is seen over and over again in various Server Admin modules. In addition to the very legitimate data presented here about the more global Info module, be sure to recognize that the purpose of this initial overview is just as much to introduce the reader to Server Admin's tendencies.

Summary view

Server Admin's standard view (discussed in the previous section) is only the beginning of its capabilities. The View menu also yields a Show Summary option, which results in a more service-oriented overview of the servers in the management list, seen in Figure 3-34.

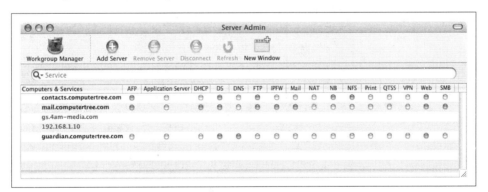

Figure 3-34. Server Admin's Summary view, accessed viâ Server Admin → View → Show Summary.

Server Admin also has a "lock view" option, which locks out configuration changes until the current administrator supplies the password; a useful option in busy environments, or in environments where junior personnel might be relegated to a monitoring role.

Preferences

Server Admin's preferences, available under the Server Admin menu (and pictured in Figure 3-35), allow for more in-depth customization of the information that's fed back to the administrator. Specifically, the status graphics can be made more or less detailed (Minimal or Advanced; the default view, Simple, is in the middle). Computer Names, rather than DNS Names, can be used to list servers, and the view can be locked automatically, requiring re-authentication for editing after a user-configurable idle time.

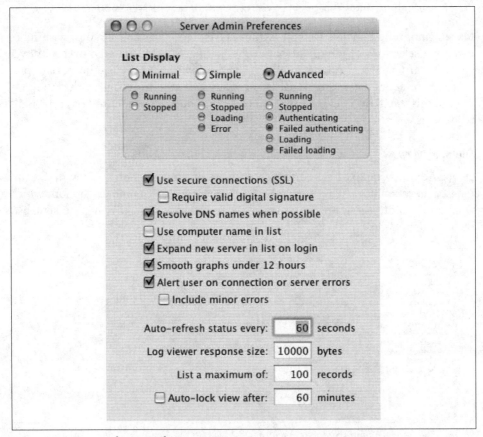

Figure 3-35. Server Admin's Preferences pane.

Server Monitor

Server Monitor is the Xserve-specific hardware-monitoring application responsible for keeping track of the physical operating environment of your server. Like Server Admin, Server Monitor is capable of managing several servers at once. Unlike Server Admin, Server Monitor does require specific hardware; it works only when Mac OS X Server is running on an Xserve. Unlike both Server Admin and Workgroup Manager, Server Monitor doesn't have a lot of options hidden in menu items; almost all of its functionality is presented up front, in the graphical user interface.

 There is little granularity to Server Monitor: it does not feature a delegation mode or any capacity for allowing access to anyone other than members of the Admin group.

That interface consists of an upper pane, from which an Xserve may be chosen for further analysis, and a lower, contextual pane that changes depending on the host and options that are selected. Both are pictured in Figure 3-36.

The upper pane contains Server Monitor's host list. Each Xserve listed has a set of icons indicating the status of that server's Info, Memory, Drives, Power, Network, Temperature, Blowers, and Security systems, each of which correspond to a tab providing more extensive information in the lower portion of the interface. As mentioned earlier, the server list may also be filtered in order to better monitor a specific server, in case you manage so many Xserves that it becomes difficult to locate a particular machine in the list, as is common in medium-to large-scale computational clusters; a market in which the Xserve is prominent.)

Finally, note the more interactive options also available in and around the computer list:

- The "Show warnings and failures only" checkbox hides any aspect of server management that's functioning properly. Anything that would normally be green isn't shown—only warnings (yellow) and failures (red).

- The "Show detailed status" checkbox shows specific details about each monitored Xserve component. For instance, if there are three hard drives in the Server, three storage icons will show up (with their appropriate status) in the monitoring list.

- The Show Log button provides a log viewer for server monitor events.

- The Edit Notifications button, covered in more depth later, allows event notifications to be sent to a designated email address.

The lower portion of Server Monitor's interface consists of a series of tabs, each of which expands on some aspect of the minimal graphical summary available in the server selection window. The first (the Info pane, pictured in Figure 3-36) provides a remarkable amount of generalized information, from the IP address to the hardware

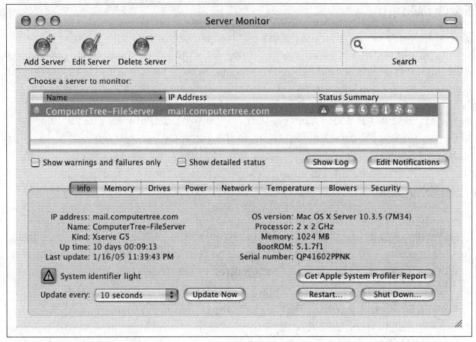

Figure 3-36. Server Monitor's user interface, including the Server List and Info pane. Note the activated System identifier light, indicated by both the depressed button in the Info pane and the grayed icon in the Server List.

serial number, installed system memory, and BootROM version. A number of more interactive options are also available, including:

Update interval
Changes the interval with which Server Monitor queries *servermgrd*.

Update Now
Forces an immediate refresh of Server Monitor data.

Get Apple System Profiler Report
Requests a variety of information about the server, similar in content to the output of the *system_profiler* command. This data is sent to the Server Monitor Log, which is automatically opened when this option is chosen.

Restart
Restarts Xserve.

Shut Down
Shuts down Xserve.

Server Monitor, like Server Admin and parts of Workgroup Manager, communicates with *servermgrd* over port 311. Its data actually comes from a daemon called *hwmond*, detailed later in this chapter. *hwmond* talks directly with the Xserve-specific monitoring hardware and updates the data available from *servermgrd*'s *servermgrd_ xserve plug-in*. Server Monitor's second tab concerns the Xserve's memory (RAM), as shown in Figure 3-37. Minimal in comparison to the Info tab, it provides information about the RAM in each of the Xserve's eight (in the case of the Xserve G5) RAM slots.

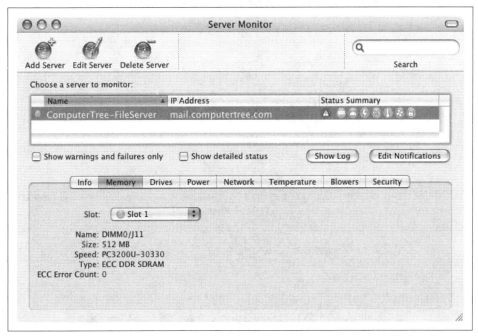

Figure 3-37. Server Monitor's Memory tab. Hardware supporting ECC RAM will display the memory errors associated with the RAM in each slot.

Drives

This tab (shown in Figure 3-38) monitors various statistics relating to the drives installed in the server. Note that, true to the nature of Server Monitor, this information does not relate to partitions or volumes, but only to the drives themselves. Chosen from a pull-down menu, each drive indicates its Capacity, Manufacturer, Bus, Drive Bay, and Bytes Written and Read since last boot.

Power

The Power section (Figure 3-39) details and graphs power output from a number of system components. It also provides a graph, from which valuable trend analysis can be obtained.

Network

The Network tab (Figure 3-40) monitors data relating to the network interfaces of the Xserve. Especially notable in this case are the graphs that monitor both the amount of data and the number of packets in and out of a particular interface.

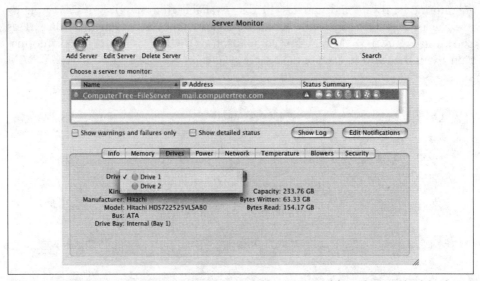

Figure 3-38. Server monitor's Drives tab makes available a variety of data about each of the drives available to the Server—both in the drive bays and otherwise attached.

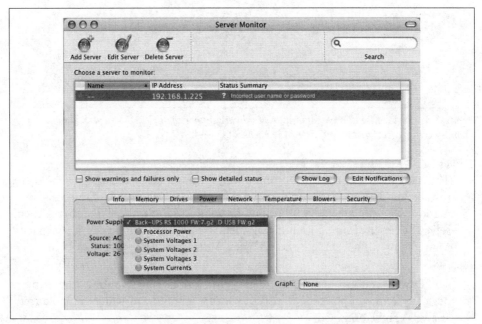

Figure 3-39. Server Monitor's Power tab. Notice that any supported USB-connected UPS shows up as another Power Supply in the pull-down menu.

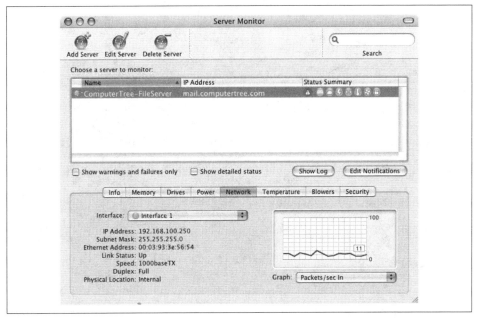

Figure 3-40. The Network tab in Server Monitor.

Temperature

This section (Figure 3-41) tracks temperature statistics; minimally, the internal ambient temperature, but also other statistics on more recent Xserve models. Once again, recent data is graphed for easier trend analysis. Temperature is particularly important in data-center and other rackmount environments, where massive amounts of cooling are required to keep room temperature cool enough for machines to operate in.

Blowers

Blower statistics (Figure 3-42) vary quite widely among Xserve models, as later Xserves sport more fans. Server Monitor tracks and graphs rotations per minute for each blower.

Security

The Security tab (Figure 3-43) exposes two pieces of data: the state of the Xserve's "lock" (a simple bolt that can be turned with an Allen wrench and, in some cases, a fingernail) and a notification indicating whether the enclosure has been accessed. Given the ease with which the "lock" can be opened (it has no specific key and can be unlocked using nearly any small tool), the former is generally not a concern. The latter is generally only triggered when the Xserve body is slid out of its case; there is an obvious switch when you open the machine.

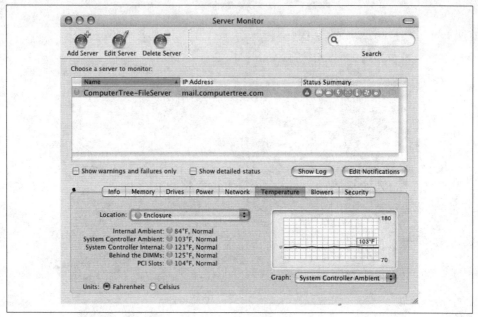

Figure 3-41. Server Monitor's Temperature tab tracks both ambient temperature and specific temperatures for several components (in either Fahrenheit or Celsius).

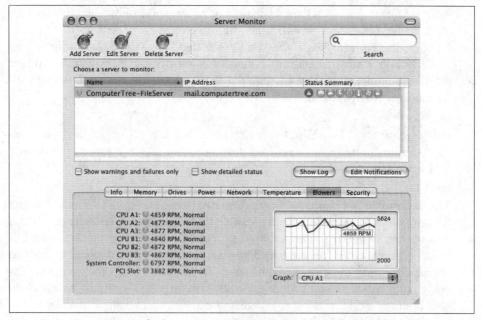

Figure 3-42. Server Monitor displays operational statistics for the many fans in the Xserve G5.

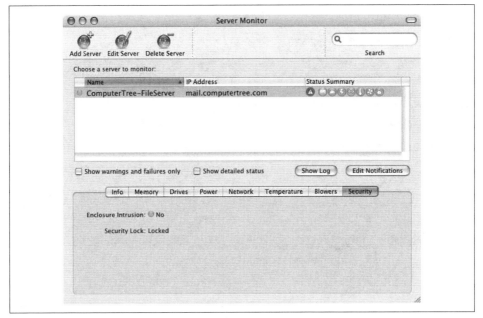

Figure 3-43. The minimal Security tab in Server Monitor.

Server Monitor notifications

An important feature of Server Monitor is the ability to send out notifications when certain system events occur. This capability is managed via the Edit Notifications button, prominent in the application's interface. These notifications are very granular in nature; administrators might choose to monitor combination of Drives, Power, Network, Temperature, Blower, or Security phenomenon.

 Server Monitor is not capable of configuring multiple notifications (differing events sent to different parties). Instead, a single notification, sent out to every listed address, is configured based on the service categories that are selected.

As seen in Figure 3-44, multiple parties can be notified, and the email can contain a customized message and priority. Perhaps most importantly, the message can be sent either from Server Monitor itself or directly from the remote server in question. In the latter case (which is important, because it's not good security policy to leave an administrative application open all the time), the *hwmond* process itself makes the outgoing SMTP connection, and the notification options are actually stored in its configuration file (*/etc/hwmond.conf*).

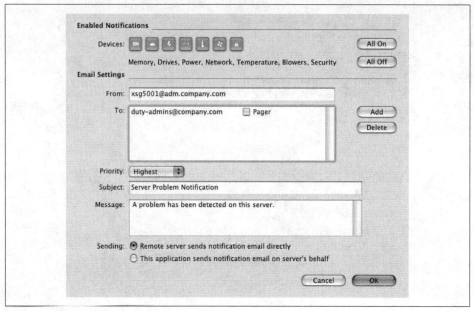

Figure 3-44. Server Monitor's interface for setting notifications.

Directory Access

It would at first appear to be a mistake to include Directory Access in a list of server administration tools. It is, after all, most commonly used to manage the Open Directory–related aspects of Mac OS X. Recall, though, that one of Mac OS X Server's design goals is complete remote management. It wouldn't do to force administrators to go sit in front of the server console just to add a new node to the Open Directory authentication path.

 Open Directory and its configuration, including more on the *DirectoryService* daemon, are covered in the Appendix.

Along these lines, Apple added (in Jaguar) a remote management capability to the Directory Access application. Specifically, it communicates with the *DirectoryService* daemon on the server in question over port 625 (Workgroup Manager also manages users over this port). You can access a remote server by choosing the Connect option from Directory Access's Server menu. This feature, called *DSProxy*, allows remote administrators to configure Mac OS X Server just as if they were running Directory Access on the local machine. Directory Access (and the DirectoryService daemon) are discussed in more depth in the Appendix.

DirectoryService knows whether to listen on port 625 according to the existence of the */Library/Preferences/DirectoryService/.DSTCPListening* file. By creating this file and restarting the *DirectoryService* daemon, it is feasible to access Mac OS X client directory data and configuration remotely.

Command-Line Tools

As Unix derivatives, Mac OS X and Mac OS X Server automatically inherit 20 years of command-line management tools. These tools have evolved mostly in response to traditional Unix administration tasks and according to traditional Unix requirements. With Mac OS X's introduction, many of these tools proved inadequate for managing Apple's new server applications and subsystems. In response, Apple began a slow evolution of its own command-line utilities to complement those more traditional tools. Panther's latest progress towards this evolution is substantial, and for the first time, command-line administration of Mac OS X Server doesn't require in-depth knowledge of the configuration mechanisms of 14 different server technologies.

This section will focus on both Apple-specific tools and traditional Unix tools that Apple has modified for their own use. The latter case is actually quite rare; Apple generally prefers cross-platform compatibility to modification of Open Source tools.

serveradmin

serveradmin is the command-line equivalent of the Server Admin application. Due to the breadth of its function and the resulting complexity in the syntax of certain options, some features are more appropriate for scripted applications. Nonetheless, it is an extremely useful tool, and its existence points to Apple's focus on the professional system administration market.

Unlike its graphical cousin, the *serveradmin* utility cannot be run as an administrator; it must be run as root. This might seem like a minor point, since by default, all administrative users can use the *sudo* utility to execute command processes as root. However, *sudo* is quite powerful, and in a highly granular, managed environment, it might be desirable to allow access to certain *serveradmin* features without allowing the user to have full root privileges. While *sudo* is flexible enough to accommodate this in advanced configuration scenarios, I feel this is too much to ask of your average Mac OS X administrator, who probably just wants to delegate some basic management functions to less-senior personnel. This lack of delegation is a common theme in many of Apple's command-line tools, most of which must be run as root.

serveradmin's simplest options—the *list*, *start*, and *stop* parameters—refer to its most basic capabilities—listing, starting and stopping particular services. See the *list* parameter in Example 3-5, and the *start* directive in Example 3-6.

Example 3-5. serveradmin's list directive. Note that the last "service" is called xserve. This reflects the command-line equivalent to the Server Monitor application.

```
xserver:~ nadmin$ sudo serveradmin list
afp
appserver
dhcp
dirserv
dns
filebrowser
ftp
info
ipfilter
mail
nat
netboot
nfs
print
privs
qtss
qtsscontents
qtssfiletransfer
signaler
smb
vpn
web
xserve
```

Example 3-6. The start directive, here used to start Samba. Stop and restart are also supported by most services.

```
xserver:~ nadmin$ sudo serveradmin start smb
smb:command = "setState"
smb:state = "RUNNING"
smb:status = 0
```

Notice the colon-delineated output in Example 3-6. This syntax is vital for constructing more complex commands and queries, and actually corresponds closely to the XML-based communications sent over the wire between Server Admin and *servrmgrd*.

The *status* and *fullstatus* directives are similarly simple: each accepting a service name as an argument, the former displaying whether a service is running and the latter displaying slightly more information, such as start time, logging configuration, and the number of current connections. More complex are the settings and command directives.

serveradmin's *settings* directive (the abbreviation *set* can also be used) reads and modifies specific setting data. This data should be in the colon-delineated, key/value syntax seen in the output of the start directive in Example 3-6.

 serveradmin might, in some cases, expose features not seen in the graphical interface. For instance, AppleFileServer's *useAppleTalk* flag. Some of these flags are unsupported by Apple, and a few don't even work (hence their unsupported nature). Try to be aware of this as you make deployment decisions.

The output of *set* can be quite verbose, and can be filtered in two ways: either by requesting a particular setting, or by parsing the output of the command with *grep* or some similar filter. For instance, the following two commands produce similar output:

```
xserver:~ nadmin$ sudo serveradmin settings afp | grep kerberosPrincipal
afp:kerberosPrincipal = afpserver/xserver.example.com@XSERVER.EXAMPLE.COM

xserver:~ nadmin$ sudo serveradmin settings afp:kerberosPrincipal
afp:kerberosPrincipal = "afpserver/xserver.example.com@XSERVER.EXAMPLE.COM"
```

The latter is probably more lightweight, since a second process doesn't have to be spawned. But either might be appropriate in certain circumstances. Setting the value of a property is very similar; in addition to specifying a particular flag, a value, offset by an = sign and enclosed in quotation marks, is also specified:

```
xserver:~ nadmin$ sudo serveradmin settings afp:kerberosPrincipal = "afpserver/
xserver.example.com@ADS.EXAMPLE.COM"
afp:kerberosPrincipal = "afpserver/xserver.example.com@ADS.EXAMPLE.COM"
```

The *command* directive (which can be abbreviated as *com*) allows service-specific commands to be issued. Due to the service-specific nature of these commands, they're covered in-depth with the actual services they affect, rather than here in the generalized management chapter.

Both the *command* and *settings* directives can also be redirected to or read from a file, as shown in Examples 3-7 and 3-8.

Example 3-7. The log level is originally set to 0…

```
xserver:~ nadmin$ sudo serveradmin settings smb:log level
smb:log level = 0
```

Example 3-8. …and then set to 3 based on the input file.+

```
xserver:~ nadmin$ cat settingsfile
smb:log level = 3
smb:auth methods = "guest opendirectory"
smb:adminCommands:homes = yes

serveradmin settings  < settingsfile
```

In fact, since the *command* directive generally outputs an array, it is most useful when passed to a file that is later parsed and used to produce an input file for further *command* statements (see Example 3-9).

Example 3-9. Re-evaluating the log level after setting it from an input file.

```
xserver:~ nadmin$ sudo serveradmin settings smb:log level
smb:log level = 3
```

One important aspect of the *serveradmin* is its role in automated setup infrastructures. Scripted environments incorporating *serveradmin* are far more capable than Apple's included automatic server configuration mechanism. One can envision a script that queries a web application server with a MAC address and, after pulling a complete configuration, sets up the server right down to specific share points and web sites. This abstracted level of scriptability—where single keywords can modify several configuration files, each with a different syntax and belonging to a different daemon—is rare in Unix system administration, which usually relies on a much lower-level ability to munge text files using tools like Perl, *sed*, and *awk*.

sharing

Data relating to share points is stored in several places in Panther. As mentioned earlier, the share record itself is stored in the local NetInfo database in the */config/ SharePoints* directory. This information can be retrieved using the *nicl . –read* command, as shown in Example 3-10. Here we're looking at some of the out-of-box options for the */Users* share.

Example 3-10. The nicl command can be used to read data in NetInfo.

```
xserver:~ nadmin$ nicl . -read /config/SharePoints/Users
name: Users
directory_path: /Users
afp_name: Users
afp_shared: 1
afp_guestaccess: 1
ftp_name: Users
ftp_shared: 1
ftp_guestaccess: 1
smb_name: Users
smb_shared: 1
smb_guestaccess: 1
smb_inherit_permissions: 0
smb_createmask: 0644
smb_directorymask: 0755
afp_use_parent_privs: 0
afp_use_parent_owner: 0
smb_oplocks: 0
smb_strictlocking: 1
amt_static_mount_path: /Network/Servers/
```

Example 3-10. The nicl command can be used to read data in NetInfo. (continued)

```
amt_is_automounted: 1
amt_is_staticMount: 0
amt_file_system: 0
amt_ds_path: LDAPv3/127.0.0.1
amt_rec_name: xserver.example.com:/Users
```

If the share is to be used as an automount, it also has to be listed in a shared domain somewhere; see Example 3-11.

Example 3-11. Using dscl to view an automount record in a shared Open Directory domain. Notice the back double back slash (\\) used to escape the slash in the /Users share.

```
xserver:~ nadmin$ dscl /LDAPv3/127.0.0.1 -read /Mounts/xserver.example.com:\\/Users
cn: xserver.example.com:/Users
mountDirectory: /Network/Servers/
mountOption: net url==afp://;AUTH=NO%20USER%20AUTHENT@xserver.example.com/Users
mountType: url
objectClass: mount top
AppleMetaNodeLocation: /LDAPv3/127.0.0.1
PasswordPlus: ********
RecordName: xserver.example.com:/Users
VFSLinkDir: /Network/Servers/
VFSOpts: net url==afp://;AUTH=NO%20USER%20AUTHENT@xserver.example.com/Users
VFSType: url
xserver:~ nadmin$
```

Previous to Panther Server, command-line creation of these share points was very difficult, given all the places data had to be written. Panther, however, brings us the *sharing* command (whose output is listed in Example 3-12), and whose basic options include:

−*l*

List shares.

−*a*

Add a share.

−*r*

Remove a share.

Example 3-12. Output from sharing −l, listing available share points and their options.

```
nadmin$ sharing -l
                    List of Share Points
name:           Groups
path:           /Groups
        afp:    {
                name:   Groups
                shared: 1
                guest access:   1
                inherit perms:  0
        }
```

Example 3-12. Output from sharing –l, listing available share points and their options. (continued)

```
ftp:    {
            name:   Groups
            shared: 1
            guest access:    1
}
smb:    {
            name:   Groups
            shared: 1
            guest access:    1
            inherit perms:  0
            oplocks:        0
            strict locking: 0
            directory mask: 493
            create mask:    420
}
```

Sharing takes a complex task and puts a comparatively simple frontend on it, making command-line administration a much simpler task than it was in the past.

Server Management Daemons

Behind the glossy ease of use of Mac OS X Server's management applications lay several daemons. Actually responsible for the work that is carried out, they are the central points through which most system administration flows, translating button-clicks, switches, and *serveradmin* flags from the administrative process to the actual configuration changes executed on the server side. This section examines each of the server management daemons, discussing their function, architecture, startup, and, in some cases, extensibility.

sshd

SSH is a secure, modern protocol designed to replace a number of less-secure remote management tools like *telnet*. Due to its flexibility, *sshd* is worth mentioning first. Because of the secure remote access it provides, most command-line management can easily be accomplished away from the server's console. Remember too that the Server Assistant application is really a graphical shell that executes some very specific commands via SSH to set up the server.

In Panther, *sshd* is started by the *xinetd* super-server, due to the existence of the */etc/xinetd.d/ssh* file (Example 3-13). While a complete examination of *xinetd* is beyond the scope of this chapter, it's worth noting that when an SSH connection comes in, *xinetd* executes the */usr/libexec/sshd-keygen-wrapper* script.

 For more information on *xinetd*, including its architecture and significance in Mac OS X, see Chapter 18.

Example 3-13. The /etc/xinetd.d/ssh file contains xinted's SSH configuration.

```
service ssh
{
        disable = no
        socket_type    = stream
        wait           = no
        user           = root
        server         = /usr/libexec/sshd-keygen-wrapper
        server_args    = -i
        groups         = yes
        flags          = REUSE IPv6
        session_create = yes
}
```

The *sshd-keygen-wrapper* script checks for the existence of various host keys, creates them if needed, and then executes *sshd*, passing any arguments to it that were passed to the *sshd-keygen-wrapper* script, as shown in Example 3-14.

Example 3-14. $@ is a built-in bash variable that stands for "all arguments passed to this script."

```
#!/bin/sh
[ ! -f /etc/ssh_host_key ]     && ssh-keygen -q -t rsa1 -f /etc/ssh_host_key     -N "" -C
" "
[ ! -f /etc/ssh_host_rsa_key ] && ssh-keygen -q -t rsa  -f /etc/ssh_host_rsa_key -N "" -C
" "
[ ! -f /etc/ssh_host_dsa_key ] && ssh-keygen -q -t dsa  -f /etc/ssh_host_dsa_key -N "" -C
" "
exec /usr/sbin/sshd $@
```

 In Jaguar, *sshd* is started by its own startup item according to the SSHSERVER flag in */etc/hostconfig*.

In most circumstances, you will want to limit *ssh* access to either admin users or some other limited membership group. (*ssh* access grants an admin user what are essentially root privileges, so I often end up creating a group that contains a subset of the admin group.) *ssh* grants fairly wide access to a system, especially next to the comparatively restricted authorization model of AFP or web services, which grant access to very limited portions of the filesystem.

 Comparing AFP to SSH is sort of like comparing apples to oranges: they serve wholly different purposes, but the fact remains that SSH generally allows more access to a server than intended by administrators, as in a default state, any valid user can *ssh* into the server.

There are a number of ways to restrict SSH access: OpenSSH is an extremely flexible tool. The easiest is to use the AllowGroups parameter in *sshd*'s configuration file, which is */etc/sshd_config*. Simply add an `AllowGroups` statement and specify a group or groups, as shown in Example 3-15.

Example 3-15. Using the cat and grep commands to examine the AllowGroups parameter in /etc/sshd_config, sshd's configuration file.

```
318116:~ mab9718$ cat /etc/sshd_config | grep AllowGroups
AllowGroups mactechs PANTHERSERVER\mac
```

servermgrd

In Panther, *servermgrd* is the mastermind behind nearly all day-to-day server management. Listening on ports 311 and 687, it carries out the work for Server Monitor, Server Admin, and parts of Workgroup Manager. This is quite a change from Jaguar, where service management was mostly the responsibility of *serversettingsd* and the Server Settings application.

 The *serveradmin* command's *list* option (covered earlier) actually reveals the full extent of *servermgrd*'s responsibility.

The underlying daemon, though, is very similar to its predecessors. All have been slightly modified versions of the Apache web server, running CGIs in response to input from their client-side counterparts. In Panther, *servermgrd* is started by the *ServerManagerDaemon* startup item (in */System/Library/StartupItems*).

servermgrd is actually spread out around the filesystem:

/etc/servermgrd
> Roughly equivalent to Apache's standard */etc/httpd* directory, *servermgrd*'s configuration file, *servermgrd.conf*, and its SSL certificate and key are stored in this directory.

/usr/share/servermgrd
> Contains the bulk of *servermgrd*, including an *html* directory that can be used to better understand what kind of queries *servermgrd* expects, a stripped-down set of Apache modules, and bundles and cgis, working together to do the actual work of *serveradmin*. Essentially, each service has a corresponding CGI and bundle.

/var/log/servermgrd
> The location of *servermgr*'s Apache-style error and SSL logs. In a default configuration, no access log is maintained.

One little-known utility is *servermgrdctl*. Very similar in nature to *apachectl*, it stops and restarts *servermgrd*. Useful parameters include:

start
stop
restart

> Fairly obvious; these parameters start, stop, and restart *servermgrd*. *start* should not be used unless you're testing unencrypted (insecure) access to *servermgrd*.

startssl

> Starts *servermgrd* with SSL. This parameter is used to start *servermgrd* in its Startup Item.

graceful

> Probably the most useful *servermgrctl* parameter in day-to-day interactive use, the *graceful* parameter restarts *servermgrd* by sending it a USR1 signal. The *config* file is automatically tested to ensure that *servermgrd*'s configuration is valid, and current open connections are maintained rather than dropped.

configtest

> Tests *servermgrd.conf* to ensure that the configuration is valid and allows *servermgrd* to run properly.

There are essentially two modifications that make knowledge of *servermgrd*'s architecture important. The first relates to SSL, and is vital to security. The second revolves around enabling the access log for better logging.

Securing servermgrd with SSL

There are certain words in technology that carry lots of excess baggage: including encryption, security, and VPN. They carry the connotations that can be easily misunderstood or misapplied, and their buzzword status ensures that somehow, somewhere, they are destined to become a checkbox on some purchasing manager's requirement list. So the question is often asked: Is the traffic encrypted? And most administrators are happy with the fact that *servermgrd* and all of its client applications use SSL out of box. However, what is less understood is that every installation of Mac OS X Server everywhere uses the same SSL certificate and key. Given an advanced sniffing package like *ssldump* (*http://www.rtfm.com/ssldump*), it is trivial to take this data maliciously. Rather than using the included certificate and key, it is highly recommended that you install your own, either self-signed or from a commercial certificate authority.

Once you've obtained your certificates, installation is not difficult. The easiest method is to name and store the new certificate and private key according to the current SSL settings indicated in */etc/servermgrd/servermgrd.conf*, effectively replacing Apple's out-of-box files. Specifically, the current directives are:

```
SSLCertificateFile /private/etc/servermgrd/ssl.crt/server.crt
SSLCertificateKeyFile /private/etc/servermgrd/ssl.key/server.key
```

Alternatively, you may edit the existing directives to reflect the location of the newly obtained files. Either way, the out-of-box SSL certificate should be replaced.

 Apple has been alerted of this vulnerability and hopefully will have fixed it by the time this book is published. For updates on the situation, refer to *http://www.pantherserver.org*, this book's errata site.

Also note that by default, Server Admin doesn't check the validity of the SSL certificate; instead, it simply trusts the server in question. To change this behavior, check the "Require valid digital signature" box in Server Admin's preferences.

Turning on servermgrd access logs

A second, fairly simple modification involves enabling access logs for *servermgrd*. In addition to the extra auditing capabilities this feature facilitates, it should be noted that logging, like several other capabilities we've covered, helps to illustrate the underlying architecture of Server Admin and *servermgrd*.

To enable the access log, uncomment the `CustomLog` directive in */etc/servermgrd/servermgrd.conf*:

```
CustomLog /private/var/log/servermgrd/servermgrd_access_log common
```

and restart the *servermgrd* process.

 Because *servermgrd* is based on Apache, its logging capabilities are extremely flexible. If you'd like to customize the access log, simply follow the same directions found in Chapter 23.

hwmond

The *hwmond* daemon is the Xserve-specific hardware-monitoring daemon. It stores its data in memory, where it is harvested by *servermgrd*'s *servermgr_xserve* plug-in. This daemon is run only on the Xserve platform. During the setup process, *hwmond* is executed with the *–t* parameter, which tests whether the hardware is supported. If it is, the process is added to *watchdog*'s watch list, so that it's started every boot.

As mentioned earlier, *hwmond* is also responsible for sending notifications configured with the Server Monitor application. This data, along with other configuration data, is stored in */etc/hwmond.conf*. *hwmond* logs to */var/log/hwmond.log*, and stores a list of devices supporting SMART (and the errors associated with them) in */etc/hwmond.SMART*. Finally, the *–s* flag can be added to *hwmond*'s invocation in the */etc/watchdog.conf* file to specify how often data is polled.

Sometimes *hwmond* is started on non-Xserve systems. While this is mostly just an annoyance, it is easy to work around by editing */etc/watchdog.conf* and changing *hwmond*'s setting from *respawn* to *off*.

DirectoryService

The *DirectoryService* daemon, which manages Open Directory, has to be given a cursory once-over here as both Directory Access and Workgroup Manager communicate with it. It will be covered in-depth in the Appendix.

CHAPTER 4

System Administration

In a way, this entire book revolves around system administration. The details, processes, and infrastructures that make up Mac OS X Server are documented—hopefully to a depth that can't be found elsewhere—specifically to enable their secure and robust management. System administration, however, is a topic of a much greater depth, and moves well beyond a mechanical understanding of how various pieces fit together, into a set of philosophies and best practices that pervade and are consistent among most aspects of the system. This chapter concerns those philosophies and trends, throwing in a few mechanical tidbits for good measure. In keeping with the spirit of this book thus far, we will examine those components specifically in the light of Mac OS X Server, especially where that differs from the practices and philosophies around other operating systems.

 Note also that these are my opinions and are, in many cases, assertions of the worst kind, with very little data presented behind them. Take them as you will, and where time and budget allow, data will be presented.

Philosophies

Most academic disciplines develop heuristics, or ways of thinking about certain types of problems. System administration (and IT in general), although it has not been widely examined in an academic context, is no different, having developed some common approaches in its young history. While these approaches are not necessarily specific to Mac OS X, and while I hope they are illustrated throughout this book, it does make sense to call at least some of them out here. Remember that there are no hard and fast, black and white rules. These are guidelines that have proven productive in many environments. This does not necessarily mean they will be applicable to yours—only that the possibility deserves analysis.

Minimize Intrusion into Existing Infrastructures

Infrastructure is developed to support certain functionality, and in general, several applications might rely on a single infrastructure element. Few applications, for instance, are useful at any scale without properly configured routing. Similarly, many separate applications (desktop logins, in-house web applications, file servers, and mail delivery, to name a few) might depend on an available and properly functioning directory server, and certain DNS conventions might be established to minimize discrepancies when managing certain classes of devices. The list is really endless. The point is that organizations develop interlocking and centralized systems in order to support other systems that meet their business goals. Significant resources are often invested into development of such environments, and systems being introduced into any organization should seek to fit in as seamlessly as feasible, interrupting as little as possible.

This is particularly the case where Apple technologies are concerned. Mac OS X has paved the way for acceptance into many environments that Apple previously could not have considered. The Macintosh is, however, still a minority platform, and it makes little sense when working to gain acceptance somewhere to ask that organization to make fundamental infrastructure changes in order to support the Mac. Such changes, because they are made to centralized, enterprise systems, are costly, and if it is costly to bring Apple technologies into an infrastructure, then those technologies have a quickly diminishing likelihood of adoption.

With Mac OS X, Apple has steadily become more friendly to such infrastructures, and has, once market realities became apparent, engineered non-intrusive solutions into the OS. Some great examples of this include:

Panther's Active Directory plug-in
> Active Directory, like nearly any directory service, fits clearly into the mold of one of those expensive, central pieces of infrastructure. Jaguar's methods for integrating Mac OS X into Active Directory, however, were often difficult to say the least, and were, when supporting a really good user experience, extremely intrusive. They often required fundamental changes to the active directory schema, and LDAP queries to the Active Directory tended to be insecure, since they did not use Kerberized LDAP like Windows clients did. In Panther, however, Apple specifically engineered a solution to work with Active Directory. At least where AD integration is concerned, Panther acts as much like a Windows client as is technically feasible. This is one definition of non-intrusive.

Use of the .local DNS namespace
> As discussed briefly in Chapter 1, when Apple initially introduced Rendezvous, its implementation of the Zeroconf standard, they architected the operating system so that all DNS queries to the *.local* namespace were dispatched to multicast DNS. Since *.local* was widely used by some of Apple's largest customers for standard (nonmulticast) DNS, this effect was problematic, to say the least. With

Panther, though, Apple engineered a mechanism (also detailed in Chapter 1) for supporting alternate query mechanisms for a particular namespace, allowing Rendezvous and enterprise *.local* implementation to coexist.

In both of these cases, Apple was confronted with significant interoperability issues and overcame them by crafting solutions that were less intrusive in nature. Systems engineered by you as a Mac OS X system administrator should take this same approach, striving to fit in, rather than stand out.

 Apple certainly isn't perfect and has only recently begun to embrace heterogeneous, non-intrusive solutions to this extent. Both of these cases got off to a slow start. Only later, after quite a bit of customer feedback, were they remedied. You most likely do not have the same luxury, and should work to ensure that your systems integrate as seamlessly as feasible.

Focus on the Needs and Business of Your Organization

Management at the head of IT infrastructures all too often tends to consist of IT experts, and not necessarily personnel with a background in the core competency of the organization in question. IT should further the needs of the organization it supports, and not necessarily the needs of IT. This lesson, while painful, is best learned early. (Curriculum developers, not server administrators, best understand the subtleties of an educational environment.) This is not to say that organizational personnel should run rampant over IT, but merely that IT should build its systems in a way that best supports the business goals of the organization. Information technology is not an island, and IT systems should help bring users closer to their professional goals and responsibilities.

Default Policy of Denial

One of the primary aspects of information technology is controlling access to resources—to files on the filesystem, to resources shared out over network protocols like HTTP and AFP or to data stored in (for instance) an LDAP directory. Every new system, however, increases complexity and decreases security of an overall infrastructure. A sane strategy, therefore, minimizes access points into any infrastructure, and supports only services required to support institutional goals. A financial organization, for instance, might not need to permit instant messaging. Similarly, services should not be enabled on the server side unless they are specifically needed. Each service, no matter how well protected and secure, is another point of entry into the system on which it is hosted (and potentially every other system in that organization). Every door built into a wall reduces the capability of that wall. Doors and walls operate towards opposite ends.

Mac OS X Server provides a lot of temptation along these lines. Interesting services like QuickTime Streaming are a click away and easy to manage. I can't stress enough, though, the need for regression testing against existing systems and a sufficiently thorough incubation period on a protected host that is accessible neither to the Internet in general nor to most other organizational hosts (since malicious intent most often arises in-house). New services should be deployed only after guidelines have been developed and justifications researched, and every new system should specifically support organizational goals.

Minimize Change, Maximize Stability

Apple supports a very feature-driven ecosystem. Much of Apple's market appeal revolves around the next big thing, the next Macworld keynote, or some surprise mid-quarter product announcement. This trend, however, doesn't necessarily exist for the benefit of information technology, and long-term, stable systems can be made difficult to maintain by the introduction of new elements and the frequency with which Apple enjoys surprising the world.

IT systems traditionally change only when such a change can be cost justified—when the benefits of change outweigh the costs. More often than not, this means the end of a vendor support cycle, or with the addition of a truly beneficial feature. My web server, though, still runs Jaguar, mainly because I've pursued several such upgrades for clients, and right now do not perceive the cost associated with porting, testing, and deployment of my web applications to be justified. Apple still issues security updates for Jaguar, and the server itself is specialized enough in purpose that none of Panther's features really appeal to me. Stable systems tend to be appreciated more than the newest feature, and at any rate, unstable and unavailable systems are far more likely to gather notice than a flashy new service.

Change to any infrastructure component—version update, feature addition, or bug fix—should be undertaken in a careful manner, bearing in mind and testing its impact on existing systems. At its most careful, this policy entails a rigorous set of processes that should be documented and adhered to for best results. Of course not every system at every scale demands this attention, but the point is that nearly any infrastructure modification can benefit from a little more structure.

Testing

The first step in making any particular change is testing. This examination, always in a nonproduction environment, often occurs in a bench area or at the desk of IT personnel. It ensures that the basic functionality of the system in question is ready for serious analysis. Testing results should be used to generate metrics for upcoming pilots, helping to determine when a pilot should be considered successful (or unsuccessful).

Pilot

Piloting involves a very limited deployment of some new infrastructure component. Pilots should include specific and measurable criteria for success, and should be used to generate plans for further deployment. Target audiences for pilots should be carefully chosen, since the systems in question are, by definition, untested. When rolling out a new image or OS release to a lab, for instance, a pilot of only a few machines (10 percent is a good number) should be first undertaken. Similarly, I often advocate isolation of IT personnel resources onto a specific server, so that it may be upgraded before other production machines. Living on a technology before general deployment allows for a familiarity that is not otherwise feasible. This familiarity, in turn, dramatically increases the likelihood of a successful rollout. Regardless of the circumstances, the pilot should be closely monitored so that the resulting data may be effectively used.

Staging

Once pilots have proven successful, deployment can be undertaken—hopefully in the context of the combined knowledge from testing and piloting. Rather than an immediate, full-scale deployment, however, this generally means deployment in stages, or waves. Staged deployment permits a more careful process, with each stage garnering more and more institutional knowledge of the system in question. As a general rule, I prefer stages of 30 to 50%, resulting in two or three stages per deployment.

Deployment and monitoring

Once a system is fully deployed, it should be continuously monitored, letting you build knowledge and prepare for its next revision or update.

Obviously, knowledge building, monitoring, and systematic testing are stressed at each point in the deployment process. The point is to be careful, to be conservative in the management of important architectures, and to carefully document the deployment process.

System Management

This section of the chapter delves into specific features and options available to support the services available in Mac OS X Server. While none fit into a specific existing chapter, all are important to day-to-day server management. These fundamental features affect the overall health of the server rather than supporting specific systems. Managing them correctly helps to support the conceptual elements outlined previously, and it is hoped, will result in a healthier server.

Software Updates

One challenge of server management common to nearly any organization or platform is that of software updates. Vendors release updated software versions, and even subtle changes in functionality or feature set can adversely affect established support infrastructures. Worse yet are new bugs, introduced unknowingly into new software versions. Either case may result in considerable downtime and lost revenue. A careful balance must be struck between secure, up-to-date software and stable, predictable systems. A careful analysis reveals three distinct phenomena in this area: major updates, like the one from 10.2 (Jaguar) to 10.3 (Panther); minor revisions, such as the one from 10.3.4 to 10.3.5, and Security Updates, issued to counter specific vulnerabilities in specific OS versions.

Software update methods

Apple includes a variety of mechanisms for accessing both minor OS versions and security updates via their Software Update infrastructure. (Generally, major OS revisions must be purchased.) Update lists are available from pre-established hosts (*swscan.apple.com* and *swquery.apple.com*), while the updates themselves are usually outsourced to companies that specialize in high-bandwidth downloads, like Akamai and AT&T. All activity—software scans and downloads—occur over port 80. Updates themselves are cryptographically signed so that bogus updates—from DNS spoofing, compromised DHCP, or any other malicious source—may be discarded. Apple includes three tools designed to help keep Mac OS X Server up-to-date:

- Command-line: Most comfortable to long-time system administrators and most friendly to managed or scripted environments is the *softwareupdate* command-line tool. Requiring root privileges, it supports all of the features of the graphical tool (discussed later) accessible in System Preferences. Although it has an accurate and well-developed manpage, many of its common options are listed in Table 4-1.

Table 4-1. Options for the softwareupdate command.

Option	Description
-l, --list	List available updates.
-i --install	Install a particular update. Can be coupled with the --a flag to install all available updates or with the --r flag to install only required updates. Automated installation is generally not recommended, for reasons enumerated earlier.
---ignored	Add specific updates to the ignored list. For more details, consult the manpage.
-d	Download updates but do not install them. Not mentioned in the manpage (as of 10.3. 5), this is an extremely useful option, allowing for offline analysis of proposed updates.

Example 4-1 is a simple shell script that checks for available updates, and downloads them.

Example 4-1. Using the softwareupdate command in a script.

```
#!/bin/sh
#
for i in `/usr/sbin/softwareupdate --list | egrep '!|\*' | awk '{print $2}'`
do
        echo $i
        echo /usr/sbin/softwareupdate -d $i
        /usr/sbin/softwareupdate -d $i
done
```

 When using Apple's command-line *softwareupdate* tool, be sure to first set the COMMAND_LINE_INSTALL environment variable:

> Xsg5:~ mab9718$ **export COMMAND_LINE_INSTALL=1**

Or, if using a *csh* derivative like *tcsh*:

> [xsg5:~] mab9718% **setenv COMMAND_LINE_INSTALL 1**

This step ensures that installers with a graphical element do not block the update process by prompting for premium upgrades or displaying other splash screens or advertisements; QuickTime is the worst offender.

Server Admin

Located in the Settings tab of the general section in Server Admin, *servermgrd*'s software update mechanism literally calls the *softwareupdate* tool. Like most graphical methods, it is a less-granular option supporting fewer features. However, it is fairly convenient and does at least allow the administrator to choose which packages should be installed. Its interface for this choice is illustrated in Chapter 3.

Perhaps most interesting about *servermgrd*'s software update is the reboot button that becomes available after an update has been successfully installed. This is generally the only method for restarting the server via Server Admin, and it is coupled with update installation. Luckily, though, this is mainly a limitation of Server Admin, and not of its underlying technology. Mac OS X Server can be rebooted via the Server Admin protocol at any time by accessing *servermgrd*'s built-in web interface, running (using HTTPS) on port 311. Choose the *servermgr_info* module as illustrated in Figures 4-1 and 4-2, which sends the proper XML (via a secured and authenticated session) to reboot the server. This capability is often present when others, such as SSH or Apple Remote Desktop access, are not working or shut down.

System Preferences and /System/Library/CoreServices/Software\ Update.app

Generally available only via Apple Remote Desktop or some other graphical remote management tool, the System Preferences application is more commonly used to manage software updates on the client version of Mac OS X. Its functionality is identical on Mac OS X Server.

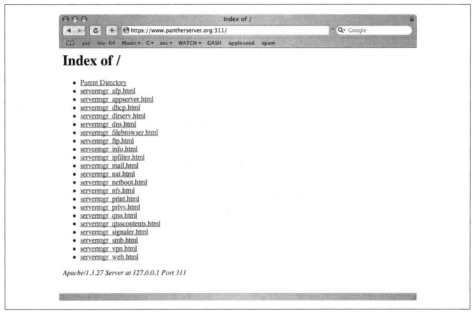

Figure 4-1. Using servermgrd's web interface.

Figure 4-2. The servermgrd-info plug-in's reboot option, which is not graphically accessible for non-Xserve hardware. The Xserve may be rebooted using Server monitor.

Minor updates

Apple issues minor OS revisions on average about every 1.9 months, with the time between updates varying from about one month to nearly four. Apple's convenient Software Update mechanism makes for a formidable temptation to simply install the

newest update available, and many administrators fall into this trap and are consequently exposed to either short-term bugs or disruptive feature-set changes.

Rather than immediately installing every available update, a few simple guidelines
will help to ease this pain:

- Monitor Mac OS X Server resources (documented later in this chapter) to determine whether the update has any known negative repercussions. Keep in mind
that your environment might be atypical in some sense and thus could be subject to issues not encountered elsewhere.

- Rather than using Apple's Software Update mechanism, manually download the
update installer package and examine it in great depth using the included utility
lsbom. *lsbom* (shown in Example 4-2) examines a packages bill of materials, documenting its payload in three fields: *path*, *stat( )* output (including filesystem
permissions),* and *owner/group UniqueID*.

*Example 4-2. Output of the lsbom command, verifying the contents of the Mac OS X Server 10.3.5
update. Only a few lines are shown here, since the ouput, at 5,755 lines, is quite verbose.*

```
[crap:~] mab9718% lsbom ./MacOSXUpdate10.3.5Patch.pkg/Contents/Archive.bom
.        41775   0/80
./Applications  40775   0/80
./Applications/Font Book.app    40775   0/80
./Applications/Font Book.app/Contents   40775   0/80
./Applications/Font Book.app/Contents/Info.plist         100664  0/80    3154    3772715790
./Applications/Font Book.app/Contents/MacOS     40775   0/80
./Applications/Font Book.app/Contents/MacOS/Font Book    100775  0/80    237432  4241228647
./Applications/Font Book.app/Contents/Resources 40775   0/80
./Applications/Font Book.app/Contents/Resources/Dutch.lproj      40775   0/80
./Applications/Font Book.app/Contents/Resources/Dutch.lproj/FBInfoView.nib       40775    0/80
./Applications/Font Book.app/Contents/Resources/Dutch.lproj/FBInfoView.nib/keyedobjects.
nib     100664 0/80    5551    439641685
./Applications/Font Book.app/Contents/Resources/Dutch.lproj/FBPreviewWindow.nib40775     0/
80
./Applications/Font Book.app/Contents/Resources/Dutch.lproj/FBPreviewWindow.nib/
keyedobjects.nib         100664  0/80    9379    2762051226
./Applications/Font Book.app/Contents/Resources/Dutch.lproj/FBPreviewWindow.nib/objects.
nib     100664 0/80    3921    2074727774
./Applications/Font Book.app/Contents/Resources/Dutch.lproj/InfoPlist.strings 100664    0/
80      632     1241940170
./Applications/Font Book.app/Contents/Resources/English.lproj    40775   0/80
./Applications/Font Book.app/Contents/Resources/English.lproj/FBInfoView.nib     40775      0/80
./Applications/Font Book.app/Contents/Resources/English.lproj/FBInfoView.nib/keyedobjects.
nib     100664 0/80    5532    3192412550
./Applications/Font Book.app/Contents/Resources/English.lproj/FBPreviewWindow.nib
40775   0/80
```

---

* This output generally consists of a five- or six-digit number. The last four digits represent file system permissions, as documented in the chmod manpage. The remaining one or two digits refer to the nature of the file—
4 for directory, 6 for block device, 10 for regular file, and 12 for symbolic link.

Careful analysis allows you to determine whether any sensitive or customized files will be overwritten and whether critical systems will be affected by the update. A busy AFP server, for instance, might want to make note of an upgrade to the AppleFileServer daemon. The command line–averse will appreciate the third-party utility Pacifist (*www.charlessoft.com*), which offers much the same functionality in a graphical environment.

Pacifist may also be used to selectively obtain certain portions of the package in order to install particular components of any update. This should be undertaken very carefully, however, since the OS itself will be in an unknown and unsupported state.

- For the high end, use a granular filesystem management tool like *radmind* (*http:// rsug.itd.umich.edu/software/radmind/*), which allows for a tremendous amount of flexibility. *radmind* is currently the only solution that allows for a complete system rollback, in case an upgrade produces unintended consequences. *radmind* documentation is beyond the scope of this book but its active and friendly community is easy to access from its site.

Major updates

It takes Apple 12 to 18 months to produce a major OS release, such as 10.3 (Panther). Most significant changes in functionality are reserved for these releases, and as a consequence each release tends to have fairly far-reaching effects, requiring organizational support mechanisms to be retooled. One example of this dramatic change can be seen in Mac OS X Server's directory services architecture, which has undergone major reorganization in nearly every OS release. See Table 4-2.

Table 4-2. Mac OS X Server's Directory Services architecture has experienced significant architectural changes from 10.0 through 10.3.

Version	Architecture
10.0 and 10.1	Shared NetInfo database
10.2	NetInfo database shared out over LDAP; Password Server for authentication
10.3	LDAP with BDB for account storage; Password Server and KDC for authentication

Because adoption of major OS revisions tends to be difficult from a support perspective, it should be undertaken with great care. Mac OS X Server in particular must be examined on a service-by-service basis, and sometimes very specific architectures must be developed in order to effectively manage the upgrade process.

 Although Apple typically includes such upgrade mechanisms as a tool to migrate from NetInfo to LDAP, they do not often scale to meet the needs of larger deployments.

An additional factor to consider is the maturity of the new OS release. Because such a high percentage of the new release tends to be code that is new and in many cases not yet widely deployed, it makes sense to approach it with skepticism. I've worked with several customers in the past, in fact, to develop specific criteria that must be met before a new OS may be deployed—usually this criteria is organization-specific, and refers to specific OS functionality. In general, I begin to consider deployment during an OS's second minor revision, and depending on the feature set that is required, proceed with pilots in the second or third revision (such as 10.3.2 or 10.3. 3). As usual, though, this should not be treated as a hard and fast rule, and actual deployment should be planned according to each organization's needs.

Security updates

Security updates were first deployed by Apple when it became apparent that certain issues would not wait for major or minor OS upgrades. They are generally engineered to address specific vulnerabilities in some component of the operating system. Security updates are themselves usually incorporated into the next minor OS release, in case the standalone updates were not, for some reason, run when they first became available.

Because their focus is so specific, security updates are generally easy to manage. The vulnerability they address should, since they are generally well-documented in the update's description, be researched and well understood. They should, like any other update, be examined carefully using *lsbom* or Pacifist, and if the update is applicable, it should generally then be applied as soon as possible. Updates that are not applicable, though, shouldn't necessarily be installed, since unwarranted modification of the OS can sometimes have unforeseen ramifications. An FTP vulnerability, for instance, doesn't necessarily have to be fixed if a server will never have FTP access enabled.

 As of this writing, Apple security updates are closely coupled with specific minor OS releases. By requiring customers to prematurely deploy minor OS releases in order to install critical security updates, Apple is painting its customers into a dangerous decision, forcing them to choose either the stability of a well-tested OS revision or the security of a patched OS.

Finally, regardless of the nature of the update in question, it makes sense to roll out system changes in a methodic and careful way. An example of this ploy is documented earlier in this chapter, moving from testing through pilots and staging and into a full deployment.

Backing Up

The science of backup in Unix operating systems is well-established and documented elsewhere. Concerns about tape rotation, scheduling, and organizational backup policy should be referred to O'Reilly's *Unix Backup and Recovery* (1999), or Prentice Hall's *Unix System Administration Handbook,* Third Edition (2000). Instead, this brief treatment of backup seeks to discuss some Mac OS X and Mac OS X Server's specific issues, along with a brief analysis of current backup products.

Mac OS X Server backup issues

Mac OS X, especially in its Server flavor, bears careful consideration where backups are concerned. Unlike most server platforms (including Windows server products) it ships with no easily accessible backup solution. Despite all its strengths, I consider this is a real downside to its deployment and a barrier to its adoption in a number of its core markets. Many server administrators need neither the complexity nor the scope of a commercial backup solution, and the lack of an equivalent to Windows Backup forces nearly all organizations deploying Mac OS X Server to spend a significant amount of money on third-party backup software.

This issue is exacerbated by the lack of a generalized tape device driver in Mac OS X and Mac OS X Server. Most Unix operating systems contain a */dev/tape* or equivalent, allowing a wide variety of common Unix utilities to be leveraged towards a backup solution. Apple's position is that such a device driver would be prohibitively complex, since tape devices are notoriously quirky and vary tremendously from vendor to vendor. While this may be true, Sun, Microsoft, and half a dozen Linux companies don't seem to have a problem with it.

A final challenge relates to the dual forked nature of HFS+. As noted many times throughout this and other documentation, most Unix utilities have evolved without the notion of dual forked files. Nowhere is this more relevant on Mac OS X and Mac OS X Server than in the backup space. Many applications still rely on documents with resource forks, and the volume of resource-ridden legacy data cannot be underestimated. This means that many well established mechanisms for backup (such as scripts using *dump*, *restore*, and *tar*) are not relevant on Mac OS X and Mac OS X Server, at least in the 10.3 environment.

tar alternatives

Although neither ships in a default install of Mac OS X, at least two versions of *tar* that support resource forks do exist. *hfstar* (*http://www.metaobject.com/Products. html*) and *xtar* (*http://www.helios.de/news/news03/N_06_03.phtml*) may both be used to effectively manage archival data on Mac OS X, including resource forks. They can be used exactly like traditional versions of *tar* (even driving remote tape drives hosted on some other OS with */dev/tape*). Most of the examples here should work with either *xtar* or *hfstar*—remember, though, they are not meant for the *tar* binary that is included with Mac OS X or Mac OS X Server. *tar* tasks include:

- Creating an archive. This most basic and common *tar* operation can be useful for archiving files. Using the *tar* and *date* commands to create a timestamped tar archive of an entire volume. Notice that the *date* command is escaped with backticks in order to make sure that its output is included in the *tar* command.

  ```
  tar -cvzf data.`date'+%m%d%y%H%M%S'` /Volumes/Data
  ```

- Moving the contents of a directory. Unix tar preserves permissions better than other mechanisms for moving files around.

  ```
  cd /Users && tar -cf - . | (cd /Volumes/NewUsers && tar -xpvf -)
  cd /Users && tar -cf - . | ssh newserver "cd /Users && tar -xpvf -"
  ```

- Dumping to a remote tape has been common practice in the Unix world for a good while now, so even though your Mac doesn't know how to drive a tape drive doesn't mean that its traditional Unix tools can't get the job done. Using *tar* over and *ssh* connection with *dd* to drive a remote tape drive. The resource fork management is all done on the Mac OS X side, and dd ensures that the data is blocked properly for the host OS.

  ```
  tar - czvf - /Users | ssh -l user remote_host dd of=/dev/tape
  ```

Commercial backup products

Slow in coming, it finally seems (halfway through the lifetime of its third major revision) that supported third-party backup products are coming to Mac OS X. Several enterprise backup vendors (among them Veritas, Legato, and Tivoli) offer Mac OS X–native clients. Additionally, a number of vendors support server-side solutions, allowing Mac OS X (using vendor-specific technology to drive tape architectures) to back up data from multiple clients. Note that this section is not meant as an exhaustive survey of backup options, but more as a survey of some of the available options.

Among the server-side offerings, the Tolis Group's BRU (Backup and Recovery Utility) comes out on top in my book. It's been a consistent player in the Unix backup marketplace for several years and was among the first commercial applications to offer Linux support. It is fast and efficient, runs totally in the background, and offers a very full feature set. BRU's downside is that its graphical interface and setup befit its heritage far more than a traditional Mac application. Its error reporting, while accurate, is tucked away behind numerous tabs and pull-down menus. There are few alert dialog boxes and, as a result, figuring out what's going wrong (and when) can be difficult during the initial setup.

 When adding new hardware to BRU Server, be sure to stop and restart the server itself after scanning for new hardware.

That said, BRU's list of features is exhaustive: unqualified support for very large volumes, staged (disk to disk to tape) backups, extensive filtering, totally remote management and pre- and post-actions (scripts or executables to be run before or after a backup operation). It is what I use and have been using ever since I bought BRU 16 for Linux to drive the tape that backed up the data my Macs deposited onto my Linux box every night.

Dantz's Retrospect (*www.dantz.com*), the perennial leader in Mac backup, is a solid contender on the low end. Sadly, however, Dantz has lost a lot of its focus on the Mac market, leaving things like automated staged backups (disk to disk to tape) to its Windows version and to BRU Server. In their haste to focus on the Windows market, Dantz has created a Mac OS 9 product that happens to run only on Mac OS X— with no remote management capabilities and weird GUI dialogs that pop up over the login window. Coupled with increasingly unfriendly licensing terms—Dantz wants you to pay more to back up Mac OS X Server, even though they do nothing to support live backups of database-driven services like Mail, NetInfo, or LDAP and MySQL—this oddness results in a picture that is not pretty and a vendor I do not like to send money to.

 One feature of Retrospect that is difficult to find elsewhere is their aggregated view of the backup history. All sessions of a Retrospect differential or incremental archive may be seen in a single view, allowing for easy selection of the newest version of every file.

Several other options bear mentioning—Bakbone (*www.bakbone.com*), another respected vendor in the enterprise backup space, recently debuted its NetVault software in both client and server versions for Mac OS X. NetVault is heavily focused on staged backups (discussed later) and features very granular management—from backup policies that provide prioritized access to backup resources to fine-grained end-user access capabilities, it is a well thought-out product. It is really too early as of this writing to make prognostications—however, while I have not yet seen it deployed at any scale that gives me a lot of confidence, it was a joy to test, and will probably have significant impact on the Mac market.

Amanda (Advanced Maryland Automatic Network Disk Archiver, *www.amanda.org*) is an Open Source *tar*-based client-server backup application that is well thought of in intuitional circles. I have not used it in Mac OS X, but I know several folks who have had luck coupling it with *hfstar* or *xtar* (and in some cases, Esbackup's dump and restore, mentioned later). Amanda has many of the features of commercial client/ server offerings and some, like Kerberos integration, that are unheard of or uncommon at the very least. An active developer and user community supports it, and if you have a Unix background, you will feel right at home. Finally, Esbackup, available from Ugsoft (*www.ugsoft.de*) is notable due to their modification of Unix dump and restore in order to support HFS+.

Backup staging

Several times now, staged backups, or disk-to-disk-to-tape backups, have been mentioned as a feature of some backup packages. The concept is pretty simple, but is nonetheless worth calling out due to its utility. In the past 15 years, disk storage has gotten progressively—sometimes remarkably—faster and larger. At the same time, disks have also dropped dramatically in price. Tape drives, although they've grown, have not evolved at nearly the same rate, and they certainly haven't gotten a whole lot cheaper. The result is that today a terabyte of space is relatively easy to obtain but very difficult to back up. Staged backups have become very popular as a workaround to this issue. Rather than being written to comparatively slow tape devices, backed-up files are initially saved to some disk based storage source (a stage disk). Clients are able to complete the backup process quickly and go on about their business, while the comparatively pokey tape drive or array can take its time working over the staged data.

> An added benefit of staging is its relatively good parallelism. It is rather easy to have multiple clients writing to a single stage disk, whereas most backup packages (in the context of relatively affordable tape devices), can back up only a single client to tape at once.

Well-implemented staged backups keep track of data no matter where it is, automatically noting when an archive has been upstaged (written to tape). This sort of transparency makes the life of any backup administrator easier, and makes staged backups a favorite tool of most larger enterprises.

Account Management

One formidable challenge as Mac OS X deployment expands in scale and scope is that of account management—adding users, groups, and computers to a directory domain. Along these lines, Apple has engineered a passable import system that's abstract enough to be applied to any type of directory node Mac OS X might interact with. This capability can be accessed graphically, using Workgroup Manager, or from the command line, using *dsimportexport* (renamed *dsimport* in later versions of Panther, since it never really did export data). This function is easy to access, from Workgroup Manager's Server menu, using the import selection, as seen in Figure 4-3.

dsimportexport offers a number of options, most of which are also available in Workgroup Manager. It takes the following general form:

```
dsimport [-g|-s|-p] /path/to/file directory-node admin  pass [O|M|I|A] [options]
```

where *directory-node* is the Open Directory node (such as */NetInfo/DefaultLocalNode* or */LDAPv3/127.0.0.1*) where the imported users should reside and where *admin* and *pass* are the credentials of an administrator in that node. Its *–p* and *–s* flags refer to

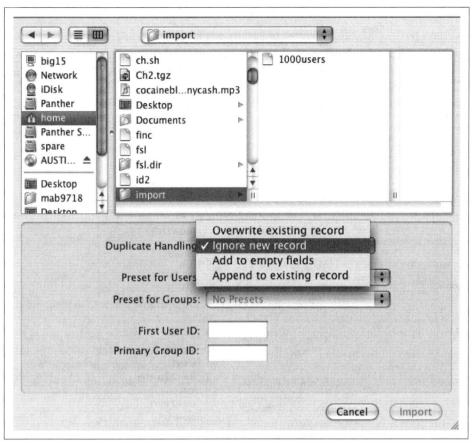

Figure 4-3. Workgroup Manager's dialog for importing user records. Duplicate records may be overwritten, ignored, appended to, or merged with duplicates. These options are identical to those of dsimportexport, and are described in more depth in Table 4-3.

specifically formatted import files from AppleShare IP and Mac OS X Server 10.X. Under most circumstances, you will be working with the –g flag, a custom character-delineated file, discussed later in this chapter. Its *O*, *M*, *I*, and *A* flags deal with duplicate handling, and are described in Table 4-3.

Table 4-3. Duplicate handling options in dsimportexport.

Option	Description
0	Overwrites existing record with that from import.
M	Granularly merges empty fields in existing record with populated fields from duplicate import. Useful for adding attributes *en masse* to existing objects.
I	Ignores duplicate object from import.
A	Granularly appends attributes from duplicate to attributes from original. This operation will result in multi-valued attributes.

A typical import, then, would look something like what's shown in Example 4-3.

Example 4-3. Using dsimportexport. A file called 100u is being added to the odm.pantherserver.org Open Directory domain. Duplicate records will be overwritten. Only a portion of the output is shown; dsimportexport shows one line of output for each record added to the domain.

```
g5:~ ladmin$ ./dsimportexport -g 100 u/LDAPv3/odm.pantherserver.org odadm !!g@#d -O
Total Bytes =9937
Total Bytes =9937
Auth err = 0
Bytes Read =234
Bytes Read =332
Bytes Read =430
```

And that's generally all you need to know. That syntax should suffice in most situations. However, *dsimport*, also supports a number of optional arguments, the most common of which are illustrated in Table 4-4.

Table 4-4. Common advanced options available in dsimportexport.

Option	Argument(s)	Description
--T	XDSStandardUser or xDSStandard-Group	Delimited import of files without the descriptive header.
--s	Integer for starting UniqueID value	Indicates the starting UniqueID value for import records without specified UniqueIDs. Avoid this if possible—in general, try to include UniqueIDs in your import record.
--recordFormat	0x0A 0x5C 0x3A 0x2C dsRecType-Standard:Users 8 RecordName AuthMethod Password UniqueID PrimaryGroupID RealName NFSHomeDirectory UserShell	Passes in an import header as a command-line option. The format of this header is discussed later in this chapter. This is somewhat cumbersome, and it's usually easiest to specify the header in the import file.
--r	PrimaryGroupID	Specifies a primary group ID for import records that lack one. In general, it is better to include a PrimaryGroupID in your import record.
--v		Verbose output.
--y, --yrnm, and --yrpwd	IP address, username, and password, respectively	Contacts Mac OS X Server remotely over the DSProxy port (625) in order to push a user import to a remote server.
--d	(in hex) End of record, escape, end of attribute and multiple value delineator characters	Specifies (in hex notation) the delineation fields normally found in the header of the import record. This is quite cumbersome and it's usually easier to specify delineators in the import file.

However it is run, *dsimportexport* leaves a descriptive log file (Example 4-4) in the *Home* directory of the user who executed the command. This log is named according to the date and time of the import. Logs are never purged automatically, and can accumulate over time on a busy system.

Example 4-4. Using the head command to see the first 17 lines of a successful user import log.

```
crap:~ mab9718$ head -17 Library/Logs/ImportExport/DSImportExport2004.0828.001157.log
DSImport Log 2004.0828.00:11:57 Number of Args = 10
DSImport Log 2004.0828.00:11:57 ======= Tool Parser Arguements ======

DSImport Log 2004.0828.00:11:57 File Path = /Users/mab9718/100users
DSImport Log 2004.0828.00:11:57 DS Node Path = /NetInfo/root
DSImport Log 2004.0828.00:11:57 User Name = mab9718
DSImport Log 2004.0828.00:11:57 User Password was supplied
DSImport Log 2004.0828.00:11:57 Dup Option = 0
DSImport Log 2004.0828.00:11:57 starting ID Num = 1025
DSImport Log 2004.0828.00:11:57 Group ID Num = 20
DSImport Log 2004.0828.00:11:57 ======= End Of Args ======

DSImport Log 2004.0828.00:11:57 Starting Delimited file import
DSImport Log 2004.0828.00:11:57 Inside DoImportDelimitedFile
DSImport Log 2004.0828.00:11:57 Auth err = 0
DSImport Log 2004.0828.00:11:58 Added a user record named: p10001.
DSImport Log 2004.0828.00:12:01 Adding Record succeeded
```

Import file format

Both Workgroup Manager and *dsimportexport* use the same type of import files, as Workgroup Manager actually calls *dsimportexport* when it needs to import data. The format of that file is actually very flexible and not extremely friendly—it requires knowledge of hexadecimal notation, as shown in Example 4-5.

Example 4-5. Using the cat command to examine a user import.

```
xserve:~ mab9718$ cat 1user
0x0A 0x5C 0x3A 0x2C dsRecTypeStandard:Users 10 RecordName AuthMethod Password UniqueID
PrimaryGroupID RealName NFSHomeDirectory UserShell Comment Keywords
p10001:dsAuthMethodStandard\:dsAuthClearText:apple:10001:20:Student 10001:/Users/p10001:/
bin/bash:this is a comment:2004,marketing
```

The first line (which in the example wraps onto two lines) consists of the following fields:

End of record marker (in hex)
Specifies that the end of an individual record has been reached. In this case, *0x0A* specifies that each record ends with a line feed.

Escape character (in hex)
This character should be used when another structural element (such as the field or value delineator) should be used in the actual value of an attribute. In our example, 0x5C specifies the "\", which is used to escape the colon in p10001's AuthMethod attribute (dsAuthMethodStandard:dsAuthClearText).

Field delineator (in hex)
> Used to separate attributes. `0x3A`, from our example, specifies the colon (:), which is used to separate attributes in an individual user record.

Multivalued delineator (in hex)
> Separates multiple values for a particular attribute, such as the two keywords in the example import record. `0x2C` specifies a comma (,). Keywords (along with comments, also represented in the example import record) are highly useful in the management of users and are described in great depth in Chapter 3.

Type of record
> Specifics what type of record is being imported. Generally prefixed with the string `dsRecTypeStandard:`, this may be any type of record that Open Directory understands, although Users, groups, computers and computer lists are the most common. For a complete listing, see the DirectoryServiceAttributes manpage.

The number of attributes per record
> Our example has 10.

The name of each attribute
> In our example, `RecordName`, `AuthMethod`, `Password`, `UniqueID`, `PrimaryGroupID`, `RealName`, `NFSHomeDirectory`, `UserShell`, `Comment`, and `Keywords`. For a complete listing of feasible attributes see the DirectoryServiceAttributes manpage.

The actual user records begin on the next line. Note that each user record, like the import file header, may wrap between lines. Each record is separated by a carriage return. Of particular interest in this example are the `AuthMethod` and `Password` attributes. Setting the latter to `dsAuthMethodStandard\:dsAuthClearText` and the former to the user's initial password allows the user's password to be added to Password Server—an important aspect of user imports.

Any number of user attributes may be added in an import. Bear in mind, though, that each additional attribute, especially at a scale of thousands of users, adds to total import time. Using the eight attributes specified in the earlier example results in an import time of about 2.5 minutes for a thousand users. Results are not linear, though, and thirty thousand users take around 26 hours. It's generally a good idea, then, to minimize the number of records in any import and to minimize the number of attributes in any large import. Large attributes, such as MCX data and the `AppleMail` attribute therefore can be added later and much more efficiently with tools like *ldapmodify*.

Another popular option for adding user accounts is Passenger, a third-party commercial application. Passenger has the added benefit of extensive text-processing capabilities, including attribute generation and multiple file format import. Although most of its features could be implemented with some shell scripting, Passenger is a good way to save time for administrators who prefer a graphical interface.

Group accounts

Management of group accounts presents a challenge that is similar to, if slightly less complex than, user management. The same import record may be used, adjusted only slightly to reflect the requirements of group accounts (see Example 4-6).

Example 4-6. Using the cat command to examine a simple group import record. Group membership is stored in the Member attribute as a list of user RecordNames.

```
g5:~ ladmin$ cat 1G
0x0A 0x5C 0x3A 0x2C dsRecTypeStandard:Groups 4 RecordName Password PrimaryGroupID
GroupMembership
newGroup:*:100:admin,p10001,skwa
```

In larger-scale deployments, it might make sense to add groups directly to Open Directory Server's LDAP interface, rather than using DirectoryService and *dsimportexport*. This is not typically feasible in user imports because the LDAP server has no way to set the user's password, which is stored in PasswordServer (and sometimes Kerberos). LDAP modifications are typically a lot faster, because they don't have to be dispatched through the *DirectoryService* daemon, and administrators from other backgrounds might be more familiar with LDIF, since it is cross-platform (see Example 4-7).

Example 4-7. This ldif file could be used with the ldapadd command to the same effect as the earlier dsimportexport record. LDAP-based modifications will typically be a lot faster than using dsimportexport. A value for the apple-generateduid attribute can be obtained with the uuidgen command. For more information relating to ldapadd and ldapmodify, see Chapter 7.

```
dn: cn=newGroup,cn=groups,dc=4am-media,dc=com
cn: newGroup
objectClass: posixGroup
objectClass: apple-group
objectClass: extensibleObject
objectClass: top
gidNumber: 100
apple-generateduid: A8FABA90-135A-11D9-A695-000A95AE7200
memberUid: admin
memberUid: p10001
memberUid: skwa
```

Computer accounts and lists

Computer accounts and lists are commonly used in Mac OS X to manage access to particular resources. A list of executive machines, for instance, might be reserved for use by a very limited group of users, or a graphics lab could be granted the right to run some licensed (and presumably expensive) application. While these capabilities are for the most part very desirable, this kind of management (based on the computer that the user is logged into) presents two formidable challenges:

- Computer accounts by themselves aren't very useful. They really have no impact on a managed Mac OS X environment until they're added to a computer list (to which managed client settings are then applied).

- Computers, when they contact an Open Directory node, search for their accounts using the MAC (hardware Ethernet) address of their built-in Ethernet; this is the case even when connecting to the network using some alternate interface, like AirPort. In order to be useful, computer accounts must correspond to real computers with real MAC addresses.

While obtaining MAC addresses is left as an exercise to the reader (you might start with your Apple Sales Rep or some automated bar code system), computers and computer lists, like users and groups, may be added to any Open Directory domain using *dsimportexport* records (see Example 4-8).

*Example 4-8. Using the cat utility to view a computer import record and a computer list creation record. Notice that the colons must be escaped, because the colon is being used as the field delineator. Alternately, a different delineator, such as the * character (hex 0x2a), could be used.*

```
g5:~ ladmin$ cat 1c.0
0x0A 0x5C 0x3A 0x2C dsRecTypeStandard:Computers 3 RecordName EnetAddress Comment
East-01:00\:0a\:95\:dp\:45\:56:East Lab
East-02:00\:0a\:95\:hf\:55\:57:East Lab
East-03:00\:0a\:95\:dg\:65\:58:East Lab
g5:~ ladmin$ cat cl.0
0x0a 0x5c 0x3a 0x2c dsRecTypeStandard:ComputerLists 2 RecordName Computers
East-Lab: East-01, East-02, East-03
crap:~ mab9718$ cat cl
0x0a 0x5c 0x3a 0x2c dsRecTypeStandard:ComputerLists 3 RecordName Computers Comment
kerb_srv2:gs.4am-media.com,xserve.4am-media.com:belch
```

 Different computer lists might have different purposes, and it is important to note that while lists of client Mac OS X systems may be named whatever is convenient, Mac OS X Server accounts, like those used to auto-configure Kerberized server services, should be named using the fully qualified domain name of the server.

Using LDAP rather than dsimportexport

Computers, like groups, do not (in Panther) have real passwords. Since computer creation doesn't require interaction with Password Server or Kerberos, it can be accomplished entirely using LDAP, which is generally faster than using *dsimportexport*. The LDIF file shown in Example 4-9 should serve as an example for use with the *ldapadd* command when adding computer lists and accounts to an Open Directory Master.

Example 4-9. An LDIF file used to add a single computer account and a single computer list. LDIF can import several types of objects at once, whereas dsimportexport cannot.

```
dn: cn=East-01,cn=computers,dc=4am-media,dc=com
cn: East-01
objectClass: apple-computer
objectClass: top
apple-generateduid: AA0137B4-136B-11D9-96D3-000A95AE7200
description: East Lab, 01

dn: cn=East-Lab,cn=computer_lists,dc=4am-media,dc=com
cn: East-Lab
objectClass: apple-computer-list
objectClass: top
apple-computers: East-01
```

Failover

New with Jaguar was an Active-Passive IP Failover mechanism, designed to let one server (or peer) take over the IP address of another in the case of a failure. The general premise is illustrated in Figure 4-4.

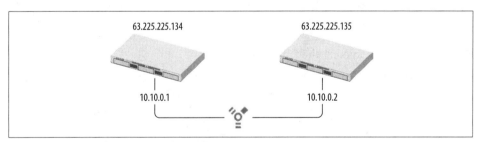

Figure 4-4. A basic IP Failover construction. The peer (63.225.225.135) will take over the IP address (63.225.225.134) of the master if it suspects that the master has failed. This model is used to demonstrate IP Failover settings later in this section.

This architecture revolves around two daemons—*heartbeatd*, running on the master, and *failoverd*, running on its peer. Both read their respective configurations from the */etc/hostconfig* file on the server on which they're running. These configuration options are documented in Table 4-5.

Table 4-5. Failover configuration directives from /etc/hostconfig. It's generally a good idea to specify a group email alias in FAILOVER_EMAIL_RECIPIENT, so that multiple people can be notified of a failure.

Daemon	Options
heartbeatd	`FAILOVER_BCAST_IPS="63.225.225.255 192.168.1.255"`

failoverd	`FAILOVER_PEER_IP=192.168.1.1`
	`FAILOVER_PEER_IP_PAIRS=en0:63.225.225.134`
	`FAILOVER_EMAIL_RECIPIENT=sysadmin_group@myschool.edu`

During normal operation, *heartbeatd*, which is started by the IP failover startup item, broadcasts every second on port 1649 to the IP addresses listed in its `FAILOVER_BCAST_IPS` */etc/hostconfig* configuration. These should usually be the broadcast addresses associated with the master's network interfaces. *failoverd*, running on the failover peer, listens for these broadcasts, and if they cease, it institutes a failover event.

 Notice that two separate networks are used in the failover process. This policy is intended to prevent false-positive failover events. If, for instance, the network switch that the master's Public interface was plugged into failed, we would not want to trigger a failover. (Obviously, a full-fledged failover event will do little to remedy the actual physical problem in this case.) So IP Failover is built to use two interfaces. In the best practice, one of those should be an interface that does not rely on extensive intermediary hardware, like a crossover cable or IP over FireWire.

The failover process

When *failoverd* detects a failure in the master, it begins a very specific set of processes, first running */usr/libexec/NotifyFailover* (in order to notify administrators specified in the `FAILOVER_EMAIL_RECIPIENT` directive) and then */usr/libexec/ProcessFailover* to complete the failover process.

ProcessFailover is actually a shell script and is, therefore, very clear about what it is doing. It logs to *syslogd*'s *daemon.error* facility and is called by *failoverd* with a specific syntax. Generalized syntax for the *ProcessFailover* command. *Interface:ip_address* refers to the Ethernet interface and IP address that the failover peer will use to provide services in the place of its master. *ProcessFailover* accepts multiple arguments, so that a peer can obtain multiple IP addresses as a result of failover.

```
ProcessFailover up|down interface:ip_address
```

ProcessFailover then performs a careful set of tasks that may be customized to suit your specific needs.

1. A test script, */Library/IPFailover/ip_address/Test* (*ip_address* being the IP that was passed to *ProcessFailover* by *failoverd*) is run if it exists. This is an optional mechanism for preventing false positive failover events. The system administrator is responsible for writing this script.

2. Any executable in */Library/IPFailover/ip_address* with the prefix *PreAcq* (pre-acquisition) is run. These are generally shell scripts designed to ensure that the failover peer is ready to obtain the master's IP address. It is generally a good practice to write a pre-acquisition script that calls the *changeip* command, as so may systems in Mac OS X are reliant on a proper IP address and hostname.

3. The address of the failover peer is changed to reflect the IP(s) specified in the FAILOVER_PEER_IP_PAIRS */etc/hostconfig* directive.

4. Any executable in */Library/IPFailover/ip_address* with the prefix *PostAcq* is executed. Generally scripts of some sort, *PostAcq* actions might commonly be used to restart processes that do not deal well with IP address changes.

Once the failover process is complete the failover peer continues to listen for the master's reappearance. If the master should appear, a failback event occurs. This process is similar to the initial failover, except in reverse. Once again, each step in the process is very structured:

1. Any executable in */Library/IPFailover/ip_address* with the prefix *PreRel* is executed. These scripts should be used to get the environment ready to failover.

2. This IP is released.

3. Any executable in */Library/IPFailover/ip_address* with the prefix *PostRel* is executed.

Note that the IP Failover mechanism in Mac OS X is capable of managing multiple interfaces. In the earlier example, only one FAILOVER_PEER_IP_PAIRS argument was specified. It is quite common, though, for a server to support multiple network interfaces, and *failoverd* is equipped to handle that case. All that is required is a second FAILOVER_PEER_IP_PAIRS argument. When a failure is detected, both pairs will be passed to the *ProcessFailover* script (Example 4-10).

Example 4-10. Managing IP Failover on multiple interfaces. In this way the fail over peer can better assume the role of a server that is providing data to multiple networks.

```
FAILOVER_PEER_IP_PAIRS=" en0:192.13.2.2 en1:10.1.0.2"
```

IP Failover is ideally suited for stateless and short-lived services, like HTTP, SMTP, and POP. Stateful protocols with longer-lived connections (like AFP) are much more likely to experience some sort of downtime, since failure events might occur while clients are connected. Although this should not dissuade you from deploying IP Failover, it is something to keep in mind.

Whenever it is available, it makes sense to prefer an application-level clustering technology over IP Failover. Application-level clustering, like that available with Apple's Open Directory Replication environment, allows for more complete solutions, including multimaster infrastructures and data synchronization.

IP Failover is an Active-Passive architecture—the failover peer, until it is needed, is largely idle. Although services may be provided by the peer, they would be subject to an interruption during and after a failover event. It is feasible to engineer around this issue using a *PostAcq* script that re-enables the peer's original IP address, but it should be noted that such an infrastructure grows more complex and difficult to maintain with each such addition.

Diskspacemonitor

One corollary to the intrusion minimization principal illustrated earlier in this chapter is that solutions—from a vendor, consultant, or IT staff—should not just minimize intrusion, but should also seek to help customers do what they are already doing more efficiently. This is well illustrated by Mac OS X Server's *diskspacemonitor* daemon, which, as its name implies, monitors available storage resources. This in itself is nothing new. System administrators have for years tweaked and hand-rolled countless *cron* jobs designed to take some action if available disk space became too low, and while it's nice of Apple to have provided such a service, other vendors have done that, too. The point is not that *diskspacemonitor* is revolutionary, but that it is a solid and consistent step in the right direction.

diskspacemonitor, which lives in */usr/sbin*, is a *cron*-driven shell script. It is typically enabled using the *on* flag:

```
[ace2:~] nadmin% sudo diskspacemonitor on
Password:
crontab: no crontab for root
```

This script adds entry into the root user's *crontab*. The following entry indicates that *diskspacemonitor* should run automatically every 10 minutes; this time with the *check* argument:

```
sudo cat /var/cron/tabs/root
# DO NOT EDIT THIS FILE - edit the master and reinstall.
# (/tmp/diskspacemonitor.22371 installed on Tue Sep 14 14:18:25 2004)
# (Cron version -- $FreeBSD: src/usr.sbin/cron/crontab/crontab.c,v 1.17 2001/06/16
03:16:52 peter Exp $)

*/10 * * * * /usr/sbin/diskspacemonitor check
```

The *check* argument, in turn, obtains a list of local disks and for each one checks the available disk space, comparing it to the *alert_threshold* and *recovery_threshold* in *diskspacemonitor*'s configuration file (*/etc/diskspacemonitor/diskspacemonitor.conf*), shown in Example 4-11.

Example 4-11. Using the cat command to examine diskspacemonitor's configuration file. Many (but not all) of diskspacemonitor's settings are stored here.

```
[ace2:~] nadmin% cat /etc/diskspacemonitor/diskspacemonitor.conf
# Config for diskspacemonitor
#

monitor_interval=10      # Check disks at this interval, in minutes

alert_threshold=75       # When a disk is this percentage full, execute
                         # the alert scripts in
                         # /etc/diskspacemonitor/action/

recovery_threshold=85    # When a disk is this percentage full, execute
                         # the recovery scripts in
                         # /etc/diskspacemonitor/action/

log_file=/var/log/diskspacemonitor.log
```

If the values established for either alert_threshold or recovery_threshold are met or exceeded for any local volume, *diskspacemonitor* takes action, executing */etc/diskspacemonitor/action/alert* or */etc/diskspacemonitor/action/recover*, respectively. The former, which has a configuration file stored at */etc/diskspacemonitor/alert.conf*, generates an email (with a subject indicating that the disk is filling up and a body consisting of the output of the *df* command) to an address specified in *alert.conf*'s to variable, as shown in Example 4-12.

Example 4-12. Using cat to examine /etc/diskspacemonitor/alert.conf, diskspacemonitor's configuration file for alert events.

```
[ace2:~] nadmin% cat /etc/diskspacemonitor/alert.conf
# Config for alert
# Arguments passed to alert (and alert.local, if
# it exists):
# - Volume name
# - Threshold
# - Percentage full
# - Log file
#
subject="DiskSpaceMonitor: Disk $1 has exceeded $2% threshold, is $3% full."
to=it-alerts@pantherserver.org
body=`df -k -l -t ufs; df -k -l -t hfs`
```

 The default *alert.conf* configuration specifies a syntax to the *df* command that will not work—the *-l* (local) and *-t* (type) options are actually exclusive, and cannot be run together. Removing the *-l* flag is probably a good idea, since all HFS or UFS partitions are by definition local.

The *recover* script (also in */etc/diskspacemonitor/action*) is typically executed at a higher-percentage disk usage—85 percent, as opposed to *alert*'s 75 percent in a default configuration. Typically, the *recover* script is used to reduce disk usage by compressing, deleting, or rolling files depending on the configuration specified in */etc/diskspacemonitor/recover.conf*.

> In a default install, */etc/diskspacemonitor/alert.conf*, */etc/diskspacemonitor/action.conf*, and */etc/diskspacemonitor/alert.conf* do not actually exist. Instead, they're copied from */etc/diskspacemonitor/action.conf.default* and */etc/diskspacemonitor/alert.conf.default*, respectively, the first time their respective scripts are run.

In addition to these Apple-supplied scripts, customized *alert* and *recover* may be manually specified (see Example 4-13). Respectively called *alert.local* and *recover.local*, these scripts should be located along with their Apple-supplied cousins in */etc/diskspacemonitor/action*.

Example 4-13. Using the cat command to examine a script I typically use to delete excess cups spool files that accumulate in /var/spool/cups. If there are more than 2,000 files there, the entire directory is deleted and recreated. This machine is not a print server and rarely (if ever) prints anything, so I can usually be assured that this data is not important.

```
[ace2:~] nadmin% cat /etc/diskspacemonitor/action/recover.local
#!/bin/sh
#this is a brute force way of doing this
if [ `/bin/ls /var/spool/cups/tmp | wc | awk '{ print $3}'` -gt 2000 ]
then
        /bin/rm -r /var/spool/cups/tmp
        /bin/mkdir -p /var/spool/cups/tmp
else
        exit 0
fi
```

diskspacemonitor must be run as root; it logs to */var/log/diskspacemonitor.log*, and supplies a little information about itself when issued the *status* directive.

watchdog

Mac OS X Server's startup process is a little bit disjointed. Different process and services are started using a number of different methodologies (illustrated in Table 4-6), and as a result it can be difficult to determine what has started where and why it was started in the first place. They are all worthy of discussion, and several are mentioned elsewhere in this book. The only one that is server-specific (doesn't exist on Mac OS X client) is *watchdog*.

Table 4-6. Mac OS X and Mac OS X Server support a number of mechanisms for starting processes.

Mechanism	Description	Services
SystemStarter	Main startup infrastructure for OS. Statically starts services, often according to configuration in /etc/hostconfig.	LDAP, NAT, IP Forwarding, servermgrd
Xinetd	Starts network services on demand. Covered in more depth in Chapter 18.	SSH, FTP
Mach_init	Starts services (generally local in nature) on demand.	diskarbitrationd, DirectoryService, WindowServer
watchdog	Starts services on boot, and (depending on its configuration) re-starts them when they become unavailable.	IMAP, Password Server

Like *diskspacemonitor*, described earlier in this chapter, *watchdog* is an Apple-provided mechanism to do what many System Administrators have pursued for many years—service monitoring. In addition to starting the services listed in its configuration file (*watchdog.conf*, seen here in Example 4-14), *watchdog* ensures, depending on its configuration, that the services it is responsible for stay running.

Example 4-14. Using cat to view /etc/watchdog.conf. The first several lines consist of documentation (comments). Only the last seven lines are actually used to manage watchdog's services. In addition to its well-documented configuration file, watchdog has an extensive manpage.

```
g5:/ odadm$ cat /etc/watchdog.conf
#
# /etc/watchdog.conf
#

# /usr/sbin/watchdog is an (AT&T) init-like process that
# launches, monitors, and relaunches critical services.
# See the watchdog man page for more information.

# The file format is familiar to most *NIX hacks:
#       The pound character (#) indicates a comment that continues
#       until the end of line.
#       White-space is ignored.
#       Each configuration line consists of the following
#       colon-delimited fields:
#               id:action:path args
# The id field is a unique identifying key for the service.
# The action field is "off", "respawn", "boot", "bootwait", or
# "now". See the man page for details of their usage.
# The path and args field is the command to execute.

# If a process quits a few seconds after launch, the process is
# considered faulty and will not be respawned. This may be caused
# by programs that daemonize themselves. To avoid this, add the
# "no-daemonize" argument to the command if one exists.

# After modifying this file, send a signal to watchdog to force
# it to reread the file. These are the special signals caught by
```

Example 4-14. Using cat to view /etc/watchdog.conf. The first several lines consist of documentation (comments). Only the last seven lines are actually used to manage watchdog's services. In addition to its well-documented configuration file, watchdog has an extensive manpage. (continued)

```
# watchdog:
#       HUP - force a re-read: Entries turned off will be terminated;
#              entries turned on will be launched; changed entries will
#              be terminated (if necessary) and relaunched; unchanged
#              entries will not be touched.
#       INT - complete restart: Terminate all children, re-read the
#              file and launch children as necessary.
#       TERM - complete shutdown: Terminate all children and exit.

pwd:respawn:/usr/sbin/PasswordService -n
PSM:respawn:/usr/sbin/PrintServiceMonitor -x     # Server Printing service
mm:off:/usr/sbin/MacintoshManagementServer -x    # Macintosh Manager service
postfix:respawn:/usr/libexec/postfix/master      # Mail services - SMTP
cyrus:off:/usr/bin/cyrus/bin/master              # Mail services - IMAP & POP
kadmind:respawn:/usr/sbin/kadmind -passwordserver  -nofork
kdc:respawn:/usr/sbin/krb5kdc -n
```

Each service entry in *watchdog.conf* consists of three fields:

```
service name:setting:command
```

- *service name* is a somewhat arbitrary tag used to identify the service in question, while *command* is much more specific, specifying the exact syntax used to start a service.

- *setting* is one of six keywords, a few of which are documented in Table 4-7. These keywords dictate how the service should be handled by *watchdog*.

- *command* is the exact command (including arguments) that should be executed.

Table 4-7. Common watchdog service configuration keywords. A few more obscure options are not listed here, and are available in watchdog's manpage.

Watchdog keyword	Description
off	Do not start process, and end it if it is running (by sending it a signal 15 and, if it does not quit, a signal 9).
bootonce	Start process, but do not attempt to keep it running.
respawn	Start the process, and restart it if it fails at some point.

watchdog, which is started by the Watchdog startup item, logs to */Library/Logs/watchdog.event.log*. A sample *watchdog* log is shown here:

```
g5:/System/Library/StartupItems odadm$ tail /Library/Logs/watchdog.event.log
2004-09-09 02:52:25 MDT Waiting for KILLed child (pid 327)
2004-09-09 02:52:25 MDT Reaped child process 327 ("/usr/sbin/PrintServiceMonitor");
quit due to signal 9.
#End-Date: 2004-09-09 02:52:25 MDT
#Start-Date: 2004-09-09 02:53:24 MDT
#Fields: date time s-comment
```

```
2004-09-09 02:53:24 MDT Started child "/usr/sbin/PasswordService" as pid 298.
2004-09-09 02:53:24 MDT Started child "/usr/sbin/PrintServiceMonitor" as pid 299.
2004-09-09 02:53:24 MDT Started child "/usr/libexec/postfix/master" as pid 300.
2004-09-09 02:53:24 MDT Started child "/usr/sbin/kadmind" as pid 301.
2004-09-09 02:53:24 MDT Started child "/usr/sbin/krb5kdc" as pid 302.
```

In addition to starting various services, *watchdog* is also responsible for maintaining Mac OS X Server's reboot timer, which is enabled using either the *systemsetup* command or the Energy Saver preference panel in System Preferences. This timer, which runs in the computer's Power Management Unit (PMU), reboots if it ever gets to 0. It is *watchdog*'s job to reset that timer, the assumption being that if the timer is not reset, then *watchdog* is not running and the server has crashed.

watchdog is easily used to start other, non-Apple services, as documented in both its manpage and the commented portions of */etc/watchdog.conf*. Processes that daemonize (move to the background) can confuse *watchdog*—it thinks they've failed, and processes that fail soon after initialization are not restarted (the assumption being that if they fail that soon after boot there's probably something wrong, and they'll probably fail again and again). So if the process in question has a *-no-daemonize* or *-foreground* option, you should be prepared to use it in *watchdog.conf*.

 Check with your developer or vendor to determine whether running your daemon in the foreground is recommended.

cron

One additional aspect of Mac OS X Server system administration is the system's use of *cron* (a traditional Unix facility for running periodic tasks). *cron* (which is started by */System/Library/StartupItems/Cron/Cron* in both Mac OS X and Mac OS X Server) checks every minute for tasks to execute. No graphical interface for it exists, and its configuration file is */etc/crontab* (shown in Example 4-15). *cron* reads this along with any per-user *crontabs* (located in */var/cron/tabs*) looking for jobs to execute. The *crontab* format is pretty straightforward, and is made up of seven tab-delineated columns representing various intervals, the user that the *cron* job should run as, and the command(s) to be executed.

Example 4-15. Using the cat command to examine cron's configuration file, which is /etc/crontab.

```
cat /etc/crontab
# /etc/crontab
SHELL=/bin/sh
PATH=/etc:/bin:/sbin:/usr/bin:/usr/sbin
HOME=/var/log
#
#minute hour    mday    month   wday    who     command
#
```

*Example 4-15. Using the cat command to examine cron's configuration file,
which is /etc/crontab. (continued)*

```
#*/5     *       *       *       *       root    /usr/libexec/atrun
#
# Run daily/weekly/monthly jobs.
#run daily script at 3:15 am every day
15      3       *       *       *       root    periodic daily

#run the weekly scripts at 4:30 on the 6th day of the week.
30      4       *       *       6       root    periodic weekly

#run the monthly script at 5:30 on the first day of every  month.
30      5       1       *       *       root    periodic monthly
```

As seen in Example 4-16, a default *crontab* on both Mac OS X and Mac OS X Server
executes the *periodic* utility. *periodic*, in turn, exists primarily to work with *cron*, con-
solidating *daily*, *weekly*, and *monthly* administrative tasks. When passed one of these
arguments (*daily*, *weekly*, or *monthly*), *periodic* executes appropriate scripts from the
/etc/periodic directory as shown in Example 4-16.

*Example 4-16. Using ls to examine various periodic tasks. The periodic utility works primarily with
cron.*

```
g5:~ ladmin$ ls /etc/periodic/*
/etc/periodic/daily:
100.clean-logs          600.daily.server
500.daily               700.daily.server.cyrus

/etc/periodic/monthly:
500.monthly             600.monthly.server

/etc/periodic/weekly:
500.weekly              600.weekly.server
```

My point in this analysis is primarily to illustrate the Mac OS X Server–specific tasks
executed by *periodic*. Illustrated in Table 4-8, they are cross-functional, impacting a
number of server services, and should serve as a template for understanding the
potential of *cron* and *periodic* as system administration tools.

*Table 4-8. Server-specific periodic tasks in a default install of Mac OS X Server. periodic is used to
manage a number of server-specific services.*

Periodic Task	Description
600.daily.server	Compresses, rolls, and deletes various log files defined in */etc/diskspacemonitor/ daily.server.conf*.
700.daily.server.cyrus	Rolls the logs for the Cyrus mail system according to the configuration established in */etc/MailServicesOther.plist*.
600.monthly.server	Empty in a default install.
600.weekly.server	Empty in a default install.

Your customized administration tasks can be added in (at a minimum) three ways—through *periodic*, directly to the system's *crontab*, or into a user-specific tab in */var/cron/tabs*. The latter two options are usually preferable, since it is feasible that Apple could replace */etc/crontab* in a future OS upgrade.

Per-user *crontabs* can be manipulated with the *crontab* utility, which opens the user's *crontab* using the executable specified in the user's EDITOR environment variable (*vi*, in a default install). It is up to the user at that point to specify a properly formatted *crontab*. *crontabs* are executed as the user they belong to, so in general system-wide administration tasks are added to root's *crontab*—both the Tolis Group's BRU backup software and Apple's *diskspacemonitor* are executed this way. *crontab*'s -*l* argument displays the currently scheduled tasks for the user. To specify a different user, add the –*u* flag.

The *periodic* scripts should be thoroughly tested and added to the appropriate (*daily*, *weekly*, or *monthly*) directories within */etc/periodic*. They are executed in the order specified by their listing in the *ls* command. Generally, this means that the script name is prepended with a number, and that the scripts are executed in numerical order.

CHAPTER 5

Troubleshooting

Troubleshooting Mac OS 9 was largely a set of black-box procedures. Recall this conversation, early in the computing experience of many Mac users: "Zap the PRAM, start up without extensions, and rebuild the Desktop." Why? "Because it fixes a lot of things."

Mac OS X is a beast of an entirely different nature. Rather than being a black box, it is, with a few exceptions, largely transparent. Rather than being closed, it is decidedly open. Rather than hiding from the user, Mac OS X's underpinnings are very near the surface, albeit under a glossy exterior. This remarkable transition fundamentally affects the act of troubleshooting. Rather than a script or a voodoo-style procedure complete with incantations, troubleshooting can now be called a way of thinking. With vastly more data available, the administrator draws vastly better conclusions about the nature of the issue at hand.

In the end, the question has to be asked: "Does troubleshooting matter?" Does the process of troubleshooting matter at all, as long as the outcome ensures that what was once broken is now fixed? I would say it does. Transparent, controlled troubleshooting leads to understanding. And better understanding contributes to architectures and systems that don't need to be fixed. So although understanding for the sake of knowledge is a worthy goal, it's not something we can advocate in a business setting. Understanding in order to foster better-built systems and lowered support costs, is.

This chapter seeks to bring academic rigor to the process of troubleshooting. In it, we'll first examine some generalized methodologies for solving problems in Mac OS X and later move into some specific tools that can be used in various stages of that framework. The goal throughout is to build an increased knowledge of the tools that work together to create the user experience we know as Mac OS X—from the fundamental data structures of the OS to the poof of the Dock.

Strategies

It's a very strange question to ask an administrator: "How do you solve problems?" Anecdotal evidence suggests that the people who gravitate towards these positions don't have to think too much about it. After all, there's hardly a wide variety of IT-centric academic disciplines, and within these disciplines there aren't many classes or research specialties that center on the process of fixing things. It seems much more likely, especially in industries where IT has not been fully professionalized, that IT staff are drawn to their positions precisely because they are particularly good at fixing things, especially under circumstances of limited knowledge. Since it is this audience I'd like to speak to, it would be presumptuous to suppose that I have all the answers. I'd like to propose instead some formalization to the process of technical analysis—frameworks in which administrators can examine and more efficiently utilize their pre-existing methodologies. Hopefully this will allow administrators, rather than simply going forward based on their natural talent, to specifically hone their already keen abilities.

Quick Fixes

All that verbiage probably seems long-winded and academic in the context of our first example, but the example's very simplicity illustrates the appropriateness of its examination in a formalized framework. We're speaking, of course, of quick fixes.

A quick fix, for the purposes of this book, is an action that can be undertaken to resolve an issue without really understanding what's wrong. Additionally, it's common for quick fixes to affect several variables at once—enough variables that individual investigation would be problematic. A good example is Mac OS X's Repair Permissions capability (see Figure 5-1).

Mac OS X itself is made up *several thousand* files; the permissions on a surprisingly large percentage of which are critical for everything from booting to proper use of AirPort. From time to time, those permissions might, for some reason, be set incorrectly. It would be exceedingly problematic to maintain a list of every critical file and manually check every one when experiencing technical issues. Such a process could be scripted, but even that is a lot to ask of your average Mac OS X administrator and it could not, at any rate, be considered an efficient use of one's time. Apple has done one better by, beginning with Mac OS X 10.2, including a Repair Permissions capability in the OS, implemented graphically by Disk Utility and on the command line by *diskutil*.

There are, however, downsides to such quick fixes. Repairing permissions—while useful—has become the same sort of panacea that zapping the parameter RAM was in Mac OS 9. All of a sudden, lots of folks (without any real quantitative evidence) claim that repairing permissions speeds booting, makes Photoshop run faster, and fixes Ethernet duplex issue; some of which are possible, but none of which should be

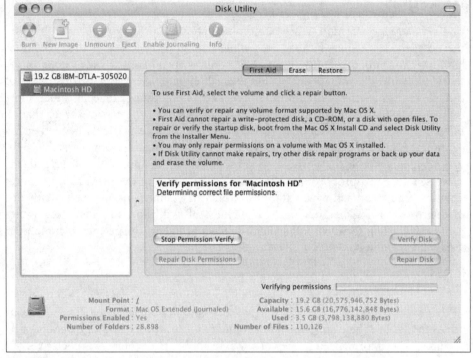

Figure 5-1. The Repair permissions interface in the Disk Utility application.

taken seriously without hard numbers. This tendency is a fundamental flaw to quick fixes.

A second issue revolves around the very nature of a quick fix. Because you won't under most circumstances, understand exactly what was broken in the first place, quick fixes tend to be vulnerable to treating the symptoms of an issue, rather than tackling the issue itself. In severe circumstances, this is akin to treating a broken arm with lots and lots of aspirin. This is certainly far from keeping with our concept of building a more fundamental understanding of the underlying system.

Obviously, nearly all Mac OS 9 system administration consisted of quick fixes. They're not all bad. It's up to the administrator to refrain from getting carried away, applying quick fixes that make little sense. A little logic is also called for—if you're running the same quick fix once or twice a day, you're probably also not seeing the bigger picture, and its probably time for a more systematic approach.

Abstraction

Modern operating systems are sufficiently complex that most operations take place at more than one level. Subsystems manage simple, smaller tasks that feed in to one another, resulting in something that the end user or system administrator is aware of.

Repairing Permissions

The permission-repairing capabilities in both *diskutil* and Disk Utility work by reading the bill of material (or *bom*) files out of selected critical package receipts in */Library/ Receipts*. The *bom* files, which are actually stored inside the *.pkg* bundles, specify the proper owner, group, and mode (permissions) for every file installed by a particular package. Repair Permissions restores files to that original, out-of-box state. BOM files checked in Repair Permissions include:

- */Library/Receipts/BaseSystem.pkg/Contents/Archive.bom*
- */Library/Receipts/Essentials.pkg/Contents/Archive.bom*
- */Library/Receipts/BSD.pkg/Contents/Archive.bom*
- */Library/Receipts/BSDSDK.pkg/Contents/Archive.bom*
- */Library/Receipts/X11User.pkg/Contents/Archive.bom*
- */Library/Receipts/X11SDK.pkg/Contents/Archive.bom*
- */Library/Receipts/Internal.pkg/Contents/Archive.bom*
- */Library/Receipts/FatLibraries.pkg/Contents/Archive.bom*
- */Library/Receipts/DevDocumentation.pkg/Contents/Archive.bom*
- */Library/Receipts/DevExamples.pkg/Contents/Archive.bom*
- */Library/Receipts/DevSDK.pkg/Contents/Archive.bom*
- */Library/Receipts/DeveloperTools.pkg/Contents/Archive.bom*
- */Library/Receipts/DevInternal.pkg/Contents/Archive.bom*
- */Library/Receipts/DevFatLibraries.pkg/Contents/Archive.bom*
- */Library/Receipts/iCal.pkg/Contents/Archive.bom*
- */Library/Receipts/iMovie.pkg/Contents/Archive.bom*
- */Library/Receipts/iPhoto.pkg/Contents/Archive.bom*
- */Library/Receipts/iSync.pkg/Contents/Archive.bom*
- */Library/Receipts/iTunes.pkg/Contents/Archive.bom*
- */Library/Receipts/MicrosoftIE.pkg/Contents/Archive.bom*
- */Library/Receipts/AdditionalFonts.pkg/Contents/Archive.bom*
- */Library/Receipts/AdditionalAsianFonts.pkg/Contents/Archive.bom*
- */Library/Receipts/EpsonPrinterDrivers.pkg/Contents/Archive.bom*
- */Library/Receipts/CanonPrinterDrivers.pkg/Contents/Archive.bom*
- */Library/Receipts/HewlettPackardPrinterDrivers.pkg/Contents/Archive.bom*
- */Library/Receipts/LexmarkPrinterDrivers.pkg/Contents/Archive.bom*
- */Library/Receipts/GimpPrintPrinterDrivers.pkg/Contents/Archive.bom*
- */Library/Receipts/ServerEssentials.pkg/Contents/Archive.bom*
- */Library/Receipts/ServerAdministrationSoftware.pkg/Contents/Archive.bom*
- */Library/Receipts/ServerFatLibraries.pkg/Contents/Archive.bom*
- */Library/Receipts/QuickTimeStreamingServer.pkg/Contents/Archive.bom*
- */Library/Receipts/ServerInternal.pkg/Contents/Archive.bom*

This is especially the case in Unix systems, which are specifically architected on the principal that many specialized tools should work together to do a more complex job. When one of these complex, multilevel systems isn't working properly, it's appropriate to examine its functionality at each fundamental level, rather than simply changing configuration or environmental variables and hoping for a different end result. This is especially the case in a heterogeneous network environment, where such variables might exists in two or three related systems and might be under the control of different branches of the IT organization in question. The best way to illustrate this principal is to walk through a couple of examples.

Name resolution: A structured approach

Hostname resolution is something most systems administrators wrestle with at one point or the other. Common tools for this include *dig*, *host*, and *nslookup*. However, it's important to understand that there are two basic parts to analysis of name resolution: analysis of the host data itself, and analysis of the system's resolver.

 Mac OS X's name resolution architecture was touched on in Chapter 1, and *lookupd* is covered in depth in the Appendix. Here wI'd like to focus on the process of fundamental analysis, rather than the technology itself.

dig, *host*, and *nsloolup* are tools that directly query the DNS service. As such, they test the configuration of a particular server or set of servers, not the configuration of the machine they're run from. The difference can be subtle, since *nslookup* queries (by default) the same server the system's resolver does, as specified in */etc/resolv.conf*.

When a process on Mac OS X needs to do host resolution (maybe Safari needs to resolve *www.apple.com* in order to query the web server there), it uses a system call available via the OS's standard C library (*libc*); probably using gethostbyname( ) whose queries are dispatched to *lookupd*. *lookupd*, as covered in Chapter 1, services that query using one of its data sources: its cache, the */etc/hosts* file, DNS, Multicast DNS, NetInfo, or Directory Services (in that order in an out-of-box Panther install).

So, if *dig*, *host*, and *nsloolup* all query DNS and not the system's resolver, how would one test the system's host resolution? At a very simple level, this is pretty straightforward. Any application that needs to convert hostnames to IP addresses probably uses the system's resolver (rather than talking directly the DNS server like *nslookup* and friends). If *ping* or your favorite web browser can't find a particular host, then you can assume something isn't working; for example:

```
fury:~ mab9718$ ping blah
ping: unknown host blah
```

A much more granular approach, however, is to use *lookupd*'s *debug* or *query* modes.

Pay attention: *lookupd* does a lot more than host resolution, and we'll use this capability time and again.

This gives us a lot of data about the host we're processing. A query is a straightforward process. The general form is:

```
lookupd -q category -a key value
```

Where *category* is, in this case, host, *key* is either ip_address or a name, and *value* is the data you want to send to the resolver. For instance:

```
fury:~ mab9718$ lookupd -q host -a name webmail.pantherserver.org

ip_address: 192.168.1.2
name: webmail.pantherserver.org

interface: 5
ip_address: 12.208.224.221
name: webmail.pantherserver.org
```

Important options for *lookupd*'s query mode include:

–q Query. Turns on query mode. Requires *category* argument and *–a* option.

–a Data to query. Requires *key* and *value* arguments.

lookupd's debug mode provides even more data. It's interactive in nature, and specified by the *–d* option:

```
fury:~ mab9718$ lookupd -d
lookupd version 320 (root 2003.08.26 04:36:20 UTC)
Enter command name, "help", or "quit" to exit
>
```

From the > prompt, a number of options are available; help is a pretty good place to start. While we'll cover a number of others throughout this book, now is not the place to discuss them all. For now we'll focus on the hostWith queries, including hostWithName, and HostWithInternetAddress, as shown in Example 5-1.

Example 5-1. Using lookupd's debug mode to query host data.

```
> hostWithName: webmail.4am-media.com
Dictionary: "FF: host webmail.pantherserver.org"
_lookup_agent: FFAgent
_lookup_validation: /etc/hosts 1063839547
ip_address: 192.168.1.2
name: webmail.4am-media.com
+ Category: host
+ Time to live: 43200
+ Age: 0 (expires in 43200 seconds)
+ Negative: No
+ Cache hits: 0
+ Retain count: 3
```

Notice that these queries give us a lot of data, including which agent, or data store, supplied it.

Coupled with a successful query from *nsloolup* and friends, a host resolution failure implies that there's something wrong with the resolver itself—not with the configuration of the data source in question, be it DNS, mDNS, Flat Files, or *DirectoryService*.

Querying Host Data

If *dig*, *host*, and *nsloolup* all query DNS, is there any way to verify data that other *lookupd* agents would use?

- mDNS: mDNS is a special case, since, rather than a dedicated agent, *lookupd* simply sends a DNS query over port 5353 to the multicast network.
- NetInfo
- Flat Files
- *DirectoryService*

The point here is that *nslookup* and friends directly query DNS and other host data, rather than relying on the system's resolver. If for some reason the data coming from *nslookup* differs from data coming from the resolver, we can typically use the discrepancy to better understand where the failure in question is occurring.

 In general, *lookupd*'s query (*q*) mode should be preferred over the interactive *d*. This is because *q* queries the running instance of *lookupd*, which has root privileges, whereas *lookupd d* runs as the user that executes it (probably having fewer rights). This makes *q* a more accurate estimate of the data available to the system.

The fundamentals of LDAP and Mac OS X Directory Services

A common task among system administrators is the integration of Mac OS X into an existing LDAP infrastructure. While an extensive coverage of Open Directory Server, Mac OS X Server's Directory Services subsystem, is actually the topic of Chapter 6, this is a good place for a a basic introduction in order to better support our discussion of troubleshooting. The basic tasks include:

network connectivity

Since directory services integration involves connectivity over a network, connectivity is a sane place to begin looking for functionality. A common method for this kind of testing is the use of the *ping* utility, which sends an ICMP echo request to a particular Internet address (see Example 5-2), presumably expecting a response, if that host is available.

Example 5-2. Ping is a common and well-known utility for testing network connectivity.

```
big15:/System/Library mab$ ping g5.pantherserver.org
PING g5.pantherserver.org (207.224.49.181): 56 data bytes
64 bytes from 207.224.49.181: icmp_seq=0 ttl=47 time=99.901 ms
^C
--- g5.pantherserver.org ping statistics ---
2 packets transmitted, 1 packets received, 50% packet loss
round-trip min/avg/max = 99.901/99.901/99.901 ms
```

In secure, modern infrastructures, however, ICMP echos are often suppressed, in order to reduce the visibility of servers to malicious parties. A better solution for testing basic connectivity might be the use of the *telnet* utility to open a connection to the port in question- in this case—LDAP, 389.

```
big15:~ mab$ telnet g5.pantherserver.org 389
Trying 207.224.49.181...
Connected to g5.pantherserver.org.
Escape character is '^]'.
^CConnection closed by foreign host.
```

While not as fundamental in its approach as *ping*, this is often the lowest form of anonymous connectivity available to a particular service.

At a more sophisticated level, a port scanner like *nmap* or Mac OS X's built-in Network Utility might also be used. Be aware, though, that port scanners are specifically disallowed on a variety of managed networks. Port scanners are covered in more depth later in this chapter.

Testing the protocol

Once it's established that the service in question is up and running, it's a good idea to use a native client of that service, rather than the OS's built-in implementation, to test it further. This is similar to the use of *nslookup* in our previous example, testing the underlying DNS service rather than the OS's resolver library. In this example, LDAP queries to find users and groups are actually made by the *DirectoryService* daemon; specifically, by its LDAP plug-in, *DSLDAPv3.dsplug*. The *ldapsearch* utility, though, is also capable of speaking LDAP, and it's a powerful utility for testing the underlying service.

```
big15:/System/Library mab$ ldapsearch -LLL -x -h g5.pantherserver.org -b "" -s
base objectclass=*
dn:
objectClass: top
objectClass: OpenLDAProotDSE
```

Important basic *ldapsearch* options:

–x

Use plain, rather than SASL authentication. SASL is an advanced authentication mechanism that's a part of the LDAPv3 protocol. While it does enhance security, it doesn't make much sense in the context of anonymous connections.

–h or –H

Host to connect to (*–h*) or LDAP URI: for instance, *ldaps://serverlexample.com:3268* (*–H*).

–D

Distinguished name to use for authentication.

–W or –w password

–W prompts for a password, while *–w* expects it as an argument.

–b

Search base.

Beyond a basic query of the LDAP service, it might also be desirable to specifically craft a query that reflects what *DSLDAPv3.dsplug* might send. (This can often be obtained from the logs of the LDAP server or the source code of the client, as shown in Example 5-3.) While this approach requires a greater depth of client-side understanding, it also yields results of a higher fidelity and can help expose very subtle client or server-side bugs.

Example 5-3. Querying the LDAP server in the same way that the LDAP plug-in would. This syntax, the result of issuing the id command, was obtained by watching the LDAP server's logs at a log level of 256.

```
big15:/System/Library mab$ ldapsearch -LLL -x -h g5.pantherserver.org -b
"cn=users,dc=4am-media,dc=com" -s sub
"(&(objectClass=inetOrgPerson)(objectClass=posixAccount)(objectClass=shadowAccount)
(objectClass=apple-user)(objectClass=extensibleObject)(|(uid=p10100)(cn=p10100)))"
dn: uid=p10100,cn=users,dc=4am-media,dc=com
uid: p10100
objectClass: inetOrgPerson
objectClass: posixAccount
objectClass: shadowAccount
objectClass: apple-user
objectClass: extensibleObject
objectClass: organizationalPerson
objectClass: top
objectClass: person
sn: 99
cn: Student 10100
loginShell: /bin/bash
uidNumber: 10100
gidNumber: 20
apple-generateduid: 5DAE5330-1BD0-11D9-B0D6-000A95AE7200
homeDirectory: /Users/p10100
authAuthority: ;ApplePasswordServer;0x416b017c4f76f4550000006900000069,1024 35
    13448610504907262984482390427259948441314746829815170032923531108027133612 98
    8770300437487030786502435192950512589005596941243326113294089693705628757 2168
    50783292809731378577114193257154105231215978009006511347873275688069613154 152
    37131757379376502789552253595365191863132122771704254232869520249819765790 969
    83 root@g5.4am-media.com:207.224.49.181
authAuthority: ;Kerberosv5;0x416b017c4f76f4550000006900000069;p10100@G5.4AM-ME
    DIA.COM;G5.4AM-MEDIA.COM;1024 35 1344861050490726298448239042725994844131474 6
```

Example 5-3. Querying the LDAP server in the same way that the LDAP plug-in would. This syntax, the result of issuing the id command, was obtained by watching the LDAP server's logs at a log level of 256. (continued)

```
829815170032923531108027133612988770300437487030786502435192950512589000559694
124332611329408969370562875721685078329280973137857711419325715410523121597
0900651134787327568806961315415237131757379376502789552253595365191863132122
717042542328695202498197657909698 root@g5.4am-media.com
userPassword:: KioqKioqKio=
```

We test in this fashion because in the course of configuration and planning, we've made certain assumptions about the LDAP service in question: its use (or lack thereof) of SSL, the credentials used to access it, the search base required, and so on. If *ldapsearch* doesn't work or returns unexpected results, we know that we need to adjust those assumptions.

Examining the client-side setup

If the data *ldapsearch* returns meets our expectations, we can let the OS run the query for itself. In Jaguar, there's no non-programmatic way to talk to Directory-Service directly. The best method is to instead use *lookupd*'s debug or query modes as shown in Example 5-4, with options modified slightly from Example 5-3.

Example 5-4. lookupd's query for a user. Note the user argument to the -q flag rather than our earlier host example.

```
g5:~ ladmin$ lookupd -q user -a name p10100

gid: 20
home: /Users/p10100
name: p10100 Student 10100
passwd: ******** ********
realname: Student 10100
shell: /bin/bash
uid: 10100
```

In Panther, the *dscl* utility is available. *dscl*, which stands for *directory services command line*, is a client to Open Directory, much like *ldapsearch* is a client of the more fundamental, less abstracted LDAP service. Simple use of *dscl* is shown in Example 5-5.

Example 5-5. dscl can be used to query Open Directory.

```
g5:~ ladmin$ dscl localhost -search /LDAPv3/127.0.0.1 RecordName p10100
Search results for dsAttrTypeStandard:RecordName
Users/p10100            dsAttrTypeStandard:RecordName = (p10100, "Student 10100")
Search results for dsAttrTypeNative:RecordName
```

While *dscl*'s results are somewhat spartan, it does provide us with a more direct method for talking to DirectoryService (rather than querying *lookupd*, which is itself a DirectoryService client.

Putting it all together

The idea throughout this process is to look for discrepancies. Hopefully you'll have understanding enough to notice inconsistent results. In general, this process won't be undertaken without some impetus—unless something is broken—and ideally somewhere in that fundamental examination you'd have found the fault you were looking for. Provided the data returned at every step seems correct, at this point you should retry whatever it was that was originally failing. In this case, perhaps you'd like to log in as a user from your LDAP directory service.

Naturally, since this is a troubleshooting strategy, it's a lot of work to go to unless there's a specific problem to solve. It is, however, a highly effective strategy for fixing what's broken. The downside, illustrated by the notes and sidebars in our examples, is that it does require a sophisticated understanding of the architecture in question.

Troubleshooting and the Scientific Method

Skepticism has long been a key aspect of Unix system administration. The tendency towards careful analysis and reasoning was vital in a time when systems were complex, finicky, and often highly customized from one site to the next. While mutual distrust would seem to be the opposite of productive, it does maximize certainty in the assumptions you're operating under. As systems have become more vendor-centric and standardized, though, and as systems administration has become less of a priesthood for many, this tendency towards skepticism has steadily been reduced. In a time when vendor certifications are an overwhelming force in the IT industry, there's a strong trend towards being spoon-fed—if for no other reason than that you can get away with it.

This tendency towards assumption and trust should be torn down from its roots. One has only to look at the unending procession of OS worms and corporate privacy violations to recognize that the vendors' assertions are built motivated by profit more often than concern. This does not mean that vendors are evil—it just means that business is founded on profit and they are doing their jobs in building shareholder wealth. The situation does not change much when dealing with one's peers. The number of technological truisms taken as scripture, because of fear, uncertainty and doubt cannot be underestimated. This phenomenon is only more prevalent in the Mac OS world, where many technologists are accustomed to the black-box, quick-fix nature of Mac OS 9.

This is an arena in which Open Source shines. Large Open Source projects are peer-reviewed and subject to analysis by a wide pool of talented programmers. Much along the lines of capitalism, self-interest motivates developers to write architecturally correct code.

Where does that leave you? How is a system administrator to differentiate among the mediocre vendor documentation, countless online HOWTOs, and general mythology surrounding various technologies in order to build and support architecturally sound systems? The answer lies in the twenty-year-old skepticism of traditional system administration.

With the scientific method, academia provides us with a consistent model for skepticism and maximization of certainty. This process has been well-established across a number of disciplines as an efficient one for weeding out spurious and incorrect ideas in favor of better-supported, more likely explanations. Its applicability to everything from sociology to finite chemistry to mechanical engineering only reiterates its generalized, rigorous nature, and its application in the IT field can have a huge impact, be it in support of the bottom line or of a controversial policy.

The Scientific Method in a nutshell

The Scientific Method can be generally summed up in these steps:

Observation

> During the observation stage, data is gathered. This data should be exact and verifiable in nature, and quantitative when feasible. For instance:

> > *"NetBoot isn't working! Help! Has anyone else been able to make it work?"*

> doesn't reflect good observation. Sure, there are issues involved. But there are several steps in the *NetBoot* process, and that observation doesn't provide much data to work with. A much better summary might be:

> > *"NetBoot isn't working. The gray Apple appears on the screen, but shortly thereafter, some strange lines appear across the screen. It was working yesterday, so I'm not sure what's changed. The server is running 10.3.2 booting a 10.3 client image produced with Carbon Copy Cloner. This is a totally consistent behavior; we came in this morning and nothing NetBoots at all."*

> Note how the latter example sought out as many details as possible. At a minimum, software versions should always be mentioned, along with the reproducibility of the issue.

Hypothesis

> A hypothesis is a tentative description or rule about observed behaviors. The idea is that if the rule accurately describes past behavior, it should also be feasible to use it to describe future behavior. A hypothesis should also include the stated assumptions that it rests upon.

> > *"NetBoot is failing during the NFS stage."*

> Assumptions: The gray Apple is drawn on the screen by the booter, so *tftp* is working.

> Since the NetBoot process is well-known and documented, we can use it as the basis for our hypothesis. This hypothesis would also be supported by data from

the system log of the server, if it were available. Specifically, we should see three *tftp* processes—for the booter, kernel, and kernel extension cache—this would strongly suggest an NFS issue, because in an NFS, rather than HTTP NetBoot scenario, it's the sole protocol used after the *tftp*s have completed.

Prediction

The rigor of the scientific method is enforced through prediction, verification, and testing. In prediction, scenarios that test the hypothesis are proposed:

> *"An NFS connection from the client to the NetBoot server—as long as it closely matches the circumstances under which NetBoot NFS connections occur—should fail."*

This prediction might be right or wrong. The important thing here isn't ego; it's getting to the bottom of the issue at hand. Note also the requirement that circumstances closely match those of a failing NetBoot. While this might seem like a common-sense requirement, it's one that is often overlooked. It means that the NFS client should have similar characteristics to the NetBoot client, including an IP address from the pool allocated to NetBoot clients.

 The central principal behind experimentation is that of *control*. It holds that across tests, circumstances should be as consistent as possible, and that only one variable should be varied at a time. This gives us a better indication that observed behavior is due to the varied circumstance, rather than some unknown error.

Verification and testing

During verification and testing, tests or experiments to verify a particular prediction are designed and executed. It is desirable to minimize variance as much as possible—in the best-case scenario, only one aspect of the test environment is varied at once. Our example—a NetBoot failure—is simple enough that it's not a particularly good example. Notice, though, our earlier requirement that the testing circumstances mirror as closely as possible the failed NetBoot, which can be considered our control instance. The following procedure might be suggested in order to test the NFS requirements of a *NetBoot* server:

Boot locally from a client on which NetBoot failed.

Ensure that the client is running the same system software as the NetBoot image, and that the client has an IP address from the range distributed to NetBoot clients.

In Terminal, enter the following commands:

```
sudo mkdir /tmp/netboot
sudo mount -t nfs 123.123.123.123:/Library/Netboot/NetBootSP0 /tmp/netboot
```

where 123.123.123.123 is the IP address of the *netboot* server. Note any errors?

Evaluation

During evaluation, the results of the testing and variation are compared to the prediction, and conclusions are drawn about not only the prediction but, also, depending on the confidence in the data, the hypothesis in question. Analysis is very important, as it's often here that intuition and creativity come into play, resulting in better hypotheses and further analysis.

Throughout the process, assumptions must be documented, because assumptions are often the keys to solving an issue. The testing must be documented and rigorous, and data must be as detailed as possible.

Tools

Mac OS X provides a wealth of tools with which to pursue troubleshooting, regardless of how you wish to pursue that goal. In this section, we'll look at some relevant options available with each tool. Although I'd like to offer an exhaustive reference, it would likely be both long and dry, so in the interest of finishing the chapter before the reader's next birthday, I'll be selective.

Many of these tools appear again later throughout the book, sometimes with different or more advanced options than shown here. This is by design. This section introduces you to the tools and provides the basics of their usage. It's my philosophy that once you're comfortable with this basic usage, incremental exposure to more advanced features is a good, comfortable way to learn.

Forensic Tools

Forensic tools help you determine what is happening, what has happened, or how a particular process works. That's a broad definition and certainly not a formal one, but it is a good way to help classify all of these tools.

 Our usage of *forensic* shouldn't be confused with a formal set of forensic analysis packages like the coroner's toolkit. Although there is some overlap, the study of computer forensics is its own science, and outside the scope of this book.

strings

Usage

```
strings filename
```

Description

The *strings* command looks for the text in a given file. While this task seems simple, its real utility comes into play when its used with binary files—like executables or binary databases—that are made up of not only of text but also of a lot of data that makes sense to Mac OS X but not to you.

These text strings can yield valuable clues about how the process in question works, including the location of its configuration files, the path to processes it might call, and helpful notes on usage. Note this partial *strings* output for the *PasswordService* command as shown in Example 5-6.

Example 5-6. The output of the strings command gives us some idea of how Password Server synchronization works.

```
g5:~ ladmin$ strings /usr/sbin/PasswordService | less
oSync: The password server on this system is decommissioned.
DoSync: cannot get the current date.
Parent
DoSync: This password server does not have replicas.
Synchronizing with "%s"
%m/%d/%Y at %r
DoSync: the next replication will occur on %s
PullStatus
DoSyncKerberosDeferrals: no database object.
DoSyncKerberosDeferrals: cannot retrieve database header.
DoSyncKerberosDeferrals: cannot find self in the replica list
DoSyncKerberosDeferrals: The password server on this system is decommissioned.
DoSyncKerberosDeferrals: cannot get the current date.
Sending Kerberos data to "%s"
/var/db/authserver/syncfile%ld.%ld.reply
```

fs_usage

Usage

```
fs_usage [pid | cmd]
```

Description

The *fs_usage* command shows in real time every file that every process on the system accesses. The system call (programming method) used to access the file is also recorded. This can be very useful in determining how a particular process works: where it stores its configuration files, when it accesses particular data, and in many cases, what it does to the file. *fs_usage* can optionally accept a numerical process ID (*pid*) or process name in order to ignore or focus solely on a particular processes (based on the inclusion of the *-e* flag or its absence, respectively). In either case, multiple arguments may be specified. For instance:

```
fs_usage -e 502 configd
```

excludes PID 502 and any process named *configd*, whereas:

```
fs_usage AppleFileService
```

shows only files accessed by *AppleFileService* (potentially staggering on a busy file server).

Perhaps most useful is a less focused usage of *fs_usage*—as an exploratory tool in the often-intuitive process of searching for relevant observations. It's often a good method for taking in a lot of data and looking for something that you're not sure you're looking for. For instance, I was once tasked with finding the mechanism behind the "Automatically log in as user" command so that it could be turned off in a scripted fashion. To obtain this data, *fs_usage* was run while the option was toggled in the System Preferences pane. It should be noted that this yielded a tremendous amount of data—and it was a lot to wade through. Ultimately, though, it was determined that the */etc/kcpassword* file was written during the process of setting the auto-login user. Additional experimentation showed that deleting the file ensured that auto-login would always be turned off; *kcpassword* contains an obfuscated version of the password of the auto-login user.

otool

Usage

```
otool [-L]
```

Description

otool is a multipurpose developer's tool with one flag that has a lot of use to system administrators. The -L flag displays the name and version of the libraries the executable in question is linked against. This requires a little explanation.

Applications are typically modular in nature; they get a lot of their functionality from chunks of prebuilt code called libraries. SSL is a good example of this. It's rather complex to implement, so instead of trying to implement it separately in every SSL-enabled application, it's implemented once in a shared library. This practice ensures consistency among SSL-enabled applications and reduces the overall amount of work associated with adding features to various applications. *otool* shows which libraries an application is linked against (see Example 5-7). This tool provides a great deal of data about an application's functionality, and can be vital in determining what elements of the OS must be present in a minimized OS installation.

Example 5-7. loginwindow is linked against several libraries.

```
[ace2:~] mbartosh% otool -L /System/Library/CoreServices/loginwindow.app/loginwindow
/System/Library/CoreServices/loginwindow.app/loginwindow:
        /usr/lib/libSystem.B.dylib (compatibility version 1.0.0, current version 63.0.0)
[ace2:~] mbartosh% otool -L /System/Library/CoreServices/loginwindow.app/Contents/MacOS/
loginwindow
/System/Library/CoreServices/loginwindow.app/Contents/MacOS/loginwindow:
```

Example 5-7. loginwindow is linked against several libraries. (continued)

```
        /System/Library/Frameworks/CoreFoundation.framework/Versions/A/CoreFoundation
(compatibility version 150.0.0, current version 263.5.0)
        /System/Library/PrivateFrameworks/DiskArbitration.framework/Versions/A/
DiskArbitration (compatibility version 1.0.0, current version 1.0.0)
        /System/Library/Frameworks/IOKit.framework/Versions/A/IOKit (compatibility version
1.0.0, current version 120.3.0)
        /System/Library/Frameworks/ScreenSaver.framework/Versions/A/ScreenSaver
(compatibility version 1.0.0, current version 1.0.0)
        /System/Library/Frameworks/ApplicationServices.framework/Versions/A/
ApplicationServices (compatibility version 1.0.0, current version 18.0.0)
        /System/Library/Frameworks/SystemConfiguration.framework/Versions/A/
SystemConfiguration (compatibility version 1.0.0, current version 53.1.0)
        /System/Library/Frameworks/Security.framework/Versions/A/Security (compatibility
version 1.0.0, current version 54.1.7)
        /System/Library/Frameworks/Cocoa.framework/Versions/A/Cocoa (compatibility version
1.0.0, current version 8.0.0)
        /System/Library/Frameworks/Carbon.framework/Versions/A/Carbon (compatibility
version 2.0.0, current version 122.0.0)
        /System/Library/Frameworks/DirectoryService.framework/Versions/A/DirectoryService
(compatibility version 1.0.0, current version 1.0.0)
        /System/Library/PrivateFrameworks/Admin.framework/Versions/A/Admin (compatibility
version 1.0.0, current version 1.0.0)
        /System/Library/Frameworks/AudioToolbox.framework/Versions/A/AudioToolbox
(compatibility version 1.0.0, current version 1.0.0)
        /System/Library/Frameworks/AudioUnit.framework/Versions/A/AudioUnit (compatibility
version 1.0.0, current version 1.0.0)
        /System/Library/Frameworks/CoreAudio.framework/Versions/A/CoreAudio (compatibility
version 1.0.0, current version 1.0.0)
        /System/Library/Frameworks/CoreServices.framework/Versions/A/CoreServices
(compatibility version 1.0.0, current version 14.0.0)
        /System/Library/PrivateFrameworks/MachineSettings.framework/Versions/A/
MachineSettings (compatibility version 1.0.0, current version 1.0.0)
        /usr/lib/libSystem.B.dylib (compatibility version 1.0.0, current version 63.0.0)
```

ps

Usage

```
ps [options]
```

Description

ps shows running processes. It is most useful with the *a* (display other users' processes as well as your own) and *x* (show background processes) flags, as shown in Example 5-8. The *ax* flag can sometimes be used in combination with *u*, which shows the user associated with a running process.

Example 5-8. The first few lines of ps output, with the a and x flags.

```
fury:~ mab9718$ ps ax
  PID  TT  STAT      TIME COMMAND
```

```
  1 ?? Ss     0:00.03 /sbin/init
  2 ?? Ss     0:01.89 /sbin/mach_init
 79 ?? Ss     0:00.93 /usr/sbin/syslogd -s -m 0
 85 ?? Ss     0:02.44 kextd
 87 ?? Ss     5:30.68 /usr/sbin/configd
 88 ?? Ss     0:02.55 /usr/sbin/diskarbitrationd
 90 ?? Ss     0:00.40 /usr/sbin/notifyd
118 ?? Ss     0:16.42 netinfod -s local
120 ?? Ss     0:24.15 update
```

Its output is generally quite verbose. In order to get very long process names to fit in the Terminal, between 1 and 3 *w* flags might be added.

lsof

Usage

```
lsof [i]
```

Description

lsof (list open files) is similar to *fs_usage*, in that it shows open files and the processes that are using them. *lsof*, however, shows a snapshot, rather than an ongoing real-time process. It is extremely verbose, and specifically designed to send its output to other tools. Its *–i* option is particularly useful and is documented in the network section later in this chapter.

lsof should be executed as root unless you want to be limited to information about processes belonging to the current user (see Example 5-9). *lsof*, in addition to helping you determine how and when a particular process latches onto a particular file, is probably the best tool for figuring out which process is keeping some volume from being unmounted.

Example 5-9. The first few lines of output from the lsof command.

```
fury:~ admin$ sudo lsof | head
Password:
COMMAND    PID   USER  FD   TYPE  DEVICE      SIZE/OFF  NODE NAME
kernel_ta    0   root  cwd  VDIR     14,9         3968     2 / (/dev/disk0s9)
init         1   root  cwd  VDIR     14,9         3968     2 / (/dev/disk0s9)
init         1   root  0r                               0x011e2f6c file struct,
                                                        ty=0x3, op=0x308fd0
init         1   root  1u   unix 0x0115e3e4          0t0 ->0x01160dc4
mach_init    2   root  cwd  VDIR     14,9         3968     2 / (/dev/disk0s9)
mach_init    2   root  0u   unix 0x01160564          0t0 ->0x01160dc4
mach_init    2   root  1w   VBAD                         (revoked)
mach_init    2   root  2w   VBAD                         (revoked)
syslogd     79   root  cwd  VDIR     14,9         3968     2 / (/dev/disk0s9)
```

ktrace

Usage

```
ktrace
```

Description

ktrace and its sibling *kdump* trace system calls and kernel I/O, giving a very detailed record of what a particular process is doing. *ktrace*'s output (viewed with *kdump*) is both verbose and oriented towards developers; more often than not, you won't understand it all unless you're a developer. It is especially important, though, for bug reports. No reproducible crash should ever be sent in to Apple as a bug report without a *ktrace*.

 ktrace is also useful for analyzing complex processes, such as login. *loginwindow* loads a lot of plug-ins and uses code from several different libraries—a lot can be learned from running *ktrace* against it during login.

To use *ktrace*, first use *ps* or some other tool to determine the PID of the daemon or tool you want to trace. *ktrace* accepts the PID as an argument to the *-p* flag. *ktrace* then begins to log, by default to a file called *ktrace.out*:

```
fury:~ admin$ sudo ktrace -p 282
Password:
```

Logging continues until it is disabled, and it can be very verbose. To turn off logging, run *ktrace* with the *-C* option:

```
fury:~ admin$ sudo ktrace -C
```

kdump is used to view *ktrace*'s output. Unless you've used *ktrace*'s *-f* flag to specify a non-default name for its output file, *kdump* doesn't require any arguments, as shown in Example 5-10.

Example 5-10. The first few lines of output for the kdump command.

```
fury:~ admin$ sudo kdump
  282 loginwindow RET    read 70/0x46
  282 loginwindow CALL   write(0x8,0xf00f19b0,0x46)
  282 loginwindow GIO    fd 8 wrote 70 bytes
      "Attempt to release a printing object without first doing a retain!!!\r
      "
```

Network Tools

The following network tools help you determine what's happening, or what has happened, with your network configuration.

netstat

Usage

    netstat *options*

Description

Depending on how you count them, *netstat* has 21 flags, which can be combined thousands of ways—most of which are useful. We're focusing on two right now, the *–r* and the *–n* flags, as shown in Example 5-11.

Example 5-11. netstat's –r flag shows the host's routing table. The addition of the –n flag avoids hostname lookup and can make the command execute faster. The IPv6 version of the routing table is not show here, but is included in the –r output.

```
fury:~ mab9718$ netstat -r
Routing tables

Internet:
Destination          Gateway           Flags  Refs     Use  Netif Expire
default              webmail.4am-media. UGSc     18      15  ppp0
10.0.2/24            link#4            UC        0       0  en1
12-208-224-221.cli   172.16.25.1       UGHS   9520    9662  en0
127                  localhost         UCS       0       0  lo0
localhost            localhost         UH       58   29232  lo0
169.254              link#5            UCS       0       0  en0
172.16.25/24         link#5            UCS       3       0  en0
172.16.25.1          0:20:6f:f:66:9    UHLW      1       0  en0     921
172.16.25.13         0:30:50:2:15:61   UHLW      0       0  en0    1181
172.16.25.15         0:30:50:2:16:f4   UHLW      0       0  en0    1199
172.16.25.49         localhost         UHS       0      10  lo0
webmail.4am-media.   192.168.1.53      UH       21    3130  ppp0
```

netstat's *–a* flag shows all open sockets on the host. This equates to showing all connections on the machine, be it between two local processes, between the local machine and a remote host, or just listening for an incoming connection. This data has important implications on a server platform—it's imperative that that you understand how data enters and exits your machine. Unexpected listening processes could indicate that your server has been compromised, and *netstat* is a good tool to help monitor for that:

```
fury:~ admin$ netstat -a
Active Internet connections (including servers)
Proto Recv-Q Send-Q  Local Address           Foreign Address         (state)
tcp4       0      0  192.168.1.53.50575      bw.4am-media.com.imap   SYN_SENT
```

The following two lines indicate a connection between two processes on the local machine, between port 631, the *ipp* (Internet Printing Protocol) port, and port

50557. Notice that from this output alone, we cannot determine which processes are involved in the socket:

```
tcp4     0     0  localhost.ipp         localhost.50557         ESTABLISHED
tcp4     0     0  localhost.50557       localhost.ipp           ESTABLISHED
tcp4     0     0  192.168.1.53.50513    idisk.mac.com.http      CLOSE_WAIT
tcp4    60     0  192.168.1.53.49751    webmail.4am-medi.imap   CLOSE_WAIT
tcp4     0     0  localhost.49513       localhost.ipp           CLOSE_WAIT
tcp4    60     0  192.168.1.53.49501    webmail.4am-medi.imap   CLOSE_WAIT
tcp4     0     0  192.168.1.53.49500    webmail.4am-medi.imap   ESTABLISHED
tcp4     0     0  192.168.1.53.49476    webmail.4am-medi.ssh    ESTABLISHED
tcp4     0     0  192.168.1.53.49423    205.188.12.44.aol       ESTABLISHED
```

The following line indicates that some process is listening in on port 5298:

```
tcp4     0     0  *.5298                *.*                     LISTEN
tcp4     0     0  *.*                   *.*                     CLOSED
tcp4    83     0  192.168.1.53.49402    webmail.4am-medi.imap   CLOSE_WAIT
```

lsof

Usage

```
lsof [-i]
```

Description

When using *lsof* with the *–i* flag (which is similar to netstat's *–a* flag), *lsof*'s *–i* flag shows all files related to network connections (see Examples 5-12 and 5-13). Also similar to *netstat* is the fact that the status of the connection is shown as well. However, remember, that in Unix, nearly everything, from processes to network connections, can be treated as a file. This feature lets *lsof* show not only connections in various states, but the processes that have those connections open—something *netstat* cannot do.

Example 5-12. lsof –i output, showing network connections.

```
fury:~ admin$ sudo lsof -i
Password:
COMMAND   PID   USER   FD   TYPE    DEVICE SIZE/OFF   NODE NAME
syslogd   79    root   4u   IPv6 0x01239f20    0t0    UDP *:syslog
```

This line and the one above it indicate that the *syslog* daemon (in the COMMAND column) is listening on all interfaces on the *syslog* port (the NAME column). The port name can be looked up in the */etc/services* file.

Example 5-13. Connections seen using lsof.

```
syslogd   79    root   5u   IPv4 0x01239e50    0t0      UDP *:syslog
configd   87    root   9u   IPv6 0x01472f20    0t0 ICMPV6 *:*
configd   87    root  10u   IPv6 0x01472e50    0t0 ICMPV6 *:*
```

Example 5-13. Connections seen using lsof. (continued)

```
configd   87    root   11u  IPv4 0x01239cb0    0t0    UDP *:bootpc
netinfod  118   root   6u   IPv4 0x01239d80    0t0    UDP localhost:netinfo-local
netinfod  118   root   7u   IPv4 0x01378d8c    0t0    TCP localhost:netinfo-local
(LISTEN)
```

Ports that don't appear in the */etc/services* file are specified by port number. In Example 5-14, you can see there's a connection established between the *netinfod* process and a process running on *localhost:796*; this happens to be the *DirectoryService* daemon, although we can't see that from this output.

Example 5-14. The first several lines of output from lsof –i.

```
netinfod  118   root   9u   IPv4 0x014fecac    0t0    TCP localhost:netinfo-local->
localhost:796 (ESTABLISHED)
netinfod  118   root   10u  IPv4 0x015b0ad8    0t0    TCP localhost:netinfo-local->
localhost:714 (ESTABLISHED)
```

The primary difference between the output of *lsof –i* and *netstat –a* is that the former does not show kernel-level connections (like NFS). These are relatively rare, though.

tcpdump

Usage

```
tcpdump [-v|-i|-s ø] [host|part|direction]
```

Description

tcpdump is a network sniffer, which means that it can read TCP/IP (and other) packets off the network in their raw form. Its basic form, *tcpdump [-vvv] –i* interface, shows connections with varying amounts of verbosity, depending on the number of *–v* flags specified, as shown in Example 5-15.

Example 5-15. Basic tcpdump usage.

```
rhp997:~ rhp$ sudo tcpdump -i en0
tcpdump: verbose output suppressed, use -v or -vv for full protocol decode
listening on en0, link-type EN10MB (Ethernet), capture size 96 bytes
20:29:43.935319 IP 64.5.69.57.ssh > c-24-9-136-68.client.comcast.net.50211: P 2119738218:
2119738410(192) ack 1470015739 win 65535 <nop,nop,timestamp 1376092642 1357539151>
20:29:43.990111 arp who-has 64.5.69.87 tell colo-vlan.cu.soltec.net
20:29:44.064345 IP c-24-9-136-68.client.comcast.net.50211 > 64.5.69.57.ssh: . ack 192 win
65535 <nop,nop,timestamp 1357539151 1376092642>
20:29:44.148562 arp who-has 64.5.69.27 tell colo-vlan.cu.soltec.net
```

tcpdump, though, can also display the contents of the packets.

Useful flags

Important *tcpdump* flags include:

–v
> Be verbose; can be used multiple times.

–i
> Use the specified interface. Requires an argument consisting of the Unix device on which you want to sniff packets. In Mac OS X, this will usually be *en0* or *en1*.

–X
> Print the contents of each packet.

–s 0
> Do not truncate packets.

You've probably noticed that *tcpdump* produces quite a bit of output. Because of this, its developers gave it a fairly easy-to-use filter syntax.

Filters

Important *tcpdump* filter options:

host
> Packets associated with the specified host. Requires a host argument.

port
> Packets associated with the specified port. Requires an argument for the port, which may be either the port's name as specified in */etc/services* or its port number.

direction
> Source (*src*) or destination (*src*): filter packets based on where they're going or coming from.

> Filters can also be based on network (as in subnet), protocol (which could be *ether*, *fddi*, *tr*, *wlan*, *ip*, *ip6*, *arp*, *rarp*, *decent*, *atalk*, *tcp*, or *udp*), or several other characteristics, all of which are covered well in *tcpdump*'s manpage.

If you wanted to see only LDAP traffic to or from the host *ldap.example.com*, you could specify the following:

```
tcpdump -i en0 -X -s 0 port ldap and host ldap.example.com or host www
```

As you might have noticed from the example, filters may also be combined using and, not, and or as conjunctions. The filters—although simple—are actually very flexible, and with just a little work, it's not hard build a *tcpdump* statement that focuses very narrowly on the traffic you're interested in.

On most wired networks, you'll be limited to seeing traffic that's either broadcast to the entire network or meant specifically for your host. This is because most modern networks are *switched*, meaning that traffic is sent only to the port where its destination host is plugged in. There are exceptions—not all networks are switched—but they grow more rare every day.

> Some people assume that switched networks are secure from network snooping. Switching, however, is a performance—not security—feature. Switches are vulnerable to ARP floods and spoofing, which could allow traffic to be sniffed.

Wireless networks, however, aren't switched, and you can generally see all network traffic—regardless of which host it's destined for.

Bear in mind that network sniffing is sometimes against policy. In particularly sensitive environments—for instance, where student or medical records are involved—even having a packet sniffer installed could be grounds for termination.

> Another highly useful network analysis tool not included in the OS is *ethereal*, which knows how to decode the hex and base64 text that many protocols use for communication. *ethereal* knows how to interpret binary *tcpdump* output files, so I often end up using *tcpdump* (because it is included in Mac OS X and nearly every other Unix OS) to grab data, then later analyzing it with *ethereal*. In this example, the output file is called *join.dump*:

```
big15:~ mab$ sudo tcpdump -w join.dump -i en1 port domain or
port 3268 or port kerberos or port kpasswd or port ldap
```

Joiners and Filters

When considering particular tools, it is important to revisit the design principles of the Unix architecture—namely, that an operating system is made up of many small, specialized tools, each of which has a special purpose, but all of which work together to do the things an OS needs to do. At a smaller scale, this is illustrated by a number of tools that get most of their worth when applied with other tools.

---

grep

Usage

```
grep {-v | -r} file_pattern filename
```

Description

grep is a generalized searching tool. In its simplest usage, it searches through a file and prints out the lines that contain a specified pattern. For instance, we can *grep* for the word *NO* in the */etc/hostconfig* file, as shown in Example 5-16.

Example 5-16. Using grep to print all the lines that contain the string NO.

```
g5:~ ladmin$ grep NO /etc/hostconfig
AUTHSERVER=-NO-
IPFORWARDING=-NO-
MAILSERVER=-NO-
NISDOMAIN=-NO-
TIMESYNC=-NO-
QTSSERVER=-NO-
WEBSERVER=-NO-
COREDUMPS=-NO-
VPNSERVER=-NO-
LDAPREPLICATOR=-NO-
```

grep's *–v* flag prints lines that *do not* contain the specified pattern, as shown in Example 5-17.

Example 5-17. grep's –v flag is essentially the opposite of grep, displaying every line that doesn't contain a particular string. In this case, it displays every line in /etc/hostconfig that does not contain NO.

```
g5:~ ladmin$ grep -v NO /etc/hostconfig
##
# /etc/hostconfig
##
# This file is maintained by the system control panels
##

# Network configuration
HOSTNAME=g5.pantherserver.org
ROUTER=-AUTOMATIC-

# Services
AFPSERVER=-YES-
AUTOMOUNT=-YES-
CUPS=-YES-
IPV6=-YES-
NETINFOSERVER=-AUTOMATIC-
NFSLOCKS=-AUTOMATIC-
RPCSERVER=-AUTOMATIC-
SMBSERVER=-YES-
DNSSERVER=-YES-
SSHSERVER=-YES-
SERVERMANAGERSERVER=-YES-
LDAPSERVER=-YES-
```

Example 5-17. grep's –v flag is essentially the opposite of grep, displaying every line that doesn't contain a particular string. In this case, it displays every line in /etc/hostconfig that does not contain NO. (continued)

```
ACFS=-YES-

ARDAGENT=-YES-
```

It's often useful to apply *grep* recursively in a particular directory in order to search through a large number of files:

```
fury:/etc mab9718$ grep -r ssh *
group:sshd:*:75:
passwd:sshd:*:75:75:sshd Privilege separation:/var/empty:/usr/bin/false
services:ssh            22/udp      # SSH Remote Login Protocol
services:ssh            22/tcp      # SSH Remote Login Protocol
services:sshell         614/udp     # SSLshell
services:sshell         614/tcp     # SSLshell
services:#                          Kazuhito Gassho <Gassho.Kasuhito@exc.epson.co.jp>
ssh_config:#            $OpenBSD:   ssh_config,v 1.16 2002/07/03 14
```

In this case, the name of the matching file is printed in the lefthand column.

grep's power goes far beyond this simple example, and even in this chapter, we'll learn a lot more about it by putting *grep* to real use. But this is a good start, and it should leave you with something to mull over if you're new to *grep*.

| (the pipe symbol)

The pipe (|) allows us to take the output of one command and send it to another command for processing. Several of the tools we've discussed are particularly verbose. On a normal system install, *ps* can have 60 lines of output. *fs_usage* can yield upwards of 300 lines per minute on a system with only a few applications running. Piping can allow that vast amount of data to be filtered (often by some of the filters included later in this section). A very common example is the search for processes belonging to a particular user:

```
fury:~ mab9718$ ps aux | grep admin
mab9718   347   1.1   0.1    18168    340 std  S+   2:54PM   0:00.01 grep admin
root      341   0.0   0.2    27844    652 p1   S    2:54PM   0:00.04 su -l admin
admin     342   0.0   0.3    18636    756 p1   S+   2:54PM   0:00.01 -su
```

sort

Usage

```
sort {-n}
```

Description

sort takes input (usually from a pipe) and—of all things—sorts it in various ways. It's also capable of merging values and checking for sordidness, but for now we're concerned with the sorting itself. This sorting is generally alphabetical in nature. *sort*'s −*n* flag sorts input numerically. So we could, for instance, take the output of the *nireport* command:

```
fury:~ mab9718$ nireport / /users uid | sort -n
-2
0
1
25
26
27
70
71
74
75
76
77
78
79
99
1024
501
1044
502
```

and *sort* the numerical UIDs on a system:

```
fury:~ mab9718$ nireport / /users uid | sort -n
-2
0
1
25
26
27
70
71
74
75
76
77
78
79
99
501
502
1024
1044
```

wc

Usage

```
wc {-c|-w-1] filename
```

Description

wc counts the characters (*–c*), words (*–w*) or lines (*–l*) in given input or file. Example 5-18 shows the use of *wc* on the */etc/password* file without any options.

Example 5-18. With no flags, wc prints line, word and character totals.

```
[ace2:~] mbartosh% wc /etc/passwd
    16     72     722 /etc/passwd
[ace2:~] mbartosh%
```

 wc's *-c* flag actually ends up counting bytes, rather than characters. For some reason on Mac OS X, this always ends up being *n+1* the number of characters. For instance:

```
fury:~ mab9718$ echo q | wc -c
2
```

q is obviously 1 character and not 2. This behavior is consistent, though, so it is easy to account for in scripts.

It is particularly useful for counting things—the number of users on a system or the number of established connections to a service—mostly because lots of commands output 1 item per line:

```
fury:~ mab9718$ nidump passwd . | wc -l
17
```

awk

Usage

```
awk options filename
```

Description

Entire books have been written about *awk*, which, according to its man page, is a "pattern-directed scanning and processing language." In its most basic form, though, *awk* is a filter, able to take input (file or pipe), and selectively print or reorder columns within. While this sounds obscure, it's actually invaluable for plucking important data out of, say, a tab-delineated file.

A very common example of how to use *awk* is for printing user names on a system, such as often for use in a shell script. Notice that the *–F* flag is used to specify the delimiter, which would otherwise be any whitespace. *nidump*'s *passwd* argument produces output that is delineated by colons, like a Unix */etc/passwd* file:

```
fury:~ mab9718$ nidump passwd .
nobody:*:-2:-2::0:0:Unprivileged User:/var/empty:/usr/bin/false
root:*:0:0::0:0:System Administrator:/var/root:/bin/sh
daemon:*:1:1::0:0:System Services:/var/root:/usr/bin/false
unknown:*:99:99::0:0:Unknown User:/var/empty:/usr/bin/false
smmsp:*:25:25::0:0:Sendmail User:/private/etc/mail:/usr/bin/false
```

That output can be piped to *awk* so that only the first column is printed; $1 here representing the first column (username):

```
fury:~ mab9718$ nidump passwd . | awk -F : '{ print $1}'
nobody
root
daemon
unknown
smmsp
```

Or, you could print the third column (the UID):

```
fury:~ mab9718$ nidump passwd . | awk -F : '{ print $3}'
-2
0
1
99
25
```

Or you could print the third and first columns in reverse order. Notice the comma between the $3 and $1 variables; without it, the two columns would run together:

```
fury:~ mab9718$ nidump passwd . | awk -F : '{ print $3, $1}'
-2 nobody
0 root
1 daemon
99 unknown
25 smmsp
```

Other Commands

Mac OS X has a number of built-in features that can aid in analysis and troubleshooting; some by design, and some simply because they reflect the open nature of the OS. This section explorers some of those, explaining instances where they're useful, and how you can use them to your advantage.

Verbosity and debugging

If you can't already tell from my over-utilization of the word, Unix has a tendency to be verbose. Most of the forensic tools demonstrated, in fact, were so verbose that their output had to be run through a filter before it was really useful.

Most utilities have verbose or debugging options—usually the *–d* or *–v* flags. When you encounter adverse issues, be sure to enable these flags to gather as much data as you can. Keep in mind, too, that these options aren't limited to interactive tools; lots of daemons employ them too. For excellent examples of this see the troubleshooting sections for *bootpd* in Chapter 12 and *slapd* in Chapter 7.

Use the source

Most of Mac OS X is Open Source. This means that the actual code used to generate the software is free for you to download and to even modify, if you so choose. This isn't anything new: FreeBSD, Linux, and many others have been Open Source since their inception. What's exciting about Mac OS X, though, is that it's commercial software from a mainstream software vendor. Open Source, in this context, is a first.

Apple calls Mac OS X's Open Sourced components Darwin. Darwin, a bootable OS in its own right, is distributed at *http://www.opendarwin.org*. When an open source component is causing an issue, it's easy enough to download the source and at least try to determine what's wrong. It's a lot easier than it sounds; some of the code is fairly simple, and most of it is documented to some extent. The important thing is to avoid being intimidated by it and to jump into the particular component you're interested in.

Obtaining Darwin Via CVS

Darwin's source code is easily available via Concurrent Versioning System (CVS), an online source code server. It can be accessed using the *cvs* command. This first requires the setting of an environment variable specifying which *cvs* server should be used.

Under *csh*-based shells like *tcsh* (the default for new users in Jaguar), use the following:

```
setenv CVSROOT :pserver:anonymous@cvs.opendarwin.org:
/Volumes/src/cvs/Apple
```

Using an *sh*-derived shell like *bash* (the default for new users in Panther), use the following:

```
export CVSROOT=:pserver:anonymous@anoncvs.opendarwin.org:
/Volumes/src/cvs/Apple
```

From there, things are the same regardless of which shell you're using:

```
cvs login
cvs co src
```

Once you enter those commands, several gigabytes of Darwin's source code download to your computer from the OpenDarwin repository on Apple's site. Of course, you might want to make sure you have enough space for Darwin's source on your drive before you embark on this mission.

Apple's Open Source isn't limited to generic Unix technologies, either. In Darwin, you'll find the up-to-date source for a variety of Apple-specific components, including Open Directory, *diskarbitrationd*, and *configd*. Source is the ultimate documentation for these technologies, which are in some cases not documented very well.

The magic Shift key

In Mac OS 9, holding the Shift key down at startup kept *extensions* (patches to the system, often supplied by third-party vendors) from loading. This trick was necessary because Mac OS 9 had no concept of privilege separation—everything, from Photoshop to the latest hack to put Christmas lights in your menubar—was run as the system.

Mac OS X has a much more robust model. Very little actually needs to run as the system, and almost nothing outside of device drivers needs to be executed in the kernel.

There are exceptions to both rules, though. Device drivers usually require a kernel extension (or *kext*), and services that require access to the entire filesystem—like backup daemons or remote-access software—still usually need to run as root. When problems arise in either of these cases, there's a safe mode, which is enabled by holding down the Shift key at startup. This does two things:

- Only extensions with a OSBundleRequired key of Local-Root in their *Info.plist* file are loaded into the kernel (via *kextd*'s *–x* option).
- Only Apple-supplied startup items are executed.

The former is due to code in the */etc/rc* script:

```
if [ "${SafeBoot}" = "-x" ]; then
    echo "Configuring kernel extensions for safe boot"
    touch /private/tmp/.SafeBoot
    kextd -x
```

/etc/rc then passes any boot options—including safe boot—to *SystemStarter*, which is responsible for managing the startup process. By editing the referenced portion of */etc/rc*, local customizations to this behavior are feasible, although it should be noted that this is not a feature of the OS that Apple supports.

Both of these behaviors appear to be similar to their Mac OS 9 counterpart. They're not, as severe, though. Starting without extensions in Mac OS 9 left you with a barely usable machine with no networking. Safe mode is more of a way to revert to a default system than it is a way to boot into a minimal one. It assumes that Apple-supplied components are not the problem. This feature is neither good nor bad—it's simply something to take into account.

Shift can also be held down during login to disable execution of login items. This is appropriate when a login item is crashing the login process or is in some other way being troublesome.

The following shell script makes a good practical joke as a login item:

```
#/bin/sh
#keep looping
while true; do
    cd /Applications
    #double-click everything
    /usr/bin/open *
    #sleep awhile
    /bin/sleep 20
    #Go back to work
    cd Utilities
    /usr/bin/open *
    /bin/sleep 30
done
```

As you can tell by reading the code, this script launches every item in the Applications folder, then goes to sleep for 20 seconds. While the user is scratching his head, wondering what the hell just happened, the system wakes back up, launches every item in the Utilities folder, and goes back to sleep for another 30 seconds. Save this one for April Fools' Day.

Logs

Another Unix tendency is towards logging. Most daemons have some kind of logging option. Apple-specific daemons tend to log to files in */Library/Logs*, while most software from the Unix world logs through *syslogd*, configured in the */etc/syslog.conf* file.

Logging, especially on a busy server, can take a significant toll on performance, so there's always a lot of data that's not actually written to the system logs. In some instances, of course, you want to gather all the data you can. This is actually quite a simple process, as long as you're comfortable using a text editor to edit the *syslog. conf* file.

Directives in *syslog.conf* take the following form of:

```
facility.level          destination
```

Where *facility* is the category or process associated with the message; *level* is one of *debug, info, notice, warning, err, crit, alert*, and *emerg* (in ascending urgency); and *destination* is the file or remote host to which messages matching that rule should be sent to. For instance, the following would send all messages to the */var/log/mail* file:

```
mail.*              /var/log/mail
```

While this would send all messages of *level alert* to a specific *loghost*:

```
*.alert              @loghost.4am-media.com
```

So, in order to catch every error from every facility, there must be an entry in *syslog. conf* that looks like this:

```
*.*                  /var/log/all.log
```

The destination actually has to exist before *syslog* logs to it, so you can use the *touch* command to create an empty file to make it happy:

```
sudo touch /var/log/all.log
```

And finally, restart *syslog*:

```
sudo killall -HUP syslogd
```

At first you might not see any extra messages; be careful, though! We've seen out-of-control software fill up a 40 GB hard drive in one night with spurious log activity that was written to the system log only due to a similar *syslog* setting. Be sure to turn this option off if you're not troubleshooting.

## PART II

Directory Services

In recent years, IT and the way that IT organizations deal with users, groups and other administrative data has changed markedly. Workgroup management has become centralized, so that user accounts and authentication data are managed on a server, rather than individually on each workstation. This concept, commonly called a *directory service*, or a *domain*, was first commercialized in the desktop market by Novell and later embraced by Microsoft.

Directory domains fit nicely with the ongoing trend of centralization in the IT industry, and have been widely adopted in the marketplace. Vendors from Microsoft to Apple to Novell to Sun have brought forward a number of directory products, and they are so important to Mac OS X that I've devoted several chapters to them. This section of the book begins with a conceptual analysis of shared directory domains and moves quickly into chapters covering specific aspects of Apple's server-side directory service offerings. Chapters in this part of the book include:

Chapter 6, *Open Directory Server*

Chapter 7, *Identification and Authorization in Open Directory Server*

Chapter 8, *Authentication in Open Directory Server*

Chapter 9, *Replication in Open Directory Server*

Additional information regarding the client-side Directory Services architecture employed by Mac OS X and Mac OS X Server is located in Appendix A.

Open Directory Server

As directory domains and centralized management have grown in importance to the IT industry, Apple has slowly but surely developed a robust and standards-based server-side directory services architecture. Panther Server represents a real milestone in that direction, with a Kerberos-LDAPv3-and SASL-based component known alternately as Open Directory, Open Directory 2, and Open Directory Server, depending on whom you ask.

 Open Directory itself is a bad case of marketing terms gone crazy—encompassing a whole suite of OS components that collectively provide a directory services architecture to Mac OS X. Open Directory Server generally refers to the server side of those components. Open Directory 2 was probably coined to differentiate Jaguar's directory service offerings (which were heavily reliant on NetInfo) from Panther's, which are more centered around LDAP. Luckily, the technology is more stable than the terminology.

The Appendix documents the client-side of Apple's Directory Services infrastructure—the processes Mac OS X and Mac OS X Server employ in order to make use of identification, authentication and authorization data. This chapter, however, begins the analysis of Mac OS X Server's Directory Service capabilities—both as a directory client and server.

Directory Services are complex. There is no getting around it. The concepts are new to many administrators and sometimes difficult to grasp. In fact, Open Directory Server Services are provided by three separate but interrelated server-side systems. OpenLDAP, an Open Source LDAP server package, is used to house and access data used to identify user, group, and machine accounts, including authorization policies and other configuration data. Password Server, an Apple-specific, standards-based and network-aware authentication authority, is Mac OS X Server's primary means of authentication for both shared and local directory domains. It is used in conjunction with MIT's Kerberos distribution in order to support a more robust, single-sign-on enabled authentication infrastructure.

Because this structure boils down to a system that is fairly complex, the task of documenting it is divided into several chapters, including:

- *Open Directory Server* (this chapter): Introduces certain conventions and the basic management of Open Directory Server, including the creation and access of Open Directory shared domains.

- Chapter 7, *Identification and Authorization in Open Directory Server*: Discusses the processing and storage of identification and authorization data in Open Directory Server.

- Chapter 8, *Authentication in Open Directory Server*: This chapter includes an in-depth analysis of Kerberos and Password Services; two parallel systems offering authentication to Open Directory clients.

- Chapter 9, *Replication in Open Directory Server*: Panther introduced a new facet to Mac OS X Directory Services—replication, which supports fault tolerance in Mac OS X Directory Services. This has lots of good data that's not available elsewhere—so be sure to take advantage of it.

If you're not already familiar with Apple's Open Directory infrastructure, you should first skip ahead to the Appendix, before going any further.

Managing Open Directory Server

Managing Open Directory Server—as opposed to managing the accounts and configuration data contained in its databases—is mostly achieved in the user interface of the Server Admin application, its command-line equivalent, *serveradmin*, and several other utilities that simplify the process of configuring the underlying services. This section of the chapter serves to introduce the reader mostly to the higher-level aspects of that interface. Some more specific configuration options are covered in later Open Directory Server chapters in a more task-oriented fashion.

Open Directory's settings are easy to locate (like all other service-specific preferences); they can be found in Server Admin's service list, as shown in Figure 6-1. This initial selection reveals several other sections available in Server Admin's righthand pane: Overview, Logs, and Settings.

The Overview, illustrated in Figure 6-2, yields a high-level look at the processes that comprise Open Directory Server. Which processes are running varies with the server's configuration. Servers that are hosting or accessing shared directory domains typically have more enabled services than those in a standalone configuration.

Absent from this list is the *DirectoryService* daemon, which is central to Directory Services on Mac OS X. If *DirectoryService* weren't running, it would be unlikely that

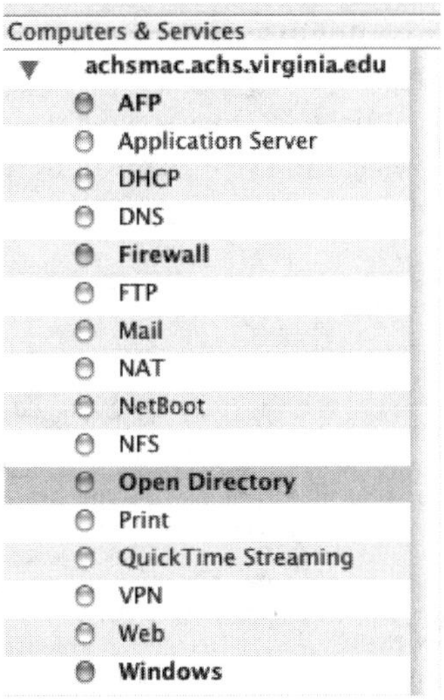

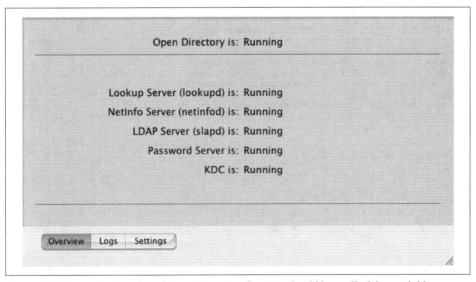

Figure 6-1. *To locate the Open Directory settings, select Open Directory from the service list of the server you wish to manage.*

Figure 6-2. *Servers hosting shared Open Directory domains should have all of the available services (lookupd, netinfod, slapd Password Server, and KDC) listed as running.*

you could have logged into Server Admin in the first place—and you'd probably have much larger issues, since it's supposed to be restarted automatically by the *mach_init* process. Still, including its status would be reassuring, for consistency's sake if nothing else. For an in-depth discussion of the *DirectoryService* daemon, see Chapter 3 and the Appendix.

The Logs portion of Server Admin's Open Directory selection (illustrated in Figure 6-3) provides access to a number of the log files associated with Open Directory Server's component processes. Its pull-down menu specifically offers access to the Directory Services Server (the *DirectoryService* daemon in its server configuration) and Password Server service and error logs, along with logs from *lookupd*, NetInfo, and LDAP.

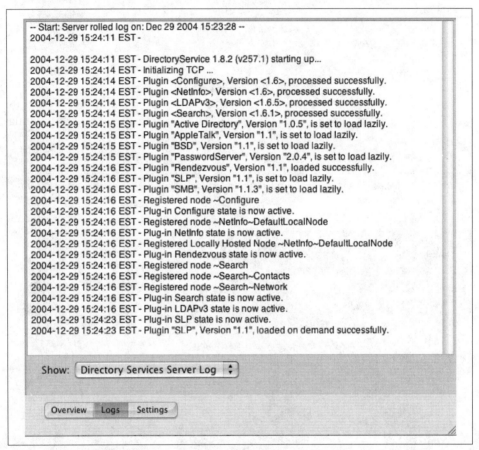

Figure 6-3. Viewing the DirectoryService server log with Server Admin.

These logs, though, are subject to Server Admin's stateless, HTTP-based query–response model, and thus aren't appropriate for some kinds of analysis, especially that of a very busy log file. Advanced administrators will want to view these logs directly, with the *tail* command or a pager like *more* or *less*. This technique has the added benefit of allowing for post-processing with a filter like *grep*. In order to facilitate this, the locations of various Open Directory logs are illustrated in Table 6-1.

Table 6-1. To enable missing or empty logs, see enabling NetInfo logging and enabling lookupd logging in the Appendix or enabling LDAP logging in Chapter 7.

Log	Filesystem location
Directory Services Server Log	/Library/Logs/DirectoryService/DirectoryService.server.log
Directory Services Error Log	/Library/Logs/DirectoryService/DirectoryService.error.log
Lookupd Log	/var/log/lookupd.log (generally empty)
NetInfo Log	/var/log/netinfo.log (generally empty)
LDAP Log	Doesn't exist out of box
Password Service Server Log	/Library/Logs/PasswordService/ApplePasswordServer.Server.log
Password Service Error Log	/Library/Logs/PasswordService/ApplePasswordServer.Error.log

Conspicuously absent from the list of logs available via Server Admin are the logs for the Kerberos server (KDC). Curiously, as of 10.3.5, even though the KDC is configured to log to */var/log/krb5kdc/kdc.log*, its messages are sent to *syslogd*, and can be seen in a default configuration in */var/log/system.log*. Chapter 8 contains directions for sending KDC logs to their own file.

The Settings section of Server Admin's Open Directory configuration is the primary graphical interface for managing Open Directory Server. The Settings section offers three other tools: General, Protocols, and Authentication. All of these interfaces are quite dynamic, and change depending on the server's configuration. The General tab is concerned mostly with the server's Open Directory role.

Roles

Roles relate to specific service configurations that support specific functionality (for instance, Open Directory Master and Open Directory Replica). These configurations are a fundamental aspect of Mac OS X Server directory services configuration. Roles are important, because the systems and services that underlie their functionality are complex and offer a wide array of configuration options. Adopting a role, which describes a very specific set of configurations, allows us to make assumptions about a server's state.

> Understanding roles is critical when building systems that will come to rely on these settings and behaviors. It would be very difficult for Apple to construct a packaged product that did not make such assumptions, precisely because there are so many options and feasible configurations. Because these modes impact strongly both the graphical management interface and the server's behavior, an understanding of each is important.

A Standalone Server (illustrated in Figure 6-4) is Apple's terminology for a server that doesn't provide or access to a shared directory domain. User records are stored in the local NetInfo database, and authentication data is stored in Password Server (PWS), which also plays an important role in Open Directory Masters.

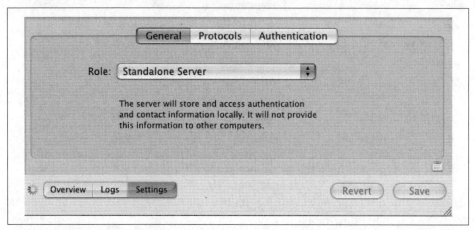

Figure 6-4. Unless otherwise configured during a server's initial setup, all Mac OS X Server installations begin in a Standalone role.

"Connected to a Directory System" (illustrated in Figure 6-5) means simply that the server is acting as a client to some directory server—possibly Mac OS X Server, but just as likely Active Directory, eDirectory, or even NIS. User accounts probably exist in that shared domain, and authentication is generally (unless Kerberos is in use) proxied through as well. This role, specifically in the context of an Open Directory Domain, is covered later in this chapter.

Even if Kerberos (single sign-on) has been configured, as of 10.3.4, Server Admin states, "Your server is not currently using Kerberos" (see Figure 6-5). This is simply incorrect. Also note that this button appears when it is inappropriate, such as when joined to an Active Directory domain (although Active Directory uses Kerberos, it is not accessed in Panther using the Join Kerberos button). For more data relating to Kerberos interoperability, see Chapter 8.

Pictured in Figure 6-6, an Open Directory Master is the centerpiece of an Open Directory Domain. In general, an Open Directory Master is running both LDAP and Kerberos servers in order to provide authentication, authorization, and identification data to network clients. An Open Directory Master is additionally assumed to contain a variety of configuration information, including LDAP and Kerberos client settings—even user records are standardized, allowing assumptions to be made about account authentication and management. This is a rather long-winded way of saying that the server is hosting a shared directory domain—something that gets examined at great depth throughout this and the subsequent three chapters.

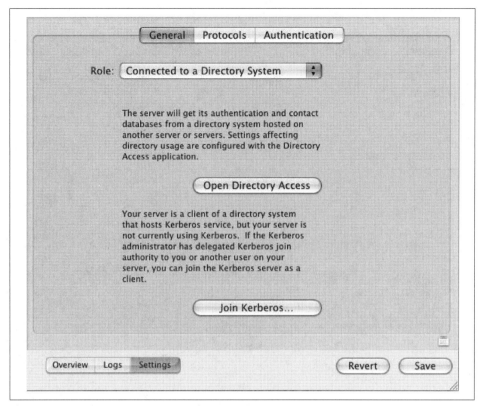

Figure 6-5. Systems that have been configured with the Directory Access application to access a nonlocal directory domain are seen as "Connected to a Directory System."

Open Directory Replicas, covered in more depth in Chapter 9 (and not pictured here), add a high availability component to Apple's Directory Services, as their name implies, they replicate data from Open Directory Masters.

 The primary difference between Open Directory Masters and Replicas is that the LDAP data on the former is writable. LDAP data on replicas is read-only.

Changing the server's role can be seen as a sort of macro operation, bringing all of the underlying services into a known state supporting that role's function. This change, achieved graphically by choosing among the available options in the Role pull-down menu, is in every case actually implemented by *servermgrd*'s *servermgrd_dirserv* plug-in, which calls the *slapconfig* utility. *slapconfig*, in turn, calls a number of other utilities, each affecting some aspect of Open Directory Server configuration. Each of these changes is detailed in more depth where appropriate; master creation later in this chapter, replica creation in Chapter 9, etc.

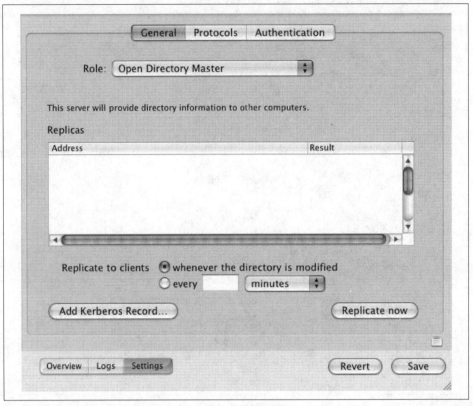

Figure 6-6. An Open Directory Master configuration.

The Protocols tab, seen in Figure 6-7, offers a set of options relating to individual Open Directory Servers and services—specifically, in 10.3, NetInfo Migration and LDAP. The former is covered in more depth in Chapter 7. The latter is used to migrate 10.2 NetInfo-based shared domains to 10.3 LDAP-based Open Directory Masters (even if you're using LDAP in Jaguar, the data is actually stored in NetInfo).

 This automated NetInfo to LDAP migration is typically unsuccessful in all but the smallest of deployments. When migrating an Open Directory Master from Jaguar to Panther, it is best to simply back up, reformat, and reinstall, either reimporting user accounts or manually scripting your own data migration.

Finally, the Authentication tab—illustrated in Figure 6-8—exposes a number of options associated with Password Server, one component of Open Directory Server's authentication mechanism. Specifically, these are global password policy options, which can be applied to all nonadmin users using a specific password server. This and other facets of Password Server are covered in more depth in Chapter 8.

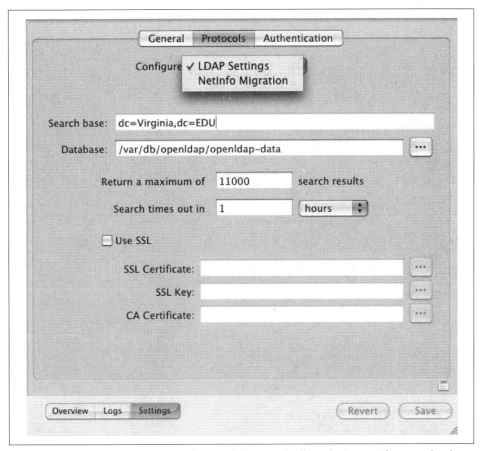

Figure 6-7. The Protocols tab seems to be one of those catch-alls in the Server Admin graphical interface, where mostly unrelated options are grouped together, mostly because there's no better place to put them. LDAP data (as seen in this example) is available only if the host is an Open Directory Master or Replica.

The Open Directory Master: Creating a Shared Open Directory Domain

In most cases, Mac OS X Server begins life after installation as a standalone server—the server itself is the only host that can access its user and group database, which is stored in the local NetInfo domain.

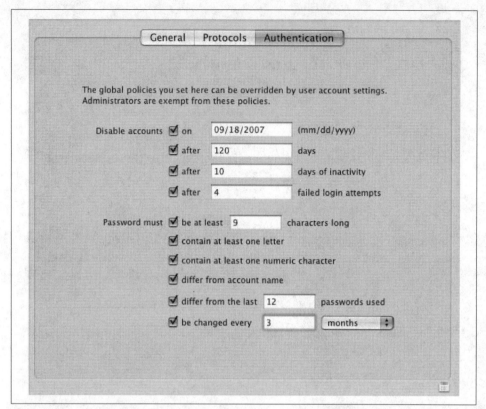

The global policies you set here can be overridden by user account settings. Administrators are exempt from these policies.

Disable accounts ☑ on 09/18/2007 (mm/dd/yyyy)

☑ after 120 days

☑ after 10 days of inactivity

☑ after 4 failed login attempts

Password must ☑ be at least 9 characters long

☑ contain at least one letter

☑ contain at least one numeric character

☑ differ from account name

☑ differ from the last 12 passwords used

☑ be changed every 3 months

Figure 6-8. The Authentication tab of Server Admin's Open Directory Setting section exposes certain global password policy options.

Although it is feasible to create an Open Directory Master immediately upon installation (as a part of the post-install configuration) it is generally a very good idea to wait until later, after all appropriate software updates have been applied. This ensures that the relatively delicate process of Master creation happens in a relatively current configuration.

In many cases this arrangement is acceptable, but by now it is hopefully apparent that centralized identity management and authentication are important directions for Apple. Customers *want* network users and the other benefits of a shared directory domain. A server that is hosting a shared domain is known as an Open Directory Master. As mentioned earlier, this status implies that both Kerberos and LDAP will be enabled on that server. Additionally, a new administrative user will be created in order to manage those shared resources.

Before a server is promoted to either master or replica, ensure that it has both forward and reverse DNS records. The host command is a good tool to use:

```
gs:~ mbartosh$ host gs.pantherserver.org

gs. pantherserver.org has address 207.224.49.180

gs:~ mbartosh$ host 207.224.49.180

180.49.224.207.in-addr.arpa domain name pointer gs.
pantherserver.org.
```

Notice that the forward and reverse addresses agree. This is vital for Open Directory Masters and Replicas. The fully qualified domain name should also match the HOSTNAME value in */etc/hostconfig*.

To promote a server graphically, first login to Server Admin and choose Directory Services Settings. In the General tab, select "Open Directory Master" from the Role pull-down menu, as shown in Figure 6-9.

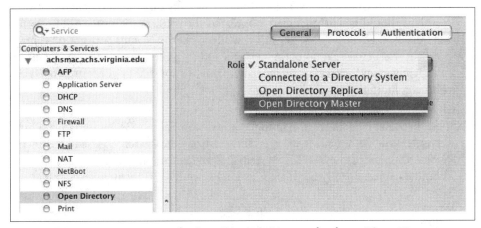

Figure 6-9. To promote a server to the Open Directory Master role, choose "Open Directory Master" from the Role pull-down in the General Tab of Server Admin's Directory Services Settings.

You will be prompted to enter some basic administrative data relating to your new Open Directory Domain, as indicated in Figure 6-10.

Administrator short name and password

This should be the first short name of an existing administrator in the server's local domain. The user must also be a password server administrator, but in Panther, this is the default setting for all admin users. Some documentation suggests that the first administrator created during the server's initial configuration must be used to promote an Open Directory Master. There is no evidence, however, that this is true, and promotion tends to work as long as the user in question is a typical administrator.

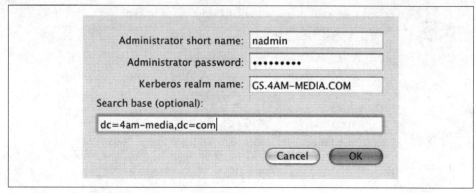

Figure 6-10. Entering basic shared domain settings.

Kerberos realm name

A realm is the basic administrative unit in Kerberos—something we'll look at in more depth in Chapter 8. It looks a lot like the fully qualified DNS name of your server (it should be automatically populated for you), but it's not. Among other differences, DNS is not case-sensitive, while Kerberos is. This convention—mapping the Kerberos realm to the server's *fqdn*—is not based on any technical requirement, and in reality, nearly any value, as long as it conforms to DNS's character limitations, will do.

Search base (optional)

This becomes the domain-naming context (or Search Base) for your LDAP server. If you do not fill it in, it is derived from the search base entered in the Network panel of the server's System Preferences application. It, too, though, should be automatically populated, as long as your DNS settings are correct.

 Once this data is entered (after pressing OK), you *must* press the Save button (in Server Admin's lower righthand corner) in order to commit the changes.

This process at first appears very simple. That appearance, however, is a testament to the work Apple has put into easing the pain of a very complex process. The actual configuration taking place is fairly complex; something easily seen when monitored from the command line. As mentioned earlier in this chapter, any change in role is actually implemented by *servermgrd*'s *servermgrd_dirserv* plug-in, using the *slapconfig* command. Luckily, *slapconfig* logs quite verbosely to */Library/Logs/slapconfig.log*, as shown in Example 6-1. This record is exceedingly useful, since errors in role changes are not reported by the Server Admin application.

Example 6-1. slapconfig's log. This report is the result of a successful master creation.

```
2004-05-23 14:58:13 -0600 - slapconfig -createldapmaster
2004-05-23 14:58:14 -0600 - Creating password server slot
2004-05-23 14:58:14 -0600 - Using generated suffix: dc=4am-media,dc=com
2004-05-23 14:58:20 -0600 - Configuring Kerberos server, realm is G5.4AM-MEDIA.COM
2004-05-23 14:58:21 -0600 - kdcsetup command output:
Contacting the Directory Server
Authenticating to the Directory Server
Creating Kerberos directory
Creating KDC Config File
Creating Admin ACL File
Creating Kerberos Master Key
Creating Kerberos Database
Creating Kerberos Admin user
WARNING: no policy specified for nadmin@G5.4AM-MEDIA.COM; defaulting to no policy
Adding kerberos auth authority to admin user
Creating keytab for the admin tools
Adding KDC & kadmind to watchdog
Adding the new KDC into the KerberosClient config record
Finished
```

Even more verbose output can be seen when running *slapconfig* manually, from the command line, outside of the context of the Server Admin application, as shown in Example 6-2.

Example 6-2. Output of the slapconfig's –createldapmaster option. The only required argument is the short name of the admin user used to create the shared domain. However, it can optionally accept specific Kerberos and LDAP values, in the form of slapconfig –createldapmaster <admin> [<search base suffix> [<realm>]].

```
g5:~ nadmin$ sudo slapconfig -createldapmaster nadmin
Password:
Creating password server slot
Using generated suffix: dc=4am-media,dc=com
Starting LDAP server
adding new entry "dc=4am-media,dc=com"
adding new entry "cn=config,dc=4am-media,dc=com"
adding new entry "ou=macosxodconfig,cn=config,dc=4am-media,dc=com"

adding new entry "cn=mcx_cache,cn=config,dc=4am-media,dc=com"
adding new entry "cn=ldapreplicas,cn=config,dc=4am-media,dc=com"
adding new entry "cn=passwordserver,cn=config,dc=4am-media,dc=com"
adding new entry "cn=users,dc=4am-media,dc=com"
adding new entry "uid=root,cn=users,dc=4am-media,dc=com"
adding new entry "cn=groups,dc=4am-media,dc=com"
adding new entry "cn=admin,cn=groups,dc=4am-media,dc=com"
adding new entry "cn=mounts,dc=4am-media,dc=com"
adding new entry "cn=aliases,dc=4am-media,dc=com"
adding new entry "cn=machines,dc=4am-media,dc=com"
adding new entry "cn=computers,dc=4am-media,dc=com"
adding new entry "cn=computer_lists,dc=4am-media,dc=com"
adding new entry "cn=locations,dc=4am-media,dc=com"
```

Example 6-2. Output of the slapconfig's –createldapmaster option. The only required argument is the short name of the admin user used to create the shared domain. However, it can optionally accept specific Kerberos and LDAP values, in the form of slapconfig –createldapmaster <admin> [<search base suffix> [<realm>]]. (continued)

```
adding new entry "cn=people,dc=4am-media,dc=com"
adding new entry "cn=printers,dc=4am-media,dc=com"
adding new entry "cn=presets_users,dc=4am-media,dc=com"
adding new entry "cn=presets_groups,dc=4am-media,dc=com"
adding new entry "cn=presets_computer_lists,dc=4am-media,dc=com"
adding new entry "cn=autoserversetup,dc=4am-media,dc=com"
Configuring Kerberos server, realm is G5.4AM-MEDIA.COM
kdcsetup command output:
Contacting the Directory Server
Authenticating to the Directory Server
Creating Kerberos directory
Creating KDC Config File
Creating Admin ACL File
Creating Kerberos Master Key
Creating Kerberos Database
Creating Kerberos Admin user
WARNING: no policy specified for nadmin@G5.4AM-MEDIA.COM; defaulting to no policy
Adding kerberos auth authority to admin user
Creating keytab for the admin tools
Adding KDC & kadmind to watchdog
Adding the new KDC into the KerberosClient config record
Finished
sso_util command output:
DoConfigure: argc = 13
Creating the service list
Creating the service principals
WARNING: no policy specified for host/g5.4am-media.com@G5.4AM-MEDIA.COM; defaulting to no
policy
WARNING: no policy specified for smtp/g5.4am-media.com@G5.4AM-MEDIA.COM; defaulting to no
policy
WARNING: no policy specified for pop/g5.4am-media.com@G5.4AM-MEDIA.COM; defaulting to no
policy
WARNING: no policy specified for imap/g5.4am-media.com@G5.4AM-MEDIA.COM; defaulting to no
policy
WARNING: no policy specified for ftp/g5.4am-media.com@G5.4AM-MEDIA.COM; defaulting to no
policy
WARNING: no policy specified for afpserver/g5.4am-media.com@G5.4AM-MEDIA.COM; defaulting
to no policy
Creating the keytab file
Configuring services
WriteSetupFile: setup file path = /temp.Qzbj/setup
Mail config file at /etc/MailServicesOther.plist updated successfully
Mail config file at /etc/MailServicesOther.plist updated successfully
Mail config file at /etc/MailServicesOther.plist updated successfully
AFP config file at /Library/Preferences/com.apple.AppleFileServer.plist updated
successfully
Hupping the AFP Server
Cleaning up
```

In reality, though, the master creation process as executed by Server Admin, *servermgrd* and *servermgrd_dirserv* is slightly (but only slightly) more idetailed. *slapconfig* is first run with the *–getstyle* flag, in order to determine its current state (role). After it is run again with its *–createldapmaster* flag, the *–getnetinfoconfig* and– *defaultsuffix* options are also called, presumably to verify the success of the master promotion.

Best Practices

Typically, folks choose an administrator when they set up their server—often calling it *admin*. They also use *admin* to create their shared domain, meaning that their Open Directory master has two users named *admin*: one in the local (NetInfo) domain, and one in the shared (LDAP) domain. Under any other circumstance, Open Directory won't allow you to create users with conflicting short names, but in this case Apple's tools inadvertently encourage it.

Confusion is exacerbated by the addition of replication to this environment. Replicas are typically created with yet another *admin* user, creating more namespace collisions and further chaos. An Open Directory domain with 12 replicas could have 12 accounts called *admin*, all of which conflict with the user called *admin* in the shared domain. Because they are all separate accounts, they can all have separate passwords, and determining which *admin* you're really authenticating as can be confusing, as illustrated in Figure 6-11.

This confusion can be avoided, however, by following a few simple guidelines, illustrated graphically in Figure 6-12:

1. Use host-specific local *admin*s. Rather than using the name *admin*, choose an *admin* name that relates in a systematic way to the hostname of the server. For instance, for a server called *rhp997.pantherserver.org*, you could use *rhp997admin*. Shorten longer hostnames so that they're manageable; for instance, *rhpadm*.

2. On the prospective master, create a user specifically for creation of the shared domain. (This is *not* the host-specific user mentioned in step 1.) So, if I were going to create an Open Directory master out of *rhp997.example.com*, I'd log in as *rhpadm* and create a second administrator, named (for instance) *nadmin*, *radmin*, or *netadm*; something to specify that this *admin* user is in the shared domain. I'd then use that user (in Server Admin or with the command-line *slapconfig* tool) to create the shared domain.

3. Finally, after the network domain is successfully created, delete the network *admin* from the local domain. This avoids the conflicting usernames otherwise typically seen in an (especially replicated) Open Directory domain.

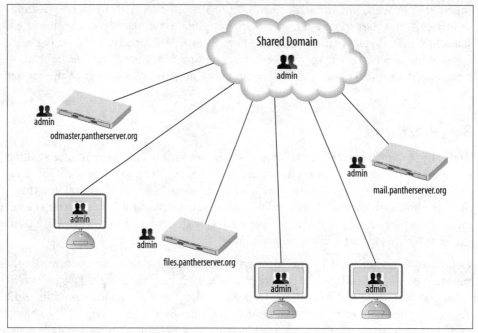

Figure 6-11. Having users with conflicting names—particularly administrative users—can result in a great deal of confusion.

 Deleting the user from the local domain (as of 10.3.5) leaves that user in the local domain's *admin* group. This allows that user (in this example, *nadmin*) to log in using Workgroup Manager, but does not allow them to make changes to the local domain using Workgroup Manager.

4. Local (nonserver) hosts are a bit of a toss up. IT staff face a temptation to user local administrators on nonserver hosts (for instance, in labs or user desktops) in order to facilitate easier management. At a minimum, this user should not be named *admin* (for all the reasons mentioned here).

   In environments where physical security is not absolute, however, where nonserver hosts might be vulnerable to theft, you should strongly consider deleting all local users. Local user passwords are stored using an NTLMv1 hash, which is not at all secure against a physical compromise. In most environments such a compromise would mean that the malicious party had access to the local admin password of all clients, which is obviously not a desirable occurrence.

Under the Hood

Behind the scenes, *slapconfig* is making some very specific configuration changes using hard-coded commands:

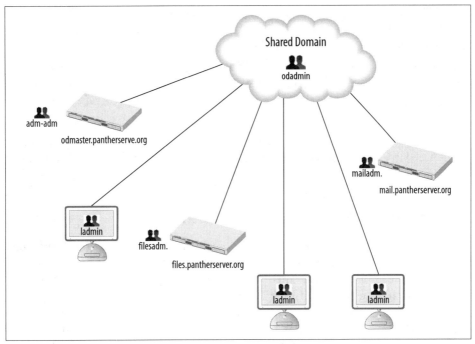

Figure 6-12. Avoiding conflicting administrative usernames in an Open Directory domain.

- Password Server slots are reserved for the local domain. This is a fairly obscure facet of Password Server architecture, and is covered in more depth in Chapter 8. Essentially, a range of Password Server IDs (128-bit hex values used to identify Password Server users) are reserved for local usage.

- Two hard-coded LDAP configuration files are copied to */etc/openldap/slapd.conf* and */etc/openldap/slapd_macosxserver.conf*. The password supplied at domain creation time is then in encrypted in a one-way MD5 hash and stored in *slapd_macosxserver.conf*'s *rootpw* setting. It is used subsequently to create the basic structure of the LDAP directory. The details of this configuration are covered in more depth in Chapter 7.

- Top-level LDAP containers are created for *user*, *group*, and *computer* accounts as well as various configuration settings.

- The *admin* used to create the domain is copied into it while a new *root* user is also created there. Both are given the password specified in the master creation dialog. The *admin* user is effectively a copy of the specified local *admin* user, and both are Password Server admins (the *root* user in the local domain has a *ShadowHash*, rather than a *PasswordServer*, authauthority).

- The *kdcsetup* command is run in order to establish the Kerberos server and create its associated configuration settings. During this process, the domain *admin* user is also given a kerberosv5 authauthority (in addition to its

AblePasswordServer authauthority). The KDC and its automated configuration settings are covered in more depth in Chapter 8.

- The *kerberosautoconfig* command is run in order to complete the server's client-side Kerberos configuration. (The server is made a client to its own KDC.)

- The *krbservicesetup* command is run in order to Kerberize services running on the Open Directory Master. *krbservicesetup* in turn calls the *sso_util* command.

Ideally, once *slapconfig* has run, a new Open Directory shared domain is available for use. No reboot should be required, although Server Admin's Open Directory Status might need to be refreshed in order to accurately reflect the currently running services.

Accessing an Open Directory Domain

The whole point behind shared directory domains is to store *user*, *group*, and *other* administrative data centrally. It makes sense, then, that servers as well as clients should make use of this data. This could be worthwhile for a number of reasons. MIT, for instance, recommends that as few services as feasible be run on any KDC. Since every Open Directory Master and Replica contains a KDC, it is a good idea to minimize the number of services running on any server supporting either one of these roles. Similarly, you might not want a public-facing web server or other high-visibility host serving as an Open Directory Master. Such a machine, however, should almost certainly participate in the shared domain in order to minimize local maintenance and to make use of domain resources.

Performance is another common impetus for differentiating server roles. LAN-based file servers might experience a tremendous I/O load, which could negatively affect the performance of Open Directory Server services (which can also lead to a fairly high load). Larger enterprises demand more servers in order to supply some base level of service to increasingly large user bases. In theory, all of these servers should participate in an Open Directory domain.

The actual configuration of Mac OS X Server to be an Open Directory Client is fairly trivial. It is, in fact, identical to the configuration of Mac OS X—in both cases, the Directory Access application is used. The one caveat is that Mac OS X Server can, in an out-of-box configuration, be configured remotely, using the connect option in Directory Access's Server menu. The resulting authentication dialog can be seen in Figure 6-13.

Once authenticated to the prospective child server, simply select the LDAPv3 plug-in in the Services pane (Figure 6-14) and either double-click it or click the Configure button. The resulting dialog allows you to access an LDAP node. Select a configuration name and specify the IP address or hostname of an Open Directory Master or Replica.

Figure 6-13. The authentication dialog from Directory Access's Server menu. As noted in Chapter 3, this operation, which communicates on the server side with the DirectoryService daemon, is protected by a 512-bit Diffie-Hellman exchange.

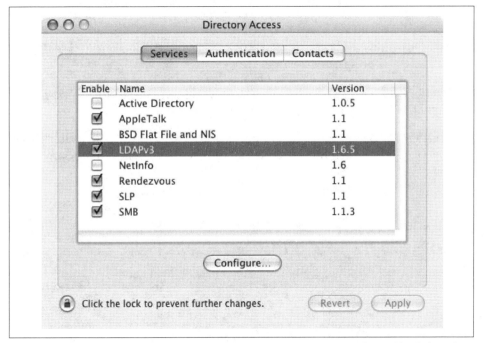

Figure 6-14. Selecting the LDAPv3 plug-in in Directory Access's Services tab. Double-clicking the plug-in's entry or selecting the Configure button exposes the plug-in's configuration interface.

Although we have not yet discussed Open Directory Replicas in any depth, keep in mind that when configuring a client or server to access an Open Directory Domain, it is best to choose the replica that is closest to the client. For instance, servers (and clients for that matter) at a branch office should generally choose that office's replica, rather than the master. This has little impact beyond the initial configuration, however.

Because we're accessing a Mac OS X Server–hosted directory domain, we're able to make some assumptions about the server's requirements, and rather than doing a lot of advanced configuration, we can simply instruct the plug-in to use standard Mac OS X LDAP mappings (mapping LDAP attributes to their Open Directory names) by choosing "Open Directory" in the "LDAP Mappings" option. If prompted for a search base (as seen in Figure 6-15) supply the one specified during creation of your Open Directory Master.

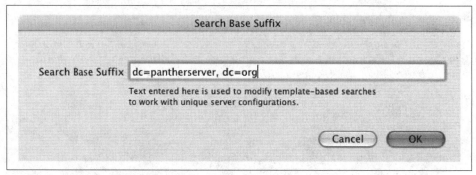

Figure 6-15. Supplying an LDAP search base. This helps the LDAP plug-in determine how to search the LDAP directory hosted on your Open Directory Master.

Next, press OK when you're ready to proceed, making sure that the Enable checkbox for the newly created node is checked. Your configuration should resemble the one found in Figure 6-16.

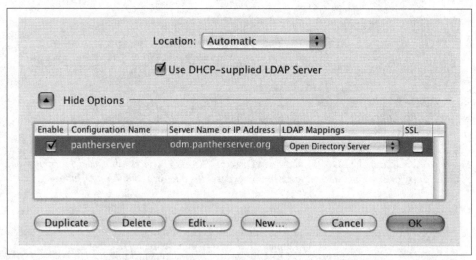

Figure 6-16. The LDAPv3 plug-in is actually capable of supporting a variety of LDAP servers and schemas. Because we're working with Open Directory Server, we can make assumptions about the server's configuration, choosing to download our settings from the server.

Now that the node (directory domain) has been successfully enabled, it must be added to the server's Authentication (or Search) path. This is accomplished with Directory Access's Authentication tab, seen in Figure 6-17.

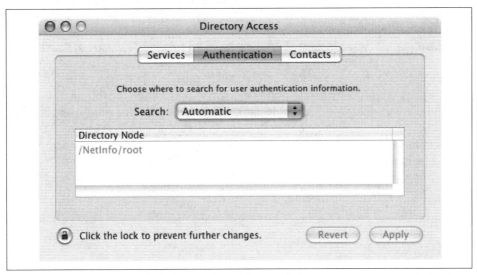

Figure 6-17. Directory Access's Authentication tab in its default state—accessing only the local directory.

From the Search pull-down menu, choose Custom Path. This enables an Add button. Selecting it should offer a choice of the node you just created, as noted in Figure 6-18.

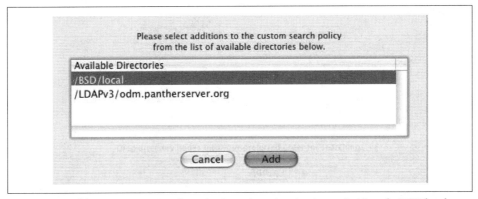

Figure 6-18. Adding an LDAPv3 node to the Server's authentication path. Note the BSD/local node, which can in most cases be ignored. It allows the server to access users and groups in the deprecated /etc files.

Once these settings are applied, the server is essentially "bound" to the parent directory. No reboot is required. Ironically enough, this same configuration can be more simply achieved using the *slapconfig* command; specifically, its *setldapstatic* flag, as shown in Example 6-3.

Example 6-3. Using slapconfig's –setldapstatic flag to enable access to a shared LDAP domain. Alternate ports and SSL usage can also be specified, using the form slapconfig–setldapstatic <IP or name> [<port> [SSL|NoSSL [<search base>]]].

```
gs:~ nadmin$ sudo slapconfig -setldapstatic g5.4am-media.com "dc=4am-media,dc=com"
```

Neither Directory Access nor *slapconfig –setldapstatic* is able to completely integrate the server in question with the target directory. They simply enable that server to access the directory's world-readable data. Deeper levels of integration are feasible, including enabling single sign-on using Kerberos. This process, which should generally be considered a requirement for member servers due to Kerberos's security and end-user feature set, is covered in more depth in Chapter 8.

## CHAPTER 7

Identification and Authorization in Open Directory Server

LDAP (the lightweight directory access protocol) plays a key role in Open Directory Server, providing identification services and some authorization data to various client-side systems. In keeping with what has become a fairly common trend in Mac OS X Server, it is supported by the Open Source OpenLDAP package. This in itself is not new; Jaguar Server also shipped with an OpenLDAP implementation. Panther, however, brings a much more standardized and securable architecture, storing its data in a fast, programmatic database rather than in NetInfo. This and other fundamental changes give Open Directory Server room to scale to hundreds of thousands of users, groups and other objects.

> Jaguar-based Open Directory Masters (which store their data in NetInfo and share it using OpenLDAP) should not have more than 10,000 objects (users, groups, and machines). Additionally note that attributes in NetInfo (such as a group's user list) are limited to 1,024 values.

This chapter begins with a generalized analysis of LDAP as a protocol, progresses into a number of aspects of OpenLDAP configuration, and ends with a look at the kind of data that can be found in most Open Directory shared domains.

LDAP: A Communication Protocol

LDAP is one of those words that's taken on a lot of baggage in the information technology field. Eager sales people have latched onto it as a sort of silver bullet, using it as a buzzword whenever feasible, promoting its standards-based nature as a solution to an endless array of challenges and issues. In the end, though, LDAP is nothing but a communication protocol; designed, as its name implies, to provide a standardized way to access data, regardless of where or how it is stored. A basic setup is shown in Figure 7-1.

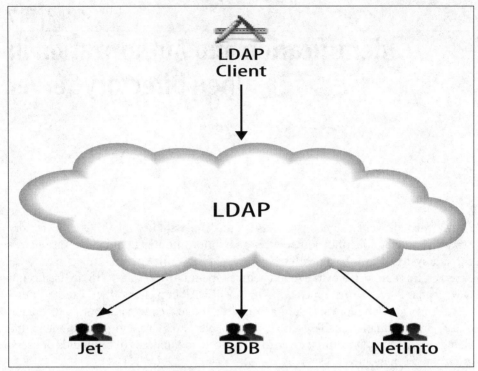

Figure 7-1. LDAP is a communication protocol that provides a standardized way to access data, regardless of where or how it is stored. This illustrates well the idea of abstraction—LDAP clients do not have to understand how to talk about BDB, NetInfo, or Jet—they simply need to know LDAP.

If the whole point of LDAP is abstraction, why is there so much excitement about 10.3's adoption of a more standardized data storage method? It boils down to three issues: standardization, performance, and security.

The most often cited aspect of this migration is probably the least important: A fairly new database (called Berkeley DB, and maintained by Sleepy Cat Software, *www. sleepycat.com*) is OpenLDAP's standard and default data storage method. Standards are good for the interoperability they provide, though, not simply because they happen to be standards. Use of Berkeley DB permits Apple to better leverage the work of the OpenLDAP community. Since LDAP's whole purpose is to insulate the client application from the nature of the back end, a standardized back end isn't as dramatic as it might seem. What makes Berkeley DB desirable, then, is not just its status as a common or standard data storage method. Much more important are the features it provides, especially when compared with NetInfo. For example:

- Berkeley DB is a high-performance data store. It is specifically tunable and much more optimized than NetInfo, and has been demonstrated to scale into the millions of entries.

- Berkeley DB supports better access controls. Regardless of the access controls imposed at the LDAP level, NetInfo will always be world-readable, through *lookupd*'s *NIAgent* if nothing else. In an out-of-box Panther install, */var/db/ netinfo/local.nidb* is not world-readable on the filesystem; *lookupd*, though, which executes as *root*, proxies full access to any local process. For more in-depth discussion of *lookupd*, see the Appendix.

These benefits are substantial as Mac OS X moves into more critical roles in larger and more diverse organizations.

LDAP Basics

This chapter is not meant to provide a definitive guide to LDAP. LDAP, although its premise is simple, is a relatively complex protocol—providing a standardized and consistent way to communicate with all those back-end data stores turns out to be harder than it sounds—and even minimal-coverage demands a lot of explanation. Because it is so important to Mac OS X Server, though, and because it is so new to many administrators, it must be given at least a light treatment. More extensive coverage may be found in *LDAP System Administration* by Gerald Carter (O'Reilly, 2003).

LDAP Is Hierarchical

LDAP directories can essentially be seen as *hierarchical databases*, with more general-ized elements at the top and more specific elements towards the bottom (as contrasted with relational databases, which support more complex relationships). This design proves useful, as lots of things in the world conform to or can be represented as some sort of hierarchy, as seen in Figure 7-2.

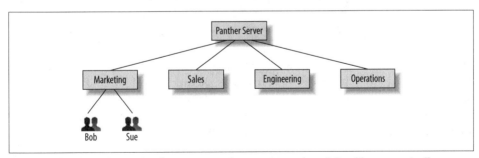

Figure 7-2. LDAP is hierarchical in nature—it has a structured, multilevel layout; typically an inverted tree.

LDAP Uses Standard Naming Conventions

A lot of the confusion around LDAP is the result of visual clutter. Because the job of providing structured and consistent access to so many diverse data stores is so complex, LDAP imposes relatively strict naming conventions, represented in Figure 7-3. Most people see things like *dc*, *ou*, and *cn* and let that get in the way of their understanding of a directory. Although the specific meaning of these terms does eventually become important (they simply refer to parts of the LDAP hierarchy, as seen in Table 7-1) they are not important the basic concept of what an LDAP Directory Domain is—a hierarchal database, usually used to represent organizational IT resources like User and Group accounts and security policy.

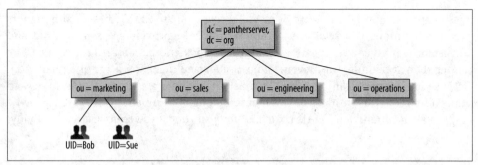

Figure 7-3. To locate data within its hierarchy, LDAP uses standardized naming conventions.

Table 7-1. Commonly seen aspects of an LDAP hierarchy.

Component	Description
dc	*Domain Component.* Commonly used to illustrate the top level (often called *search base* or *directory context*) of a directory.
ou	*Organizational Unit.* Similar in purpose to a container, an oU is supposed to represent some unit of an organization (like the marketing department).
cn	*Common Name.* Used to identify everything from user accounts to containers (like Users).

Specifically, in Mac OS X Server (rather than describing a typical organization), LDAP is used as a hierarchical representation of the kind of Data an OS needs to support directory services. A limited view of this hierarchy, containing commonly used aspects, can be seen in Figure 7-4. A more detailed analysis of Open Directory Data can be found towards the end of this chapter.

LDAP Terminology

In order to add to this basic understanding of LDAP, it's important to establish some basic terminology:

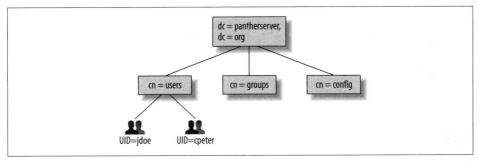

Figure 7-4. The organization of LDAP in Mac OS X Server conforms to the hierarchy imposed by Open Directory.

Distinguished Name

Distinguished Name (DN) refers to the fully qualified LDAP name of a particular object (beginning with its most specific element, up through the directory's search base). DNs can be used to identify anything that exists in an LDAP directory—commonly (but not limited to) users, groups, computers, or automounts, as shown in Figure 7-5.

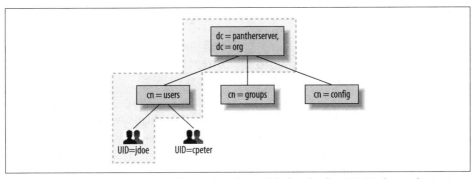

Figure 7-5. A Distinguished name refers to the fully qualified path of an LDAP object—beginning with the most specific element.

A distinguished name is usually specified by prepending the LDAP path of an object with *dn:*.

```
dn: uid=jdoe,cn=Users,dc=pantherserver,dc=org
```

Relative Distinguished Name (RDN)

Relative Distinguished Name refers to the portion of a DN that differentiates it from its peers. In the previous example, consider the fact that there might be several user objects in the *cn=Users* container. So *uid=jdoe*, which differentiates *jdoe*'s account from everything else in that container, is the RDN.

Search Base

Search Base, as its name implies, provides a base, or context for all objects in a particular directory; the search base is included in every distinguished name in the LDAP domain.

Case sensitivity is one of those confusing aspects of LDAP. Actual LDAP data may be case-sensitive, depending on how the schema for that data is defined (schema is covered in more depth later in this chapter). Structural components of the LDAP directory, however, should case-insensitive—*uid=jdoe,cn=Users,dc=local* should be equivalent to *UID=jdoe,CN=Users,DC=local*.

OpenLDAP

OpenLDAP (the software package Apple uses to provide LDAP services on Mac OS X Server) began life as an offshoot of the University of Michigan's original LDAP code. Since then, it has been actively maintained by the OpenLDAP foundation (*www.openldap.org*) towards the goal of providing a standards-compliant and reasonably capable LDAP infrastructure. It is a deep and feature-rich software package that has a number of important architectural components, from daemons to client applications, utilities, configuration files and data stores. For organizational purposes, our discussion of OpenLDAP is split roughly along these lines. Server-side components are discussed first, followed by the utilities and applications used to maintain and query LDAP data.

A Word on Contacts

One very common application of LDAP is as a sort of network-available address book. Although this is feasible in an Open Directory environment (all the right schema is there), this is not something Apple's tools are currently oriented towards, and is something I've chosen currently to forgo documenting in this book.

For a more complete coverage of OpenLDAP in this role, see *LDAP System Administration* (O'Reilly, Gerald Carter, 2003).

Managing OpenLDAP with Server Admin

Some of OpenLDAP's basic options are available in Server Admin's graphical interface—specifically, from the LDAP Settings pull-down menu in the Protocols tab of the Open Directory Module, illustrated in Figure 7-6. Here the location of the actual LDAP data can be changed (presumably to store it on a more reliable or higher-performance volume), the maximum number of search results and the search timeout can be set. SSL settings, discussed in more depth in the "OpenLDAP Security" section of this chapter, can also be managed.

Search Base, or Directory Context, is also visible, although it may not be edited. Changing the Search Base is a very involved process, usually not required, and not covered in this title.

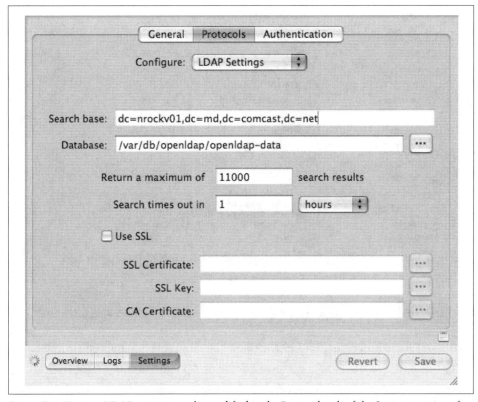

Figure 7-6. Various LDAP settings can be modified in the Protocols tab of the Settings portion of Server Admin's Open Directory module.

The how and why of changing the Search Base boils down to the fact that it is embedded in each and every entry in the LDAP database. Changing it requires dumping the database to a flat file, batching a change, and basically recreating the database. The reason that this isn't usually necessary is that the search base really doesn't do anything besides provide a naming context for the directory. End users will usually never even see it, and although it is originally based on the DNS domain of the server, this is a matter of convention, and the two are not tightly coupled—changing the server's DNS domain name won't make the search base less functional.

Changing the LDAP data store location (seen in Figure 7-7) is as simple as specifying a new directory in the file selection dialog that results from clicking the ellipsis (...) button. Ironically, this dialog has no provision for creating a new directory—that has to be done using SSH, ARD, or some other protocol.

Most settings available in the LDAP portion of the Protocols tab can also be set on the command line using the *serveradmin* command, as shown in Example 7-1.

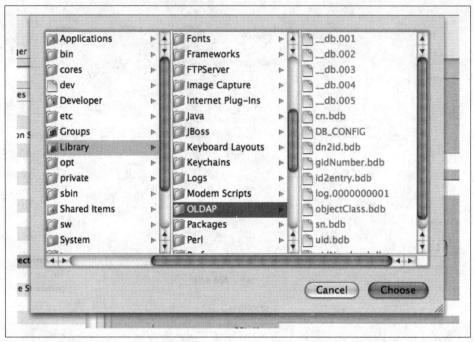

Figure 7-7. Choosing a new location for LDAP data. The data is conveniently copied to the new location.

Example 7-1. Using serveradmin to modify various settings also available graphically. In the first case, LDAP data is being moved to a new location. In the second, maximum search results are specified.

```
g5:~ ladmin$ sudo serveradmin settings dirserv:LDAPSettings:LDAPDataBasePath =
"/Library/OLD2"
dirserv:LDAPSettings:LDAPDataBasePath = "/Library/OLD2"
g5:~ ladmin$ sudo ls !$
sudo ls "/Library/OLD2"
DB_CONFIG      __db.003      cn.bdb         id2entry.bdb    sn.bdb
__db.001      __db.004      dn2id.bdb      log.0000000001  uid.bdb
__db.002      __db.005      gidNumber.bdb  objectClass.bdb uidNumber.bdb
g5:~ ladmin$ sudo serveradmin settings dirserv:LDAPSettings:maxSearchResults = "15000"
dirserv:LDAPSettings:maxSearchResults = "15000"
```

Server Architecture

OpenLDAP's server-side components provide standardized access to directory data. *slapd*, OpenLDAP's LDAP server daemon, listens for connections on port 389 and, if SSL is configured, port 636. It's started by the */System/Library/StartupItems/LDAP* startup item if the LDAPSERVER flag is set to -YES- in */etc/hostconfig*; this value is normally set as a part of the master or replica creation process. Some important server-side components, many of which are discussed in more depth later, are documented in Table 7-2.

Table 7-2. Important aspects of Mac OS X Server's LDAP infrastructure.

Daemon location	Description
/usr/libexec/slapd	The OpenLDAP server daemon.
/usr/libexec/slurpd	The OpenLDAP replication daemon.
/etc/openldap/slapd.conf	OpenLDAP's default configuration file.
/etc/openldap/slapd_macosxserver.conf	Apple-specific *slapd* configuration file. All Open Directory shared domains are defined here.
/System/Library/StartupItems/LDAP/	Startup Item for *slapd* and *slurpd*.
/var/db/openldap/	Default directory for LDAP data.
/etc/openldap/schema/	Default location of schema files. Note especially *apple.schema*, containing schema definitions for Open Directory.

slapd options

The *slapd* daemon itself, as mentioned previously, is started by the LDAP startup Item; specifically, with the sytax *slapd –h "ldap:// ldaps:///"*. The *–h* flag with its arguments specifies that *slapd* should attempt to listen on both *ldap* and *ldaps* (LDAP over SSL) ports on every active network interface. Unless SSL is properly configured, the *ldaps* directive fails, leaving *slapd* listening only on port 389. SSL configuration is covered in more depth later in this chapter, in the "OpenLDAP Security" section.

Since runtime directives override settings specified in *slapd*'s configuration file, this can be a convenient place for localized customization, with the caveats that:

*   This information won't be replicated and must be manually configured on any Open Directory Replicas (for more information relating to replication, see Chapter 9).
*   Since this is an Apple-supplied file, it might be overwritten during a system upgrade.

Upgrade issues are covered in more depth in Chapter 4. Common enhancements to *slapd*'s startup include running *slapd* as an underprivileged (non-*root*) user (which is beyond the scope of this title) and more granular control of SSL options.

slapd.conf

An out-of-box standalone Mac OS X Server install contains a single LDAP server configuration file (*/etc/openldap/slapd.conf*) configured to access OpenLDAP's NetInfo back end (*back-netinfo*). Under most circumstances, this file is unused, and is replaced when Mac OS X Server's role is changed to an Open Directory Master or Replica. The resulting *slapd.conf* uses an include directive to call a second configuration file, */etc/openldap/slapd_macosxserver.conf*. An analysis of these files is one very effective way to get a good overview of OpenLDAP's capabilities on Mac OS X Server.

slapd configuration files are likely to contain sensitive information—from the encrypted, LDAP-specific *rootdn* credentials (mentioned later in this section) to the plain-text password used to update Open Directory replicas. For this reason all *slapd* configuration files should be readable only by the user that *slapd* will be executed by. In a default configuration, this is *root*, as shown here:

```
#
# See slapd.conf(5) for details on configuration options.
#
# This file should NOT be world readable.
#
```

The *include* directive, as its name implies, is used to add files to *slapd*'s configuration. A number of *include* directives are used to add several schema definitions to an Open Directory Master. These files define the kind of data that is permitted in the LDAP directory; for instance, specifying which attributes users must have.

```
include          /etc/openldap/schema/core.schema
include          /etc/openldap/schema/cosine.schema
include          /etc/openldap/schema/nis.schema
include          /etc/openldap/schema/inetorgperson.schema
include          /etc/openldap/schema/misc.schema
include          /etc/openldap/schema/samba.schema
include          /etc/openldap/schema/apple.schema
```

Related schema definitions are generally stored in their own files, which are separate from *slapd*'s configuration for manageability reasons and because of their complexity. The default set of definitions are listed in Table 7-3.

Table 7-3. The schema files included in a default Open Directory Master slapd configuration.

Schema file	Description
core.schema	Includes schema defined in RFCs 2252 (LDAPv3) and 2256 (X.500 user schema for LDAPv3).
cosine.schema	Schema defined in RFC 1274, a suggested naming scheme for x.500's Internet pilot. Some aspects of this schema are required to support later schemas.
nis.schema	Supports RFC 2307, which originally proposed a method for supplying NIS data via LDAP. NIS is no longer widely deployed, but the attributes and object classes defined in RFC 2307 are the most widely adopted method for providing Unix account data to LDAP clients. Some aspects, such as the *homeDirectory* and *uidNumber* attributes, are used by Mac OS X.
inetorgperson.schema	Implements RFC 2798, which defines some attributes and object classes useful in the support of Internet-enabled organizations. While this concept now seems quaint (what organization isn't "Internet-enabled?," it was a novel idea at the time.
misc.schema	A mixed bag of works-in-progress and ad hoc schema added to support a particular need. Currently most of these relate to *sendmail*'s LDAP support, which is not something Mac OS X makes use of.
samba.schema	Supports a number of LDAP-enabled features of Samba, the Open Source package used to support Windows and other SMB clients.
apple.schema	Apple's schema, containing Apple-specific object classes and attributes. Whenever feasible, Apple has re-used existing LDAP data definitions. In some cases, though, no existing definitions met Apple's need. *apple.schema* is discussed in more depth later in this chapter.

Access control lists (ACLs), like replication, are not defined in the LDAP standard, and thus are implemented differently on different LDAP server platforms. This unused comment is a placeholder for disabling read access to directories that contain sensitive data. (ACLs are discussed in more depth in the "OpenLDAP Security" section of this chapter.)

```
# Define global ACLs to disable default read access.
```

Some features of OpenLDAP, such as referrals, are not used in Mac OS X Server and thus are beyond the scope of this book:

```
# Do not enable referrals until AFTER you have a working directory
# service AND an understanding of referrals.
```

The *.pid* and *.args* file arguments specify the location *slapd* and *slurpd* will use to record certain runtime data—namely, their process IDs and any arguments that are passed to them:

```
#referral          ldap://root.openldap.org

pidfile                 /var/run/slapd.pid
argsfile                /var/run/slapd.args
replica-pidfile         /var/run/slurpd.pid
replica-argsfile        /var/run/slurpd.args
```

replicationinterval, which is used by *slurpd* rather than *slapd*, is the number of seconds that *slurpd* waits to check its replication log for changes. (This is discussed in more depth in Chapter 9.) It is also an Apple-supplied option, and is not present on other platforms.

```
replicationinterval    3
```

The loglevel directive specifies which events should be sent to *syslog*. It is generally a cumulative value. This means that each type of message has a different integer associated with it, and that when their values are combined, the cumulative log level can be described by the resulting total:

```
loglevel               32768
```

The default loglevel of 32768, however, is an exception to this rule, and results in the least-verbose logging that OpenLDAP is capable of. These log component log levels are described in Table 7-4.

Table 7-4. Various OpenLDAP messages and their associated component log levels.

Value	Message
1	Trace function calls
2	Debug packet handling
4	Heavy trace debugging
8	Connection management
16	Print out packets sent and received

Table 7-4. Various OpenLDAP messages and their associated component log levels. (continued)

Value	Message
32	Search filter processing
64	Configuration file processing
128	Access control list processing
256	Stats log connections/operations/results
512	Stats log entries sent
1024	Print communication with shell backends
2048	Entry parsing

Keep in mind that more intense levels of logging result in higher *slapd* loads—this is the reason Apple chose 327688 as a default. It's generally best to either turn off logging or to use a fairly light log level unless gathering data for some specific reason. Also note that simply having a loglevel directive won't result in useful LDAP logs; loglevel specifies what data is sent to *syslogd*. *syslogd* also needs to be instructed as to what it should do with that data. This is best accomplished the *slapconfig* utility's *–enableslapdlog* flag, which creates */var/log/slapd.log* and adds a *LOCAL4.*;LOCAL4. debug* parameter to */etc/syslog.conf*, indicating that *slapd*'s data should be sent to the newly created file. *slapconfig* also restarts *syslogd* to make it aware of its new configuration.

sizelimit limits the number of entries returned to LDAP queries. This is done primarily for security reasons, to ensure that very large LDAP queries do not place an undue load on the server. It can also make certain aspects of system administration difficult, since it means that some larger directories can never be retrieved fully via LDAP.

```
sizelimit      11000
```

The *limits* directive may be used to work around this limitation, specifically granting more broad capabilities to specific users. This approach is discussed in more depth later in this chapter. sizelimit can also be set in Server Admin's graphical interface or using the *serveradmin* command-line utility.

gentlehup, which is not enabled in a default configuration, is a setting that allows *slapd* to keep existing connections open when it's issued a *HUP* (hang up) signal. This capability is unused in Mac OS X Server.

```
gentlehup      off
```

Open Directory Server ships with schemachecking disabled, making the earlier discussion of schemas somewhat moot for now, at least in the context of a default Mac OS X Server configuration. Schema checking may generally be turned on (it is turned off for legacy reasons), but your mileage may vary, since this is not an Apple-supported configuration.

```
schemacheck    off
```

These sample security restrictions are disabled (commented out). They are provided in the OpenLDAP distribution's default *slapd.conf* file as guidance for system administrators. Similar concepts are discussed in more depth in the "OpenLDAP Security" section, later in this chapter.

```
# Sample security restrictions
#
#   Disallow clear text exchange of passwords
# disallow bind_simple_unprotected
#
#       Require integrity protection (prevent hijacking)
#       Require 112-bit (3DES or better) encryption for updates
#       Require 63-bit encryption for simple bind
# security ssf=1 update_ssf=112 simple_bind=64

# Sample access control policy:
#       Allow read access of root DSE
#       Allow self write access
#       Allow authenticated users read access
#       Allow anonymous users to authenticate
# Directives needed to implement policy:
#access to dn.base="" by * read
#access to *
#       by self write
#       by users read
#       by anonymous auth
#
# if no access controls are present, the default policy is:
#       Allow read by all
#
# rootdn can always write!
# Some settings are maintained in slapd_macosxserver.conf,
# which is updated by Server Admin. Put your own changes in
# this file.
```

Finally, an include directive is used again, this time to refer to the configuration file containing the Open Directory domain definition:

```
include /etc/openldap/slapd_macosxserver.conf
```

The *slapd_macosxserver.conf* file generally contains configurations specific to the Open Directory Master's shared domain. For the sake of completeness, it is also documented here:

```
#
# See slapd.conf(5) for details on configuration options.

# This file should NOT be world readable.
# This file is maintained by Server Admin.
#
```

Access controls in OpenLDAP are extremely flexible. These grant access to the userPassword, apple-user-authenticationHint, and apple-user-picture attributes, so that any user may change these details of their own account. The last ACL grants write access to the entire directory to the members of the *admin* group, and preserves read access for everyone else, including anonymous users. Access Controls are covered in the "OpenLDAP Security" section of this chapter.

```
# Access Controls
access to attr=userPassword
        by self write
        by group/posixGroup/memberUid="cn=admin,cn=groups,dc=4am-media,dc=com" write
        by * read
access to attr=apple-user-authenticationHint
        by self write
        by group/posixGroup/memberUid="cn=admin,cn=groups,dc=4am-media,dc=com" write
        by * read
access to attr=apple-user-picture
        by self write
        by group/posixGroup/memberUid="cn=admin,cn=groups,dc=4am-media,dc=com" write
        by * read
access to *
        by group/posixGroup/memberUid="cn=admin,cn=groups,dc=4am-media,dc=com" write
        by * read
```

The database directive indicates the beginning of an OpenLDAP datastore definition. Its bdb flag indicates that back-bdb should be used to maintain and store the directory data:

```
########################################################################
# bdb database definitions
########################################################################

database        bdb
```

The suffix directive identifies the naming context (search base) of the directory. Changing this value, which is visible in the LDAP Settings pull-down menu in the Protocols tab of Server Admin's Open Directory Settings section, is a long process that involves rebuilding the entire LDAP database.

```
suffix          "dc=4am-media,dc=com"
```

rootdn and rootpw specify the credentials that have full administrative control over the database definition within which they are located. These directives are perhaps inaptly named, as they actually have little relation the system's *root* user, other than that in a default configuration, both tend toward having the same password. In most cases, rootpw will be the CRAM-MD5 hash of the password used to create the shared domain.

```
rootdn          "uid=root,cn=users,dc=4am-media,dc=com"
rootpw          {SMD5}VJstMhAodTPA4vqMPLvbXfp5I+Y=
```

sasl-regexp establishes rules that help determine how SASL authentication requests, which generally take the form of *uid=username,cn=auth*, should be matched to distinguished names. Remember: authentication and identification are two distinct concepts that are largely unrelated to one another without some sort of glue. The sasl-regexp directive serves as that glue. Generally it takes the form *sasl-regexp* *<search pattern> <replacement pattern>*. Regular expressions are far beyond the scope of this book, but these are very lenient rules that map the UID (RecordName) of an incoming request to a very structured location within the users container of the domain; the parenthesis around the UID in the search pattern indicates that it should be used in the replacement string as $1. These settings should not be modified, unless Password Server users have been stored somewhere other than the users container. SASL authentication is discussed briefly later in the "OpenLDAP Security" section of this chapter.

```
sasl-regexp
        uid=(.*),cn=.*,cn=.*,cn=auth
        uid=$1,cn=users,dc=4am-media,dc=com
sasl-regexp
        uid=(.*),cn=.*,cn=auth
        uid=$1,cn=users,dc=4am-media,dc=com
```

The password-hash setting is left in the bdb definition in order to support legacy users with a ;basic; authauthority. Supporting userPassword (known to Open Directory as Password) in this way, however, violates the separation of authentication and identification data established in rules listed in the Appendix. Since userPassword, like the rest of the LDAP directory, is world-readable, storing encrypted passwords in it would be very bad practice. This generally isn't an issue, since most users in a shared domain will have Password Server and/or Kerberos authentication authorities.

```
# use crypt passwords to support older clients
password-hash    {CRYPT}
password-crypt-salt-format  "%.2s"
```

The directory directive specifies where on the server's filesystem the bdb data is stored. This may be changed in Server Admin or using the *serveradmin* tool, but the data must be manually copied to the new location as specified earlier in this chapter.

```
# The database directory MUST exist prior to running slapd AND
# should only be accessible by the slapd/tools. Mode 700 recommended.
directory        /var/db/openldap/openldap-data
```

checkpoint operations flush all LDAP data to disk and write a record to back-bdb's current transaction log. Mac OS X Server's default configuration specifies that this happen every 10 megabytes or 60 minutes, whichever occurs first.

```
# checkpoint the database every 10MB of logging and every 1 hour
checkpoint       10240 60
```

The LDAP protocol supports several specific types of searches—at a basic level, presence (pres), equality (eq), approximate (approx), and substring (sub). Indices help to accelerate specific types of searches for specific attributes. Any common searches should be indexed. This process is discussed in the next section.

```
# Indices to maintain
index   cn,sn,uid           pres,eq,approx,sub
index   uidNumber,gidNumber     eq
index   objectClass         eq
```

OpenLDAP Performance

Mac OS X Server's out-of-box OpenLDAP configuration supports adequate performance characteristics for most organizations. Larger directories, however, can benefit from one or more of several performance enhancement techniques, listed here in order of ascending difficulty.

The cachesize parameter indicates how many recently searched entities should remain in an in-memory cache. In most cases, as long as available memory permits, this number should be set to the total number of distinct distinguished names present in the directory (users, groups, computer account presets, configurations, and so on). The default value of 1000 (which *slapd* uses unless it is overridden in the configuration file) should be suitable for many smaller organizations.

```
cachesize12000
```

As covered briefly during our analysis of the *slapd.conf* configuration file, indexes increase the performance of specific searches on specific attributes, and should be maintained for most common searches. This change isn't as simple as adding an index parameter to *slapd_macosxserver.conf*. Since indices are generated on the fly, as attributes are added, new indices (if they're going to apply to existing objects) must be built from scratch, using the *slapindex* command; which requires first stopping the LDAP server, and thus implies a service unavailability.

One common unindexed query is an equality search for memberUid, the ldap attribute that corresponds to both Open Directory's Member and GroupMembership attributes. memberUid is typically multivalued, with one instance for each member of every group in an Open Directory domain. In other words it's used to keep track of group membership, something commonly pursued due to Unix's pervasive use of the *initgroups()* system call. To index memberUid equality searches, an additional index directive should be added to *slapd_macosxserver.conf*:

```
index memberUid eq
```

and the indices musto be rebuilt, as shown in Example 7-2.

Example 7-2. Rebuilding OpenLDAP's indices. Notice that the LDAP server is stopped before this occurs.

```
g5:~ nadmin$ sudo SystemStarter stop LDAP
Welcome to Macintosh.
Startup complete.
Hangup
g5:~ nadmin$ sudo slapindex
g5:~ nadmin$ sudo SystemStarter start LDAP
Welcome to Macintosh.
Initializing network
Starting LDAP server
Startup complete.
Hangup
g5:~ na
```

A final and much more difficult performance measure involves setting the bdb cache, which instructs OpenLDAP's back-bdb to use a certain amount of RAM for storage of both its back-end data store and full indices. The difficulty doesn't lie, however, in the configuration itself, which is as simple as adding an appropriate set_cachesize argument to the */var/db/openldap/openldap-data/DB_CONFIG* file.

It's actually the conspicuous absence of two tools (as of Panther) that makes this action rather difficult. set_cachesize is persistent across reboots, and requires that the *db_recover* tool be run before a changed (or even nondefault) value may take effect. *db_recover*, part of the Berkeley DB software distribution, is not included in Mac OS X or Mac OS X Server. Neither is *db_stat*, which is useful (although not required) for determining exactly what the most efficient set_cachesize value is.

DB_Config is stored wherever the LDAP data is stored. If you've moved your LDAP data to a faster or more reliable filesystem, the *DB_Config* file has been moved too, and is no longer in */var/db/openldap/opendlap-data*.

 Since set_cachesize in essence tells *slapd* how much *bdb* data should be loaded into RAM, it is feasible to simply specify a value that is equal to the amount of space taken up by the entire database. This value, however, is generally higher than what is required for optimum performance.

Until Apple includes the DB tools, I've made them available at *www.4am-media.com/downloads*. An exact recipe for their use is well beyond the scope of this book. Details, however, may be obtained on the OpenLDAP mailing list archives (*www.openldap.org/lists/openldap-software/200311/msg00469.html*) and from the *README* file of the tools packaged referenced here.

OpenLDAP Security

When considering the security aspects of OpenLDAP on Mac OS X, it's important to remember that Apple considers directory data (as opposed to authentication data) public and nonsensitive. Since directories, in the case of Open Directory Server, are largely a replacement for the world-readable */etc/passwd* file; this is not considered to be a vulnerability. This setup fails to take into account the fact that */etc/passwd* isn't usually available over the network, but in a general sense, the analogy is accurate. Unix tools that depend on *libc* calls like *getpwnam()* for identification assume that identification data is always available to local processes.

The first and easiest method of limiting access to directory data, then, is to limit anonymous LDAP access. This is achieved with a disallow_bind_anon parameter in one of *slapd*'s configuration files. Such a configuration limits access to directory data to authenticated (and therefore hopefully legitimate) LDAP connections, regardless of the ACLs that are established in the directory.

Local processes running on Open Directory clients will still need access to directory data. Because of this, each client must, in the case of a `disallow_bind_anon` configuration, store credentials with which to access the directory. Functionally in Mac OS X and Mac OS X Server this is done by embedding the credentials in */Library/Preferences/ DirectoryService/DSLDAPv3PlugInConfig.plist*. This data is maintained by the Directory Access application. Credentials located in this file are then used to establish an authenticated LDAP bind to the Open Directory Master or Replica.

Access controls, a common and critical aspect of most LDAP infrastructures, are designed to limit access to the attribute level in very granular ways. Because (as mentioned briefly earlier) they are not part of the LDAP standard, Mac OS X's access controls are specific to OpenLDAP. They're defined using the *access* parameter, specifically in the form of:

```
access to <what> <by whom> <access level>
```

This simple formula, however, is not as straightforward as it seems. All three variables can be defined in a number of ways, the discussion of which is well beyond the context of this chapter. For more detailed analysis, see *LDAP System Administration* (O'Reilly; Carter; 2003). Our examination of access controls focuses on the specific examples provided in an out-of-box Open Directory Master configuration. Let's take another look at the first entry in that portion of *slapd_mcosxserver.conf*, in Example 7-3.

Example 7-3. One of the four access controls specified in slapd_mcosxserver.conf. Notice that all aspects of the directive do not have to be on the same line. Convention specifies, in fact, that each portion of the directive appear on its own line for clarity.

```
access to attr=userPassword
      by self write
      by group/posixGroup/memberUid="cn=admin,cn=groups,dc=4am-media,dc=com" write
      by * read
```

This is not a sophisticated example. Write access to the userPassword attribute is given to self, meaning whichever user is authenticated to the directory. This ensures that *;basic;* (crypt hash) users, if for some reason they exist in the shared domain, can change their own password.

As noted earlier, there should generally be no *;basic;* users in a shared LDAP domain, and their existence constitutes a security risk. Access controls may be added limiting read access to userPassword, but this breaks certain Open Directory assumptions and requires further configuration.

A second *<by whom>* variable also grants write access—this time to members of the admin group. The third and final definition enables world readability for everyone.

apple-user-authenticationHint and *apple-user-picture* receive similar treatment, since they too are user-configurable aspects of the user record. The fourth and final directive, however, is key to defining the character of Open Directory Server's identification and authorization platform, granting write access to every object and attribute in the directory (*) to members of the admin group, as well as read access to everyone (see Example 7-4).

Example 7-4. The fourth and final access directive in slapd_macosxserver.conf grants write access to the admin group and specifies that the entire directory is world-readable.

```
access to *
        by group/posixGroup/memberUid="cn=admin,cn=groups,dc=4am-media,dc=com" write
        by * read
```

It should be obvious from these examples that OpenLDAP supports several levels of access. The ones presented here are very basic: read and write. They, along with the others are documented in Table 7-5.

Table 7-5. OpenLDAP access levels.

Level	Description
none	No access.
auth	May be used to perform bind operations using the entity (usually some sort of password attribute). The user provides a perspective value and the server returns a yes/no. Not widely used in Mac OS X as most authentication takes place using Password Server.
compare	Similar to *auth* with the exception that it can be used with nonbind operations.
search	Needed in order to apply search filters to a particular entity.
read	Allows entity defined in *<by whom>* to read entity in question.
write	Entity in *<by whom>* has write access.

An important aspect of OpenLDAP access controls is their cumulative nature. Later, more intrusive access implies all previous levels (someone with write access also has read, search, compare, and auth; someone with compare access can also auth). It is also worth pointing out that access controls use a "first match wins" strategy. Evaluation of access controls stops when the first matching rule is located. This means that the ordering of the *<by whom>* statements is very important.

Another popular method of securing LDAP transaction is the use of SSL. Because SSL encrypts all LDAP traffic over the wire, it serves a slightly different purpose from *disallow_bind_anon* and access controls by protecting legitimate traffic from malicious snooping. SSL is often employed in concert with simple authenticated binds in an effort to protect user passwords that are sent over the network. SSL configuration is a bit simpler than it was in Jaguar, due to the addition of a graphical interface for specification of SSL certificate, key, and Certificate Authority files, as seen in Figure 7-8. Values for these settings are stored in the `TLSCertificateFile`, `TLSCertificateKeyFile`, and `TLSCACertificateFile` settings (respectively) in *slpapd_macosxserver.conf* file. In addition to being set graphically, these options can also be specified using the *serveradmin* command.

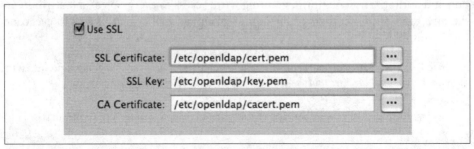

Figure 7-8. Graphically specifying SSL settings for OpenLDAP. If a certificate for another service on the Open Directory Master has already been established, then these settings may refer to that certificate (as long as the common name for both services corresponds to the hostname). For more information regarding SSL, see Part V, Security Services.

Under most circumstances, SSL-enabled clients must have a Certificate Authority file that corresponds to the one used to sign (or verify) the Certificate the server presents to them. This is a basic facet of SSL security.

LDAP clients in Mac OS X, however, perform no such verification, instead trusting any certificate that's sent to them. It is not clear why Apple has chosen this configuration, but it can be corrected by changing the `TLS_REQCERT` flag in */etc/openldap/ldap.conf* from `NEVER` to `ALWAYS`.

A key weakness of LDAP is its authentication model. Previous to Panther, Mac OS X Server was capable of servicing only simple LDAP binds, which imply sending connection credentials (the distinguished name and password used to bind) over the wire. Largely due to the authenticated nature of LDAP replication, support for SASL's CRAM-MD5 authentication method was added to *slapd* in Panther. This capability, which is fairly standard among OpenLDAP implementations on other platforms, allows connections to be authenticated without requiring that passwords be sent over the wire. SASL authentication in Mac OS X Server leverages Password Server, and is discussed in more depth in Chapter 8.

The limits directive constitutes an exceedingly flexible method for limiting any combination of either the amount of time (in seconds) expended for or the total number of results returned from a particular search. It takes the general form of `limits <by whom> <limits>`. Multiple limit definitions may be enforced. At a simpler level, note the following example, which allows searches initiated by members of the *admin* group to return an unlimited number of entries. This technique can be very useful in the execution of administrative scripts, which would otherwise fail to return a complete listing of the directory due to the sizelimit parameter.

```
limits group/posixGroup/memberUid="cn=admin,cn=groups,dc=4am-media,dc=com" size=none
```

Troubleshooting

Most *slapd* troubleshooting is pursued using client-side tools, illustrated later in this chapter. The *slapd* daemon itself, however, may also be executed in debug mode, using the *–d* flag. The resulting data is functionally identical to the data sent to *syslogd* at the same loglevel (*slapd –d 256* produces the same output as a a *slapd.conf loglevel* of 256; the former is sent tothe terminal screen stdout, while the latter is sent to *syslog*). The *–d* flag, however, can be useful for temporary, quick troubleshooting (as shown in Example 7-5), when the process of enabling *slapd*'s logs, changing the *loglevel*, and so on, might prove more labor-intensive than necessary.

Example 7-5. Starting slapd in debug mode. Notice that several slurpd-specific directives are ignored by slapd. Notice also that the LDAP service is first stopped (if it is running) by executing the SystemStarter command.

```
g5:~ nadmin$ sudo SystemStarter stop LDAP
Welcome to Macintosh.
LDAP server is not running.
Startup complete.
Hangup
g5:~ nadmin$ sudo /usr/libexec/slapd -d 256
bdb_initialize: Sleepycat Software: Berkeley DB 4.1.25: (December 19, 2002)
/etc/openldap/slapd.conf: line 22: unknown directive "replica-pidfile" outside backend
info and database definitions (ignored)
/etc/openldap/slapd.conf: line 23: unknown directive "replica-argsfile" outside backend
info and database definitions (ignored)
/etc/openldap/slapd.conf: line 24: unknown directive "replicationinterval" outside backend
info and database definitions (ignored)
bdb_db_init: Initializing BDB database
slapd starting
```

OpenLDAP: Utilities and Tools

OpenLDAP also ships with a number of tools and utilities useful for manipulation of LDAP data. The LDAP commands mostly use a common set of options, documented in Table 7-6. These commands are used in a variety of capacities throughout this book. The following entries should serve as a brief introduction:

ldapadd/ldapmodify
    These are actually the same tool with lightly differing syntax depending on how it is called. These two utilities modify data in an LDAP directory. Data is generally added from an *ldif* file, a specially formatted text file often used with LDAP data (Example 7-6).

Example 7-6. Using ldapadd. Notice that a fully qualified distinguished name (specified using the –D flag) is required for authentication. The contents of the input.ldif file are being added to the directory hosted on ldap.example.com.

```
ldapadd -x -h ldap.examplde.com -D "uid=admin,dc=example,dc=com" -W -f input.ldif
```

ldapsearch

Searches an LDAP directory. *ldapsearch* has a powerful and somewhat complicated filter mechanism, as shown in Example 7-7.

Example 7-7. Using ldapsearch. The ldap.example.com host is being searched for a record with a uid of jde.

```
ldapsearch -x -h ldap.example.com -b "dc=example,dc=com" uid=jdoe
```

ldapdelete

Deletes a particular entry from the LDAP directory. *ldapdelete*, like *ldapadd*, is often used in conjunction with an *ldif* file.

Table 7-6. Options common to ldapsearch, ldapdelete, ldapadd, and ldapmodify.

Option	Description
–x	Use simple authentication (rather than SASL). Insecure unless performed over SSL, and usually unnecessary, as OpenLDAP on Mac OS X supports SASL CRAM-MD5 authentication. Useful primarily in the context of anonymous connections.
–h	Connect to a particular server.
–D	Connect using the following distinguished name.
–b	Search base.
–W	Prompt for password.
–f	Use the following file.

While the *ldap* commands operate using the LDAP protocol, the *slap* commands (*slapcat*, *slapadd*, and *slapindex*) differ in that they communicate specifically and directly with the LDAP database. Because they operate on the database itself, they should be run when the LDAP server is either stopped or in read-only mode:

slapcat

Reads the LDAP database directly, accessing the data source specified in OpenLDAP's configuration file. *slapcat* produces an LDIF file, as shown in Example 7-8.

Example 7-8. Using slapcat to read an LDAP database. Notice that the LDAP server is stopped first, and that sudo must be used to gain root privileges and read the database off the filesystem.

```
g5:~ nadmin$ sudo SystemStarter stop LDAP
Welcome to Macintosh.
LDAP server is not running.
Startup complete.
```

Example 7-8. Using slapcat to read an LDAP database. Notice that the LDAP server is stopped first, and that sudo must be used to gain root privileges and read the database off the filesystem. (continued)

```
Hangup
g5:~ nadmin$ sudo slapcat -l pantherserver.ldif
g5:~ nadmin$ sudo SystemStarter start LDAP
Welcome to Macintosh.
LDAP server is not running.
Startup complete.
Hangup
```

slapadd

Writes to the LDAP database directly. The performance benefit, when compared to *ldapadd*, is up to 50 percent. The LDAP protocol is optimized for reads, and write performance tends to suffer. *slapadd* is particularly useful for adding a large amount of data to the directory (see Example 7-9).

Example 7-9. Using slapadd to add an LDIF file to the LDAP directory. This method is much faster than using ldapadd, because it does not suffer from the overhead of the LDAP protocol, but is rather written directly to the database. This is not a good way to add accounts, however, as the LDAP server has no access to Password Server, where user authentication data is stored.

```
g5:~ nadmin$ sudo SystemStarter stop LDAP
Welcome to Macintosh.
LDAP server is not running.
Startup complete.
Hangup
g5:~ nadmin$ sudo slapadd -l pantherserver.ldif
g5:~ nadmin$ sudo SystemStarter start LDAP
Welcome to Macintosh.
LDAP server is not running.
Startup complete.
Hangup
```

LDAP Data and Open Directory Server

One of the great strengths of Open Directory is its consistency. As established earlier in this chapter, LDAP is a communications protocol that makes directory data available in a consistent and standards-based way. The LDAP standards, however, don't even begin to describe how that data should be used with various applications (like mail or file servers) or even what kind of data should be available in any particular directory. That's where Open Directory comes in, allowing us to make assumptions about everything from the way the LDAP server is configured to the type and format of data in user records.

Knowledge of this data is rather important in order to foster a more complete understanding of the services that Open Directory provides. LDAP data in an Open Directory Master can be broken down roughly into three categories.

Identification

Used to identify user, group, and computer accounts.

Authorization

Authorization data specifies what a user is allowed to do. Some Authorization data in Mac OS X—specifically, data relating to the Managed Client (MCX) capabilities in the OS—is stored in Open Directory Domains.

Configuration

Certain applications and services are able to access configuration data stored in Open Directory.

The lines aren't always clear, though. Authorization (unlike authentication) data is often stored in the *user*, *group*, or *computer_list* record itself, in the MCXFlags and MCXSettings attributes. In order to gain a better understanding, it is necessary to take a deeper look and examine the data available via LDAP in an Open Directory Domain.

Apple's LDAP Schema

The kind of data permitted (or required) to exist in an LDAP directory is known as the directory's *schema*. Schema is more important than it might immediately seem—keep in mind that an LDAP directory is a central infrastructure component. Because so many critical systems come to depend on a directory, it is important to make sure that the data stored there is valid. The canonical example of this importance in the context of Mac OS X system administration is a Jaguar bug that caused *loginwindow* to crash if the user logging in had a UniqueID (numerical uidNumber) that was something other than an integer. Because of this badly formed user data, the user logging in was presented with a command-line environment and an effective UID of 0—*root*. That bug is fixed now, but it does underscore the importance of good directory data. Directory schema helps to ensure that directory data will meet the requirements of directory-enabled applications.

 The attentive reader will recognize the fact that (in Panther) Apple currently has schema enforcement turned off. This is done because LDAP in Open Directory has to support directory data that has evolved over the course of nearly a decade. Some of that data originated before the idea of schema was applied to directory services. Apple is carefully moving towards a time when schema enforcement may be enabled.

Apple's schema is defined on every Mac OS X and Mac OS X Server host at */etc/openldap/schema/apple.schema*. Apple-specific objects and attributes are defined in this file. This schema may also be used with other directory products (like Active Directory or iPlanet). This schema is, however, subject to change—not something that is popular in large-scale directory deployments, and something that is difficult in Active Directory. So proceed with caution.

Schema enforcement mainly has two components—requirements for the format (or syntax) of object attributes and the specifications defining precisely which attributes certain types objects are permitted to have. There are other aspects to schema management but they are less relevant to this analysis.

At a basic level, both components are straightforward. The *loginwindow* crash described earlier would not have happened if schema enforcing UniqueID's integer format had been enforced, and it is easy to see why a user account without a short name would be less than optimal. From an implementation perspective, however, both sets of requirements may become a little more complex. The former—attribute format—is established in the attribute's definition in the schema file, specifically in the SYNTAX directive. OpenLDAP uses a set of predefined set of SYNTAX values specified with numerical object identifiers. In Example 7-10, 1.3.6.1.4.1.1466.115.121.1. 27 specifies an integer value. Other common SYNTAX values are described in Table 7-7.

Example 7-10. The definition of uidNumber in /etc/openldap/schema/apple.schema. Apple uses uidNumber to meet Open directory's UniqueID attribute requirements.

```
attributetype ( 1.3.6.1.1.1.1.0 NAME 'uidNumber'
     DESC 'An integer uniquely identifying a user in an administrative domain'
     EQUALITY integerMatch
     SYNTAX 1.3.6.1.4.1.1466.115.121.1.27 SINGLE-VALUE )
```

Table 7-7. Common LDAP schema SYNYAX (format) values.

SYNTAX value	Numerical object identifier	Description
1.3.6.1.4.1.1466.115.121.1.26	IA5string	Simple character set—a subset of ASCII, does not include non-Latin characters.
1.3.6.1.4.1.1466.115.121.1.15	DirectoryString	Capable of supporting Unicode characters.
1.3.6.1.4.1.1466.115.121.1.27	Integer	Integer.
1.3.6.1.4.1.1466.115.121.1.5	Binary	Binary data, such as actual photo data.

The second set of schema requirements, which specify the attributes particular objects are permitted (or required) to have, can be seen in various *objectclass* definitions, and also in the schema file. (An *objectclass* is essentially a grouping that describes a particular type of object—an *objectclass* defining user accounts is illustrated here.) After *objectclasses* are defined, they may be applied to specific LDAP objects, requiring those objects to conform to their data specifications. Every attribute assigned to a particular object typically must be either permitted or required (MAY and MUST directives, respectively) by one of the *objectclasses* it belongs to. In this way, we can be sure LDAP entries contain the data required to meet the demands of relevant directory-enabled applications (see Example 7-11).

Example 7-11. The apple-user objectclass. Notice that no MUST attributes are specified in this class.

```
objectclass (
        1.3.6.1.4.1.63.1000.1.1.2.1
        NAME 'apple-user'
        SUP top
        AUXILIARY
        DESC 'apple user account'
        MAY ( apple-user-homeurl $ apple-user-class $
                apple-user-homequota $ apple-user-mailattribute $
                apple-user-printattribute $ apple-mcxflags $
                apple-mcxsettings $ apple-user-adminlimits $
                apple-user-picture $ apple-user-authenticationhint $
                apple-user-homesoftquota $ apple-user-passwordpolicy $
                apple-keyword $ apple-generateduid $ authAuthority $
                acctFlags $ pwdLastSet $ logonTime $ logoffTime $
                kickoffTime $ homeDrive $ scriptPath $ profilePath $
                userWorkstations $ smbHome $ rid $ primaryGroupID ) )
```

Examining LDAP Data

Nearly any LDAP client—either from the command line, or graphically, as pictured in Figure 7-9—may be used to query Open Directory's LDAP services (this standardized data access is, once again, the whole point behind LDAP). The best place to start this exploration is at the top level of the directory, as shown in Example 7-12. Notice the scope (–s argument) of one, resulting in a view solely of the top level of the directory. Notice also the use of SASL CRAM-MD5 authentication. Since this data is all world-readable, there's no particular reason to authenticate the connection, other than to demonstrate that it is feasible.

Example 7-12. Using ldapsearch to enumerate the top-level containers of Open Directory Server.

```
g5:~ nadmin$ ldapsearch -LLL -H "ldap://g5.4am-media.com" -b "dc=4am-media,dc=com" -D
"uid=nadmin,cn=users,dc=4am-media,dc=com" -W -s one
Enter LDAP Password:
SASL/CRAM-MD5 authentication started
SASL username: nadmin
SASL SSF: 0
dn: cn=config,dc=4am-media,dc=com
cn: config
objectClass: container

dn: cn=users,dc=4am-media,dc=com
cn: users
objectClass: container

dn: cn=groups,dc=4am-media,dc=com
cn: groups
objectClass: container

dn: cn=mounts,dc=4am-media,dc=com
```

```
cn: mounts
objectClass: container

dn: cn=aliases,dc=4am-media,dc=com
cn: aliases
objectClass: container

dn: cn=machines,dc=4am-media,dc=com
cn: machines
objectClass: container

dn: cn=computers,dc=4am-media,dc=com
cn: computers
objectClass: container

dn: cn=computer_lists,dc=4am-media,dc=com
cn: computer_lists
objectClass: container

dn: cn=locations,dc=4am-media,dc=com
cn: locations
objectClass: container

dn: cn=people,dc=4am-media,dc=com
cn: people
objectClass: container

dn: cn=printers,dc=4am-media,dc=com
cn: printers
objectClass: container

dn: cn=presets_users,dc=4am-media,dc=com
cn: presets_users
objectClass: container

dn: cn=presets_groups,dc=4am-media,dc=com
cn: presets_groups
objectClass: container

dn: cn=presets_computer_lists,dc=4am-media,dc=com
cn: presets_computer_lists
objectClass: container

dn: cn=autoserversetup,dc=4am-media,dc=com
cn: autoserversetup
objectClass: container
```

It is important to note that the overall structure of a shared Open Directory Domain (as opposed to other directory products) is fairly rigid. Users, groups and computers and other specific data types are generally kept in their respective containers and

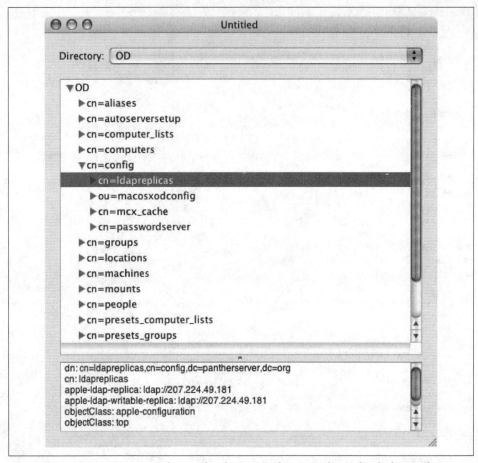

Figure 7-9. Using LDaper, a popular graphical LDAP tool, to view the top level of Open directory Server's LDAP data.

nowhere else, and there is little delegation of administrative privileges within the actual domain The structure of the domain itself is not meant, as of Panther, to reflect the structure of the organization, and on the whole, that structure is not meant for modification. Each top-level container is documented in Table 7-8.

Table 7-8. Top level containers in an out-of-box Open Directory Master's LDAP configuration.

Container	Description
Config	Domain-wide configuration data.
Users	User accounts
Groups	Group Accounts
Mounts	Mount records stored for the *automount* daemon. Mount records are discussed in more depth in Chapter 14.

Table 7-8. Top level containers in an out-of-box Open Directory Master's LDAP configuration. (continued)

Container	Description
Aliases	Usage unclear. Possible an LDAP replacement for NetInfo's */aliases* directory, which was used to house *sendmail* aliases.
Machines	NetInfo-style machine records. Not generally used in shared domains.
Computers	Computer accounts are stored here, and must exist before they are added to computer lists (much like users must exist before they can be added to groups).
Computer_lists	Computer lists, which are used to enforce managed client settings at the machine level, are stored here.
Locations	Purpose unclear. Probably replacement for NetInfo's */locations* directory, which does not exist in a default configuration.
People	Not currently used. Probably meant to hold contact (rather than account) data.
Printers	Used to house printers that are advertised via Open Directory. These printers are discussed in more depth in Chapter 19.
presets_users	Presets are used in Workgroup Manager to assign specific settings to newly created accounts. Presets for user accounts are stored in this container. Presets are covered in more depth in Chapter 4.
Presets_groups	Presets for group accounts are stored in this container
preset_computer_lists	Presets for computer are stored in this container.
autoserversetup	Directory-based automatic server configuration record. Server-specific configurations are stored according to the MAC address of the servers in question. This mechanism is discussed in more depth in Chapter 2.

All except for cn=config are fairly straightforward and well-defined, as shown in Example 7-13. Config, however, is a place where just about anything relating to server configuration can be stored. In the local domain this means serial numbers, Share Points and some service-specific configurations. In the shared domain, however, this data is usually limited to domain-wide replica, Kerberos, MCX and *PasswordServer* configurations. These items are discussed in more depth in their respective chapters.

Example 7-13. Using ldapsearch to enumerate the entries in the config container of a shared Open directory Domain.

```
g5:~ nadmin$ ldapsearch -LLL -x -h g5.4am-media.com -b "cn=config,dc=4am-media,dc=com" dn
dn: cn=config,dc=4am-media,dc=com

dn: ou=macosxodconfig,cn=config,dc=4am-media,dc=com

dn: cn=mcx_cache,cn=config,dc=4am-media,dc=com

dn: cn=ldapreplicas,cn=config,dc=4am-media,dc=com

dn: cn=passwordserver,cn=config,dc=4am-media,dc=com
```

Example 7-13. Using ldapsearch to enumerate the entries in the config container of a shared Open directory Domain. (continued)

```
dn: cn=KerberosKDC,cn=config,dc=4am-media,dc=com

dn: cn=KerberosClient,cn=config,dc=4am-media,dc=com
```

LDAP tools can also be used to examine specific objects within these various top-level containers. This is a fairly basic operation, and is demonstrated in numerous examples throughout this book, including here in Example 7-14.

Example 7-14. Using ldapsearch to retrieve the user nadmin's user record. Notice that this search was performed anonymously.

```
g5:~ nadmin$ ldapsearch -LLL -x -H ldap://g5.4am-media.com -b "dc=4am-media,dc=com"
uid=nadmin
dn: uid=nadmin,cn=users,dc=4am-media,dc=com
uid: nadmin
objectClass: inetOrgPerson
objectClass: posixAccount
objectClass: shadowAccount
objectClass: apple-user
objectClass: extensibleObject
objectClass: organizationalPerson
objectClass: top
objectClass: person
sn: 99
userPassword:: KioqKioqKio=
homeDirectory: /Users/nadmin
gidNumber: 501
cn: nadmin
apple-user-picture: /Library/User Pictures/Animals/Butterfly.tif
apple-generateduid: 3E949E61-B407-11D8-84DC-000A95AE7200
authAuthority: ;ApplePasswordServer;0x40bce1e03e6d22d50000000300000003,1024 35
 1730650903837838322545995698493842475315882825662429469836846262203114620893
 2592878819220561534532705573399929009017307861451367803020447470171935098537
 1225158654972143108391573596837423525568759138045816844345245721588947386169
 6754705379972845521821187923031185488311524566553385005497987683056656965172
 17 93 root@g5.4am-media.com:207.224.49.181
authAuthority: ;Kerberosv5;0x40bce1e03e6d22d50000000300000003;nadmin@G5.4AM-ME
 DIA.COM;G5.4AM-MEDIA.COM;1024 35 1730650903837838322545995698493842475315882
 8256624294698368462622031146208932592878819220561534532705573399929009017307
 8614513678030204474701719350985376122515865497214310839157359683742352556875
 9138045816844345245721588947386169675470537997284552182118792303118548831152
 4566553385005497987683056656965172 1793 root@g5.4am-media.com:207.224.49.181
loginShell: /bin/bash
uidNumber: 501
```

## CHAPTER 8

Authentication
in Open Directory Server

It should be evident by now that Mac OS X Server has a very broad scope and encompasses a wide variety of services. Because these services and the protocols they implement have all evolved separately (and sometimes towards conflicting goals), they require a nearly equally wide variety of authentication mechanisms. Each of these mechanisms, in turn, has technological requirements associated with it, fostering a number of management and synchronization challenges. Towards these challenges, Apple has architected a fairly robust, standards-based authentication platform, leveraging a homegrown, multiprotocol authentication service called Password Server and MIT's Kerberos distribution. This chapter examines both of these architectures in depth, from the underlying services to their graphical and command-line administrative interfaces.

PasswordService (SASL)

Password Server is Panther Server's authentication workhorse. In addition to being a vital component of Open Directory Server, in a default configuration it also supports authentication of accounts in Mac OS X Server's local NetInfo domain.

 In most circumstances, the only non–Password Server user in any Panther Server installation is the *root* user in the local domain, which has a ShadowHash authentication authority (or *authauthority*, for short). For more information on ShadowHash authentication, see the Appendix, and *Running Mac OS X Panther* (O'Reilly, 2004). (ShadowHash authentication is more widely used in Mac OS X than Mac OS X Server.)

Originally designed as a more secure alternative to storing password hashes in the user's record, *PasswordService* is based on SASL, (the Simple Authentication and Security Layer) a protocol for negotiating authentication methods. Password Server supports a number of authentication protocols, or Mechanisms (illustrated in Table

8-1), each generally oriented towards one or more server-side applications (Windows Services, for instance, rely on NTLMv1 and LANMANAGER). Despite Panther's marketing focus on Kerberos, it is safe to say that Password Server, from a statistical standpoint, is used much more widely. Not all services are Kerberized, and those that aren't always configured to properly support Kerberos.

Table 8-1. Password Server supports a variety of authentication methods.

Method	Application	Format
NTLMv1 (SMB-NT)	Samba	Hash
LANMANAGER (SMB-LAN-MANAGER)	Samba (older clients)	Hash
MS-CHAPv2	PPTP VPN Server	Plain
CRAM-MD5	IMAP (Cyrus)	Hash
WEBDAV-DIGEST	Web Services (Apache)	Hash
APOP	POP (Cyrus)	Plain
DHX (Diffie-Hellman Exchange)	Password Server password changes[a]	Hash
DIGEST-MD5	Many plain-text protocols.	Hash

[a] Although *AppleFileService* (the daemon that implements the Apple Filing Protocol) uses DHX for authentication, it does not use Password Server's DHX implementation, and instead rolls its own.

Most of the mechanisms supported by Password Server fit into the general heading of challenge-response authentication (see Figure 8-1). This means that rather than sending passwords over the network, the client and server begin with a shared secret—commonly the password, or a one-way hash of the password, perform a set of mathematical operations on it, and then compare the result of that operation over the wire. It is mathematically exceedingly difficult to derive the original password from the eventual result sent over the network, and if the results are identical, then the password is most likely correct.

The downside of supporting so many authentication methods is that, in general, each requires its shared secret to be stored in its own format. The generation of all of those hashes (in addition to any Kerberos password operations) makes setting passwords on Mac OS X Server somewhat slower than it is on other platforms.

The overall security of your server is theoretically weakened with each new supported authentication method, since each provides another path of entry into the system. This is especially the case with APOP, MS-CHAPv2, and LANMANAGER—the first two because they require the password to be stored in clear text (rather than as a hash) and the latter because it is trivial to compromise over the network. It stands to reason, then that the number of available mechanisms should be minimized. Mechanisms can be enabled and disabled with the NeST utility, documented later in this chapter. All mechanisms are enabled by default Panther install. This configuration differs from Jaguar on two levels, where Password Server had to be

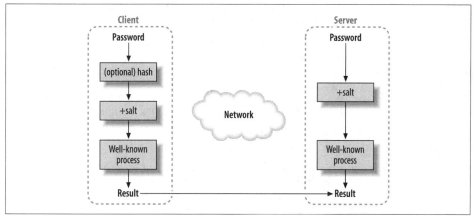

Figure 8-1. The use of challenge-response mechanisms is a proven method for securing network authentication.

manually enabled and where APOP was typically disabled even once Password Server had been turned on.

Password Server Architecture

Few Password Server options are configurable graphically; those that are mostly relate to password policies, and are described in more depth in "Password Server Policies," later in this chapter. The daemons, data stores, and configuration files don't necessarily share this simplicity. Password Server is a capable and sophisticated infrastructure component with a number of interrelated components. Several of its architectural aspects are described in Table 8-2.

Table 8-2. Important files and executables in the Password Server architecture.

Location	Description
/usr/sbin/PasswordService	The Password Server daemon.
/Library/Preferences/com.apple. passwordserver.plist	Password Server configuration file.
/var/db/authserver/authservermain	The main Password Server database.
/var/db/authserver/authserverfree	List of free (reusable) slots in the Password Server database.
/var/db/authserver/authserverreplicas	List of Password Server replicas.
/var/db/authserver/authserverreplicas.local	Local list of Password Server replicas (maintained by DirectoryService's Password Server Plug-in).

In Panther, *PasswordService* (the daemon that implements Password Server) is started by the *watchdog* daemon according to the pwd entry in */etc/watchdog.conf*, as shown in Example 8-1. The *PasswordService* listens on ports 106 (3COM-TSMUX, commonly used to support the highly insecure *popasswd* protocol) and 3659 (*apple-sasl*). For more information on watchdog, see Chapter 4.

Example 8-1. Using the grep command to read the Password Server entry from /etc/watchdog.conf. PasswordService's –n flag keeps it from daemonizing (moving into the background). This flag is required for processes managed by watchdog.

```
rhp997:~ rhp$ grep PasswordService /etc/watchdog.conf
pwd:respawn:/usr/sbin/PasswordService -n
```

The Password Server associates sets of hashes (also called a *slot*) with users using a 128-bit hexadecimal (base16) ID visible in the user record's *AuthenticationAuthority*[*] attribute and seen in the output of *mkpassdb*'s *–dump* flag.

Although the disconnect between the concepts of identification and authentication has been stressed at some length throughout this book, it is worth revisiting here. The user's *AuthenticationAuthority* attributes are the glue that ties their account (identification data) in the directory in question to one or more of the many authentication services Mac OS X is capable of utilizing. In fact, in the case of Password Server, two users' *AuthenticationAuthority* attributes may be switched, allowing one user to authenticate using another's password (*john* would be required to supply *susie*'s password in order to authenticate as himself). This loose coupling of identification and authentication has certain system administration applications, and thus, is covered here.

Password Server's treatment of administrative users (who can make changes to password server's database and to whom Password Server policies are not applied) is worth mentioning, as it differs strongly from that of the rest of the OS. In general, users are authorized to perform administrative tasks by virtue of their membership in the admin group. This authorization, though, does not allow a user to administer the password server.

In some cases, the host on which the Password Server is running might not actually be a member of the domain making use of its authentication data, making group membership determinations impossible.

Instead, Password Server administration is authorized by virtue of the `isAdminUser` policy on the Password Server ID listed in the user's *AuthenticationAuthority* attribute. This setting can be viewed by opening a telnet connection to one of Password Server's ports and issuing a *GETPOLICY* command for the Password Server ID in question. This ID can be obtained by viewing the user record, either from a host accessing the directory data or directly, by using the *ldapsearch* command. In the

---

[*] In keeping with this book's convention, *AuthenticationAuthority* is Open Directory's term for this user attribute. In NetInfo it is called *authentication_authority*, while in Apple's LDAP schema it is known as *authAuthority*.

case of administrative users, the *GETIDBYNAME* command may also be sent to Password Server in order to obtain their Password Server ID (see Example 8-2).

Example 8-2. Using telnet to mine Password Server for data. Password policies are discussed in more depth later in this chapter.

```
g5:~ nadmin$ telnet 207.224.49.181  106
Trying 207.224.49.181...
Connected to 207.224.49.181.
Escape character is '^]'.
+OK ApplePasswordServer 10.1.0.0 password server at 207.224.49.181 ready
GETIDBYNAME nadmin
+OK 0x40bce1c03e6d22d50000000300000003;0x40bce1bc3e6d22d50000000200000002
GETPOLICY 0x40bce1e03e6d22d50000000300000003
+OK isDisabled=0 isAdminUser=1 newPasswordRequired=0 usingHistory=0
canModifyPasswordforSelf=1 usingExpirationDate=0 usingHardExpirationDate=0 requiresAlpha=0
requiresNumeric=0 expirationDateGMT=4294967295 hardExpireDateGMT=4294967295
maxMinutesUntilChangePassword=0 maxMinutesUntilDisabled=0 maxMinutesOfNonUse=0
maxFailedLoginAttempts=0 minChars=0 maxChars=0 passwordCannotBeName=0 isSessionKeyAgent=0
```

This separate authorization interface allows for the creation of password-only administrators, capable of changing only passwords and password policies but not of administering the server or the directory domain. Although this is not promoted by Apple it is a very common request, and a virtual requirement in decentralized organizations.

 Do bear in mind that if this Password Server administrator is malicious and technically adept they might change the password of an existing administrator in an unauthorized fashion, gaining access to that account's administrative capabilities. This change would be rather easy to detect, as the administrator in question would notice that his password had been changed, and all such operations are logged.

Creation of such an administrator is fairly simple. Any pre-existing Password Server administrator may use the *pwpolicy* command (Example 8-3), covered in more depth later in this chapter, to promote any other Password Server user to administrator status.

Example 8-3. Using pwpolicy to promote a pre-existing Password Server user to administrative status.

```
g5:~ nadmin$ pwpolicy -a nadmin -u p10019 -setpolicy isAdminUser=1
Password:
```

Making use of these new capabilities, however, proves very difficult. Most of Apple's graphical tools assume that a directory administrator is also a Password Server administrator, and that all Password Server administrators will also be members of an admin group. Password Server–only administrators cannot use any of these tools to manage Password Server data. *pwpolicy*, however, can be called from a web page, streamlining this process for inexperienced password administrators. This, though, does expose the user's new password (*notapple* in Example 8-4) to malicious viewing of the server's process listing. Further scripting solutions, such as using the *expect* scripting language in order to keep the password out of the process listing, are left as an exercise to the reader.

Example 8-4. Using p10019's credentials to change the password of another user. The groups command is used to verify that p10019 is not in the admin group.

```
g5:~ p10019$ pwpolicy -a p10019 -u p10018 -setpassword notapple
Password:
g5:~ p10019$ groups
staff
```

Password Server Policies

Password Server Policies, introduced with Jaguar, allow restrictions to be placed on the quality of user passwords. Panther added several new password policies (such as a *password history*) and introduced the concept of global policies, which, rather than being applied on a per-user basis, are enforced for to all non-admin users in a particular Password Server database. These policies are described in Table 8-3.

Table 8-3. Password policies available in Password Server.

Policy	Password Server string	Description	Level
Allow user to log in	isDisabled	Disables login of a particular user. Especially useful in the scripting of automatic account maintenance functions.	Per-user
Disable on date	UsingExpirationDate, expirationDateGMT	Disable on particular date.	Both
Disable after *n* days	maxMinutesUntilDisabled	Disable after a particular number of days.	Global
Disable after *n* days of inactivity	maxMinutesOfNonUse	Disable account if user does not authenticate during a given period of time.	Both
Disable after *n* failed login attempts	maxFailedLoginAttempts	Disable account after a set number of authentication failures.	Both
Allow user to change password	canModifyPasswordforSelf	Allows the user to change own password. Novice users—for instance, elementary school students—might not be allowed to modify their passwords.	Per-user
Require Change at login	newPasswordRequired	Require a user to change their password upon successful authentication.	Per-user
Require Change every *n* days	maxMinutesUntilChangePassword	Requires a periodic password change.	Per-user
Password must be at least *n* characters long	MinChars	Establishes minimum password length.	Global
Password must contain at least one letter	RequiresAlpha	Requires at least on alphabetic character in the user name.	Global

Table 8-3. Password policies available in Password Server. (continued)

Policy	Password Server string	Description	Level
Password must contain at least one numeric character	`requiresNumeric`	Requires at least one numeric character in the user name.	Global
Password must differ from account name	`passwordCannotBeName`	Password must not be the same as account name.	Global
Password must differ from the last *n* passwords used	`usingHistory`	Password must differ from a configurable number of previous passwords. Since passwords themselves might not be recoverable, this list is established using hashes of previous passwords.	Global

Both global and per-user policies may be retrieved by telneting to one of Password Server's ports (Example 8-5). GETPOLICY, as seen earlier, retrieves policies associated with a specific Password Server ID. GETGLOBALPOLICY, on the other hand, results in the global policy.

Example 8-5. Reading Password Server's local policy using Telnet.

```
mab9718s-Computer:~ mab9718$ telnet g5.4am-media.com apple-sasl
Trying 207.224.49.181...
Connected to g5.4am-media.com.
Escape character is '^]'.
+OK ApplePasswordServer 10.1.0.0 password server at 207.224.49.181 ready
GETGLOBALPOLICY
+OK usingHistory=5 usingExpirationDate=0 usingHardExpirationDate=1 requiresAlpha=1
requiresNumeric=1 expirationDateGMT=4294967295 hardExpireDateGMT=1095490800
maxMinutesUntilChangePassword=86400 maxMinutesUntilDisabled=43200 maxMinutesOfNonUse=7200
maxFailedLoginAttempts=10 minChars=8 maxChars=0 passwordCannotBeName=1
```

Global policies are set either using the *pwpolicy* command, discussed in more depth later in this chapter, or using the Authentication tab of Server Admin's Open Directory Settings interface, illustrated in Figure 8-2.

Per-user policies, although they are also stored in password server's database, are managed mostly in Workgroup Manager user record → Advanced tab → Options button , seen in Figure 8-3.

The scope of a particular policy—whether it is global, per-user, or available as both—is strictly a graphical convention. Any policy may be applied to any user's Password Server account (as shown in Example 8-6), even those that are available only globally in the graphical interface.

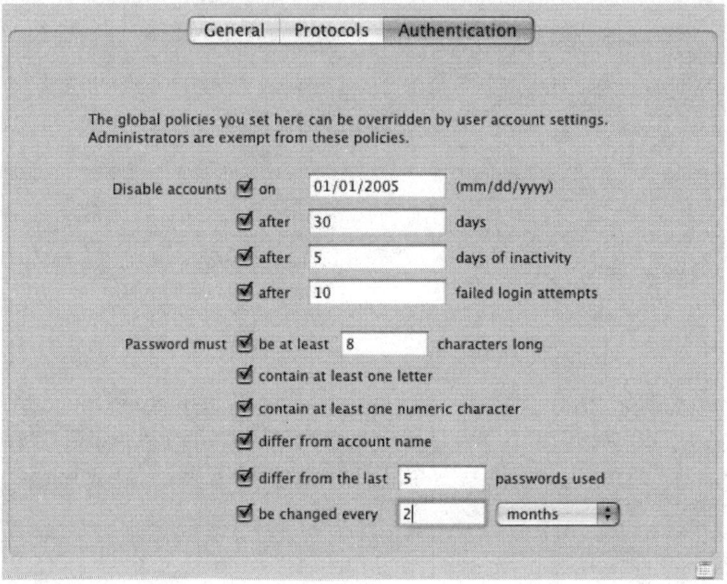

Figure 8-2. Server Admin's interface for setting global password policies. The serveradmin command-line tool could also be used towards this task, but pwpolicy, described later, is really more appropriate and less abstracted.

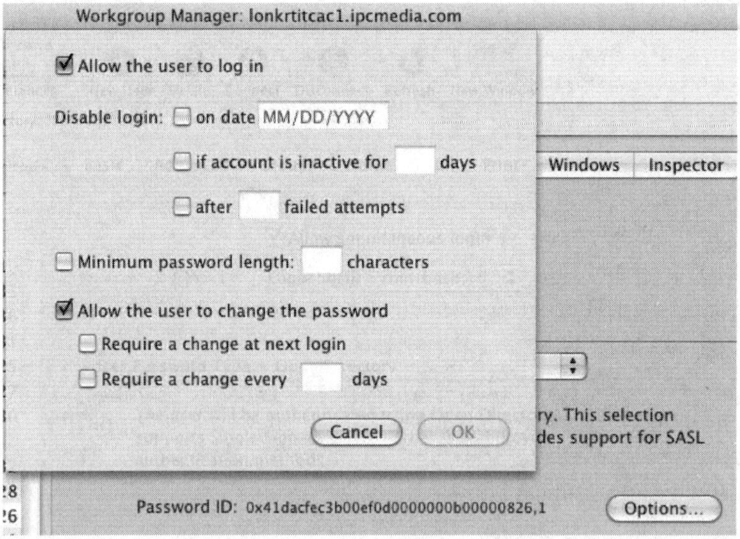

Figure 8-3. Using Server Admin to set per-user password server policies.

Example 8-6. pwpolicy can apply any policy to any Password Server principal—even one, like alphabetic character requirement, that is available only as a global policy in the graphical interface.

```
g5:~ nadmin$ pwpolicy -a nadmin -u p10016 -setpolicy requiresAlpha=1
Password:

g5:~ nadmin$ pwpolicy -u p10016 -getpolicy
isDisabled=0 isAdminUser=0 newPasswordRequired=0 usingHistory=0 canModifyPasswordforSelf=1
usingExpirationDate=0 usingHardExpirationDate=0 requiresAlpha=1 requiresNumeric=0
expirationDateGMT=12/31/69 hardExpireDateGMT=12/31/69 maxMinutesUntilChangePassword=0
maxMinutesUntilDisabled=0 maxMinutesOfNonUse=0 maxFailedLoginAttempts=0 minChars=0
maxChars=0 passwordCannotBeName=0 isSessionKeyAgent=0
```

Password Server and public-private key-pairs

Another important component of Password Server is its use of public key cryptography. Every Password Server has a 1024-bit RSA key pair, the public aspect of which is available in the */config/passwordservice* record in the shared domain in question and in each user's *AuthenticationAuthority* attribute. This public key is used to encrypt data in such a way that only legitimate Password Servers (which hold the corresponding private key) can decrypt it. This is particularly handy in the case of replication. Since replication partners all share the same key-pair, it can use it to encrypt and decrypt data sent among themselves.

> Most academic interest in Password Server is its ability to serve as a public key infrastructure. Each Password Server principal has a key-pair associated with it, and any authenticated user can, using programmatic means, ask Password Server to encrypt data in such a way that only a specific user—again using programmatic means—can decrypt it. This public key infrastructure is not highly promoted by Apple in Panther, and is used primarily in the *autoconfiguration* mechanism used to Kerberize servers in an Open Directory domain. This process is discussed later in this chapter, "Integrating Kerberos: Kerberizing Mac OS X Server services."

Password Server Tools

Like most other aspects of Mac OS X Server, *PasswordService* can be managed with command-line utilities that ship with the system. In fact, in almost every case, these tools provide functionality that isn't available in any graphical interface. This section of the chapter examines those tools.

pwpolicy

Used illustratively at several points earlier in this chapter, *pwpolicy*, as the name implies, uses the Password Server protocol to make changes to Password Server policies and passwords. It follows the general form shown in Example 8-7.

Example 8-7. A general form for pwpolicy. Note that the –a flag specifies a Password Server admin, and that this does not necessarily imply membership in the admin group of any directory domain.

```
pwpolicy -a admin name -u username "command"
```

Available options include:

–getglobalpolicy

Provides output, demonstrating the global password policies. The same data can be obtained by telneting to Password Server and issuing the *GETGLOBALPOLICY* command, illustrated earlier in this chapter.

–setglobalpolicy

Provides functionality identical to Server Admin's interface for setting global policy.

–getpolicy

Displays a user's password policies, similar to the *GETPOLICY* Telnet example earlier in the chapter.

–setpolicy

Sets a user's password policies.

–setpassword

Sets a user's password, as demonstrated earlier in this chapter.

Policy strings, used with the set policy options, are documented earlier in Table 8-3. Examples 8-8, 8-9, and 8-10 demonstrate specific *pwpolicy* usages.

Example 8-8. Using pwpolicy to change the global password policy. Notice that a successful pwpolicy command doesn't provide much feedback.

```
gs:~ nadmin$ pwpolicy -a nadmin -setglobalpolicy "minChars=4 maxFailed-LoginAttempts=3"
Password:
```

Example 8-9. Attempting to use pwpolicy to modify the password policies of a non–Password Server user. The syntax of the command is otherwise correct.

```
gs:~ nadmin$ pwpolicy -a nadmin -u s10001 -setpolicy "minChars=4 maxFailed-⏎
LoginAttempts=3"
Password:
s10001 is not a password server account.
gs:~ nadmin$
```

Example 8-10. Using pwpolicy to prevent a user from changing his or her password. While this is not a tremendously secure practice, it is common among organizations with very young constituents, such as elementary schools.

```
gs:~ nadmin$ pwpolicy -a nadmin -u p10001 -setpolicy "canModifyPasswordforSelf"Password:
```

mkpassdb

New with Panther, *mkpassdb* performs a number of administrative operations directly on the Password Server database. It actually supports several very different functions—from adding new administrator accounts to creation and destruction of the Password Server database itself. Some of its more useful supported options can be seen in Table 8-4.

Table 8-4. Common mkpassdb flags.

Flag	Description/Usage
mkpassdb -b -u *username* -p	Add *username* to the Password Server database.
mkpassdb -a -u *username* -p	Add a new administrator to the Password Server database.
mkpassdb -dump	Dump user IDs, public keys, and replica data from Password Server database.
mkpassdb -list	List supported authentication methods.
mkpassdb -key	Display Password Server's public key.

mkpassdb can also manage the Password Server replication interval and Password Server global policies. When called without arguments, its default behavior is to attempt to create a new database, failing if another already exists. Additionally, it supports several undocumented (and presumable unsupported) flags:

–setkerberos

Used when a user changes their password through Kerberos. The *kadmin* daemon calls *–setkerberos* to inform the Password Server that the modification date of the password has been changed (see Example 8-11).

Example 8-11. The –setkerebros flag usually won't be called by an end user. It is included here mostly because it is not documented elsewhere.

```
gs:~ nadmin$ sudo mkpassdb -setkerberos johnd EXAMPLE.COM
```

–setkeyagent

Sets the key agent for the VPN service (see Example 8-12). This user has the authority to request PPTP session keys as any other password server user. For more discussion of PPTP see Chapter 21.

Example 8-12. mkpassdb –setkeyagent is called by the vpnaddkeyagentuser command.

```
gs:~ nadmin$ sudo mkpassdb -setkeyagent vpn_keyuser
```

–backupdb

Backs up the Password Server database (see Example 8-13).

Example 8-13. Useful in automation of staged backups, mkpassdb's –backupdb flag is not widely documented.

```
gs:~ nadmin$ sudo mkpassdb -backupdb /var/backups/
/bin/cp /var/db/authserver/authserverfree /var/backups/
/bin/cp /var/db/authserver/authservermain /var/backups/
/bin/cp /var/db/authserver/authserverreplicas /var/backups/
/bin/cp /var/db/authserver/authserverreplicas.local /var/backups/
/bin/cp /var/db/authserver/authserverreplicas.saved /var/backups/
```

-mergedb

> This is *–backupdb*'s counterpart, merging the running Password Server with a backed up database (see Example 8-14).

> *Example 8-14. mkpassdb's –mergedb flag is used in conjunction with –backup.*
>
> ```
> g5:~ ladmin$ sudo mkpassdb -mergedb ./bakdb/authservermain
> ```

NeST

The NetInfo Setup Tool, or *NeST*, was originally written to set up and tear down shared NetInfo domains. *NeST* was at the right place at the right time to absorb some of the functionality needed to manage Password Server. Its Password Server–related options and usage are outlined in Table 8-5.

Table 8-5. NeST can be used to administer various aspects of the Password Server.

NeST Options	Description
NeST -getprotocols	Display enabled authentication methods.
NeST -setprotocols <sasl mech name> <on|off>	Modify list of enabled authentication methods.
NeST –NOpasswordserver	Disable Password Server.
NeST -hostpasswordserver *username*	Enable Password Server, making *username* a Password Server admin.

The *–NOpasswordserver* and *–hostpasswordserver* options can often be used to work around a corrupted Password Server entry; the admin user named will be given a new password server ID. *NeST* also plays a role in replication, covered in Chapter 9.

Kerberos: MIT KDC

Kerberos is a network authentication protocol designed around the concept of mutual, initial distrust. In practical terms, it is paranoid, and that paranoia is what makes it so very applicable to this particular period of nearly pervasive and almost universally insecure public networks. Three conceptual aspects of Kerberos are worth mentioning in order to lay the groundwork for more complete understanding:

- Kerberos is a shared secret mechanism. Because both the authentication service (called a *key distribution center*, or KDC; essentially, the Kerberos server) and the client share a secret, the user's password never has to be sent over the wire. The downside of shared secret mechanism is that the authentication service— because it must store those secrets in a recoverable format—can be vulnerable to compromise. More security across the network implies an authentication server that is sensitive to local access.

- Kerberos is paranoid. It assumes that every Kerberos packet will be captured and attacked. This paranoia leads to some complexity, which Apple has, overall, done a great job of mitigating.
- Kerberos is a single sign-on technology, meaning that once a user has authenticated to the authentication service (KDC) the user does not need to authenticate once again in order to access a Kerberized service in the same domain. This aspect of Kerberos makes it popular with end users.

In versions of Mac OS X leading up to Panther, Apple worked with MIT to ensure that Mac OS X and at least some Mac OS X Server services had some basic level of compatibility with Kerberos. Users could utilize Kerberos to authenticate at login and at least some server services were able to access some KDCs. Beginning with Panther, however, Kerberos has become Apple's preferred authentication platform, providing with Mac OS X Server both a much improved level of service compatibility and a complete KDC that is well integrated with the rest of Open Directory services. Although not all Mac OS X Server services are Kerberized, this represents a large investment on Apple's part, and should be taken as a signal of Apple's support going forward.

Kerberos Basics

Despite Kerberos's widespread adoption as a part of Active Directory, it is not widely understood. In fact, because its operational characteristics are new to so many administrators, a portion of this chapter is devoted to understanding the protocol itself. This differs, somewhat, from our approach to other protocols. The treatment, though, is admittedly light. For more on Kerberos, refer to *Kerberos: The Definitive Guide* (O'Reilly, 2003).

Kerberos terms

Certain vocabulary is required before any discussion of Kerberos or its applications can be pursued.

Realm

> The basic administrative unit of a Kerberos infrastructure. A realm is to Kerberos as a domain is to DNS. In fact, realm names are by convention capitalized versions of DNS names—MIT's Kerberos realm is *MIT.EDU*. Since Mac OS X is often deployed by large, heterogeneous customers with pre-existing Kerberos realms, Apple has chosen instead to use the Open Directory master's fully qualified domain name (*server.example.com*) as the default label for Open Directory realms.

Principal

Kerberos entity. Much like a Password Server slot, Kerberos principals have one or more secrets, or hashes, associated with them. Principals may generally be associated with users, hosts, or services, as illustrated in Table 8-6.

Table 8-6. Labeling host principals as something that differs from a service principal is somewhat dubious, since host principals often act as service principals.

Principal type	Example	Description
User	jon@PANTHERSERVER.ORG	Used to authenticate users.
Service	smtp/mail.pantherserver.org@PANTHERSERVER.ORG	
Host	host/homes.pantherserver.org@PANTHERSERVER.ORG	

KDC

Key Distribution Center. The authentication server.

Ticket

An authentication token. Tickets are not by themselves useful, and must be accompanied by authenticators, discussed later in this section.

TGT

Ticket-granting ticket. Initial token sent to a Kerberos client in response to an authentication attempt. The TGT, when used in conjunction with the right authenticator, allow the Kerberos client to obtain tickets for other services.

Service ticket

Ticket granting access to a particular purpose. Service tickets are associated with service principals.

Encryption type

When principals (user, service, or host) sets their password, they are not stored for further use. Instead they are encrypted with one or more one-way algorithms. The results are stored and later used as shared secrets between the KDC and the Kerberos client. These algorithms, which tend towards standardization among Kerberos implementations, are known as encryption types.

Authenticator

An authenticator consists of a timestamp encrypted with a *session key*, or *shared secret*. The ability to use this key provides a high level of assurance that a client is legitimate, since session keys are generally sent over the network encrypted with secrets known only by legitimate clients.

The Kerberos exchange

The Kerberos exchange—the actual conversation between the Kerberos client and the KDC (and later between the Kerberos client and the Kerberized service) can appear mind-bending at first glance. Be patient, and draw it out for yourself if you need to. Each step in that conversation has an established name, useful to system administrators primarily due to the fact that it is used to illustrate the requests that the KDC records in its logs. The entire process is summarized in Figure 8-4.

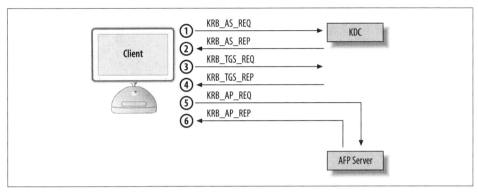

Figure 8-4. An overview of the Kerberos exchange.

Steps 1 and 2 occur when a client has decided that it needs a TGT. This is usually during the login process but might also be due to an attempt to access a Kerberized service.

1. KRB_AS_REQ (*Kerberos Authentication Service Request*): The Kerberos client sends a user principal name to the KDC requesting authentication.

2. KRB_AS_REP (*Kerberos Authentication Service Reply*): The KDC sends back a two-part message, consisting of a TGT and a session key to be shared between the it and the client. The session key is encrypted with a key that is derived from the user's password. The TGT is encrypted with a different key, known only to the KDC. It contains a number of relevant pieces of data, including the user principal name that requested it, a timestamp, and a second copy of the session key that accompanies it. If the client is able to successfully decrypt the session key (presumably because the supplied password is correct), it is considered successfully authenticated.

 Steps 3 through 6 represent a client's attempt to access a Kerberized service. They assume that a TGT and corresponding session key have already been obtained and stored in the credentials cache. These credentials are used to prove the client's identity later in the Kerberos process. The client needs a service ticket and session key for each Kerberized service it attempts to access.

3. KRB_TGS_REQ (*Kerberos Ticket Granting Service Request*): When a client wishes to access a Kerberized service, it sends the principal name associated with the service to the KDC along with its TGT and an authenticator. As mentioned earlier, this authenticator consists of a timestamp encrypted with the session key obtained in the KRB_AS_REP—the session key itself is not sent over the wire. The TGT, since it

is already encrypted in such a way that only the KDC may access it, is not encrypted again.

4. KRB_TGS_REP (*Kerberos Ticket Granting Service Reply*): If the KDC recognizes the TGT returned to it in KRB_TGS_REQ, and if that TGT matches the session key used to generate the accompanying authenticator, the KDC is reasonably sure that the requesting client is legitimate, and will respond with a successful KRB_TGS_REP. This two-part message consists of a service ticket for the service principal requested in KRB_TGS_REQ and a second session key. In order to ensure that only legitimate clients may obtain it, this second session key is encrypted with the first session key, already shared between the KDC and the client.

 After a successful KRB_TGS_REP, the client has two more items in its credential cache: a Service ticket, which can be decrypted only by the KDC or service, and another session key, specifically corresponding to the service ticket. The client then uses these new credentials to access the Kerberized service—which is really the point of this entire exercise.

5. KRB_AP_REQ (*Kerberos Authentication Protocol Request*): The Kerberos client sends the service ticket and an authenticator to the Kerberized service. Remember that the client initially obtained this service ticket from the KDC (in KRB_TGS_REP), and that the service ticket is encrypted with a secret shared by the KDC and the Kerberized service, so that no other party can decrypt it. Among other things, the service ticket contains a copy of the session key that the client uses to create the accompanying authenticator. If the session key and the authenticator match (much the same way that they must in KRG_TGS_REQ) then the Kerberized Service can be reasonably confident that the client is who it says it is.

 The Kerberized service is able to decrypt the service ticket only because it shares a secret with the KDC. In Mac OS X, that shared secret is usually stored on the server in the */etc/krb5.keytab* file, which should be considered sensitive, since any party possessing it can impersonate the service in question by decrypting legitimate service tickets.

6. KRB_AP_REP (*Kerberos Authentication Protocol Reply*): Once the service verifies the authenticity of the authenticator and service ticket, it may consider the client authenticated. However, bear in mind that that this is a one-way verification. The Kerberized service has done nothing to verify its authenticity to the client, and a malicious or spoofed service may simply accept KRB_AP_REQ regardless of its authenticity, expecting the client to then send it sensitive data. To protect against this, the client may request mutual authentication, meaning that the Kerberized service must reply with yet another authenticator—a timestamp encrypted with the supposedly shared session key. This would ensure successful decryption of the

service ticket, since this is the only way for the Kerberized service to legitimately obtain the session key.

Admittedly, Kerberos is complex; complex enough that it is, given the page size constraints of this book, it is difficult to represent graphically—the text in the graphic would have to be really, really small. This complexity is due to a thorough paranoia, which can be seen as only healthy in an untrusted network environment. The rest of this chapter examines the KDC side implementation of Kerberos in Mac OS X Server.

 Most Kerberos messages are not recorded in any log in a default configuration of Mac OS X Server. In order to get *syslog* to send them to their own file (for easier processing), make the following changes to */etc/syslogd.conf*:

1. Add an *auth.** directive to */etc/syslogd.conf*. This requires *root* privileges:

   ```
   auth.*/var/log/krb.log
   ```

2. Create the log file you just specified in */etc/syslogd.conf*:

   ```
   sudo touch /var/log/krb.log
   ```

3. Restart *syslogd*:

   ```
   sudo killall -HUP syslogd
   ```

The KDC should then proceed to log to the file you specified in step 1.

Securing Kerberos

In a default configuration, any host with access to the KDC's Kerberos service (port 88, typically UDP) can attempt to authenticate, sending KRB_AS_REQ. The KDC typically responds with KRB_AS_REP, trusting that only legitimate users will be capable of decrypting the included session key (which is encrypted using a hash of the user's password). This tack ignores the possibility, though, that the response may be attacked—that malicious clients might attempt to brute-force the decryption of the session key, employing a dictionary attack or popular cracking algorithm. In order to thwart this kind of attack, the Kerberos V protocol introduced preauthentication. This setup requires that the client send a recognizable authenticator (in this case, a timestamp encrypted with a hash of the user's password) to the KDC before KRB_AS_REP is sent back across the network. Since the KDC also stores a hash of the user's password, it can have a high confidence level that the client does indeed know the password if the authenticator is legitimate. Preauthentication must be set individually on each principal using the *kadmin local* command's *modify_principal* flag: kadmin.local -q "modify_principal +requires_preauth user@REALM.COM" (preauthentication may also be specified for service principals). The script shown in Example 8-15 could be used to enable preauthentication for every user principal a realm.

Example 8-15. In a default configuration, this script (when executed on an Open Directory Master) adds a preauthentication requirement to every user in the realm.

```
#!/bin/sh
for i in `sudo /usr/sbin/kadmin.local -q list_principals | /usr/bin/egrep -v
'afpserver|ftp|host|kadmin|krbtgt|pop|smtp|root|imap|K/M'`
do
    echo /usr/sbin/kadmin.local -q "modify_principal +requires_preauth $i"
done
```

Kerberos and Mac OS X Server

Apple includes with Mac OS X Server a fairly standard version of MIT's Kerberos 1.3.1 distribution. In fact, Apple prides itself on having left Kerberos unmodified. Some of the architectural components of that distribution are documented in Table 8-7.

Table 8-7. Components of Mac OS X's Kerberos infrastructure.

Kerberos file	Description
/usr/sbin/krb5kdc	The KDC daemon. *krb5kdc* provides the Kerberos 5 authentication service. It is essentially read-only, servicing various authentication requests.
/usr/sbin/kadmind	The MIT Kerberos administration daemon. *kadmind* is the portal through which all changes to the Kerberos and policy databases are made—from password changes to the addition and deletion of principals. In a replicated environment, *kadmind* runs only on the Open Directory Master.
/var/db/krb5kdc/kdc.conf	The configuration file for both *krb5kdc* and *kadmind*.
/var/db/krb5kdc/principal	The Kerberos database. It contains all of the keys (hashed passwords) in the realm. The file itself is encrypted with a key stored in */var/db/krb5kdc/.k5.REALMNAME.COM*.
/var/db/krb5kdc/.k5.REALMNAME.COM	Key used to encrypt the Kerberos database.
/var/db/krb5kdc/kadm5.acl	Access control list for *kadmind*. Lists specific Kerberos principals along with the administrative actions they are allowed to perform. In Mac OS X, its configuration is simple, granting all administrative privileges to the account used to create the shared domain.
/var/db/krb5kdc/kadm5.keytab	File containing keys that correspond to *kadmin*'s keys in the Kerberos database. These keys—secrets shared between *kadmind* and *krb5kdc*—allow *kadmind* to administer the Kerberos database.
/var/db/krb5kdc/principal.kadm5	Administrative database. Contains policy information, such as Kerberos's password complexity requirements. Should not be used in Mac OS X Server without a relatively complete understanding of the KDC's integration with Password Server, covered later in this chapter.
/var/db/krb5kdc/principal.kadm5.lock	*kadmind*'s lock file. If this file *does not* exist, *kadmind* won't write to the Kerberos database.

MIT's Kerberos distribution also includes a number of utilities, useful for both administering and accessing the KDC:

kadmin and kadmin.local

> *kadmin* is the main utility for adding and manipulating objects in the Kerberos database; it relies on access controls established in the *kadm5.acl* file to determine who is authorized to make changes. *kadmin.local* is its heavy-handed forceful cousin that, when executed as *root*, ignores all access controls and writes directly to the Kerberos and policy databases.

kdb5_util

> Performs low-level maintenance on the Kerberos database. Probably most useful in its *dump* and *load* directives, which can be used to backup and restore a Kerberos database. *kdb5_util* well illustrates the security limitations of Kerberos; the keys it reveals can be utilized maliciously to impersonate accounts in the KDC. This makes access to any KDC (Open Directory Masters or Replicas) very sensitive.

kinit and kdestroy

> *kinit* uses user principal credentials to get a TGT, essentially implementing KRB_ AS_REQ. *kdestroy* destroys any current tickets.

klist

> Lists any current tickets. Its *–k* flag also allows for examination of any keys in the keytab file (used to secure communication between a Kerberized service and the KDC), if it exists.

ktutil

> Used to maintain keytab files. Typically this means combining keytabs so that a server can support more than one Kerberized service.

It should be noted that MIT's distribution—being a reference implementation produced by the same organization that maintains the Kerberos protocol itself—is as standard as it gets. One of the great strengths and weaknesses of Kerberos, though, is that the protocol itself is very open—sometimes to the point of being vague. The Kerberos standards, for instance, say nothing about administration—the creation and maintenance of principals in the Kerberos database. MIT provides *kadmind* and its associated utilities for that purpose, but because there is no standard for them, they will not interoperate with other KDCs (for instance Active Directory's). Replication also comes under this nonstandard umbrella, although it's less important to Mac OS X Server, which leverages its Password Server to replicate Kerberos principals.

Kerberos Configuration

Open Directory KDC's are generally configured when the Open Directory Master is first promoted. Aside from specifying the name of the Kerberos realm during that process, there are no KDC configuration options are exposed in the graphical user interface. A wide range of options, however, are discussed in *kdc.conf*'s manpage, which describes the KDC's configuration file. A sample file is presented here, interrupted by line-by-line documentation. *kdc.conf* is used by both *krb5kdc* and *kadmind*.

```
## This file autogenerated by KDCSetup from (null) ##
[kdcdefaults]
```

Kerberos operates on port 88, typically using UDP rather than TCP.

```
    kdc_ports = 88
```

The [realms] section of *kdc.conf* describes the realms that the KDC is responsible for. Open Directory Masters are responsible typically for only one realm, which is by convention named after the fully qualified domain name of the Open Directory Master.

```
[realms]
        ODM.PANTHERSERVER.ORG = {
```

kadmind typically listens on port 749.

```
        kadmind_port = 749
```

Tickets have a finite lifetime, so that the likelihood of a successful dictionary attack is greatly reduced—it is likely that the amount of time necessary to successfully compromise a ticket would be significantly longer than the default 10-hour lifetime. Renewable tickets balance security and convenience, allowing any valid ticket to be renewed for a particular period—in the default case, one week.

```
        max_life = 10h 0m 0s
        max_renewable_life = 7d 0h 0m 0s
```

Kerberos uses a variety of algorithms to encrypt data. master_key_type specifies the method used to encrypt the Kerberos database. The two enctype entries specify the algorithms used to produce the keys that will be used as shared secrets between the KDC and its clients.

```
        master_key_type = des3-hmac-sha1
        supported_enctypes = des3-hmac-sha1:normal arcfour-hmac-md5:normal
des-cbc-crc:normal des-cbc-crc:v4
        kdc_supported_enctypes = des3-hmac-sha1:normal arcfour-hmac-md5:
normal des-cbc-crc:normal des-cbc-crc:v4
```

The KDC relies on a number of files, the purposes of which are described earlier in this chapter. Many must be explicitly defined in *kdc.conf*.

```
        acl_file = /var/db/krb5kdc/kadm5.acl
        admin_keytab = /var/db/krb5kdc/kadm5.keytab
        database_name = /var/db/krb5kdc/principal
    }
```

Logging statements seem to be ignored, and logging messages are instead sent to *syslogd*, as described earlier in this chapter.

```
[logging]
        kdc = FILE:/var/log/krb5kdc/kdc.log
        admin_server = FILE:/var/log/krb5kdc/kadmin.log
```

Integrating Kerberos: Kerberizing Mac OS X Server services

Open Directory Masters and Replicas Kerberize their services at promotion time, so that AFP, FTP, SMTP, SSH, POP, and IMAP all support single sign-on. Not all servers, though, are Open Directory Masters or Replicas, and in fact for both security and performance reasons, the number of replicas should be minimized, leaving several common instances of non-Kerberized servers participating in an Open Directory domain:

Home directory servers

> File services, particularly when supporting home directory usage, can impose a significant load on any server. Typically in environments with many users, several home directory servers may support a single Open Directory domain. It's desirable in that context to support single sign-on, so that users do not have to reauthenticate to access file services resources.

Scientific computing clusters

> Administration of the large number of hardware nodes associated with a computational cluster can prove troublesome. Enabling single sign-on lessens that burden and streamlines the administration process.

Single sign-on is not typically enabled at configuration time for these servers. The reason is subtle but significant. In Panther, since all directory data (generally stored in the Master's LDAP server) is world-readable, computers participating in the domain, including servers, do not have to be trusted in any way. Most connections to the domain are not authenticated. Since no username or password has to be supplied in order to join the domain, Kerberos, which generally requires administrative authorization to be set up, cannot be configured. Because of this, most servers participating in the domain see a message that looks something like Figure 8-5 in the General tab of Server Admin's Open Directory section.

Unfortunately, joining Kerberos is not as simple as clicking the Join Kerberos button, and while the underlying technology and infrastructure is very well done, the graphical user interface leaves a lot to be desired.

Recall that in order to communicate securely, a Kerberized service must share a secret with the KDC, and that this secret is generally stored in the */etc/krb5.keytab* file on the server in question. Because these secrets are extremely sensitive, much of joining Kerberos revolves around getting the keytab securely to the server that is to be Kerberized. The first step is not choosing the Join Kerberos button, but actually creating a computer account in the shared domain for the server to be Kerberized, illustrated in Figure 8-6. This step is accomplished using Workgroup Manager. It's a good idea to create a computer list specifically for servers. This list can be used for other purposes later, such as limiting console logins to members of the domain admin group.

Once the computer account is created, Kerberos data can be added to it. The terminology Apple uses to describe this process varies, depending on the interface, between "Creating a Kerberos Record" and "Delegating Kerberos Join." Effectively

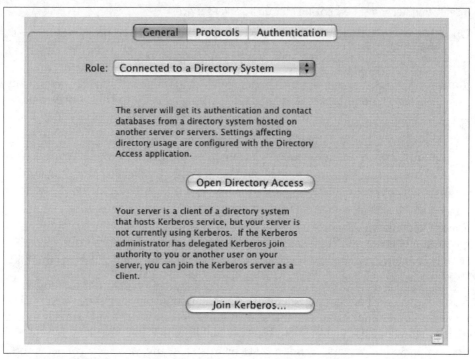

Figure 8-5. The deceptively simple Join Kerberos button tempts us with its hopeful-looking ellipsis…

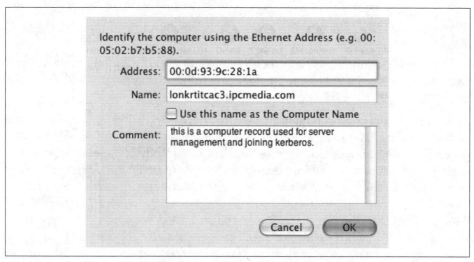

Figure 8-6. Adding computer accounts for use with single sign-on. Be sure in this case to use the server's fully qualified domain name in the Name field.

what happens is that a keytab and its associated service principals are created and stored securely in the computer record of the server to be Kerberized. This is accomplished *on the Master*, in the General pane of the Open Directory section of Server Admin, using the Add Kerberos Record button. Clicking the Add Kerberos button reveals the dialog seen in Figure 8-7. After specifying an administrative name and password for the shared domain, a computer record and list of delegated administrators must be chosen. The delegated administrators will be later permitted to complete the Kerberos join process, moving the keytab from the shared domain to the member server described in the computer record. This allows services on that server can communicate securely with the KDC, supporting Kerberos authentication and single sign-on.

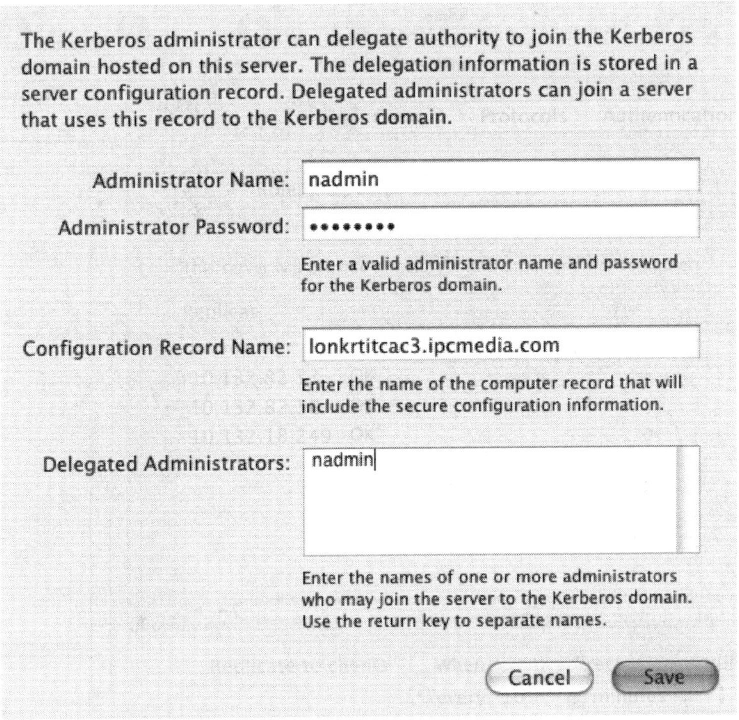

The Kerberos administrator can delegate authority to join the Kerberos domain hosted on this server. The delegation information is stored in a server configuration record. Delegated administrators can join a server that uses this record to the Kerberos domain.

Administrator Name: nadmin

Administrator Password: ••••••••

Enter a valid administrator name and password for the Kerberos domain.

Configuration Record Name: lonkrtitcac3.ipcmedia.com

Enter the name of the computer record that will include the secure configuration information.

Delegated Administrators: nadmin

Enter the names of one or more administrators who may join the server to the Kerberos domain. Use the return key to separate names.

Cancel   Save

Figure 8-7. The Kerberos delegation interface. A keytab is created and stored securely in the named configuration record in such a way that only the delegated administrators may retrieve it.

This interface is among the most cumbersome in Mac OS X Server—rather than allowing you to choose among compatible (fully qualified) computer records, it forces you to specify one. Rather than making use of the convenient Users and Groups picker seen elsewhere in Server Admin, it forces you to type in multiple user names manually, and at no point does it validate the data you've entered. You can specify totally incorrect data—users and computer records that don't exist and an incorrect password—and press Save, and this dialog box happily presents much the same behavior that it would if that data were correctly entered.

Adding a Kerberos record ends up calling the *sso_util* command on the Open Directory Master, specifically using its *generateconfig* flag, as shown in Example 8-16.

Example 8-16. Using sso_util to create a secure configuration record. This record will later be used to Kerberize services on g5.4am-media.com.

```
sso_util generateconfig -r GS.4AM-MEDIA.COM -R g5.4am-media.com -f /LDAPv3/127.0.0.1 -U
nadmin -a nadmin -p
```

sso_util, in this case, calls *kadmin.local* and *ktutil* to create service principals and their associated secrets in the KDC, produce a *keytab* file using those principals, and securely store that *keytab* in the world-readable LDAP directory; specifically, in the Computer record. The latter is accomplished by first encrypting the *keytab*, and then leveraging Password Server's little-known public key cryptography infrastructure to encrypt that key in such a way that only the specified delegated administrators can decrypt it. The resulting data is stored in the computer's XMLPlist attribute, seen in Example 8-17. The data tag, which contains the encrypted *keytab* file, is shortened (indicated by the ellipsis), due to its extreme length.

Example 8-17. Using dscl to view the Kerberos configuration data created in the graphically driven Kerberos delegation process documented earlier.

```
gs:~ nadmin$ dscl /LDAPv3/127.0.0.1 -read /Computers/g5.4am-media.com XMLPlist
XMLPlist: <?xml version="1.0" encoding="UTF-8"?>
<!DOCTYPE plist PUBLIC "-//Apple Computer//DTD PLIST 1.0//EN" "http://www.apple.com/DTDs/
PropertyList-1.0.dtd">
<plist version="1.0">
<dict>
        <key>comment</key>
        <string>Record created by nadmin on 2004-07-17 21:28:16 -0600</string>
        <key>configData</key>
        <data>
        kKV4BVOVie4XaBBb1Qo+UomigdShosAyE75VuaIfa/CkBhAFBkFM5euO62qT+JUnuiel
        k4UNBT1kUnICeGekwL4/nhXebCMh5urrusRFCszJeJGPPg+SmpLrAHP6KknAYPHeoTvS
        ...
        </data>
        <key>configDataHash</key>
        <string>QjwuLBBdLe4ISTDB1rOGsNt95/U=</string>
        <key>recipientList</key>
        <array>
                <dict>
                        <key>key</key>
        <string>b8OGIjiU3tWSJYmEuCSS9OgsiFfgmSNwkCDvNfHeVnKV</string>
                        <key>shortName</key>
                        <string>nadmin</string>
                </dict>
        </array>
</dict>
</plist>
```

This completes the Kerberos delegation process; the resulting modified Computer record sits there, unused, in the directory until the Join Kerberos process, where we began this discussion, is executed. The specific tags of the XMLPlist attribute are documented in Table 8-8.

Table 8-8. Data included in the XMLPlist attribute of a computer record.

Key	Description
Comment	Data about the creation of the secure record.
configData	The configData key contains the encrypted version of the server's *keytab* file.
configDataHash	A signature of the configData.
recipientList	recipientList is actually an array, consisting of a list of short names authorized to decrypt the configData along with their own encrypted version of the key used to encrypt it.

On the server that is to be Kerberized, Server Admin must finally be used to complete the Kerberos join process. Any administrator delegated in the record creation process may click the Join Kerberos button (Figure 8-5). The resulting dialog (illustrated in Figure 8-8) is relatively simple, prompting for the name and password of a delegated administrator.

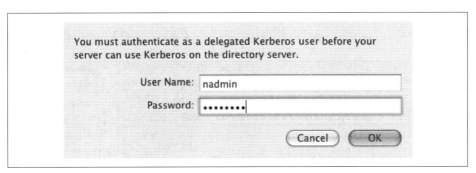

Figure 8-8. Credentials of a delegated administrator are required in order to make use of single sign-on.

Once again, this dialog calls the *sso_util* command, this time (on the member server, rather than on the Master) with its *useconfig* option, as shown in Example 8-18.

Example 8-18. sso_util's useconfig option searches the shared domain for a computer record and uses the secure configuration data in the XMLPlist attribute to build an appropriate keytab file.

```
sso_util useconfig -u -a nadmin -p
```

This command essentially uses the provided credentials to access and decrypt the secure configuration record stored in the XMLPlist attribute of the server's computer account, decodes the *keytab* file, and installs it onto the now Kerberized server. The success of this process can be gauged with the *klist* command's –*k* flag, which examines the *keytab* file, as shown in Example 8-19.

Example 8-19. Using klist to examine the keytab file. Notice that due to the sensitive nature of the keytab, this operation requires root privliges. Klist's –e flag additionally displays the encryption types associated with each key.

```
g5:~ nadmin$ sudo klist -ke
Password:
Keytab name: FILE:/etc/krb5.keytab
KVNO Principal
---- --------------------------------------------------------------------
   3 host/g5.4am-media.com@G5.4AM-MEDIA.COM (Triple DES cbc mode with HMAC/sha1)
   3 host/g5.4am-media.com@G5.4AM-MEDIA.COM (ArcFour with HMAC/md5)
   3 host/g5.4am-media.com@G5.4AM-MEDIA.COM (DES cbc mode with CRC-32)
   3 smtp/g5.4am-media.com@G5.4AM-MEDIA.COM (Triple DES cbc mode with HMAC/sha1)
   3 smtp/g5.4am-media.com@G5.4AM-MEDIA.COM (ArcFour with HMAC/md5)
   3 smtp/g5.4am-media.com@G5.4AM-MEDIA.COM (DES cbc mode with CRC-32)
   3 pop/g5.4am-media.com@G5.4AM-MEDIA.COM (Triple DES cbc mode with HMAC/sha1)
   3 pop/g5.4am-media.com@G5.4AM-MEDIA.COM (ArcFour with HMAC/md5)
   3 pop/g5.4am-media.com@G5.4AM-MEDIA.COM (DES cbc mode with CRC-32)
   3 imap/g5.4am-media.com@G5.4AM-MEDIA.COM (Triple DES cbc mode with HMAC/sha1)
   3 imap/g5.4am-media.com@G5.4AM-MEDIA.COM (ArcFour with HMAC/md5)
   3 imap/g5.4am-media.com@G5.4AM-MEDIA.COM (DES cbc mode with CRC-32)
   3 ftp/g5.4am-media.com@G5.4AM-MEDIA.COM (Triple DES cbc mode with HMAC/sha1)
   3 ftp/g5.4am-media.com@G5.4AM-MEDIA.COM (ArcFour with HMAC/md5)
   3 ftp/g5.4am-media.com@G5.4AM-MEDIA.COM (DES cbc mode with CRC-32)
   3 afpserver/g5.4am-media.com@G5.4AM-MEDIA.COM (Triple DES cbc mode with HMAC/sha1)
   3 afpserver/g5.4am-media.com@G5.4AM-MEDIA.COM (ArcFour with HMAC/md5)
   3 afpserver/g5.4am-media.com@G5.4AM-MEDIA.COM (DES cbc mode with CRC-32)
```

One final aspect of the Kerberos Join process is the configuration of individual Mac OS X Server processes to recognize the newly installed service keys. This data is added to AFP, FTP, and Mail configurations (*/Library/Preferences/com.apple.applefileserver*, */Library/FTPServer/Configuration/ftpaccess*, and */etc/MailServicesOther.plist*, respectively). OpenSSH does not require a service principal to be specified, and instead assumes the use of a host principal derived from the server's fully qualified domain name.

Remember that although the underlying configuration architecture (*sso_util*) works quite well, the graphical interface is, ironically, more difficult to use, providing neither a list of Kerberized servers nor any meaningful feedback when single sign-on is incorrectly configured. To make matters worse, neither the Join Kerberos button, nor its warning text of "Your server is a client of a directory system that hosts a Kerberos service, but your server is not currently using Kerberos..." goes away once a server has been successfully configured. Virtually the only way to ensure correct configuration is to use the *klist* command as illustrated previously and to actually test single sign-on by attempting a connection.

Putting It All Together

As you might expect, use of multiple authentication authorities (both Kerberos and Password Server) presents a real problem in terms of data consistency. It's easy to imagine a scenario where a user's password might be one thing in Password Server's database and another in the KDC's. This, though, is only one of the many issues that Apple has had to surmount in order to facilitate a mostly seamless and well-integrated server architecture. It, along with several other issues, is summarized in Table 8-9.

Table 8-9. Summary of challenges associated with integration of Open Directory Server technologies.

Integration challenge	Apple's response
KDCs are difficult to deploy and maintenance of Kerberos principals can be complex.	Mac OS X Server includes a bundled KDC and automated setup tools. It's integrated with Directory Services so that user principals are created when users are.
Kerberos doesn't support legacy authentication methods.	Password Server is bundled with Mac OS X Server in order to support legacy authentication methods required by services that are not Kerberized.
Kerberos-client configuration tends to be difficult and command-line–oriented.	Kerberos clients are automatically configured based on a directory record.
Multiple authentication databases can get out of sync.	Both *kadmind* (the Kerberos Administration daemon) and PasswordService know how to update user records in each others' databases.
Kerberos replication is very complex, and is not standardized among Kerberos implementations.	Kerberos leverages Password Server replication.
Kerberos is an authentication mechanism, and its relationship with identification data (user accounts) is not defined in the Kerberos standard.	Apple has established a consistent convention for associating user principals with user accounts using the *AuthAuthority* user attribute.

The first challenge Apple faced was the difficulty of KDC deployment. The initial setup and day-to-day management of a Kerberos realm can both be quite difficult and command-line–oriented. Apple overcame this by including a full MIT KDC in Mac OS X Server. It's automatically configured to work with Open Directory, so that when users are created in LDAP, they're created in Kerberos, too. This step is accomplished using the *kdcsetup* command, shown in Example 8-20 and Table 8-10.

Example 8-20. kdcsetup, as used to set up an Open Directory Master. kdcsetup's options are documented in Table 8-10.

```
/usr/sbin/kdcsetup -f /LDAPv3/127.0.0.1 -w -a nadmin -p
```

Table 8-10. kdcsetup is called during Open Directory Master creation by the slapconfig utility. It can also be run manually, either outside the context of Master creation or to repair a failed promotion process.

Flag	Option	Description
−f	Directory node	Create a master KDC and write the kerberosKDC and KerberosClient configuration records to the specified directory node. Used during Master creation.
−c	Directory node	Create a clone KDC, based on the kerberosKDC configuration record in the specified domain.
−w	Auto-start *krb5kdc* and *kadmind*.	Adds *kadmind* and *krb5kdc* to *watchdog.conf*.
−a	Admin Name	The RecordName (short name) of an administrator authorized to make changes to the directory node specified in the −f or −c argument.
−p		
−v	1–6	

Additionally, setup was standardized enough that some assumptions could be made about initial configuration options, allowing that process to become fairly transparent to most administrators. This automated Server-side infrastructure is complimented by a client-side autoconfiguration mechanism. When *loginwindow* finds a ;Kerberosv5; *AuthAuthority* in a user record, the *kerberosautoconfig* command is automatically called by *mach_init*, as shown in Example 8-21.

Example 8-21. The ;Kerberosv5; AuthAuthority, which serves the dual purpose of Kerberos autoconfiguration and association of a user account with a specific Kerberos user principal. The user's AuthAuthority attribute is the glue that binds authentication and identification together.

```
;Kerberosv5;0x41007c772f2bb2cf0000000300000003;nadmin@GS.4AM-MEDIA.COM;GS.4AM-MEDIA.
COM;1024 35
15345326445168027393996655490490721615368531299530672912502250870913646125686886595154543
63577505502469615333578648502669058540950116707897517428009563736817604024451255700505771
00380148741388983635716639905012153782390796493189351294183659447397409497257680215383981
8969475833430224656027866765787351108583937 root@gs.4am-media.com:207.224.49.180
```

kerberosautoconfig, which is examined in more depth in Table 8-11, reads the */Config/KerberosClient* configuration record out of the Open Directory node where the user was located, and uses it to create a valid Kerberos configuration file on the client at */Library/Preferences/edu.mit.Kerberos*.

Table 8-11. kerberosautoconfig options. Pre-existing configuration files are overwritten only if an autogeneration header (indicating kerberosautoconfig has already run) exists and if the generation_id of that header is less than the generation_id indicated in the KerberosClient record.

Flag	Option	description
−f	Directory node	Specifies which Open Directory node should be used for Kerberos configuration. A KerberosClient configuration record must exist in the specified directory domain.
−o	Output directory	The directory the *edu.mit.Kerberos* file should be saved to. The default choice is */Library/Preferences*.

Table 8-11. kerberosautoconfig options. Pre-existing configuration files are overwritten only if an autogeneration header (indicating kerberosautoconfig has already run) exists and if the generation_ id of that header is less than the generation_id indicated in the KerberosClient record. (continued)

Flag	Option	description
−r	Realm name	
−m	Master KDC	
−u	Force an update of the *edu.mit. Kerberos* configuration file.	
−v	Verbose	Specifices a level of verbocity.

This automatic configuration mechanism can also be leveraged outside of an Open Directory, by manually adding KerberosClient data to a directory domain hosted on some other platform. The format of that record is documented in Example 8-22.

Example 8-22. Using dscl to read a KerberosClient configuration record in a shared Open Directory domain. The KerberosClient record is created by the kdcsetup command in order to aid in automated client configuration. Notice that dscl shows both the native (LDAP) and standard (Open Directory) names for the configuration record's attributes.

```
mab9718s-Computer:~ mab9718$ dscl -u nadmin -p gs.4am-media.com -read /LDAPv3/127.0.0.1/
Config/KerberosClient
Password:
apple-xmlplist: <?xml version="1.0" encoding="UTF-8"?>
<!DOCTYPE plist PUBLIC "-//Apple Computer//DTD PLIST 1.0//EN" "http://www.apple.com/DTDs/
PropertyList-1.0.dtd">
<plist version="1.0">
<dict>
        <key>edu.mit.kerberos</key>
        <dict>
                <key>domain_realm</key>
                <dict>
                        <key>.pantherserver.org</key>
                        <string>ODM.PANTHERSERVER.ORG</string>
                        <key>pantherserver.org</key>
                        <string>ODM.PANTHERSERVER.ORG</string>
                </dict>
                <key>libdefaults</key>
                <dict>
                        <key>default_realm</key>
                        <string>ODM.PANTHERSERVER.ORG</string>
                </dict>
                <key>realms</key>
                <dict>
                        <key> ODM.PANTHERSERVER.ORG </key>
                        <dict>
                                <key>KADM_List</key>
                                <array>
                                        <string>odm. pantherserver.org </string>
                                </array>
                                <key>KDC_List</key>
```

Example 8-22. Using dscl to read a KerberosClient configuration record in a shared Open Directory domain. The KerberosClient record is created by the kdcsetup command in order to aid in automated client configuration. Notice that dscl shows both the native (LDAP) and standard (Open Directory) names for the configuration record's attributes. (continued)

```
                            <array>
                                    <string> odm. pantherserver.org </string>
                            </array>
                    </dict>
            </dict>
        </dict>
        <key>generationID</key>
        <integer>1515194755</integer>
</dict>
</plist>

cn: KerberosClient
objectClass: apple-configuration top
AppleMetaNodeLocation: /LDAPv3/127.0.0.1
PasswordPlus: ********
RecordName: KerberosClient
XMLPlist: <?xml version="1.0" encoding="UTF-8"?>
<!DOCTYPE plist PUBLIC "-//Apple Computer//DTD PLIST 1.0//EN" "http://www.apple.com/DTDs/
PropertyList-1.0.dtd">
<plist version="1.0">
<dict>
        <key>edu.mit.kerberos</key>
        <dict>
                <key>domain_realm</key>
                <dict>
                        <key>.pantherserver.org</key>
                        <string>ODM.PANTHERSERVER.ORG</string>
                        <key>pantherserver.org </key>
                        <string> ODM.PANTHERSERVER.ORG </string>
                </dict>
                <key>libdefaults</key>
                <dict>
                        <key>default_realm</key>
                        <string> ODM.PANTHERSERVER.ORG </string>
                </dict>
                <key>realms</key>
                <dict>
                        <key> ODM.PANTHERSERVER.ORG </key>
                        <dict>
                                <key>KADM_List</key>
                                <array>
                                        <string> pantherserver.org </string>
                                </array>
                                <key>KDC_List</key>
                                <array>
                                        <string> pantherserver.org </string>
                                </array>
                        </dict>
                </dict>
```

Example 8-22. Using dscl to read a KerberosClient configuration record in a shared Open Directory domain. The KerberosClient record is created by the kdcsetup command in order to aid in automated client configuration. Notice that dscl shows both the native (LDAP) and standard (Open Directory) names for the configuration record's attributes. (continued)

```
            </dict>
            <key>generationID</key>
            <integer>1515194755</integer>
</dict>
</plist>
```

Finally, note that *kerberosautoconfig* is capable of producing a minimal configuration file with no *KerberosClient* record at all, by manually specifying its *–r* and *–m* options. If there is a pre-existing *edu.mit.Kerberos* file, the *–u* flag must be specified, as shown in Example 8-23.

Example 8-23. Using kerberosautoconfig to create a fairly generic Kerberos configuration.

```
mab9718s-Computer:~ mab9718$ sudo kerberosautoconfig -v 2 -u -r REALM.COM -m ↵ master.
realm.com
```

Password Server and Synchronization

As mentioned previously, Password Server was introduced in Jaguar primarily to support various challenge–response authentication protocols, since Kerberos, despite its proactive security model, is not well integrated into some server services. This introduction, however, presents a large issue. Kerberos and Password Server maintain separate authentication databases, and it was going to be a challenge to get them to stay synchronized. In order to achieve this, Apple first modified *PasswordService* to understand how to use the *kadmin.local* tool to set Kerberos passwords and (some) policies. When password or policy change requests come in to *PasswordService*, it invokes *kadmin.local* in order to update the Kerberos database. Since all changes to Kerberos principals have to go through *kadmind*, it makes sense to use it as the conduit for synchronization between the two systems.

 Not all Password Server policies are propagated to the KDC. In fact, right now, the only per-user policy that is propagated seems to be *require password change every n days*. Policy synchronization (as limited as it is) is one way. No KDC policies are propagated to Password Server.

Passwords can also be set via Kerberos, though. This means that Apple also had to supply a way for changes to be propagated from the Kerberos database to the Password Server. This was achieved through the addition of a *–passwordserver* flag to *kadmind*, the Kerberos administrative daemon. This enables *kadmind* to execute the *mkpassdb* command, updating Password Server passwords to match those in the KDC, as shown in Figure 8-9. Kerberos policies, however, are not replicated to the

Password Server database, minimizing the utility of the KDC's policy capabilities when deployed on Mac OS X Server.

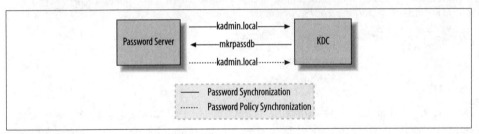

Figure 8-9. *Passwords enjoy a two-way synchronization between Password Server and the MIT KDC. Password policies, however, such as length requirements and expiration, are only synchronized from the Password Server to the KDC.*

## CHAPTER 9

Replication in Open Directory Server

Jaguar's Open Directory infrastructure, while viable for smaller organizations, suffered from one nearly debilitating flaw. The Open Directory Master itself was a single point of failure. And clients, upon that failure, had a very negative user experience. Simple things, like a Finder file listing or starting Terminal, could take two or three minutes, and the login process, which worked only for local users, could be excruciating. Clients were very tightly coupled to the directory services infrastructure, and that infrastructure consisted of a single server, subject to all of the hardware failures and network outages that implies. With Panther, however, Apple has introduced a stable and fault-tolerant replication infrastructure designed to meet the needs of a modern directory service. While not without flaws, it is a great step forward, and it deserves much of the credit for Panther's acceptance in increasingly critical Directory Service roles.

 Open Directory Replication also parallels a common trend in highly available systems, relying on application level clustering and numerous parallel hosts rather than the massively redundant single systems of the mainframe age.

This chapter examines that replication architecture, discusses the implications of the design choices that formed it, and describes best practices associated with its deployment.

Creating an Open Directory Replica

Creation of an Open Directory Replica is, on a fundamental level, very similar to creation of an Open Directory Master. The KDC is enabled, LDAP server started, and the Password Server reconfigured—all with the added complexity of ensuring these systems are synchronized. The underlying process is actually quite complex, and Apple has done a remarkable job of simplifying the actual act of configuration, which is, at a graphical level, nearly trivial.

Graphical Configuration

Graphical configuration of an Open Directory Replica is pursued in the Open Directory Settings interface of the Server Admin application. To create a replica, choose "Open Directory Replica" from the Role pull-down menu. The resulting dialog box (Figure 9-1) prompts for the location (IP address or hostname) of the Master, along with the *root* and *admin* passwords.

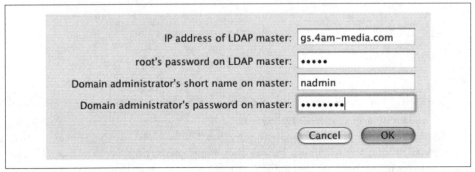

Figure 9-1. Configuring an Open Directory Replica using Server Admin.

Replication setup has several caveats that must be respected in order for the process to be successful:

- DNS: Replicas, like Masters, house a KDC. So (also like Masters) functioning forward and reverse DNS resolution is a requirement.

- SSH: The SSH protocol is heavily used in the Replica creation process—specifically SSH logins as *root* using password authentication. As a security measure, *root* SSH logins are often disallowed and password authentication is often disabled, favoring other authentication mechanisms, such as Kerberos (GSSAPI) or Identity Keypair. During the replica creation, root SSH logins using password authentication must be enabled.

- Serial Number: Open Directory Masters must have a serial number that differs from the Open Directory Replica. You should probably do this from a legal perspective too. Reusing serial numbers is not allowed by Apple's license agreement for Mac OS X Server.

The administrator you specify must be a Password Server administrator on the Master. Note that you must press the Save button (in the bottom righthand corner of Server Admin) to commit these changes.

The replication setup process should take a couple minutes for a small directory and much longer as the number of user, group, and computer accounts grows. At its conclusion, the Settings pane should reflect the server's new status. As with the Open Directory Master, all services in Server Admin's Open Directory status should be marked as running, as seen in Figure 9-2.

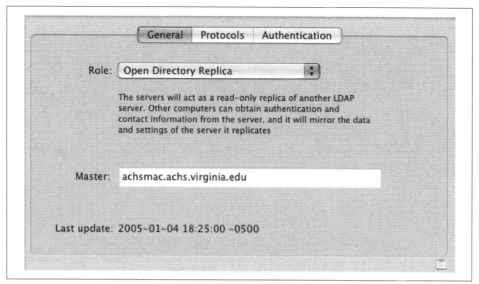

Figure 9-2. The General pane of the Settings section of Server Admin's Open Directory module following successful replica creation.

The Open Directory Master should also notice that it has a new replica, seen in the General tab of the Settings section of Server Admin's Open Directory module, seen in Figure 9-3.

The Replica Status is rarely anything but OK. A number of things can be going wrong—including severe and long-lived replication failures— and the status still says OK. The replica can be powered down for hours and it still shows up as OK. So don't hesitate to pursue further analysis if something doesn't seem right but Server Admin insists that it's OK.

Command-Line Configuration

The graphical configuration actually invokes *slapconfig*, the same underlying utility used to create Open Directory Masters. *slapconfig* itself, despite the underlying complexity of this process, is not difficult to use, and provides very good feedback concerning replica creation as shown in Example 9-1.

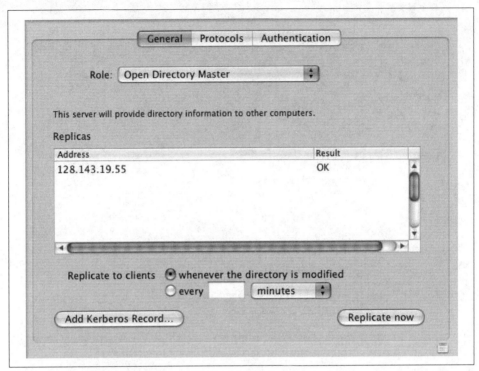

Figure 9-3. The Open Directory Master displays a list of replicas in the General pane of the Open Directory Settings section of Server Admin.

Example 9-1. slapconfig's replica creation process.

```
g5:~ ladmin$ sudo slapconfig -createreplica gs.4am-media.com nadmin
Root Password For Master LDAP Server:
nadmin's Password:
Warning: Permanently added 'gs.4am-media.com,207.224.49.180' (RSA) to the list of known
hosts.
nadmin's Password:
1 Destroying local LDAP server
You must have a network administrator's name & password to remove a KDC
from the directory
sso_util command output:
shutting down kadmind
kadmind shut down
shutting down kdc
kdc shut down
removing kdc database files
LDAP server is not running.
NeST command output:

2 Stopping master LDAP server
Warning: Permanently added 'gs.4am-media.com,207.224.49.180' (RSA) to the list of known
hosts.
3 Copying master database to new replica
```

Example 9-1. slapconfig's replica creation process. (continued)

```
4 Updating master configuration
5 Restarting master LDAP server
Starting LDAP server
6 Updating local replica configuration
7 Starting new replica
Starting LDAP server
8 Starting replicator on master server
Starting LDAP replicator
Configuring Kerberos server, realm is GS.4AM-MEDIA.COM
9 Enabling password server replication
NeST command output:


10 Enabling local Kerberos server
kdcsetup command output:
Contacting the Directory Server
Authenticating to the Directory Server
Creating Kerberos directory
Creating KDC Config File
<CFArray 0x300fe0 [0xa01900e0]>{type = immutable, count = 1, values = (
      0 : <CFDictionary 0x305e00 [0xa01900e0]>{type = mutable, count = 0, capacity = 4,
pairs = (
)}
)}
Adding KDC to watchdog
Adding the new KDC into the KerberosClient config record
Finished
sso_util command output:
DoConfigure: argc = 13
Creating the service list
Creating the service principals
WARNING: no policy specified for host/g5.4am-media.com@GS.4AM-MEDIA.COM; defaulting to no
policy
add_principal: Principal or policy already exists while creating "host/g5.4am-media.
com@GS.4AM-MEDIA.COM".
WARNING: no policy specified for smtp/g5.4am-media.com@GS.4AM-MEDIA.COM; defaulting to no
policy
add_principal: Principal or policy already exists while creating "smtp/g5.4am-media.
com@GS.4AM-MEDIA.COM".
WARNING: no policy specified for pop/g5.4am-media.com@GS.4AM-MEDIA.COM; defaulting to no
policy
add_principal: Principal or policy already exists while creating "pop/g5.4am-media.com@GS.
4AM-MEDIA.COM".
WARNING: no policy specified for imap/g5.4am-media.com@GS.4AM-MEDIA.COM; defaulting to no
policy
add_principal: Principal or policy already exists while creating "imap/g5.4am-media.
com@GS.4AM-MEDIA.COM".
WARNING: no policy specified for ftp/g5.4am-media.com@GS.4AM-MEDIA.COM; defaulting to no
policy
add_principal: Principal or policy already exists while creating "ftp/g5.4am-media.com@GS.
4AM-MEDIA.COM".
```

Example 9-1. slapconfig's replica creation process. (continued)

```
WARNING: no policy specified for afpserver/g5.4am-media.com@GS.4AM-MEDIA.COM; defaulting
to no policy
add_principal: Principal or policy already exists while creating "afpserver/g5.4am-media.
com@GS.4AM-MEDIA.COM".
Creating the keytab file
Configuring services
WriteSetupFile: setup file path = /temp.tPFF/setup
Mail config file at /etc/MailServicesOther.plist updated successfully
Mail config file at /etc/MailServicesOther.plist updated successfully
Mail config file at /etc/MailServicesOther.plist updated successfully
AFP config file at /Library/Preferences/com.apple.AppleFileServer.plist updated
successfully
Cleaning up
g5:~ ladmin$
```

Regardless of whether Server Admin is used or *slapconfig* is called directly, the Replica creation process leaves very good logs behind in */Library/Logs/slapconfig.log* (shown in Example 9-2). While not as complete as *slapconfig*'s output, it is an invaluable diagnostic tool.

Example 9-2. slapconfig's replica creation log.

```
2004-08-01 18:31:07 -0600 - slapconfig -createreplica
2004-08-01 18:31:20 -0600 - 1 Destroying local LDAP server
2004-08-01 18:31:20 -0600 - sso_util command output:
shutting down kadmind
kadmind shut down
shutting down kdc
kdc shut down
removing kdc database files
2004-08-01 18:32:20 -0600 - NeST command output:

2004-08-01 18:32:20 -0600 - 2 Stopping master LDAP server
2004-08-01 18:32:24 -0600 - 3 Copying master database to new replica
2004-08-01 18:32:38 -0600 - 4 Updating master configuration
2004-08-01 18:32:41 -0600 - 5 Restarting master LDAP server
2004-08-01 18:32:45 -0600 - 6 Updating local replica configuration
2004-08-01 18:32:45 -0600 - 7 Starting new replica
2004-08-01 18:32:47 -0600 - 8 Starting replicator on master server
2004-08-01 18:32:51 -0600 - Configuring Kerberos server, realm is GS.4AM-MEDIA.COM
2004-08-01 18:33:07 -0600 - 9 Enabling password server replication
2004-08-01 18:34:11 -0600 - NeST command output:

2004-08-01 18:34:11 -0600 - 10 Enabling local Kerberos server
2004-08-01 18:34:13 -0600 - kdcsetup command output:
Contacting the Directory Server
Authenticating to the Directory Server
Creating Kerberos directory
Creating KDC Config File
<CFArray 0x300fe0 [0xa01900e0]>{type = immutable, count = 1, values = (
```

Example 9-2. slapconfig's replica creation log. (continued)

```
        0 : <CFDictionary 0x305e00 [0xa01900e0]>{type = mutable, count = 0, capacity = 4,
pairs = (
)}
)}
Adding KDC to watchdog
Adding the new KDC into the KerberosClient config record
Finished
2004-08-01 18:34:14 -0600 - sso_util command output:
DoConfigure: argc = 13
Creating the service list
Creating the service principals
WARNING: no policy specified for host/g5.4am-media.com@GS.4AM-MEDIA.COM; defaulting to no
policy
add_principal: Principal or policy already exists while creating "host/g5.4am-media.
com@GS.4AM-MEDIA.COM".
WARNING: no policy specified for smtp/g5.4am-media.com@GS.4AM-MEDIA.COM; defaulting to no
policy
add_principal: Principal or policy already exists while creating "smtp/g5.4am-media.
com@GS.4AM-MEDIA.COM".
WARNING: no policy specified for pop/g5.4am-media.com@GS.4AM-MEDIA.COM; defaulting to no
policy
add_principal: Principal or policy already exists while creating "pop/g5.4am-media.com@GS.
4AM-MEDIA.COM".
WARNING: no policy specified for imap/g5.4am-media.com@GS.4AM-MEDIA.COM; defaulting to no
policy
add_principal: Principal or policy already exists while creating "imap/g5.4am-media.
com@GS.4AM-MEDIA.COM".
WARNING: no policy specified for ftp/g5.4am-media.com@GS.4AM-MEDIA.COM; defaulting to no
policy
add_principal: Principal or policy already exists while creating "ftp/g5.4am-media.com@GS.
4AM-MEDIA.COM".
WARNING: no policy specified for afpserver/g5.4am-media.com@GS.4AM-MEDIA.COM; defaulting
to no policy
add_principal: Principal or policy already exists while creating "afpserver/g5.4am-media.
com@GS.4AM-MEDIA.COM".
Creating the keytab file
Configuring services
WriteSetupFile: setup file path = /temp.tPFF/setup
Mail config file at /etc/MailServicesOther.plist updated successfully
Mail config file at /etc/MailServicesOther.plist updated successfully
Mail config file at /etc/MailServicesOther.plist updated successfully
AFP config file at /Library/Preferences/com.apple.AppleFileServer.plist updated
successfully
Cleaning up
```

Behind the Scenes: Dissecting Replica Creation

Replica creation, because it involves three services running on two hosts, operates on a very tight sequence of events.

1. An SSH connection is established (using the *ssh_command* utility in */System/ Library/ServerSetup*) to verify that the supplied *root* password is correct.

2. If an LDAP server or KDC is currently running on the prospective replica, they are destroyed. Note that an existing *keytab* file (*/etc/krb5.keytab*) must, as of 10.3.5, be removed or moved aside by hand.

3. Another SSH connection is established to the master, this time to stop the master's LDAP server using *SystemStarter*. LDAP data cannot be reliably copied if the LDAP server is running in read-write mode.

4. The Master's LDAP data is copied to the replica using the *scp* command. This includes both the actual LDAP database (*/var/db/openldap/openldap-data*) and the LDAP configuration files in */etc/openldap*.

5. The Master's LDAP configuration (*/etc/openldap/slapd_macosxserver.conf*) is updated to reflect its new replica. Specifically a *replicahost* directive, discussed later in this chapter, is added.

6. Another SSH connection is established in order to restart the Master's LDAP server.

7. The replica's LDAP configuration files are updated to reflect the fact that it is a replica. Its *rootdn* is changed to reflect the credentials stored in its *replicahost* entry on the Open Directory Master; in this way the Open Directory Master has full write access to its replica.

8. The LDAP server (*/usr/libexec/slapd*) is started on the replica.

9. The LDAP replication daemon (*/usr/libexec/slurpd*), if it is not already running, is started on the master.

10. Kerberos is configured on the replica. This process includes first copying over the entire contents of the master's Kerberos directory (*/var/db/krb5kdc*) and then running the *kdcsetup* command with its *c*, or clone option. *kdcsetup*, which is documented in more depth in Chapter 8, in turn calls *kdb5_util* to set up the new KDC.

11. The replica's single sign-on environment is configured using *sso_util*'s configure flag. This process is nearly identical to the single sign-on configuration of an Open Directory master, and is documented in more depth in Chapter 8.

12. The *mkpassdb* command (with the *-zoq -s n' -e n -n Replican''* syntax, specified in Table 9-1) is used to set up the replica's Password Server. Password Server replication is then begun. Local password server slots are replicated to the master; each replica is given a range of 500, starting a Password Server slots to support users in its local domain.

Table 9-1. mkpassdb options used to establish a Password Server replica. The –s and –z flags are not covered in mkpassdb's man page.

Flag	Description	Argument
–z	"Create a Replica"; nearly impossible to use interactively.	(Typically not seen.) This flag tells *mkpassdb* to prompt for the Password Server public and private keys, which during replica creation are supplied by the NeST utility.
–o	Overwrite the existing database.	
–q	Be less verbose.	
–e	Expand the database by *n* slots. Generally *n* increased by 500 for every pre-existing replica or master. So the third replica generally has an –e value of around *2000*.	*2000* (an integer)
–s	Start this replica's data at the *n*th slot, which is about 500 less than the –e argument, so each Replica gets around 500 slots for local use.	*1500* (an integer)
–n	The replica's name. Generally *Replica n ' '*, where *n ' '* is the number of replicas.	*Replica3*

The Replication Process

Once a replica is established, ongoing replication can proceed. This is not as simple as it sounds, since it actually involves the three distinct services that comprise Open Directory Server, each having to some extent a distinct replication process and architecture and each deserving a thorough treatment here. This matter is made more complex by the multimaster nature of Password Server replication and because Apple's KDC replication is closely tied to its Password Server–KDC synchronization process.

LDAP Replication

Replication is not defined in the LDAP standard, and various LDAP implementations, if they support replication at all, tend to differ somewhat in their approach. Open Directory Server, since it uses OpenLDAP, follows OpenLDAP's single-master model—a single writable master pushes updates out to its replicas using standard LDAP write operations. Replicas, in turn, are configured to accept updates from only that master.

The architecture behind this process is actually fairly straightforward. The Master's LDAP server records all changes that are made to it according to the replogfile entry in */etc/openldap/slapd_macosxserver.conf* file. In Mac OS X, this file is usually located at */var/db/openldap/openldap-slurp/replication.log*.

Don't expect to get a meaningful replication history from the replication log. It is maintained dynamically, and entries such as those seen here are expunged from the file as soon as *slurpd* processes them.

These changes are read by the *slurpd* replication daemon and written to its temporary buffer (*/var/run/openldap-slurp/replica/slurpd.replog*) and from there pushed out to replicas using the credentials (identity and password) recorded in the replica host entry of the previously mentioned *slapd_macosxserver.conf* (see Example 9-3).

The security-conscious among you will initially balk at the storage of sensitive credentials in clear text in a service's configuration file. This is required, however, since the credentials are used to authenticate to the replica.

Example 9-3. Using the grep command to view the replogfile and replicahost entries in slapd_macosxserver.conf. These entries are added as a part of the replica creation process. Note the specification of a SASL CRAM-MD5 authentication. This method prevents passage of clear-text LDAP credentials during the replication process.

```
g5:/ odadm$ sudo grep rep /etc/openldap/slapd_macosxserver.conf
replogfile      /var/db/openldap/openldap-slurp/replication.log
replica host=207.224.49.180:389 bindmethod=sasl credentials=updater846481064
saslmech=CRAM-MD5 authcId=updater1389711348
```

Corresponding entries exist on each replica, allowing the master to push out these changes. The credentials specified in the Master's replicahost setting are used as the rootdn entry in the replica in question. rootdn (shown in Example 9-4 and covered in more depth in Chapter 7), is basically an administrative LDAP identity with full control of the local database (and is not a system user account).

Example 9-4. Using the cat and grep commands to view the rootdn setting of an Open Directory Replica. The Replica's rootdn setting corresponds to the credentials listed in the Master's replicahost entry, allowing slurpd on the Master to push out LDAP changes to each replica.

```
gs:/ odadm$ sudo grep root /etc/openldap/slapd_macosxserver.conf
rootdn  uid=updater1389711348,cn=users,dc=4am-media,dc=com
rootpw  updater846481064
```

The frequency of these updates is controlled by the Master's replicationinterval setting, again located in */etc/openldap/slapd.conf*. This interval is set (along with Password Server's replication interval) in the General tab of Server Admin's Open Directory Settings section, partially pictured in Figure 9-4. These and other files used in the LDAP replication process are described in Table 9-2.

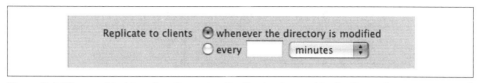

Figure 9-4. The graphical interface for setting Replication interval in the General settings section of the Master's Open Directory Server Admin module. Choosing "whenever Directory is modified" sets a replication interval of 3 seconds.

Table 9-2. Other key files in the OpenLDAP replication infrastructure. Like other files in /var/run, these are dynamic, and not preserved between boots.

File	Description
/var/run/openldap-slurp/replica/replica-status	File containing the last-modified date and status of each replica.
/var/run/openldap-slurp/replica/slurpd.replog	slurpd's buffer, where changes are stored until they can be written to replicas.
/var/run/openldap-slurp/10.1.1.3:389.rej	Host-specific rejection log; each replica has one. Changes written to this log are permanently discarded and must be reapplied manually in order to keep from being lost.

Password Server Replication

Password Server replication is, unlike LDAP replication, a multimaster operation. This means that changes to passwords and password policies can be made from any replica and will be written back to all other replicas, rather than having to go through a single master. The architecture is, again, fairly simple. All replicas talk to all other replicas, and in all cases, the most recent update wins. Because of this, the system time in any replication domain (or group of replicas) should probably be set using a time server. Allowing for time zone differences (as with many other Unix infrastructures, timestamps occur in GMT), replication will not occur if the system time is out of sync.

A list of Password Server replicas for a particular domain is stored in the */Config/ passwordserver* configuration record's `PasswordServerList`. This record (shown in Example 9-5) is used later to generate */var/db/authserver/authserverreplicas.local*, the client-side configuration file for Open Directory's Password Server plug-in.

Example 9-5. Using the dscl command to the passwordserver config record's PasswordServerList attribute in an Open Directory Master. Notice that each Password Server has two hex values specifying the beginning and ending PasswordServer IDs.

```
xs1:~ ladmin$ dscl /LDAPv3/127.0.0.1 -read /Config/passwordserver PasswordServerList
PasswordServerList: <?xml version="1.0" encoding="UTF-8"?>
<!DOCTYPE plist PUBLIC "-//Apple Computer//DTD PLIST 1.0//EN" "http://www.apple.com/DTDs/
PropertyList-1.0.dtd">
<plist version="1.0">
<dict>
        <key>ID</key>
```

```
            <string>DD553D7F76CAEC53976C313511C6C539</string>
            <key>Parent</key>
            <dict>
                    <key>DNS</key>
                    <string>10.1.0.1</string>
                    <key>IDRangeBegin</key>
                    <string>0x000000000000000000000000000000001</string>
                    <key>IDRangeEnd</key>
                    <string>0x0000000000000000000000000000001f5</string>
                    <key>IP</key>
                    <string>10.1.0.1</string>
            </dict>
            <key>Replicas</key>
            <array>
                    <dict>
                            <key>IDRangeBegin</key>
                            <string>0x00000000000000000000000000000209</string>
                            <key>IDRangeEnd</key>
                            <string>0x000000000000000000000000000003fd</string>
                            <key>IP</key>
                            <string>10.1.0.2</string>
                            <key>ReplicaName</key>
                            <string>Replica1</string>
                    </dict>
            </array>
            <key>Status</key>
            <string>AllowReplication</string>
</dict>
</plist>
```

Replication may occur either on a change (called *on dirty*, since the replicas are out of sync) or on a particular interval, specified in the graphical interface. Intervals less than 30 minutes result in *on dirty* behavior. The interval is global, applying to all replicas. This is to say that specific replicas may not be given individual intervals—a feature that might be useful when some, but not all, replicas live across slow or unreliable networks. It might be nice to have some replicas that were updated less frequently than others.

> Replication interval may, however, be set independently for Password Server (not affecting LDAP) using the *mkpassdb* command's *–setreplicationinterval* flag. Changes, though, are replicated throughout a replication group, and therefore applied to all replicas.

When replication does occur, it depends on the 1024-bit RSA key-pair shared by all Password Server replicas. The public key is used to propagate a session key specific to that particular exchange. When a replica comes online after some period of downtime, it attempts to contact every other replica in the domain. Each replica maintains a list of the most recent update it has received from every other replica (in /var/db/authserver/authserverreplicas), and accepts only updates, that post-date those in that list. Any update pre-empted by a more recent update is discarded. Password Server elements relating to replication are listed in Table 9-3.

Table 9-3. Password Server elements relating to replication.

File and Directory Records	Description
/Library/Logs/PasswordService/ApplePasswordServer.replication.log	Password Server replication log.
/var/db/authserver/authserverreplicas	List of Password Server Replicas, including slots assigned to them for local use.
/Config/passwordserver	Directory record used to configure Password Server clients.

Kerberos Replication

Kerberos, like LDAP, has no standardized method of replication; instead, most Kerberos distributions roll their mechanism. Since Apple leverages MIT's distribution, it might make sense to also leverage MIT's replication mechanism. This approach, though, ignores the relatively complex nature of that infrastructure, and instead, Apple has integrated Kerberos replication into Password Server's replication architecture. (You will recall from Chapter 8 that Password Server and the KDC synchronize with one another.)

When replication is initialized, the KDC data files are *scp*'d (secure copy, using SSH) from the Master over to the new replica (see Figure 9-5). Once replication begins, however, the local Password Server running on the replica simply updates the KDC using the *kadmin.local* command whenever it receives a password or policy change. This process is identical to the synchronization process on the master, detailed in Chapter 8. Where replica-side synchronization differs is in the area of Kerberos-initiated changes. On the master, such changes are written directly to the KDC and then propagated out to the Password Server according to *kadmind*'s *–passwordserver* flag. *kadmind*, however, runs only on the master; so replica-side changed using the *kadmin* or *kpasswd* protocols must first be sent to the master, rather than being implemented locally on the replica. The master then propagates these changes back out to its replicas using the Password Server protocol. This means that if the master is unavailable, changes using the Kerberos protocol may not be made.

Graphical Replication Management

When viewing an Open Directory Master's configuration using Server Admin, one obvious option is the "Replicate now" button, seen in Figure 9-6. It calls *slapconfig* with its *–replicatenow* option.

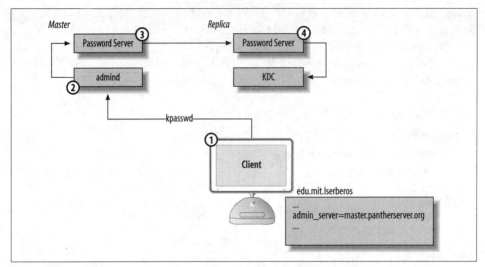

Figure 9-5. Replica-side changes using Kerberos are first sent to the kadmind process running on the Master, and then propagated out using password server.

Figure 9-6. The "replicate now" button, located in the General tab of Server Admin's Open Directory Settings section.

slapconfig, in turn, restarts the Master's LDAP server using the LDAP startup item. This action prompts the *slurpd* daemon to flush any queued changes to its replicas. Password Server replication is also triggered at this time.

Client-Side Replica Discovery

Replica discovery, like replication itself, actually takes place on three separate levels, separately for Password Server, LDAP, and Kerberos. On reboot, network change (including and unsleep operations) and logout *DirectoryService* daemon re-evaluates its list of replicas. In general, the first replica to respond wins, and that replica is strongly preferred until replicas are re-evaluated. The details, however, vary according to the protocol in question, and, in fact, it is entirely feasible that any one client might be using three different replicas for LDAP, Password Server, and Kerberos services.

LDAP Replica Discovery

LDAP replica discovery is a function of the client-side LDAPv3 Open Directory plug-in. Since it is open sourced as a part of the Darwin project, its behavior is rather easy to divine. On replica evaluation, it tries to contact every replica listed in its configuration file (*/Library/Preferences/DirectoryService/DSLDAPv3PlugInConfig.plist*) in the Replica Hostname key, as shown in Example 9-6.

Example 9-6. The Replica Hostname key from the LDAPv3 Open Directory Plug-in's configuration file. Any write operations are transparently redirected to the host listed in the Writeable Hostname List key.

```
<key>Replica Hostname List</key>
    <array>
        <string>10.1.0.2</string>
        <string>192.168.1.3</string>
        <string>10.1.3.2</string>
    </array>
```

Specifically, the hosts are contacted (using an LDAP bind operation) sequentially, with a delay of only a few milliseconds between each query. If none respond, each is queried again, this time with a slightly longer delay. If no replicas respond, the search is abandoned. Once a replica is chosen, the plug-in is rather stubborn about choosing another one, and tries to contact an unavailable replica for a relatively long time, resulting in brief hangs in some applications. The actual duration of this timeout—the attempt to contact an established replica that has become unavailable—varies, and is basically 1m15s + the timeout specified in the Connection Times Out field of the LDAPv3 plug-in. In the rare event that the established replica is available but unreachable via LDAP (perhaps due to a crash of that service), the transition to a new replica is, ironically, much faster, and takes about a half second.

 Unless there is signifigant network latency between an Open Directory Master and its clients, LDAP replicas will almost never be used under normal circumstances. This is because replicas are always queried in the same order (according to the Replica Hostname List) and the Master is always first. In order to prevent this behavior, some sites employ firewall rules, limiting LDAP connections to relevant subnets and forcing clients to use particular replicas.

Write operations, such as when a user changes their authentication hint or when an administrator modifies a user's mail record, are transparently redirected using the *DirectoryService* Proxy protocol to the master (which is specified by a Writable Hostname key in *DSLDAPv3PluginConfig.plist*). LDAP referrals were not used because their credentials handling was not considered robust enough.

Password Server Replica Discovery

Open Directory's client-side Password Server plug-in is, like its LDAPv3 counterpart, an open source component. Although its lack of a graphical configuration element in the Directory Access application makes it a lesser-known entity, it is similarly easy to analyze. On replica evaluation, the Password Server plug-in, like its LDAPv3 counterpart, attempts to contact every password server listed in a configuration file (*/var/db/authserver/authserverreplicas.local*) that is, like that of the LDAPv3 plug-in, constructed from data in the directory.

 During the course of replica discovery, the Password Server client-side plug-in queries each replica literally with the string "What do you know?" Available replicas respond with "How was your weekend?"

Password Server replicas are contacted in sequence, with a delay of only a few milliseconds between each attempt (which takes place initially using UDP, in Panther using the *apple-sasl* port). The first server to respond is used, but (unlike an LDAPv3 Replica) is not cached. A new Password Server replica might be chosen for every authentication operation.

Kerberos Replica Discovery

Kerberos replica (KDC) discovery, unlike its Password Server and LDAPv3 counterparts, is not implemented in an Open Directory plug-in. It is, instead, a part of the Kerberos distribution that MIT partners with Apple to develop. KDCs are contacted in the order they are listed in the Kerberos configuration file (*edu.mit.Kerberos*, which is usually, but not always, in */Library/Preferences* or */etc/krb.conf*). KDC are contacted virtually simultaneously, and the first one to respond is used for that authentication operation. As with the Password Server plug-in, KDC choice is not cached, and the KDC list is re-evaluated for each Kerberos operation.

Replication Best Practices

Open Directory replication in Mac OS X server is a seamless and relatively straightforward process that adds a lot of value to Apple's Directory Services platform. It is, however, focused architecturally on deployments that are much smaller than those in which we find it deployed in the real world. In general, it is best to keep each replica as close to the clients it is meant to service as is feasible. Directory Services are important, network links often unreliable, and clients very unhappy when their directory server cannot be located. It is important, though, (and difficult) to balance the need for redundancy with budget constraints and the overall scalability of the architecture.

How Many Replicas?

The question of replica sizing is probably the most commonly asked in replica deployment. Not surprisingly, the answer tends to be "It Depends." In general, each site in an organization should have $n+1$ replicas; n being the number of replicas required to support the site in question.

 "Site" (in this case) can be defined as "a group of hosts that share a relatively fast connection," such as a school or remote office. Multiple sites, in this usage, are connected by relatively slow links, such as leased lines, T1s or microwave connections.

The troublesome fact is that n will vary tremendously from site to site, organization to organization, and according to the type of organization (a K–12 district on a semester schedule looks very different from a resource utilization standpoint than one on a block schedule). Both, in turn, differ tremendously from the usage seen in a publishing firm, yet all are core Apple constituencies). An Open Directory LDAP server will support an absolute maximum of around 1,000 connections (as of 10.3.4; previous to that the number was 255). Not every directory-bound client, however, will have an ongoing LDAP connection, since idle connections are, in a default installation, dropped after five minutes of inactivity.

Also note that several LDAP queries might take place in a multiplexed fashion across a single LDAP connection, resulting in a tremendously varied server load, depending on the type of data being queried. Managed client XML attributes, for instance, are extremely large when compared with the traditional elements of a user record.

The truth is that a typical site might be supported by a single directory server. Under ideal circumstances every site would have at least one Replica and one Master. Very large deployments, more and more common as Apple's visibility increases, are certainly an exception, and may require multiple replicas to handle their base load, before any redundancy comes into play.

IP Services

IP services can be generally classified as the basic services on which other services depend. They provide the infrastructure and foundation needed to support client configuration and basic network connectivity, and without them the network would be a much less friendly (and in some cases useless) place. This part of the book examines Apple's DNS, DHCP, and NAT services along with *xinetd*, which serves as a server-side infrastructure responsible for maintaining and running several of these services.

Whether Mac OS X Server is the center of your network or must integrate with an existing heterogeneous environment, its implementation is vital to a successful deployment. This section examines administration best practices along with the daemons and configuration mechanisms that work together to ensure consistency and stability of these fundamental services.

Chapters in this part of the book include:

xinetd

Early in Unix history, hardware resources were expensive: so expensive, in fact, that several users typically shared one really big piece of hardware. So expensive that every single process running on that hardware was audited meticulously, so that no extraneous processes took up system resources. Out of this conservation-focused environment, *inetd*, *xinetd*'s precursor, was born. The large, shared computing environments of the time typically supported several network services: *finger*, *telnet*, *ftp*, and *rlogin*, among others. Rather than having to keep all of these daemons running all of the time, *inetd* would listen on the service's port and then start the appropriate daemon when connections were established, thus conserving resources and managing access to the system.

inetd served the Unix world well; it was a central point through which connections to the system were established. And it made sense in a time of increasing security concerns to add some basic support for access controls into the infrastructure, and over time, as hardware resources became cheaper, this became *inetd*'s central role—providing security for the services it managed.

This evolution eventually produced *xinetd*, a completely rewritten facility that, like *inetd*, managed a set of services in the OS. Unlike *inetd* though, *xinetd* is specifically architected with security in mind. It plays an increasing role in Panther Server as well as Panther client, and like much of the OS, supports a deep set of features that can easily be leveraged by system administrators.

Configuration

Since *xinetd* is actually a structural element in Mac OS X Server (it provides a foundation other services make use of) it's not readily configurable in any centralized graphical interface. Instead, its configuration is mostly accomplished using the interfaces for enabling and disabling specific services that it's responsible for. When you turn on FTP in Server Admin, it's ultimately modifying *xinetd*'s configuration.

The days when *inetd* was responsible for nearly *every* connection to a system are largely over. In 10.3.2, Mac OS X Server uses *xinetd* only for *ftp*, *bootps* (DHCP and NetBoot), *tftp*, and *ssh*.

One exception is the command-line utility *service*. Located at */sbin/service*, it is actually a shell script that manages *xinetd*'s configuration files. Outside of its utility for managing *xinetd*, it's also a well-written example of a shell script that manages text files. The syntax for its intended purpose is fairly simple:

```
service service [--list stop start]
```

For instance, to start FTP, use the following command:

```
[ace2:~] nadmin% sudo service ftp start
```

Or, to list all services (notice that this doesn't require *root* privileges):

```
[ace2:~] nadmin% service --list
auth
bootps
chargen
chargen-udp
comsat
daytime
daytime-udp
echo
echo-udp
exec
finger
ftp
ftp.darwin
login
ntalk
shell
telnet
tftp
time
time-udp
```

service is the only way (short of manually editing the configuration files and restarting *xinetd*) to start several services that Apple does not support in the graphical interface. Note, however, that most of these services (such as *telnet*) are unsupported for security reasons, and generally should not be used.

Architecture

xinetd itself lives in */usr/sbin*, and it's started at boot time by the IPServices startup item:

```
##
    # Internet super-server.
    ##
```

```
ConsoleMessage "Starting internet services"
xinetd -inetd_compat -pidfile /var/run/xinetd.pid
```

In keeping with *inetd*'s resource-conservative nature, *xinetd* exits if it does not find any enabled services. When an *xinetd*-enabled service is started, Apple's configuration tools (based on *service*) are smart enough to start *xinetd* if it is not running already.

In a default configuration, *xinetd* is started with two flags: *–inetd_compat* and *–pidfile*. The former specifies that *inetd*'s configuration file (*/etc/inetd.conf*) should be read in addition to *xinetd*'s. As the option implies, this is for the sake of compatibility, since many administrators are accustomed to editing *inetd.conf* to enable services. The latter—a common option for many daemons—writes *xinetd*'s numerical process ID to the specified file, */var/run/xinetd.pid*. Some other useful options are specified in Table 10-1.

Table 10-1. Useful startup options for xinetd. For other less-common options, see the xinetd manpage.

Flag	Option	Description
–d	debug	Used to run *xinetd* in debug mode. Typically called from a command prompt rather than the startup script, the –*d* flag is useful in troubleshooting.
–stayalive		Changes *xinetd*'s default behavior, so rather than exiting if no services are enabled, it stays running.

xinetd's configuration file (*/etc/xinetd.conf*) establishes some defaults, and then specifies */etc/xinetd.d* as an *includedir* (a directory in which every file is included into the daemon's configuration). By convention, each file in *xinetd*'s *includedir* contains the configuration for a different service, as shown in Example 10-1.

Example 10-1. The /etc/xinted.d directory contains a separate file for each service xinetd manages. Note that in Mac OS X Server, some of these services are not typically managed by xinetd.

```
mab9718:~ mbartosh$ ls /etc/xinetd.d/
auth          daytime-udp    ftp        smb-direct    time
bootps        echo           login      smbd          time-udp
chargen       echo-udp       nmbd       ssh
chargen-udp   eppc           ntalk      swat
comsat        exec           printer    telnet
daytime       finger         shell      tftp
```

The granularity of this configuration mechanism allows each service to have very different settings. This is really the heart of *xinetd*—its rich set of per-service configuration options. We'll use SSH in Example 10-2, and then later examine some advanced options that can be applied to any of the services.

Example 10-2. The /etc/xinetd.d/ssh file contains xinted's ssh configuration.

```
mab9718:~ mbartosh$ cat /etc/xinetd.d/ssh
service ssh
{
        disable = no
        socket_type     = stream
        wait            = no
        user            = root
        server          = /usr/libexec/sshd-keygen-wrapper
        server_args     = -i
        groups          = yes
        flags           = REUSE IPv6
        session_create  = yes
}
```

- The most important directive is the `disable=no` flag. This apparent double negative indicates that the service should be enabled, and that *xinetd* should listen on the service's port (the port associated with the service listed in the service flag). What this basically means is that SSH is turned on—this is the default configuration for Mac OS X Server.

- `socket_type` specifies what kind of connection is required for the service (`dgram` and `stream` are the most common; the former implies UDP, or stateless connections; the latter, stateful, persistent protocols), and user indicates what user ID the server runs as. Because *xinetd* runs as *root*, it can force a process to run as any other user.

- `wait` generally has a value of yes for single-threaded services, which means that *xinetd* will start the server, and the server will then stop handling requests until the server stops or dies. A wait value of no indicates that the server is multi-threaded. In this case, *xinted* continues to handle requests. Generally, a `socket_type` of `dgram` has a `wait=yes` value, while stream `socket_types` have a `wait=no` value.

- The server directive specifies that the process will be executed when an SSH connection is received. Generally, this is the server daemon—but SSH makes a good example since it provides an exception to this tendency. Instead of launching *sshd*, *xinetd* executes the */usr/libexec/sshd-keygen-wrapper* shell script, shown in Example 10-3.

Example 10-3. The $@ is a built-in bash variable that stands for "all arguments passed to this script."

```
#!/bin/sh
[ ! -f /etc/ssh_host_key ]     && ssh-keygen -q -t rsa1 -f /etc/ssh_host_key      -N "" -C
""
[ ! -f /etc/ssh_host_rsa_key ] && ssh-keygen -q -t rsa  -f /etc/ssh_host_rsa_key -N "" -C
""
[ ! -f /etc/ssh_host_dsa_key ] && ssh-keygen -q -t dsa  -f /etc/ssh_host_dsa_key -N "" -C
""

exec /usr/sbin/sshd $@
```

That script, in turn, checks for the existence of various host keys (which are required for *sshd*'s public key cryptography), creating them if they're not available, and then executing *sshd*, passing any arguments to it that were passed to the *sshd-keygen-wrapper* script.

 In Jaguar, *sshd* is started by its own startup item according to the SSHSERVER flag in */etc/hostconfig*.

Obviously, though, *xinetd*'s SSH configuration file includes a number of other directives, and *xinetd* is capable of many more that Apple does not currently leverage. These per-service options relate to everything from security and denial of service concerns to basic TCP/IP connectivity. In keeping with previous convention, we won't list every single option here; the manpage does a good job of that. Instead we'll highlight particularly useful directives, talking a little about their practical application.

General

The following are general options for use with *xinetd*:

id

> Used to differentiate the server; useful when more than one server might provide a particular service, or when a server supplies more than one protocol. By default, *id* is the same as the service name.

env

> The *env* operator lets the administrator specify values that should be added to the shell environment before a process is executed. Some services use environment variable to keep track of specific settings. This option is for them.

passenv

> Similar to *env*, the arguments to *passenv* are added to the shell environment of the service in question before it starts. Rather than being specified in the configuration file, however, these values are instead passed from *xinted*'s environment.

port

> If a service's port can't be located in */etc/services* (based on its *service* operator) it must be specified in the *port* directive.

redirect

> Sends the connection to another host. Useful when the server is not visible to clients initiating the connection; for instance, on a NAT network. The syntax is: redirect = (*IP* or *hostname*) (*port*). For example:
>
> ```
> redirect = 192.168.1.1 10143
> ```

bind/interface

These two synonyms specify an interface for the service to bind to. Useful when a service should be available on one physical network—perhaps a trusted, private link—but not another. *xinetd*'s default behavior is to listen on all interfaces.

banner

The filesystem path to the file that's always printed upon an attempted connection. Often used for legal reasons to specifically state who should and should not be attempting to contact a particular service.

banner_success

The filesystem path to the file that contains the text sent to a remote host (the manpage uses the technical term "splat" to describe this transaction) upon successful login. Often used for legal reasons to specify acceptable behavior once access to a service is confirmed.

banner_fail

The filesystem path to the file that contains the text sent to a remote host upon unsuccessful connection attempts.

groups

Controls group access rights of the service. Must be set to "yes" on Mac OS X Server and many other BSD systems.

server_args

Determines which arguments are sent to the server. For instance, if your FTP server accepts a *–k* flag (to force Kerberos authentication), you could specify the following in its *xinetd* configuration file in order to pass that flag to it on startup:

```
server_args       = -k
```

log_on_success

Specifies what data is logged when a service is successfully started and once that service has exited and its session. This can be very useful for trend analysis. Be careful, though—on a busy server, logs can grow quickly. *log_on_success* is controlled using several variables, specified in Table 10-2.

Table 10-2. Variables used to control the data xinetd logs.

Option	Description
PID	Process ID of server spawned by *xinetd*
HOST	The address of the remote host initiating the connection
USERID	The user ID of the remote user
EXIT	Logs the exit status of the server spawned by *xinetd*
DURATION	The duration of the session
TRAFFIC	The total traffic in bytes; only applicable to redirected services

protocol

The network protocol (as specified in */etc/services*) supplied by the service.

umask

Sets inherited Umask for the service (in standard octal form). This determines the permissions given to files created by the services.

Mac OS X Specific

The following options for *xinetd* are Mac OS X specific:

mdns

Disables or enables registration of a service with Multicast DNS (the naming protocol behind Rendezvous).

session_create

If set to *yes*, xinetd uses the Security Framework to created a new *mach_init* context for each new connection it spawns. This prevents users from using *mach_init*'s automatic startup capabilities to hijack other system services.

Security Related

The following options for *xinetd* are security-related:

log_on_failure

Determines what information is logged when a server for some reason can not start. This is typically due to an authorization failure but might also occur if the server is under too heavy a load to service the request. *log_on_failure* uses a set of variables (described in Table 10-3) to standardize this logging.

Table 10-3. Variables used with xinetd's log_on_failure directive to determine which data should be logged when a service is unable to start.

Value	Description
HOST	Address of the remote host.
USERID	The id of the remote user.[a]
ATTEMPT	Logs the fact that an attempt to connect occurred. ATTEMPT is implied by any other.

[a] Logs the user ID of the remote user, using the RFC 1413 identification protocol.

only_from

Specifies which hosts or networks should be allowed to access a specific service. The syntax to specify hosts can get very complex. At a basic level, hostnames along with numeric IP's may be specified, including CIDR notated networks.

no_access

A black list. These hosts or networks may never access the specified service. *no_access* uses the same syntax for specifying hosts that *only_from* uses.

access_times

Determines what time a particular resource may be accessed. The time is specified with the form hour:min-hour:min. For instance to allow access to a service from 8 am to 5 pm, a value of 8:00-17:00 would be indicated.

instances

Specifies the maximum instances of the service. IP address. Takes any integer or the string UNLIMITED as an argument.

nice

Sets the priority with which the service will run. The range of the value is from -20 to 20. Lower values mean that the service will have a higher priority access to CPU resources.

per_source

A more granular version of the instances option, *per_source* specifies the maximum instances of the service per client IP address. Like *instances*, *per_source* takes any integer or the string UNLIMITED as an argument.

cps

Limits the rate of incoming connections. Requires two arguments—the first is the maximum number of connections per second. Connections in excess of this will be denied. The second is the number of seconds to wait before re-enabling the service.

## CHAPTER 11

DNS

A case could be made for nomination of DNS as the most taken for granted service in a modern network. Without it, the Internet is effectively "broken," as many hapless tech support veterans will gladly tell you. Email, web browsing, streaming video and the iTunes Music Store are all dead in the water without the ability to translate cryptic IP addresses to more palatable hostnames, and the irony is that the vast majority of Internet end users have no idea what it is.

Directory Services adds another suite of functionality that is effectively useless without name resolution—both Microsoft's Active Directory and Apple's Open Directory rely on healthy DNS records. Even more important are the concepts of accuracy, and DNS security; a lack of DNS is actually preferable to bad DNS, which could result in submittal of credit card numbers or other valuable data into sites that are not legitimate.

 The first question to ask yourself, though, is "Do I really need to run my own DNS server?" Many ISPs provide DNS services for their customers, and Apple's tools are not easy or full-featured enough to really insulate the administrator from DNS's complexity. Unless you have a deep background in DNS administration, it's best to let someone more qualified handle it.

Mac OS X employs the BIND (Berkeley Internet Name Domain) package for DNS services. Probably the widest distributed DNS package in existence, BIND can be complex to maintain. This chapter provides an adequate treatment of BIND's underlying configuration in addition to its analysis of Apple's graphical DNS management tools. It also seeks to provide conceptual advice regarding certain BIND configuration options.

Graphical Interface

The irony is that (as important as DNS has always been) until Panther, Mac OS X Server had effectively no graphical DNS management utility. Although you could turn the DNS Server on and off without use of the command line, you couldn't set up zones, add host records, or change any configuration options without use of a text editor. Panther goes one step further, providing a graphical interface for the editing of DNS configuration files. Examine this statement carefully. Panther does not deliver an intuitive, easy method for configuring DNS. The user is still required to know a good bit about DNS. As a BIND veteran of six years, I had to manually configure the *named* configuration file and manually create a zone before I really understood what Apple expected in its graphical options.

 named is the actual DNS server employed by the BIND package.

Like other services, DNS is configuration accessible in Server Admin's list of services. Like other services, it initially offers an overview listing the service's status, the number of zones currently hosted on the server, and some other data. This interface is seen in Figure 11-1.

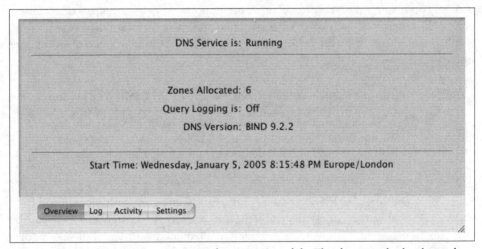

DNS Service is: Running

Zones Allocated: 6
Query Logging is: Off
DNS Version: BIND 9.2.2

Start Time: Wednesday, January 5, 2005 8:15:48 PM Europe/London

Overview Log Activity Settings

Figure 11-1. The overview pane in Server Admin's DNS module. This data can also be obtained with the serveradmin command's status dns and fullstatus dns arguments.

Also available are DNS logs and a summary of current activity, seen in Figures 11-2 and 11-3.

```
Jan 05 20:41:46.307 zone 0.1.10.in-addr.a/IN: journal rollforward completed successfully: no journal
Jan 05 20:41:46.567 zone 0.1.10.in-addr.a/IN: loaded serial 2005010501
Jan 05 20:41:46.568 zone_timer: zone 0.1.10.in-addr.a/IN: enter
Jan 05 20:41:46.568 zone_maintenance: zone 0.1.10.in-addr.a/IN: enter
Jan 05 20:41:46.568 zone_timer: zone mabaleb.org/IN: enter
Jan 05 20:41:46.568 zone_maintenance: zone mabaleb.org/IN: enter
Jan 05 20:41:46.568 zone_timer: zone version.bind/CH: enter
Jan 05 20:41:46.568 zone_maintenance: zone version.bind/CH: enter
Jan 05 20:41:46.569 zone_loaddone: zone 0.0.127.in-addr.arpa/IN: enter
Jan 05 20:41:46.569 zone 0.0.127.in-addr.arpa/IN: loaded
Jan 05 20:41:46.569 zone 0.0.127.in-addr.arpa/IN: journal rollforward completed successfully: no journal
Jan 05 20:41:46.569 zone 0.0.127.in-addr.arpa/IN: loaded serial 2005010502
Jan 05 20:41:46.569 zone_timer: zone authors.bind/CH: enter
Jan 05 20:41:46.569 zone_maintenance: zone authors.bind/CH: enter
Jan 05 20:41:46.569 zone_loaddone: zone 4am-media.com/IN: enter
Jan 05 20:41:46.570 zone 4am-media.com/IN: loaded
Jan 05 20:41:46.570 zone 4am-media.com/IN: journal rollforward completed successfully: no journal
Jan 05 20:41:46.570 zone 4am-media.com/IN: loaded serial 2005010501
Jan 05 20:41:46.570 zone_timer: zone 4am-media.com/IN: enter
Jan 05 20:41:46.570 zone_maintenance: zone 4am-media.com/IN: enter
Jan 05 20:41:46.570 zone_timer: zone 0.0.127.in-addr.arpa/IN: enter
Jan 05 20:41:46.570 zone_maintenance: zone 0.0.127.in-addr.arpa/IN: enter
Jan 05 20:41:46.571 zone_loaddone: zone localhost/IN: enter
Jan 05 20:41:46.571 zone localhost/IN: loaded
Jan 05 20:41:46.571 zone localhost/IN: journal rollforward completed successfully: no journal
Jan 05 20:41:46.571 zone localhost/IN: loaded serial 44
Jan 05 20:41:46.572 zone_loaddone: zone pantherserver.org/IN: enter
Jan 05 20:41:46.572 zone pantherserver.org/IN: loaded
Jan 05 20:41:46.572 zone pantherserver.org/IN: journal rollforward completed successfully: no journal
Jan 05 20:41:46.572 zone pantherserver.org/IN: loaded serial 2005010501
Jan 05 20:41:46.572 zone_timer: zone localhost/IN: enter
Jan 05 20:41:46.572 zone_maintenance: zone localhost/IN: enter
Jan 05 20:41:46.572 zone_timer: zone pantherserver.org/IN: enter
Jan 05 20:41:46.572 zone_maintenance: zone pantherserver.org/IN: enter
Jan 05 20:41:46.572 zone pantherserver.org/IN: sending notifies (serial 2005010501)
Jan 05 20:41:47.659 received control channel command 'status'
Jan 05 20:41:49.712 received control channel command 'stats'
Jan 05 20:41:52.716 received control channel command 'status'
```

```
Overview   Log   Activity   Settings
```

Figure 11-2. Using Server Admin to examine DNS logs, which are located at a path specified in the Settings panes, discussed later in this chapter.

The logging data is gathered from the file specified in the logging section of the DNS Settings tab, while the data in the Activity pane comes from the output of the *rndc* command. The same data can be gathered directly with the following syntax:

```
xserver:~ nadmin$ sudo rndc -s 127.0.0.1 -p 54 status
number of zones: 4
debug level: 0
xfers running: 0
xfers deferred: 0
soa queries in progress: 0
query logging is OFF
server is up and running
```

or parsed from the rather verbose output of *serveradmin*'s *dns fullstatus* query.

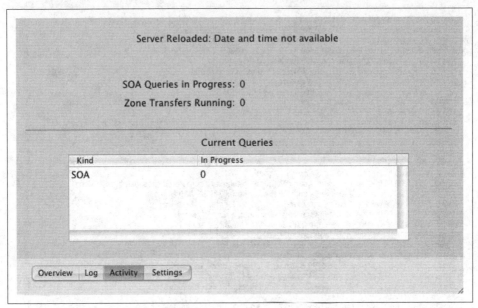

Server Reloaded: Date and time not available

SOA Queries in Progress: 0
Zone Transfers Running: 0

Current Queries

Kind	In Progress
SOA	0

Overview   Log   **Activity**   Settings

Figure 11-3. The Activity pane of Server Admin's DNS module provides data about current DNS queries. Since DNS connections are short-lived, your server has to be pretty busy before much shows up here.

 Ironically, as of 10.3.2, logged data is still dispatched to *syslog*, despite a default setting pointing it to */Library/Logs/named.log*. A DNS setting (any setting; we generally change the log level) must be toggled and then saved before the destination file is created, used, and displayed in Server Admin.

All graphical configuration of DNS is accomplished via the Settings tab of Server Admin's DNS plug-in. It exposes enough of a subset of BIND's functionality to be useful in most basic configurations. The General tab, illustrated in Figure 11-4, deals transfers and recursion, two important facets of DNS security.

Enabling the "Allow: Zone transfers" checkbox (its default state) permits other machines to query zones hosted on your DNS server for a complete list of hosts. This setting is generally very bad, since it allows malicious parties to enumerate every machine in your domain. Generally, zone transfers should be restricted to backup DNS servers, and DNS-sec should be used to verify their identity cryptographically. Some of these precautions are covered in "Advanced Configuration," later in this chapter, and are not configurable in the graphical interface.

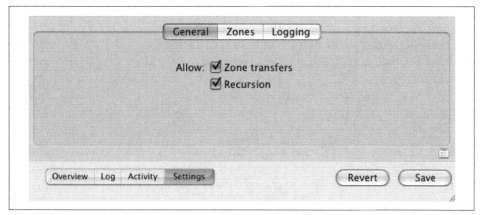

Figure 11-4. A few minimal options are available to the DNS server in the General pane of Server Admin's DNS module.

 If you don't have a backup DNS server, zone transfers should not be not allowed at all.

Turning on recursion (another default configuration) allows *named* to consult the DNS hierarchy for queries it is not authoritative for—generally meaning for zones not hosted on the server. This setting is essentially required if you want to act as a DNS server for a LAN.

 The previous sentence is not strictly the truth. If there is another DNS server that you have access to, you can set yours up to proxy queries towards it with a *forwarders* statement in the global section of your DNS server's configuration file (*/etc/named.conf*, described later in this chapter). Your server essentially forwards any queries it isn't authorized for to the specified server. The forwarder, though, must have recursion turned on. There is no way to set up a global forwarder in the graphical interface, so this falls under the increasingly large "Advanced Configuration" heading later in this chapter.

It is also considered a security risk to recursion in some cases. The first and most likely is that it exposes the server to a feasible denial-of-service attack. In essence, DNS clients are sending your server off on a task, and it is possible that answering a high number of complex DNS queries could either exhaust system resources or result in a failure condition for *named*. The second concern relates to the fairly frequent rate of BIND vulnerabilities that can result in (among other things) DNS cache poisoning. In some circumstances, certain versions of BIND, when sent to resolve a recursive query, can accept data from a server that is not authoritative for a particular domain.

This at first sounds innocuous, but bear in mind the implications if someone is able to supply the wrong address for *www.mybank.com*, or an online retailer, or any one of several high-volume financial entities on the Internet—PayPal comes to mind. These vulnerabilities are patched fairly quickly, and Apple does an OK job of getting patched software into Security Updates. However, it's generally a good idea to disable recursion if you don't need it, or to limit it to trusted clients. This limitation cannot be achieved graphically, and is covered in "Advanced Configuration" later this chapter.

A significant annoyance in Jaguar's DNS implementation related to log data. Rather verbose in a default configuration, it was all sent to *syslog*, resulting in frequent log entries. Although it was feasible to change *named*'s logging behavior, it could not be accomplished in the GUI. Panther greatly improves on this behavior. Covered briefly earlier in the chapter, the Logging tab (Figure 11-5) dictates where *named*'s logging data should be stored, and which log data should be displayed.

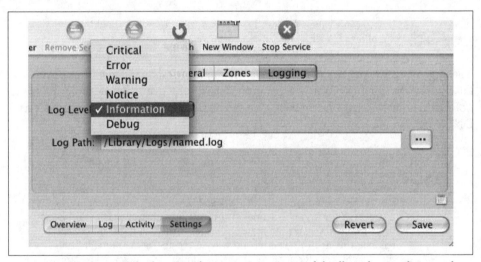

Figure 11-5. The logging tab of Server Admin's DNS Settings module allows for specification of DNS log location and level.

You might recognize from Chapters 4 or 5 that Critical, Error, Warning, Notice, Information, and Debug are standard *syslog* log levels. Despite the graphical interface, all logging data in a default configuration is sent to *syslog*, just like it was in Jaguar. By modifying and then saving any of these values, however, it can be sent elsewhere and its verbosity can be reduced, saving hard disk space and time spent pursuing the logs.

The Zones tab, illustrated in Figure 11-6, is where the real work of Server Admin's DNS interface occurs. Here zones are created and managed, hosts are associated with IP addresses, and an acceptable amount of chaos reigns, due to the slightly awkward interface.

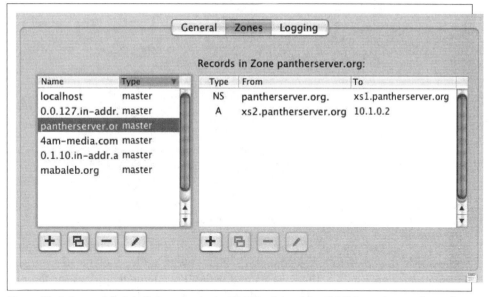

Figure 11-6. Server Admin's Zones pane in the DNS module—Mac OS X Server's central interface for editing DNS data.

The left pane lists zones hosted on the server. The right pane changes contextually, displaying the host data in the selected zone. Vague icons at the bottom of each window hint at (but are not explicit about) what might be accomplished if they are accessed. This is not an interface designed to ease DNS administration. Unless you already know what @ means in the context of DNS—much less what NS, PTR, and *in-addr.arpa* signify—it's not going to help you much. What it does accomplish, though, is to hide the complex syntax of the actual DNS configuration files, which can be very picky about the placement of brackets and semicolons. While I'd like to see a more complete solution, this is in itself fairly helpful.

 You probably get the idea that I'm not the biggest fan of this interface. It disturbs me when administration is easier in Windows 2000 than it is on Mac OS X Server.

The plus (+) button, or *add*, adds an appropriate object to either pane; a zone on the left, and a host on the right. Adding a zone produces yet another dialog that is extremely vague and, unless you are very seasoned in the management of DNS, quite counterintuitive. In order to alleviate this confusion, I've provided accurate examples in Figure 11-7.

Zone Name refers specifically to the namespace of the zone you are creating. This is intuitive enough for forward zones, which map IP addresses to names. As illustrated in Figure 11-7, the Zone Name for *example.com* is, of all things, *example.com*. For

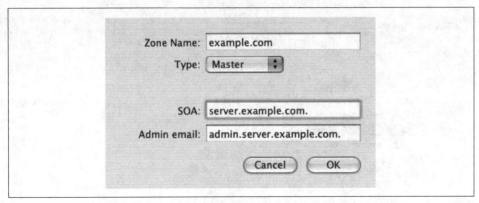

Zone Name:	example.com
Type:	Master
SOA:	server.example.com.
Admin email:	admin.server.example.com.

Cancel   OK

Figure 11-7. Unlike most of Apple's well-crafted interfaces, Server Admin's DNS settings provide no examples of which data should be entered into each field.

reverse zones, which map IP addresses to DNS names, it is quite complex, consisting of the suffix *in-addr.arpa* prepended with the network address of the IP range *in reverse order*. For instance, the zone name for the IP to name mappings for the private address range *192.168.1.1/24* would be *1.168.192.in-addr.arpa*.

> Almost every other interface for management of DNS autogenerates the consistent but confusing name for a reverse zone. For that matter, most DNS management tools make a much more clear differentiation between forward and reverse zones, and make sane assumptions for the user when one or the other is specified.

The Type pull-down menu is actually quite powerful, as it contextually controls the rest of the zone creation interface and differentiates among three types of zones. It has three choices: Master, Slave, and Forward. The Master selection, illustrated in Figure 11-7, also prompts for other data. Since the master bears ultimate responsibility for a DNS namespace or IP range, it must contain the most complete data. Neither forward nor slave zones have this need for initially complete data. Since they get their data elsewhere, they do not need it to be specified at their creation.

SOA, or *start of authority*, should, in most cases be populated with the DNS name of the server that will be hosting the zone. Keep in mind that the name you enter must be defined elsewhere. If *server.example.com* is the SOA for the *example.com* zone, then *server.example.com* must also have an A, or address record, elsewhere in the zone. It is entirely feasible that the server hosting a zone is not defined within it. This is commonly the case for hosting companies, which might host DNS for a number of organizations—*dns.provider.com* might be the SOA for *client1.com*, *client2.com*, and *timewasters.org*.

Slave Zones and DNS Masters

Slave zones are replicas of DNS Masters. As is the case in most master-subordinate infrastructures, their most important role is one of redundancy. Slaves periodically query masters in order to ensure that accurate DNS data is always available.

Unfortunately, forward zones are not so clear-cut. Common terminology indicates that forward zones (as mentioned previously) are set up to support forward queries—mapping hostnames to IP addresses. This, though, is not the forward indicated in the zone creation panel. Instead the interface lets the administrator create a zone that is literally of the type forward in the DNS configuration file. The server will forward queries for the selected domain to another server. Unfortunately, both uses of forward are correct. It's just confusing. Just keep in mind that Server Admin's interface does not differentiate between reverse and forward zones (both are type Master), and you'll be fine.

SOA actually refers to a number of options, two of which happen to be MNAME, the name of the server that will be hosting the zone, and RNAME, the administrator's email. Other values not configurable from the graphical interface include serial number (used to keep masters and slaves in sync), and refresh, retry, and time-to-live values. Apple assumes default values for these settings, the implications of which are discussed later in the chapter.

Admin Email seems straightforward enough until you realize that it expects *named*'s odd format for mail addresses. Instead of using an @ symbol (which has special meaning in *named*'s configuration files) to differentiate between the username and domain, a period (.) is used, with the assumption that the first period-delineated field is the username and subsequent fields are the host and/or domain portions of the address.

Clicking OK adds the zone to Server Admin's DNS graphical configuration. It is not saved to your server, though, until you choose to save it by clicking on the Save button in the lower right corner of the user interface. Once a zone is added, the other vague icons below the left pane (illustrated in Figure 11-8) can be used to Add, Clone, Delete, or Edit it (respectively, from left to right).

Figure 11-8. Buttons for adding, cloning, deleting, and editing DNS Zones.

Once a zone is selected in the left pane, records can be added to it using the right pane and its identical set of vague buttons (once again, Add, Clone, Delete, and Edit, respectively.) The behavior of the Add button changes, depending on what kind of zone is selected. Forward and slave zones can only have forward and master servers, respectively. The Add button's behavior enforces this convention, resulting in a very simple interface (seen in Figure 11-9) when adding hosts to either a slave or forward zone.

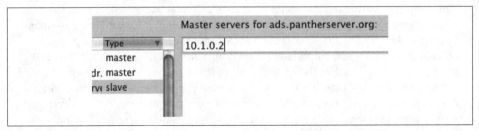

Figure 11-9. Hosts added to Forward zones can only be forward servers. The odds that you'll need a forward zone are relatively low.

Master zones, however, have several options, because, as mentioned earlier, they are the ultimate source for all authoritative DNS data, and DNS data can be quite diverse. Master record creation options, seen in Figure 11-10, reflect this diversity.

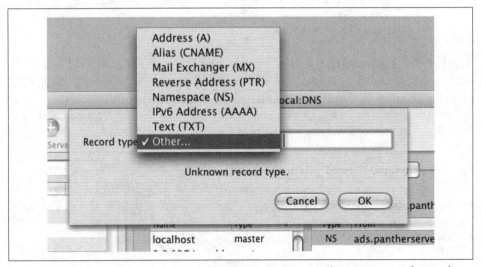

Figure 11-10. Options for creating a record in a master DNS zone. These options are discussed in more depth in Table 11-1. Realistically, you will most commonly deal with A records and pointers.

A pull-down menu allows the new object's type to be specified. DNS zones can contain lots of data, and specifying an object's type allows for that data to be better used and organized. Table 11-1 should give some background into the creation of these records. To understand what they actually look like in the DNS configuration files, see the "Configuration Storage" section later in the chapter.

Table 11-1. Note once again that neither example values nor plain-text explanation of the fields are given in the graphical interface.

Type	Description
A	A, or Address records map names to IP addresses; for instance, *gs.example.com* to *192.168.1.1*. They are used to locate hosts in order to establish connections with them.
CNAME	Alias, or CNAMEs, are a way to associate multiple hostnames with a single host. They are used rather than assigning multiple A records to a single IP.
MX	Mail Exchange records identify which hosts are responsible for a domain's mail.
PTR	Pointer, or PTR records, map IP addresses to names; for instance, *192.168.1.1* to *gs.example.com*. The opposite of A records, they are often used as a sort of ad hoc security mechanism and by certain protocols to determine a DNS name for certain hosts.
NS	Name Service records identify the DNS servers responsible for a specific zone.
AAAA	AAAA records are like A records, except that instead of using IPv4 addresses, they use IPv6. IPv6 is still rarely deployed, so you probably won't have to use this option.
TEXT	TEXT records provide the ability to associate some text—for instance, versioning information or a telephone contact number—with a host or domain name.
Other...	Other, user-defined record types; could be used to add service (SRV) records.

In a way that's consistent with the zone creation process, the record creation dialog (demonstrated in Figure 11-11) adjusts according to the type value that's selected. Note that this does not mean it necessarily adjusts intelligently—MX records, for instance, don't really map from anything to anything else; they specify which host or hosts accept mail for the domain.

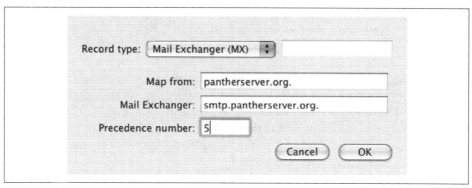

Figure 11-11. Keep in mind that there should be multiple MX records in a domain. This policy allows for redundancy—if one mail server is down, mail should be sent to the backup, or next lowest priority server. The lower the value, the higher a MX record's priority actually is, so that a priority of 1 is higher than a priority of 5.

Configuration Storage

As mentioned briefly earlier, Mac OS X Server uses Berkeley Internet Name Domain (BIND v.9.2.2) to provide DNS services. BIND is a widely deployed open source reference implementation of the DNS protocol provided by the Internet Software Consortium (ISC). Because of its prevalence, there's a large body of material available relating to its deployment. Our goal is to distill that material into the elements that are most useful in the context of Mac OS X Server's requirements and common deployment scenarios. Luckily, Apple's minimal graphical DNS tools do not do anything weird or nonstandard with BIND's configuration files. Perhaps more surprising is that Apple's tools respect many manual changes to the files, making manual configuration a lot simpler than it could be.

Files, Directories, and Daemons

One constant among open source software is its tremendous flexibility. Almost any setting can be overridden either at runtime or compile time, when the software was built. BIND is certainly no exception, and almost nothing we say here can be applicable 100 percent of the time to 100 percent of BIND installations. Unless otherwise noted, everything here refers to the out-of-box configuration options Apple has chosen for BIND in Mac OS X 10.3.

 With the possible exception of *sendmail*, BIND is likely the single most picky common network daemon. Its syntax must be exact, and it is fairly odd. Brackets are required in strange places, semicolons in others, and if they're not there, BIND *will* fail. Be very careful when you manually edit BIND's files.

The BIND package consists of a number of utilities and developmental libraries, but its actual name server is the *named* daemon. Its primary configuration file is */etc/named.conf*. This file specifies *named*'s default global options and enumerates the zones that it is responsible for. Rather than try to explain the file in its entirety, we've taken the *named.conf* we produced in the "Graphical Interface" section earlier and commented it heavily for better understanding:

```
// // Declares control channels to be used by the rndc utility.
// It is recommended that 127.0.0.1 be the only address used.
// This also allows non-privileged users on the local host to manage
// your name server.
//
controls {
        inet 127.0.0.1 port 54 allow {any; };

};
```

named's options are specified in the options section of the *named.conf* file:

```
options {
```

By convention, the directory where zone files are stored is */var/named*:

```
        directory "/var/named";
```

Recursion is enabled:

```
            recursion true;
            /*
             * If there is a firewall between you and nameservers you want
             * to talk to, you might need to uncomment the query-source
             * directive below.  Previous versions of BIND always asked
             * questions using port 53, but BIND 8.1 uses an unprivileged
             * port by default.
             */
```

Optionally, specify the source port for DNS queries:

```
            // query-source address * port 53;
        };
```

The template *named.conf* file includes a caching-only nameserver configuration (capable of serving as a DNS server for a LAN). This configuration is not disabled when zones are added to the configuration:

```
    //
    // a caching only nameserver config
    //
```

The period (.) zone defines the root nameservers, which are listed in the *named.ca* file:

```
zone "." IN {
        type hint;
        file "named.ca";
};
```

Zone data for the *pantherserver.org* domain (which is a master zone) is defined in the */var/named/pantherserver.org.zone* file:

```
zone "pantherserver.org" IN {
        file "pantherserver.org.zone";
        type master;
};
```

Zone data for the *ads.pantherserver.org* domain (which is a slave to the 10.1.0.5 master) is located in the */var/named/ads.pantherserver.org.bak* file:

```
zone "ads.pantherserver.org" IN {
        file "ads.pantherserver.org.bak";
        masters {
                        10.1.0.5;
                };
        type slave;
};
```

A logging channel called *_default_log* is established, which sends debug messages to the file */Library/Logs/named.log*:

```
logging {
        channel _default_log {
                file "/Library/Logs/named.log";
                severity debug;
                print-time yes;
        };
        category default {
                _default_log;
        };

};
```

Each zone defined in *named.conf* has its own data file in the location specified by the directory flag in *named.conf*'s options section. Once again, rather than attempting to explain every option available in the file, we've taken one of the zone files that we configured graphically and commented it heavily in order to explain its function. Because this file is the result of Apple's graphical configuration mechanism, it is rather simple. For more sophisticated examples, see "Advanced Configuration," later in this chapter.

The time-to-live setting establishes a global (per-zone) time-to-live setting. This setting specifies how long other DNS servers should cache data from the *pantherserver. org* zone:

```
$TTL 86400
```

The Start of Authority (SOA) in the *pantherserver.org* domain establishes default domain settings and specify both the master server for the domain (MNAME) and administrative email address associated with the domain (RNAME):

```
pantherserver.org.                              SOA    xs1.
pantherserver.org.  admin.new.com.  (
                                     2004100601   ;    serial
                                     3h       ;   refresh
                                     1h       ;   retry
                                     1w       ;   expiry
                                     1h       ) ;    minimum
```

xs1 is the nameserver (NS) for the *pantherserver.org* domain:

```
pantherserver.org.                              IN     NS     xs1.
pantherserver.org.
```

smtp.pantherserver.org handles mail for the *pantherserver.org* domain, with a priority of 5:

```
pantherserver.org.                              IN     MX     5      smtp.
pantherserver.org.
```

When *named* is started on Mac OS X Server, the DNSSERVER flag in */etc/hostconfig* is changed from -NO- to -YES- by *servermgrd*'s *servermgr_dns* plug-in. The DNS startup item (in */System/Library/StartupItems*), which starts *named* if it is specified in */etc/ hostconfig*, is then run with a start flag, and if all goes well, *named* is off and running.

Troubleshooting

Much is made of BIND's complexity, and its history of vulnerabilities and misconfiguration testifies to the fact that its deployment should not be taken lightly. With a good knowledge of DNS, though, mere mortals can maintain their own name server. Troubleshooting, as is the case with many other Unix daemons, is really a matter of gathering and processing data about the environment within which it is running. This is where BIND excels, providing a much better environment than its reputation would imply.

Tools

A number of tools for exploring the DNS hierarchy exist in common use. The most common of these, now deprecated in favor of *dig*, is *nslookup*. Both tools ship with BIND, and both tools are well documented elsewhere. The *host* tool, however, is not, and since its output is rather friendly as command-line tools go, we'll focus on it on our examples. All of these tools have in common the fact that they query the DNS hierarchy directly, rather than relying on Mac OS X's *resolver* (which lives as a part of *lookupd*) to do it for them.

host is very simple to use. To look up a forward record (obtain an IP address from a name), type *host hostname*, where *hostname* is the host you'd like to resolve:

```
mab9718:~ mbartosh$ host www.apple.com
www.apple.com is an alias for www.apple.com.akadns.net.
www.apple.com.akadns.net has address 17.254.0.91
```

The case of *www.apple.com* is fairly complex, and host takes care of it rather succinctly, stating that *www.apple.com* is an alias (CNAME) for *www.apple.com.akadnc.net*, which has an address of 17.254.0.91. *host* can also do reverse lookups and service lookups, among other things, as shown in Example 11-1. Host is also used to enumerate Kerberos SRV (service) records in the ads.pantherserver.org domain, which is usually associated with Active Directory. Administrators accustomed to the verbosity of dig and nslookup may be comforted by host's *–v* flag, which yields similar output.

Example 11-1. Using the host command to look up a reverse record for 192.168.1.2.

```
mab9718:~ mbartosh$ host 192.168.1.2
2.1.168.192.in-addr.arpa domain name pointer xs2.pantherserver.org.
mab9718:~ mbartosh$ host -t SRV _kerberos._udp.ads.4am-media.com
_kerberos._udp.ads.pantherserver.org SRV 0 100 88 dc01.ads.pantherserver.org.
_kerberos._udp.ads.pantherserver.org SRV 0 100 88 w2k.ads.pantherserver.org.
```

Most of the issues encountered during *named* configuration revolve around BIND's complex configuration syntax. It is very easy to forget a semi-colon or to close a bracket, or to leave a global directive in the wrong portion of the file. Tracking down such an issue would be difficult, as with Example 11-2, were it not for the fact that *named* tells you where to look for your error.

Example 11-2. named's log is very good for helping to identify potential errors.

```
Oct  7 01:10:59 localhost named[22192]: starting BIND 9.2.2
Oct  7 01:10:59 localhost named[22192]: using 1 CPU
Oct  7 01:10:59 localhost named[22192]: loading configuration from '/private/etc/named.
conf'
Oct  7 01:10:59 localhost named[22192]: /private/etc/named.conf:10: missing ';' before
'options'
Oct  7 01:10:59 localhost named[22192]: loading configuration: failure
Oct  7 01:10:59 localhost named[22192]: exiting (due to fatal error)
```

In *vi*, finding the error is as easy as opening the *named.conf* file, typing in number of the line referenced in the error, and pressing Return. This command jumps the edit cursor to the appropriate line. So while BIND's configuration file is indeed difficult, this difficulty is somewhat offset by its verbose error log.

Another common error revolves around the termination of fully qualified domain names in bind's zone files. *named* assumes that unless a name is terminated with a period (.) it is not fully qualified; thus, an MX record that looked like this:

```
    IN  MX 10 mail.example.com
```

could be returned with a doubled domain name:

```
    mbartosh$ host -t MX example.com
    example.com mail is handled by 10 mail.example.com.example.com
```

This problem, though, is fairly easy to correct—periods are easy to add—so it's typically resolved quickly and with little pain.

Finally, it is worth mentioning that *named* can be run in the foreground rather than as a daemon. This approach is quite useful for debugging of new configurations, and quite simple to do: call the –g flag. Between a careful analysis of *named*'s logs and liberal use of *named*'s –g flag, there are few issues that can escape a little scrutiny.

Advanced Configuration

You've probably guessed by now that BIND offers an amazing array of configuration choices—most of which Apple has wisely chosen to leave to the command line. A graphical interface that encompassed all of them would be amazingly complex and cumbersome. There are a few options, however, that are very common, and easy enough that I'd like to see graphical equivalents added.

Running As an Underprivileged User

In an out-of-box Mac OS X Server installation, *named*, after it is started, runs as *root*. This is quite common among older, Unix-based processes that need to listen to listen for connections, since root privileges are mostly required to listen on a port below 1025. Unfortunately, though, BIND has a legacy of fairly frequent vulnerabilities. If a malicious party is able to compromise a service, such as *named*, that's running as *root*, there is a very good chance that the malicious party will end up with *root* privileges on the system. Frequent vulnerabilities in this case mean an increased likelihood of a root-level compromise of your server. This is obviously a bad thing.

To lessen the chances of this happening, the ISC introduced a *–u*, or user, flag to *named*. The *–u* flag means that *named* starts as *root*, obtains its root-privileged socket, and then sets its UID to that of an underprivileged user (or at least one with fewer privileges than *root*). The process is a little more roundabout than changing *named*'s startup item. Because the daemon is no longer running as *root*, it's necessary to make sure that it can access the files it needs to access, and determining which files those are can be a long process:

1. The first thing we'll do is create a user for *named* to use. We could leverage a pre-existing system account, but since security is our biggest concern, we want to do everything in our power to eliminate the possibility of unduly permissive permissions. The user will be in the local NetInfo database, since it will have no need to access network domain resources.

   ```
   xserver:~ nadmin$ sudo nicl . -create /users/named
   xserver:~ nadmin$ sudo nicl . -create /users/named uid 53
   ```

   named's default group is *daemon*. This is done so *named* can write its process ID to the */var/run* directory.

   ```
   xserver:~ nadmin$ sudo nicl . -create /users/named gid 1
   xserver:~ nadmin$ sudo nicl . -create /users/named passwd "*"
   xserver:~ nadmin$ sudo nicl . -create /users/named home /var/named
   xserver:~ nadmin$ sudo nicl . -create /users/named shell /bin/false
   ```

   A more restrictive solution involves changing the location *named* uses to write its file. This is accomplished with the pid-file directive in *named*'s global options, and would usually be accomplished by creating a specific group for the newly created *named* user. If you do this, be sure to change the references to */var/run/named.pid* in the BIND startup item so that they reflect the file's new location.

2. Change permissions on the *named* directory so that *named* can write its statistics file there. Since *named* is a part of the *daemon* group, we'll add write permissions at the group level:

   ```
   xserver:~ nadmin$ sudo chown :daemon /var/named
   xserver:~ nadmin$ sudo chmod g+w !$
   xserver:~ nadmin$ sudo chmod g+w /var/named
   ```

These commands allow *named* to write its statistics file. Note the use of !$, which is a time-saving variable on the command line that refers to the last argument of the previous command. Since the file or directory (in this case, */var/named*) receiving the action is often the last argument, this is often a convenient way to perform several actions on the same filesystem object while saving lots of typing.

3. If you have specified a logfile for *named*, change permissions on it so that the user you created can write to it:

```
xserver:~ nadmin$ sudo chown named /Library/Logs/named.log
```

This step is optional, and might be customized if you have chosen to log to another location.

4. Test, using *named*'s *–g* flag:

```
nadmin$ sudo named -u named -g
Feb 26 00:11:14.870 starting BIND 9.2.2 -u named -g
Feb 26 00:11:14.871 using 1 CPU
Feb 26 00:11:14.880 loading configuration from '/private/etc/named.conf'
Feb 26 00:11:14.882 listening on IPv4 interface lo0, 127.0.0.1#53
Feb 26 00:11:14.884 listening on IPv4 interface en0, 192.168.1.10#53
Feb 26 00:11:14.892 command channel listening on 127.0.0.1#54
Feb 26 00:11:14.894 ignoring config file logging statement due to -g option
Feb 26 00:11:14.898 zone 0.0.127.in-addr.arpa/IN: loaded serial 2004022101
Feb 26 00:11:14.900 zone localhost/IN: loaded serial 43
Feb 26 00:11:14.901 running
```

5. Supposing *named* started successfully, you can now modify the BIND startup item to start with the *–u* flag. This change can be accomplished with your favorite text editor, changing the StartService function from this:

```
StartService ()
{
    if [ "${DNSSERVER:=-NO-}" = "-YES-" ]; then
        ConsoleMessage "Starting named"
        named
    fi
}
```

to this:

```
StartService ()
{
    if [ "${DNSSERVER:=-NO-}" = "-YES-" ]; then
        ConsoleMessage "Starting named"
        named -u named
    fi
}
```

Finally, test your modification by manually running the BIND startup item, taking care that DNSSERVER's flag in the file */etc/hostconfig* has been changed from -NO- to -YES-.

> Unfortunately, in 10.3.5, Server Admin's "Start Service" option—both in the graphical interface, and via the *serveradmin* command's *start* flag—circumvent the BIND startup item. So they'll start BIND, but they ignore the options you've specified. (At startup, your options are run correctly.)
>
> The easiest way to work around this is to stop *named* with the *rndc* utility (*sudo rndc –s 127.0.0.1 –p 54 stop*) and start it by calling the startup item manually (*sudo /System/Library/StartupItems/BIND/BIND start*).

Forwarders

Establishing a domain-specific forwarder—a server that passes requests for hosts in a particular domain on to another, specific server—is easily accomplished in Server Admin's interface. As specified earlier, all you have to do is create a zone with a type of "Forward" (as seen in Figure 11-12) and add to it the IP of another server that is authoritative for the zone in question—this is the only type of record that Server Admin allows you to add to a forward zone. Unfortunately, this is a relatively uncommon configuration, especially when compared with global forwarders, which are not configurable in the graphical interface.

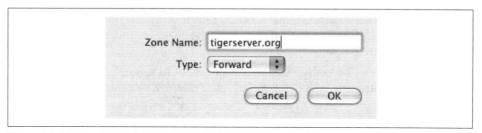

Figure 11-12. Setting up a forward zone for the tigerserver.org domain. Queries to tigerserver.org will be dispatched to a specific server.

Global forwarders—to which all nonauthoritative queries are dispatched—are arguably more useful, and not configurable in the graphical interface. Commonly used to artificially separate private LAN namespaces from their public counterparts, global forwarders allow an administrator to override settings for a particular domain or domains while forwarding all other DNS requests to another server. They are for most purposes the opposite of forward zones, covered earlier.

The reasoning behind the inclusion of domain-specific forwarding and the exclusion of global forwarding is unclear, since the latter is arguably much more widely deployed.

In this case, the *named.conf* file must be edited, and a `forwarders` directive must be added to the options section. The directive itself looks something like this:

```
forwarders {
            192.168.1.1;
            10.1.0.1;
        };
```

Notice that every opened bracket has a corresponding closing bracket, and that the directive itself (and every value inside of it) is terminated with a semicolon (;). After *named.conf* is modified in this way, *named* must be restarted.

Change Root (chroot)

Change rooting (or *chrooting*) extends on the security advantages offered by running *named* as an underprivileged user. It is another way of limiting which files a process has access to, this time by tricking *named* into thinking that a particular, protected directory is the root of the filesystem. If *named* thinks that */var/chroot/named* is */*, then it won't be able to find */Users*, */System*, or any other filesystem that is critical to any other daemon. This is commonly referred to as a "jail." Even if it were compromised, it wouldn't be able to do any damage outside of its *chroot*'d environment.

Setting up *chroot* is not difficult, but it doesn't do much good unless configured in conjunction with running as an underprivileged user.

 Because *root* can typically break a *chroot* jail, so be sure to set up an alternate user (as specified earlier) before contemplating *chroot*.

1. Create the *chroot* jail: the directory on the filesystem that *named* will be confined to. This step requires creation of an alternate device filesystem, since *named* cannot see */dev* when its running in the jail.

```
xserver:~ nadmin$ sudo mkdir -p /chroot/named/private/etc
xserver:~ nadmin$ sudo mkdir -p /chroot/named/private/var/run
xserver:/chroot/named nadmin$ sudo chown :daemon !$
sudo chown :daemon private/var/run
xserver:/chroot/named nadmin$ sudo chmod g+w !$
sudo chmod g+w private/var/run
xserver:~ nadmin$ sudo mkdir -p /chroot/named/dev
xserver:~ nadmin$ sudo mount_devfs devfs /chroot/named/dev
```

Note the !$ convention: this is a built-in shell variable that means "the last argument of the previous command." It is useful for performing a number of operations on the same file or directory, without having to re-type the file or directory's name over and over again.

2. Copy *named*'s configuration into the jail:

```
xserver:~ nadmin$ sudo ditto /private/var/named /chroot/named/private/var/named
xserver:~ nadmin$ sudo cp /etc/named.conf /chroot/named/ private/etc/
xserver:~ nadmin$ sudo cp /etc/rndc.key !$
```

3. Finish setting up the jail so it closely resembles the directory structure outside of the jail. This ensures that *named* starts up in the sort of environment Apple built it for, easing configuration and minimizing unknown variables.

```
xserver:~ nadmin$ cd /chroot/named/
xserver:/chroot/named nadmin$ sudo ln -s private/var var
xserver:/chroot/named nadmin$ sudo ln -s private/etc/ etc
xserver:/chroot/named nadmin$ cd
xserver:~ nadmin$
```

4. Set up a symbolic link, so that Mac OS X Server's management tools can find the files they're supposed to manage:

```
xserver:~ nadmin$ sudo mv /private/var/named /private/var/named.bak
xserver:~ nadmin$ sudo ln -s /chroot/named/private/var/named /private/var/named
xserver:~ nadmin$ sudo mv /etc/named.conf /etc/named.conf.bak
xserver:~ nadmin$ sudo ln -s /chroot/named/private/etc/named.conf ⏎
/private/etc/named.conf
xserver:~ nadmin$ sudo mv /chroot/named/private/etc/rndc.key ⏎
/chroot/named/private/etc/rndc.key.bak
xserver:~ nadmin$ sudo ln -s /chroot/named/private/etc/rndc.key ⏎
/private/etc/rndc.key
```

5. Test your configuration with *named*'s *–g* flag:

```
xserver:/chroot/named nadmin$ sudo named -g -u named -t /chroot/named
        Mar 07 20:00:08.897 starting BIND 9.2.2 -g -u named -t /chroot/named
        Mar 07 20:00:08.902 using 1 CPU
        Mar 07 20:00:08.915 loading configuration from '/private/etc/named.conf'
        Mar 07 20:00:08.921 listening on IPv4 interface loO, 127.0.0.1#53
        Mar 07 20:00:08.950 listening on IPv4 interface en0, 10.1.0.2#53
        Mar 07 20:00:08.977 ignoring config file logging statement due to -g option
        Mar 07 20:00:09.011 zone 0.0.127.in-addr.arpa/IN: loaded serial 1997022700
        Mar 07 20:00:09.019 zone localhost/IN: loaded serial 42
        Mar 07 20:00:09.022 running
```

6. Once your test is successful, you can modify the BIND Startup Item again, this time to reflect the *–t /chroot/named* flag in addition to the already enabled *–u* flag. Additionally, *named*'s devfs needs to be made available before *named* starts in its *chroot*. This means adding the mount_devfs command you executed earlier either to the BIND startup item or to */etc/rc*, where */dev* is mounted. Neither is a best-case scenario; the former requires maintenance, probably needing to be reset after major upgrades, while the latter needs extra logic to ensure that the

filesystem is not already mounted (assuming that you plan to restart *named* between boots). That logic could be something as simple as:

```
if [ `/sbin/mount | /usr/bin/grep devfs | wc -l` -lt 2 ]; then
    /sbin/mount_devfs devfs /chroot/named/dev
fi
```

Naturally, customized in the case that you are running more than one *chroot*'d daemon requiring access to */dev*. All said, you might consider adding the mount command to */etc/rc*, since that's where Apple mounts the system's */dev*.

 Once again, note that Server Admin won't honor options set in BIND's startup item when stopping and restarting the daemon. To work around this, use *rndc* to stop BIND and its startup item to start it, identically to what I did with the *–u* option earlier in the chapter.

Limiting Zone Transfers

Earlier in the chapter, zone transfers were discussed. Zone transfers are the principal method for moving zone data from a DNS master to its slave servers. The mission-critical role of DNS has probably been discussed enough in this text to indicate that zone transfers are a fairly important part DNS redundancy.

Allowing zone transfers to DNS slaves is required—but allowing them to arbitrary hosts is a bad idea, since they are a virtual map of your infrastructure. Server Admin's interface (its "Allow Zone transfers" checkbox) does not have the granularity necessary to support this kind of selectiveness. Instead, the *named.conf* file must be edited in order to specify which hosts are authorized to perform transfers.

To limit zone transfers, add an `allow-transfers` statement to */etc/named.conf*'s options section, as follows:

```
allow-transfer { ip_address_1; ip_address_2; };
```

where `ip_address_1` and `ip_address_2` are the actual IP addresses of the slave server(s).

 In addition to supplying a list of IP addresses, a CIDR network address or wildcard statement (192.168.1.*) may also be specified in *named*'s allow-transfer directive.

Views

A common difficulty that arises in the deployment of DNS is the need to provide different data to different clients—for either security or organizational reasons; see Figure 11-13 as one possible example.

Views were added to BIND 9 for just this purpose—so that a single name server could provide differing host data, depending on where a query originated. In order to implement views, *named.conf* must be edited directly, as Mac OS X's graphical inter-

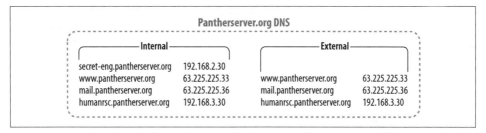

Internal		External	
secret-eng.pantherserver.org	192.168.2.30	www.pantherserver.org	63.225.225.33
www.pantherserver.org	63.225.225.33	mail.pantherserver.org	63.225.225.36
mail.pantherserver.org	63.225.225.36	humanrsc.pantherserver.org	192.168.3.30
humanrsc.pantherserver.org	192.168.3.30		

Figure 11-13. External DNS clients do not need to be aware of humanresc.pantherserver.org or secret-eng.pantherserver.org.

face does not support them. The configuration, though, is not difficult, as seen in Figure 11-13.

Access Control Lists (ACLs) should first be defined using the acl directive, in the form of acl *aclname {address-definition;};*, where *aclname* is a tag given to identify the acl, and address-definition is any address, cinder block, hostname, or one of four built-in definitions, listed in Table 11-2.

Table 11-2. BIND 9's built-in address variables

Definition	Matches
any	Matches any query.
none	Matches no queries.
localhost	Matches queries originating from the DNS server itself.
localnets	Matches queries originating from one of the networks the server has access to.

The first ACL to match wins, so order is important. In this case, anything not matching the 192.168.1.1:225.225.225.0 network gets the access specified for the ACL called external:

```
//Define an access control list called office
acl locoffice{ 192.168.1.0/24; };

//Define an access control list called external
acl external { any; };
```

Specific views (to which ACLs will be applied) must then be defined using the view directive. Each view may have its own set of global options. In this example, for instance, recursion is turned on for the office view. The view directive defines a version of the DNS namespace that will be made available to a specific set of clients. Its general syntax is:

```
view viewname {
    match-clients {acl;};
    options
    zone(s)
};
```

where *viewname* is a tag used to identify the view, acl is a previously defined acl, *options* are anything that would otherwise appear in the global options section, and *zone(s)* are otherwise normally defined zones visible only to that view. For example:

```
//Define the office view
view "office " {

    //associate the  view called office with the acl called office
    match-clients { locoffice; };

    //allow recursion in the office view.
    recursion yes;

    //Define a zone available only to the office view.
    zone "example.com" {
      type master;
      //It is good practice to keep all zones for a particular view together in a
      //specific directory- in this case /var/named/office
      file "office/db.example.com";
    };
      zone "private.example.com" {
       type master;
       file "office/db.private.example.com";
      };
};
```

A view (called external) is then defined and applied to the ACL (as defined earlier), which is also called external:

```
//Define a view called external.
view "external" {

    //associate the view called external with the acl called external
    match-clients { external; };

    //Do not allow recursion  in the external view
    recursion no;

    //Define a zone visible only to the office view
    zone "example.com" {
      type master;
      file "external/db.example.com";
    };

};
```

> In this example, differing views of the *example.com* zone are presented, depending on the source address of the query. Although not required, it is good practice to keep zone files organized by view, so that all zones for a particular view are stored in the same directory.

This is a general set of guidelines, covering only the most basic and common cases of view deployment. For a more in-depth analysis, including advanced matching options see the *BIND 9 Administrator's Reference Manual* (*www.bind9.net/Bv9ARM. html*).

 Views are an all-or-nothing feature. If you use views for one of your zones, you must use views for all of your zones. Unfortunately, despite their utility, use of views will break Server Admin's ability to manage DNS in 10.3.5. *servermgrd*'s DNS plug-in can not deal with BIND configurations that it does not understand, and the views directive throws it for a loop.

CHAPTER 12

DHCP

People with a background in networking often overestimate the simplicity of adding a host to the network. Someone accustomed to configuring Internet access can bang out an IP, subnet mask, router, and DNS server in mere seconds, probably without thinking too much and maybe even weighing internal metrics (like lists of available IP addresses) on the fly in their head. For the end user, though the dazzling array of numbers and dots can be quite confusing. And this only covers basic network configuration options—in a modern, mature, network it's likely that users also need to access several components of the infrastructure, from WINS servers to LDAP or Net-Info domains.

It's probably no surprise that Dynamic Host Configuration Protocol (DHCP) fulfills these requirements quite well. Mac OS X Server employs Apple's homegrown service *bootpd* to supply (among other things) DHCP services. This breaks slightly with Mac OS X Server's tendency to leverage open source software. For the moment, at least, it's necessary (or at least convenient) in order to provide NetBoot to Mac OS X clients.

Graphical Configuration

Apple's graphical configuration mechanism for DHCP is in Server Admin, in the DHCP module. Like all Server Admin modules, DHCP defaults to a Status tab (seen in Figure 12-1) that illustrates the current state of the service. In this case, that's limited to the number of clients, service start time (actually the time when *xinetd*'s *bootps* service was enabled), and the timestamp of the most recent client database update.

DHCP's Log tab (seen in Figure 12-2) displays DHCP log data as recorded in the system log (*/var/log/system.log*). Server Admin's HTTP-based request-response cycle might not be fast enough to keep up with the large volume of log data, so you might want to view it using the tail command, which displays the last 10 lines of a file. The logging characteristics are configurable, and are discussed later in this chapter.

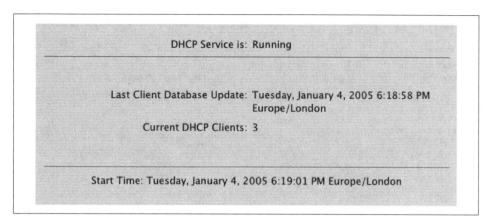

Figure 12-1. Basic data relating to the DHCP service.

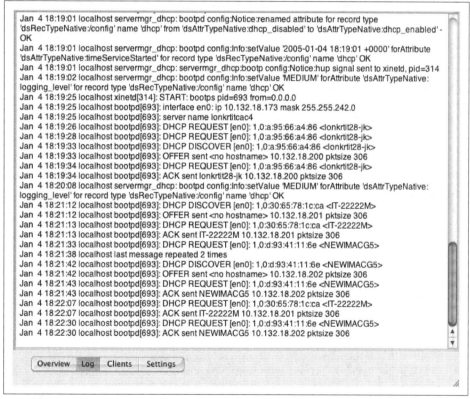

Figure 12-2. Viewing the log for the bootpd daemon.

The Clients pane (Figure 12-3) displays all current DHCP clients; that is, clients who have an outstanding lease. This data is parsed directly from the */var/db/dhcpd_leases* file, which is maintained as clients obtain their leases from the server.

Computer Name	Ethernet ID	Client ID	IP Address	Lease	
NEWIMACG5	0:d:93:41:11:6e		10.132.18.202	23:56	
IT-22222M	0:30:65:78:1c:ca		10.132.18.201	23:55	
lonkrtit28-jk	0:a:95:66:a4:86		10.132.18.200	23:53	

Number of clients: 3

Overview   Log   Clients   Settings

Figure 12-3. The Clients view of Server Admin's DHCP module.

Mac OS X's DHCP service is configured using the Settings pane of Server Admin's DHCP wodule, which has two subsections available via their respective tabs: Logging (Figure 12-4) and Subnets (Figure 12-5). It is worth pointing out that this interface is very new in Panther Server, and that it differs significantly from DHCP configuration in Jaguar. Controlling DHCP logging is fairly simple; there are only three choices in the Logging pane: Low (errors only), Medium (errors and warnings), and High (all events). When saved, this data is written directly to NetInfo as an attribute of the *netinfo://config/dhcp* directory.

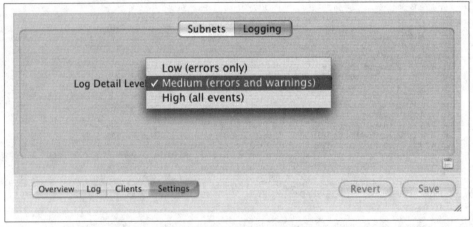

Figure 12-4. Setting logging levels for DHCP Services on Mac OS X Server. This setting also determines the log level for NetBoot, which uses the same daemon (bootpd).

The following code uses *nicl* to read the DHCP configuration stored in NetInfo:

```
xserver:~ nadmin$ nicl . -read /config/dhcp
name: dhcp
logging_level: MEDIUM
dhcp_enabled: en0
```

bootpd's global options are stored as attributes of the /config/dhcp directory in NetInfo. This location is also the home of a number of advanced functions that cannot be set in the GUI. For more information, see "Advanced Configuration," later in this chapter.

The Subnets tab actually has a somewhat misleading name. Apple uses the name "subnet" for what other DHCP servers would commonly refer to as a *scope*—a single set of IP addresses (along with the options associated with them) from which clients are assigned addresses.

In fact it is entirely feasible that a single logical subnet—lets use 192.168.1.0/24 as an example—might have two or more of Apple's "subnets" associated with it: one with a range of 192.168.1.10–20 and a second with a range of 192.168.1.50–100. This is the only way to achieve this kind of granularity, where a set of addresses is reserved for static assignment. In order to avoid this confusion, we'll use the term "range" from here on to describe these entities.

In a default configuration (illustrated in Figure 12-5), every server already has one preassigned (but disabled) DHCP range. Since the DHCP service is not running, and since the range is disabled anyway, this configuration isn't even slightly risky. The existing range (which is based on the initial configuration of *en0*) is there solely for the sake of convenience.

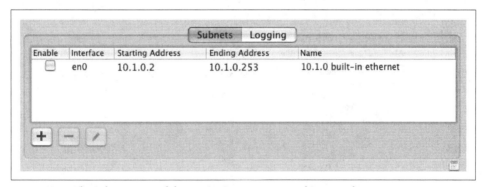

Figure 12-5. The Subnets pane of the DHCP Settings section of Server Admin.

The range can be examined more closely (or edited) either by double-clicking it, or by selecting it and then clicking the Edit (pencil) button in the pane's lower lefthand corner. The resulting interface is where the bulk of the DHCP configuration choices are implemented. It has four parts: General, DNS, LDAP, and WINS.

The General tab (seen in Figure 12-6) establishes the range's basic, required values: the beginning and ending addresses of the range, the router, which interface this range should be provided on, and the lease time. Subnet Name is simply a tag given to help identify that particular range.

 Lease time is a very site-specific setting. Setting the lease time too long invites exhaustion of the available IP range. For example, imagine a pool of 20 IPs with a three-month lease time. If the twenty-first machine requesting a lease happens to come three weeks into the life if the server, that machine is denied an IP address. Obviously, high-volume DHCP servers with fairly limited resources should keep lease times relatively short. On the other hand, some services, especially legacy services deployed on older systems, depend on either static or relatively static IP addresses. This design would seem to prefer longer lease times. In general, you should try to keep lease times as short as possible, since DHCP traffic doesn't provide a lot of network overhead.

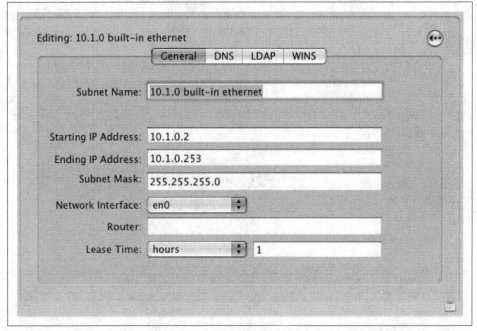

Figure 12-6. General options for the default range. Notice that a router is not initially supplied, and must be entered manually.

 Under most circumstances, there should only be one DHCP server on any physical network range. If you are configuring a DHCP server, be sure you are not in conflict with any pre-existing infrastructure components (such as a campus DHCP server).

At any time, in any of the range's configuration panes, clicking the back arrow button in Server Admin's upper right corner (seen in Figure 12-7) returns to the main DHCP configuration pane and its list of subnets. New ranges may be added with the Add (+) button, and existing ones may be edited or deleted, with the Pencil and Minus (−) buttons, respectively.

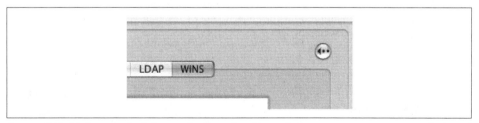

Figure 12-7. Clicking the back button from any DHCP configuration pane returns you to the list of ranges.

While not required, providing DNS settings to DHCP clients is highly recommended, because it's unlikely that end users will have an understanding of DNS configuration. The DNS tab of the scope record (seen in Figure 12-8), appropriately enough, accomplishes this task quite nicely. Its configuration is very straightforward, and in fact, values will be auto-populated with any DNS servers and search bases the server is itself using.

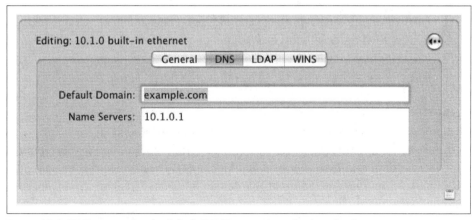

Figure 12-8. DNS settings for the default DHCP range. Initial values for these settings are assumed, based on the server's network settings.

Pictured in Figure 12-9, the LDAP tab allows for population of Directory Services autoconfiguration data (via Option 95, a standard part of the DHCP specification; see *www.iana.org/assignments/bootp-dhcp-parameters* for details). Clients obtain this data automatically from their DHCP lease rather than having to be configured manually. The data entry is simple enough, and is described in Table 12-1. You cannot, however, arbitrarily enter the address of just any LDAP server. The requirements are stringent, and are centered around configuration data commonly available in an Open Directory Master.

 Specifically, the client requests the *ou=macosxodconfig,cn=config* object below the provided search base. It is expected to contain an XML configuration for the client's LDAPv3 plug-in. This data can be maintained using the Directory Access's "Write to Server" option, discussed in *Running Mac OS X Panther* (O'Reilly, 2004).

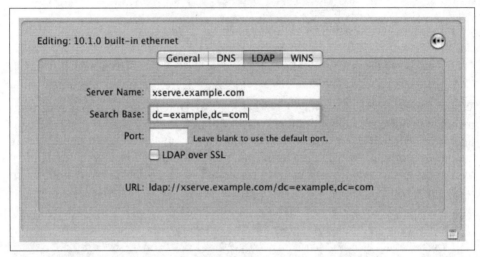

Figure 12-9. Setting LDAP options in a DHCP range.

Table 12-1. Options for specifying an LDAP server in DHCP Option 95.

Option	Description
Server Name	The name or IP address of the Open Directory–compatible LDAP server.
Search Base	The location below which a properly specified *ou=macosxodconfig,cn=config* path must be located.
Port	Under most circumstances, should be left blank. The *ldap://* prefix assumes the default *ldap* port. If SSL is enabled, the *ldap* changes to *ldaps*, and port 636 is assumed. The Port option itself should be used only if a nonstandard port is specified.
ssl	Allows for the specification of *ldaps* connections. The server must be specifically configured to support this, and out-of-box Panther clients ship with an insecure *ldaps* client configuration.

Mac OS X no longer obtains its LDAP configuration from DHCP in an out-of-box configuration. This feature was considered a security risk, because users are not generally accustomed to verifying whether their DHCP server is malicious, and because accessing a directory domain in this fashion means effectively granting local access to the person running the DHCP server and Open Directory master. "Use DHCP-Supplied LDAP Server" must be manually enabled for each client using the LDAPv3 plug-in's configuration in the Directory Access application.

The Windows Internet Name Service (WINS) is Microsoft's implementation of the NetBios Naming Service—a method for translating network names to network addresses—like DNS, except Microsoft-specific and not widely used outside of older versions of Windows. New in Panther, the DHCP Service's WINS tab (Figure 12-10) allows Mac OS X Server to supply WINS configuration data to DHCP clients. This is a standard method of operations in the Windows world, saving a lot of configuration time and effort. WINS options are described in Table 12-2.

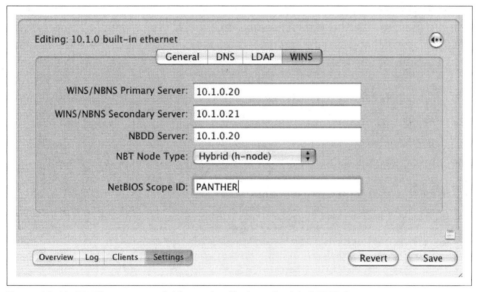

Figure 12-10. WINS options available graphically from Apple's DHCP Server.

 Mac OS X clients are not able to taka advantage of automatically supplied WINS servers. For more information regarding NetBIOS DHCP options, see *http://www.microsoft.com/windows2000/en/server/help/ sag_DHCP_add_OptionsNetBIOS.htm.*

Table 12-2. WINS options.

Option	Description
WINS/NBNS Primary Server	The primary WINS server.
WINS/NBNS Secondary Server	The secondary WINS server.
NBDD Server	The NetBIOS Datagram Distribution server. Generally the same machine as the WINS server, a NBDD server acts as a centralized distribution point for NetBios packets.
NBY Node Type	Choice of Not Set, Broadcast, Peer, Mixed, or Hybrid. Determines what sort of browsing policy should be used.
NetBIOS Scope ID	Similar to an SLP scope or AppleTalk zone. Defines a namespace for NetBIOS clients to use.

In all cases, subnet-specific data is stored in a subdirectory of the previously mentioned *netinfo://config/dhcp*:

```
G5:~ ladmin$ nicl . -list /config/dhcp/subnets
93          EF2B03A5-64D3-11D8-880A-00306558D4E6
```

Notice that each object in the NetInfo database has a number associated with it. Called a directory ID, this number can be used rather than a path or name to identify that particular object. This approach is especially useful when the object in question has a long or unwieldy name.

 NetInfo directory IDs are not available when using *dscl*, because it communicates with Open Directory (via the *DirectoryService* daemon) rather than working directly with NetInfo directly, like *nicl* does.

In this case, you can use the directory ID so you don't have to type out some long command (*nicl . –read /config/dhcp/subnets/EF2B03A5-64D3-11D8-880A-00306558D4E6*) just to see the set of configuration options associated with the default range:

```
g5:~ ladmin$ nicl . -read 89
name: EF2B03A5-64D3-11D8-880A-00306558D4E6
net_address: 192.168.1.0
net_mask: 255.255.255.0
descriptive_name: Built-in Ethernet
dhcp_router: 192.168.1.1
selected_port_name: en0
dhcp_domain_name: 4am-media.com
lease_min: 3600
lease_max: 3600
net_range: 192.168.1.2 192.168.1.30
client_types: bootp
dhcp_domain_name_server: 64.5.64.21
dhcp_nb_over_tcpip_node_type: 8
dhcp_nb_over_tcpip_name_server: 10.1.0.20 10.1.0.21
dhcp_nb_over_tcpip_dgram_dist_server: 10.1.0.20
dhcp_nb_over_tcpip_scope: PANTHER
dhcp_ldap_url: ldap://xs1.pantherserver.org/dc=pantherserver,dc=org
```

Starting DHCP by pressing the "Start Service" button in the menubar is the equivalent of running *sudo service bootps start*. The disable flag in */etc/dinetd.d/bootps* is changed to NO, and *xinetd* loads the service. When a DHCP, *bootpd*, or NetBoot (BSDP) request comes in, *xinetd* spawns *bootpd* in order to service it. If *bootpd* is idle for five minutes (if no appropriate requests come in), the service is shut down.

Troubleshooting

bootpd, like many other daemons, sends verbose logs to */var/log/system.log*, as seen here:

```
Mar  9 12:24:40 localhost bootpd[6342]: DHCP DISCOVER [en0]: 1,0:3:93:63:89:e2
<dhcp211>
Mar  9 12:24:40 localhost bootpd[6342]: OFFER sent dhcp211 10.1.0.211 pktsize 345
Mar  9 12:24:41 localhost bootpd[6342]: DHCP REQUEST [en0]: 1,0:3:93:63:89:e2
<dhcp211>
Mar  9 12:24:41 localhost bootpd[6342]: DHCP DECLINE [en0]: 1,0:3:93:63:89:e2
Mar  9 12:24:51 localhost bootpd[6342]: DHCP DISCOVER [en0]: 1,0:3:93:63:89:e2
<dhcp211>
Mar  9 12:24:51 localhost bootpd[6342]: OFFER sent <no hostname> 10.1.0.211↵
pktsize 345
Mar  9 12:24:52 localhost bootpd[6342]: DHCP REQUEST [en0]: 1,0:3:93:63:89:e2
<dhcp211>
Mar  9 12:24:52 localhost bootpd[6342]: ACK sent dhcp211 10.1.0.211 pktsize 345
```

If this isn't verbose enough for you, *bootpd* can also be run in debug mode, which keeps the daemon in the foreground and outputs even more protocol data. To accomplish this, *bootpd* must first be disabled in *xinetd*'s service list (because *xinetd* doesn't know how to start it in the foreground) as follows:

```
mab9718:~ mbartosh$ sudo service bootps stop
mab9718:~ mbartosh$ sudo /usr/libexec/bootpd -d
```

Finally, from a client-side perspective, note the *ipconfig* command's *getpacket* option, which displays lease data for a particular network interface. Its syntax requires the specification of a network interface—usually *en0* for built-in Ethernet and *en1* for AirPort. This command is highly valuable when examining the functionality of any DHCP server:

```
cbig15:~ mab$ ipconfig getpacket en1
op = BOOTREPLY
htype = 1
dp_flags = 0
hlen = 6
hops = 0
xid = 841999999
secs = 0
ciaddr = 0.0.0.0
yiaddr = 192.168.1.101
siaddr = 0.0.0.0
giaddr = 0.0.0.0
chaddr = 0:d:93:7d:27:82
```

```
sname =
file =
options:
Options count is 9
dhcp_message_type (uint8): ACK 0x5
renewal_t1_time_value (uint32): 0x708
rebinding_t2_time_value (uint32): 0xc4e
lease_time (uint32): 0xe10
server_identifier (ip): 192.168.1.4
subnet_mask (ip): 255.255.255.0
router (ip_mult): {192.168.1.1}
domain_name_server (ip_mult): {192.168.1.4}
end (none):
```

Advanced Configuration

bootpd has a number of features not available in the graphical interface. Some of the more useful are discussed in the sections that follow.

DHCP and bootpd Static Bindings

One very common feature request is the ability to limit a particular machine to a particular IP address by associating its MAC address with a particular IP in the DHCP server's configuration. *bootpd* accomplishes this by accessing data stored in the Net-Info database, a machine record that stores both pieces of data. A valid record looks something like this:

```
mab9718:~ mbartosh$ nicl . -read /machines/imac05-hlms
name: imac05-hlms
ip_address: 10.1.0.5
en_address: 00:0d:93:7d:27:82
```

Such a record can be created with the following set of commands:

```
mab9718:~ mbartosh$ sudo nicl . -create /machines/imac05-hlms ip_address 10.1.0.5
mab9718:~ mbartosh$ sudo nicl . -create /machines/imac05-hlms en_address⏎
00:0d:93:7d:27:82
```

or by adding the proper data with NetInfo Manager, as seen in Figure 12-11.

In any case, the contentious issue is really two-fold. Managing hundreds of machines in this way is cumbersome, requiring the manipulation of a lot of data (including the MAC address of every client). Secondly, keep in mind that this is not the only place that data might have to be managed. Computer accounts (discussed in Chapter 4), serve a very similar purpose—management of client data. In a worst-case scenario, every computer you manage might have two entries: one in the shared LDAP directory in */Computers*, and one in the local NetInfo domain in */machines*.

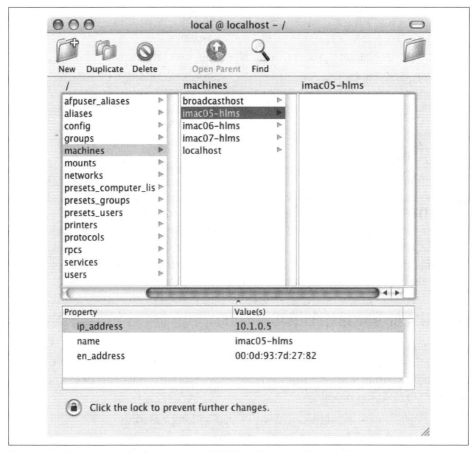

Figure 12-11. Viewing and editing custom DHCP bindings with NetInfo Manager.

Supplying Other DHCP Options

In addition to LDAP, WINS, and DNS options, *bootpd* is able to supply a number of other options described by the Internet Assigned Numbers Authority (IANA). These are added to specific subnets using either NetInfo Manager or command-line NetInfo tools. They are described in Table 12-3.

Table 12-3. DHCP options available to bootpd.

Option	Description
dhcp_netinfo_server_address *(option 112)*	The IP address of the NetInfo parent
dhcp_netinfo_server_tag *(option 113)*	The NetInfo tag or database label existing on the parent named in option 113
dhcp_url *(option 114)*	The default URL to present in a web browser
dhcp_time_offset *(option 2)*	The number of seconds offset from GMT

Table 12-3. DHCP options available to bootpd. (continued)

Option	Description
dhcp_network_time_protocol_servers *(option 42)*	NTP servers available for use
dhcp_smtp_server *(option 69)*	SMTP servers available to the local subnet
dhcp_pop3_server *(option code 70)*	The local POP3 server
dhcp_nntp_server *(option 71)*	Local newsgroup servers

ISC's dhcpd

It's common for Unix administrators familiar with the ISC's DHCP server (*dhcpd*) to use it instead of *bootpd*. ISC *dhcpd* offers a number of options not available in *bootpd*, and it can even be patched to support NetBoot (*www.macosxhints.com/article.php?story=20021017055337617*). However, be aware that this trick invalidates Apple's graphical configuration tools, and that you'll be largely on your own when making configuration changes. On the other hand, ISC *dhcpd* is configurable with Webmin, a web-based systems management utility (*www.webmin.com*).

Compilation and Installation

ISC *dhcpd* is not included with Mac OS X Server. If you'd like to use it, you'll have to obtain and build it yourself. This requires that the Developer Tools be installed on the machine you're working from. The latest version of *dhcpd* can be located from *www.isc.org/index.pl?/sw/dhcp/*.

1. The distribution must first be downloaded and unpacked:

```
mab9718:~ mbartosh$ curl -O ftp://ftp.isc.org/isc/dhcp/dhcp-3.0pl2.tar.gz
  % Total    % Received % Xferd  Average Speed          Time          Curr.
                                 Dload  Upload Total   Current  Left   Speed
100  844k  100  844k     0      0  35840      0  0:00:24  0:00:24  0:00:00 35489
mab9718:~ mbartosh$ tar -xzf dhcp-3.0pl2.tar.gz
```

2. It is then necessary to configure the software, using the *configure* script that ships in the distribution directory. *configure* gathers data about your system and build environment and sets up the build environment accordingly. Only a portion of its output, which is extremely verbose, is recorded here:

```
mab9718:~ mbartosh$ cd dhcp-3.0pl2
mab9718:~/dhcp-3.0pl2 mbartosh$ ./configure
System Type: darwin
Making links in common
Making links in minires
Making links in dst
Making links in omapip
Making links in server
Making links in client
Making links in relay
Making links in dhcpctl
```

3. After *configure* has run, we can compile the software. This is done with the *make* command. Its output is also rather verbose—here I list only the first and last few lines:

```
mab9718:~/dhcp-3.0pl2 mbartosh$ make
Making all in common
cc -g  -I/Users/mbartosh/dhcp-3.0pl2  -I/Users/mbartosh/dhcp-3.0pl2/includes -
Ddarwin -Wall -Wno-unused -Wno-implicit -Wno-comment -Wno-uninitialized -Wno-
switch -Werror -pipe      -c -o raw.o raw.c
sed -e "s#ETCDIR#/etc#g" -e "s#DBDIR#/var/db#g" \
        -e "s#RUNDIR#/var/run#g" < omshell.1 >omshell.man1
nroff -man omshell.man1 >omshell.cat1
```

4. If you have been building the software on a client, it is now time to upload it to the server:

```
mab9718:~/dhcp-3.0pl2 mbartosh$ cd
mab9718:~ mbartosh$  tar -czf dhcp-built.tgz dhcp-3.0pl2
mab9718:~ mbartosh$ scp dhcp-built.tgz nadmin@192.168.1.2:
nadmin@192.168.1.2's password:
dhcp-built.tgz                              100% 5041KB  81.3KB/s   01:01
```

5. The software is installed with the *make* command; this time, though, it is passed an *install* argument. Again, the output is quite verbose, so I only show the first and last few lines here:

```
mab9718:~/dhcp-3.0pl2 mbartosh$ sudo make install
Password:
Installing in common
for dir in /usr/share/man/cat5; do \
  foo=""; \
  for bar in `echo ${dir} |tr / ' '`; do \
    foo=${foo}/$bar; \
    if [ ! -d $foo ]; then \
...
done
install -c -m 444 omshell /usr/bin
chmod 755 /usr/bin/omshell
install -c  omshell.cat1  \
                        /usr/share/man/cat1/omshell.0
mab9718:~/dhcp-3.0pl2 mbartosh$
```

Configuration and Administration

Unless you're using Webmin, you'll need to configure *dhcpd* manually, using its configuration file, */etc/dhcpd.conf*. While a complete analysis is beyond the scope of this chapter, the following example mirrors the graphical configuration of Apple's *bootpd* daemon seen earlier in this chapter:

```
# /etc/dhcpd.conf
# invoke: /usr/sbin/dhcpd en0
# don't foget to "touch /var/db/dhcpd.leases"

default-lease-time 600;
```

```
max-lease-time 7200;
option subnet-mask 255.255.255.0;
option broadcast-address 10.0.0.255;
option routers 10.0.0.1;
option domain-name-servers 10.1.0.1;
option domain-name "example.com";
option ldap-server "ldap://xserve.example.com/dc=example,dc=com";
option netbios-name-servers 10.1.0.20, 10.1.0.21;
option netbios-node-type 8;
option netbios-dd-server 10.1.0.20;
option netbios-scope PANTHER;

subnet 10.0.0.0 netmask 255.255.255.0 {
  range 10.1.0.2 10.0.0.253;
}
```

CHAPTER 13

NAT

Last in our analysis of Mac OS X Server's fundamental network services is Network Address Translation (NAT), which allows the server to share its public network access with multiple clients that usually reside on a private, nonroutable network. In this way, several computers can share a single network connection. This concept is illustrated in Figure 13-1.

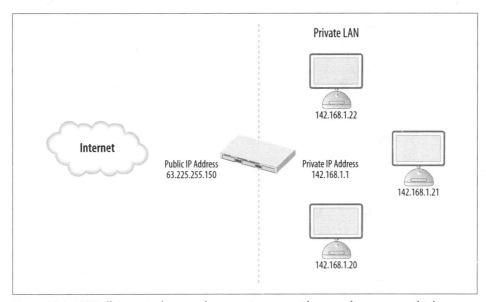

Figure 13-1. NAT allows a single network connection to provide network access to multiple computers.

NAT is a fairly basic function of TCP/IP, and even the minimal hardware requirements for Mac OS X Server specify a machine that is more than capable of providing NAT services on all but the highest-bandwidth links. NAT is such a simple function, in fact, that the question must be asked: why use a $2,000–$5,000 piece of hardware to accomplish what can be done just as easily with a $100 appliance? This is a valid question and there are several valid answers, but in general, if NAT is employed, I'd generally rather use an appliance built specifically for it. Personally, I use Mac OS X Server's NAT capabilities, but this is mainly to ensure that I have a good understanding of them.

Managing NAT

NAT's graphical configuration can be found, appropriately enough, in the NAT module of Server Admin. Owing to the simplicity of NAT, it is very minimal. The Overview pane (seen in Figure 13-2) displays the state of the service, as well as the current number of TCP, UDP, and ICMP links.

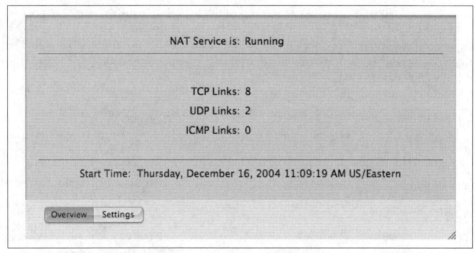

Figure 13-2. The NAT service overview displays the number of current NAT-supported connections.

This same data can be gathered with the *serveradmin* command:

```
[ace2:~] nadmin% sudo serveradmin fullstatus nat
nat:command = "getState"
nat:activeTCP = 5
nat:activeUDP = 7
nat:state = "RUNNING"
nat:logPaths:natLog = "/var/log/alias.log"
nat:readWriteSettingsVersion = 1
nat:devices:_array_index:0:device = "en7"
nat:devices:_array_index:0:name = "PCI Ethernet Slot 2, Port 5"
nat:devices:_array_index:1:device = "en0"
nat:devices:_array_index:1:name = "Built-in Ethernet"
nat:setStateVersion = 1
nat:startedTime = "2004-10-09 02:15:15 -0600"
nat:activeICMP = 0
```

Enabling NAT is as easy as choosing a network interface to share in the Settings pane of Server Admin's NAT module (illustrated in Figure 13-3). This should be the public interface—the one connected to the Internet, rather than to the private LAN.

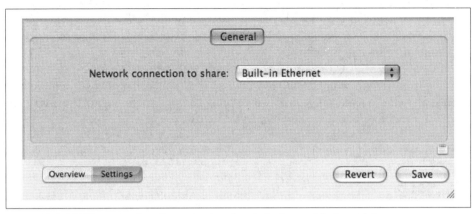

Figure 13-3. NAT's minimal configuration interface in its Server Admin module.

Once NAT is configured, the service can be started. Clients on the private network should list the private interface of the server in the router field of their network configuration, as illustrated in Figure 13-4. This kind of configuration is usually best accomplished automatically, using DHCP.

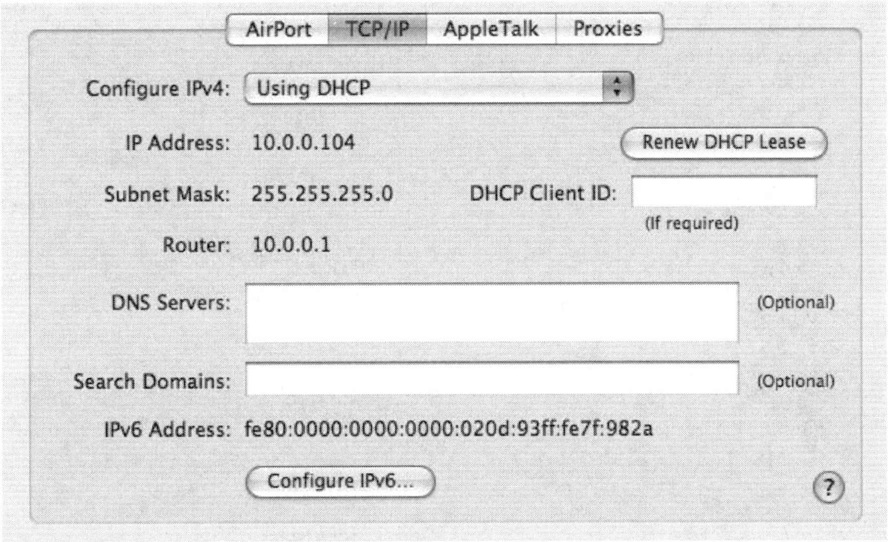

Figure 13-4. Clients use the NAT server as a router, as listed in the Network pane of the System Preferences application.

Architecture

NAT services in Mac OS X Server are provided by the *natd* daemon in conjunction with *ipfw* (Mac OS X and Mac OS X Server's packet filter, or firewall, which is covered in more depth in Chapter 21). *natd* is started by the NAT startup item according to the NATSERVER setting in */etc/hostconfig*. This startup item uses the *serveradmin* command to start *nat* (specifically, with the */usr/sbin/serveradmin --start nat* command). *serveradmin*, in turn, instructs *servermgrd* to read */etc/nat/natd.plist* and to produce from it */etc/nat/natd.conf.apple*, which is a standard *natd* configuration file. Finally, the *natd* daemon is started with the *–f* flag, instructing it to use *natd.conf.apple* for its configuration, as shown in Example 13-1.

Example 13-1. Apple's configuration plist for natd. servermgrd's servermgr_nat plug-in. servermgr_ nat reads in this file and produces from it /etc/nat/natd.conf.apple.

```
<?xml version="1.0" encoding="UTF-8"?>
<!DOCTYPE plist PUBLIC "-//Apple Computer//DTD PLIST 1.0//EN" "http://www.apple.com/DTDs/
PropertyList-1.0.dtd">
<plist version="1.0">
<dict>
        <key>verbose</key>
        <true/>
        <key>clamp_mss</key>
        <true/>
        <key>deny_incoming</key>
        <false/>
        <key>dynamic</key>
        <true/>
        <key>interface</key>
        <string>en0</string>
        <key>log</key>
        <true/>
        <key>log_denied</key>
        <false/>
        <key>proxy_only</key>
        <false/>
        <key>reverse</key>
        <false/>
        <key>same_ports</key>
        <true/>
        <key>unregistered_only</key>
        <false/>
        <key>use_sockets</key>
        <true/>
</dict>
</plist>
```

A firewall rule is enabled when NAT is started, diverting all traffic that goes across external interface to the *natd* process (the firewall must be enabled in order for NAT to work), as shown in Example 13-2.

Example 13-2. NAT uses an ipfw divert rule to send all traffic that touches the external interface to the natd process.

```
[ace2:~] nadmin% sudo ipfw show | grep divert
Password:
00010  2320783    971323335 divert 8668 ip from any to any via en0
```

natd then processes the packets, proxying them when appropriate, and, when it receives the reply, sends it back to the original client. This process is illustrated in Figure 13-5.

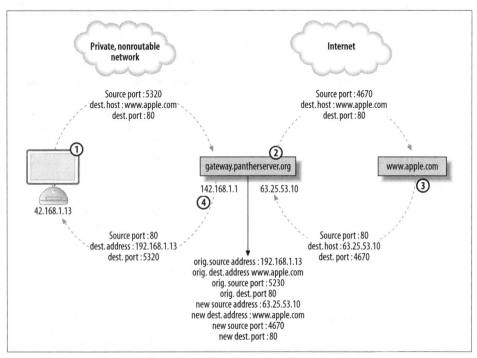

Figure 13-5. NAT operates by keeping a table of source and destination ports, proxying connections to and from the private network.

Advanced Configuration

Despite its simplicity and the limited nature of its graphical configuration interface, NAT has quite a bit of functionality that Apple hasn't chosen to make available. To get a good idea of this extra capability, peruse its manpage. Some of these options, however, are available with a little command-line editing. As seen earlier, Server Admin and *servermgrd* maintain an XML file at */etc/nat/natd.plist* that describes some of the most typical options.

Several other NAT options are inactive but available, however, as described in */etc/nat/natd.plist.default*. By editing */etc/nat/natd.plist*, an administrator may make use of these options. They, together with the default options, are described in Table 13-1. A fairly complete sample configuration follows.

Table 13-1. Commonly used options from natd.plist.

Option	Value	Description
interface	String; device name for public interface, for instance, *en1*	
alias_address	String; IP address of public interface	
dynamic	Boolean (true or false)	When set to true, *natd* automatically adjusts for changes to the IP address on the public interface.
log	Boolean (true or false)	Log to */var/log/alias.log*.
log_denied	Boolean (true or false)	Log denied incoming packets to *syslog*.
log_facility	String	Facility to use when sending data to *syslog*. Can be any facility specified in */etc/syslog.conf*.
deny_incoming	Boolean (true or false)	Specifies to not pass unsolicited packets back to the internal network. This setting helps to protect hosts in the private address space, while still allowing for the legitimate connections that they initiate.
unregistered_only	Boolean (true or false)	Allow only outgoing packets from private address spaces (10.0.0.0/8, 172.16.0.0/12, and 192.168.0.0/16). This setting helps to ensure that the connections are legitimate and not spoofed.
punch_fw	Dictionary; *basenumber:count*	Punch holes in an *ipfw*-based firewall for active-mode FTP and IRC connections. A maximum of *count* rules, starting at rule number *basenumber*, will be used. For more information on *ipfw* rule ordering, see Chapter 20.
proxy_rule	Dictionary; port *xxx*; server *a.b.c.d:yyyy*	Transparent proxy. Outgoing packets on port *xxx* will be redirected to server *a.b.c.d* on port *yyyy*. Useful, for instance, in order to force internal clients to use a web proxy.
Proxy_only	Boolean (true or false)	Specifies to *only* do transparent proxy. Do not do normal NAT.
redirect_port	Array; a set of several values: proto (protocol), targetIP, targetPortRange, aliasIP, aliasPortRange.	Establishes a rule specifying that traffic on a particular port be redirected to another host. Usually used to make a service running on a host in the private access space publicly available.
redirect_address	Array; a set of two values: localIP and publicIP.	Set up Static NAT, which establishes a one-to-one relationship between an internal and external IP.

The most commonly used *natd* options—redirect_port and proxy_rule—are illustrated in Example 13-3, which is a simplified version of the one used in my office—I redirect so many ports that including them all here is probably redundant.

Example 13-3. My natd.plist file. Portions that differ from Apple's default installation are commented.

```
<?xml version="1.0" encoding="UTF-8"?>
<!DOCTYPE plist PUBLIC "-//Apple Computer//DTD PLIST 1.0//EN" "http://www.apple.com/DTDs/
PropertyList-1.0.dtd">
<plist version="1.0">
<dict>
    <key>clamp_mss</key>
    <true/>
    <key>deny_incoming</key>
    <false/>
    <key>dynamic</key>
    <true/>
    <key>interface</key>
    <string>en0</string>
    <key>log</key>
    <true/>
    <key>log_denied</key>
    <false/>
    <key>proxy_only</key>
    <false/>
```

Port 3389 (Microsoft Remote Desktop Protocol) is redirected to my internal Windows domain controller:

```
    <key>redirect_port</key>
    <array>
        <dict>
            <key>aliasIP</key>
            <string>24.9.136.68</string>
            <key>aliasPortRange</key>
            <string>3389</string>
            <key>proto</key>
            <string>tcp</string>
            <key>targetIP</key>
            <string>192.168.1.4</string>
            <key>targetPortRange</key>
            <string>3389</string>
        </dict>
    </array>
```

All outgoing SMTP is proxied to a single SMTP server. I don't actually have this rule, but I thought it would make a good example, as this sort of thing is a common request:

```
    <key>proxy_rule</key>
    <array>
            <dict>
            <key>port</key>
            <string>25</string>
            <key>server</key>
            <string>smtp-out.4am-media.com:25</string>
            </dict>
```

```
    </array>
        <key>reverse</key>
        <false/>
        <key>same_ports</key>
        <true/>
        <key>unregistered_only</key>
        <false/>
        <key>use_sockets</key>
        <true/>
    </dict>
    </plist>
```

The result of these settings can be viewed with the *serveradmin* command, as shown here:

```
[ace2:~] nadmin% sudo /usr/sbin/serveradmin --command nat:command=readSettings
nat:command = "readSettings"
nat:readStatus = 0
nat:configuration:deny_incoming = no
nat:configuration:log_denied = no
nat:configuration:clamp_mss = yes
nat:configuration:reverse = no
nat:configuration:log = yes
nat:configuration:proxy_only = no
nat:configuration:dynamic = yes
nat:configuration:use_sockets = yes
nat:configuration:interface = "en0"
nat:configuration:unregistered_only = no
nat:configuration:same_ports = yes
nat:configuration:redirect_port:_array_index:0:proto = "tcp"
nat:configuration:redirect_port:_array_index:0:targetPortRange = "3389"
nat:configuration:redirect_port:_array_index:0:aliasPortRange = "3389"
nat:configuration:redirect_port:_array_index:0:aliasIP = "24.9.136.68"
nat:configuration:redirect_port:_array_index:0:targetIP = "192.168.1.4"
```

as well as by viewing */etc/nat/nat.conf.apple*. Generally, the NAT service needs to be stopped and restarted so that its configuration file may be written correctly from *natd.plist*. *natd* keeps a log at */var/log/alias.log*, but there's generally not a whole lot there that's interesting or useful. Other *natd* options including use_sockets, same_ports, redirect_proto, in_port, out_port, port, target_address, and clamp_mss are not as common, and are documented in *natd*'s manpage.

PART IV

File Services

Mac OS X Server seeks to be a universal file service platform, and is capable of serving a single file system out over AFP (Apple Filing Protocol), SMB (Server Message Block, or Samba), NFS (Network File System), and FTP (File Transfer Protocol). This part of the book devotes a chapter to each of these services after first touching on Share Point, Automount, and Home Directory management in Chapter 14, *File Services Overview*. This part of the book wraps up with an overview of Mac OS X Server's Print Services.

Chapters in this part include:

Chapter 14, *File Services Overview*
Chapter 15, *Apple Filing Protocol*
Chapter 16, *Windows File Services*
Chapter 17, *FTP*
Chapter 18, *Network File System*
Chapter 19, *Print Services*

File Services Overview

Although the trend is slowly changing with the tremendous diversity of features that Mac OS X Server now provides, Apple server products have traditionally focused strongly on file services. Often displaced in the mid-1990s, as Windows servers broadened their reach into more and more of the niche markets that Apple focused on at the time, these services are poised to make a real comeback in the 10.3 and 10.4 timeframe, with a deepening featureset and an underlying OS that is relatively secure and robust.

Mac OS X Server seeks to be a universal file service platform, and is capable of serving a single filesystem out over AFP, SMB, NFS, and FTP (Apple Filing Protocol, Server Message Block, Network File System, and File Transfer Protocol, respectively). This section devotes an in-depth chapter to each of these services after touching on Share Point, Automount and Home Directory management in this introductory text.

Share Points

A Share Point (or share) is a portion for the Server's filesystem that has been made available to network clients using a file-sharing protocol. The focus of Mac OS X Server's File Sharing capabilities is its ability to easily manage multiple protocols across any given share point. Management of share points takes place primarily in Workgroup Manager's Sharing section (illustrated in Figure 14-1). Here share points are defined, service-specific share point options are specified, and Network Mounts (automatically mounted network shares, otherwise known as *automounts*) are defined.

Selection of a Share Point contextually populates the General tab of Workgroup Manager's right pane with service-agnostic data about that share point, including the privileges granted to the Owner, the Group, and "Everyone." In Panther (unlike AppleShare IP), the Owner must be a user and Group setting must specify a group—a group may not be the owner of a share.

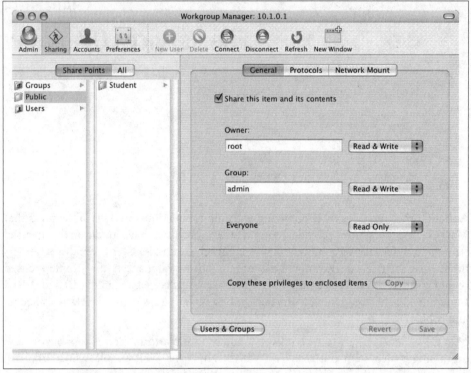

Figure 14-1. Workgroup Manager's Sharing section (discussed briefly in Chapter 3) is the center of Mac OS X Server's Share Point Management capabilities. When its Sharing option is first selected, Work Group Manager defaults to a General view of all defined Share Points.

Users and Groups from any directory domain your server has access to may be accessed by clicking the Users & Groups button. Users and Groups may be dragged from this well and dropped into the Owner and Group fields for the selected share point. This interface may also be used to manager ownership and permissions for files and directories within the share point.

This pane also presents an option to "Copy these privileges to enclosed items." As of 10.3.5, this option copies both ownership and permissions recursively to every item enclosed by the selected directory.

Arguably, "Everyone" should actually say "Everyone Else" since both Owner and Group privileges take precedence over "everyone" access. These levels correspond to User, Group, and Other (U-G-O) permissions seen on the command line. For a more in-depth discussion of permissions, see *Running Mac OS X Panther* (O'Reilly, 2004).

The Protocols tab (illustrated partially in Figure 14-2) reveals a pull-down menu used to set service-specific (AFP, SMB, FTP, and NFS) options for the selected share. These options are covered in the chapters relating to their respective protocols.

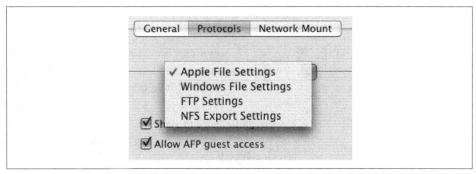

Figure 14-2. The Protocols tab of Workgroup Manager's Sharing section allows management of service-specific options for the selected share.

Finally, the Network Mount option allows the currently selected share to be mounted on demand in a particular directory domain. This setting is required for shares on which network-available home directories will be housed and is very useful for making resources—such as fonts or shared applications—available to multiple computers and users. Automounts are discussed extensively later in this chapter.

Managing Share Points

A default installation Mac OS X Server has three shares defined: /Users, /Groups, and /Shared Items/Public. All have guest access turned on by default, and all are located on the system's boot drive. While this might be acceptable in very limited circumstances, most administrators will want to make some modifications. It's a good idea to keep nonsystem resources somewhere other than the boot drive; not every share point should be available via every service; and guest access should generally not be enabled.

 Guest access is enabled on out-of-box shares. Unless the services themselves are turned on during initial configuration, though, this has little impact on security. Services should not generally be activated during initial server configuration, since software and security updates have not yet been applied.

The administrator created during initial configuration has a Home directory on the /Users share point, so if you wish to allow that user to log in to the directory domain and access a network Home directory, you must either leave the initial Users share defined, move the Home directory to another share (for which the ditto or hfstar commands are is a good choices), or simply recreate it. In any case, the /Users share is mostly disposable, and not all that useful if there are higher-performing or more reliable filesystems available.

 It is also feasible to mount those higher performance resources at /Users using the *fstab* file and *diskarbitrationd*. See Chapter 2 for details.

/Groups and /Shared Items/Public are both empty in an out-of-box install and may be unshared and probably deleted. If you're interested in Mac OS X's client-management capabilities, though, you will probably want to have one or more group share points defined somewhere.

Unsharing Items

To un-share an item using the Workgroup Manager:

1. Open Workgroup Manager's Sharing section.
2. Select the share point in the Share Points tab.
3. Uncheck the "Share this item and its contents" checkbox in Workgroup Manager's right pane.
4. Click the Save button.

Defining new shares

More often than not, you'll want to define new shares once your server is configured. This is accomplished using the All tab in Workgroup Manager's Sharing section, which allows the entire contents of the server's installed hard drives to be browsed. When the folder to be shared has been located, you simply select it, click the "Share this item and its contents" box, and then choose Save. That folder is now effectively a share point, and will be listed in the Share Points tab. Unless otherwise configured, it will take on the default settings for all new share points, including:

- Guest access is enabled for all services.
- AFP, SMB, and FTP access are enabled.
- NFS access is disabled.
- The share is not mounted automatically.

Careful administrators, rather than simply enabling a share point, will cull through the options available for each service, changing their default values to reflect local policy and security needs before clicking on "Save."

Most other open-and-save dialogs (where the paradigm of browsing the filesystem was really perfected) feature a "new folder" option. This is not the case with Panther's Workgroup Manager. If you want to share out a new folder, you must first create it with another tool— either the finder (locally or using Remote Desktop) or via SSH, using the *mkdir* command.

Once saved, the share point definition is buffered to the *netinfo://config/SharePoints* directory, where it is stored on a per-share point basis. This data can be viewed either using either *dscl* (Example 14-1) or any NetInfo utilities (*nidump*, *nicl*, or *niutil* all work). In some cases, this is the data's final destination; *AppleFileServer*, for instance, reads its share data directly out of NetInfo. Other services (such as FTP and SMB) make use of configuration files generated from this data, as described later in their respective chapters.

Example 14-1. Using dscl, first to list all share points and then to read the default options for the new sw sharepoint.

```
g5:~ nadmin$ dscl . -list /SharePoints
Groups
Public
sw
Users
g5:~ nadmin$ dscl . -read /SharePoints/sw
afp_guestaccess: 1
afp_name: sw
afp_shared: 1
afp_use_parent_owner: 0
afp_use_parent_privs: 0
directory_path: /sw
ftp_guestaccess: 1
ftp_name: sw
ftp_shared: 1
smb_createmask: 0644
smb_directorymask: 0755
smb_guestaccess: 1
smb_inherit_permissions: 0
smb_name: sw
smb_oplocks: 0
smb_shared: 1
smb_strictlocking: 1
AppleMetaNodeLocation: /NetInfo/DefaultLocalNode
RecordName: sw
```

The sharing Command

In addition to Workgroup Manager's graphical mechanism for share point management, Apple also includes its command-line driven cousin, the *sharing* command. Although its syntax is somewhat confusing and not really conducive to day-to-day management, it is quite functional, as shown in Example 14-2. The *sharing* command's three basic flags are listed in Table 14-1.

Example 14-2. The sharing command's –l flag lists established share points. Its output is limited here due to the command's verbosity.

```
g5:~ ladmin$ sharing -l

                List of Share Points
name:          Users
path:          /Users
      afp:     {
               name:   Users
               shared: 1
               guest access:   1
               inherit perms:  0
      }
      ftp:     {
               name:   Users
               shared: 1
               guest access:   1
      }
      smb:     {
               name:   Users
               shared: 1
               guest access:   1
               inherit perms:  0
               oplocks:        0
               strict locking: 1
               directory mask: 493
               create mask:    420
      }
```

Table 14-1. Command-line flags available to the sharing command. Sharing may be used to manipulate share points from the command line.

Flag	Description	Syntax
–a	Create a new share point.	*sharing –a /Shared\ Items/newshare*
–e	Edit an existing share point.	*sharing –e Users*
–r	Remove a share point.	*sharing –r Groups*
–l	List share points.	*sharing –l*

When used to share out a directory, the –a flag creates a new share point that is (unless otherwise specified) given the same set of default options as share points created in Workgroup Manager's graphical interface. –a accepts as an argument the full path to the directory to be shared, while –e and –r (edit and remove) expect the share name, rather than its filesystem path. A number of modifier flags may be used with the –a and –e options to specify protocol-specific share point options. These are covered in depth in the AFP, SMB, and FTP chapters.

Automounts

Once the share itself is defined it is very easy to request that it be automounted. When the share is selected in the Share Points tab of Workgroup Manager's Sharing section, click on the Network Mount tab (pictured in Figure 14-3) and enable the "Create a mount record for this share point" checkbox. Next, choose a directory domain within which to share it (authenticating as a domain administrator if prompted), choose a protocol, define its role using the Use For list, and you're done.

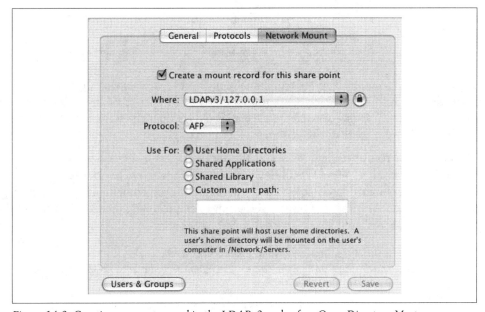

Figure 14-3. Creating a mount record in the LDAPv3 node of an Open Directory Master.

To automount a share point:

1. Select the share in the Share Points tab of Workgroup Manager's Sharing section.
2. Click the Network Mount tab in Workgroup Manager's right pane.
3. Click the "Create a mount record for this share point" checkbox.
4. Choose a directory domain in which the Share should be mounted automatically.
5. Select the protocol that clients should use to mount the share. The graphical interface allows you to select either AFP or NFS. SMB automounts (which are not supported outside the Active Directory plug-in) are discussed later in this chapter. Generally, choose AFP.
6. Select a role for the Share Point. These roles are discussed in Table 14-2.

Table 14-2. An analysis of automount behavior in 10.3.5. This behavior is subject to change, and has changed in the past in some minor OS releases.

Role	Description
User Home Directories	Share is mounted at */private/automount/Network/Servers/hostname/sharename* and a symbolic link is established from */private/automount/Network/Servers/hostname* to */Network/Servers/hostname*. For a more in-depth discussion of Home directories, see "Supporting Home Directories," later in this chapter.
Shared Applications	Share is mounted at */private/automount/Network/Applications* and symbolically linked to */Network/Applications*.
Shared Library	Share is mounted at */private/automount/Network/Library* and symbolically linked to */Network/Library*.
Custom Mount Path	Share is mounted at path specified by administrator. Path must exist ahead of time on client.

Typically, clients within the shared domain must reboot in order to register the newly defined automount. New automounts may also be registered by restarting the *automount* daemon, being sure to preserve all the flags that it is started with according to the NFS startup item; this requires a lot of care, though

The *automount* record itself is stored in the shared domain that is specified in the Network Mount tab's "Where" pull-down menu. Much like a network user, this setting allows it to be made available to every computer in the domain. The raw record itself can be seen with the *dscl* utility (shown in Example 14-3), or with Workgroup Manager's Inspector menu.

Example 14-3. Using the dscl utility to examine a mount record. Notice the use of the double backslash to escape the forward slash in the name of the mount record itself. This mount record corresponds to the one created in Figure 14-2.

```
g5:~ nadmin$ dscl /LDAPv3/127.0.0.1 -read /Mounts/g5.4am-media.com:\\/Users
cn: g5.4am-media.com:/Users
mountDirectory: /Network/Servers/
mountOption: net url==afp://;AUTH=NO%20USER%20AUTHENT@g5.4am-media.com/Users
mountType: url
objectClass: mount top
AppleMetaNodeLocation: /LDAPv3/127.0.0.1
PasswordPlus: ********
RecordName: g5.4am-media.com:/Users
VFSLinkDir: /Network/Servers/
VFSOpts: net url==afp://;AUTH=NO%20USER%20AUTHENT@g5.4am-media.com/Users
VFSType: url
```

Although only AFP and NFS are available in the choice of automount protocols in 10.3.3, SMB automounts, including SMB home directories, are supported as of that software update. The process to create an SMB automount record is not complex. The easiest method is to start with a valid AFP record and modify it to accurately reflect the host and share point that should be automatically accessed. A template SMB mount record is demonstrated in Example 14-4, and is also available for download from the book's web site (*www.pantherserver.org*).

Example 14-4. A mount record for an SMB share point. When added to a directory domain, this record will allow the HOMES share on w2k.pantherserver.org to be mounted on demand using SMB.

```
{
  "name" = ( "mounts" );
  CHILDREN = (
    {
      "vfstype" = ( "url" );
      "opts" = ( "url==smb://AUTH=NO%20USER%20AUTHENT@w2k.pantherserver.org/HOMES",↵
"net" );
      "name" = ( "w2k:/HOMES" );
      "dir" = ( "/Network/Servers" );
    }
  )
}
```

Automount Schema

Like user records, automount records have certain attributes that are required in order for them to be recognized by the Operating System. These attributes will be called different things depending on where they're stored. Table 14-3 translates among Open Directory, NetInfo, and Apple's LDAP implementation in order to facilitate manual configuration of automount records.

Table 14-3. Even though they all contain precisely the same data, automount attributes in various directory services are called different names.

Open Directory	NetInfo	LDAP	Example
RecordName	name	cn	`xs1.pantherserver.org:/Users`
VFSLinkDir	dir	mountDirectory	`/NetworkServers`
VFSType	vfstype	mountType	`url`
VFSOpts	opts	mountOptions	`Net, url==afp://;AUTH=NO%20USER%20AUTHENT@`

Guest Access and Automounts

A common issue relating to automounted share points is the assumed requirement of guest access. Because automounted shares are typically mounted automatically on demand, and since it doesn't make sense to store credentials in the automount record (the directory domain is typically world-readable, and posting passwords to a world-readable location is usually a bad idea), and finally since the string AUTH=NO%20USER%20AUTHENT often appears in the automount record, many administrators assume that guest access is and has always been required for automounted AFP and SMB share points. This myth has apparently been exacerbated by some at Apple. This does not make it any more correct.

Allowing anonymous access where it is not required for business or organizational purposes, much less requiring it, is tremendously bad security practice. It is true that enabling guest access for automounts masks several common automount misconfigurations. Correlation, though, does not imply causality, and careful testing will always result in more accurate descriptions of a system's behavior. These principles should help to guide you in automount planning. Guest access is not required for an automounted share:

- If the automounted share point houses home directories for Jaguar or Panther clients, guest access does not have to be enabled. As of 10.2, guest access is never required for network home directory shares. The user's home directory is mounted (or remounted) using the credentials supplied by the user at login.

 If guest access is not enabled on the home directory share, personal web sites (in the users' *Sites* directory) will not be available unless the web server is running on the home directory server. This functionality is typically not critical, and is not worth enabling guest access where it would not otherwise be available.

- If the AFP server on which the share resides supports Kerberos authentication, guest access is never required. In some cases, the removal of the `;AUTH=NO%20USER%20AUTHENT` string from the automount record might be required. This step breaks older, non-Kerberized clients; this requirement (which is inconsistent, to say the least) is considered a bug.

These two circumstances describe the vast majority of automount scenarios. At the same time, certain less common deployments do require guest access:

- If the automounted share point is housing home directories for 10.0 or 10.1 clients, guest access is required. For reasons that are not very relevant now, 10.0 and 10.1 were unable to use AFP network home directories unless the share on which they were housed allowed guest access.
- If the AFP server on which a non–home directory share resides does not support or is not configured to use Kerberos authentication, guest access is required. (The non–home directory part is important; as mentioned earlier, home directories are mounted with the credentials of the user logging in.)

Basically, if Kerberos authentication isn't enabled on the file server (there is no Open Directory or Active Directory shared domain, and no third-party KDC is available) *and* the share does not house Jaguar or Panther home directories, guest access is probably required in order to make the file share automatically available to hosts in the shared domain. Luckily, these circumstances are increasingly rare, and in most cases, guest access can be disabled.

Storing automounts in the local domain: stealth infrastructure

Sometimes no shared domain is available to host mount records, either because the domain schema is too strictly defined or because there simply isn't a shared directory service in place. One possible solution is to store automount records in the client's local NetInfo domain, rather than in a shared directory. This approach is especially common in circumstances where clients are managed through a centralized imaging process, since the mount only has to be set up once, on the master image, rather than on each individual machine.

In order to assist in this process, I've included a template dump file (see Example 14-5) of a local NetInfo database's */mounts* directory.

Example 14-5. An automount record in nidump format. This file can be edited to reflect your local environment and then reloaded into the local NetInfo database.

```
{
  "name" = ( "mounts" );
  CHILDREN = (
    {
      "vfstype" = ( "url" );
      "opts" = ( "url==afp://AUTH=NO%20USER%20AUTHENT@homes.pantherserver.org/HOMES",
"net" );
      "name" = ( " homes.pantherserver.org:/HOMES" );
      "dir" = ( "/Network/Servers" );
    }
  )
}
```

 You can download the *mountdump* shell script using the following command:

```
curl -O http://www.4am-media.com/mountdump
```

This script can be edited to suit your local environment and then loaded into the local NetInfo database of the clients that should access the *automount* using the *niload* command, as shown here:

```
mab9718:~ mbartosh$ sudo niload -r /mounts . < mountdump
```

If the edited mount has been successfully integrated, the query shown in Example 14-6 should be successful.

Example 14-6. Querying lookupd for mounts. Mounts stored in NetInfo might show up twice, since they are located once using lookupd's niagent and once using dsagent. For more information on lookupd's agents, see the Appendix.

```
mab9718:~ mbartosh$ lookupd -q mount

dir: /Network/Servers
name: g5:/Users
opts: url==afp://AUTH=NO%20USER%20AUTHENT@g5.4am-media.com/Users net
vfstype: url

dir: /Network/Servers
name: g5:/Users
```

Example 14-6. Querying lookupd for mounts. Mounts stored in NetInfo might show up twice, since they are located once using lookupd's niagent and once using dsagent. For more information on lookupd's agents, see the Appendix. (continued)

```
opts: url==afp://AUTH=NO%20USER%20AUTHENT@g5.4am-media.com/Users net
vfstype: url
```

The automount should be fully functional either on reboot or after restart of the automount daemon.

```
big15:~ mab$ cat record
{
  "vfstype" = ( "url" );
  "opts" = ( "url==afp://AUTH=NO%20USER%20AUTHENT@afp.pantherserver.org/HOMES", "net"
);
  "name" = ( "afp.pantherserver.org:/HOMES" );
  "dir" = ( "/Network/Servers" );
}
big15:~ mab$ sudo nicl . -create /mounts/afp.pantherserver.org:\\/HOMES
Password:
big15:~ mab$ sudo niload -r /mounts/afp.pantherserver.org:\\/HOMES . < record
```

Troubleshooting Automounts

Automounts have proven to be one of the more contentious aspects of user management in Mac OS X. They are delicate—especially when used as home directories—and depend on accurate data and service configuration. The first step when troubleshooting *automount* issues is to ensure that the operating system is aware of their existence. This step is easily accomplished by using *dscl* or *lookupd* to query the Open Directory responder chain, as shown in Example 14-7.

Example 14-7. Using lookupd's query mode to locate all available mount records.

```
g5:~ ladmin$ lookupd -q mount -a allMounts

dir: /Network/Servers/
name: g5.pantherserver.org:/Users
opts: net url==afp://;AUTH=NO%20USER%20AUTHENT@207.224.49.181/Users
vfstype: url

dir: /Network/Applications
name: g5.pantherserver.org:/Applications
opts: url==afp://;AUTH=NO%20USER%20AUTHENT@207.224.49.181/Applications
vfstype: url
```

Automounts are managed and sometimes mounted by the *automount* daemon, which is started by the NFS Startup Item. Luckily, it is fairly verbose when called in debug mode, so it is feasible to *ssh* into a client machine and run it manually in order to gather data about any problems you might encounter. This operation is made slightly more complex in Panther, as two instances of *automount* are actually running. One manages automatically mounted filesystems (which we're interested in), while the other, using *automount*'s *–nsl* flag, manages the Finder's somewhat idio-syncratic browsing behavior (which I avoid as much as possible). For this reason, we have to look at the process listing before we start killing things (Example 14-8).

Example 14-8. Using the ps and grep commands to search for automount processes.

```
mab9718:~ mbartosh$ ps auxwww | grep automount
root       427  0.0  0.1   28972   684 ??  Ss   Mon03PM   0:00.09 /usr/sbin/automount
-f -m /Network -nsl
root       430  0.0  0.1   28972   688 ??  Ss   Mon03PM   0:00.07 /usr/sbin/automount
-f -m /automount/Servers -fstab -mnt /private/var/automount/Network/Servers -m /automount/
static -static -mnt /private/var/automount
mbartosh  2645  0.0  0.1   18172   344 std S+   4:09PM    0:00.00 grep automount
```

From the output of *ps*, we can infer that we should kill the *automount* with the pro-cess ID (PID) of 430. We can then restart it, adding the *–d* (or debug) flag, in order to get more in-depth data about *automount*'s behavior. Both of these operations require *root* privileges, provided by the *sudo* command; see Example 14-9.

Example 14-9. Killing the automount daemon and restarting it in debug mode.

```
mab9718:~ mbartosh$ sudo kill 430
mab9718:~ mbartosh$ sudo /usr/sbin/automount -d -f -m /automount/Servers -fstab -mnt
/private/var/automount/Network/Servers -m /automount/static -static -mnt /private/var/
automount
automount[2655]: automount version 57
automount[2655]: Host Info: mab9718.local darwin 7.2 ppc (big endian)
automount[2655]: handle_deferred_requests: completing forked mount.
automount[2655]: Initializing map "-fstab" parent "/automount" mountpt "Servers"
automount[2655]: New (FstabMap) mount: mab9718.local:/ on ...
automount[2655]: New (FstabMap) mount: g5:/Users on /Network/Servers...
automount[2655]: ***** Found url string afp://AUTH=NO%20USER%20AUTHENT@g5.4am-media.com/
Users
automount[2655]: New (FstabMap) mount: g5:/Users on /Network/Servers...
automount[2655]: Creating intermediate directory automount...
automount[2655]: Creating intermediate directory Servers...
automount[2655]: Mounting map -fstab on /automount/Servers
automount[2655]: Mounted -fstab on /automount/Servers
automount[2655]: Initializing map "-static" parent "/automount" mountpt "static"
automount[2655]: Creating intermediate directory automount...
automount[2655]: Creating intermediate directory static...
automount[2655]: Mounting map -static on /automount/static
automount[2655]: Mounted -static on /automount/static
automount[2655]: Starting service
```

When the automounted portion of the filesystem is accessed, the mount is triggered, and the automount proceeds. Much data can be gathered here if things aren't going right. The important thing to remember is to perform this analysis while remaining as true to the original circumstances of the failure as possible. If the mount failure occurs on login, then you'll need to *ssh* into the client, begin *automount*'s debug ses-sion, and log in graphically.

Supporting Home Directories

The term *Home directory* has different implications in different situations. For users accessing a standalone server, a Home directory might simply be their user folder—a convenient place to store files, available by connecting to some file server somewhere using SMB or AFP. For users accessing a *shared directory domain* (such as Active Directory or Open Directory Server), a Home directory is much more, carrying with its user settings and documents, and acting as the center of the user's computing environment. Mac OS X Server's interface for Home directory management (the Home tab of the User Record in the Accounts section) reflects this to some extent.

Users records in the Server's local domain (Figure 14-4) are automatically given a list of local share points below which their home directory may be located. The resulting filesystem path, seen in the Home field, is stored in the user record's NFSHomeDirectory attribute.

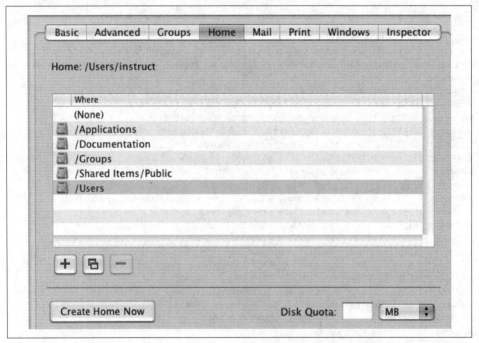

Figure 14-4. Home directory locations for users in a server's local domain are chosen from a list of local share points. Home directories may be created below any share point.

User records stored in a shared directory domain, however, are assumed to have a type of Network, and (rather than being offered a list of share points) are offered a list of *automounts* available in their domain, as seen in Figure 14-5. The resulting Home directory data is stored in the user record's NFSHomeDirectory attribute (as a filesystem path indicated in the Home field) and in the `HomeDirectory` attribute (as structured XML specifying the server and share point below which the Home directory may be located). Because these Home directories exist on automatically mounted shares, they should be available to any computer that is accessing the directory domain.

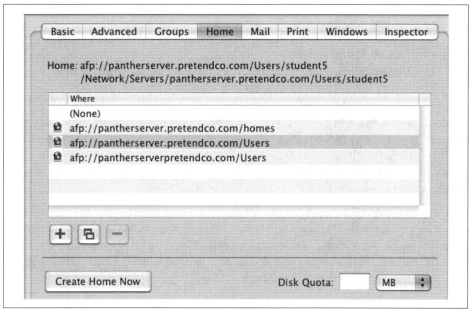

Figure 14-5. User accounts listed in a nonlocal directory domain are graphically allowed to have home directories on any automount located in the same shared domain as the user.

Virtual home directory shares

In Jaguar, lots of people went to the effort to implement an unsupported flag in the AFP server configuration that provided for virtual home directory shares. When a user logged in, rather than just being presented with a share point called Users (within which there could be hundreds of home directories), they'd see a share named the same as their username that provided access directly to their Home directory. For the sake of posterity, that flag was:

```
[ace2:~] mbartosh% sudo nicl . -create /config/AppleFileServer use_home_dirs 1
```

This feature proved so popular that Apple made this the default behavior in Panther Server. However, they did so with one fatal flaw that still exists in 10.3.3: the AFP server won't grant virtual share access to a user's Home directory unless it decides that they have a Home directory type of Network, something that Workgroup Manager makes very difficult when the user is not in a shared domain. Worse yet, the old flag has been deprecated and no longer works. Help is here, though.

The AFP server makes its oddly chosen determination based on the presence of NFSHomeDirectory and HomeDirectory attributes in the user record.

 As specified earlier, NFSHomeDirectory and HomeDirectory are the Open Directory names for two attributes typically used to support network Home directories.

NFSHomeDirectory actually has nothing to do with networking at all, much less NFS; it is simply the filesystem path to the user's Home directory. It typically looks something like */Network/Servers/g5. example.com/Users/bob*.

HomeDirectory is an XML *plist* containing the URL that's used at login time to build the path specified in NFSHomeDirectory.

When the user exists in a nonlocal domain, this is easy to accomplish in Workgroup Manager's interface; simply choose from the shares listed in the Home tab of the user's record (as seen earlier in Figure 14-5). Because the Home location is chosen from among automounted shares, the network data that *AppleFileServer* uses to determine that virtual shares should be available is populated.

No such option exists for users in the local domain, though. Instead, if you're looking for a graphical solution, you must click the + button at the lower-left corner of the user's Home tab. Once there, use the manual Home directory specification interface (shown in Figure 14-6) to enter data that points to a valid Home directory and register with the AFP server set as *network*.

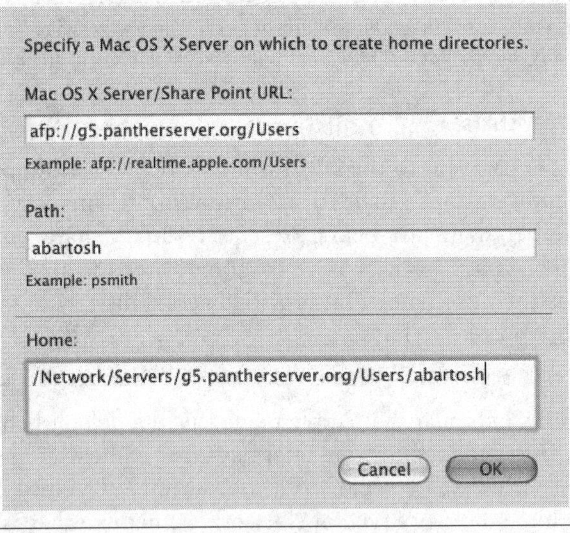

Specify a Mac OS X Server on which to create home directories.

Mac OS X Server/Share Point URL:

afp://g5.pantherserver.org/Users

Example: afp://realtime.apple.com/Users

Path:

abartosh

Example: psmith

Home:

/Network/Servers/g5.pantherserver.org/Users/abartosh

Cancel   OK

Figure 14-6. Using the manual home directory specification interface to create HomeDirectory and NFSHomeDirectory attributes that will result in successful advertisement of virtual home directory shares.

Since the data that needs to be in the user record is rather predictable, the shell script shown in Example 14-10 can be used to make the same change.

Example 14-10. This script populates Home directory data for users in the local domain, so that when they connect to the server via AFP, they will have the option of mounting a virtual home directory share.

```
#!/bin/sh
for i in `/usr/bin/ nireport . /users home | /usr/bin/ awk -F / '{ print $3 }' | /usr/bin/
egrep -v
'root|nobody'daemon|unknown|smmsp|lp|postfix|eppc|mysql|sshd|qtss|cyrus|mailman|appserver
'`
do
        nicl . -create /users/$i home /Network/Servers/`hostname`/Users/$i
        nicl . -create /users/$i home_loc "<home_dir><url>afp://`hostname`:/Users</url>
<path>$i</path></home_dir>"
done
```

 For now, Home directories for Mac OS X clients must live below a share point. Windows allows user Home directories to be on a virtual share. Although a user may connect to a file server and mount their Home directory there as a virtual share, they may use it in that form as a network Home directory as well. The share it lives under must also be available.

Home directories in /Volumes

Mac OS X and Mac OS X Server (as noted in Chapter 1) typically mount non-boot volumes in the */Volumes* directory. This feature presents several difficulties, all centered around the fact that the NFSHomeDirectory attribute (a filesystem path to a user's Home directory) is effectively limited to 89 characters. As shown here in Example 14-11, notice that the *automount* record contains a reference to */Volumes*.

Example 14-11. This automount record contains a reference to /Volumes. This reference is meaningless to AFP clients, which can see only filesystem resources contained below a particular share (/Volumes is not contained inside the share).

```
pantherserver:~ instruct$ dscl /LDAPv3/127.0.0.1 -read ↵
/Mounts/pantherserver.pretendco.com:\\/Volumes\\/tarbosh\\/homes
cn: pantherserver.pretendco.com:/Volumes/tarbosh/homes
mountDirectory: /Network/Servers/
mountOption: net url==afp://;AUTH=NO%20USER%20AUTHENT@pantherserver.pretendco.com/homes
mountType: url
objectClass: mount top
AppleMetaNodeLocation: /LDAPv3/127.0.0.1
PasswordPlus: ********
RecordName: pantherserver.pretendco.com:/Volumes/tarbosh/homes
VFSLinkDir: /Network/Servers/
VFSOpts: net url==afp://;AUTH=NO%20USER%20AUTHENT@pantherserver.pretendco.com/homes
VFSType: url
```

This reference exists solely to allow users with Network Home Directories to log in locally to the server. The *automount* daemon creates a symbolic link from the root of the filesystem, as shown in Example 14-12, to */Network/Servers/hostname* to ensure that network users get a consistent view of available resources regardless of where they log in from (locally on the server or remotely on the client).

Example 14-12. This symbolic link allows users logging in locally to the server to access share points contained in /Volumes.

```
pantherserver:~ instruct$ ls -la /Network/Servers/
total 2
dr-xr-xr-x  1 root  wheel  512 26 Jan 11:39 .
drwxr-xr-x  4 root  admin  136 25 Jan 08:33 ..
lrwxr-xr-x  1 root  wheel  512 25 Jan 16:50 pantherserver.pretendco.com -> /
```

Given the amount of headache this step ends up causing, that logic is debatable—very few users should typically be allowed to log into a server locally, and of that small group, few will have network Home directories. Unfortunately, though, all automounts created graphically with Workgroup Manager display this odd behavior. The updated automount record, shown in Example 14-13, reduces the overall length of the user's Home directory path, still allowing remote users to login successfully using network Home directories.

Example 14-13. This amended automount record functions identically to the first one presented in this section—with the exception that it shortens the path to the user's home directory. Existing users must have their home directories (which will be preserved) reassigned to the modified share for the shorter path name to take effect.

```
pantherserver:~ instruct$ dscl /LDAPv3/127.0.0.1 -read /Mounts/pantherserver.pretendco.
com:\\/homes
cn: pantherserver.pretendco.com:/homes
mountDirectory: /Network/Servers/
mountOption: net url==afp://;AUTH=NO%20USER%20AUTHENT@pantherserver.pretendco.com/homes
mountType: url
objectClass: mount top
AppleMetaNodeLocation: /LDAPv3/127.0.0.1
PasswordPlus: ********
RecordName: pantherserver.pretendco.com:/homes
VFSLinkDir: /Network/Servers/
VFSOpts: net url==afp://;AUTH=NO%20USER%20AUTHENT@pantherserver.pretendco.com/homes
VFSType: url
```

The easiest way to make this change is to use Workgroup Manager's All Records tab. While viewing the shared domain, choose the Accounts section. Choose the All Records tab (with the target icon) and from the resulting pull-down menu choose Mounts. A list of all available automount records in the shared domain should be visible in Workgroup Manager's right pane. Select the RecordName attribute of the mount record in */Volumes* and click the Edit (pencil) button at the bottom of the right pane. In the resulting dialog (shown in Figure 14-7), change the attribute's value so that it no longer refers to the full filesystem path of the share point and instead refers simply to the share name. Note that once this change is made, the home directory data of all user records with home directories on the share in question must be updated to reflect the change. The easiest way to do this is usually using a batch change in Workgroup Manager.

Figure 14-7. In this example, the share's RecordName attribute was modified to refer to the name of the share point (homes) rather than the full path to the share point (/Volumes/tarbush/homes). The dscl command could also be used toward this purpose.

If for some reason it is important to support local console logins on the server specifically for users with Home directories on this modified mount record, you may create a symbolic link from the share point's path to the root of the filesystem, as shown in Example 14-14.

Example 14-14. Creating a symbolic link to from the share in /Volumes to /sharename will allow users with network home directories to log in locally to the server.

```
pantherserver:~ instruct$ sudo ln -s /Volumes/tarbosh/homes /homes
Password:
pantherserver:~ instruct$
```

Because / is already linked to *Network/Servers/hostname*, this step has the effect of creating a path to */Network/Servers/hostname/homes*. This is the same path that AFP clients end up using when supporting Network Home directories for users with Home directories on that share point.

CHAPTER 15

Apple Filing Protocol

First developed in-house by Apple to run on the AppleTalk network stack, the Apple Filing Protocol (AFP) has undergone a long transformation—first to TCP/IP and then from the single-user Mac OS 9 to the more robust requirements of Mac OS X. It has simultaneously scaled from running on a serial line through increasingly robust Ethernet technologies up through now-common gigabit connections. Despite Apple's evolution towards more open and standardized practices, AFP is—for better or for worse (mostly for better)—still Apple's primary and preferred file sharing protocol.

This chapter examines Apple's AFP implementation, especially noting the evolution of its treatment of user identification and permissions management. As always, a great amount of care is taken to hold this discussion at an appropriate depth, hopefully bringing to bear an analysis that can not be found elsewhere.

 In its lifetime, AFP has seen several major revisions, the most recent of which is 3.1. Notable in AFP 3.1 are improvements to disconnect and reconnect behavior and better support for shared directory service domains. AFP 3.0 brought other important features that are roughly analogous to the features of HFS+: support for files larger than 2 GB, Unicode filename support, and per-file (rather than per-directory) permissions. For a long time, Panther Server was the only product that offered an AFP 3.1 installation. More recently, Novell Netware 6.5, Group Logic's ExtremeZIP 4.0, and the Open Source Netatalk project have added AFP 3.1 support.

AFP Management: Server Admin

AFP, like most other Mac OS X Server Services, can be graphically configured with the Server Admin application, under the AFP module of the server that is being managed. Also very similar to other available services are the options found in this interface: Overview, Logs, Connections, Graphs, and Settings. The overview pane (seen in Figure 15-1) supplies basic information about the state of the service—current throughput, the status of guest access, the number of current connections, and the service's start time. This information is also available using the *serveradmin* command.

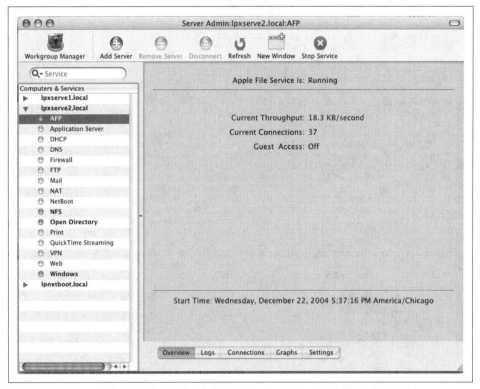

Figure 15-1. Most of the data available in AFP's Overview tab can be obtained with the serveradmin command's fullstatus and status directives.

The Logs pane (seen in Figure 15-2) grants access to the AFP service's logs, which are actually located in */Library/Logs/AppleFileService*. The error and access logs (*AppleFileServiceError.log* and *AppleFileServiceAccess.log*, respectively) are rolled (archived) periodically according to settings located in the service's Settings tab, discussed later in the chapter. The graphical interface does not offer any kind of filtering, making it necessary sometimes to access the logs directly using the *ssh* and *tail* commands—the logs grow too fast for the graphical interface to keep up. Keep in mind that not all undesirable behavior is considered an error. Incorrectly set permissions, for instance, will not show up in the error log, as their enforcement does not constitute an error on the part of the service. This means it is important to monitor both sets of logs carefully..

```
IP 192.168.1.153 - - [04/Jan/2005:12:20:26 -0600] "Wakeup by activity: moroschan" 0 0 0
IP 192.168.1.153 - - [04/Jan/2005:12:20:26 -0600] "Sleep request: moroschan" 0 0 0
IP 192.168.1.153 - - [04/Jan/2005:12:20:26 -0600] "Wakeup by activity: moroschan" 0 0 0
IP 192.168.1.116 - - [04/Jan/2005:12:24:00 -0600] "OpenFork 031.Assess_Gr8_C4.eps" 0 0 0
IP 192.168.1.116 - - [04/Jan/2005:12:24:00 -0600] "OpenFork 031.Assess_Gr8_C4.eps" 0 0 0
IP 192.168.1.116 - - [04/Jan/2005:12:26:55 -0600] "OpenFork .DS_Store" 0 0 0
IP 192.168.1.116 - - [04/Jan/2005:12:26:56 -0600] "OpenFork .DS_Store" 0 0 0
IP 192.168.1.116 - - [04/Jan/2005:12:26:56 -0600] "OpenFork .DS_Store" 0 0 0
IP 192.168.1.116 - - [04/Jan/2005:12:26:56 -0600] "OpenFork .DS_Store" 0 0 0
IP 192.168.1.116 - - [04/Jan/2005:12:26:56 -0600] "OpenFork Copy of ISBN.xls" 0 0 0
IP 192.168.1.116 - - [04/Jan/2005:12:26:56 -0600] "OpenFork 7_1.pdf" 0 0 0
IP 192.168.1.116 - - [04/Jan/2005:12:26:56 -0600] "OpenFork 7_22.pdf" 0 0 0
IP 192.168.1.116 - - [04/Jan/2005:12:26:56 -0600] "OpenFork 7_29.pdf" 0 0 0
IP 192.168.1.116 - - [04/Jan/2005:12:26:56 -0600] "OpenFork FYI.doc" 0 0 0
IP 192.168.1.116 - - [04/Jan/2005:12:26:56 -0600] "OpenFork PRICING.doc" 0 0 0
IP 192.168.1.116 - - [04/Jan/2005:12:26:56 -0600] "OpenFork VOYAGES pricing 2.xls" 0 0 0
IP 192.168.1.116 - - [04/Jan/2005:12:27:20 -0600] "OpenFork loyola kewpie.tif" 0 0 0
IP 192.168.1.116 - - [04/Jan/2005:12:27:20 -0600] "OpenFork loyola snowman.tif" 0 0 0
IP 192.168.1.116 - - [04/Jan/2005:12:27:20 -0600] "OpenFork Travel Cover 4_title page.psd" 0 0 0
IP 192.168.1.116 - - [04/Jan/2005:12:27:20 -0600] "OpenFork Travel Cover 4_VIE logo.psd" 0 0 0
IP 192.168.1.116 - - [04/Jan/2005:12:27:20 -0600] "OpenFork VIE ship art FNL.psd" 0 0 0
IP 192.168.1.116 - - [04/Jan/2005:12:27:20 -0600] "OpenFork VIE_title page LOGO copy.eps" 0 0 0
IP 192.168.1.116 - - [04/Jan/2005:12:27:20 -0600] "OpenFork VIE_title page LOGO.eps" 0 0 0
IP 192.168.1.156 - - [04/Jan/2005:12:28:57 -0600] "Login dhaliwal" 0 0 0
IP 192.168.1.156 - - [04/Jan/2005:12:29:07 -0600] "OpenFork .DS_Store" 0 0 0
IP 192.168.1.156 - - [04/Jan/2005:12:29:08 -0600] "OpenFork FindingGod_DOVE_white.eps" 0 0 0
IP 192.168.1.156 - - [04/Jan/2005:12:29:08 -0600] "OpenFork FindingGod_LOGO_white.eps" 0 0 0
IP 192.168.1.156 - - [04/Jan/2005:12:29:08 -0600] "OpenFork i_19020_FG_DirGuide_P6.qxd" 0 0 0
IP 192.168.1.156 - - [04/Jan/2005:12:29:08 -0600] "OpenFork FindingGod_DOVE_white.eps" 0 0 0
IP 192.168.1.156 - - [04/Jan/2005:12:29:08 -0600] "OpenFork FindingGod_DOVE_white.eps" 0 0 0
```

Show   ✓ Access Log
       Error Log

Overview   Logs   Connections   Graphs   Settings

Figure 15-2. The Logs pane offers access to the AFP Access and Error logs.

The AFP Server's logging is particularly poor. Although file access logging is relatively complete, things like preference processing, startup directives, and granular authentication operation analysis are not available anywhere in the Server logs

Illustrated in Figure 15-3, the Connections pane displays all current AFP connections, sortable by username, type (TCP or AppleTalk), IP address, connection time, or idle time. Administrators may disconnect users using or send an AFP pop-up message using the Disconnect and Send Message buttons, respectively. The Stop button stops the AFP Service, disconnecting all users after a specified amount of time.

The *serveradmin* command can also be used to disconnect users, although the syntax is cumbersome, to say the least. First, to obtain a list of connected users, use the *getConnectedUsers* command directive, as shown in Example 15-1.

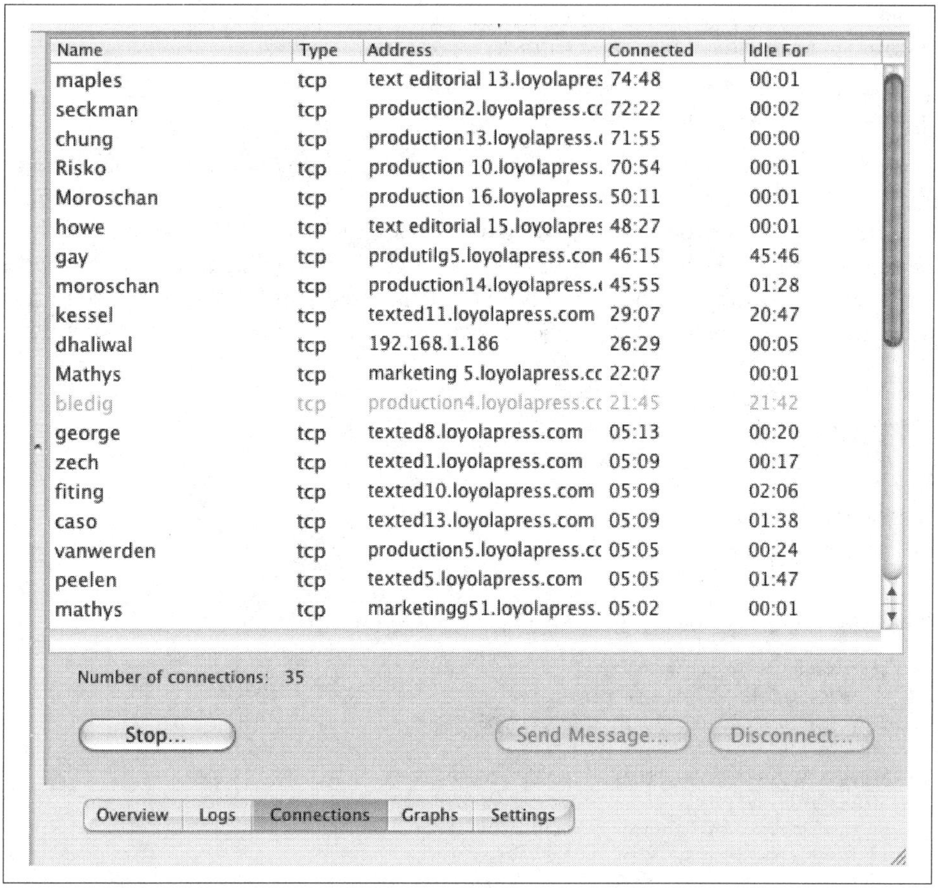

Name	Type	Address	Connected	Idle For
maples	tcp	text editorial 13.loyolapres	74:48	00:01
seckman	tcp	production2.loyolapress.cc	72:22	00:02
chung	tcp	production13.loyolapress.(	71:55	00:00
Risko	tcp	production 10.loyolapress.	70:54	00:01
Moroschan	tcp	production 16.loyolapress.	50:11	00:01
howe	tcp	text editorial 15.loyolapres	48:27	00:01
gay	tcp	produtilg5.loyolapress.con	46:15	45:46
moroschan	tcp	production14.loyolapress.(	45:55	01:28
kessel	tcp	texted11.loyolapress.com	29:07	20:47
dhaliwal	tcp	192.168.1.186	26:29	00:05
Mathys	tcp	marketing 5.loyolapress.cc	22:07	00:01
bledig	tcp	production4.loyolapress.cc	21:45	21:42
george	tcp	texted8.loyolapress.com	05:13	00:20
zech	tcp	texted1.loyolapress.com	05:09	00:17
fiting	tcp	texted10.loyolapress.com	05:09	02:06
caso	tcp	texted13.loyolapress.com	05:09	01:38
vanwerden	tcp	production5.loyolapress.cc	05:05	00:24
peelen	tcp	texted5.loyolapress.com	05:05	01:47
mathys	tcp	marketingg51.loyolapress.	05:02	00:01

Number of connections: 35

Stop...   Send Message...   Disconnect...

Overview   Logs   Connections   Graphs   Settings

Figure 15-3. The Connections interface yields a lot of data about current AFP connections. A certain amount of service management is also available, as users may be manually disconnected.

Example 15-1. Using serveradmin to list connected users. This output can be quite verbose, because an array (group of settings) is returned for each connected user.

```
[ace2:~] nadmin% sudo serveradmin command afp:command=getConnectedUsers
Password:
afp:command = "getConnectedUsers"
afp:state = "RUNNING"
afp:timeStamp = "2004-10-16 11:54:33 -0600"
afp:usersArray:_array_index:0:lastUseElapsedTime = 69
afp:usersArray:_array_index:0:disconnectID = 0
afp:usersArray:_array_index:0:sessionID = 3
afp:usersArray:_array_index:0:minsToDisconnect = 0
afp:usersArray:_array_index:0:flags = 0
afp:usersArray:_array_index:0:state = 1
afp:usersArray:_array_index:0:loginElapsedTime = 79
afp:usersArray:_array_index:0:name = "ghydle"
afp:usersArray:_array_index:0:serviceType = "afp"
```

Example 15-1. Using serveradmin to list connected users. This output can be quite verbose, because an array (group of settings) is returned for each connected user. (continued)

```
afp:usersArray:_array_index:0:ipAddress = "192.168.1.144"
afp:usersArray:_array_index:0:sessionType = "tcp"
```

The user(s) is disconnected with the *disconnectUsers* command directive. This command requires an array for input, meaning you have to use the *serveradmin* command somewhat interactively, as shown in Example 15-2. Each line ends with a carriage return. Don't forget to press Control-D when you're finished, because that's a very Mac-like thing to do. In reality I've never actually used this capability in the wild; it's just too much typing for such a simple task, and it doesn't always work.

Example 15-2. Using serveradmin to disconnect one or more connected AFP users requires cumbersome syntax.

```
[ace2:~] nadmin% sudo serveradmin command
afp:command = disconnectUsers
afp:message = you are terminated
afp:minutes = 0
afp:sessionIDsArray:_array_index:0 = sessionID3
```

Disconnecting a user results in some fairly verbose output:

```
afp:command = "disconnectUsers"
afp:messageSent = "you are terminated "
afp:timeStamp = "2004-10-16 12:08:31 -0600"
afp:timerID = 2
afp:usersArray:_array_index:0:lastUseElapsedTime = 907
afp:usersArray:_array_index:0:disconnectID = 0
afp:usersArray:_array_index:0:sessionID = 3
afp:usersArray:_array_index:0:minsToDisconnect = 0
afp:usersArray:_array_index:0:flags = 0
afp:usersArray:_array_index:0:state = 1
afp:usersArray:_array_index:0:loginElapsedTime = 917
afp:usersArray:_array_index:0:name = "mbartosh"
afp:usersArray:_array_index:0:serviceType = "afp"
afp:usersArray:_array_index:0:ipAddress = "192.168.1.144"
afp:usersArray:_array_index:0:sessionType = "tcp"
afp:usersArray:_array_index:1:lastUseElapsedTime = 867
afp:usersArray:_array_index:1:disconnectID = 0
afp:usersArray:_array_index:1:sessionID = 4
afp:usersArray:_array_index:1:minsToDisconnect = 0
afp:usersArray:_array_index:1:flags = 0
afp:usersArray:_array_index:1:state = 1
afp:usersArray:_array_index:1:loginElapsedTime = 868
afp:usersArray:_array_index:1:name = "ghydle"
afp:usersArray:_array_index:1:serviceType = "afp"
afp:usersArray:_array_index:1:ipAddress = "24.8.7.222"
afp:usersArray:_array_index:1:sessionType = "tcp"
afp:status = 0
```

The Graphs pane, useful for trend analysis, is capable of showing graphically either the average number of connected users or the average data throughput for a specified period of time, from 1 hour to 7 days in the immediate past. It can be seen in Figure 15-4. This command is especially useful for locating specific periods of time that might be worth pursuing in the service logs (for instance, a spike in file-sharing activity, or an unexpected drop-off in the number of connected users).

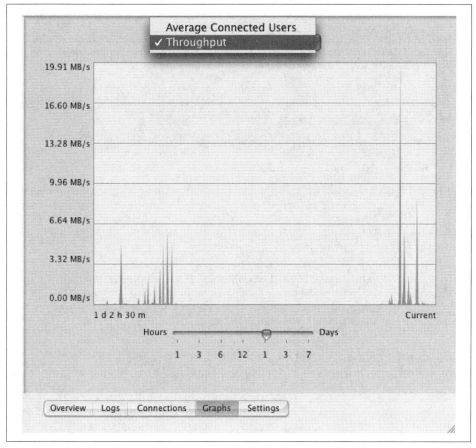

Figure 15-4. The Graphs portion of Server Admin's AFP management interface.

Server Admin's AFP Settings tab reveals the primary interface for changing the configuration of the AFP Server, separated into General, Access, Logging, and Idle Users panes. The General tab (illustrated in Figure 15-5) is really a somewhat random grouping of options, where AppleTalk and Rendezvous service registration (allowing the server to be browsed using enabled protocols) are configured and where a logon greeting may be set. Remember that enabling AppleTalk browsing here has no effect if the AppleTalk protocol is not enabled on one of the Server's network interfaces.

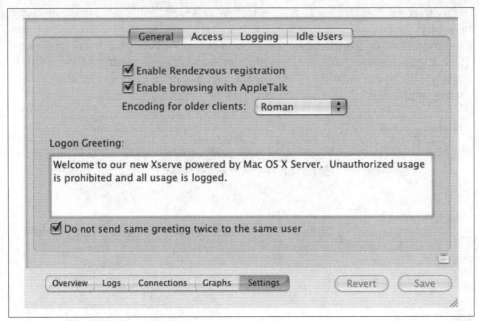

Figure 15-5. The General tab is home to several AFP Service options that do not appear to belong anywhere else. Logon greetings are generally considered annoying by users, and complicate deployment of network home directories.

AppleTalk can be enabled on only one interface at a time. Personally I do not like these ad hoc, broadcast, or multicast-based browsing technologies, and prefer a more structured, directory-based approach to making resources easily available.

Finally, Encoding specifies a text encoding for older clients that are not able to make use of AFP's Unicode support—typically pre–Mac OS X.

The Access tab, pictured in Figure 15-6, appropriately enough, controls various aspects of access to the server's AFP service. Authentication may be one of Standard (typically a Diffie-Hellman exchange, known as DHX), Kerberos, or Any Method, in which case the server should try to negotiate the most secure option that the client supports. It is generally safe to choose Any Method, the default selection. However, especially where clients from several unrelated Kerberos realms interface, it might be appropriate to specify Standard. The AFP client in Mac OS X will attempt to negotiate Kerberos authentication if the server claims to support it, even if the client and server are in different realms that are not configured to work together. This isn't a bad thing necessarily; it's just the way Kerberos works. There is no way to know whether the domains trust one another (share cross-realm principals) until authentication is attempted. If they don't, though, the user will be prompted twice—once for

Kerberos authentication, and then again for standard—regardless of whether the Kerberos authentication was successful.

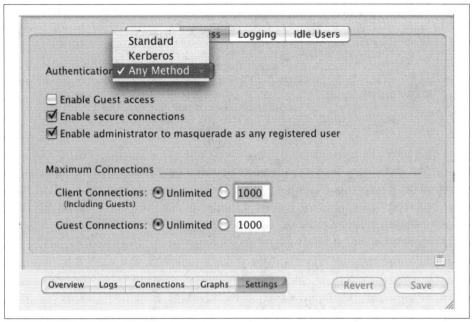

Figure 15-6. The Access pane of Server Admin's AFP settings controls various characteristics of the AFP service relating to access. The maximum number of simultaneous connections may also be configured here.

This sounds alarming but actually makes quite a bit of sense. The Kerberos dialog attempts to authenticate user to the Kerberos realm, after which, presumably, the Kerberos-enabled server could be accessed using single sign-on. Since the server and client are in unrelated realms, however, Kerberos authentication to the AFP server fails, even if authentication to the domain has succeeded. Since "Any Method" is chosen, the AFP server then falls back to standard (generally secure) authentication methods.

The "guest access" checkbox allows for anonymous connections to the AFP service. This isn't as bad as it sounds—guest access can be overridden at the share level. Enabling it here simply gives you the option of later enabling it on a per-share basis.

Secure Connections

Another option in the Access pane of Server Admin's AFP settings interface is the "Enable secure connections" checkbox. AFP has supported relatively secure authentication methods for several years now; however, until Jaguar, the rest of the connection—the actual data sent over the wire—could not be easily encrypted or protected in any way. The Secure Connections option enables the AFP connection from Jaguar or newer clients to be tunneled over the SSH protocol, so that malicious parties cannot successfully intercept it. Allowing secure connections means that if the client requests such a tunnel, it may be used.

> There is currently no way to require that all connections must be secure. Enterprising minds will suggest disallowing incoming connections on port 548, so non-tunneled connections are not successful. Unfortunately, though, initial contact on port 548 is required in order to negotiate use of SSH.

Keep in mind that encryption brings with it at least some overhead, and in the case of tunneling AFP, this load can become quite noticeable on high-bandwidth links. Using secure connections is, for practical purposes, not feasible on 10base-T or faster networks. The overhead is too severe. The idea is that such high bandwidth links tend to be local and tend to be trusted, and that the relatively tiny amount of bandwidth available across the Internet or a WAN becomes a performance bottleneck long before the overhead of encryption.

In order to support SSH-tunneled AFP (in addition to enabling secure connections on the server side), clients must specifically request it using the Options button in the AFP authentication dialog, which is pictured in Figure 15-7. The resulting Options interface is illustrated in Figure 15-8.

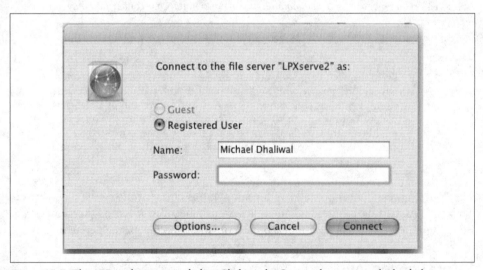

Figure 15-7. The AFP authentication dialog. Clicking the Options button reveals the dialog pictured in Figure 15-8.

Figure 15-8. The AFP connection interface's Options dialog reveals a number of mostly security-related options.

In the Options dialog, users are able to add their password to their keychain (a mostly client-side feature, discussed in more depth in O'Reilly's *Running Mac OS X Panther*), disallow Clear Text Passwords, request warning when clear-text authentication is going to be used and (finally) permit secure, SSH-based connections.

Keep in mind that permitting SSH-secured connections means that you must permit users to have SSH access to the server. Since SSH grants a far wider scope of access than AFP (which specifically limits user access to particular share points), this change should be undertaken with great care, and only if users are highly trusted. Typically, I limit SSH access to either the *admin* group or, in larger organizations, a subset of the *admin* group. For more information on limiting access to SSH, see Chapter 3.

A final option in the Access tab is user masquerading, a controversial feature that has made its way in and out of Apple AFP servers for years, depending on whether customers had requested it as a feature or reported it as a security issue. Masquerading allows any user to use any administrator's password to log in over AFP. This can be quite handy when an administrator wishes to examine a user's environment first-hand, but becomes quite messy when some member of the admin group has chosen a trivial, common, or worse yet, blank password, with which any user may log in as any other user. This feature is enabled by default, so unless you explicitly need it, it should probably be disabled. This feature is limited to logging in over AFP, and is not applicable to any other service, including console (*loginwindow*) logins.

The Logging tab in the AFP module's settings section (illustrated in Figure 15-9) allows access to the logging settings of the AFP server. It is capable of providing a tremendous amount of information about actual connections, including login and logout events, file creation and access, and directory (folder) creation and deletion events. The logging is so verbose, in fact, that on a busy file server the access logs can grow quite large. To remedy this, a log archival feature is exposed in the graphical interface. At the specified interval, the log is labeled with a date, compressed using the *gzip* command, and stored in the same directory as the active logs.

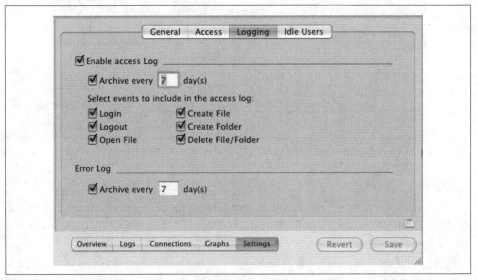

Figure 15-9. The logging settings of Mac OS X Server's AFP service.

To view compressed logs, use the *zcat* command as follows:

```
[ace2:~] nadmin% zcat /Library/Logs/AppleFileService/
AppleFileServiceAccess.log\09.26.04.gz | less
!!Log File Created On: 9/18/2004 19:19:44 261:6:1 GMT
**** - - [18/Sep/2004:19:19:44 -0700] "Mounted Volume mirBak" 6 0 0
**** - - [19/Sep/2004:22:39:24 -0700] "Mounted Volume boot" 0 0 0
**** - - [19/Sep/2004:22:39:24 -0700] "Mounted Volume fink" 1 0 0
**** - - [19/Sep/2004:22:39:24 -0700] "Mounted Volume alt" 2 0 0
**** - - [19/Sep/2004:22:39:24 -0700] "Mounted Volume pxn" 3 0 0
**** - - [19/Sep/2004:22:39:24 -0700] "Mounted Volume nod" 4 0 0
**** - - [19/Sep/2004:22:39:24 -0700] "Mounted Volume Data" 5 0 0
**** - - [19/Sep/2004:22:39:26 -0700] "DiskArbStart -" 0 6695 0
IP 63.227.125.24 - - [20/Sep/2004:12:50:44 -0700] "Login mbartosh" 0 0 0
IP 63.227.125.24 - - [20/Sep/2004:12:50:57 -0700] "OpenFork .DS_Store" 0 0 0
IP 63.227.125.24 - - [20/Sep/2004:12:51:18 -0700] "OpenFork current" 0 0 0
```

Error logs, which typically show little aside from AppleTalk initiation errors (because the AFP server ships with AppleTalk browsing enabled, even though the AppleTalk protocol itself isn't turned on in a default installation), have their own logging interval but are otherwise treated identically These archives are never purged in 10.3.3, and even though modern hard drive capacities make it unlikely that these logs alone would cause a shortage of disk space, it might make sense for the sake of thoroughness to store them on a nonsystem partition.

 Also be sure to reference the *diskspacemonitor* facility built in to Mac OS X Server, which is discussed in more depth in Chapter 4. *diskspacemonitor* alerts you if available disk space drops below a certain threshold, and takes corrective action if it drops below a second (higher) threshold.

What the AFP server does not log effectively, however, are startup, shutdown and connection establishment events, which can be quite useful in many deployments. For an example of the kind of depth I'd like to have, see the "Troubleshooting" section later in this chapter.

Pictured in Figure 15-10, the Idle Users tab—again accurately named—allows for customization of the AFP server's behavior when certain classes of users (guests, authenticated users, and administrators) have been idle. Customized messages may be sent to the user at disconnect time, and specific disconnect allowances can be made for sleeping clients.

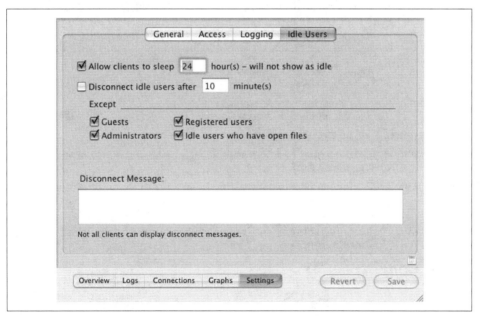

Figure 15-10. The Idle User settings allow for granular specification of idle disconnect behavior for several types of users.

AFP Server Preferences

Most of *AppleFileServer*'s global options are saved by Server Admin and *servermgrd*'s *servermgrd_afp* plug-in to */Library/Preferences/com.apple.AppleFileServer.plist.* (For a more in-depth analysis of *servermgrd*, see Chapter 3.) Some of those settings are discussed in Table 15-1. Options already documented elsewhere in the chapter, along with those that are self-explanatory, are not reviewed.

Table 15-1. Settings stored in /Library/Preferences/com.apple.AppleFileServer.plist. It is safe to assume that only settings available in the graphical interface or mentioned in Apple Kbase articles are actually supported. Obvious options—like the path to log files—are not covered here.

Option	Description	Sample value
TCPQuantum	Server's maximum amount of data that can be sent in one request.	`262144`
admin31GetsSp	Using AFP version 3.1 or better, show administrators share points when they connect. If set to False, Administrators see all server volumes.	`True`
adminGetsSp	Using AFP versions before 3.1, show administrators share points when they connect (rather than all the volumes mounted on the server).	`False`
afpTCPPort	Change the port used by AppleFileServer.	`548`
allowRootLogin	Permit the root user—if it is enabled—to log in via AFP.	`False`
clientSleepOnOff	Determines whether clients should be allowed to sleep.	`True`
clientSleepTime	Amount of times clients are permitted to sleep if *clientSleepOnOff* is enabled.	`24`
CreateHomeDir	On log in, create home directories for users who are supposed to have home directories on this server.	
enforce_unix_access	-waiting on reply-	`False`
kerberosPrincipal	The service principal that the server should use when authenticating Kerberos.	*afpserver/g5.4am-media.com@G5.4AM-MEDIA.COM*
loggingAttributes	Lists filesystem access events that should be recorded in the access log.	`LogCreateDir`, `logCreateFile`, `logDelete`, `logLogin`, `logLogout`, `logOpenFork`
noNetworkUsers	Turns permissions mapping on and off, as discussed later in this chapter.	`False`

Table 15-1. Settings stored in /Library/Preferences/com.apple.AppleFileServer.plist. It is safe to assume that only settings available in the graphical interface or mentioned in Apple Kbase articles are actually supported. Obvious options—like the path to log files—are not covered here. (continued)

Option	Description	Sample value
permissionsModel	Describes how the AFP server enforces ownership. This is separate from the inherit permissions versus Unix behavior discussed later in this chapter.	classic_permissions (default, same as AFP 2.x/Mac OS 9.x): Any user can change the owner or group of an item they own to any other user.
		unix_with_classic_admin_permissions (Unix-style, but administrator has *root* power): *root* and administrator can change the owner of an item to any other user. Any user can change any file they own to any group they are a member of.
		unix_permissions (strict Unix): Only *root* can change the owner of an item to any other user. Any user can change any file they own to any group they are a member of. Only *root* can change to any group.
recon1SrvrKeyTTLHrs	Time-to-live (in hours) for the server key used to generate reconnect tokens.	168
recon1TokenTTLMins	Time-to-live (in minutes) for a reconnect token.	10080
reconnectFlag	Who should be allowed to reconnect.	No_admin_kills, none, all
reconnectTTLInMin	Time-to-live (in minutes) for a disconnected session waiting reconnection	1440
specialAdminPrivs	Allows extended read access to admin users, allowing them to access resources that filesystem permissions would otherwise restrict access to. This access, however, is read-only.	False
tickleTime	Frequency with which AFP tickles should be sent in order to determine whether client is still connected. Tickets are retried before the connection is considered dead.	30
updateHomeDirQuota	Instructs *AppleFileServer* to request the *apple-user-homequota* attribute of users logging in. If the user's Home directory resides on that server, the quota for the volume on which the Home directory is located will be updated.	True
useAppleTalk	Allows AppleTalk connections (rather than simply using AppleTalk as a service discovery mechanism).	False

The *serveradmin* utility is the complete command-line equivalent of the graphical Server Admin application. As such, it can be extremely useful for performing remote command-line management tasks in Mac OS X Server. Using it to change settings is not intuitive, but is at least consistent, as shown here in Example 15-3.

Example 15-3. Using the serveradmin command to specify a Kerberos principal for the AFP server. Virtually any option in com.apple.AppleFileServer.plist can be managed using this syntax: serveradmin settings afp:setting = "value".

```
sudo serveradmin settings afp:kerberosPrincipal = "afpserver/xserver.4am-media.com@ADS.
4AM-MEDIA.COM"
```

AFP Management: Workgroup Manager

While the global options for the AFP service are managed in Server Admin, per-share options are managed in Workgroup Manager, in the AFP portion of the Protocols tab mentioned in the introduction to Part IV. Appropriately, choosing Apple File Settings from the pull-down menu in that interface reveals AFP-specific options for the selected share, illustrated in Figure 15-11. All of the options available in this interface are stored in the share point's record, in the local NetInfo domain of the server.

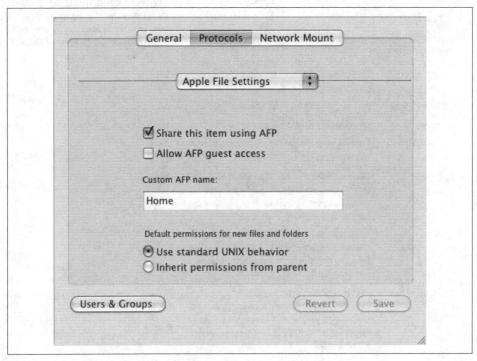

Figure 15-11. AFP-specific options for share points.

Most of the per-share options in this dialog are fairly straightforward:

Share this item using AFP

Makes the selected share available for AFP. It is good security policy to minimize exposure by making resources available only when they specifically need to be. If, for instance, a share point contains data that is useful only to clients using Windows, it makes no sense to make it available via AFP. Additionally, some cross-platform file access issues still exist, meaning that deployment can be simplified if a resource is accessed using as few protocols as feasible. Default value for new share points: enabled.

Allow AFP guest access

Allows anonymous (guest) users to access this resource. This is generally a bad idea unless specific business organizational or business reasons exist for allowing guest access. Default for new share points: enabled.

Custom AFP name

Specifies a custom name for this share when it is browsed or mounted. Default value for a new share point: share is advertised using the name of its topmost folder.

Default permissions for new files or folders

Standard Unix behavior or inherited permissions from parent. Until Mac OS X 10.2, the permissions for files and folders created on an AFP share always inherited their permissions from the folder that contained them: if that folder were group writable, other files and folders created within it would be as well. This option is illustrated in Figure 15-12.

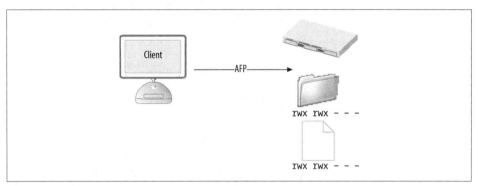

Figure 15-12. Until 10.2, newly created files and folders on an AFP share inherited permissions from their parent directory.

Beginning in 10.2, however, Apple changed the behavior of the AFP server to be more Unix-like—rather than inheriting permissions, newly created files and folders would be assigned specific permissions, regardless of the permissions of their parent. More exactly, files and directories were created with a *umask* of 022, meaning that while owners could read, write or execute anything they created, groups and users could only read those files, as shown in Figure 15-13.

This change produced quite a stir, since many Apple Server customers depended on the ability to support group-writable resources, and Jaguar initially did not have this capability. The inflexible 022 *umask* did not allow for it. In order to meet these needs, 10.2.2 introduced this option—to choose either the older, inherited behavior or the newer, *umask*-based one.

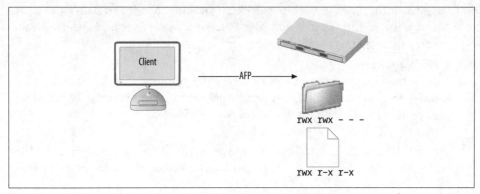

Figure 15-13. When Jaguar was introduced, new files and folders on AFP shares—rather than inheriting permissions—were specifically made group and world readable, while the owner was given full read/write access.

These per-share options can be both specified and viewed using a variety of command-line utilities. As noted in the introduction to Part IV, the *sharing* command's *–l* (list) flag is a good place to start. Recall also that *sharing*'s *–a* and *–e* flags allow for manipulation of share point data (adding and editing share points, respectively). *–a* and *–e* also accept a number of options, the AFP-specific potions of which are illustrated in Table 15-2.

Table 15-2. These sharing flags and their associated arguments are useful in the management of AFP share point data.

Flag	Description
–A	Specify an AFP-specific name for the share point.
–s	Used to enable a share point for a service or services. Requires a three-digit argument consisting of 0s and 1s (0 for disabled, 1 for enabled). The first digit represents AFP, the second SMB, and the third FTP.
–g	Enables or disables group access. Like *–s*, requires a three-digit argument consisting of 0s and 1s (0 for disabled, 1 for enabled). The first digit represents AFP, the second SMB and the third FTP.
–i	The inherit privileges option. Only applicable to AFP and SMB. Requires a two-digit argument consisting of 0s and 1s (0 for disabled, 1 for enabled). The first digit represents AFP, the second SMB.

Share settings themselves can be examined with any tool capable of reading the local NetInfo database: *nicl*, *dscl*, and *nidump* are all capable (Example 15-4).

Example 15-4. Using nicl to read options on the Users Share Point. The grep command is used to filter for AFP-specific options.

```
rhp997:~ rhp$ nicl . -read /config/SharePoints/Users | grep afp
afp_name: Users
afp_shared: 1
afp_guestaccess: 1
```

Architecture

AppleShare services are provided by the *AppleFileServer* daemon, which lives in the file */System/Library/CoreServices/AppleFileServer.app* and is symbolically linked to the file */usr/sbin/AppleFileServer*. It is started by the AppleShare Startup Item (*/System/Library/StartupItems/AppleShare*) if the AFPSERVER flag in */etc/hostconfig* has a value of -YES-. When run in the foreground (using its –d flag), *AppleFileServer* does not offer any better logging or debug messaging. Its –v flag, shown in Example 15-5, causes it to print its version and then exit.

Example 15-5. AppleFileServer's minimal man page describes its –d (fail to daemonize) and –v (version) options.

```
big15:~ mab$ AppleFileServer -v
afpserver-468.12
```

AFP services may also be started (or stopped) using the *serveradmin* command, as shown in Example 15-6.

Example 15-6. Using serveradmin, first to stop, and then to restart the AFP service. This is generally necessary after changes are made to the AFP Server's configuration file (either manually or using the serveradmin command). Changes made in the Server Admin graphical interface automatically.

```
[ace2:~] nadmin% sudo serveradmin stop afp
afp:command = "setState"
afp:state = "STOPPED"
afp:timeStamp = "2004-10-16 09:45:00 -0600"
afp:status = 0

[ace2:~] nadmin% sudo serveradmin start afp
afp:command = "setState"
afp:state = "RUNNING"
afp:status = 0
```

Permissions Mapping

AFP evolved from an environment that did not have the concept of multiple users, much less numeric user IDs or shared directory domains. Because of this lack, its adaptation to the more modern environment fostered by Mac OS X has required the bridging of those gaps. One of the biggest of these changes has been the migration to a true multiuser operating system. Since the server and the client don't always exist in the same shared directory domain, a method had to be established to represent permissions on the server's filesystem in a way that accurately reflected the client's level of access. Apple's approach is documented in Figure 15-14.

Because *bob* know's *bsmith*'s password, we assume that he is authorized to access anything that *bsmith* has access to. The client is not aware of a user account called *bsmith*, and would otherwise not know who to assign privileges to. Since *bob* logged

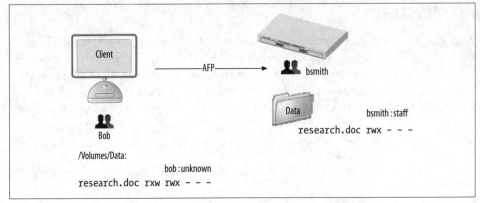

Figure 15-14. In this example, the local user "bob" is logging into a departmental AFP server with his institutional username: bsmith.

into the AFP server using the name *bsmith*, the AFP client maps those permissions, giving *bob* access to everything that the server says *bsmith*, as shown in Examples 15-7 and 15-8.

Example 15-7. bsmith's home directory as seen locally from the server.

```
[ace2:/Volumes/Data] nadmin% ls -la /Users/bsmith/
total 8
drwxr-xr-x  11 bsmith   staff  374 16 Oct 21:34 .
drwxrwxr-t  18 root     admin  612 16 Oct 21:34 ..
-rw-r--r--   1 bsmith   staff    3 16 Oct 21:34 .CFUserTextEncoding
drwx------   3 bsmith   staff  102 16 Oct 21:34 Desktop
drwx------   3 bsmith   staff  102 16 Oct 21:34 Documents
drwx------  17 bsmith   staff  578 16 Oct 21:34 Library
drwx------   3 bsmith   staff  102 16 Oct 21:34 Movies
drwx------   3 bsmith   staff  102 16 Oct 21:34 Music
drwx------   3 bsmith   staff  102 16 Oct 21:34 Pictures
drwxr-xr-x   4 bsmith   staff  136 16 Oct 21:34 Public
drwxr-xr-x   6 bsmith   staff  204 16 Oct 21:34 Sites
```

Example 15-8. bsmith's home directory as seen over an AFP connection, mounted by the user bob. Since no user called bsmith exists in the client's local NetInfo domain, permissions for bsmith must be mapped to bob.

```
Last login: Sat Oct 16 21:37:02 on console
Welcome to Darwin!
big15:~ bob$ ls -la /Volumes/Users/bsmith/
total 16
drwxr-xr-x  11 bob  unknown  330 16 Oct 21:34 .
dr-xr-xr-x  18 bob  unknown  568 16 Oct 21:34 ..
-rw-r--r--   1 bob  unknown    3 16 Oct 21:34 .CFUserTextEncoding
drwx------   3 bob  unknown  264 16 Oct 21:34 Desktop
drwx------   3 bob  unknown  264 16 Oct 21:34 Documents
drwx------  17 bob  unknown  534 16 Oct 21:34 Library
drwx------   3 bob  unknown  264 16 Oct 21:34 Movies
```

Example 15-8. bsmith's home directory as seen over an AFP connection, mounted by the user bob. Since no user called bsmith exists in the client's local NetInfo domain, permissions for bsmith must be mapped to bob. (continued)

```
drwx------  3 bob  unknown  264 16 Oct 21:34 Music
drwx------  3 bob  unknown  264 16 Oct 21:34 Pictures
drwxr-xr-x  4 bob  unknown  264 16 Oct 21:34 Public
drwxr-xr-x  6 bob  unknown  264 16 Oct 21:34 Sites
```

In order to achieve this mapping, *bsmith*'s full set of access (every privilege granted to him, either via group membership or due to ownership) is mapped to *bob*, the locally logged-in user. Client-side Other and Group permissions, when mapping is enabled, are mapped as well—both (confusingly enough) to the permissions granted to Other server-side. This concept is illustrated in Figure 15-15.

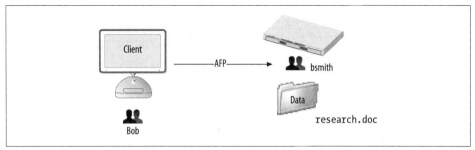

Figure 15-15. bsmith's full set of permissions (combined user and group access) is mapped to bsmith. Other permissions on the server are mapped to both Group and Other fields on the AFP client.

With 10.2, the AFP Server became better able to cope with shared directories and a Unix-like environment. Specifically (and as shown in Examples 15-9 and 15-10), if the RecordName and UniqueID of the user logging in matches the RecordName and UniqueID of the account used to log into the server, the client and server assume that they share a user and group database.

Example 15-9. ghydle's home directory as seen locally from the server. Notice the output of the id command, which will match what is seen on the client.

```
xsg5:~ tadmin$ id ghydle
uid=1025(ghydle) gid=20(staff) groups=20(staff)
xsg5:~ tadmin$ ls -la /Users/ghydle/
total 8
drwxr-xr-x  11 ghydle  staff  374 17 Oct 00:10 .
drwxrwxr-x   6 root    admin  204 17 Oct 00:10 ..
-rw-r--r--   1 ghydle  staff    3 17 Oct 00:10 .CFUserTextEncoding
drwx------   3 ghydle  staff  102 17 Oct 00:10 Desktop
drwx------   3 ghydle  staff  102 17 Oct 00:10 Documents
drwx------  17 ghydle  staff  578 17 Oct 00:10 Library
drwx------   3 ghydle  staff  102 17 Oct 00:10 Movies
drwx------   3 ghydle  staff  102 17 Oct 00:10 Music
drwx------   3 ghydle  staff  102 17 Oct 00:10 Pictures
```

Example 15-9. ghydle's home directory as seen locally from the server. Notice the output of the id command, which will match what is seen on the client. (continued)

```
drwxr-xr-x   4 ghydle   staff  136 17 Oct 00:10 Public
drwxr-xr-x   6 ghydle   staff  204 17 Oct 00:10 Sites
```

Example 15-10. ghydle's home directory as seen over an AFP connection, mounted on the client. Notice the output of the id command, which matches what is seen on the server. Because the client and server agree on the RecordName and UniqueID of the user logging in, actual filesystem permissions are reflected on the client, rather than the mapped permissions seen in the earlier example.

```
Big15:~ ghydle$ id ghydle
uid=1025(ghydle) gid=20(staff) groups=20(staff)
Big15:~ ghydle$ ls -la /Volumes/Users/ghydle/
total 8
drwxr-xr-x  11 ghydle   staff  374 17 Oct 00:10 .
drwxrwxr-x   6 root     admin  204 17 Oct 00:10 ..
-rw-r--r--   1 ghydle   staff    3 17 Oct 00:10 .CFUserTextEncoding
drwx------   3 ghydle   staff  102 17 Oct 00:10 Desktop
drwx------   3 ghydle   staff  102 17 Oct 00:10 Documents
drwx------  17 ghydle   staff  578 17 Oct 00:10 Library
drwx------   3 ghydle   staff  102 17 Oct 00:10 Movies
drwx------   3 ghydle   staff  102 17 Oct 00:10 Music
drwx------   3 ghydle   staff  102 17 Oct 00:10 Pictures
drwxr-xr-x   4 ghydle   staff  136 17 Oct 00:10 Public
drwxr-xr-x   6 ghydle   staff  204 17 Oct 00:10 Sites
```

Unfortunately, this behavior can have unforeseen consequences. Because people tend to follow very similar naming conventions, there's a high probability of namespace collision. (For instance, a great many organizations would give me a short name of *mbartosh*, *bartoshm*, or *m.bartos*.) On the vast majority of Mac OS X installs (every one that uses Apple's Setup Assistant), the first user created has a UniqueID of 501. These two tendencies together increase the risk of assuming a shared domain when one does not exist, as illustrated Examples 15-11 through 15-15.

Example 15-11. The user mbartosh exists on the client and has a UniqueID of 1025. Sequentially, this is usually the second UniqueID assigned to a user in a shared domain, the first being 1024, which is assigned to the admin user used to create the domain. In this case, mbartosh is such a user, and has been cached in the local domain.

```
mab9718:~ mbartosh$ id mbartosh
uid=1025(mbartosh) gid=20(staff) groups=20(staff), 79(appserverusr),
80(admin), 81(appserveradm)
```

Example 15-12. The server is also aware of a user with the RecordName of mbartosh and a UniqueID of 1025. This server, however, does not participate in any shared domain. Notice that mbartosh is a member of the 4am group on this server (with a UniqueID of 1029).

```
[ace2:~] mbartosh% id mbartosh
uid=1025(mbartosh) gid=20(staff) groups=20(staff), 1025(info),
1026(post-rap), 1027(adm), 1028(mu-AD), 1029(4am), 1030(vpn)
```

Example 15-13. When viewed locally from the server, we can see that the user mbartosh should have write access to the 0418MB file, due to mbartosh's membership in the 4am group.

```
[ace2:~] mbartosh% ls -la /Volumes/nod/MYOB\ Folder/in\ use/0418MB
-rwxrwx--x  1 ghydle  4am  3866624 17 Apr 00:44 /Volumes/nod/MYOB
Folder/in use/0418MB
```

Example 15-14. But when seen from the client—mounted over AFP—permissions mapping is assumed. The client has no idea who the user 1044 or group 1029 is, though, because these exist only in the local domain of the server.

```
mab9718:~ mbartosh$ ls -la /Volumes/4am/MYOB\ Folder/in\ use/0418MB
-rwxrwx--x  1 1044  1029  3866624 17 Apr 00:44 /Volumes/4am/MYOB Folder/in
use/0418MB
```

Example 15-15. So when mbartosh tries to access the file over AFP, access is denied.

```
mab9718:~ mbartosh$ ditto /Volumes/4am/MYOB\ Folder/in\ use/0418MB .
ditto: /Volumes/4am/MYOB Folder/in use/0418MB: Permission denied
```

Luckily, Apple has anticipated this issue, and has included a flag that can be set manually in */Library/Preferences/com.apple.AppleFileServer.plist* turning this feature off. This can be accomplished using the *defaults* or *serveradmin* commands (see Example 15-16 for an example using the *serveradmin* command), or by editing the file manually. In either case, the AFP server should be restarted.

Example 15-16. Using the serveradmin command to change the AFP Server's configuration, turning on permission mapping globally. The AFP server then needs to be restarted.

```
xsg5:~ tadmin$ sudo serveradmin settings afp:noNetworkUsers = yes
afp:noNetworkUsers = yes
```

Once this flag has been set, *mbartosh* is able to remount the share and then properly access the file. Permissions are mapped, reflecting *mbartosh*'s true authorization,

Integration

AFP Services in Mac OS X can be integrated into various types of shared directory domains with varying amounts of ease. Active Directory integration is specifically covered on the following site: *http://www.4am-media.com/sso/*. Enabling single sign-on in an Open Directory shared domain is documented in Chapter 8.

Troubleshooting

The single most useful tool I've discovered for looking into issues with AFP connectivity is actually AFP client logging. While the AFP server does a great job of logging access events (like file creation and deletion), it doesn't do such a great job of closely monitoring log-in and server start-up events. The login process doesn't just "happen"; it's a complex, multistep negotiation, and the AFP server doesn't return much aside from a success or error code.

Enter the AFP client libraries, which, ironically enough, have the capability to be extremely verbose. To enable AFP client logging, follow these steps:

1. Ensure that logging is turned on in *~/Library/Preferences/. GlobalPreferences. plist*; that's the *Library/Preferences. GlobalPreferences.plist* file within the user's Home directory. The important keys (shown in Example 15-17) are afp_debug_ level (which can be anywhere from 1 to 8) and afp_debug_syslog which when set, ensures that the output is sent to syslog.

Example 15-17. Using the defaults command to view AppleShare client configuration. The –g flag specifies the global domain, stored in ~/Library/Preferences/.GlobalPreferences.plist.

```
mab9718:~ mbartosh$ defaults read -g com.apple.AppleShareClientCore
{
    "afp_authtype_show" = 0;
    "afp_cleartext_allow" = 1;
    "afp_cleartext_warn" = 1;
    "afp_debug_level" = 6;
    "afp_debug_syslog" = 1;
    "afp_keychain_add" = 0;
    "afp_keychain_search" = 1;
    "afp_login_displayGreeting" = 1;
    "afp_mount_defaultFlags" = 0;
    "afp_prefs_version" = 0;
    "afp_reconnect_allow" = 1;
    "afp_reconnect_interval" = 10;
    "afp_reconnect_retries" = 12;
    "afp_ssh_allow" = 0;
    "afp_ssh_force" = 0;
    "afp_ssh_require" = 0;
    "afp_ssh_warn" = 0;
    "afp_voldlog_skipIfOnly" = 0;
}
```

If the configuration is not satisfactory, it can be enabled with the command shown in Example 15-18. This command can also be used to modify its default log level.

Example 15-18. Using the defaults command to set up logging for AppleShare client libraries.

```
defaults write -g com.apple.AppleShareClientCore -dict-add afp_debug_syslog
-boolean  YES
```

2. Modify */etc/syslog.conf* to contain the following line:

```
*.debug            /var/log/debug.log
```

3. Create log file specified in Step 2; in this case, that's */var/log/debug.log*:

```
mab9718:~ mbartosh$ sudo touch /var/log/debug.log
```

4. Restart *syslogd*:

```
mab9718:~ mbartosh$ sudo killall -HUP syslogd
```

Depending on the specified debug level, when you connect an enormous amount of debug data can be provided—enough that we can only show a portion of it here in Example 15-19.

Example 15-19. A portion of the extremely verbose access available to the AFP client.

```
Apr 24 09:00:19 mab9718 /System/Library/CoreServices/Finder.app/Contents/MacOS/Finder:
Looking at ^MClient Krb v2
Apr 24 09:00:19 mab9718 /System/Library/CoreServices/Finder.app/Contents/MacOS/Finder:
Looking at ^DDHX2
Apr 24 09:00:19 mab9718 /System/Library/CoreServices/Finder.app/Contents/MacOS/Finder:
Adding ^DDHX2
Apr 24 09:00:19 mab9718 /System/Library/CoreServices/Finder.app/Contents/MacOS/Finder:
Looking at    DHCAST128
Apr 24 09:00:19 mab9718 /System/Library/CoreServices/Finder.app/Contents/MacOS/Finder:
Adding  DHCAST128
Apr 24 09:00:19 mab9718 /System/Library/CoreServices/Finder.app/Contents/MacOS/Finder:
Looking at ^V2-Way Randnum exchange
Apr 24 09:00:19 mab9718 /System/Library/CoreServices/Finder.app/Contents/MacOS/Finder:
Looking at ^PCleartxt Passwrd
Apr 24 09:00:19 mab9718 /System/Library/CoreServices/Finder.app/Contents/MacOS/Finder:
Adding ^PCleartxt Passwrd
Apr 24 09:00:19 mab9718 /System/Library/CoreServices/Finder.app/Contents/MacOS/Finder:
Looking at ^ONo User Authent
Apr 24 09:00:19 mab9718 /System/Library/CoreServices/Finder.app/Contents/MacOS/Finder:
^DDHX2
Apr 24 09:00:19 mab9718 /System/Library/CoreServices/Finder.app/Contents/MacOS/Finder:
DHCAST128
Apr 24 09:00:19 mab9718 /System/Library/CoreServices/Finder.app/Contents/MacOS/Finder:
^PCleartxt Passwrd
Apr 24 09:00:19 mab9718 /System/Library/CoreServices/Finder.app/Contents/MacOS/Finder:
TUAMHandler::ChooseBestUAM
Apr 24 09:00:19 mab9718 /System/Library/CoreServices/Finder.app/Contents/MacOS/Finder:
Choosing ^DDHX2
Apr 24 09:00:19 mab9718 /System/Library/CoreServices/Finder.app/Contents/MacOS/Finder:
SharedVolumeEnumerator::Count
Apr 24 09:00:19 mab9718 /System/Library/CoreServices/Finder.app/Contents/MacOS/Finder:
SharedVolumeEnumerator::FetchVolumeList Fetching the volume list  fSessionRef = 0
```

CHAPTER 16

Windows File Services

Apple Server products are not deployed in a homogeneous world consisting solely of Mac OS X–based clients. The opposite is true—in most cases, Apple's products are minority players, and in many environments interoperability with Windows clients and infrastructures is probably the single most important set of features of Mac OS X and Mac OS X Server. Along these lines, Apple has bundled Samba—a highly successful open source package for providing a variety of native services to Windows clients. Samba in Mac OS X though differs in several aspects to Samba on other platforms. This chapter focuses both on those differences and on the infrastructures Apple has put into place to both integrate Samba with the rest of Mac OS X Server and simplify its management.

Managing Windows Services: Server Admin

Global options for Windows Services can be managed and monitored using Server Admin, in the Windows section of the selected server. Since Windows services (aside from having a different constituency) serve much the same purpose as AFP, you'll notice that the two have similar options. Displaying a summary that is similar to that of many other services in Server Admin, Overview (seen in Figure 16-1) lists the current number of accesses and the status of both guest access and logging, along with the service's start time.

The data available in the Overview portion of Server Admin's SMB module is a happy medium between the *serveradmin* utility's Spartan *status smb* and slightly more verbose *fullstatus smb* directives, as shown here:

```
[ace2:~] nadmin% sudo serveradmin status smb
Password:
smb:command = "getState"
smb:state = "RUNNING"
[ace2:~] nadmin% sudo serveradmin fullstatus smb
smb:command = "getState"
smb:guestAccess = "NO"
```

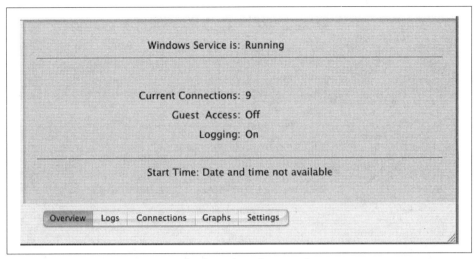

Figure 16-1. The Overview pane supplies basic data about Windows services.

```
smb:logging = "YES"
smb:currentConnections = 0
smb:currentThroughput = 0
smb:state = "RUNNING"
smb:logPaths:fileServiceLog = "/var/log/samba/log.smbd"
smb:logPaths:nameServiceLog = "/var/log/samba/log.nmbd"
smb:readWriteSettingsVersion = 1
smb:setStateVersion = 1
smb:startedTime = ""
```

The Logs interface, seen in Figure 16-2, provides access to two logs: Windows File Services Log and Windows Name Services Log, stored at */var/logs/samba/log.smbd* and */var/logs/samba/log.nmbd*, respectively. You'll probably be most interested in the File Services Log. As is the case with most other logging features in Server Admin, there is no filtering ability in this interface, and it is limited by Server Admin's HTTP request/response model, so logging in via SSH and using the *tail* utility might provide better results. Additionally, note that Samba is capable of more in-depth logging than is exposed in the user interface. For details, see the Logging section of Windows settings, descibed later in this chapter.

A basic view of established SMB connections can be seen in the Connections section (Figure 16-3), sortable by user name, originating IP address, and connection time. Users may also be disconnected using the Disconnect button in the lower right corner of the interface.

Historical statistics gathered from the SMB service are consolidated into the Graphs interface, which gives a graphical representation of the average number of connected user for any period of time from one hour to seven days in the past. This can be seen in Figure 16-4. Unlike the AFP Service, average throughput for Windows services are not available.

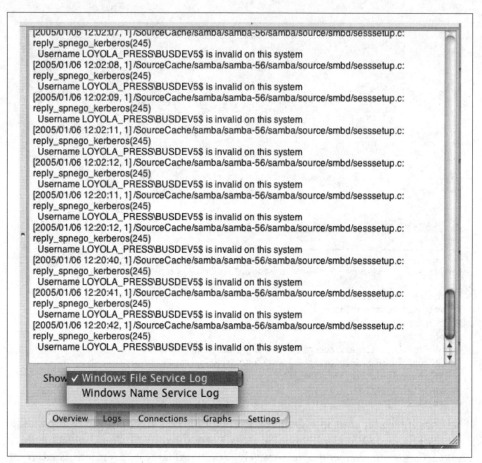

```
[2005/01/06 12:02:07, 1] /SourceCache/samba/samba-56/samba/source/smbd/sesssetup.c:
reply_spnego_kerberos(245)
  Username LOYOLA_PRESS\BUSDEV5$ is invalid on this system
[2005/01/06 12:02:08, 1] /SourceCache/samba/samba-56/samba/source/smbd/sesssetup.c:
reply_spnego_kerberos(245)
  Username LOYOLA_PRESS\BUSDEV5$ is invalid on this system
[2005/01/06 12:02:09, 1] /SourceCache/samba/samba-56/samba/source/smbd/sesssetup.c:
reply_spnego_kerberos(245)
  Username LOYOLA_PRESS\BUSDEV5$ is invalid on this system
[2005/01/06 12:02:11, 1] /SourceCache/samba/samba-56/samba/source/smbd/sesssetup.c:
reply_spnego_kerberos(245)
  Username LOYOLA_PRESS\BUSDEV5$ is invalid on this system
[2005/01/06 12:02:12, 1] /SourceCache/samba/samba-56/samba/source/smbd/sesssetup.c:
reply_spnego_kerberos(245)
  Username LOYOLA_PRESS\BUSDEV5$ is invalid on this system
[2005/01/06 12:20:11, 1] /SourceCache/samba/samba-56/samba/source/smbd/sesssetup.c:
reply_spnego_kerberos(245)
  Username LOYOLA_PRESS\BUSDEV5$ is invalid on this system
[2005/01/06 12:20:12, 1] /SourceCache/samba/samba-56/samba/source/smbd/sesssetup.c:
reply_spnego_kerberos(245)
  Username LOYOLA_PRESS\BUSDEV5$ is invalid on this system
[2005/01/06 12:20:40, 1] /SourceCache/samba/samba-56/samba/source/smbd/sesssetup.c:
reply_spnego_kerberos(245)
  Username LOYOLA_PRESS\BUSDEV5$ is invalid on this system
[2005/01/06 12:20:41, 1] /SourceCache/samba/samba-56/samba/source/smbd/sesssetup.c:
reply_spnego_kerberos(245)
  Username LOYOLA_PRESS\BUSDEV5$ is invalid on this system
[2005/01/06 12:20:42, 1] /SourceCache/samba/samba-56/samba/source/smbd/sesssetup.c:
reply_spnego_kerberos(245)
  Username LOYOLA_PRESS\BUSDEV5$ is invalid on this system
```

Show ✓ Windows File Service Log
        Windows Name Service Log

Overview | Logs | Connections | Graphs | Settings

Figure 16-2. Logs for the Windows File and Naming services are available in the logging portion of Server Admin's SMB module.

The Settings section of Server Admin's Windows services reveals a contextual tabbed interface used for establishing Windows services' global settings. Its General tab (Figure 16-5) offers a set of basic options, all of which correspond to parameters in Samba's configuration file (*/etc/smb.conf*, discussed in more depth later in this chapter):

Role: Standalone Server, Domain Member, or Primary Domain Controller
This option relates to hosting Windows NT–style log-ins on an Open Directory master, and is discussed in more detail in Chapter 26.

Description
Corresponding to the server string value in */etc/smb.conf*, this is an arbitrary string used to describe the server. This is set to Mac OS X in an out-of-box install.

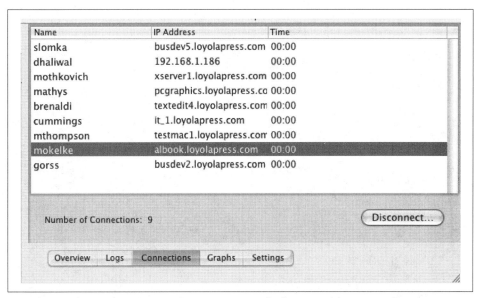

Name	IP Address	Time
slomka	busdev5.loyolapress.com	00:00
dhaliwal	192.168.1.186	00:00
mothkovich	xserver1.loyolapress.com	00:00
mathys	pcgraphics.loyolapress.co	00:00
brenaldi	textedit4.loyolapress.com	00:00
cummings	it_1.loyolapress.com	00:00
mthompson	testmac1.loyolapress.com	00:00
mokelke	albook.loyolapress.com	00:00
gorss	busdev2.loyolapress.com	00:00

Number of Connections: 9   Disconnect...

Overview   Logs   Connections   Graphs   Settings

Figure 16-3. The Windows Services Connections pane displays currently connected users.
Troublesome users may be disconnected.

Computer Name

Corresponding to the netbios name value in */etc/smb.conf*, this is the name used to browse for the server on Windows networks or using Windows browsing technologies. It should in most cases correspond to the unqualified portion of the server's hostname; this aids in configuring Samba to support single sign-on, as documented in Chapter 27.

Workgroup

Corresponding to the workgroup value in */etc/smb.conf*, this is the name of the NT-style workgroup in which the server is advertised for browsing. Workgroups are a loose, voluntary affiliation used to organize computers advertising Windows services for browsing. You do not have to do anything to join a workgroup other than advertise yourself as a part of it, and a new workgroup is created simply by configuring a single computer to belong to it. The default configuration for the Workgroup in Mac OS X and Mac OS X Server is WORKGROUP. This configuration is identical to most Windows variants.

Oddly enough, the Workgroup value becomes important when integrating with Active Directory (AD). The Workgroup value must be changed, then, to reflect the NT-style domain emulated by that Active Directory's PDC emulator—each AD, even in native mode, emulates an NT4 Primary Domain Controller for backwards compatibility. This step also aids in supporting Single Sign-on from Active Directory clients.

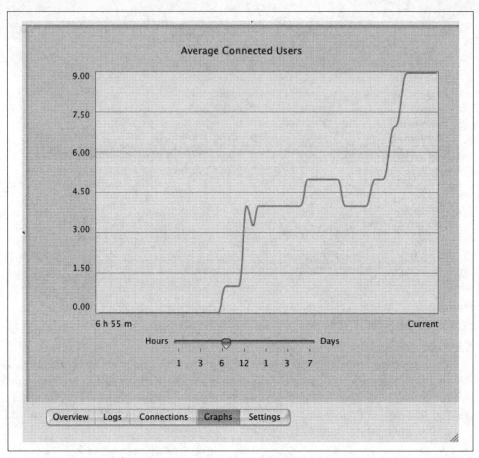

Figure 16-4. Historical data concerning the number of simultaneously connected users is available in the SMB module's Graphs interface.

The Access tab—similar to its cousin in AFP—controls two settings related to accessing the service (see Figure 16-6). Guest access may be enabled here (it is disabled in a default configuration) and the number of client connections can be limited. Ten-user Mac OS X Server licenses are limited to ten simultaneous SMB connections, no matter what this number is set to. Guest access is implemented using *smb.conf*'s map-to-guest parameter. A value of Never (the default) means that unrecognized users such as guest are never allowed to log in. When *Guest* is enabled, map-to-guest is given a value of Bad User, which (confusingly) means that unrecognized users like guest are mapped to the account specified in the guest account parameter. In Mac OS X and Mac OS X Server, this is the user called *unknown* (see Example 16-1).

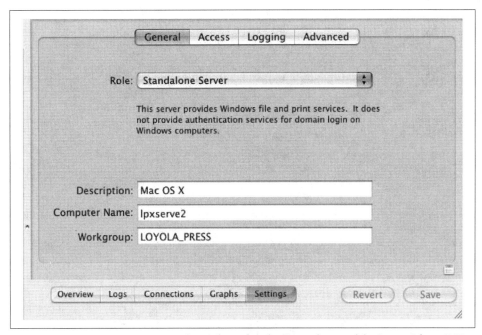

Figure 16-5. Basic SMB settings may be configured in the General pane of the Server Admin SMB module's Settings interface.

Example 16-1. Guest connections in Samba, when they're enabled, are mapped to the user unknown. Samba uses lookupd to identify users.

```
g5:~ ladmin$ lookupd -q user -a name unknown

_writers_passwd: unknown
change: 0
expire: 0
gid: 99
home: /var/empty
name: unknown
passwd: *
realname: Unknown User
shell: /usr/bin/false
uid: 99
```

Client connection limitations are implemented using *smb.conf*'s *max smbd* processes directive, which is set to 0 (which ironically equates to unlimited) in an out-of-box install.

A minimal interface to Samba's logging capabilities is available in the Logging tab, allowing the administrator to choose Low, Medium, or High logging, as shown in Figure 16-7. This corresponds to *smb.conf* "log level" settings of 0, 1, and 2, respectively (described in Table 16-1). These log levels, however, provide a depressing and limited view of Samba's rich logging capabilities. Other Samba log levels offer an amazing amount of data.

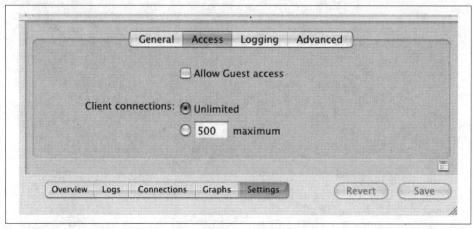

Figure 16-6. The Access pane essentially controls guest access and limits simultaneous connections.

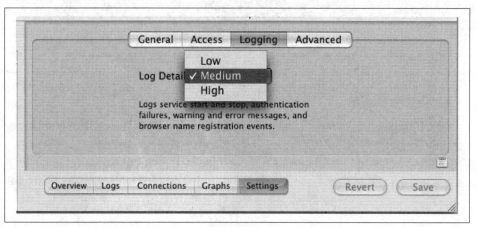

Figure 16-7. Server Admin's SMB logging capabilities ignore the great depth of data made available by the Samba package.

Table 16-1. Log levels that are available graphically using Server Admin.

Log level	smb.conf log level setting	Description
Low	0	Logs errors and warnings only. No file-access events are logged.
Medium	1	Logs service start and stop, authentication failures, warnings and error messages, and browser name registration events.
High	2	Logs file-access events, start and stop, authentication failures, warnings and error messages, and browser name registration events.

In the course of troubleshooting or initially setting up windows services, I've found log levels up to 5 very useful, especially when integrating Samba with Active Directory or NT domains. To temporarily support these higher log levels, edit */etc/smb. conf*'s log level parameter to 3, 4, or 5 and restart SMB using the Server Admin application or the *serveradmin* utility. Keep in mind, though, that the next time a configuration change is saved in Server Admin, *smb.conf* is rewritten and the changes will not be respected.

> In Jaguar, all changes to *smb.conf* could potentially be overwritten any time the configuration was changed or any time SMB services were started using Server Settings (Server Admin's predecessor). This situation was extremely frustrating to experienced Samba administrators and Apple customers seeking to get more out of Windows services than was offered in the graphical interface.
>
> In Panther *smb.conf* is still overwritten. However, many changes that do not affect graphically configured options are preserved as of 10.3.3. Comments are not preserved, and the organization of the files options might be changed—again frustrating experienced administrators, accustomed to well managed and neatly commented configuration files. But functionally the file may usually be modified, and those modifications will be consistently used to change the behavior of Windows services.

The Advanced pane of Server Admin's Windows settings (Figure 16-8), exposes a variety of (mostly unrelated) options.

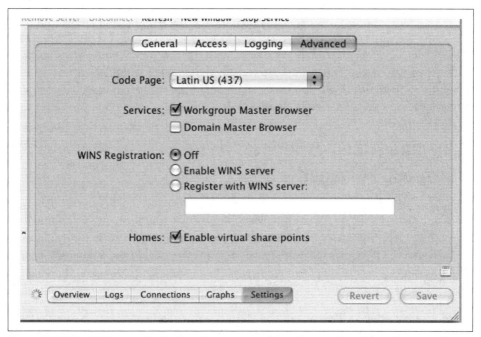

Figure 16-8. The SMB service's Advanced settings pane contains a variety of mostly unrelated (and not terribly advanced) functions.

The Code Page setting refers to the text encoding that should be used for files on the server's share points (Latin, Kanji, etc.). Strictly speaking, changing this should not be required for newer clients—they speak Unicode, as does Samba 3. For older clients, though, it is important to specify the correct code page.

 Note that even though *smb.conf* does not contain a Unicode parameter, it is enabled by default in the Samba distribution. Its status can be seen with the *testparm* command:

```
g5:~ nadmin$ testparm -v | grep unicode
            unicode = Yes
```

The Workgroup Master Browser and Domain Master Browser checkboxes enable the *local master* and *domain master* parameters in */etc/smb.conf*. A local master consolidates locally announced SMB services into a single list in order to reduce the amount of broadcast traffic that would otherwise occur while multiple clients browsed for resources. Setting local master to *yes* (the default configuration) does not mean, though, that Mac OS X Server automatically becomes the local master. It simply means that it participates in the local browser election, winning unless there is a Windows NT 4.0, 2000, or 2003 Domain Controller on the same subnet.

Checking the Domain Master Browser box causes Samba to claim the role of domain master browser for the workgroup specified in the General tab. This means that that per-subnet local master browsers sends their local browse lists to the server, and then requests a consolidated, authoritative, Workgroup-wide browse list back in return. Thus, when local clients contact the local master, they actually see a workgroup-wide list of resources. This option should not be enabled if there is a pre-existing Windows NT or Windows 2000 or 2003 domain controller, but will be enabled automatically if Mac OS X Server is set up as a PDC.

Managing Windows Services Using Workgroup Manager

While the global options for the SMB service are managed in Server Admin, per-share options are managed in Workgroup Manager, in the Protocols tab, shown in Figure 16-9. Appropriately, choosing Windows File Settings from the pull-down menu in that interface reveals SMB-specific options for the selected share.

In general, these options map directly to commonly used features of the underlying Samba package:

Share this item using SMB
    Allows the share to be accessed over SMB. Sets the *smb_shared* attribute in the share's record in NetInfo (*netinfo://config/SharePoints/sharename*) to 1 and creates a share entry in */etc/smb.conf* conforming to the other *smb*-specific parameters that have been established.

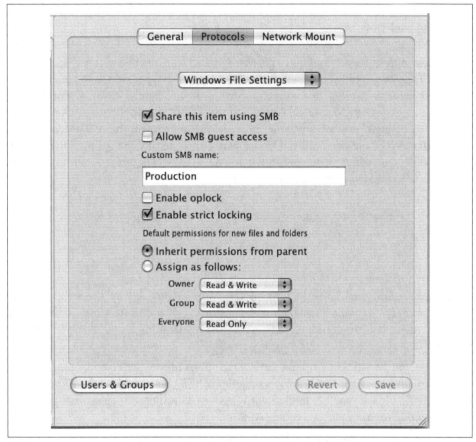

Figure 16-9. SMB-specific options on the /Users share in a default, out-of-box configuration.

Allow SMB guest access

Allow guest access to this share point. When set, this sets the *guest ok* parameter to "1" in that share's definition in */etc/smb.conf*. However, unless guest access is also enabled globally (in Server Admin), *guest ok* remains set to 0, despite what is reflected in the graphical interface. As of 10.3.3, an error condition is feasible wherein the *guest ok* parameter for a particular share may remain set to 0 after guest access has been enabled globally, if it was enabled for that share before it was enabled globally. This is remedied by disabling, saving and then re-enabling guest access on that share after it has been enabled globally.

Custom SMB name

Specify a custom name for this share when it is accessed via SMB. The shares name in Samba is typically established in the shares definition, rather than being derived from its path, which is stored in a separate *smb.conf* parameter. It is only by convention that Mac OS X derives the former from the latter. Setting this feature changes the share definition to reflect a different name. For more information relating to share definitions, see the commented *smb.conf* file later in this chapter.

Enable oplock

Enable opportunistic locking, an SMB-specific feature that involves local caching of the entire file. This feature can have impressive performance benefits—up to 30 percent faster performance, according to the Samba team. Unfortunately no other service in Mac OS X (including the OS itself) supports oplocks, and clients accessing shares via any other protocols won't respect them. This could lead to data loss or file corruption. Oplocks are controlled by the `oplocks` attribute in */etc/smb.conf*, which is set according to the share's *smb_oplocks* setting in NetInfo. They are disabled by default.

 Irix and Linux Kernels version 2.4 or higher both support oplocks.

Enable strict locking

A more traditional Unix locking mechanism. Controlled by the strict locking attribute in */etc/smb.conf*, which is set according to the share's *smb_strictlocking* attribute in NetInfo. Strict locking is enabled by default.

Default permissions for new files and folders

Allows for the "inherit from parent" permissions model preferred by many workgroup administrators and newly available to AFP clients in 10.2.2. Alternatively, a specific umask may be defined with "Assign as follows" (rather than the hard-coded 022 umask enforced by the AFP server).

Share settings themselves can be examined with any tool capable of reading the local NetInfo database—*nicl*, *dscl*, and *nidump* are all are capable (see Example 16-2). The actual per-share options are written (by *servermgrd* or the *sharing* command) to the share point's record in the local NetInfo domain.

Example 16-2. Using nicl to read options on the Users Share Point. The grep command is used to filter for SMB-specific options.

```
g5:~ ladmin$ nicl . -read /config/SharePoints/Users | grep smb
smb_shared: 1
smb_guestaccess: 1
smb_name: Users
smb_inherit_permissions: 0
smb_createmask: 0644
smb_directorymask: 0755
smb_oplocks: 1
smb_strictlocking: 1
```

Share options are then flushed by *servermgrd_smb* to */etc/smb.conf*. These per-share options can be both specified and viewed using a variety of command-line utilities.

As noted in Chapter 14, the *sharing* command's *–l* (list) flag is a good place to start. Recall also from that introduction that *sharing*'s *–a* and *–e* flags allow for manipulation of share point data (adding and editing share points, respectively). The flags *–a* and *–e* also accept a number of options, the *smb*-specific portions of which are illustrated in Table 16-2.

Table 16-2. These sharing flags and their associated arguments are useful in the management of AFP share point data.

Flag	Description
–S	Specify an SMB-specific name for the share point.
–s	Enable a share point for a service or services. Requires a three-digit argument consisting of 0s and 1s (0 for disabled, 1 for enabled). The first digit represents AFP, the second SMB, and the third FTP.
–g	Enables or disables group access. Like –s, requires a three-digit argument consisting of 0s and 1s (0 for disabled, 1 for enabled). The first digit represents AFP, the second SMB, and the third FTP.
–i	The inherit privileges option. Applicable only to AFP and SMB. Requires a two-digit argument consisting of 0s and 1s (0 for disabled, 1 for enabled). The first digit represents AFP, the second SMB.
–c	Specify a file creation mask for *smb*. The default value is 644, meaning that the owner will be able to read and write, while the group and everyone else will be permitted to read.
–d	Specify a folder creation mask for *smb*. The default value is 755, meaning that the owner will be able to read, write, and execute, while the group and everyone else will be able to read and execute.
–o	Enable oplocks. Accepts an argument *og 0* for disabled oplocks and *1* for enabled oplocks.
–t	Enable strict (POSIX) locks. Accepts an argument of 0 for disabled and 1 for enabled.

When using the *sharing* command, you must manually flush SMB options to */etc/smb.conf* using the *serveradmin* command (see Example 16-3).

Example 16-3. The serveradmin's command syncPrefs directive may be used to flush settings in NetInfo to the smb.conf file.

```
g5:~ ladmin$ sudo serveradmin command smb:command=syncPrefs
Password:
smb:command = "syncPrefs"
smb:status = 0
```

In 10.2, changes made in Server Settings were buffered initially in NetInfo, in the *netinfo://config/SMBServer* directory. When the service was started or stopped, those changes were flushed to the */etc/smb.conf* file. While this really didn't constitute a change to Samba, it is worth mentioning, because it interfered with traditional management techniques like the SWAT web-based Samba Administration tool. In 10.3, however, changes in Server Admin, as soon as they're committed, are written to */etc/smb.conf* by the *servermgrd_smb* plug-in.

netinfo://config/SMBServer still seems to exist, containing only a *code_page* setting, corresponding to */etc/smb.conf*'s dos charset parameter. Changes to Server Admin, though, seem to be saved to the configuration file directly, rather than being buffered.

Architecture

Windows services are provided in the Samba package using the *smbd* and *nmbd* daemons—for file and print access and name services, respectively. They are started by the Samba startup item according a -YES- flag on the SMBSERVER setting in */etc/hostconfig*. As mentioned previously in the chapter, *smbd* and *nmbd* share the */etc/smb.conf* configuration file, as shown in Example 16-4. Ironically, Mac OS X Server's configuration subsystem (specifically servermgrd's servermgrd_smb plug-in) rewrites existing *smb.conf* files, preserving changes that do not ocnflict with graphical settings, but discarding file comments.

Example 16-4. A well-commented /etc/smb.conf file.

```
#defines the global section
[global]
    #The workgroup or NT domain the server is associated with. Should be set to the
    #name of the emulated NT domain when working with AD.
    workgroup = 4AM
    #The charset that samba will use to print  messages.
    display charset = UTF-8-MAC
    #command used to pass print jobs to the print server
    #SMB printing is covered in more depth in the printing chapter.
    print command = /usr/sbin/PrintServiceAccess printps %p %s
    #the command used to delete print  jobs
    lprm command = /usr/sbin/PrintServiceAccess remove %p %j
    #parameter defining samba's security model. Set to ads when integrating with
    #Active Directory
    security = user
    #the user used access services and resources when logged in over SMB as guest
    guest account = unknown
    #controls whether or not encrypted authentication will be negociated. The
    #method by which this occurs in Mac OS X and Mac OS X Server differs from other
    #platforms, as described in the Apple's changes heading later in this chapter.
    encrypt passwords = yes
    # how  printer  status  information should be parsed
    printing = BSD
    #unused; used only when security is set to domain or server
    allow trusted domains = no
    preferred master = no
    lppause command = /usr/sbin/PrintServiceAccess hold %p %j
    netbios name = g5
    wins support = no
    max smbd processes = 0
```

Example 16-4. A well-commented /etc/smb.conf file. (continued)

```
    printcap =
    server string = Mac OS X
    lpresume command = /usr/sbin/PrintServiceAccess release %p %j
    client ntlmv2 auth = no
    domain logons = no
    lpq command = /usr/sbin/PrintServiceAccess jobs %p
    passdb backend = opendirectorysam guest
    dos charset = CP437
    unix charset = UTF-8-MAC
    auth methods = guest opendirectory
    local master = yes
    use spnego = no
    map to guest = Never
    domain master = no
    printer admin = @admin, @staff
    log level = 0
[homes]
    read only = no
    comment = User Home Directories
    browseable = no
[Groups]
    comment = macosx
    inherit permissions = no
    path = /Groups
    directory mask = 0755
    map archive = no
    guest ok = 1
    read only = no
    create mask = 0644
```

Apple's Changes to Samba

Apple was the first Unix vendor to embrace Samba 3, and many of the shortcomings in Jaguar's Samba implementation (such as the lack of PDC support and the totally rewritten *smb.conf* file) have been overcome in Panther. Apple has done a good job of living by the mantra of "Open Source Made Easy," contributing its source changes back to the Samba project. Those changes revolve primarily around authentication.

Password Server Integration

Windows supports a variety of authentication mechanisms of vastly varying security. The four most common where file sharing is concerned are documented in Table 16-3.

Table 16-3. Authentication mechanisms available to Windows SMB clients. With version 3, the Samba team added NTLMv2 support to smbd. Password Server, though, does not have this support in 10.3.3.

Mechanism	Minimum Supported OS	Description
LANMAN	Windows 3.1	Trivial to compromise, based on a case-normalized, maximum-14-character password.
NTLMv1	Windows NT 4	Identical in strength to LANMAN if the password is less than seven characters, NTLMv1 is not considered secure by Microsoft.
NTLMv2	Windows NT 4 Service Pack 4	Not supported by Mac OS X Server, NTLMv2 is the only relatively secure Windows authentication method outside of Active Directory.
Kerberos	Windows 2000	Considered fairly secure.

All of these authentication methods require hashes of the password to be stored in different formats. One of the biggest issues with Samba integration on Unix platforms is generating and securely storing these hashes.

 A hash is just one way of saying that the password is encrypted. Because storing clear-text passwords is probably a bad idea, passwords are hashed in such a way that the original clear text password is difficult to obtain. Windows and Mac OS X require different hashing mechanisms.

Windows authentication mechanisms require passwords to be stored in methods that the traditional Unix */etc/passwd* files did not support. Because Unix password hashes tended to use the DES *crypt( )* algorithm, they could not be easily reversed, which would be required in order to generate the Windows hashes. The easiest solution seemed to be to transmit user credentials in the clear. This, of course, was horrible security practice. In time, procedures to store LANMAN and NTLMv1 passwords were developed, usually by storing all three hashes (Unix and Windows) at password change or user creation.

In order to avoid synchronization issues, Apple modified Samba so that it is capable of authenticating against Password Server. All necessary hashes are stored in one network available authentication system rather than having to be maintained on the server itself. This has the added advantage of centralizing authentication in a managed domain. The downside is that Apple's Samba is fairly difficult to build outside of Apple's internal build process, so porting these changes to new or updated versions of Samba depends largely on Apple—although they commit their changes back to the Samba group, those changes depend on software that isn't open source or a build environment that is difficult to construct from open source components. This also means that traditional LDAP integration mechanisms in Samba will not usually work with Mac OS X Server, since they depend on storage of Windows hashes in the LDAP directory.

Useful Utilities

The Samba suite ships with a number of utilities that assist with setup and day-to-day management. Some of those are documented here, along with the most common options:

testparm

> The oddly pronounced *testparm* analyzes the server's *smb* configuration—command-line flags, specified parameters, and compiled-in default options—looking for conflicts and reporting and discrepancies. The *–v* flag is required in order to display compiled-in default settings. *testparm* is demonstrated earlier in this chapter, in the note discussing Unicode and Samba.

smbutil

> A useful utility for performing a number of administrative tasks (Example 16-5). Common options include:
>
> *lc*
>
>> Looks cool. Actually meant to list connections, but does not appear to work.
>
> *lookup*
>
>> Resolve a host's IP using NetBIOS naming.
>
> *status [server]*
>
>> Similar to *lookup*, resolves a *server* and displays its workgroup.
>
> *view //[workgroup;][user[password]@] server*
>
>> Enumerate resources available on a particular *server*.

Example 16-5. Using smbutil to list available resources on G5. The lc (list connections) directive, listed in the manpage, does not appear to work.

```
g5:~ ladmin$ smbutil -v view //g5
kextload: extension /System/Library/Extensions/smbfs.kext is already loaded
Password:
Share          Type      Comment
-------------------------------
Documentation  disk      macosx
Users          disk      macosx
Applications   disk      macosx
IPC$           pipe      IPC Service (Mac OS X)
ADMIN$         pipe      IPC Service (Mac OS X)
ladmin         disk      User Home Directories

6 shares listed from 6 available
```

Troubleshooting

The good news is that Samba on Mac OS X is similar enough to Samba on other platforms that many of the same troubleshooting methodologies (often using utilities documented in this chapter) are generally applicable. The bad news is that Mac OS X is different enough in some regards—also documented here—that troubleshooting can be difficult.

Samba apparently still uses *libc getpw()* calls (such *as getpwnam()* and *getpwent()*) to look up users. The *libc* calls are serviced by *lookupd*, which (unless the users are in the local NetInfo database) dispatches them to the *DirectoryService* daemon. Because Samba spawns at least one process per connection, this is particularly hard on *lookupd*. Apple recommends changing *lookupd*'s maximum thread value from 64 to 128, as shown in Example 16-6.

Example 16-6. Changing lookupd's Maxthreads value to 128.

```
sudo dscl . -create /locations/lookupd Maxthreads 128
```

SMB Share Point Permissions Restrictions

In Mac OS X 10.3.3, the entire path to the share must be readable by the system user that is attempting to access it. For example, the path in Figure 16-10 would not be technically feasible for sharing via Windows services. The path shown in Figure 16-11 would be.

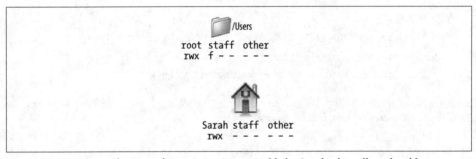

Figure 16-10. Because the Users directory is not executable by Sarah, she will not be able to access another user's home directory via Windows Services.

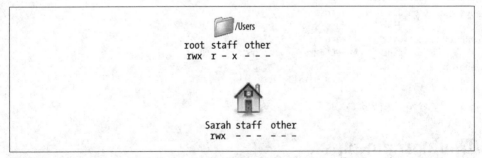

Figure 16-11. Sarah is a member of the staff group, which can execute the Users directory. Because of this, Sarah is able to access her home directory over SMB.

Integration

Since Samba is designed primarily to integrate with Windows infrastructures, it tends to follow less generalized guidelines than other services. In fact, Samba is incapable of interoperating with non-Windows KDCs in its current release (3.03, included in 10.3.3). Although later versions of samba do support Kerberos outside of Active Directory, it is not clear when Apple will adopt this functionality. Samba, then, is one of the few Mac OS X Server Services that won't support single sign-on with an Apple Open Directory master. Integration with Windows infrastructure is covered here: *http://www. macdevcenter.com/pub/a/mac/2003/12/09/active_directory.html.*

CHAPTER 17
FTP

As simple as it is ubiquitous and insecure, the File Transfer Protocol (FTP) is one of the most popular methods for cross-platform file transfers in use today. Multiple FTP clients (both command-line and graphical) are included in Mac OS X and in Windows, and it is integrated into a variety of other software packages like Macromedia Dreamweaver and Adobe GoLive. It is also, in most cases, tremendously insecure, sending the user's name and password unencrypted over the network. Its popularity, though, along with the fact that there are no common, secure, feature-compatible alternatives, makes it an important part of Mac OS X Server.

Managing FTP with Server Admin

Global options for the FTP service can be managed and monitored using Server Admin, in the FTP module of the selected server. Displaying a summary that is similar to that of many other services, the Overview section (seen in Figure 17-1) lists the current number of connections and the status of both guest access and logging, along with the services' start time. It also introduces a concept seen again and again throughout the service, differentiating between authenticated and anonymous connections.

Much of this data can also be seen with the *serveradmin* command's *fullstatus ftp* argument, as shown in Example 17-1.

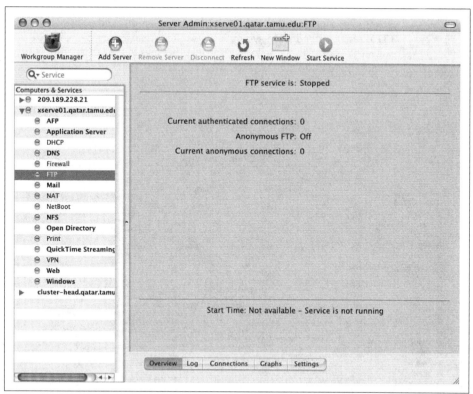

Figure 17-1. FTP's Overview is similar to that of most other Server Admin services. Current connections are displayed separately for authenticated and anonymous (guest) connections.

Example 17-1. Using serveradmin's fullstatus ftp argument to gather basic data about FTP services.

```
g5:~ nadmin$ sudo serveradmin fullstatus ftp
ftp:command = "getState"
ftp:anonymousAccessPermitted = "NO"
ftp:state = "RUNNING"
ftp:realConnectionCount = 0
ftp:logPaths:transferLog = "/Library/Logs/FTP.transfer.log"
ftp:anonymousConnectionCount = 0
ftp:readWriteSettingsVersion = 1
ftp:setStateVersion = 1
ftp:startedTime = "2004-05-01 19:25:00 -0600"
```

Logs for Mac OS X's FTP services can sometimes be viewed using the Log section of Server Admin's FTP management interface, illustrated in Figure 17-2. The verbosity of these logs is controlled in the Log tab of the FTP Settings section, discussed later in this chapter. As is the case with many Server Admin log viewers, this feature does not support any sort of filtering and is limited by *servermgrd*'s HTTP request-response model. It might make more sense to view the files directly, with the *tail* command over an SSH session.

In a default configuration, the FTP server logs to both */Library/Logs/FTP.transfer.log* and */var/log/system.log*, sending transfer (upload and download) messages to the former and all other logs to the latter. This is the case even though the graphical configuration states they are all being sent to */Library/Logs/FTP.transfer.log*.

Figure 17-2. Server Admin's ftp logs. Not all relevant data is available in this interface; many FTP logs are sent to the system log (/var/log/system.log).

The FTP Connections interface (Figure 17-3), like that of many other services, displays current connections to the server, sortable by Name, Type (Authenticated or Anonymous), originating address and current Activity. Once again, real (authenticated) and guest users are segregated—not only by type, but also due to the way the user's name is represented. Real users are identified by their RecordName, while anonymous connections display the email address users are asked to supply as a password. Unlike SMB and AFP connection management interfaces, though, clients may not be manually disconnected as of 10.3.5.

The *serveradmin* command, as shown here, can be used to view the same connection data available in Server Admin's FTP Connections tab:

Figure 17-3. The Connections interface displays information about currently logged-in users. Unlike similar interfaces that support AFP and SMB management, FTP users may not be disconnected.

```
g5:~ nadmin$ sudo serveradmin command ftp:command = getConnectedUsers
ftp:command = "getConnectedUsers"
ftp:timeStamp = "2004-05-02 13:22:33 -0600"
ftp:usersArray:_array_index:0:sessionID = 11156
ftp:usersArray:_array_index:0:userType = "real"
ftp:usersArray:_array_index:0:userName = "nadmin"
ftp:usersArray:_array_index:0:userCommand = "IDLE"
ftp:usersArray:_array_index:0:ipAddress = "gs.pantherserver.org"
ftp:usersArray:_array_index:1:sessionID = 11155
ftp:usersArray:_array_index:1:userType = "anon"
ftp:usersArray:_array_index:1:userName = "ambrlyn@mac.com"
ftp:usersArray:_array_index:1:userCommand = "IDLE"
ftp:usersArray:_array_index:1:ipAddress = "c-24-9-140-74.client.comcast.net"
```

Illustrated in Figure 17-4, the Graphs section (which could be more accurately called Graph, since there is only one) displays graphically the number of connected users over historical periods ranging from 1 hour to 7 days. As with other graphing interfaces in Server Admin, this tool is useful for a quick and intuitive summary of recent usage trends.

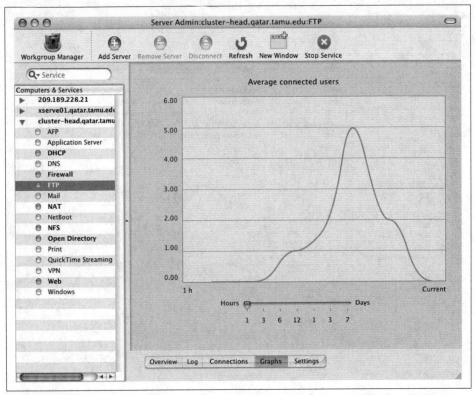

Figure 17-4. Like its Windows services counterpart, the FTP graph illustrates the average number of connected users over the immediately past 1 hour to 7 days.

Selection of the Settings section yields a choice of several tabs used to change the behavior and configuration of the FTP service. Most of the data in all of these interfaces is written by *servermgrd*'s *servermgrd_ftp* plug-in directly to the FTP server's configuration file, */Library/FTPServer/Configuration/ftpaccess*. *ftpaccess* is discussed in more depth in the *ftpaccess* section, later in this chapter.

The General tab, seen in Figure 17-5, exposes a number of options relating to Access, authentication, file conversion and the server's basic behavior. Most are fairly straightforward:

Disconnect client after n failures

The *loginfails* option in the *ftpaccess* file. This option, as the name implies, disconnects any session that has failed to authenticate the specified number of times. The user must open another FTP connection in order to attempt authentication again. This is a fairly common security measure available to most network services. The default value is 3.

FTP administrator email address

The email option in *ftpaccess*. This address is provided in order to facilitate communications with someone with administrative authority for the service. It is represented with the %E variable in FTP messages. For a complete list of variables, see Table 17-1 later in this chapter.

Authentication method

Specifies which authentication methods are available. This setting corresponds to the auth_level directive in the *ftpaccess* file. Allowed values are *both*, *gssapi* (Kerberos), and *standard*. Standard is essentially clear text—the username and password are sent over the network without encryption. In most cases, the authentication method should be set to Kerberos. This setting will allow anonymous access (if it is enabled) but require authenticated users to use Kerberos rather than sending their password over the network. The out-of-box default is *both*.

> Even though both Kerberos and standard authentication methods are enabled by default, Kerberos authentication cannot proceed unless the server is a part of a Kerberos realm and has a valid FTP service record. Additionally, not all FTP clients support Kerberos authentication. For more information on Kerberos integration, see "Securing FTP," later in this chapter.

Allow a maximum of n authenticated or anonymous users

When enabled, these place limits on the number of authenticated and/or anonymous connections (see Example 17-2). This restriction is implemented using a set of user classes established in *ftpaccess*. The details of this configuration are discussed in more depth in the *ftpaccess* section later in this chapter.

Example 17-2. The class and limit directives used in /Library/FTPServer/Configuration/ ftpaccess to limit access by authenticated and anonymous connections.

```
class      realusers    real *
class      anonusers    anonymous  *

limit      realusers    50     Any /Library/FTPServer/Messages/limit.txt
limit      anonusers    50     Any /Library/FTPServer/Messages/limit.txt
```

Enable anonymous access

Selection of this checkbox authorizes anonymous connections to the server. This corresponds to the anonFTP setting in *ftpaccess*, and is disabled in a default configuration. Out of the box, guest access to FTP is globally disabled using this setting.

The "Enable MacBinary and disk image auto-conversion" checkbox is the most perplexing of Server Admin's General FTP settings—mostly because (as of 10.3.4) it does not do what it says it does. File conversion is a good idea, and it's not new with

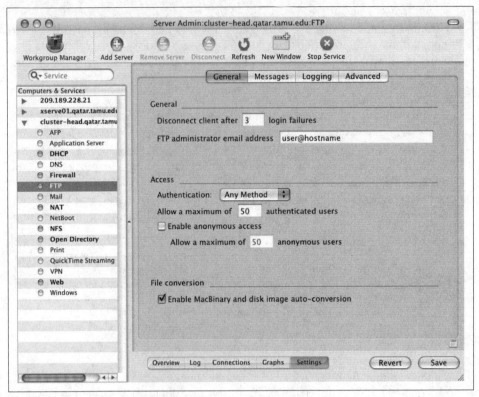

Figure 17-5. The General tab of Server Admin's FTP Settings tab is home to a variety of settings.

Mac OS X Server—other FTP platforms have offered similar technologies for years. Example 17-3 shows an FTP directory that contains several files.

Example 17-3. Command-line FTP clients typically work in a way that is similar to an interactive login shell. In this case, the ls command, when executed over ftp, lists the contents of the notes directory.

```
ftp> ls notes
227 Entering Passive Mode (192,168,1,1,74,152)
150 Opening ASCII mode data connection for directory listing.
total 1192
-rw-r--r--  1 1025  1029     272 Jul 23  2003 README
-rw-------  1 1025  1029  142421 Jul 18  2003 ktrace.out.1
-rw-------  1 1025  1029  139826 Jul 18  2003 ktrace.out.2
-rw-------  1 1025  1029  208957 Jul 18  2003 ktrace.out.3
-rw-r--r--  1 1025  1029    9300 Jul 18  2003 loginwindow.crash.log
-rw-r--r--  1 1025  1029   78434 Jul 23  2003 notes-20030723a.tar.gz
-rw-r--r--  1 1025  1029    2040 Jul 18  2003 syslog.1
-rw-r--r--  1 1025  1029    2253 Jul 18  2003 syslog.2
-rw-r--r--  1 1025  1029     243 Jul 18  2003 syslog.3
226 Transfer complete.
```

FTP doesn't widely support any good standards for recursion—there's no way to get the entire directory. Instead, the client can simply request an archive of the directory, or, optionally, a compressed archive, as shown in Example 17-4.

Example 17-4. Requesting file conversion using Mac OS X's built-in ftp client. File conversion isn't limited to directories—files may be processed as well. Directories simply make a good example.

```
ftp> get notes.tar
local: notes.tar remote: notes.tar
227 Entering Passive Mode (192,168,1,1,74,209)
150 Opening BINARY mode data connection for /usr/bin/gzip -cd notes.tar.gz.
226 Transfer complete.
522240 bytes received in 00:00 (2.67 MB/s)
```

The FTP server knows, based on the extension and the file name that's requested, how to process the file or directory in order to meet the client's request (the server's rules are specified in the *ftpconversions* file, covered in more depth later in this chapter). Mac OS X Server takes this process further, adding on-the-fly disk image and BinHex (*.bin*) file conversions, both designed to facilitate transfer of files containing resource forks.

Not all clients support file conversion, though. The server would be more than happy to process files if they were requested, but there aren't any standards for communicating these capabilities. In order to work around this, Mac OS X Server supports an *influence_listings* directive in *ftpaccess*, which artificially appends a *.bin* to the listing any file with a resource fork. (The file name isn't actually changed—it just appears that way when viewed over FTP.) This feature allows the client to specifically request an encoded file, and works around the fact that there is no other way for the client to be aware of the server's conversion capabilities.

Rather than actually disabling File conversion, turning off the "Enable MacBinary and disk image auto-conversion" checkbox simply sets *ftpaccess*'s *influence_listings* directive to *no*. This setting does not prevent clients from requesting file conversions—it just prevents the server from announcing the capability in its file listings.

While often desirable in cross-platform environments because most Windows clients don't always know what to do with *.bin* files (and can't use resource forks, anyway), this does not alleviate the resource allocation and denial of service concerns inherent to file conversion. For a more in-depth discussion, including methods for disabling file conversion, see the *ftpconversions* section, later in this chapter.

The Messages pane of Server Admin's FTP Settings section, illustrated in Figure 17-6, allows two of the most commonly used FTP messages—banner and welcome—to be edited and managed graphically. The banner message, specified in *ftpaccess* by the *banner* directive and living at */Library/FTPServer/Messages/banner. txt*, is displayed during the connection process, immediately before the user is prompted for a username and password.

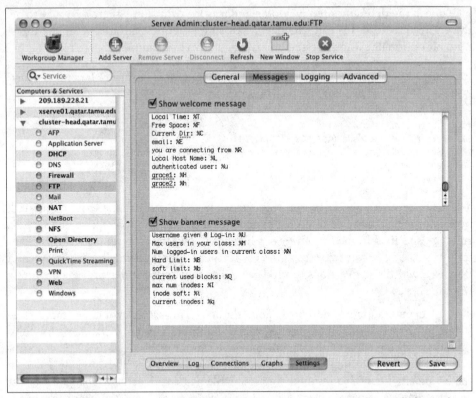

Figure 17-6. The Message pane of Server Admin's FTP Settings allows for the control of two of xftpd's status messages. The variables used in this configuration are described in Table 17-1.

The welcome message, specified by one of several message directives, is stored in */Library/FTPServer/Messages/welcome.txt*. It is displayed immediately after a successful login. These and other messages support a number of cookies, or variables, that once included in the message files will be interpreted on the fly when sent to clients. This method is usually in order to better communicate the current state of the server. Rather than having to hard-code this data, requiring periodic manipulation of the message files, it is dynamically generated. Table 17-1 contains a listing of these variables; see Example 17-5 for usage of some of these variables.

Table 17-1. Cookies (variables) available in various FTP banner and message files.

Variable	Description
%T	Server's local time
%F	Free space on partition of current directory
%C	Current directory
%E	Email of maintainer, as specified by the email directive of the *ftpaccess* file

Table 17-1. Cookies (variables) available in various FTP banner and message files. (continued)

Variable	Description
%R	Remote hostname
%L	Local hostname
%u	Username determined by authentication
%U	Username given at login time
%M	Maximum number or allowed users in the current class
%N	Number of logged-in users in the current class
%B	Hard limit imposed on the number of disk blocks allocated
%b	Preferred (soft) limit on the number of allocated blocks
%Q	Current block count
%I	Maximum number of allocated inodes
%i	Soft limit on the number of allocated inodes
%q	Current number of allocated inodes
%H	Grace period for disk quota overage
%h	Grace period for inode overage

Example 17-5. Using variables in the welcome message and banner text. No quotas are set on the FTP server in this example, so quota-related variables show up as having a value of %?.

```
big15:~ mab$ ftp 192.168.1.1
Connected to 192.168.1.1.
220-Username given @ Log-in:
220-Max users in your class: 50
220-Num logged-in users in current class: 0
220-Hard Limit: %?
220-soft limit: %?
220-current used blocks: %?
220-max num inodes: %?
220-inode soft: %?
220-current inodes: %?
220-
220 ace2.4am-media.com FTP server (Version:  Mac OS X Server 10.3.2 - +GSSAPI) ready.
Name (192.168.1.1:mab): p10001
331 Password required for p10001.
Password:
230-No directory! Logging in with home=/
230-Local Time: Fri Oct 22 21:40:53 2004
230-Free Space: Fri Oct 22 21:40:53 2004
230-Current Dir: /Library/FTPServer/FTPRoot
230-email: user@hostname
230-you are connecting from 192.168.1.103
230-Local Host Name: ace2.4am-media.com
230-authenticated user: [unknown]
230-grace1: %?
230-grace2: %?
230-
```

Example 17-5. Using variables in the welcome message and banner text. No quotas are set on the FTP server in this example, so quota-related variables show up as having a value of %?. (continued)

```
230 User p10001 logged in.
Remote system type is UNIX.
Using binary mode to transfer files.
ftp>
```

The Logging tab of Server Admin's FTP Settings tab, seen in Figure 17-7, specifies which access events should be logged. Administrators may choose from among Uploads, Downloads, FTP commands, and Rule violation attempts, specified granularly, depending on whether they originated from anonymous or authenticated connections.

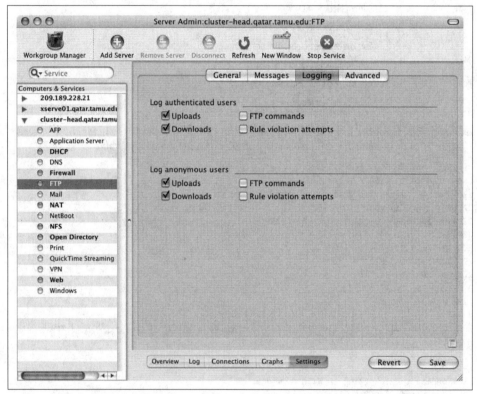

Figure 17-7. The Logging tab of Server Admin's FTP Settings section. It is pictured in its default state.

This interface is somewhat misleading, however, as it actually refers to two separate logs: */Library/Logs/FTP.transfer.log* and */var/log/system.log*. Uploads and downloads (transfers) are sent to *FTP.transfer.log*, while FTP commands and Rule violation attempts are sent to *syslog*. There is no indication of this difference in either the graphical interface or the server's included documentation.

It is only by deduction that I've arrived at these conclusions. No differentiation is made among transfer, command, and security logging statements in *ftpaccess*.

A big problem with some FTP implementations is that they assume any authenticated user should be authorized to see any world-readable portions of the filesystem. This is not always desirable, and generally FTP services are *chroot*'d, or limited to certain directories. Instead of seeing the true contents of the filesystem root (/), *chroot*'d clients can see only the directories they are limited to.

 chroot( ) is not a concept that is limited to FTP. For more discussion of *chroot*, see Chapter 11.

Mac OS X is no exception, and the Advanced tab of Server Admin's FTP Settings specifies two options (seen in Figure 17-8) that together determine what the server's *chroot* environment will look like: these are the "Authenticated users see" and "Authenticated user FTP root" pop-up menus.

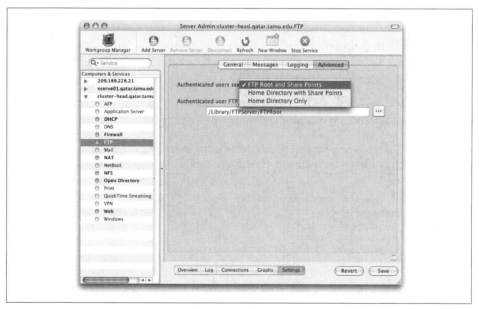

Figure 17-8. The Advanced tab of Server Admin's FTP Settings tab controls the FTP Server's chroot behavior. Both of these options work in concert with the per-share FTP options that are established using Workgroup Manager.

Usually, all users, (when accessing the server via FTP) are limited to the FTP root directory. This default makes the graphical interface somewhat unclear, since it specifically labels this directory *authenticated* users FTP root. In actuality, the directory that is specified in the graphical interface is used to populate two *ftpaccess* variables—*defrootdir* and *anonymous-root*. The matter is only made more complex by the fact that authenticated users might not always see it, depending on the "Authenticated users see" setting. This interaction is documented in Table 17-2. The point, though, is to limit users to a specific portion of the filesystem, so that they are not able to access any system files.

Table 17-2. Observed behaviors with various combinations of the "authenticated users see" and "authenticated users FTP root" settings.

Setting	Authenticated users see	Anonymous users see
FTP Root and Share Points (default)	FTP Root and Share points with FTP enabled. Users are logged in into their home directories, if they live on a share point.	FTP Root and Share Points with both FTP and guest access enabled.
Home Directory with Share Points	Contents of home directory, with a virtual link called FTPRoot, allowing access to the FTP Root and FTP-enabled Share Points.	FTP Root and Share Points with both FTP and guest access enabled.
Home Directory Only	Contents of home directory, with a broken virtual link to FTP Root.	FTP Root, with no access to any share points, regardless of whether guest access is enabled on them.

The "Authenticated users see" item, which corresponds to *ftpaccess*'s *chroot_type* option, controls whether authenticated users will see the FTP Root, and whether or not Share Points are made accessible via FTP.

As with other services, FTP settings may also be set and viewed using the *serveradmin* command's settings directive (see Example 17-6).

Example 17-6. Using serveradmin to view FTP settings and to enable guest access. Ironically, since guest access does not require sending a username and password over the network, it is often the only suitable use for FTP.

```
[ace2:~] nadmin% sudo serveradmin settings ftp
ftp:logSecurity:anonymous = no
ftp:logSecurity:guest = no
ftp:logSecurity:real = no
ftp:authLevel = "ANYMETHOD"
ftp:logToSyslog = no
ftp:maxAnonymousUsers = -1
ftp:welcomeMessage = "ftp is insecure, do not use it."
ftp:showBannerMessage = no
ftp:anonymousAccessPermitted = no
ftp:loginFailuresPermitted = 5
ftp:maxRealUsers = -1
ftp:anonymous-root = "/Library/FTPServer/FTPRoot"
ftp:chrootType = "STANDARD"
ftp:showWelcomeMessage = no
ftp:logTransfers:anonymous:inbound = no
```

Example 17-6. Using serveradmin to view FTP settings and to enable guest access. Ironically, since guest access does not require sending a username and password over the network, it is often the only suitable use for FTP. (continued)

```
ftp:logTransfers:anonymous:outbound = no
ftp:logTransfers:guest:inbound = no
ftp:logTransfers:guest:outbound = no
ftp:logTransfers:real:inbound = no
ftp:logTransfers:real:outbound = no
ftp:enableMacBinAndDmgAutoConversion = yes
ftp:ftpRoot = "/Library/FTPServer/FTPRoot"
ftp:logCommands:anonymous = no
ftp:logCommands:guest = no
ftp:logCommands:real = no
```

Settings values may also be adjusted using *serveradmin* (see Example 17-7).

Example 17-7. Using serveradmin to configure the FTP service to change the maximum number of permitted login failures.

```
[ace2:~] nadmin% sudo serveradmin settings ftp:loginFailuresPermitted = 3
ftp:loginFailuresPermitted = 3
```

Managing FTP Using Workgroup Manager

While the global options for the FTP service are managed in Server Admin, per-share options are managed in Workgroup Manager, in the Protocols tab mentioned earlier in the chapter. Appropriately, choosing FTP from the pull-down menu in that interface reveals FTP-specific options for the selected share, as illustrated in Figure 17-9. They are rather brief—a custom share name may be specified, guest access may be allowed or disallowed and FTP access may be disallowed for the share.

These per-share options are stored in the local NetInfo database, in the *ftp_shared*, *ftp_guestaccess*, and *ftp_name* attributes of the share's entry in */config/sharepoints*. As shown here, you can use *nicl* to view the FTP-specific attributes of the *sw* share; *nicl*'s output is piped to *grep* in order to filter it for *ftp*:

```
g5:~ nadmin$ nicl . -read /config/SharePoints/sw | grep ftp
ftp_shared: 1
ftp_guestaccess: 1
ftp_name: sw
```

Items that are *ftp_shared* have a symbolic link into the FTP Root specified in Server Admin's Advanced FTP Settings tab. Adding a custom name simply changes the name of that symlink, as shown in Example 17-8.

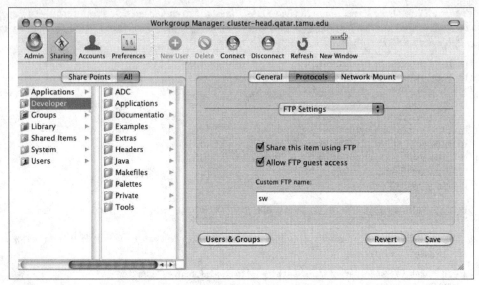

Figure 17-9. Share-specific options for Mac OS X Server FTP services. Guest access may be controlled on a per-share basis, and custom share names may be specified.

Example 17-8. FTP shares are simply links into the specified FTP Root directory. Custom FTP share names simply change the name of that symlink.

```
g5:~ nadmin$ ls -la /Library/FTPServer/FTPRoot/
total 32
drwxrwxr-x  6 root    admin  204  1 May 19:26 .
drwxrwxr-x  7 root    admin  238 17 Apr 08:54 ..
lrwxr-xr-x  1 root    admin    7  1 May 19:26 Groups -> /Groups
lrwxr-xr-x  1 root    admin   20 17 Apr 09:26 Public -> /Shared Items/Public
lrwxr-xr-x  1 root    admin    6 17 Apr 09:26 Users -> /Users
lrwxr-xr-x  1 root    admin    3  1 May 19:26 sw -> /sw\
```

Disabling guest access to a share breaks that share's symlink when anonymous users connect. Authenticates users, however, still have access to the resource, as shown in Example 17-9.

Example 17-9. Anonymous access is disabled for the "sw" share.

```
ftp> ls /
502 'EPSV': command not understood.
227 Entering Passive Mode (207,224,49,181,60,190)
150 Opening ASCII mode data connection for directory listing.
total 32
drwxrwxr-x  1 0   80   68 May  1 19:26 Groups
drwxrwxr-x  1 0   80   68 Apr 17 09:26 Public
drwxrwxr-x  1 0   80  374 Apr 17 09:26 Users
lrwxr-xr-x  1 0   80    3 May  1 19:26 sw -> ???
226 Transfer complete.
ftp>
```

As with other services, the entire set of FTP options may also be configured using the *sharing* command-line utility. As noted in the introduction to Part IV, the *sharing* command's *–l* (list) flag is a good place to start. Recall also from that introduction that *sharing*'s *–a* and *–e* flags allow for manipulation of share point data (adding and editing share points, respectively). The *–a* and *–e* flags also accept a number of options, the AFP-specific portions of which are illustrated in Table 17-3.

Table 17-3. These sharing flags and their associated arguments are useful in the management of AFP share point data.

Flag	Description
–F	Specify an FTP-specific name for the share point.
–s	Enables a share point for a service or services. Requires a three-digit argument consisting of 0s and 1s (0 for disabled, 1 for enabled). The first digit represents AFP, the second SMB, and the third FTP.
–g	Enables or disables group access. Like *–s*, requires a three-digit argument consisting of 0s and 1s (0 for disabled, 1 for enabled). The first digit represents AFP, the second SMB, and the third FTP.
–i	The inherit privileges option. Applicable only to AFP and SMB. Requires a two-digit argument consisting of 0s and 1s (0 for disabled, 1 for enabled). The first digit represents AFP, the second SMB.

Architecture

Apple's FTP services are provided by *xftpd*, a modified version of Washington University's *wu-ftpd*. *xftpd* is started by *xinetd*, as described in Chapter 10. Most of its configuration options are stored in several files, all located in */Library/FTPServer/Configuration*, which are described in Table 17-4. *xtfpd* itself, along with many of these files, has extensive manpages.

Table 17-4. FTP configuration files stored in /Library/FTPServer/Configuration.

File	Description
ftpaccess	Discussed earlier in the chapter, *ftpaccess* is *xftpd*'s main configuration file, containing most of the options specified in Server Admin.
ftpconversions	Contains *xftpd*'s rules for file conversion, discussed briefly earlier.
ftpgroups	Allows or denies access to FTP services for specific groups.
ftphosts	Allows or denies access to FTP services for specific hosts.
ftpusers	Allows or denies access to FTP services for specific users.

Each file in this directory has a corresponding *.default* file (for instance, *ftpaccess. default*). Manual changes should be made to the *.default* file as well as to the file itself, and should be made only to settings that are not available in the user interface. This ensures that any manual changes are not overwritten. The default installed Configuration directory itself is also duplicated in */Library/FTPServer/Configuration. installed*, ensuring that the server's configuration can always be restored to its default state.

ftpaccess: Advanced Options

ftpaccess, as covered previously in this chapter, is *xftpd*'s main configuration file, and all changes made in Server Admin are reflected there. Server Admin, though, exposes only a few of its features, and many more may be accessed by manually editing the file. Remember that any change to *ftpaccess* requires that the *ftp* service be restarted. Graphical changes made through Server Admin will prompt the user for this restart. Manual changes made with *serveradmin*, or by editing the configuration file, should be accompanied by the *serveradmin stop ftp* and *serveradmin start ftp* commands.

This class directive assigns all real users (real *) and all anonymous users (anonymous *) to the realusers and anonusers classes, respectively. These classes are then used with the limit directive to control the maximum number of clients allowed to access the server at a particular time (in this case, Any means that the limit is always enforced). The limit directive additionally points to the *limit.txt* document, which is presented to users when the limit established for their class has been met or exceeded. *limit.txt* can be customized to reflect any specific site-wise policies, but in its default state is rather minimal, as shown in Example 17-10.

Example 17-10. Defining limits for particular ftp classes. Classes may also be defined according to the source address of the connection. As of 10.3.4, this feature is not covered in ftpaccess's manpage.

```
class          realusers     real *
class          anonusers     anonymous  *

limit          realusers     50      Any /Library/FTPServer/Messages/limit.txt
limit          anonusers     50      SaSu|Any1800-0600 /Library/FTPServer/Messages/
limit.txt
```

ftpaccess uses the time conventions first established in Unix-to-Unix Copy (UUCP), a protocol that hasn't been used much in a long time). The format is as follows:

Any
> Refers to all days and all times

Mo, Tu, We, Th, Fr, Sa, Su
> Days of the week.

0000–2359
> Military time (on a 24-hour, rather than 12-hour, scale). 0000 is midnight (12 a.m.), 1200 is noon (12 p.m.), and 1600 is 4 p.m., etc.

Time conventions can be combined, and the pipe (|) serves as a logical *or*, so in the anonusers limit specified earlier, the restriction is enforced on both Saturday and Sunday, and from 6 p.m. to 6 a.m. every other day.

The banner directive lists the file whose contents are sent to any clients before they are prompted for a username and password. It is covered in more depth earlier in this chapter:

```
banner         /Library/FTPServer/Messages/banner.txt
```

The readme parameter, which is not configurable in the graphical interface, checks for the specified file (*README*, in this case) and notifies the user that the file exists and when it was last modified. readme takes the form of:

```
readme <path> {<when> {<class>}}
```

The first parameter checks for a *README* file at login. The second specifies that the check should be run any time the current working directory is changed. Both specify a relative path to the *README* file, so that each current working directory may have its own.

```
readme          README* login
readme          README* cwd=*
```

Similar to the readme parameter, message specifies a file whose contents will be displayed to the user at certain events, the difference being that users are simply notified of the file specified in readme, whereas the contents of the message file are actually sent to the client. The first message parameter corresponds to the welcome message specified in the Messages tab of Server Admin's FTP Settings section. (This feature is mentioned earlier in the chapter.) The second specifies that (if it exists) the contents of the *message.txt* file in any directory will be sent to any user as soon as they transfer to that directory.

```
message         /Library/FTPServer/Messages/welcome.txt login
message         message.txt     cwd=*
```

defrootdir and chroot_type, as discussed earlier, correspond to the "Authenticate users see" and "Authenticated user FTP root" section options in the Advanced tab of Server Admin's FTP Settings, and are discussed earlier in the chapter.

```
defrootdir      /Library/FTPServer/FTPRoot
chroot_type     standard
```

sjis sets Kanji code to shift JIS. This is used to support Japanese localization:

```
sjis            no
```

keepalive sets the TCP SO_KEEPALIVE option for FTP data sockets, meaning that FTP data connections are kept alive even if it looks like the client has gone away (such as during network disconnects or sleep events):

```
keepalive       yes
```

As discussed earlier, the loginfails option corresponds to the "Disconnect after *n* login failures" option in the General tab of Server Admin's FTP Settings tab.

```
loginfails      3
```

passwd-check doesn't actually affect authenticated users. Instead, it controls the checks performed on the *password* sent when anonymous users log in. Its default state, set here, simply warns users if they do not supply an RFC822-compliant email address (*user@domain.com* or *user@host.domain.com*). A more severe option, which would deny login to users who did not supply a validly formatted address, is commented out.

The passwd-check option does not actually ensure that the supplied email address is valid. It simply checks the format; so at best this is a weak method of enforcement that depends on the user's honesty.

```
passwd-check      rfc822  warn
# passwd-check    rfc822  enforce
```

chmod, delete, overwrite, rename, and umask granularly disallow these specific FTP operations to specific types of users. In this case, they are used to further restrict the access that anonymous users have to FTP resources. For more information on allowing anonymous uploads, see the discussion on upload, coming up next.

```
chmod         no    anonymous
delete        no    anonymous
overwrite     no    anonymous
rename        no    anonymous
umask         no    anonymous
```

upload specifies a directory that permits people to upload files to the FTP server. In these simple examples, it takes the form of:

```
upload ftproot directory yes|no user group permissions dirs|nodirs
```

These options are detailed in Table 17-5.

Table 17-5. FTP's upload options.

Option	Value	Description
upload	upload	Identifies the upload directive
ftproot	/Library/Logs// FTPServer/FTPRoot	The root of the FTP server
directory	/uploads	Directory within the FTP root to which this directive should apply
yes|no	yes	Label, determining whether this tool is a positive or negative
user	ftp	User who will own uploaded files
group	Daemon	Group with which newly created files will be associated
permissions	0666	Permissions assigned to uploaded files and directories within the specified portion of the FTP root
dirs|nodirs	nodirs	Determines whether FTP clients are allowed to create new directories in the portion of the filesystem indicated in the directive

More complex options are available. Note the *ftpaccess* manpage for details.

```
upload  /Library/FTPServer/FTPRoot /uploads yes ftp daemon 0666 nodirs
upload  /Library/FTPServer/FTPRoot /uploads/mkdirs yes ftp daemon 0666 dirs 0777
```

The compress and tar options enable conversion capabilities for the given class of user (in this case, all, meaning all classes). The actual implementation of those features is left up to the definitions in the *ftpconversions* file, covered in more depth later in this chapter.

```
compress        yes         all
tar             yes         all
```

Three separate log statements occur in this file, corresponding to the four types of logging specified in the Logging tab of Server Admin's FTP Settings section. (transfers includes both uploads and downloads; referred to as inbound and outbound in the log parameter—although both can be specified separately.) The real and anonymous options mean that both authenticated and guest connections will be logged.

```
log transfers anonymous,real inbound,outbound
log     security        real,anonymous
log     commands        real,anonymous
```

 As mentioned earlier, transfers (uploads and downloads) are logged to */Library/Logs/FTP.transfer.log*, whereas security and commands are sent to *syslog*.

shutdown specifies the path to file that is checked regularly to determine whether any FTP shutdowns are scheduled. If one is, the user is notified, and new logins are optionally denied after a specified period before the scheduled downtime.

```
shutdown        /Library/FTPServer/Messages/shutdown.txt
```

The email parameter is set by the FTP administrator email address option in the General tab of Server Admin's FTP Settings section, and is discussed earlier:

```
email user@hostname
```

krb5_principal is an Apple-specific directive specifying the name of the service ticket required for Kerberos authentication. This setting must match a service principal available in the KDC. *wu-ftpd*'s built-in Kerberos integration is not very robust, so in this case it was extended by Apple. For more data relating to Kerberos and Mac OS X Server's FTP Services, see "Using Kerberos," later in this chapter.

```
krb5_principal  ftp/g5.pantherserver.org@G5.pantherserver.org
```

An alternate root for anonymous (guest) users can be specified using the anonymous-root parameter. In a default install, this setting is the same directory as defroot:

```
anonymous-root  /Library/FTPServer/FTPRoot
```

anonFTP is an Apple-specific flag allowing anonymous access to the server. Its value corresponds in part to the "Enable anonymous access option" in FTP's General Settings pane (discussed earlier), although enabling that checkbox might also influence other *ftpaccess* settings:

```
anonFTP yes
```

influence_listings controls whether files with resource forks are displayed with a *.bin* extension. This setting is discussed in more depth as a part of the "Enable

MacBinary and disk image auto-conversion" option in FTP's General Settings pane, earlier in this chapter:

```
influence_listings     no
```

auth_level is controlled by the Authentication option in FTP's General Settings pane, and is discussed earlier in this chapter:

```
auth_level      both
```

ftpconversions

The *ftpconversions* file governs the behavior of *xftpd*'s file-conversion capability, which is discussed briefly earlier in the chapter. In general terms, each file extension (suffix) a line describing what should be done when it is requested. Each line consists of colon-delimited fields and takes the following form:

```
strip prefix: strip postfix: addon prefix: addon postfix: external command: types:
options: description
```

Those fields are documented in Table 17-6. Specific conversions may be disabled by commenting out their entry in the *ftpconversions* file.

Table 17-6. The ftpconversions file determines how particular types of files should be handled. These examples specify the handling of a Mac OS X application (.app), which is really a special directory.

Field	Description	Example
Strip prefix	Not currently supported.	Not currently supported
Strip postfix (suffix)	Original, preconversion file extension.	*.app*
Addon prefix	Not currently supported.	Not currently supported
Addon postfix (suffix)	New file extension.	*.dmg*
External command	The command that is executed to run the conversion. Accepts a variable—%s—that specifies an input file.	*/usr/bin/mkdmg - -s %s*
Types	Specifies whether this conversion is allowed for files, directories, or both. T_REG specifies files, while T_DIR specifies directories.	T_REG|T_DIR
Options	Typically unused.	
Description	Text string identifying the file that is produced by this conversion.	DISKIMAGE

Example 17-11 shows the *ftpconversions* file. Notice that the ability to create disk imaged is disabled. To make ensure that this change is preserved through graphical configuration changes, both *ftpfileconversions* and *ftpfileconversions.default* should be edited.

Example 17-11. The ftpconversions file.

```
#:.mpkg: :.dmg:/usr/bin/mkdmg - -s %s:T_REG|T_DIR::DISKIMAGE
# :.pkg: :.dmg:/usr/bin/mkdmg - -s %s:T_REG|T_DIR::DISKIMAGE
# :.rtfd: :.dmg:/usr/bin/mkdmg - -s %s:T_REG|T_DIR::DISKIMAGE
```

Example 17-11. The ftpconversions file. (continued)

```
# :.app: :.dmg:/usr/bin/mkdmg - -s %s:T_REG|T_DIR::DISKIMAGE
# :   :  :.dmg:/usr/bin/mkdmg - -s %s:T_REG|T_DIR::DISKIMAGE
  :    :  :.bin:/usr/bin/macbin -e %s:T_REG::MACBINARY
:.Z:  :   :/usr/bin/compress -d -c %s:T_REG|T_ASCII::UNCOMPRESS
  :    :  :.Z:/usr/bin/compress -c %s:T_REG::COMPRESS
:.gz:  :   :/usr/bin/gzip -cd %s:T_REG|T_ASCII::GUNZIP
  :    :  :.gz:/usr/bin/gzip -9 -c %s:T_REG::GZIP
  :    :  :.tar:/usr/bin/tar -cf - -- %s:T_REG|T_DIR::TAR
  :    :  :.tZ:/usr/bin/tar -cf - -- %s | compress -c :T_REG|T_DIR::TAR+COMPRESS
  :    :  :.tar.Z:/usr/bin/tar -cf - -- %s | compress -c :T_REG|T_DIR::TAR+COMPRESS
  :    :  :.tgz:/usr/bin/tar -cf - -- %s | /usr/bin/gzip -c :T_REG|T_DIR::TAR+GZIP
  :    :  :.tar.gz:/usr/bin/tar -cf - -- %s | /usr/bin/gzip -c:T_REG|T_DIR::TAR+GZIP
  :    :  :.crc:/usr/bin/cksum %s:T_REG::CKSUM
```

ftphosts, ftpgroups, and ftpusers

ftphosts, *ftpgroups*, and *ftpusers* control which hosts, groups and users are allowed to access the FTP server. In most cases, these capabilities are redundant, as this access can also be controlled using *xinetd*, as described earlier. *ftpusers* and *ftpgroups* are simple enough that they really don't need illustration; users and groups referenced in them (one per line) are not allowed access via FTP. *ftphosts* is only slightly more complex. It consists of three fields, the last of which is optional: allow/deny, username, and one or more host address specifications. Example 17-12 shows a default *ftphosts* file as installed with Mac OS X Server, with one additional entry, denying anonymous login to the 10.*x* class A network.

Example 17-12. The format of the ftphosts file is fairly straightforward.

```
# Example host access file
#
# Everything after a '#' is treated as comment,
# empty lines are ignored

   allow   bartm    somehost.domain
   deny    fred     otherhost.domain 131.211.32.*
# the following  an example not provided in the default file:
deny        anonymous    10.0.0.0/8
```

Securing FTP

For reasons that are difficult to pin down, while the developers of other basically insecure TCP/IP-based protocols (such as IMAP, POP, and SMTP) were busy extending their standards in order to support secure authentication mechanisms, FTP remained basically unchanged for several years. The result is a widely supported and easy-to-use protocol that is, in the vast majority of circumstances, deployed insecurely. This section explores some options for securing FTP.

Using Kerberos

Built in to Mac OS X Server is the ability to support Kerberos authentication and transport encryption for FTP services.

 FTP is the only service in Panther Server that reuses the session key to encrypt the data stream (in addition to protecting the authentication process).

If it is a member server in an Open Directory domain (this requires configuration above and beyond joining the Domain using Directory Access; see Chapter 9 for details), or if a third-party KDC (Active Directory and MIT have been tested) is available, Kerberos may be used, both to ensure that the user's name and password are never sent over the wire and to protect the data sent between the client and server. General requirements for Kerberized FTP access include:

- A valid *edu.mit.Kerberos* or *krb5.conf* file must exist on the server. For a more in-depth discussion of Kerberos, see Chapter 9.
- The server must have a *keytab* containing at least host and ftp service principals.
- The ftp principal must be manually specified in the krb5_principal directive of the */Library/FTPServer/Configuration/ftpaccess* file. This setting, unlike that of the AFP server, is not available to the *serveradmin* command.

This feature is configured automatically when an Open Directory Master is created or when member servers are joined to the domain, but must be manually set up if the server is participating in a non–Mac OS X Server Kerberos realm. Integration with Active Directory is specifically covered in Chapter 27.

 A real downside to this approach is the relatively small list of Kerberized FTP clients. Mac OS 9 and Mac OS X clients may use Fetch (*www.fetchsoftworks.com*). Windows clients may use (among a few others) Filezilla (*http://filezilla.sourceforge.net*).

FTP Tunneled over SSH

Alternatively, FTP may be tunneled over SSH. Since SSH is encrypted over the wire, it protects the otherwise-vulnerable unencrypted data. This capability—the tunneling of other TCP-based protocols—is built into SSH, and the SSH client and server know how to forward packets to the appropriate destination. The most common type of SSH tunnel is called "local," as illustrated in Figure 17-10.

Despite its relative complexity, configuring an SSH tunnel isn't difficult, and is very similar to other SSH commands, as shown in Example 17-13. The options used in Example 17-13 are discussed in Table 17-7.

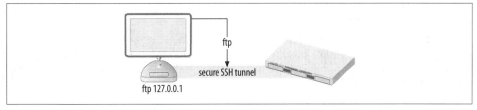

Figure 17-10. Insecure protocols like FTP may sometimes be tunneled over SSH.

Example 17-13. Because FTP uses at least two ports, both must be forwarded. In this case, the tunnel is dropped in 90 seconds if it is not used.

```
tigre:~ 4am$ sudo ssh -L 20:odm.pantherserver.org:20 -f mb@odm.pantherserver.org sleep 90
mb@odm.pantherserver.org's password:
tigre:~ 4am$ sudo ssh -L 21:odm.pantherserver.org:21 -f mb@odm.pantherserver.org sleep 90
mb@odm.pantherserver.org's password:
tigre:~ 4am
```

Table 17-7. Options used to tunnel FTP traffic over SSH.

Option	Description
-L 20:odm.pantherserver.org:20	Use local to remote tunneling (–L). Specifically, forward port 20 on 127.0.0.1 to port 20 on *server.example.com*.
-f	Put the tunnel in the background.
mb@odm.pantherserver.org	Use the credentials of the user *mb*.
sleep 90	Execute the sleep command on the server. This option holds the tunnel open for 90 seconds. Any FTP connections will subsequently keep the tunnel open until they are manually terminated, either by logging out or due to the server's timeout.

A final option is to create a persistent tunnel. Rather than using the sleep 90 command on the foreign host, the –N flag is used to specify that no command should be executed. This creates a persistent background tunnel that must be manually killed on logout (using the *killall ssh* command is a good choice).

```
tigre:~ 4am$ sudo ssh -L 20:odm.pantherserver.org:20 -f -N mb@odm.pantherserver.org
mb@odm.pantherserver.org's password:
tigre:~ 4am$ sudo ssh -L 21:odm.pantherserver.org:21 -f -N mb@odm.pantherserver.org
```

Keep in mind that in all of these cases, this type of tunnel forwards local traffic—on the client's loopback interface—to some foreign destination. In order to use the tunnel, the local client software needs to connect to 127.0.0.1. This is the whole point of a local tunnel; local traffic is forwarded to the remote server, as shown in Example 17-14.

Example 17-14. The system's loopback interface is used to establish a connection tunneled over SSH. sshd, in turn, forwards that connection to the target host.

```
tigre:~ 4am$ sudo lsof -i | grep ftp
ssh      2172 root    7u  IPv6 0x02ab4e80      0t0    TCP localhost:ftp-data (LISTEN)
ssh      2174 root    7u  IPv6 0x02ab4b20      0t0    TCP localhost:ftp (LISTEN)
tigre:~ 4am$ ftp localhost
Trying ::1...
Connected to localhost.
220--------------------------------------------------------------------------------
220                     unauthorized access prohibited
220 odm.pantherserver.org FTP server (Version:  Mac OS X Server 10.3.2 - +GSSAPI) ready.
Name (localhost:mb): mb
331 Password required for mb.
Password:
230--------------------------------------------------------------------------------
                        Welcome !
230--------------------------------------------------------------------------------
230-
230 User mb logged in.
Remote system type is UNIX.
Using binary mode to transfer files.
ftp>
```

A downside to this approach is that users must have SSH access to the server in question. SSH access in itself is difficult to limit, and effectively gives much more access to the server than FTP alone would.

 Some FTP servers validate incoming connections, ensuring that the source address in the FTP request matches the actual client address. In the case of an SSH tunnel, this step means the connection will be denied. The server thinks the client is local (since it is coming from the *sshd* process), but the packets themselves, originally created on the remote client, claim the client's IP address. This mismatch could, under other circumstances, mean that the connection is spoofed, so it is denied. This kind of checking must be disabled for SSH-tunneled FTP to work.

Secure FTP (sftp)

sftp, which is not actually related to FTP at all, but is instead part of the SSH protocol, is a final option. Because it leverages SSH encryption and authentication, it is secure over the wire, and because it is built to emulate FTP, it is relatively user-friendly. Its biggest limitations stem from the fact that it is not compatible with any pure FTP clients—although some graphical FTP clients do support *sftp*—and that it is not generally feasible to *chroot()* it (limit client's view of the filesystem to certain directories). *sftp* is enabled in a default install of Mac OS X, according to the Subsystem sftp /usr/libexec/sftp-server directive in */etc/sshd_config*.

Be aware, however, that there is no really easy way to limit clients from access to the majority of the server's filesystem. SSH-based protocols were not designed to be *chroot*'d, and this is one square peg that will not easily fit into its round hole.

 Search Google for chroot + shh for more details and information.

CHAPTER 18

Network File System

With roots deep in Mac OS X's Unix predecessors and cousins, the Network File System (NFS) is widely used and understood in the Unix world, and a virtual requirement for integration with Unix environments. Additionally, though, some Mac OS X Server services (such as NetBoot) also rely on it, and it fits well in some file sharing roles for which AFP and SMB are not appropriate. Regardless of whether or not you support Unix clients, NFS is worth understanding. This chapter examines NFS services in Mac OS X Server. They don't differ much from an administrative perspective from similar services offered on other Unix platforms—other than an occasional tendency to be quirky.

 It is worth admitting at the beginning that NFS in Mac OS X Server could use some tweaking. Despite that, it is mostly functional and has come a very long way from Jaguar server's implementation (and Cheetah's before that). Although Mac OS X Server would not currently make much sense as a single-purpose large scale NFS server, nothing should dissuade you from taking advantage of its NFS server in addition to any other services you might be deploying.

The NFS (In)security Model

There's no getting around it—NFS is old. Like SMTP and so many other protocols, it was designed at a time when the network was a much more trusted entity, when only trusted parties had administrative access to hosts on the network, and when the population of the Internet was much, much lower than it is today. Like a gullible neighbor with no tools left in his garage, NFS is just too trusting. Its problems begin with the fact that most NFS implementations, rather than supporting user-based authorization, simply maintain lists of hosts permitted to mount particular shares. Since IP addresses are relatively easy to spoof, this does not amount to a reliable security architecture.

NFS shares are commonly known as *exports*. The terms are used here interchangeably to more closely identify with Mac OS X Server's management tools and terminology.

This issue is exacerbated by the NFS server's assumption that the server and its clients share a user and group database. A user with the UniqueID 501 on the server is assumed to have the same file access rights as the user with UniqueID 501 on the client. The server trusts the client to actually authenticate that user. This model is described in Figure 18-1.

 Some NFS implementations have been extended to support security features that either have not been entirely standardized or are just not supported in Mac OS X and Mac OS X Server.

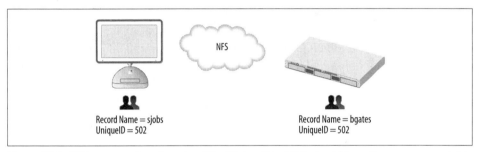

Figure 18-1. NFS assumes that the user with a UniqueID of 502 should have the same access rights as the user with a UniqueID of 502 on the client, even though in reality they are not the same user.

Ten years ago, when only system administrators could create users and when */etc/ passwd* files were regularly maintained in parallel (so that user RecordNames and UniqueID's were always consistent among hosts), this might have been an acceptable, if slightly short-sighted, security model. Today it is virtually unworkable.

One principal downside of this behavior is a UniqueID mismatch (see Figure 18-2). Legitimate users, because their UniqueIDs differ on the client and the server, may be denied access, whereas illegitimate users may have access to files that they should not have, because their UniqueID happens to match that of another user on the server. What is worse is that anyone with administrative access to such a client might specifically create a user to match UniqueIDs with a server user, maliciously exploiting this behavior. Despite these shortcomings, NFS is a viable and common protocol when it is secured properly.

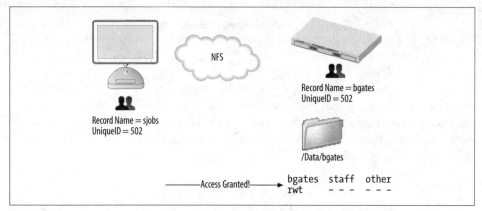

Figure 18-2. UniqueID mismatches are a common pitfall in NFS deployment.

Managing NFS with Server Admin

The NFS options available in Server Admin, unlike options for other protocols, are rather minimal. This is probably because few NFS settings are global in nature, and most are manipulated on the share level, in Workgroup Manager. In fact, there's not even an NFS start or stop option. Instead, NFS is started whenever it is enabled for any share point. The Overview tab, which illustrates the state of various NFS-related daemons, is indicated in Figure 18-3.

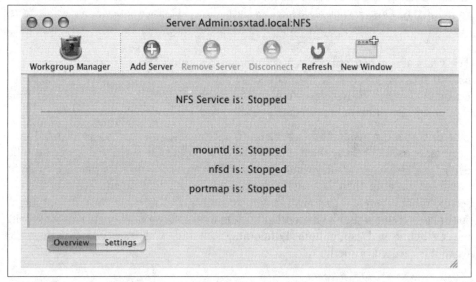

Figure 18-3. The Overview section of Server Admin's NFS management interface reveals the state of several NFS-related daemons.

As is the case with most Server Admin services, the data from the Overview pane can also be obtained from the *serveradmin* command-line utility, as shown in Example 18-1.

Example 18-1. Using serveradmin to obtain state data about Mac OS X Server NFS services.

```
[ace2:~] nadmin% sudo serveradmin fullstatus nfs
nfs:command = "getState"
nfs:mountd = "STOPPED"
nfs:nsfd = "STOPPED"
nfs:rpc.statd = "STOPPED"
nfs:state = "STOPPED"
nfs:readWriteSettingsVersion = 1
nfs:portmap = "STOPPED"
nfs:rpc.lockd = "RUNNING"
```

Settings (the only other choice in Server Admin's NFS interface, illustrated in Figure 18-4) exposes only one pane, called General. Its options (see Table 18-1) are rather limited—the number of daemons and their supported protocols are configurable.

 In fact, the number of daemons is limited to a value between 4 and 20. Since each daemon can service multiple clients, this value does not imply a specific limitation on the number of NFS connections.

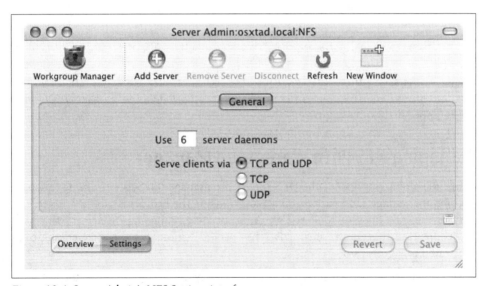

Figure 18-4. Server Admin's NFS Settings interface.

Choosing the TCP and UDP option is commonly the most compatible protocol choice. Clients that support only UDP will request it, and offering TCP access (which is more reliable, but often slower) will not prevent that.

Table 18-1. Default options passed to the NFS Server in Mac OS X.

Option	Description
-t	Serve TCP NFS clients.
-u	Serve UDP NFS clients.
-n 6	Start six NFS servers. Servers are multithreaded, so this option does not limit the server to six clients.

These options are written to NetInfo, in the */config/nfsd* directory; see Example 18-2.

Example 18-2. Using dscl to examine NFS settings. nicl or niutil could also be used, both directly examining the NetInfo database.

```
g5:~ nadmin$ dscl . -read /config/nfsd
arguments: -t -u -n 6
AppleMetaNodeLocation: /NetInfo/DefaultLocalNode
RecordName: nfsd
```

They can also be viewed by using the *serveradmin* utility. Some command output, which searches other directory nodes for configuration, has been removed from this output:

```
g5:~ nadmin$ sudo serveradmin command nfs:command=readSettings
nfs:command = "readSettings"
nfs:readStatus = 0
nfs:configuration:useTCP = yes
nfs:configuration:useUDP = yes
nfs:configuration:nbDaemons = 6
nfs:dsConfiguration:localNodePath = "/NetInfo/DefaultLocalNode"
...
```

These options, in turn, are read by the NFS Startup Item (*/System/Library/ StartupItems/NFS*), which, if no options are present, defaults to the *–t –u –n 6* options specified in this example.

Managing NFS with Workgroup Manager

While the global options for the NFS service are managed in Server Admin, per-share options are managed in Workgroup Manager, using the Protocols tab mentioned earlier (in the introduction to Part IV). Appropriately, choosing NFS from the pull-down menu in that interface reveals NFS-specific options for the selected share, as illustrated in Figure 18-5.

NFS is the only service for which access to a newly created share is disabled. This is for security reasons; as mentioned earlier, its shares are exported to a specific list of hosts rather than to a specific list of users or groups.

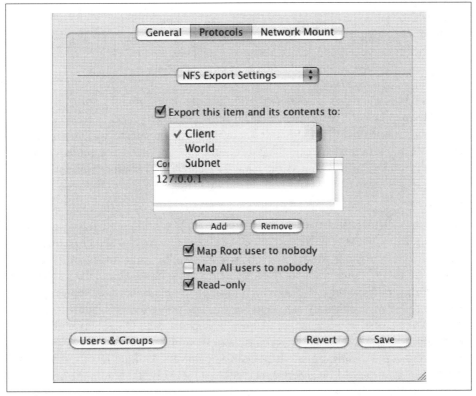

Figure 18-5. Workgoup Manager's per-share options control NFS access and security features on a per-share basis.

Since this security model is relatively weak, it makes sense to ensure that administrators specifically enable it.

These access controls are defined in Workgroup Manager's options. Be aware, however, that IP addresses are easy to spoof, and that access to NFS protocols should be limited at the network level as well, so that requests come only from physical networks known to be trusted.

Access to any share may be limited to a specific list of hosts, to a particular subnet, or to the world. Subnet access is specified using the network address (the subnet's address with all the host bits set to 0; for instance, 192.168.1.0 for that Class C subnet) and subnet mask. Granting world access allows unlimited, unauthenticated access to the share in question, and should be used only with extreme caution, preferably in conjunction with one or more of the available security options.

As of Mac OS X Server 10.3.4, attempting to specify world access to multiple NFS shares on the same partition (although permitted in the graphical interface) results in errors. Only one NFS share per partition may have world access. This is a limitation of the Mac OS X NFS service, not of the user interface or of NFS in general.

Workgroup Manager also exposes two NFS security management options relating to UniqueID mapping. As mentioned earlier, an NFS Server generally trusts clients to inform it of the UniqueID of the user accessing a file or directory. The server then assumes that the user in question has the same UniqueID on the server, and that access to the file can be granted or denied based on this shared user list and the underlying filesystem permissions.

This isn't a good assumption. Every user initially created on a Mac OS X client, for example, has a UniqueID of 501. It is unlikely that most of the millions of users with the UniqueID of 501 should be authorized to access a particular server resource. Yet under NFS's permissions model, they all would be. This behavior is an issue especially if the client claims that the user accessing a file has a UniqueID of 0, which always corresponds to *root*. It is a tremendously bad idea to trust a client, especially one (due to NFS's lax authorization model) validated only by its IP address, to grant or deny root access on your server. Along these lines, Mac OS X Server (like most other NFS servers) allows for server-side suppression of requests for root access. When a process running on a client claims to have a UniqueID of 0, the server squashes (that is the technical term!) this request, and instead grants the access that would be given to the user *nobody* (UniqueID –2). Root access is effectively mapped to that of *nobody*. This is enabled on a per-share basis by the "Map Root user to *nobody*" checkbox.

A more complete solution (but one invalidating multiple user access to the share) involves mapping all requests to the user *nobody*. Every user, no matter what their UniqueID is, always has the access granted to the user *nobody*. This access is enabled on a per-share basis by the "Map All users to *nobody*" checkbox.

The downside of both of these security measures is that is that certain processes cannot access the resource in question. In the case of squashing root access, this applies to almost all server services, which generally run as *root*. An alternative, exposed by the Read-only checkbox, enforces read-only access to the share, regardless of the underlying filesystem permissions. Exposure to malicious access is reduced since the filesystem cannot be written to, but permissions may still be used to enforce different access controls for different users and groups.

All of the per-share NFS options in Workgroup Manager are saved to the server's local NetInfo domain. Unlike AFP, SMB, and FTP services, however, they are not buffered into protocol-specific options in the share's entry in *netinfo://config/SharePoints*. Instead they are written directly to *netinfo://exports*, which is read both by the NFS Startup Item (in order to determine whether or not NFS Services should be started) and by the *mountd* and *nfsd* process, which are covered in more depth later in this chapter.

```
g5:~ nadmin$ dscl . -read /exports/\\/sw
AppleMetaNodeLocation: /NetInfo/DefaultLocalNode
RecordName: /sw
VFSOpts: ro mapall=nobody network=192.168.1.0 mask=255.255.255.0
g5:~ nadmin$ nicl . -read /exports/\\/sw
name: /sw
opts: ro mapall=nobody network=192.168.1.0 mask=255.255.255.0
```

Each option in Workgroup Manager corresponds to a different NetInfo attribute. These attributes, along with their abstracted Open Directory names, appear in Table 18-2.

Table 18-2. *Analysis of NFS share points and their directory attributes. For more information on Open Directory's abstraction and naming, see the introduction to Part II and the Appendix.*

NetInfo attribute name	Open Directory attribute name	Description
name	RecordName	Name of the share
opts	VFSOpts	Space-delineated strings describing share options
clients	clients	List of individual clients authorized to access share

The VFSOpts attribute (or opts, as seen directly in NetInfo) consists of a number of space-delimited strings (listed in Table 18-3), each corresponding to one of the options available in Workgroup Manager.

Table 18-3. *Strings in the opts attribute of NFS share points, along with their Workgoup Manager equivalencies*

Workgroup Manager option	VFSOpt/opt string	Description
Read-only	ro	Forces the filesystem to be mounted read-only, regardless of the underlying permissions.
Map Root user to nobody	maproot	Map root-level access to some other user. Workgroup manager allows mapping only to the user *nobody*.
Map All users to nobody	mapall	Map all access to some other user. Workgroup manager allows mapping only to the user *nobody*.
Export this item and its contents to: Subnet	network, *or* mask	Used together to allow access for some subnet.

Keep in mind that the final access list is determined by a combination of the clients attribute of the share point and the network and mask strings in its opts attribute. World access is assumed if the clients list is nonexistent or empty and no network or mask setting exists in opts. Mac OS X's NFS service is incapable of allowing a combination of subnet and specific client access to be granted simultaneously. If such a configuration exists, the share won't be available via NFS.

This combination of access rights—granted both using the share's clients attribute and network and mask values in its VFSOpts attribute, is not allowed by the NFS

Service as of 10.3.4 (even though there are very valid reason to use such a configuration), as shown here:

```
[ace2:~] nadmin% nicl . -read /exports/\\/Volumes\\/Data\\/lantest
name: /Volumes/Data/lantest
opts: ro mapall=nobody network=192.168.1.0 mask=255.255.255.0
clients: 207.224.49.181
```

Similarly, several other options are recognized by *nfsd*, even though they aren't accessible in the Workgroup Manager's user interface. These options may be set by using command-line tools like *dscl* and *nicl* or by a third-party graphical tool like NFS Manager (*www.bresink.de/osx/NFSManager.html*), and will be respected by the NFS Server. Subsequent share management using Workgroup Manager, however, will rewrite the entire share entry and lose this custom configuration, so in practice it is probably best to store shares that are configured outside the scope of Workgroup Manager in the */etc/exports* file, discussed later in this chapter.

NFS File Locking

Before Panther was available, integrating Panther with some NFS clients was problematic, due to the lack of file locking support in Apple's NFS implementation. Specific applications written with file locking in mind would fail to launch when running environmental sanity checks. NFS file locking is now enabled in a default configuration of Mac OS X Server if the NFS Startup Item locates any exports, either in NetInfo or in */etc/exports* (discussed next). If for some reason NFS locks need to be disabled, the best way is to manually comment out the NFSLOCKS portions of the NFS Startup Item. This technique was helpful in early versions of Panther, which sometimes displayed incompatibilities with NFS clients from other OSes. These issues seem to have been fixed in 10.3.4.

/etc/exports

Unix hosts have traditionally stored NFS sharing configuration data in the */etc/exports* file. Mac OS X's NeXT and OPENSTEP predecessors moved away from that tendency and towards NetInfo and the centralized, object-oriented administration it provided—and in fact most NFS Shares are still configured there. For compatibility, though, Apple preserved the ability to read NFS Shares from */etc/exports*. This is part of an overall trend to preserve standard Unix administration practices, but more than that, provides a method for setting up sharing options that are not available in Workgroup Manager's graphical interface and will not be discarded when other options are changed. (NetInfo-based NFS shares are rewritten when their configuration is changed graphically and customizations made manually are not preserved.)

As of 10.3.4, it appears that administrators must choose to either store exports in NetInfo, where they can be managed using Workgroup Manager, or store them in /etc/exports, where they can be managed manually. If the /etc/exports file even exists, all mounts in NetInfo are ignored by the NFS Service.

/etc/exports follows a simple format, illustrated using Example 18-3. In this case, the two shares managed earlier have been migrated to /etc/exports, where some custom options have been added.

Example 18-3. An /etc/exports file, mapping all permissions for the /sw share to the user monty, rather than nobody.

```
/sw  -ro -mapall=monty 127.0.0.1 192.168.1.1 10.1.0.1
/Users  -ro -mapall=nobody -network=192.168.1.2 -mask=255.255.255.0
```

Template /etc/exports entries can be dumped into flat file format using the *nidump* command (see Example 18-4). Be sure to remove the original share to avoid duplicate entries.

Example 18-4. Using nidump to migrate NFS Shares to /etc/exports. The orginal shares are then deleted from the NetInfo database.

```
g5:~ nadmin$ sudo su root -c "nidump exports . > /etc/exports"
g5:~ nadmin$ sudo nicl . -destroy /exports/\\/sw
g5:~ nadmin$ sudo nicl . -destroy /exports/\\/Users.
```

When adding NFS Shares manually, it should be feasible to run the *SystemStarter* command to announce the new resource that is available. However, *sudo SystemStarter restart NFS* does not appear to do the trick. Instead, the *mountd* daemon should be sent a HUP signal, as follows:

```
sudo killall -HUP mountd
```

Servers

In keeping with the standard Unix philosophy of using lots of small, specialized processes that work well together, NFS services in Mac OS X are actually provided by several different daemons, including *mountd*, *nfsd*, *rpc.lockd*, and *rpc.statd*.

mountd services mount attempts from NFS clients, allowing or denying connection attempts based on the source IP of the request. Using the /usr/sbin/slp_reg utility, *mountd* also advertises share points over SLP—a service location protocol that predates Rendezvous. This is a function specific to Apple's NFS Service. It writes also its process ID to /var/run/mountd.pid, but otherwise tells us very little about its state or what it is doing. In particular, it does not log reasons for mount denials. It does, however, have an undocumented debug mode that is useful for analysis of its startup. This mode is invoked with the –d flag, as shown in Example 18-5.

Example 18-5. mountd's startup process is well documented in its debug mode.

```
g5:~ nadmin$ sudo killall mountd
g5:~ nadmin$ sudo mountd -d
Debug Enabled.
Getting export list.
get_exportlist: freeing old exports...
get_exportlist: freeing old groups...
record_hostname: hostnamearray[0] = 'g5.pantherserver.org'.
record_hostname: hostnamearray[1] = '192.168.1.15'.
unregistering URL nfs://g5.pantherserver.org/
/usr/sbin/slp_reg exit status 0
unregistering URL service:x-file-service:nfs://g5.pantherserver.org/
/usr/sbin/slp_reg exit status 0
unregistering URL nfs://192.168.1.15/
/usr/sbin/slp_reg exit status 0
unregistering URL service:x-file-service:nfs://192.168.1.15/
/usr/sbin/slp_reg exit status 0
Getting mount list.
Here we go.
```

nfsd is the actual NFS Server. Once *mountd* allows a mount request, *nfsd* actually services file access. *nfsd* does not appear to have any debugging options, as of 10.3.4.

rpc.lockd and *rpc.statd* work together to provide NFS file locking. They are started before *mountd* and *nfsd* as a part of the NFS Startup Item. *rpc.lockd* is the actual file-locking daemon, and as such keeps track of which files are held locked by which hosts. *rpc.statd* keeps track of those hosts, so that if they're no longer on the network, their locks may be purged. It assumes after 24 hours that a monitored host that has disappeared is gone permanently. Both have much more robust logging capabilities than either *nfsd* or *mountd*; however, because each must be started at boot time, the best way to access them is to add the –d flag to both in the NFS Startup Item itself.

Utilities and Troubleshooting

One of the biggest limitations of Mac OS X's NFS server is that *mountd* doesn't log very well. Because of this, determining why access to an NFS resource has been denied can be more difficult than it should be.

NFS is based on the Sun RPC protocol, and as such can be monitored to some extent with the *rpcinfo* command. RPC can be though of as a sort of service discovery mechanism, alerting clients to the ports on which particular RPC-enabled services are running. Unless both *nfsd* and *mountd* are listed, connections to the server will not work. *rpc.statd* and *rpc.lockd* also make themselves available via RPC, and file locking support requires their presence. *rpcinfo*'s –*p* flag probes a host in order to monitor its services, as shown in Example 18-6.

 RPC is often considered a security risk; don't be surprised if attempts to probe remote hosts result in a refused connection.

Example 18-6. Using rpcinfo's –p flag to probe for RPC-enabled services on g5.pantherserver.org. portmap is the process responsible for managing RPC port assignments.

```
[bw:~] mbartosh% rpcinfo -p g5.pantherserver.org
   program vers proto   port
    100000    2   tcp    111  portmapper
    100000    2   udp    111  portmapper
    100021    1   udp   1015  nlockmgr
    100021    3   udp   1015  nlockmgr
    100021    4   udp   1015  nlockmgr
    100021    1   tcp    982  nlockmgr
    100021    3   tcp    982  nlockmgr
    100021    4   tcp    982  nlockmgr
    100024    1   udp    999  status
    100024    1   tcp    981  status
    100005    1   udp    992  mountd
    100005    3   udp    992  mountd
    100005    1   tcp    742  mountd
    100005    3   tcp    742  mountd
    100003    2   udp   2049  nfs
    100003    3   udp   2049  nfs
    100003    2   tcp   2049  nfs
    100003    3   tcp   2049  nfs
```

The *showmount* command queries a particular NFS server and shows data about its status, including which shares are exported, and which hosts have mounted which share. Other options are documented in *showmount*'s manpage, but the –*e* option (shown in Example 18-7) can be very useful.

Example 18-7. showmount's –e and –a options. The former displays exported shares, and is useful in determining whether the server is configured properly. The latter shows which hosts are accessing which shares.

```
mab9718:~ mbartosh$ showmount -e g5.pantherserver.org
Exports list on g5.pantherserver.org:
/sw                       127.0.0.1 207.224.49.179 10.1.0.1
/Users                    192.168.1.2
mab9718:~ mbartosh$ showmount -a g5.pantherserver.org
All mount points on g5.pantherserver.org:
207.224.49.179:/sw
```

## CHAPTER 19

Print Services

It's hard to determine what to say about Mac OS X Server Print Services. They're there, after all—there's a module devoted to them in Server Admin, and they have a complete management interface, including a suite of options available using the *serveradmin* command. In my time working with Mac OS X Server, however, I have rarely seen them used. Which is unfortunate. Apple lost a lot of server-side market share to Windows NT 4 specifically because it (at the time) offered a rich set of print queue management capabilities.

So it would make sense for print services to be of a very high quality in Panther, because much of Panther's marketing goals seem to revolve around replacing NT servers (which are, when they still exist, at the far end of their life cycle). This has not been the case. With little real quota support and a very weak authentication model, Panther Server Print Services remain one of the least robust portions of what is otherwise a (mostly) dynamic and full-featured server platform. Nonetheless, they will be examined in great depth in this chapter, specifically with an eye towards the future, and the underlying architecture that Apple is moving towards.

Managing Print Services

Mac OS X Server Print Services are capable of controlling access to (sharing out) PostScript printers that are accessible via AppleTalk LPR or USB. Printer queues hosted on Mac OS X Server may then be accessed by clients using LPR, AppleTalk, or SMB protocols, as illustrated in Figure 19-1. Print Services management is achieved primarily using the Printing Module of Server Admin, although per-user print settings are typically managed in Workgroup Manager. This section analyzes both aspects of Print Services management and monitoring. Before print queues may be managed and shared, however, they must be created.

Why Use a Print Server?

It's important to understand precisely what print services really offer, and to establish realistic expectations about any infrastructure you build.

A good principle to keep in mind is that of control. Server software is typically a lot more flexible than a printer's firmware, and a server typically has a lot more CPU power to spare in order to add features to existing printing protocols. These differences provide a much greater level of control over the printing process than what is typically available from printers themselves.

- **Faster spooling:** Print jobs leave the client faster. Printers are linear in nature and in most cases can print only one page at a time. To be at all effective, network printers typically have some amount of system memory where incoming jobs can be stored until they can be printed. Servers typically have more system memory than printers, allowing more jobs to be spooled without waiting for a comparatively limited printer.

- **Redundancy:** Multiple printers can typically be added to a queue, meaning that a printer can fail (an all-too-common part of this most mechanical aspect of IT) while clients may keep printing.

- **Access control:** Because print server software is a part of Mac OS X Server, it can theoretically take advantage of Open Directory identification, authentication, and authorization services. Unfortunately, we'll see that this link is weak in Panther, but in general it is something you'd expect to see in a Print Server.

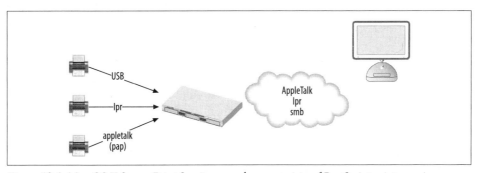

Figure 19-1. Mac OS X Server Print Services can share a variety of PostScript printers using AppleTalk, LPR, or SMB. Yes, an AppleTalk printer could simply be shared using AppleTalk.

Adding Printer Queues

Mac OS X Server Printing Services share out existing system print queues via LPR, SMB, and AppleTalk. To be shared out, the print queues must first exist. Towards this purpose, three practical methods are available. The most common is to use the Print Setup Utility (*/Applications/Utilities*), just as you would in order to add a printer for the server's local use. This is simple enough that it's not something worth spending a lot of time on. It is assumed that most readers will have installed a printer before. Less known, however, and worth noting here, is the method of creation of printer classes, pictured in Figure 19-2. Printer classes allow multiple printers to be added to a single queue, increasing the queue's reliability and throughput (as noted earlier in the chapter).

As noted earlier, only PostScript printers available via AppleTalk, LPR, or USB may be managed using Mac OS X Server Print Services. Confusingly, any other local printers also show up in Mac OS X Server's administrative interfaces. Despite their appearance, they may not be used as queues for Mac OS X Server. This anomaly is noted where appropriate throughout this chapter.

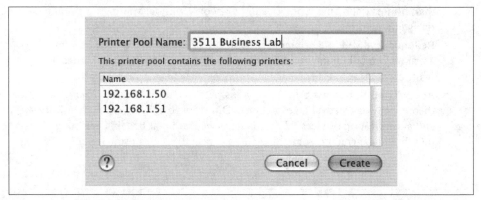

Figure 19-2. To create a printer class (cluster), select two or more existing printers and choose Pool Printers… from the Printer Setup Utility's Printers menu. Printers should be the same model.

It would not do, however, to force server administrators to log into the server locally in order to add printer queues for sharing. A minimal interface for queue creation is also available in Server Admin's printer settings, discussed later in this chapter. Pictured in Figure 19-3, it is much less capable than the Printer Setup Utility.

Finally, we have the *lpadmin* command-line utility. Covered in depth later, it is essentially an administrative interface to the Common Unix Printing System (CUPS), the underlying architecture Apple uses to actually print in Mac OS X and Mac OS X Server. In Example 19-1, CUPS is used to create a local printer that may later be shared out using Server Admin.

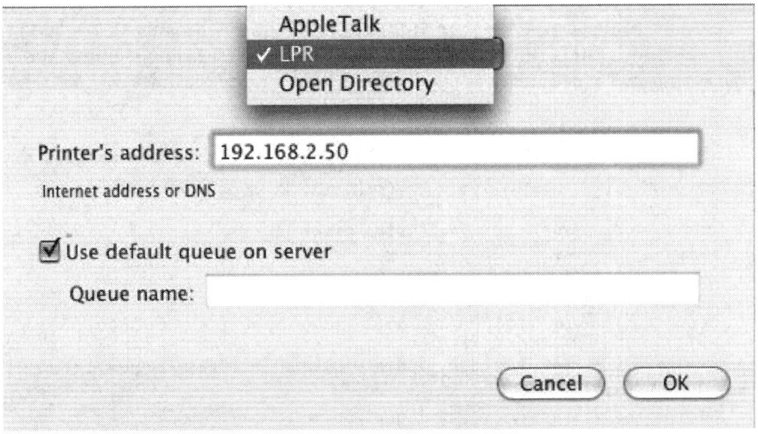

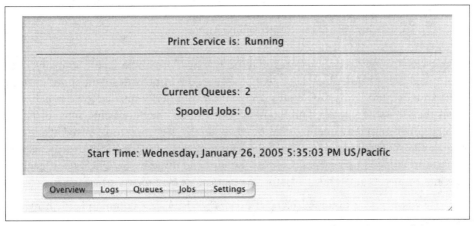

Figure 19-3. To add a printer queue remotely using Server Admin, select the + icon in the Queues tab of the Settings portion of the Print module.

Example 19-1. The lpadmin command can add local printer queues that may then be shared out using Server Admin. This printer uses HP's socket protocol.

```
sudo lpadmin -p laserjet6L -E -v socket://10.1.36.221:4010 -m laserjet
```

Server Admin and Printing

As with most other Mac OS X Server services, a number of options are available for Print Services monitoring and administration. This first, Overview (shown in Figure 19-4), is very similar to other Overview panes seen elsewhere in Server Admin.

Figure 19-4. An overview of Printing Services is available in Server Admin. The state of the service is available, as is its start time. Also seen is the number of print queues and the total number of queued jobs.

The print service may be stopped at any point in time using Server Admin's Stop button (not pictured) or the *serveradmin* command's *stop* and *start* directives.

A more complete picture of the Print Server's configuration and state can be obtained with the *serveradmin* command's *fullstatus* directive, as shown here:

```
xsg5:~ tadmin$ sudo serveradmin fullstatus print
print:command = "getState"
print:currentJobs = 4
print:currentQueues = 1
print:state = "RUNNING"
print:logPaths:logPathsArray:_array_index:0:path = "/Library/Logs/PrintService/
PrintService.server.log"
print:logPaths:logPathsArray:_array_index:0:name = "SYSTEMLOG"
print:logPaths:logPathsArray:_array_index:1:path = "/Library/Logs/PrintService/
PrintService.192.168.1.55.job.log"
print:logPaths:logPathsArray:_array_index:1:name = "192.168.1.55"
print:pluginVers = "1.0.38"
print:readWriteSettingsVersion = 1
print:setStateVersion = 1
print:startedTime = "2004-10-24 23:58:37 -0600"
```

Print Server logs—both global in nature and per-queue—can be seen in the Logs section of Server Admin's Print module (Figure 19-5). As with other Server Admin log-viewing interfaces, this view is subject to the HTTP-based request/response cycle of Server Admin and *servermgrd*, so it often makes more sense to view the logs directly. Global and per-queue logs are both stored in */Library/Logs/PrintService*.

 Not seen in Server Admin's interface are logs for CUPS, the underlying technology generally used to actually print files. CUPS's logs (in */var/logs/cups*) are discussed later in this chapter.

In Mac OS X Server, Print Services may be managed on three levels: globally, per-queue, and per-job. The Queues interface (Figure 19-6) provides data about current system queues, including their status, the current number of queued jobs, which protocols they are shared over, and what kind of printer they are being sent to. Additionally, once selected, queues may be individually stopped and started using the stop and start buttons in the lower right corner of the interface. Queues may also be started and stopped using the *serveradmin* command directive *SetQueState*. It is cumbersome enough that it's not particularly practical for day-to-day use.

Identical data can be obtained using the *PrintServiceAccess* command, as shown in Example 19-2.

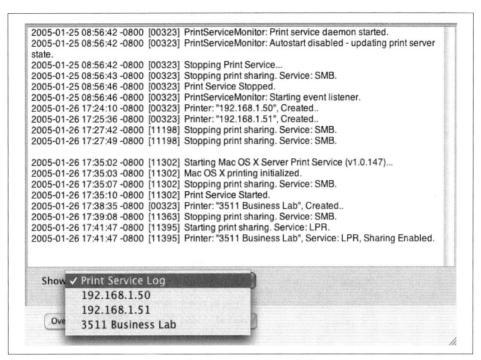

Figure 19-5. Server Admin's interface for viewing Print Services logs.

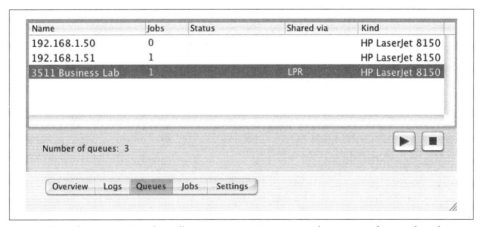

Figure 19-6. The Queues interface allows existing print queues to be monitored, started, and stopped. Note that every system print queue will be listed in this interface, even if it may not be shared out using Mac OS X Server.

Example 19-2. Using PrintServerAccess to obtain information on all system print queues. Individual queues may be specified, but in this case the dash argument (–) specifies all queues.

```
pantherserver:~ instruct$ PrintServiceAccess info -
                                          Shared       Cover
Name                    LPR Name          LPR SMB State Page
----------------------  ----------------  --- --- ------ -----
192.168.1.50            192.168.1.50      NO  NO  Active OFF
192.168.1.51            192.168.1.51      NO  NO  Active OFF
3511 Business Lab       3511 Business Lab YES NO  Active OFF
```

The Jobs portion of Server Admin's Printing module (Figure 19-7) allows individual jobs to be monitored and managed. Jobs may be paused, restarted, or deleted on an individual basis, allowing server administrators to restrict very large jobs that might be in the queue. Jobs for a particular queue are viewed together; the pictured pull-down menu permits queue-by-queue job monitoring.

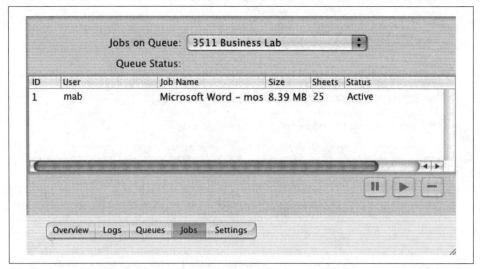

Figure 19-7. Individual jobs may be paused, resumed, or deleted using the three buttons pictured in the bottom right corner of the interface.

A list of running jobs may also be obtained using the serveradmin command's get-Jobs command directive, as shown in Example 19-3. This output is quite verbose on a busy server; this example consists of one currently spooled job. While it is also feasible to pause and delete jobs using serveradmin, the process is very cumbersome.

Example 19-3. Using the serveradmin command to list currently printing jobs.

```
pantherserver:~ instruct$ sudo serveradmin command print:command=getJobs
print:command = "getJobs"
print:queueNamesArray:_array_index:0 = "192.168.1.50"
print:queueNamesArray:_array_index:1 = "192.168.1.51"
print:queueNamesArray:_array_index:2 = "3511 Business Lab"
print:jobsArray:_array_index:0:jobCount = 0
```

Example 19-3. Using the serveradmin command to list currently printing jobs. (continued)

```
print:jobsArray:_array_index:0:jobQueueStatus = ""
print:jobsArray:_array_index:0:jobQueueName = "192.168.1.50"
```

Once again, though, the *PrintServerAccess* command offers a friendlier alternative (see Example 19-4). *PrintServerAccess* also allows jobs to be easily held or removed from the command line, but the behavior is often unpredictable.

Example 19-4. Using PrintServerAccess to monitor print jobs. A specific queue may be specified, but in this case the – argument displays jobs from all queues.

```
pantherserver:~ instruct$ PrintServiceAccess jobs -

Rank  Owner   Job      Files                                      Total Size
1st   mab     1        Microsoft Word - mosxserve_ch19_print.doc  8802304
bytes

Rank  Owner   Job      Files                                      Total Size
1st   mab     1        Microsoft Word - mosxserve_ch19_print.doc  8802304
bytes
```

Settings for Mac OS X Server Print Services can be manipulated in the Settings portion of Server Admin's Print module. Settings are divided among three panes: General, Logging, and Queues. The General pane, seen in Figure 19-8, simply contains a setting for the default LPR queue—the printer queue to which LPR jobs are sent if a specific queue is not requested. It is a good idea to set up a low-cost printer as default LPR queue (rather than the expensive new plotter with costly consumables).

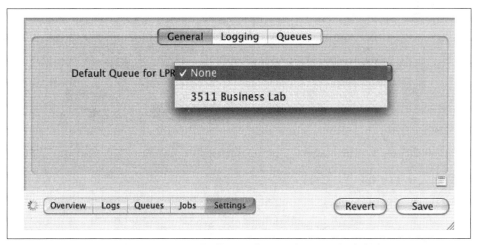

Figure 19-8. The General pane is minimal, allowing for specification of a default LPR queue.

The Logging tab of Server Admin's Print Settings (Figure 19-9) is similarly minimal, specifying separate archival intervals for the server and per-queue (jobs) logs. As mentioned earlier, these settings apply to the logs located in */Library/Logs/ PrintService*.

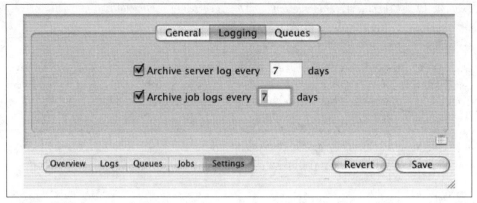

Figure 19-9. The jobs interval applies to all queues on the server in question. Individual archival intervals may not be specified for busier queues.

The Queues portion of Server Admin's Print Settings (see Figure 19-10) is the heart of queue management in Mac OS X Server. Its initial view is straightforward; it simply lists existing system queues.

All system queues are listed here, even those that may not be shared out with Mac OS X Server.

Double-clicking on a queue reveals a much more full-featured analysis of that queue's capabilities, seen in Figure 19-11.

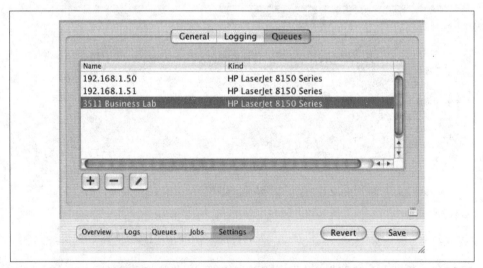

Figure 19-10. Print queues may be managed using the Queues interface in Server Admin's Print Settings module. Clicking the new (+) button in the lower left corner reveals Server Admin's queue-creation dialog, seen earlier in Figure 19-3.

Specific queue options are available in the queue management interface (Figure 19-11). The Printer and Kind settings are not modifiable, and are specified when the queue is created (queue creation is discussed later in this chapter). The Sharing Name is modifiable, and controls the name used to advertise the queue across any enabled protocols. Each available protocol may then be chosen, making the queue accessible to compatible clients. Choosing SMB is a special case. In addition to being noted in the Printing Services preferences, queues available via SMB are also specified in *etc/smb.conf*, the Windows Services configuration file.

> Quotas may also be enabled on a per-queue basis in the queue management interface. Keep in mind that extra work must be undertaken in order to ensure that quotas are not bypassed. This step is discussed later in this chapter.

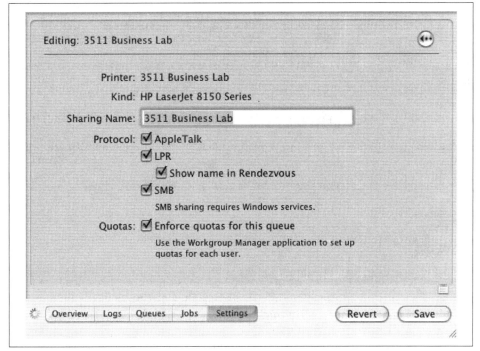

Figure 19-11. Server Admin's queue management interface. LPR queues may be advertised using Rendezvous.

All Print Services settings may be viewed and set using the *serveradmin* command's settings directive (shown in Example 19-5). Due to the way their configuration data is stored, Print Services are probably the least accessible of all of Mac OS X Server's services, often requiring manipulation of a long printer ID array.

Example 19-5. Using the serveradmin command's settings directive to view Print Services configuration data in Mac OS X Server.

```
xsg5:~ tadmin$ sudo serveradmin settings print
print:serverLogArchiveIntervalDays = 7
print:lprQueues:_array_index:0 = "192.168.1.55"
print:queuesArray:_array_id:D463AA93-6777-AE94-F028-317C5CBBE153:quotasEnforced = yes
print:queuesArray:_array_id:D463AA93-6777-AE94-F028-317C5CBBE153:sharingList:_array_index:
0:service = "LPR"
print:queuesArray:_array_id:D463AA93-6777-AE94-F028-317C5CBBE153:sharingList:_array_index:
0:sharingEnable = yes
print:queuesArray:_array_id:D463AA93-6777-AE94-F028-317C5CBBE153:sharingList:_array_index:
1:service = "SMB"
print:queuesArray:_array_id:D463AA93-6777-AE94-F028-317C5CBBE153:sharingList:_array_index:
1:sharingEnable = yes
print:queuesArray:_array_id:D463AA93-6777-AE94-F028-317C5CBBE153:sharingList:_array_index:
2:service = "PAP"
print:queuesArray:_array_id:D463AA93-6777-AE94-F028-317C5CBBE153:sharingList:_array_index:
2:sharingEnable = yes
print:queuesArray:_array_id:D463AA93-6777-AE94-F028-317C5CBBE153:shareable = yes
print:queuesArray:_array_id:D463AA93-6777-AE94-F028-317C5CBBE153:defaultJobPriority =
"NORMAL"
print:queuesArray:_array_id:D463AA93-6777-AE94-F028-317C5CBBE153:printerName = "192.168.1.
55"
print:queuesArray:_array_id:D463AA93-6777-AE94-F028-317C5CBBE153:defaultJobState =
"PENDING"
print:queuesArray:_array_id:D463AA93-6777-AE94-F028-317C5CBBE153:printerURI = "lpd://192.
168.1.55/"
print:queuesArray:_array_id:D463AA93-6777-AE94-F028-317C5CBBE153:registerRendezvous = yes
print:queuesArray:_array_id:D463AA93-6777-AE94-F028-317C5CBBE153:printerKind = "Generic
PostScript Printer"
print:queuesArray:_array_id:D463AA93-6777-AE94-F028-317C5CBBE153:sharingName = "192.168.1.
55"
print:defaultLprQueue = "192.168.1.55"
print:serverLogArchiveEnable = yes
print:jobLogArchiveIntervalDays = 7
print:jobLogArchiveEnable = yes
```

Regardless of how they are set, Print Services' settings (including per-queue configurations) are stored in the local NetInfo database. They can be viewed with any tool capable of reading NetInfo, such as *nicl* (as shown in Example 19-6).

Example 19-6. Using nicl to read Print Services configuration out of the local NetInfo database. Due to the verbosity of this output only a portion is shown.

```
xsg5:~ tadmin$ nicl . -read /config/PrintService_Local
name: PrintService_Local
PrintServiceInfoText: ATTR     printservice_ServerState       BOOL    TRUE
ATTR    printservice_ServerAutoStart    BOOL    TRUE
ATTR    printservice_ServerLogURL       STRN    /Library/Logs/PrintService/PrintService.
server.log
ATTR    printservice_ServerStartTime    DATE    20041024235837
ATTR    printservice_ServerDefaultQueueEnable  BOOL    TRUE
```

Example 19-6. Using nicl to read Print Services configuration out of the local NetInfo database. Due to the verbosity of this output only a portion is shown. (continued)

```
ATTR    printservice_QueueName    STRN    192.168.1.55    D463AA93-6777-AE94-F028-
317C5CBBE153
ATTR    printservice_QueueLPRName    STRN    192.168.1.55    D463AA93-6777-AE94-F028-
317C5CBBE153
ATTR    printservice_QueueLPRShare    BOOL    TRUE    D463AA93-6777-AE94-F028-
317C5CBBE153
ATTR    printservice_QueueLPRRegister    BOOL    TRUE    D463AA93-6777-AE94-F028-
317C5CBBE153
ATTR    printservice_QueueSMBShare    BOOL    TRUE    D463AA93-6777-AE94-F028-
317C5CBBE153
ATTR    printservice_QueuePAPShare    BOOL    TRUE    D463AA93-6777-AE94-F028-
317C5CBBE153
ATTR    printservice_QueueHoldState    BOOL    FALSE    D463AA93-6777-AE94-F028-
317C5CBBE153
ATTR    printservice_QueueCoverPage    BOOL    FALSE    D463AA93-6777-AE94-F028-
317C5CBBE153
```

PrintServiceAccess

Seen thus far in several examples, the *PrintServiceAccess* command has a rich set of capabilities, some of which have not yet been covered. *PrintServerAccess* has no manpage, but its usage statement is quite good, and is included in Example 19-7 as further documentation.

Example 19-7. Most aspects of print queue management can be controlled with PrintServiceAccess.

```
rhp997:~ rhp$ PrintServiceAccess help
Usage: PrintServiceAccess <command>
General commands:
  help                    Display this message.
  version                 Display version of application.
Server commands:
  autostart               Enable server autostart flag.
  noautostart             Disable server autostart flag.
  getautostart            Display state of autostart flag.
  smbqueues               Display smb queue list.
  queues                  Display queue list.
  smbqueues               Display smb queue list.
  lprqueues               Display lpr queue list.
Queue commands:
  info [ <queue> | - ]    Display information for queue ("-"=all).
  pause <queue>           Suspend printing on queue.
  resume <queue>          Resume printing on queue.
  printps <queue> <file>  Print postscript file on queue.
  jobs [ <queue> | - ]    Display job list for queue ("-"=all).
Job commands:
  hold <queue> <job>      Indefinite hold for job.
```

```
until <queue> <job> <time> Hold job until time (yyyymmddhhmmss).
release <queue> <job>      Enable normal printing for job.
priority <queue> <job> <#> Set job priority to number <#>.
remove <queue> <job>       Remove job from queue.
```

Managing Print Services with Workgroup Manager

In a way that is similar other Mac OS X Server services, the Print Services per-user configuration (which relates in Panther entirely to print quotas) is managed using Workgroup Manager, in the Print pane of each user record. In this interface, print quota settings may be set globally (for all queues), specified on a per-queue basis, or disabled entirely (the default setting). Global print quotas, seen in Figure 19-12, limit the total number of pages printed across all printers for a certain configurable period of time. In both cases, a Restart Print Quota button is available, capable of setting print counts for the current period back to 0.

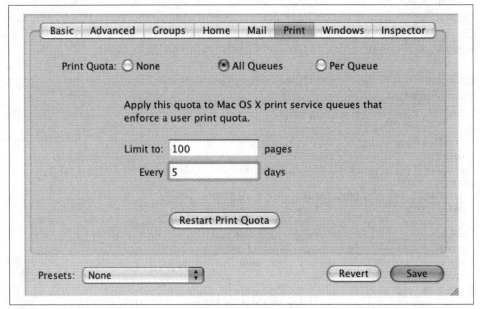

Figure 19-12. Print quotas may be specified globally for all queues. Quota usage may be reset (set to zero) using the Restart Print Quota button.

The interface for specification of per-queue quotas (seen in Figure 19-13) is very similar, differing only in that it provides a pull-down list of printers, offering separate quota settings for each one.

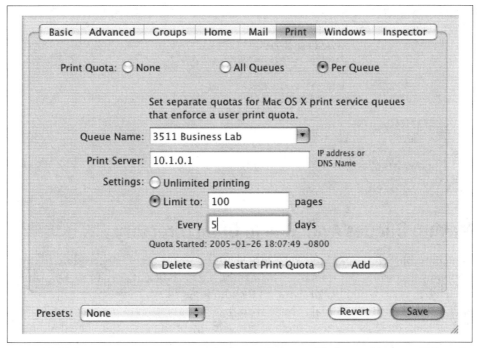

Figure 19-13. Per-queue print quotas may also be specified using Workgroup Manager. Unlimited printing may optionally be specified for specific queues.

Print quota configuration data is stored first in the user's record in XML *plist* format, in the `PrintServiceUserData` attribute, shown in Example 19-8. It is later saved on a per-user basis into the NetInfo database of the server hosting the print queue in question.

Example 19-8. Print quota data is copied from the user record in the shared domain into the local domain of the print server.

```
xsg5:~ tadmin$ nicl . -list /printserviceusers
170        mab
172        mb
xsg5:~ tadmin$ nicl . -read /printserviceusers/mab
name: mab
appleprintservice: <?xml version="1.0" encoding="UTF-8"?>
<!DOCTYPE plist PUBLIC "-//Apple Computer//DTD PLIST 1.0//EN" "http://www.apple.com/DTDs/
PropertyList-1.0.dtd">
<plist version="1.0">
<dict>
        <key>lastmod</key>
        <date>2004-10-25T06:15:25Z</date>
        <key>quotastats</key>
        <dict>
                <key>default</key>
                <dict>
```

```
                        <key>lastmod</key>
                        <date>2004-10-25T06:15:25Z</date>
                        <key>printed</key>
                        <integer>26</integer>
                        <key>start</key>
                        <date>2004-10-25T06:07:31Z</date>
                </dict>
        </dict>
        <key>version</key>
        <integer>1</integer>
</dict>
</plist>
```

Making Queues Available in Open Directory

Printers published to an Open Directory shared domain become accessible to every computer accessing that domain. This can be a very efficient way to make printers available to a large number of users, as they no longer have to be specifically configured on each machine. A major issue with this configuration in Panther (unlike Jaguar) is that there is no easy method for adding printers to the shared domain. Instead, printers must be added manually, using *dsimportexport*, Workgroup Manager's Inspector, the *dscl* utility, or any other tool capable of writing either to Directory Services or to the underlying directory service. The format for this record is demonstrated in Table 19-1.

Table 19-1. Only LPR printers may be published to the shared Open Directory domain.

Attribute	Description
RecordName	The name users will see when they browse for the printer.
PrinterLPRHost	The IP address or hostname of the printer.
PrinterLPRQueue	(Optional) If the queue you wish to advertise is not the printer's default queue, you may specify a particular queue using the PrinterLPRQueue attribute.
PrinterModel	The printer model, obtained from the ModelName attribute in the printer's PPD file.

This file could be used with *dsimportexport* to add a printer to the shared Open Directory domain, as described in Chapter 4. The command syntax would be something along the lines of:

```
dsimportexport -g importfile /LDAPv3/odm.pantherserver.org username password -O
```

which results in the following output:

```
0x0A 0x5C 0x3A 0x2C dsRecTypeStandard:Printers 4 RecordName PrinterLPRHost
PrinterLPRQueue PrinterModel
office_color:192.168.1.4:less_quality:HP9000
```

Quotas and Authentication

One issue with Print Services in Mac OS X is the lack of authentication in Apple's LPR and PAP (AppleTalk printing) implementations. Without authentication, the only thing tying a job to a specific user is the printing software's assertion that a job belongs to a specific user. Malicious users, especially users with administrative access to printing clients, can easily work around this safeguard by creating a local user that the server has no quota for. SMB print services do support authentication and are not subject to this limitation.

Print Services Architecture

Panther's Print Services are a hybrid, with the legacy *PrintServicesMonitor* process limiting access to newer-style CUPS queues. Each aspect of this system is discussed in this section.

PrintServicesMonitor

Most of the features of Mac OS X Server Print Services are implemented in the *PrintServicesMonitor* process, which is started by *watchdog* according to its entry in */etc/watchdog.conf*, as shown in Example 19-9.

Example 19-9. Using the grep command to examine the Printing Services entry in /etc/watchdog. conf. The watchdog daemon ensures that the PrintServiceMonitor starts with its –x (don't daemonize) flag. For more information on watchdog, see Chapter 4.

```
xsg5:~ tadmin$ grep Print /etc/watchdog.conf
PSM:respawn:/usr/sbin/PrintServiceMonitor -x    # Server Printing service
```

PrintServicesMonitor itself does not accept print jobs directly from clients. Instead, *lpd*, *atprintd*, and *smbd* accept (respectively) incoming LPR, AppleTalk, and SMB connections. *lpd* is a modified version of the OpenBSD *lpd* daemon, while *atprintd* is a homegrown Apple tool. Both are designed to work specifically with *PrintServiceMonitor*. Windows Services must be running in order to support SMB printing. Windows print jobs are accepted from clients by the *smbd* daemon and submitted to *PrintServicesMonitor* using the *PrintServicesAccess* tool, as specified in */etc/smb.conf* (shown in Example 19-10).

Example 19-10. Using grep to examine the Windows printing settings in /etc/smb.conf. %p and %j are smb.conf-specific variables referring to the service's path (in this case, a queue) and the print job in question.

```
[ace2:~] nadmin% grep lp /etc/smb.conf
      lprm command = /usr/sbin/PrintServiceAccess remove %p  %j
      lppause command = /usr/sbin/PrintServiceAccess hold %p  %j
```

Example 19-10. Using grep to examine the Windows printing settings in /etc/smb.conf. %p and %j are smb.conf-specific variables referring to the service's path (in this case, a queue) and the print job in question. (continued)

```
lpresume command = /usr/sbin/PrintServiceAccess release %p  %j
lpq command = /usr/sbin/PrintServiceAccess jobs %p
```

Incoming jobs are sent to the appropriate queue (which lives in */var/spool/ PrintService*) for subsequent processing.

CUPS

Once *PrintServiceMonitor* obtains print jobs from *atprintd*, *smbd*, or *lpd* it checks for any quota restrictions and submits the job to CUPS over IPP (TCP port 631). CUPS processes those jobs according to its architecture, pictured in Figure 19-14.

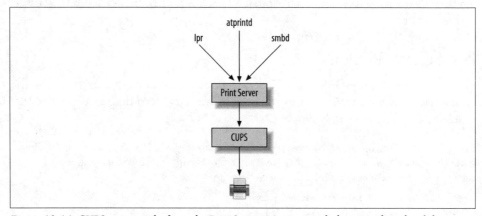

Figure 19-14. CUPS accepts jobs from the PrintServiceMonitor via lpd, atprintd, and smbd.

CUPS is a widely accepted and commonly deployed part of the Unix world. Its modular and extensible nature is well-suited to the constantly evolving world of print media, and its support for the next-generation Internet Printing Protocol (IPP) makes it ideal for Apple's core markets. In fact, CUPS doesn't really need *PrintServiceMonitor* at all. Its IPP implementation already supports sophisticated authentication, security, and quota management features.

CUPS PPDs

CUPS is designed around the idea of printer descriptions (called PPDs). CUPS PPDs are not limited to PostScript printers. CUPS uses PPDs to describe any printer, specifying the filters and back-ends required to successfully print to them. PPDs, which may live anywhere on the filesystem (although they're typically located in */Library/Printers/ PPDs* or */System//Library/Printers/PPDs*), are copied into */etc/cups/ppd* and renamed to reflect the name given to the queue when it is created. Each printer in */etc/cups/ppd* has a corresponding entry in */etc/cups/printers.conf*.

Internet Printing Protocol (IPP)

Much of Apple's dominance in printing markets was due to the AppleTalk's Printer Access Protocol (PAP). PAP provided in the late 1980s what few printing protocols provide today—automatic discovery of printer capabilities and state, seamless print services browsing, and an overall ease of use. PAP supports a wide variety of messaging, robust error handling, and lots of other things users like. Its problem, though, is that (being an AppleTalk protocol) it does not use a TCP connection. AppleTalk as a network protocol is difficult to manage and is being or has been phased out in most places, including at Apple. Without AppleTalk, there is no PAP. The problem that arises is that existing TCP/IP-based printing protocols simply don't provide PAP's deep set of capabilities.

Enter the Internet Printing Protocol (IPP). IPP, defined in RFC 2567, seeks to provide many of the features of PAP to TCP/IP clients. In Panther, Mac OS X clients do not use IPP to access Mac OS X Server Print Services, but its announced importance to Apple means that it bears mentioning here, and its importance will only grow in the future. IPP in Mac OS X and Mac OS X Server is implemented by CUPS.

CUPS configuration

CUPS is configured very consistently among Mac OS X Server deployments. No graphical management options really affect CUPS configuration. It is, however, a full-featured architecture that is worth exploring. Most of its configuration files live in */etc/cups*. A full analysis is beyond the scope of this book (there are plenty of good CUPS references out there), but Table 19-2 contains a brief overview of the most commonly used files.

Table 19-2. CUPS configuration files.

File	Description
cupsd.conf	The main CUPS configuration file.
apple.convs	Describes available CUPS filters—the file format they accept (such as Mac OS X Core Graphics PDF), the file format they produce (such as raster) and their relative weight, or performance impact.
apple.types	MIME types CUPS is capable of printing. Generally jobs are PDFs produced by Apple's Core Graphics subsystem. Often in the context of Print Services, though, they're PostScript files produced by remote printing clients.
classes.conf	Describes available printer classes (pools).

Most of *cupsd.conf* is commented out. In Panther, Apple doesn't take advantage of most of CUPS options (like SSL-protected printing or authenticated IPP). The few enabled are documented here. Where feasible, CUPS uses Apache-like configuration semantics, because they are familiar to a wide variety of administrators.

`ServerName` specifies the fully-qualified domain name of the server. Since CUPS in Mac OS X is mostly designed to accept jobs from local processes, this is set to the loopback address:

```
ServerName 127.0.0.1
```

`LogLevel` determines what logging data is used in CUPS's logs. It corresponds from a management standpoint to *syslogd* log levels, supporting values of `none`, `warn`, `error`, `info`, `debug`, or `debug2`. The default value of `info` is often sufficient for day-to-day operations, while the `debug` level is typically used during setup or troubleshooting. `debug2` is most often used by developers. CUPS logs are discussed in more depth later in this chapter.

```
LogLevel info
```

The maximum number of simultaneous jobs to support is indicated in the `MaxCopies` directive:

```
MaxCopies 10000
```

`ConfigFilePerm` indicates the filesystem permissions of all configuration files written by the *cupsd* daemon:

```
ConfigFilePerm 0644
```

The `BrowseShortNames` directives controls the format of printer names, determining whether they'll accept short (*printer*) or long forms (*printer@server*):

```
BrowseShortNames No
```

`BrowseAllow` allows incoming CUPS browse packets (UDP 631). In this case, any local subnet is accepted by the loopback interface; all other browse packets are denied:

```
BrowseAllow 127.0.0.1
BrowseAllow @LOCAL
BrowseDeny All
```

`ImplicitClasses`, if set, automatically creates a pool (class) when identical printers are discovered:

```
ImplicitClasses Off
```

`SystemGroup` specifies which group should be permitted to perform system-level (administrative) tasks:

```
SystemGroup admin
```

`Location` blocks specify access controls. They are relative to the `DocumentRoot` that supports CUPS web-based administration (*/usr/share/doc/cups*). Because no path is specified, this default ACL applies to the entire `DocumentRoot`:

```
<Location />
Order Deny,Allow
Deny From All
Allow From 127.0.0.1
</Location>
```

CUPS web administration

The CUPS web interface (while worth mentioning) is not covered in great depth here. To reach it, open a web browser and point it to *http://127.0.0.1:631*, as illustrated in Figure 19-15. It may be used towards a variety of administration purposes. Be careful that you do not overwrite any configuration that Apple's print management architecture relies on.

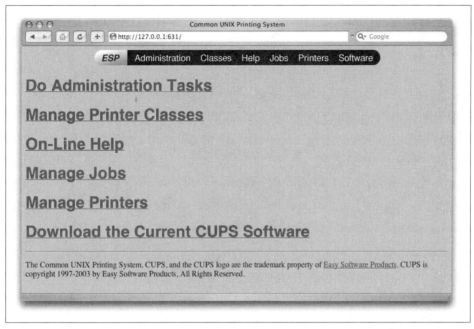

Figure 19-15. CUPS provides a convenient web interface. Use it with care so you don't overwrite configurations that Apple's software depends on.

CUPS logs

Not available in the graphical interface, CUPS logs (located in */var/spool/cups*) can be vital to any diagnosis relating to the printing process. Discussed briefly earlier, they are located in */var/log/cups*; both access and error logs are available.

```
xsg5:~ tadmin$ ls /var/log/cups/
access_log      access_log.0    error_log
```

CUPS logs are far more useful for diagnosing the printer's interaction with the OS than the *PrintService* logs, which are largely used to monitor incoming *lpr*, Apple-Talk, and SMB jobs.

## PART V

Security Services

Security is like driving a really nice (but really high maintenance) car. There is really no end to the process of analysis, tweaking, and engineering required to keep your server or organization safe and secure. In fact, the word *process* is really key. Secure systems, because they are forced to interact with an ever-changing set of environmental characteristics, are much more of a process than a destination. An infrastructure can never really be called *secure*. Instead, we refer to the relative confidence levels associated with the ongoing process of building a secure system.

This part of the book concerns itself with Security Services—specific services within Mac OS X Server designed to help increase the confidence that your server is secure (or securely interacting with your organization's IT environment). These services are required because security is a rather late architectural requirement for server products. Most protocols examined in this book were engineered at a time when the Internet was a far friendlier place. Getting them to function securely in a modern IT environment—as you all know—can be quite the challenge.

Chapters in this part of the book include:

Chapter 20, *The Mac OS X Server Firewall*
Chapter 21, *Virtual Private Networks*

The Mac OS X Server Firewall

The term "firewall" can take a variety of meanings, but we will start with a general definition of purpose: a firewall exists to help enhance the security of the firewall operator's resources. These resources generally include computers, data, bandwidth, and employee productivity. Computer networks can be complex, and perhaps sometimes as much of a liability as an asset. Firewalls are a great way to help limit the liabilities surrounding network-related resources.

This chapter follows a bottom-up approach. It starts by discussing exactly what a firewall does and how it does its thing. I identify various reasons to implement a firewall, along with discussion of how the firewall service is positioned in Mac OS X Server by Apple. Mostly, the chapter focuses on the specifics of the firewall service in Panther Server, and the ways it is different from firewalls on other platforms.

From there, the chapter examines the default firewall configuration, how that configuration is loaded at startup and stored on disk, and of course how to modify that configuration using Server Admin and various command-line tools. This chapter does not attempt to teach all the fundamentals of routing or firewall theory, but it does attempt to aid the novice or advanced administrator in understanding, configuring, and maintaining the firewall.

A Firewall's Place in Network Communication

A good way to achieve an understanding of how network communication works from end to end is to analyze each of the logical components required for effective communication. An abstracted description of this process is provided by something called the Open Systems Interconnection (OSI) Reference Model (see Figure 20-1).

Without going into excruciating detail on the OSI Reference Model, it is important to note that firewalls operate at a specific place within this model, and the implementation and administration of a firewall is more or less independent of other areas in the model. For example, it doesn't matter which specific Ethernet card is in use on a

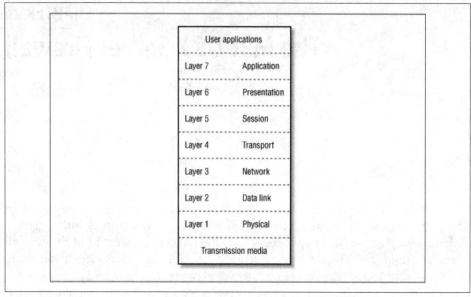

User applications

Layer 7	Application
Layer 6	Presentation
Layer 5	Session
Layer 4	Transport
Layer 3	Network
Layer 2	Data link
Layer 1	Physical

Transmission media

Figure 20-1. The OSI Reference Model. Firewalls operate at layers 3 and 4.

server, or what sort of data is passing through the network. This model exists to help achieve a high degree of transparency or abstraction between layers. As long as the various layers in the model interact in well-defined and agreed-upon ways, the specific nature of a given component does not matter. The layers in the model help clearly define the logical functions required for effective network communication, which helps ensure compatibility.

In a generic example of network communication between two computers attached to the same physical network, information flows from Layer 7 down to Layer 1 on one computer, at which point it is transported across some physical medium, arrives at the destination computer, and moves from Layer 1 back up to Layer 7. At each layer, different pieces of software or hardware operate on the data and pass it to the next layer.

Network communication is facilitated in large part by protocol suites, or stacks. On the Internet, the primary protocol suite is IP (Internet Protocol), which exists at the Network layer (Layer 3). IP provides a means by which computers can be distinguished from other computers; in a word, addressing. This is also where route selection occurs; using IP it is possible to know whether another computer is on a local network. This feature provides criteria used to determine where to send data to get it closer to the destination. The Transport layer (Layer 4) includes subprotocols of IP such as TCP or UDP, and the firewall has the ability to inspect these protocols as well.

Before we can understand how a firewall does its job, it's important to understand what data looks like at Layers 3 and 4 of the OSI reference model, because this is where firewalls do their work.

Packet-Switched Networking

A useful method of describing the nature of the Internet (and packet-switched networks in general) is by comparison to *circuit-switched* (sometimes called *connection oriented*) networks. The telephone system is a good example of a circuit-switched network. In a circuit-switched network, there is a dedicated channel (in most familiar cases, represented by a physical line) that is used for the duration of a conversation. All communication during that conversation travels along the same physical path between the two endpoints. Because the channel is dedicated, it can be used for only one connection at a time.

In a packet-switched network, by contrast, the transmission medium (perhaps also a physical line) is not dedicated to a single connection, and may be used to facilitate many conversations with different endpoints at once. The information payload is broken up into chunks and sent across the network in small pieces. In order to share the transmission medium between multiple conversations, packet-switched networks require a way to identify which data belongs to which conversation so that it can be routed correctly. Another important attribute of packet-switched networks is that the physical path taken by any given packet can change at any time for a variety of reasons. Given the meshed nature of the Internet, this design can provide some degree of fault tolerance, allowing data to be routed around problem areas (such as a fiber cut). On the Internet, there is no guarantee that a packet will reach its destination, and so reliability mechanisms are implemented in Layer 4 (the Transport layer), most notably by Transmission Control Protocol (TCP).

The term *packet* is the name given to data at Layer 3 of the OSI model. A general term for logical chunks regardless of layer is *protocol data unit*, or PDU; at Layer 3, PDUs are called packets. Other examples of packets are parcels that move through the postal system, or even automobiles on the road. In each case, there are units that move throughout the system, sharing the transmission medium with other units that may have a different source or destination, and being routed based primarily on the destination.

In the case of the Internet, and the OSI reference model in general, another important function is *encapsulation*. This process adds a *header* to the data unit. A header contains information about the payload of the unit, and is prepended to the unit itself. Familiar examples of encapsulation include the address labels placed on a package to be snail-mailed, the wrapping placed around the package, and perhaps a smaller box around the item inside the package.

Information being sent from a computer flows down from Layer 7 to Layer 1, and each layer encapsulates the data handed to it from the above layer by adding a header. Once the data reaches the destination machine, it travels from Layer 1 to Layer 7, and at each layer, the appropriate header is decapsulated and interpreted by protocols operating in that layer. A given header is generally used only by protocols that operate at the same or adjacent layer in which that header was added. For example, an IP firewall pays attention to headers used only at Layers 3 and 4 (see Figures 20-2 and 20-3). A firewall does its job by acting upon information found in packet headers.

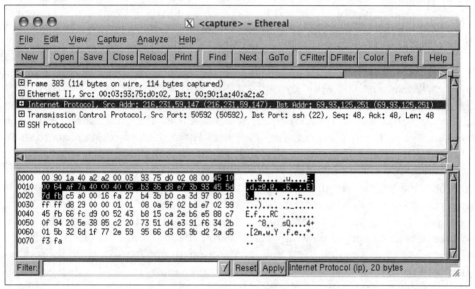

Figure 20-2. An Ethernet frame containing an IP packet of type TCP; in this case, part of an SSH session. The IP header portion is highlighted.

Filtering Packets

A *packet filter* is a more specific term than *firewall*, because it reveals more about the inner workings: it operates at Layer 3, filtering packets. In the case of Mac OS X and Mac OS X Server, the packet filter in use is called *ipfw*, which stands for *IP Firewall*. Other packet filters vary in supported features and administration details, but the general idea is the same. This chapter focuses squarely on *ipfw*, as that's what Apple includes.

ipfw operates by inspecting each packet as it moves through the system, inbound and outbound. After each packet inspection, *ipfw* consults a list of rules. The rules each have a number, and are evaluated in ascending order until a rule is found that fits, or *matches* the packet. Once a rule matches, that rule's action is taken, and *ipfw* moves on to the next packet, starting back at the beginning of the rule set. A basic rule has

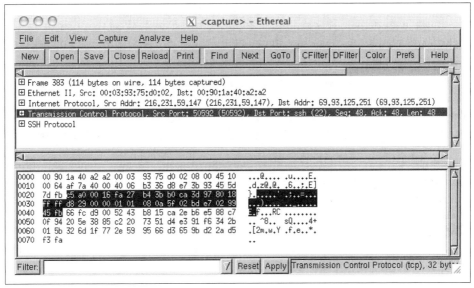

Figure 20-3. Same Ethernet frame as in Figure 20-2, but with the TCP header highlighted.

three primary functional components: rule number, action, and criteria used to match packets to the rule. The list of available criteria and actions is somewhat long; however, effective firewall configurations are often relatively simple.

Perhaps the best place to begin understanding how packet filter rules work is by looking at the default rules that ship with Mac OS X Server. We'll cover how to view and set rules shortly, but for now, open a Terminal window and execute the following command to produce a list of the current rules:

```
andre@core[~] sudo ipfw show
01000 0 0 allow ip from any to any via lo0
01010 0 0 deny ip from any to 127.0.0.0/8
01020 0 0 deny ip from 224.0.0.0/4 to any in
01030 0 0 deny tcp from any to 224.0.0.0/4 in
12300 0 0 allow tcp from any to any 22 in
12301 0 0 allow udp from any to any 22 in
12302 0 0 allow tcp from any to any 311 in
12303 0 0 allow tcp from any to any 625 in
12304 0 0 allow tcp from any to any 687 in
12305 0 0 allow icmp from any to any in icmptype 0
12306 0 0 allow igmp from any to any in
63200 0 0 deny icmp from any to any in icmptype 0
63300 0 0 deny igmp from any to any in
65000 0 0 deny tcp from any to any in setup
65535 0 0 allow ip from any to any
```

The number in the first column is the rule number (remember that rules are evaluated in ascending order). The second and third columns are counters that represent the number of packets and bytes matched by each rule. The counters are all empty because the firewall service is not yet enabled. The remaining elements specify the action (allow or deny in this example), followed by an expression that defines which packets will match the rule. Note that some of the rules include more elements than others, while some rules look very similar to each other.

These are the default firewall rules used in Panther Server. A recommended form for a packet filter rule set is to allow only the desired packets to pass, and then deny what isn't wanted by using a "catchall" rule that would match everything that isn't expressly allowed by a higher-priority rule. This approach is evident in the structure of the default rule set. It is a secure default that approximates the security of being behind a NAT router, though it does stop short of the "default deny" commonly found at the end of packet filter configurations; we "allow" instead. Any incoming TCP connections except those that facilitate remote administration of the server are blocked. The default rule set also allows our server to make unrestricted outgoing connections, the responses to which are allowed; for example, an admin logs into the console and hits a remote web site. This packet filter rule set is a secure and functional default for Mac OS X Server.

> All traffic is allowed when the firewall is disabled, and it is disabled by default. However, the firewall is only a first line of defense. Just because traffic is not blocked at the network layer doesn't mean that it can't be denied at higher layers. A well-configured server is pretty secure without a firewall, because just about every service provides ways to control who can access that service.

As an introduction to understanding *ipfw* packet filter rules, let's take a close look at the default rule set:

01000
> This rule allows any IP packets on the interface *lo0*, which is the local loopback interface. *lo0* is a virtual interface that is used only to send traffic between services running on the local machine. This rule is first because many packets match this rule, and we want those packets to be dispatched as quickly as possible.

01010
> Deny any IP packets being sent to the address 127.0.0.1 (the address of the local loopback). We know that any legitimate local traffic would have been matched by the first rule, so anything that matches this rule is treated as an attempt by an external source to spoof the IP of the local loopback, and is dropped.

01020
> Drop any incoming IP traffic (IP includes TCP, UDP, and ICMP) originating from a multicast address. Multicast traffic that you might want (such as Rendezvous) originates from other hosts, not from the 224/4 range.

01030

Drop any incoming TCP traffic sent to a multicast address. Multicast traffic that you might want (Rendezvous) is UDP, not TCP, so it will not be blocked by this rule.

12300 through 12304

These rules "poke holes" for essential services for remote administration. These are SSH (port 22), Server Admin (311 and 687), and *DirectoryService* (625, provides remote directory access). These rules are here so that you can enable the firewall service without changing the default configuration. Plus, it doesn't lock you out.

12305

Allow incoming ICMP (Internet Control Message Protocol, one of IP's subprotocols) echo replies from anywhere, which allows *ping* responses back in. There are several types of ICMP packets; type 0 is "echo reply," which is the response a host will send after receiving an "echo request" (aka ping).

12306

Allow incoming ICMP, used by multicast-enabled routers to track multicast group membership.

63200

Deny incoming *ping* replies. Apple considers this rule and the next two unmodifiable, and they support the "allow what you want and deny everything else" mindset. In the case of the default rule set, this rule should never match, due to rule 12305. This rule is here to disallow *ping* functionality unless it is explicitly allowed by a higher-priority rule. As a side note, this seems like a strange thing to do, as this rule won't stop the server from being pinged from elsewhere; it only stops *us* from being able to see *ping* results.

63300

Deny incoming ICMP (but this traffic is allowed by a higher-priority rule in the default rule set).

65000

Block any incoming TCP packets that are attempting to establish a new session. The "setup" option at the end causes this rule to match only TCP packets that are attempting to open a new TCP session. This rule's result is similar to what happens in a NAT situation; TCP sessions that traverse the firewall are allowed only if initiated from inside the network.

So far, we have seen only fairly basic *ipfw* rules. The actions in these rules have been only allow or deny, though there are other actions. Table 20-1 lists the other actions that can be taken, with short descriptions of each.

Table 20-1. Rule actions for ipfw.

Action	Description
allow	Let the packet through
deny	Don't allow the packet
unreach	Deny the packet and try to notify the sender that it was denied
reset	Deny the packet and send a TCP reset (similar to unreach)
count	Update counters (useful for collecting stats/reporting)
check-state	Used for stateful packet inspection
divert	Send packet to another port on the local machine
tee	Send a copy of the packet to another port on the local machine
fwd	Used for transparent proxying
skipto	Jump to a specific *ipfw* rule number

Of the available packet-matching criteria, so far we have used most of them: source or destination IP address, IP protocol, TCP/UDP port number, direction (in or out), one of the IP options (setup), one of the ICMP types (*icmptype 0*), and interface specification (*lo0*). This is generally enough for a basic packet filter configuration. The full list of criteria for matching packets that can be used with *ipfw* is found in Table 20-2.

Table 20-2. Packet matching criteria for ipfw.

Criteria	Description
Transmit and receive interface	Most commonly *en0*, *en1*, *en2*, etc.
Direction	In or out
Source and destination IP address	Possibly masked to include ranges
Protocol	TCP, UDP, ICMP, etc.
Source and destination port	Lists, ranges, or masks
TCP	Flags
IP	Fragment flag
IP	Options
ICMP	Types
User ID	ID of the socket associated with the packet

Further information about the syntax of an *ipfw* command is provided later, though not every option available is covered. Refer to *ipfw*'s manpage or other texts focused on packet filtering for more general information, as we focus mostly on the things that are specific to Panther Server.

The Mac OS X Firewall Service

With a basic understanding of how a packet filter works, we can look closely at how it is used as part of the Firewall service in Mac OS X Server. As mentioned previously, *ipfw* provides our core packet-filtering functionality. Mac OS X Server adds value to *ipfw* by providing a GUI (and command-line) interface for configuring and monitoring *ipfw*, and also by providing useful (and relatively conservative) defaults.

Of all the things that a packet filter *can* do, Apple seems to have some pretty specific things in mind for the Firewall service in Mac OS X Server. Panther Server's Firewall service is targeted at protecting the server on which it is running. Configuring a firewall for this purpose is very different from configuring a firewall designed to sit at the border between a network and the Internet. Mac OS X Server is simply not well-suited for the tasks normally performed by a dedicated firewall.

For example, Mac OS X Server needs to be rebooted for things like software updates, and does a fairly poor job of routing packets during the reboot. Surely you could configure Mac OS X Server as a router and then never touch it so that it wouldn't have to be rebooted, but that means no software updates. Just because Mac OS X Server *can* act as a router; that does not mean it's the most cost-effective or functional solution. Trying to shoehorn Apple's Firewall service into performing duties that it wasn't intended to provide is generally not a good idea.

Apple also includes a Network Address Translation (NAT) service that works in conjunction with the firewall. This service could be used to provide Internet access to a workgroup by allowing the workstations to share the server's IP address. While the NAT service does work, better results may be found with the average $40 NAT router. The bottom line is that it's a very good idea to use dedicated network hardware, and not a personal computer, to perform critical network functions like routing. This reduces network downtime due to computer maintenance such as software updates.

I will focus on using Apple's Firewall service for protection of services running on our server, and not to do routing or NAT for other computers.

The firewall startup process

Before examining how the firewall is configured, first let us carefully look at how (and whether) the Firewall is initialized at boot time. We'll walk through the process exactly as it is undertaken by the system, in rather excruciating detail:

1. The */etc/rc* script is invoked, early after powering on, by the *init* process. Starting at line 92 of */etc/rc*, the files */etc/sysctl-macosxserver.conf* and */etc/sysctl.conf* are loaded. The latter does not exist by default, and may include directives described in the former, and any other site-specific *sysctl* configuration. The parameters described in *sysctl-macosxserver.conf* allow the administrator to set a bandwidth limit for ICMP traffic (this step may help mitigate some denial-of-service

attacks), adjust the TCP window size (possibly useful for obtaining higher throughput on local networks), and finally implement some ways to make your packet filter a bit more stealthy by not responding to incoming connection attempts for a service that is not being offered (and optionally logging those attempts).

2. *kextd* is started at line 129 of */etc/rc*. *kextd* and loads kernel extensions, including */System/Library/Extensions/IPFirewall.kext*. This extension provides the kernel-resident portions of *ipfw*, which constitute the core of the packet-filtering engine in Mac OS X.

3. At the very end of */etc/rc*, *SystemStarter* is invoked. *SystemStarter* is responsible for executing the startup scripts stored under the directory */System/Library/StartupItems* (and optionally */Library/StartupItems*). Most startup scripts look at the values of the variables defined in the */etc/hostconfig* file to determine whether to take action. Settings in *hostconfig* are generally maintained by the admin tools, but can also be switched by hand. The following is a list of firewall-related startup items and their functions:

   - *Network* startup item: If IPFORWARDING is set to YES in the *hostconfig* file, then the *Network* startup item enables IP forwarding with the command *sysctl -w net.inet.ip.forwarding=1*. IP forwarding is needed for NAT to work.

   - *IPAliases* startup item: If IPALIASES is set to YES and the IP aliases config file exists at */etc/IPAliases.conf*, the specified interface aliases is loaded and activated. This is useful when the server needs to bind more than a handful of addresses.

   - *IPFilter* startup item: This one does several things, and comprises the bulk of the firewall initialization, including:

     1. The *StartService* block is the first to get executed, and it begins by disabling the firewall. As of Mac OS X Server 10.3, there is an *ipfw* "kill switch" in the kernel, accessible via the *sysctl* command. The *Disable()* function uses the command *sysctl -w net.inet.ip.fw.enable=0* to disable *ipfw*.

     2. The *Reload* function in the *IPFilter* script is then called, which executes a function called CopyDefaultConfig—this function is defined toward the top of the IPFilter script. CopyDefaultConfig makes sure that all required firewall configuration files are present, and if they are not, it creates new default config files from the Apple-supplied defaults stored in */etc/ipfilter*. The defaults are:

        ```
        ip_address_groups.plist.default
        ipfw.conf.default
        standard_services.plist.default
        ```

     3. The *Reload* function then loads (but does not activate) the firewall rules stored in */etc/ipfilter* using a *serveradmin* command:

        ```
        serveradmin command ipfilter:command=reloadFW
        ```

The rules are loaded from the *ipfw.conf* and *ipfw.conf.apple* files.

4. If `IPFILTER` is set to `YES` in */etc/hostconfig*, or if the `DefaultEnable` variable at the top of thpe *IPFilter* script is set to `YES`, the *StartService* block calls the *Enable* function.

5. The *Enable* function activates the firewall in the kernel by flipping the firewall's *sysctl* kill switch using the command *sysctl –w net.inet.ip.fw. enable=1*. This step activates the rules that were previously loaded.

Configuring the Firewall with the General Pane

This is the easy part. Server Admin makes it very painless to accomplish the goal of enhancing the network security of services running on your server by restricting access to those services based on the IP address of the connecting computer. The mechanics of how *ipfw* rules are formatted, ordered, and all the various actions and matching criteria are great to know about, but only a small subset of that knowledge is necessary to understand how to configure the firewall using Server Admin. By giving the Firewall Service a fairly specific purpose, Apple is able to make many of the configuration choices for us, which means we only have to think about two essential variables for each rule.

First is the IP Address Group, which is a way to specify which hosts will be affected by a rule. The address groups each have a name and a list of one or more elements that specify either an IP address or a range of addresses, expressed in CIDR notation. There are three address groups by default. First is 10-net, which actually applies to 10.0.0.0/24 only (and not the much larger 10/8, which is one of the ranges reserved for private networks). In the General Settings pane of the Firewall Service, double-click 10-net to see the field that contains the list of addresses that fall within this address group. Selecting an address in the list triggers some text describing exactly which hosts fall within the range, if the item is a network mask instead of a single IP. The second default address group is 192.168.0.0/16, and finally a group called "any," the address for which uses the special keyword "any," which naturally would apply to any host. The "any" address group cannot be deleted or changed, as it needs to exist as a catchall. It is very important when creating custom address groups to specify network masks that include all four octets. For example, though 10/8 is conventionally a valid way to say 10.0.0.0/8, this will not work properly here. Failure to supply all four octets will result in malformed rules.

The second bit of configuration required to create a basic *ipfw* rule using Server Admin is to specify the service to allow. Services are differentiated by their TCP or UDP port numbers, and Server Admin includes a handy list of common services and their associated ports (see Figure 20-4). For each service listed, there is but one solitary checkbox. When checked, hosts in the selected address group are allowed to access the chosen service. It's that simple.

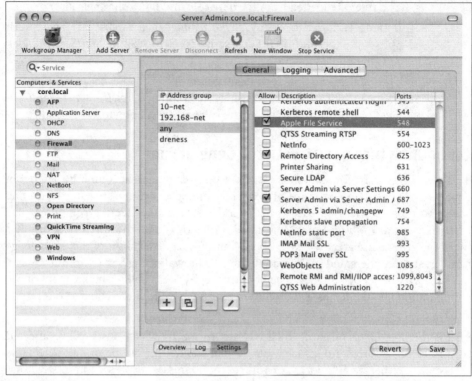

Figure 20-4. Server Admin's list of common services and their associated ports.

For example, if you wanted to provide access to Apple File Service (AFP) only to other hosts in our subnet, you would create an address group for that subnet, hit the Allow checkbox for Apple File Service in that address group, but not allow AFP for the "any" address group. When you apply the changes, the Firewall Service automatically orders the rules so that they'll be applied in the order that makes sense. In this case, the "allow" rule for AFP access for our new address group would appear before the rule that disallows all incoming TCP connections (rule 65000).

Creating rules in this manner works for poking holes as in the earlier example, but the inverse seems to not function as described in the Network Services PDF (part of the Mac OS X Server documentation). For example, if we decided to allow AFP access by default, we would check the Apple File Server checkbox for the "any" address group. We should then be able to create a new address group and *not* allow AFP service for that group. The result should be that AFP service is allowed for all hosts except those in the new address group. Denying access to services in this way seems to not work at all using the General pane. It's tempting to think that the lack of the "Allow" checkbox implies a "Deny," but this does not jibe with the Network Services PDF documentation. The good news is that it's not too hard to achieve this goal; it requires either using the Advanced configuration pane, or writing the rules by hand in the traditional *ipfw* format.

"Allow" rules created in the General pane of the Firewall settings are stored in the file */etc/ipfilter/ip_address_groups.plist* as XML dictionaries in the rules array for an address group. Example 20-1 shows the definition of the address group 192.168-net, along with one rule that is configured for that group. The string associated with the name key in the rules array (afpovertcp) refers to a specific network service defined in */etc/services*.

Example 20-1. A snippet from the ip_address_groups.plist file.

```
...
<dict>
    <key>_id_</key>
    <string>192.168-net</string>
    <key>addresses</key>
    <array>
        <string>192.168.0.0/16</string>
    </array>
    <key>name</key>
    <string>192.168-net</string>
    <key>readOnly</key>
    <false/>
    <key>rules</key>
    <array>
        <dict>
            <key>action</key>
            <string>allow</string>
            <key>name</key>
            <string>afpovertcp</string>
        </dict>
    </array>
</dict>
...
```

Configuring the Firewall with the Advanced Pane

While the General pane makes it easy to poke holes for common services, it cannot be used to create "deny" rules—as of 10.3.7, the Network Services PDF is wrong about this. For example, if there were a global allow for SSH in the any address group, we could not use the General pane to restrict SSH access from a particular address group. Instead, we can use the Advanced pane to create the deny rule.

Click the Advanced pane of the Firewall Settings window to see the list of Advanced rules. Note that some of the default rules are visible here. These rules are stored in the file */etc/ipfilter/ip_address_groups.plist*, along with the rules created in the General pane. These rules are broken into two sections, though that is not visible by looking at the Advanced pane. The first four rules appear very early in the rule set (see rules 1000 through 1030, described previously), while the last three enabled rules appear at the end of the rule set (rules 63200 through 65000).

Also note that several of these rules are not modifiable, because the value of the key readOnly is set to true for some of the rules in *ip_address_groups.plist*. It is generally advisable to leave the read-only rules in place. Finally, note the last rule, which is not enabled by default. This rule would deny any incoming UDP packets not expressly allowed by a higher-priority rule (such as one configured via the General pane). Enabling this rule will break lots of things, including DNS lookups performed from our server against external servers. It is recommended to leave this rule disabled unless you plan on creating specific allow rules for all necessary incoming UDP traffic. Allowing "Domain Name Service" in the "any" address group only allows external DNS resolvers to query name services hosted on the server, and would not allow lookups against external servers from our server if this last rule were enabled.

To begin the process of adding a new Advanced rule, click the + button. Here in the Advanced pane, we have more granular control over the rules we create. Let's examine each of the available elements, starting at the top:

Action

Most commonly Allow or Deny. Choose "Other" to manually enter one of the other actions (described in the *ipfw* manpage).

Protocol

Usually TCP or UDP, but other common options that can be manually entered include "ICMP" (used for pings) and "IP", which includes both TCP and UDP, but cannot be used if any ports are specified later.

Service

This is the list of services contained in the file */etc/ipfilter/standard_services.plist*. Selecting a service from this menu fills in the value for the destination port. This is the port used by the service to receive data from a client.

Log all packets matching this rule

Any packets that match will be recorded in the main system log (*/var/log/system.log*). By default, only the first 1000 matches are logged per rule.

Source address

Use this menu to select one of the address groups. This rule will match packets coming from the selected address group. Note that when specifying an IP or netmask that's not in one of the address groups (by choosing "Other" from the Source Address menu), be sure to specify all four octets if entering a netmask (e. g., 10.0.0.0/8 and not 10/8). Select "any" to match packets regardless of source.

Source port

Source ports are generally chosen dynamically in an incremental fashion to uniquely identify the local endpoint of an outgoing connection, so that return traffic makes it back to the client that issued the connection, even if multiple such clients are in use at the same source IP address. Due to the dynamic nature of the source port, it is not very useful for our purposes, so generally this field should be left empty.

Destination address
> Chose an address group from the list in order to match packets sent to that address group, or enter a custom address or netmask by choosing "Other."

Destination port
> This corresponds to the "well known" port numbers that are not chosen dynamically, and generally correspond to specific services. This field is automatically populated when selecting from the Service menu above. For a list of common ports and their associated services, see the file */etc/services*.

Interface
> Chose "In" to match only incoming packets, "Out" to match only outgoing packets, or "Other" to specify a network interface. In this case, the rule will only match packets that traverse the specified interface. Interfaces are expressed using the BSD style interface name, such as *en0*. To see a list of available interfaces, use the *ifconfig* command. Leave this field empty to match packets regardless of direction or interface.

Once all the necessary elements have been specified, click OK, and then Save. Once the firewall is finished reloading, the rule should re-order itself to appear between the two default blocks of rules. If other advanced rules are added, the order in which they will appear in the *ipfw* rule set is determined by their order in this list. Drag and drop your custom advanced rules to re-order them.

Be careful not to drag any custom rules above the rule that is in the fourth position by default (rule 1030). As of 10.3.7, there is currently a bug that causes this rule to become corrupted if it is reordered and the configuration is saved a few times.

Configuring the Firewall from the Command Line

There are a few good reasons to configure *ipfw* rules from the command line. One reason is if you already have a set of traditionally formatted *ipfw* rules that you wish to use. Another would be to administer firewall settings remotely from a machine that doesn't have Apple's admin tools installed, but that does have an SSH client. Finally, some administrators might wish to bypass Apple's Firewall methodology entirely, and maintain *ipfw* completely outside of Server Admin/*servermgrd*, due to a couple quirks that will be addressed here.

In order to understand these quirks, let's take a step-by-step look at how the firewall service generates and applies rules stored in the configuration files (this process is documented in */etc/ipfilter/ipfw.conf*). This series of events occurs whenever the firewall is reloaded. A reload is triggered by saving a change via Server Admin, altering firewall settings using *serveradmin* from the command line, a reboot, or manually with the following command:

```
sudo serveradmin command ipfilter:command=reloadFW
```

1. *ipfw* is disabled and all rules are flushed, leaving the server unprotected until the rules can be reapplied and *ipfw* is re-enabled.

2. The *ipfilter* module of *servermgrd*, which forms the backend of the firewall service, generates an *ipfw* rule set from the configuration specified in Server Admin, which is stored on disk in the file */etc/ipfilter/ip_address_groups.plist*. Any pending changes made via Server Admin to rules defined in that file are written out. The generated rules are then written out to */etc/ipfilter/ipfw.conf.apple*, along with a date stamp in the comments.

3. The rules in */etc/ipfilter/ipfw.conf.apple* are loaded into *ipfw* in the order shown in the file, but do not take effect yet because *ipfw* is still disabled.

4. If the NAT service is enabled, the divert rule required for NAT is loaded but does not take effect until *ipfw* is enabled.

5. Any custom rules defined in */etc/ipfilter/ipfw.conf* are loaded into *ipfw*, but do not take effect until *ipfw* is enabled. This is where *ipfw*-savvy admins may place their own handwritten rules.

6. If the firewall is supposed to be enabled (according to the IPFILTER variable in */etc/hostconfig*, which is maintained by *servermgrd*), *ipfw* is activated by *servermgrd* by flipping a *sysctl* bit (*net.inet.ip.fw.enable*), which activates the firewall.

Astute readers may note that mention was made no less than three times that rules being loaded do not take effect until *ipfw* is re-enabled. Unfortunately, *ipfw* rules are loaded extremely slowly in Mac OS X Server as of Panther. This fact is exposed in */var/log/system.log*, which receives a play-by-play of what's going on with the firewall service. After the firewall is reloaded, there will be a record of the length of time that was required to load the rules; for example:

```
Oct 31 15:34:10 core servermgr_ipfilter: ipfw config:Info:Finished applying generated
rules in 14007 ms
```

In this instance, *ipfw* took 14 seconds to load 17 rules, which is a *really* long time. By contrast, a pokey ol' OpenBSD 3.4 machine loads 23 rules in exactly 0.01 seconds (though it is using *pf* and not *ipfw*; *ipfw* is about this fast elsewhere).

```
floe# time pfctl -f /etc/pf.conf
pfctl -f /etc/pf.conf  0.01s user 0.00s system 102% cpu 0.010 total
floe# pfctl -s rules | wc -l
      23
```

 Mac OS X 10.2 did not have this sluggishness with *ipfw*, and at this time it's not clear when this problem will go away.

Obviously, this pace can cause problems. For example, if you depend heavily on deny rules being in place, then any reload of the firewall causes exposure of the server for however long it takes to load the rules. The more rules there are, the longer it takes to load them. For example, a rule set of 182 rules takes 72 seconds to load on a 400 MHz G4. This also causes big problems with the NAT service, for the brave few that actually use the NAT service in the first place. Because all rules are flushed, this includes the divert rule which is the linchpin of a functional NAT setup. When this rule is flushed, all connections through NAT are destroyed. NAT'd clients will have no Internet access until the firewall is finished reloading, and any persistent sessions will have to be recreated.

So then, with all that in mind, let's take a look at some ways to configure *ipfw* from the command line to allow us to bypass these quirks. The old-fashioned way is to use the *ipfw* command in the Terminal, as *root*. For example:

```
sudo ipfw add 2000 deny ip from 1.2.3.4 to any
```

This command would add a rule in position 2000 that denies all traffic from the host 1.2.3.4. A very important thing to note here is that when directly interacting with *ipfw*, *the firewall reload process does not occur*. This feature is beneficial because the existing *ipfw* rules continue to function even as this single new rule is added. Also, this is a much faster way to make changes since only one rule is being loaded instead of the entire rule set. To see the active rule set, use the following command :

```
sudo ipfw show
```

The general form of a basic *ipfw* rule is as follows:

```
ipfw add rule_number action protocol from source to destination
interface options
```

which breaks down as follows:

- *rule_number* should be some unique number used to determine rule order.
- *action* is typically allow or deny.
- *protocol* is typically udp, tcp, or ip (ip is a superset that includes tcp, udp, and all others listed in the */etc/protocols* file).
- *source* and *destination* can be expressed as a single IP address (such as 1.2.3.4) or a netmask (such as 216.231.59.1/24).
- *interface* can be in or out to match packets based on their direction, or via interface to match packets traversing only the specified interface, such as *en0*.
- *options*, of which there are quite a few—such as setup, which matches only packets used to initiate TCP connections, or keep-state, which is used to create stateful filtering rules.

There is a lot of flexibility when creating *ipfw* rules manually, but just about everything not already mentioned is beyond the scope of this text. See the *ipfw* manpage or Google for more information.

To delete rules from the active rule set, use the following command, where 2000 is the number of the rule to be deleted:

```
sudo ipfw delete 2000
```

One problem with using *ipfw* to add rules from the command line is that the rule is not stored in the *ipfw* configuration on disk, so the next time the firewall is reloaded, this rule is no longer enforced. In order to make rules added in this manner stick, they should also be added to the */etc/ipfilter/ipfw.conf* file. Any rules defined in this file are loaded as part of the normal firewall reload process. Placing rules in this file is the recommend method for integrating traditionally formatted *ipfw* rules into Mac OS X Server's Firewall configuration.

There is another way to add *ipfw* rules from the command line that utilizes the underrated *serveradmin* command-line tool. *serveradmin* is great for many reasons, although in the case of the firewall service, it's actually much more difficult to create or modify rules using *serveradmin* than it is to use traditional command-line methods.

Like the GUI Server Admin, using *serveradmin* to manage the firewall also causes a full firewall reload. Another drawback is that a lot more typing is required than the traditional method. On the plus side, rules added via *serveradmin* are stored in the firewall configuration on disk, so they'll stick beyond a reload, and will be visible in the Advanced pane of the Firewall settings in Server Admin. The steps required to add the rule in the previous example are as follows:

```
andre@core[~] sudo serveradmin settings
ipfilter:rules:_array_id:2000 = create
ipfilter:rules:_array_id:2000:action = "deny"
ipfilter:rules:_array_id:2000:protocol = "ip"
ipfilter:rules:_array_id:2000:source = "1.2.3.4"
ipfilter:rules:_array_id:2000:destination = "any"
ipfilter:rules:_array_id:2000:enabled = "yes"
^D
```

The array ID number (in this case, 2000) becomes the *ipfw* rule number used to determine the rule's position in the list. After hitting return on the last line, type Control-D. This command tells *serveradmin* that you're finished entering the rule, and then initiates the firewall reload process. The shell will appear to hang for some time while it waits for the *serveradmin* command to exit. This is the same delay encountered after clicking Save in Server Admin.

Some other useful attributes are log and readOnly, each of which can be set to either yes or no. readOnly cause the rule to appear in Server Admin as a nonmodifiable rule. Once a rule has been created in this manner, it is possible to change the values of individual keys. For example, to make the rule read-only:

```
sudo serveradmin settings
ipfilter:rules:_array_id:2000:readOnly = "yes"
^D
```

All the attributes of a rule managed by *serveradmin* can be retrieved as follows:

```
andre@core[~] sudo serveradmin settings ipfilter:rules:_array_id:2000
ipfilter:rules:_array_id:2000:source = "1.2.3.4"
ipfilter:rules:_array_id:2000:protocol = "ip"
ipfilter:rules:_array_id:2000:destination = "any"
ipfilter:rules:_array_id:2000:action = "deny"
ipfilter:rules:_array_id:2000:enabled = yes
ipfilter:rules:_array_id:2000:readOnly = yes
```

Rule Order

If your required firewall configuration can be supplied without leaving the General pane of Server Admin (which should be the case for most people if they are using the Firewall Service for its intended purpose), then the rule ordering is handled automatically. When adding rules via the Advanced pane or via the command line (using either *ipfw* or *serveradmin*), a rule number must be specified that determines the order in which the rule appears in the final rule set. The following is a list of the default rule numbers, and what each range is used for:

10
> Divert rule, if NAT is enabled.

1000 through 1030
> First four rules in Advanced pane (these rules were described previously).

1040 through x
> User-defined advanced rules. Drag and drop these rules if there is a need to control their order relative to other user-defined advanced rules.

12300 through x
> "Allow" rules, defined in the General pane that permit access to specific services.

63200 through 6553
> Read-only rules that appear at the bottom of the Advanced pane. According to the Network Services PDF (part of the server docs), other rules are added here as needed by specific services. For example, if a shared NetInfo domain is detected, a rule is added to allow access to port 111 via TCP and UDP.

The logic behind the rule ordering goes something like this (once again, remember that rules are evaluated in order, and the first match is the one that affects a packet): Start by diverting all packets to the *natd* program if NAT is enabled. Packets processed by *natd* are re-injected into the *ipfw* rule chain directly after the *natd* divert rule. Next, allow all local traffic. This rule appears early because there will be a lot of such traffic. Next are the anti-spoofing and broadcast control rules. After that come user-defined advanced rules, which are typically used to deny packets that would otherwise be allowed by a lower-priority rule. Then come the allow rules for specific services, as configured in the General pane. Finally, the read-only rules at the end close things up, mostly by denying incoming TCP connections in rule 65000. This step denies any incoming TCP connections not explicitly allowed by a higher-priority rule.

When creating rules manually, it's up to you to specify a rule number that makes sense. If it is a deny rule, make sure it appears before the rule that would otherwise allow the traffic, and vice versa. In general, try to keep rules that will match more frequently higher in the list. This strategy will decrease the average time it takes a packet to find a matching rule.

The order in which rules are loaded is also significant, and is in fact different from the order indicated by the rule numbers. *ipfw* allows for rules to be inserted at any rule number, in any order. The rules generated from the XML property list */etc/ipfilter/ip_address_groups.plist* are written to */etc/ipfilter/ipfw.conf.apple* in standard *ipfw* format and loaded into *ipfw* in the order they appear in the file. The first group of rules loaded are those defined in the General pane of the firewall settings, followed by the rules in the upper group of the Advanced pane (1000–1030), followed by the rules in the lower group of the Advanced pane (63200–65000), followed by any user-defined rules in the Advanced pane (if any), and finally the user-defined rules in */etc/ipfilter/ipfw.conf* (if any).

The key point is that the two sets of user-defined rules are loaded last. In the event that a malformed rule is encountered while the firewall is loading, it stops loading the remaining rules and an error is written to the system log. If the firewall was enabled before the reload began, it is re-enabled now. This load order ensures that even in the event of a problem rule, all but the remaining user-defined rules will still be in effect.

Configuration Examples

Here are some common scenarios in which you may need to employ the Firewall service, including instructions for configuring the firewall to meet the needs of that scenario.

Example 1

Scenario. The server has a public IP address and should allow incoming access only to services necessary for remote administration. All other incoming TCP connections should be dropped, and any sessions initiated from the server should be allowed.

Action. To enable the Firewall Service, open Server Admin, connect to the server, select the Firewall Service from the list on the left and click the "Start Service" button in the toolbar. Alternatively, from the command line, issue *sudo serveradmin start ipfilter*. The default firewall settings meet the needs of this scenario.

Example 2

Scenario. Same as Example 1, except that the server should also provide access to Apple File Service to any host that connects.

Action. With the Firewall Service selected in the "Computers and Services" list, click the Settings button near the bottom of the window, verify that the General pane is selected, click the "any" address group, and select the "Allow" checkbox for Apple File Service. Click Save. Alternatively, from the command line, add the following rule to the end of */etc/ipfilter/ipfw.conf*:

```
add 5000 allow tcp from any to any 548 in
```

Reload the firewall configuration with the command:

```
sudo serveradmin command ipfilter:command=reloadFW
```

Example 3

Scenario. Same as in Example 2, except that the server should also provide access to the Web Service only to hosts in the 216.231.59.1/24 network.

Action. In the General Settings pane, click the + button below the list of address groups to create a new address group. Name the group, then double-click the field that contains "any" and type 216.231.59.1/24, then click "OK." Verify that the new address group is selected in the IP address group list, then select the "Allow" checkbox for Web Service. Verify that Web Service is not allowed for the "any" address group and click Save. Alternatively, from the command line, add the following rule to *ipfw.conf* and then reload the firewall:

```
add 5010 allow tcp from 216.231.59.1/24 to any 80 in
```

Example 4

Scenario. Same as in Example 3, except the server should also deny access to the Apple File Service from hosts in the 192.168.0.0/16 network.

Action. Click the Advanced pane, then click the + button to begin adding a new Advanced rule. Set Action to Deny, Protocol to TCP, Service to Apple File Service, choose the 192.168-net address group from the Source Address menu, leave source port empty, set the Destination Address menu to "any," verify that Destination Port is set to 548, and leave Interface unset (the menu should be set to "Other..." and the field next to it should be empty). Click OK, select the "Enabled" checkbox for the new rule, then click Save. Alternatively, from the command line, add the following to rule *ipfw.conf* and reload the firewall:

```
add 5020 deny tcp from 192.168.0.0/16 to any 548 in
```

Example 5

Scenario. Same as Example 4, except that the server should also log all disallowed incoming TCP connection attempts.

Action. As *root*, open */etc/ipfilter/ip_address_groups.plist* with your favorite text editor. Search for the text 65000, which is the rule that denies incoming TCP connections. Find the log key in that rule's dictionary, and change the value from false to true. Save the file. Trigger a reload of the firewall using the following command:

```
sudo serveradmin command ipfilter:command=reloadFW
```

Enabling logging for rule 65000 can also be accomplished in one step via *serveradmin*, with this command, which automatically reloads the firewall:

```
sudo serveradmin settings ipfilter:rules:_array_id:65000:log = yes
```

Reporting and Monitoring

There are three primary outlets of information and status for the firewall: command-line tools like *ipfw* and *serveradmin*, the Overview pane in the Firewall Service in Server Admin, and the system log, */var/log/system.log*.

A list of the current firewall rules can be obtained with the following commands:

```
sudo ipfw list
sudo ipfw -t show
```

The second form also includes the number of matched packets and bytes for each rule, as well as the time stamp at which the rule was last matched. The contents of the Overview pane for the firewall service in Server Admin are roughly equivalent to *ipfw show*, but cannot be counted on to be entirely up to date, even when pounding the refresh button in the toolbar.

The *serveradmin* command is also useful for gathering information about the firewall, as is *sysctl*. Both of these commands return the on or off state of the firewall service:

```
sudo serveradmin status ipfilter
sudo sysctl net.inet.ip.fw.enable
```

The main system log, */var/log/system.log*, is used by the firewall for two purposes: to log messages about the firewall service as a whole, generated by the *servermgr_ipfilter* module of *servermgrd*, and also to log individual rules that are flagged for logging. The kernel generates rule log entries. It is good practice to follow the system log when working with the firewall:

```
tail -f /var/log/system.log
```

The Logging pane for the firewall service in Server Admin contains only a couple of items:

- The "Enable logging" checkbox is a master switch for rule logging only, and does not disable the log entries generated by *servermgrd*. Additionally, all allow or deny rule matches may be logged.

- The "Log only 1000 packets" field is for setting the maximum log threshold for each rule. Once the indicated number of matches has been made against a given rule, a message stating this fact is logged. No further packets matching that rule are logged until the firewall is reloaded.

Any rule changes made via Server Admin cause a reload (as would a reboot), though stopping and starting the service does not reset the log thresholds (as that does not reload the firewall). To manually reset the log thresholds (and counters) without making any rule changes, use the following command:

```
sudo ipfw zero
```

Managing the Firewall Service

The firewall service can be started and stopped in three ways: clicking the Start or Stop button for the firewall service in Server Admin, or by using either of the following two command-line methods:

```
sudo serveradmin start ipfilter
sudo serveradmin stop ipfilter

sudo sysctl -w net.inet.ip.fw.enable=1
sudo sysctl -w net.inet.ip.fw.enable=0
```

These last two methods are functionally equivalent (except that the *serveradmin* command is logged twice, once by *servermgrd* and once by *sudo*), and are aware of changes made by each other. Though rules may be added and removed while the firewall is disabled, they will not take effect. This *sysctl* kill switch enables the firewall to be turned on or off quickly because it does not require going through the firewall reload process.

The entire rule set can be flushed, returning the firewall to the default state where it allows all traffic—this approach bypasses *servermgrd*, and so does not affect the stored firewall configuration, which makes it only a temporary solution:

```
sudo ipfw flush
```

To manually a trigger a full firewall reload, use the following command:

```
sudo serveradmin command ipfilter:command=reloadFW
```

This initiates the chain of events detailed earlier in this chapter in "Configuring the Firewall from the Command Line," resulting in a synchronization of the in-kernel firewall state to the configuration stored on disk. Other *ipfilter*-specific *serveradmin* commands in addition to *reloadFW* include:

- *getStandardServices*, which returns the list of common services and protocols stored in the file */etc/ipfilter/standard_services.plist*.
- *getIPAddressGroups*, which returns all address groups and their configured rules, as well as the Advanced rules.
- *getLogPaths*, which displays the path to the log file.

Resetting the firewall service to factory defaults is also easy, because any missing configuration files will automatically be created from templates as the service starts. This is handled at boot time by the IPFilter startup item, and also by *servermgrd* whenever the *reloadFW* command is issued. The firewall can be reset to its default state using this small shell script:

```
#!/bin/sh
cd /etc/ipfilter
sudo rm ip_address_groups.plist ipfw.conf.apple \
ipfw.conf standard_services.plist
echo "firewall config whacked, reloading..."
sudo serveradmin command ipfilter:command=reloadFW
```

The entire Server Admin portion of the firewall configuration can be dumped and loaded in a couple ways—remember that this does not include rules defined in */etc/ipfilter/ipfw.conf* or rules declared manually with *ipfw*. From the GUI Server Admin, drag the tearoff icon at the bottom right corner of any Firewall Settings window to the Desktop. This saves an XML-formatted *plist* very similar to what is stored in */etc/ipfilter/ip_address_groups.plist*. To load the configuration back in, drag it into the Settings window from the Desktop.

 The command *sudo serveradmin settings ipfilter > fw_dump* creates a file that contains the same rule definitions. Due to the way that multi-value data structures are fed to *serveradmin*, this dump file is not suitable for re-importing, but could be used as a template to create such a file. See *serveradmin*'s manpage for more details.

Considerations for IPv6

None of this applies to IPv6, which is enabled by default in Mac OS X Server. All IPv6 traffic is accepted. If this default is a concern, you should disable IPv6 in the Network preference pane, or with the following command:

```
sudo networksetup -setv6off <networkservice>
```

<networkservice> is one of the items returned by *sudo networksetup –listallnetworkservices*. For example, *sudo networksetup –setv6off "Built-in Ethernet"* (note the quotes).

## CHAPTER 21

Virtual Private Networks

Virtual Private Networks (VPNs) allow remote users an incredible amount of freedom to utilize sensitive internal IT resources by creating an encrypted "tunnel" between the client machine and your local area network. While VPNs have been around for quite some time, they have just recently been approachable by any but the largest organizations, as they have usually involved a fair amount of complexity and extensive hardware or software requirements. Mac OS X Server solves a lot of those issues by providing industry-standard VPN solutions that can used by Macintosh, Windows, and Linux/Unix clients alike with a minimum effort.

One of the hardest part of truly understanding the concept of a VPN is distinguishing a VPN from other types of encrypted connections. Secure Shell (SSH) and Secure Socket Layer (SSL) are both common types of encrypting a specific connection between a client and a server, but they are not really examples of a VPN. Both fail the VPN definition on two accounts:

- Neither usually protects more than one connection. For example, when using SSL to protect your mail connection, you are only protecting that specific mail connection, not all mail connections and certainly not all traffic that your client is sending.

- SSH or SSL will not give the client machine a presence on the remote network. When using a VPN, a client machine actually receives an IP address that is local on the remote network.

Naturally, there are exceptions to both of these circumstances in which a VPN differs from SSH and SSL. Before PPTP become popular, many admins leveraged SSH's tunneling capabilities and tunneled a PPP connection through SSH. This method is very similar to using L2TP over IPSec. However, it couples the VPN to the SSH connection and allows users to connect over SSH, which may be a violation of a site's security policy. It is also not as robust as L2TP over IPSec, as it is primarily designed for host-to-host connections, rather than network-to-network connections.

A PPP-over-SSH VPN is usually a home-grown solution, as few firewall and software vendors implement it. However, Apple used PPP over SSH for their own VPN solution when OS X was first released since there were no other VPN clients available for the platform.

Another type of VPN that is more common with commercial applications is to use SSL to tunnel a PPP connection. Some implementations of this aren't really a VPN but are really an SSL-secured web-based virtual desktop. This type of VPN is easier to get through network firewalls, as it uses the normal HTTPS port (443) to communicate. OpenVPN, *http://openvpn.sourceforge.net*, is an example of this type of VPN.

VPN Protocols

Mac OS X Server supports two major VPN standards: PPTP and L2TP over IPSec (L2TP/IPSec). Both enjoy extensive client-side support and both offer a relatively high level of confidence from a security perspective. Each must be examined in some depth in order to determine which is most appropriate for any organization.

PPTP

PPTP or Point-to-Point Tunneling Protocol, which works by encrypting a standard serial PPP connection between the client and the server, is the older of the two protocols and is being phased out in many locations in favor of newer standards.

Much like a dial-up PPP connection, this method gives the client an IP address in the server's LAN, allowing the client to be a part of the LAN security policies, as opposed to a remote connection coming in from the Internet.

PPTP was heavily promoted by Microsoft when Windows NT Server was released. However, over the years, a number of security flaws were discovered in this protocol. PPTP also commonly used rather weak encryption algorithms, or even none at all! Recently, though, all known flaws with PPTP have been overcome. It is still not the most secure VPN by any means, but if you maintain 128-bit encryption, it will

---

provide significant protection for you client connections from all but the most determined of attackers.

PPTP, being the older protocol, is sometimes your only choice, as your client machines are not recent enough to support newer protocols. In addition to clients, you may also need to support PPTP since some older network equipment will only support it too.

L2TP over IPSec

L2TP over IPSec is the more advanced protocol, but also requires a more robust network and more modern operating system. It is based off of the Internet Protocol Security (IPSec) suite that is part of the IPv6 standard.

IPSec is incredibly complicated to support. In an effort to make it as flexible as possible, a number of different options have been added to make it be robust enough to survive years of use. One downside of this flexibility is authentication—there is no built-in standard way of authenticating a specific user. Instead, the suite simply provides a way of setting up an encrypted connection. Determining whether a client machine is authorized to use that connection is beyond IPSec's scope. Many current IPSec implementations, including Cisco VPNs, use a mechanism called *xauth* to verify a client's credentials. *xauth* is an extension to the IPSec protocol and has not been ratified by the working group yet. As such, the IPSec stack in OS X, which is based off of the Kame IPv6 implementation (*http://www.kame.net*) does not support the *xauth* extension.

To get around this and still allow client authentication, Microsoft and Apple have decided to use an L2TP connection, which wraps a point-to-point protocol (PPP) connection to provide the client authentication. So, think of L2TP/IPSec as a heavily encrypted layer around a very common and unsecured PPP connection. This approach, known as L2TP/IPSec, has been ratified by the IETF (Internet Engineering Task Force) and has achieved a high level of acceptance in the market.

This is an important concept to keep in mind as you are viewing the IPSec settings in Mac OS X. The default configuration will happily allow any correctly configured remote system to successfully negotiate a secure IPSec connection. Once that connection is established, the client must then successfully authenticate to the L2TP service, which would normally be an unencrypted protocol.

L2TP/IPSec is fully supported on Mac OS X and Mac OS X Server and v10.3. Windows machines as of Windows 2000 or newer also support this connection type. Recently a number of hardware and software vendors have followed Microsoft's lead and begun supporting this particular implementation of IPSec as well.

Server Configuration

All graphical VPN configurations for Mac OS X Server are accomplished through the VPN module of Server Admin. The Overview tab (pictured in Figure 21-1) shows you what VPN types are enabled and whether the service is running. It also tells you what types of VPNs your server is currently configured to support and how many current connections there are for each type.

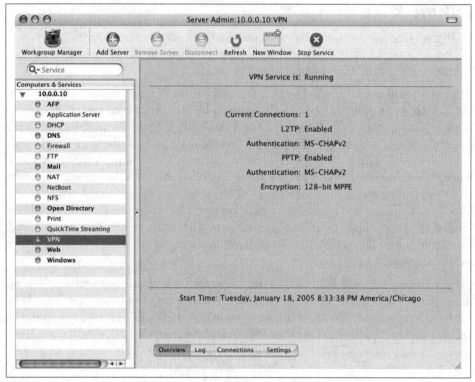

Figure 21-1. The Overview screen for Server Admin's VPN module.

The Log viewer (Figure 21-2) shows you the log found at */Library/Logs/VPNService*, which contains messages from */var/log/ppp/vpnd.log*. As is typical of logs made available via Server Admin, this interface is subject to *servermgrd*'s HTTP request-response cycle, and does not scale to support truly busy servers.

The Connections tab (Figure 21-3) enumerates all currently connected VPN clients. You'll be able to see whether the client is using PPTP or L2TP/IPSec, what internal IP address the client was given, and how long the client has been connected.

This same data is available using the *serveradmin* command's *getConnectedUsers* flag, as with other services; for example:

```
serveradmin command vpn:command = getConnectedUsers
```

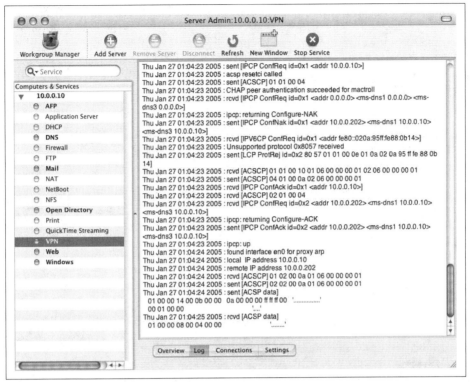

Figure 21-2. The Log view of the VPN module of Server Admin.

There is no way to disconnect a specific client without shutting down the entire service and disconnecting all clients.

The Settings section of the VPN module reveals three further tabs (General, Logging and Client Information), allowing you to specify how your VPN connections are setup. Its General tab, seen in Figure 21-4, contains global settings for both PPTP and L2TP/IPSec services. Although they're located in the same graphical interface, the settings for the two services mutually are exclusive, and don't really affect each other.

Configuring L2TP/IPSec

Checking the "Enable L2TP over IPSec" box launches *raccoon* (the IPSec daemon supplied by the Kame suite, which Apple leverages to supply L2TP services) and an instance of *vpnd* with the *–i com.apple.ppp.l2tp* flag. Since *vpnd* is used for both the L2TP/IPSec and PPTP VPNs, the *–i* flag determines which part of the configuration

Figure 21-3. The Connections screen of the VPN module of Server Admin.

file it uses and as such determines whether it is a L2TP/IPSec or PPTP instance of *vpnd*.

The General tab of the Settings pane of the Server Admin VPN module (see Figure 21-4) allows you to enable and configure general settings for both L2TP/IPSec and PPTP VPNs. To restrict access to the L2TP VPN to a specific group, you can use the Users and Groups button to expose your available groups and then drag that group over to the field, or you can type the group in manually. After enabling L2TP over IPSec you must supply a *shared secret*. This "secret" is used by any L2TP client as it establishes an IPSec connection through which the L2TP connection is tunneled. This secret—since it must be shared by every user connecting via L2TP—is not really a secret, and does not necessarily need to be treated with the same care as an actual user password.

It is feasible to preconfigure the VPN configuration of highly managed Mac OS X clients, so that the IPSec shared secret does not have to be known by every user in an organization. Be aware, however, that this measure is largely obfuscation, and anyone with local access and sufficient motivation will be able to retrieve it.

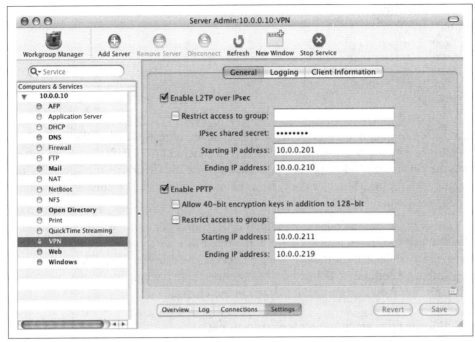

Figure 21-4. The General tab of the Settings pane of the VPN module in Server Admin.

The secret is stored in the System keychain *(/Library/Keychains/System.keychain)*, and you can view it (once it is set) by using either the Keychain Access utility or the *security* command, as shown in Example 21-1. There is no flag to the security command allowing for a more granular analysis of the system keychain, so the output of the command on your system might have more entries.

Example 21-1. Using the security command to retrieve the IPSec shared secret from the System keychain.

```
[ace2:~] nadmin% sudo security dump-keychain -d
keychain: "/Library/Keychains/System.keychain"
class: "genp"
attributes:
    0x00000007 <blob>="com.apple.net.racoon"
    0x00000008 <blob>=<NULL>
    "acct"<blob>="com.apple.ppp.l2tp"
    "cdat"<timedate>=0x32303034303932333033333730375A00  "20040923033707Z\000"
    "crtr"<uint32>=<NULL>
    "cusi"<sint32>=<NULL>
    "desc"<blob>=<NULL>
    "gena"<blob>=<NULL>
    "icmt"<blob>=<NULL>
    "invi"<sint32>=<NULL>
    "mdat"<timedate>=0x32303034303932333033333730375A00  "20040923033707Z\000"
    "nega"<sint32>=<NULL>
```

```
    "prot"<blob>=<NULL>
    "scrp"<sint32>=<NULL>
    "svce"<blob>="com.apple.net.racoon"
    "type"<uint32>=<NULL>
data:
"apple"
```

You'll need to supply a range of IP addresses to be used by the L2TP clients. This range must not be in use by any other service, including DHCP. The VPN server gives the clients an IP address from that list, allowing the clients a virtual presence on the server's network. There can only be as many concurrent L2TP clients as you have IP addresses in this range.

The rest of the settings in this tab pertain to PPTP connections and will be covered later. The changes you make in the GUI are all stored in *vpnd*'s preference file (*/Library/ Preferences/SystemConfiguration/com.apple.RemoteAccessServers.plist*). Because *vpnd* is responsible for both L2TP/IPSec and PPTP services, both configurations may be located in this file. PPTP options are discussed later in this chapter.

L2TP/IPSec and com.apple.RemoteAccessServers.plist

The best way to understand precisely how *vpnd* works is to undertake a careful and thorough analysis of its configuration file. For this, we'll use the *cat* command to peer inside the *com.apple.RemoteAccessServers.plist* file:

```
bitey:/Library/Preferences/SystemConfiguration root# cat com.apple.
RemoteAccessServers.plist

        <key>Servers</key>
        <dict>
                <key>com.apple.ppp.l2tp</key>
                This key starts the L2TP/IPSec section.
                <dict>
                        <key>DNS</key>
```

The DNS search domains and DNS servers given to the client are specified in the `OfferedSearchDomains` and `OfferedSearchAddresses` keys:

```
                        <dict>
                                <key>OfferedSearchDomains</key>
                                <array/>
                                <key>OfferedServerAddresses</key>
                                <array>
                                        <string>10.99.37.26</string>
                                </array>
                        </dict>
```

This key sets what group is allowed to use the L2TP/IPSec VPN; in this example, no groups are specified:

```
<key>DSACL</key>
<dict>
        <key>Group</key>
            <string></string>
</dict>
<key>IPv4</key>
<dict>
        <key>ConfigMethod</key>
        <string>Manual</string>
        <key>DestAddressRanges</key>
```

This section is the range of IP addresses that L2TP clients receive on a first-come, first-serve basis:

```
<array>
        <string>10.99.37.40</string>
        <string>10.99.37.49</string>
</array>
<key>OfferedRouteAddresses</key>
```

The OfferedRouteAddresses section defines a private route for the VPN clients (discussed later):

```
<array>
        <string>10.99.37.0</string>
</array>
<key>OfferedRouteMasks</key>
<array>
        <string>255.255.255.0</string>
</array>
<key>OfferedRouteTypes</key>
<array>
        <string>Private</string>
</array>
</dict>
```

This dictionary indicates what type of interface to generate for this connection. As you can see, the heart of an L2TP VPN is a PPP connection:

```
<key>Interface</key>
<dict>
        <key>SubType</key>
        <string>L2TP</string>
        <key>Type</key>
        <string>PPP</string>
</dict>
<key>L2TP</key>
```

This section defines the entry in the System keychain that holds the L2TP shared secret, as entered in Server Admin:

```
<dict>
    <key>IPSecSharedSecret</key>
        <string>com.apple.ppp.l2tp</string>
        <key>IPSecSharedSecretEncryption</key>
        <string>Keychain</string>
```

```
                            <key>Transport</key>
                            <string>IPSec</string>
                    </dict>
                    <key>PPP</key>
```

Basic PPP settings to define PPP authentication and compression:

```
                    <dict>
                            <key>ACSPEnabled</key>
                            <integer>1</integer>
                            <key>AuthenticatorPlugins</key>
                            <array>
                                    <string>DSAuth</string>
                            </array>
                            <key>AuthenticatorProtocol</key>
                            <array>
                                    <string>MSCHAP2</string>
                            </array>
                            <key>IPCPCompressionVJ</key>
                            <integer>0</integer>
                            <key>LCPEchoEnabled</key>
                            <integer>1</integer>
                            <key>LCPEchoFailure</key>
                            <integer>5</integer>
                            <key>LCPEchoInterval</key>
                            <integer>60</integer>
                            <key>Logfile</key>
                            <string>/var/log/ppp/vpnd.log</string>
                            <key>VerboseLogging</key>
                            <integer>1</integer>
                            <key>_UI_DSACLEnabled</key>
                            <false/>
                    </dict>
                    <key>Server</key>
```

General VPN server configuration, including which file to log to and the maximum number of concurrent VPN connections:

```
                    <dict>
                            <key>Logfile</key>
                            <string>/var/log/ppp/vpnd.log</string>
                            <key>MaximumSessions</key>
                            <integer>128</integer>
                            <key>VerboseLogging</key>
                            <integer>1</integer>
                    </dict>
            </dict>
```

racoon.conf

The actual IPSec configuration is handled mainly in two files: */etc/racoon/racoon.conf* and */etc/racoon/remote/anonymous.conf*. The first, *racoon.conf*, defines a number of basic IPSec configurations. While you can make changes here, there is little reason that you would want to do so. Primarily, this file is used to establish basic server settings:

```
# $KAME: racoon.conf.in,v 1.17 2001/08/14 12:10:22 sakane Exp $

# "path" must be placed before it should be used.
# You can overwrite which you defined, but it should not use due
# too confusing.
path include "/etc/racoon" ;
```

The include statement here allows third-party utilities to add their own connection settings into */etc/racoon/remote/* without needing to worry about Server Admin changing them. However, since Server Admin configures the "anonymous" configuration, all third-party configurations must specify IP addresses of the clients for the configuration to be used.

```
# Allow third parties the ability to specify remote and
# sainfo entries by including all files matching
# /etc/racoon/remote/*.conf
include "/etc/racoon/remote/*.conf" ;
```

The path pre_shared_key setting, as its name implies, determines the path to the *pre-shared key* (PSK) file. In most instances of *racoon*, this is where the PSK is stored in plain text. Starting with 10.3, Apple enabled *racoon* to use the System keychain; as mentioned earlier, it can be viewed (given the proper authorization) using the *security* command or with Keychain Access.

```
# search this file for pre_shared_key with various ID key.
path pre_shared_key "/etc/racoon/psk.txt" ;
```

The *path* certificate directive determines where your x509 certificates are stored. IPSec, as configured through Server Admin, uses the pre-shared key (instead of certificates) to authorize users to set up an encrypted connection. Using certificates for L2TP/IPSec connections requires deviating from the Apple GUI on both Mac OS X Server and client, as you'll need to reconfigure the *pppd* daemon, a procedure that is not recommended for any but the most hardened of admins. Hopefully Apple will include support for L2TP/IPSec certificates in future releases of Mac OS X Server.

```
# racoon looks for the certificate file in the directory,
# if the certificate/certificate request payload is received.
path certificate "/etc/cert" ;
```

The log setting specifies which messages should be sent to *syslogd*, which is discussed more in Chapter 5:

```
# "log" specifies logging level.  It is followed by either
# "notify", "debug", or "debug2".
#log debug;
```

Padding allows the packet's payload to be a multiple of the bit level of the encryption, and should not generally be modified:

```
# "padding" defines some parameter of padding.
# You should not touch these.
```

```
padding
{
        maximum_length 20;      # maximum padding length.
        randomize off;          # enable randomize length.
        strict_check off;       # enable strict check.
        exclusive_tail off;     # extract last one octet.
}
```

The listen directive determines what interfaces you want *racoon* to listen on. It's conceivable that you would want to limit this list to just the public interfaces on your server, specifically the interface you have designated for VPN traffic. Having *racoon* listen on other interfaces poses little security risk, since you need to be both encrypted and authenticated to connect. However, some admins may feel that the mere presence of a listener on that port gives too much information away to possible attackers.

```
# if no listen directive is specified, racoon will listen to all
# available interface addresses.
Listen

{
        #isakmp ::1 [7000];
        #isakmp 202.249.11.124 [500];
        #admin [7002];          # administrative's port by kmpstat.
        #strict_address;        # required all addresses must be bound.
}
```

The "timer" block establishes some basic timeouts used by *racoon*. The counter and interval options determine how many times—separated by the count—*racoon* will attempt to connect to a remote system. Since clients are connecting to your server, rather than the reverse, this setting is rather irrelevant on the server.

The phase1 and phase2 timeouts specify how long *racoon* will attempt to get the two phases of IPSec running. The 30-second default setting should be more than enough for almost all situations.

```
# Specification of default various timer.
Timer

{
        # These value can be changed per remote node.
        counter 10;             # maximum trying count to send.
        interval 3 sec;  # interval to resend (retransmit)
        persend 1;              # the number of packets per a send.

        # timer for waiting to complete each phase.
        phase1 30 sec;
        phase2 30 sec;
}
```

With the exception of the sample IPv6 configuration, the rest of the *racoon.conf* file has been commented out. The IPv6 configuration establishes policies for connecting to the server on the IPv6 loopback address ::1. The IPv4 configuration is stored in the *anonymous.conf* file (located in */etc/racoon/remote*). If you have need to support IPv6 clients, you should create a new configuration file—specific to their connection—in */etc/racoon/remote*.

```
# anonymous entry is defined in /etc/racoon/remote/anonymous.conf
#
#remote anonymous
#{
#        #exchange_mode main,aggressive;
#        exchange_mode aggressive,main;
#        doi ipsec_doi;
#        situation identity_only;
#
#        #my_identifier address;
#        my_identifier user_fqdn "macuser@localhost";
#        peers_identifier user_fqdn "macuser@localhost";
#        #certificate_type x509 "mycert" "mypriv";
#
#        nonce_size 16;
#        lifetime time 1 min;     # sec,min,hour
#        initial_contact on;
#        support_mip6 on;
#        proposal_check obey;     # obey, strict or claim
#
#        proposal {
#                encryption_algorithm 3des;
#                hash_algorithm sha1;
#                authentication_method pre_shared_key ;
#                dh_group 2 ;
#        }
#}

remote ::1 [8000]
{
        #exchange_mode main,aggressive;
        exchange_mode aggressive,main;
        doi ipsec_doi;
        situation identity_only;

        my_identifier user_fqdn "macuser@localhost";
        peers_identifier user_fqdn "macuser@localhost";
        #certificate_type x509 "mycert" "mypriv";

        nonce_size 16;
        lifetime time 1 min;     # sec,min,hour

        proposal {
                encryption_algorithm 3des;
                hash_algorithm sha1;
                authentication_method pre_shared_key ;
```

```
                dh_group 2 ;
        }
}

#
# anonymous entry is defined in /etc/racoon/remote/anonymous.conf
#
#sainfo anonymous
#{
#        pfs_group 1;
#        lifetime time 30 sec;
#        encryption_algorithm aes, 3des ;
#        authentication_algorithm hmac_sha1;
#        compression_algorithm deflate ;
#}

# sainfo address 203.178.141.209 any address 203.178.141.218 any
# {
#        pfs_group 1;
#        lifetime time 30 sec;
#        encryption_algorithm des ;
#        authentication_algorithm hmac_md5;
#        compression_algorithm deflate ;
# }

sainfo address ::1 icmp6 address ::1 icmp6
{
        pfs_group 1;
        lifetime time 60 sec;
        encryption_algorithm 3des, cast128, blowfish 448, des ;
        authentication_algorithm hmac_sha1, hmac_md5 ;
        compression_algorithm deflate ;
}
```

anonymous.conf

The *anonymous.conf* file configures all incoming connections that have not already been explicitly listed by IP address or x509 certificate in other configuration files. In a default configuration, this description includes all incoming L2TP/IPSec connections, and you'll never have another configuration.

The remote block establishes all the settings for phase1 of the IPSec connection. During phase1, public key infrastructure (PKI) is used to establish the identity of the two machines and to securely negotiate the symmetric cipher used in phase2.

    remote anonymous

The exchange_mode determines phase1's exchange mode:

- aggressive mode is slightly faster, fewer packets, but sends the identifier in the clear as the encryption has not been set up yet.

- main mode takes more packets, but takes greater care in protecting the identifier:

```
{
exchange_mode main;
```

The `lifetime time` determines the time-out for setting up the `phase1` connection between the client and the server. `phase1` is used only to begin the IPSec connection; once the connection is established, `phase2` settings are used.

```
doi ipsec_doi;
situation identity_only;
shared_secret keychain "com.apple.ppp.l2tp";
nonce_size 16;
lifetime time 3600 sec;
```

When set to `obey`, the server acquiesces to the settings for `phase2` timeouts and algorithms proposed by the client. A setting of `strict` causes the server to reject timeouts proposed by the client if they are longer than the server has been configured for. Also, the server will reject the connection if the proposed algorithms are not accepted by the server's configuration.

`claim` attempts to negotiate a timeout between the two systems using the shorter of the two times. The algorithms proposed by the client, however, must still be accepted by the server's configuration.

```
initial_contact on;
support_mip6 on;
proposal_check claim;
```

The `proposal` block determines the `phase1` settings that will be used to securely negotiate the `phase2` connection between the client and the server. The algorithm is defaulted to `3des`, or triple-DES, which is a secure encryption type. The *hash* algorithm defaults to `sha1`, a very modern hashing algorithm and the highest encryption hash-type supported by *racoon*. The *authentication_method* is set to `pre_shared_key`, as opposed to `rsasig`, which would denote the use of x509 certificates.

Finally `dh_group` sets up which Diffie-Hellman exchange type to use. Groups 1, 2, and 5 are available. These groups correspond to modp768, modp1024 and modp1536, respectively. The higher the number, the more secure the exchange. However, keep in mind that more computational power is used as the number increases. Group 2 is generally the most common group you'll see being used. If you have specified the `aggressive` mode, both the server and client must have this setting configured the same. Otherwise the two will attempt to negotiate a group.

```
proposal {

encryption_algorithm 3des;
hash_algorithm sha1;
authentication_method pre_shared_key;
dh_group 2;
}
}
sainfo anonymous
```

The final configuration block completes *racoon*'s phase2 configuration:

```
{
lifetime time 3600 sec;
encryption_algorithm aes, 3des;
authentication_algorithm hmac_sha1, hmac_md5;
compression_algorithm deflate;
}
```

A number of directives can affect phase2's behavior, including:

- pfs_group is similar to the dh_group for phase1; it establishes the phase2 Diffie-Hellman exchange mechanism.

- This lifetime time determines how long phase2 uses the same key. The default on Mac OS X is 3,600 seconds, which means that the entire phase2 connection between the client and server is rekeyed every 60 minutes. Anyone who was able to decipher your VPN communication would have to start from scratch whenever this timeout occurs.

- encryption_algorithm is similar to the encryption algorithm for phase1, but is used only in phase2. As with all settings in phase2, you are able to supply multiple types supported by your machine. Mac OS X uses the Advanced Encryption Standard (AES, a 128-bit algorithm) and 3des again here. This is the algorithm that defines phase2's *encapsulated security payload* (ESP), which actually encrypts the packets.

- authentication_algorithm is similar to the authentication algorithm being used in phase1. This is used for the *authentication header* (AH) settings to certify that the packets are coming from either the client or the server. This setting prevents man-in-the-middle attacks.

- The compression_algorithm directive enables the client and server to compress their communications. This directive is similar to use of the –C flag with an SSH connection.

The Connection Process

When an L2TP client initially connects to the server, an IPSec connection is made on port 500, using protocol 50 (ESP), to the server where *racoon* is listening.

As soon as communication has been secured by IPSec, the *vpnd* process (running with the *–i com.apple.ppp.l2tp* flag to specify it as the L2TP/IPSec server) spawns a *pppd* process to handle the actual PPP connection.

Configuring PPTP

PPTP configuration is very similar to the L2TP setup. You are able to enable or disable the PPTP service by checking or unchecking the "Enable PPTP" box in the General tab of the VPN module of Server Admin (Figure 21-5). When you enable the PPTP server, an instance of *vpnd* is launched with the *–i com.apple.ppp.pptp* flag, listening on port 1723. (If both PPTP and L2TP/IPSec are enabled, then two instances of *vpnd* will be running.)

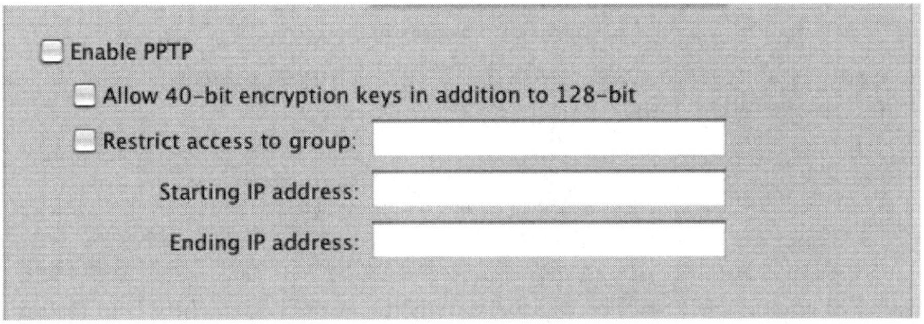

Figure 21-5. The PPTP portion of Server Admin's General VPN settings.

Next, you are given the option to permit 40-bit encryption. PPTP usually uses a 128-bit SHA key to encrypt sensitive data; however, you won't need this unless you are using older clients that can't support the 128-bit key by default. PPTP access may also be granted to a specific group, which is again very similar to the L2TP configuration.

The changes you make in Server Admin are stored in the *vpnd* preference file (*/Library/Preferences/SystemConfiguration/com.apple.RemoteAccessServers.plist*). Changes for specific PPTP connections appear under the *com.apple.ppp.pptp* key.

```
<key>com.apple.ppp.pptp</key>
```

DNS settings for the VPN clients are stored in the `OfferedSearchDomains` and `OfferedSearchAddresses` keys. These are setup in the Client Information settings in Server Admin's VPN module. By default, these keys are the same as for the L2TP/IPSec clients.

```
                    <dict>
                            <key>DNS</key>
        <dict>

                                    <key>OfferedSearchDomains</key>
                                    <array/>
                                    <key>OfferedServerAddresses</key>
                                    <array>
                                            <string>10.99.37.26</string>
                                    </array>
                            </dict>
```

The group, if any has been specified, that's authorized to use the PPTP VPN is specified in the DSACL key:

```
                <key>DSACL</key>
    <dict>
                    <key>Group</key>
                    <string></string>
        </dict>
        <key>IPv4</key>
        <dict>
                    <key>ConfigMethod</key>
                    <string>Manual</string>
                    <key>DestAddressRanges</key>
```

The IP address range to be used for the PPTP client's virtual presence on the server's network may be found in the DestAddressRanges key:

```
            <array>
                    <string>10.99.37.50</string>
                    <string>10.99.37.59</string>
            </array>
            <key>OfferedRouteAddresses</key>
```

A listing of any private or public routing statements as defined in the Client Information settings in Server Admin:

```
            <array>
                    <string>10.99.37.0</string>
            </array>
            <key>OfferedRouteMasks</key>
            <array>
                    <string>255.255.255.0</string>
            </array>
            <key>OfferedRouteTypes</key>
            <array>
                    <string>Private</string>
            </array>
        </dict>
        <key>Interface</key>
        <dict>
                    <key>SubType</key>
                    <string>PPTP</string>
                    <key>Type</key>
                    <string>PPP</string>
        </dict>
        <key>PPP</key>
```

These settings determine the PPP configuration. They specify that MSCHAPv2 will be used for authentication and that MPEE will be used for encryption. Many of these options are passed to the *pppd* daemon when it is spawned by *vpnd* during the PPTP connection process:

```
        <dict>
                    <key>ACSPEnabled</key>
                    <integer>1</integer>
```

```
                              <key>AuthenticatorPlugins</key>
                              <array>
                                    <string>DSAuth</string>
                              </array>
                              <key>AuthenticatorProtocol</key>
                              <array>
                                    <string>MSCHAP2</string>
                              </array>
                              <key>CCPEnabled</key>
                              <integer>1</integer>
                              <key>CCPProtocols</key>
                              <array>
                                    <string>MPPE</string>
                              </array>
                              <key>IPCPCompressionVJ</key>
                              <integer>0</integer>
                              <key>LCPEchoEnabled</key>
                              <integer>1</integer>
                              <key>LCPEchoFailure</key>
                              <integer>5</integer>
                              <key>LCPEchoInterval</key>
                              <integer>60</integer>
```

The logfile that the PPP service sends information to is specified in the Logfile key:

```
                              <key>Logfile</key>
                              <string>/var/log/ppp/vpnd.log</string>
```

The setting of 1 means that 128-bit keys are enabled:

```
                              <key>MPPEKeySize128</key>
                              <integer>1</integer>
```

while a setting of 0 means that 40-bit keys are not enabled:

```
                              <key>MPPEKeySize40</key>
                              <integer>0</integer>
                              <key>VerboseLogging</key>
                              <integer>1</integer>
                              <key>_UI_DSACLEnabled</key>
                              <false/>
                        </dict>
                        <key>Server</key>
                        <dict>
                              <key>Logfile</key>
                              <string>/var/log/ppp/vpnd.log</string>
```

The logfile used by the PPTP server:

```
                              <key>MaximumSessions</key>
                              <integer>128</integer>
```

The maximum number of concurrent PPTP connections is noted in the VerboseLogging key:

```
                              <key>VerboseLogging</key>
                              <integer>1</integer>
```

```
                    </dict>
              </dict>
        </dict>
```

MPEE

PPTP uses Microsoft Point-to-Point Encryption (MPEE, a Microsoft-developed encryption protocol) to protect the underlying PPP connection. The encryption key for PPTP is based on a hash of the user's password. To create this hash, the *vpnd* server needs access to the user's MSCHAPv2 hash, which is stored in the Password Server. Usually the Password Server does not allow the hash to be given out since having the hash makes cracking the password much easier. To get around this, Apple has created the MPEE user, which can retrieve the hash from the Password Server.

If you use the *pwpolicy* command to get the MPEE user's password policy, you'll find it has a isSessionKeyAgent=1 flag set, as shown here:

```
bitey:~ mactroll$ pwpolicy -u vpn_000d939c1aac -getpolicy
isDisabled=0 isAdminUser=0 newPasswordRequired=0 usingHistory=0
canModifyPasswordforSelf=1 usingExpirationDate=0 usingHardExpirationDate=0
requiresAlpha=0 requiresNumeric=0 expirationDateGMT=12/31/69 hardExpireDateGMT=12/31/
69 maxMinutesUntilChangePassword=0 maxMinutesUntilDisabled=0 maxMinutesOfNonUse=0
maxFailedLoginAttempts=0 minChars=0 maxChars=0 passwordCannotBeName=0
isSessionKeyAgent=1
```

The *vpnd* server, which runs as *root*, has access to the MPEE user's password, which is stored in the System keychain (*/Library/Keychains/System.keychain*, the same location that the IPSec shared secret is kept). After authenticating the incoming connection, the *vpnd* server authenticates as the MPEE user to the Password Server and retrieves the VPN user's MSCHAPv2 hash. From this it computes the MPEE encryption algorithm for the user and proceeds to encrypt the PPTP connection.

An MPEE user needs to be in the directory domain that your VPN user is. For example, to support LDAP users authenticating to the VPN server, you'll need an MPEE user in the LDAP domain as well. The MPEE user is in the local NetInfo domain by default; however, in systems that have been upgraded from early versions of 10.3, you might not have an MPEE user in your LDAP domain. If that's the case, you'll need to run the following command to add the user to the LDAP database on your server:

```
sudo /usr/sbin/vpnaddkeyagentuser /LDAPv3/127.0.0.1
```

You will also need to use this command if your users are hosted in an LDAP domain on another server. Use the same command, but target the other LDAP node.

> ## The PPTP Connection Process
>
> When a PPTP client connects, it establishes a connection to port 1723, using protocol 47 (GRE) on the server where the PPTP instance of *vpnd* is listening. *vpnd* then spawns a *pppd* process to handle the actual connection, and then goes back to listening for new, incoming PPTP connections.

Logging

Server Admin's Logging tab (Figure 21-6) allows you to enable or disable verbose logging. Again you can use the "Log" tab at the bottom to view the log, which defaults to */var/log/ppp/vpnd.log*.

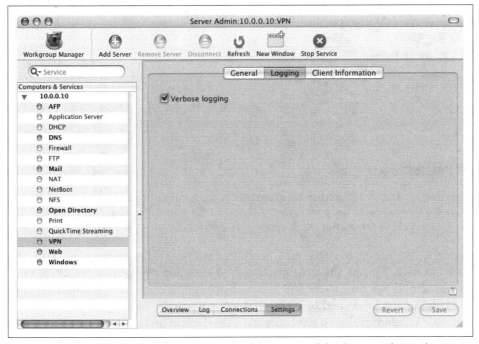

Figure 21-6. The Logging tab of the Settings pane of the VPN module of Server Admin. There isn't much to see here, but verbose logging can be instrumental when troubleshooting connection problems.

Client Information

Because both L2TP and PPTP clients have a virtual presence on your server's LAN, they'll need DNS information supplied to them. You are able to enter multiple DNS servers and search domains, which will be used by the clients after they have made the VPN connection. All this is done through the Client Information pane of Server Admin's VPN module, as shown in Figure 21-7.

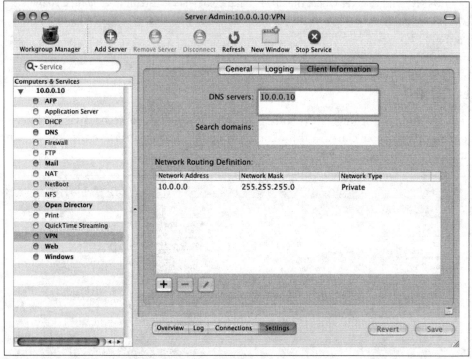

Figure 21-7. The Client Information tab of the Settings pane of the VPN module in Server Admin allows you to set up public and private routing definitions for your VPN clients. You can also specify here the DNS servers and search domains the clients will use.

Once the connection is established, the client uses the VPN connection as its primary interface. This means that by default, all outgoing traffic from the client goes through the VPN tunnel to the VPN server before going out to the Internet. In many cases, this is not the desired behavior. Instead, it would be more appropriate—and a better use of bandwidth—to send only traffic to the remote LAN through the VPN.

The "Network Routing Definition" box allows you to customize this behavior. Keep in mind that the routing information you specify here is applied globally to all clients coming in over either VPN type.

There are two possible types of routing statements here, public and private:

- A *private network* forces all traffic going to that network through the VPN connection. By default the whole Internet is installed as a private network. However, many people choose to specify just their internal LAN as a private network, allowing all other traffic to go across the normal connection method the client has already established.

- A *public network* definition explicitly denies traffic going to that network from going across the VPN connection. Instead, traffic is sent to the Internet using whatever connection the client had established before it connected to the VPN.

To assign a private network definition, click the + button beneath the Network Routing Definition box, and then enter the network address and networkmask. Then use the pull-down menu to specify whether the connection is public or private.

 If you specify a private network, you do not need to specify the rest of the Internet as public. The VPN server tells the client to route all non-private traffic normally.

Internet Connect

Client machines use the Internet Connect application (located in the *Applications* folder of a default Mac OS X client install) to create VPN connections. Under the File menu in Internet Connect, select "Create a new VPN connection." You'll then have the option of setting up either an L2TP/IPSec or a PPTP VPN.

The default screen, shown in Figure 21-8, does not allow you to specify the shared secret for this connection. If you need to enter a shared secret, use the Configuration pull-down menu and select "Edit Configurations" at the bottom of the menu. Now you will be able to supply a descriptive name for the connection, the server's address (either IP address or FQDN), your username, your password (which is stored in the user's Keychain), and the L2TP/IPSec shared secret (which will also be stored in the user's Keychain).

Figure 21-8. Editing a configuration for an L2TP/IPSec connection in Internet connect allows you to specify the Shared Secret and other settings.

If you are using RSA SecurID tokens, you can specify RSA SecurID here. However, you must also enable the VPN server to use RSA SecurID. Refer to Apple's KBase (article 107699) for more information on this (*http://www.apple.com/support*).

The process of configuring a PPTP connection (shown in Figure 21-9) is very similar. Create a new PPTP connection instead of L2TP/IPSec when prompted. Again, use the Configuration pull-down menu to edit configurations. This allows you to specify a descriptive name, your VPN server's IP address or FQDN, your username, and password (which is stored in the user's Keychain), and your encryption type.

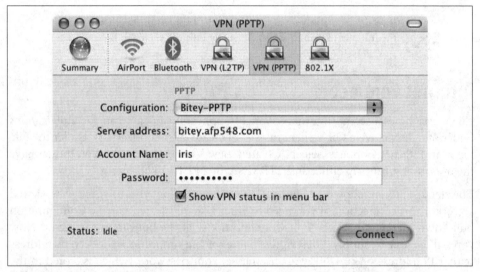

Figure 21-9. Setting up a PPTP connection in Internet Connect.

While setting the encryption type to Automatic should work in most cases, I have found that forcing it to 128-bit gives you the best security.

Once you have configured either type of VPN, you'll find a new entry in the Network Port Configuration of your Network preference pane. This entry allows the VPN to work and should not be deleted.

 To add additional VPN connections after the first one, don't use the "New VPN Connection" menu. Instead, just edit your current configuration and add a new configuration for the new VPN connection.

To connect to the VPN, just use the Connect button in Internet Connect. This moves the VPN configuration to the top of the Network Ports Configuration in the Network preference panel, and makes the connection to the VPN server.

You can make sure your connection worked by using the *netstat* command to check your client machine's routing table.

```
MacTrolls-Computer:~ mactroll$ netstat -rn
Routing tables

Internet:
Destination      Gateway              Flags  Refs       Use  Netif Expire
default          192.168.1.1          UGSc     25        22  en0
10.99.37/24      ppp0                 USc       1         0  ppp0
64.5.69.56       192.168.1.1          UGHS   1827      2237  en0
127              127.0.0.1            UCS       0         0  lo0
127.0.0.1        127.0.0.1            UH       17    181054  lo0
169.254          link#4               UCS       0         0  en0
192.168.1        link#4               UCS       2         0  en0
192.168.1.1      0:c:41:3c:be:5c      UHLW      8        17  en0    1127
192.168.1.10     127.0.0.1            UHS       1       174  lo0
192.168.1.19     127.0.0.1            UHS       0         0  lo0
192.168.1.255    ff:ff:ff:ff:ff:ff    UHLWb     0        32  en0
```

If the VPN connected successfully, you should see a *ppp0* connection and any private routes you supplied in the Client Information settings.

Other Considerations

Here are some additional thoughts to consider when it comes to Rendezvous networks, subnets, and authentication:

Rendezvous

When you make a VPN connection, you have a virtual *presence* on the remote network, but that is not enough for Rendezvous services. This means that iChat, iTunes music sharing, and other mDNS-based services won't be able to find each other. This is especially vexing when you are using Rendezvous to find your backup clients and would like your VPN users to be backed up. To compound this situation, there seems to be no easy way to assign a specific IP to a specific VPN user.

Subnets

It is important that you maintain unique private subnets between your VPN clients and your server. It is all too common for network administrators to use a 192.168.1.0/24 subnet for multiple locations. If your VPN client is on a local network that has the same numbering scheme as the remote VPN network, it won't be able to route through the VPN because the client will attempt to connect to the local side of the tunnel instead of the remote side.

When setting up your networks, it's a good idea to custom-configure your hardware network appliances to make sure that your subnets are unique. Remember that the 172.16.0.0/12 subnet range is reserved for private use, but is rarely used.

Authentication

Both the L2TP/IPSec and the PPTP VPNs use MSCHAPv2 for authentication to the *pppd* service. You won't be able to authenticate VPN users if they have either crypt or shadow hash passwords, or if you disable Password Server's MSCHAPv2 method using the NeST command.

A second authentication issue arises if you are accessing an Active Directory domain using Mac OS X's Active Directory Plug-in. The Active Directory plug-in uses either Kerberos or the *ntlm_auth* utility to authenticate users and does not support the MSCHAPv2 password hash required by *vpnd*. Therefore, you won't be able to use AD users with a Mac OS X Server–hosted VPN.

## PART VI

Internet Services

"Internet Services" refers to a loose grouping of functionality commonly deployed and available to users across the Internet. This isn't to say that these services (Mail, Web, and Java application deployment) aren't ever deployed within an organization; they commonly are. More than anything the terminology is historical in nature. In Mac OS X Server 10.0 and 10.1's Server Admin application, Mail and Web Services were grouped under the Internet Services tab. Java Application Services, because they are commonly deployed to support Web platforms, seemed like a good fit. My examination of Mac OS X Server has always followed Apple's organization as closely as possible, and the trend continues today. In general, though, Internet Services do have at least two things in common:

Internet Services typically deal with small bits of data.
> It is common to see AFP, SMB, and other file services move large files about— big graphics, video files and large disk images. Internet Services more commonly deal with smaller files, typically mail messages and HTML.

Internet Services are sensitive to latency.
> Because files are small and requests frequent (loading Apple's current home page requires at least n http connections), Internet Services are typically sensitive to latency issues.

Internet Services in Mac OS X are also (unlike generalized service categories examined elsewhere in this book) entirely open source in nature. Every actual service is implemented using an open source tool available on other platforms. This provides an excellent opportunity for more in-depth chapters that examine the configuration infrastructures Apple has employed in order to add value to the Mac OS X Server platform.

Chapters in this part of the book include:

Chapter 22, *Mail Services*
Chapter 23, *Web Services*
Chapter 24, *Application Servers*

Mail Services

Mail is perhaps the most consistently business-critical Internet application in use today. There are few enterprises that do not rely on it, at the very least leveraging it as a primary communication medium. This popularity, though, also lends itself to exposure—and in the case of mail services, exposure has meant abuse. Fighting spam (unsolicited mail messages) and mail-based worms and viruses now accounts for some of the largest IT expenditures yearly.

 Email is amazingly popular—so much that it can probably be called the killer app of the Internet age thus far. This is most likely due to its familiar paradigm. It doesn't take much of an intellectual leap to understand the sending of a message—even a multimedia message— to someone else. It's something that humanity has been doing for a long time, and contrasted with the Web or online chat forums, it is a very novice-friendly concept. This simplicity, though, is only skin-deep—the sending of a message from one user to another actually employs a number of systems and services that must work together.

In versions leading up to Panther, Mac OS X Server used AppleMailService, a workgroup mail server that was ported to Mac OS X from Mac OS 9 and AppleShare IP. While easy to maintain and configure, it didn't scale to large deployments. Perhaps more important, though, was its feature set. In recent years, a number of open source spam- and virus-checking solutions have come to dominate that marketplace. Apple-MailService, due to its proprietary nature, was unable to leverage those solutions, leaving Mac administrators in a difficult spot.

Panther represents a radical departure from this architecture, utilizing powerful and scalable open source solutions that are managed by a familiar and simple graphical interface. Additionally, because of its open nature, Panther Server is now able to make use of a variety of value-added solutions for mail filtering. This chapter will delve below the interface, examining both the underlying processes included with Mac OS X Server and several alternatives that provide different feature sets. We'll also examine add-on products allowing for filtering, spam management, and web-mail access.

Mail Protocols

This chapter is not meant as an in-depth survey of mail history, protocols, or architectures. It is, instead, an analysis of Mac OS X Server's Mail Services. Such an analysis, however, cannot take place without at least a basic understanding of constituent mail service protocols. Such a basic knowledge of SMTP, POP, and IMAP is hopefully provided in this section.

SMTP

The Simple Mail Transfer Protocol (SMTP) is the protocol used to send email—both among mail servers and from *mail user agents* (MUAs)—such as Mail.app, Eudora, or Entourage—to outgoing mail servers. It is implemented by a class of daemons known as *mail transfer agents* (MTAs). A typical set of SMTP interactions is documented in Figures 22-1 and 22-2.

1. After composing a message, a client uses its MDA to send it. The MDA uses SMTP to contact the server listed as its outgoing mail server.

Figure 22-1. SMTP is used to send mail to its destination.

2. The outgoing SMTP server examines the message. If its To: field contains the fully qualified domain name of a host (*user@mail.pantherserver.org*), a second SMTP connection is established, delivering the message. More typically, though, messages are addressed to a user in a particular DNS domain (*user@pantherserver.org*). In that case, the MTA queries DNS, looking for the domain's MX (mail exchanger) records. MX records indicate a host that is authorized to accept mail for a particular domain, as shown in Example 22-1.

Example 22-1. Mail Exchanger (MX) records determine which computer handles mail for a particular domain.

```
tigre:~ mb$ host -t MX pantherserver.org
pantherserver.org mail is handled by 5 smtp.pantherserver.org.
```

The MTA then contacts that host and sends the message to its final destination.

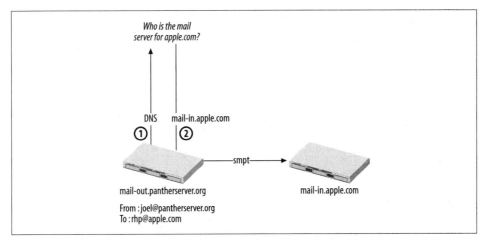

Figure 22-2. In the simplest case, an SMTP server relays mail to its final destination. This is a generalization; there are often intermediary relay filters, and proxies.

3. The mail is accepted by the destination server (commonly after Virus and Spam Filtering). It usually sits there, waiting for delivery, which is implemented using other protocols and daemons.

POP

The Post Office Protocol (POP) is an older (but still very common) mail delivery protocol. POP is very simple and lightweight. MUAs typically use POP to download messages from a user's mail server. Messages are typically deleted from the server at that point; they may be left in place, but the mail server itself has no concept of the message being read or unread. This is a determination that is made on the client side, and multiple POP clients accessing the same data store have no way of knowing which messages have been viewed by other clients. POP is also relatively hard to secure, and uses TCP port 110.

IMAP

Designed around the limitations of POP, the Internet Mail Access Protocol (IMAP) is a heavier-weight, more full-featured mail delivery protocol. Messages are generally stored on a server, although most IMAP clients permit client-side caching to aid disconnected mobility. Message state is also stored on the server side. Any authorized IMAP client may determine whether a particular message has been viewed, replied to, or forwarded. IMAP clients and servers typically support a variety of user authentication methods, and IMAP runs over TCP port 143.

Graphical Management

Bundled mail services in Mac OS X include IMAP, POP3, SMTP Webmail, and Mailing List capabilities. Although actually implemented with a variety of underlying daemons, Mac OS X Mail Services are consolidated into a management interface that is consistent with both earlier versions of the mail server and current management models established by other services (for instance, per-user settings are managed in Workgroup Manager, while global, server-specific options are managed in Server Admin). This consistency is one of the keys to the ease with which the Panther transition may occur.

Server Admin

Global monitoring and options for SMTP, IMAP, POP, Webmail, and Mailing List services can be located in the Server Admin application, in the Mail module. In keeping with other Mac OS X Server services, the initial view of Mail Services consists of an Overview, listing the global state of Mail Services as well as the state of their various component protocols. This interface is illustrated in Figure 22-3.

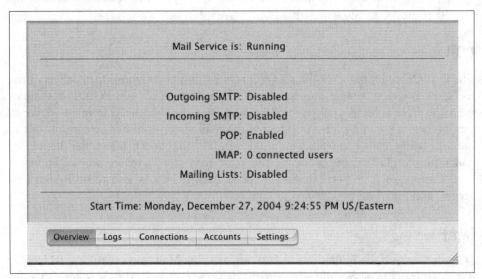

Figure 22-3. Note that in an out-of-box configuration, even after starting Mail Services, SMTP, POP, IMAP, and Mailing Lists are all disabled. This default state ensures the most granular default security possible. Each service must be enabled separately.

Various mail logs show up, appropriately enough, in the Logs tab of Server Admin's Mail Service (much as they do for nearly every other service Server Admin manages).

These logs can be seen in Figure 22-4. IMAP, various list-related, POP, and SMTP logs are available via the pop-up menu in the lower left corner. Table 22-1 describes the location on the filesystem and the purpose of each of these logs.

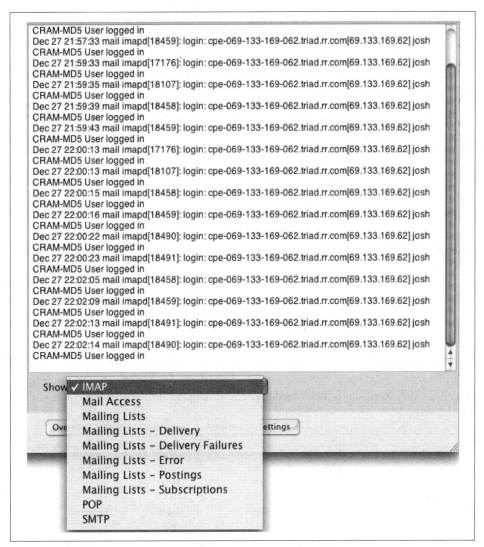

Figure 22-4. Several mail service logs are available.

Table 22-1. As with other Server Admin Log interfaces, it is often helpful, particularly on busy servers, to view these logs using the tail command, rather than Server Admin. The verbosity of the SMTP, IMAP, and POP logs may be adjusted in the Mail Settings tab.

Log	Location	Description
IMAP	/var/log/mailaccess.log	IMAP and POP status messages are both sent to *mailaccess.log*. Choosing IMAP limits the messages displayed specifically to IMAP.
Mail Access	/var/log/mailaccess.log	IMAP and POP status messages are both sent to *mailaccess.log*. Choosing Mail Access displays the entire log.
Mailing Lists	/private/var/mailman/logs/qrunner	*qrunner* is the engine behind Mailman; this is its log.
Mailing Lists—Delivery	/private/var/mailman/logs/smtp	Mailman's SMTP log records successful SMTP transactions.
Mailing Lists—Delivery Failures	/private/var/mailman/logs/smtp-failure	The SMTP failure log contains records of unsuccessful SMTP connections.
Mailing Lists—Error	/private/var/mailman/logs/error	Generic mailing list errors are written to this file.
Mailing Lists—Postings	/private/var/mailman/logs/post	Posts to Mailman-hosted lists are recorded here.
Mailing Lists—Subscriptions	/private/var/mailman/logs/subscribe	New Mailman subscriptions are logged to the subscribe file.
POP	/var/log/mailaccess.log	IMAP and POP status messages are both sent to *mailaccess.log*. Choosing POP displays only POP messages from that file.
SMTP	/var/log/mail.log	All SMTP activity is noted in *mail.log*.

Pictured in Figure 22-5, the Connections tab displays current connections, sortable by username, IP address, connection type, number of sessions, or session length. Note that this interface does not display SMTP connections—only IMAP and POP are shown.

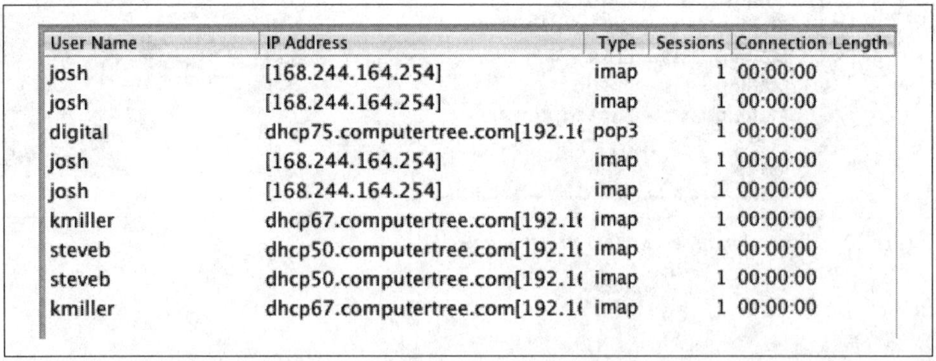

User Name	IP Address	Type	Sessions	Connection Length
josh	[168.244.164.254]	imap	1	00:00:00
josh	[168.244.164.254]	imap	1	00:00:00
digital	dhcp75.computertree.com[192.16	pop3	1	00:00:00
josh	[168.244.164.254]	imap	1	00:00:00
josh	[168.244.164.254]	imap	1	00:00:00
kmiller	dhcp67.computertree.com[192.16	imap	1	00:00:00
steveb	dhcp50.computertree.com[192.16	imap	1	00:00:00
steveb	dhcp50.computertree.com[192.16	imap	1	00:00:00
kmiller	dhcp67.computertree.com[192.16	imap	1	00:00:00

Figure 22-5. The Connections portion of Server Admin's Mail module displays a wide variety of information concerning current mail IMAP and POP activity.

This disk utilization of individual mail server accounts can be monitored with the Accounts tab, and, similarly to the Connections tab, sorted based on a variety of data, including Username, Quota, Disk Space Used, percent free, and mail store location. Most of these settings, since they're implemented on a per-user basis, are managed in Workgroup Manager. The Accounts tab is pictured in Figure 22-6.

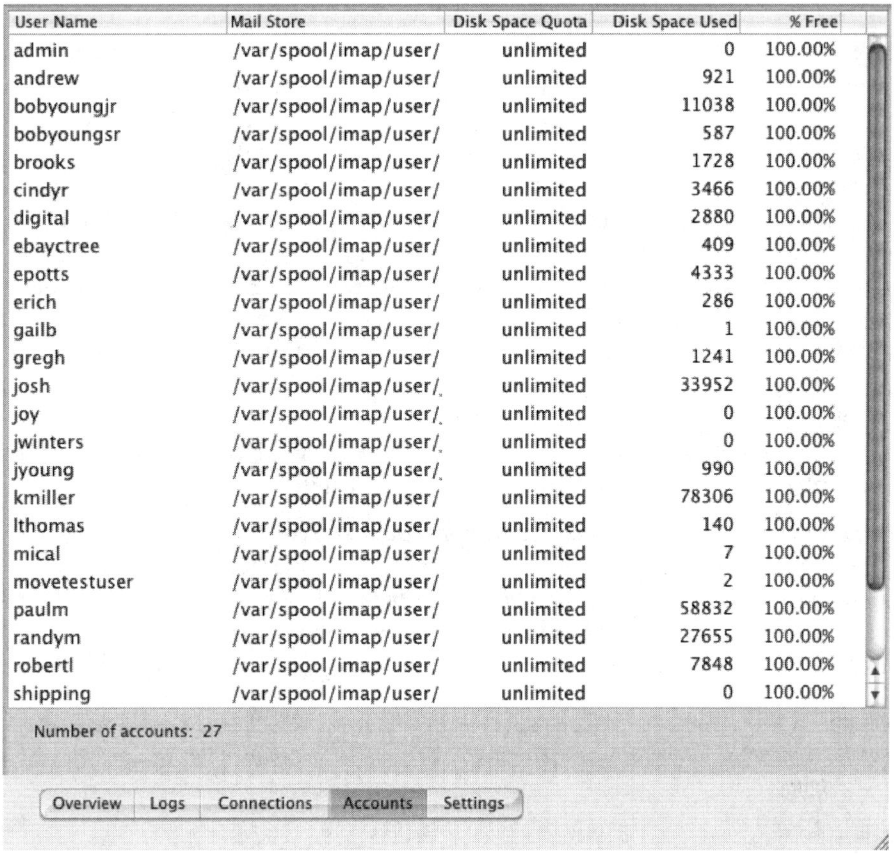

User Name	Mail Store	Disk Space Quota	Disk Space Used	% Free
admin	/var/spool/imap/user/	unlimited	0	100.00%
andrew	/var/spool/imap/user/	unlimited	921	100.00%
bobyoungjr	/var/spool/imap/user/	unlimited	11038	100.00%
bobyoungsr	/var/spool/imap/user/	unlimited	587	100.00%
brooks	/var/spool/imap/user/	unlimited	1728	100.00%
cindyr	/var/spool/imap/user/	unlimited	3466	100.00%
digital	/var/spool/imap/user/	unlimited	2880	100.00%
ebayctree	/var/spool/imap/user/	unlimited	409	100.00%
epotts	/var/spool/imap/user/	unlimited	4333	100.00%
erich	/var/spool/imap/user/	unlimited	286	100.00%
gailb	/var/spool/imap/user/	unlimited	1	100.00%
gregh	/var/spool/imap/user/	unlimited	1241	100.00%
josh	/var/spool/imap/user/	unlimited	33952	100.00%
joy	/var/spool/imap/user/	unlimited	0	100.00%
jwinters	/var/spool/imap/user/	unlimited	0	100.00%
jyoung	/var/spool/imap/user/	unlimited	990	100.00%
kmiller	/var/spool/imap/user/	unlimited	78306	100.00%
lthomas	/var/spool/imap/user/	unlimited	140	100.00%
mical	/var/spool/imap/user/	unlimited	7	100.00%
movetestuser	/var/spool/imap/user/	unlimited	2	100.00%
paulm	/var/spool/imap/user/	unlimited	58832	100.00%
randym	/var/spool/imap/user/	unlimited	27655	100.00%
robertl	/var/spool/imap/user/	unlimited	7848	100.00%
shipping	/var/spool/imap/user/	unlimited	0	100.00%

Number of accounts: 27

Overview   Logs   Connections   **Accounts**   Settings

Figure 22-6. The Accounts portion of Server Admin's Mail module provides a per-user analysis of mail resource usage. Mail quotas are entirely separate from filesystem quotas.

This same data can be obtained by using the *serveradmin* command, as shown here:

```
serveradmin command mail:command = getUserAccounts
```

Be aware that both this interface and the equivalent *serveradmin* command currently give out (as of 10.3.3) at a fairly small number of user accounts—around 200, in my testing. If this interface is accessed or this command run, the *servermgr_mail* process will consume up to 80 percent of available CPU resources. It remains stuck in this state until either it returns data (an outcome with vanishing probability as the number of accounts increases), or until the process is killed.

Don't be surprised if a full list of your mail-enabled users is not available. A mail account is not created for users until mail arrives for them or they check their mail for the first time. The reason for this is twofold. Firstly, in a modern, centralized directory services infrastructure, it is likely that the server hosting user accounts (Open Directory Master, Active Directory Domain Controller, or an other directory server) is not the same machine hosting mail for that account. Both mail and directory services tend to be very I/O intensive, so it makes sense to host them on separate servers when load starts to increase. Also worth noting, however, is the history of Cyrus, the MDA (Mail Delivery Agent) that Mac OS X Server uses to host POP3 and IMAP services. It was originally designed as a closed system, catering to ISPs and large institutions not wanting to give system login accounts to the many mail users they supported. While Mac OS X Server administrators are far more likely to run more integrated, less specialized systems, this does mean that we get the benefits that come with a mail system that feasibly scales into the millions of users.

The Settings tab exposes the configuration options used to control the behavior of Mac OS X Mail Services. Simple enough to ease the migration of AppleMailServer administrators from Jaguar to Panther, it exposes only a fraction of the capabilities inherited from Cyrus, Postfix, and Mailman, the specific packages responsible for IMAP and POP, SMTP, and Mailing Lists, respectively (as described in Table 22-2).

Table 22-2. Component open source packages that make up Mac OS X Server's Mail Services. WebMail is managed graphically as a part of Web Services, rather than in the Mail module of Server Admin.

Protocol	Package
SMTP	Postfix (*www.postfix.org*)
POP	Cyrus IMAP (*http://asg.web.cmu.edu/cyrus/imapd*)
IMAP	Cyrus IMAP (*http://asg.web.cmu.edu/cyrus/imapd*)
Mailing Lists	Mailman (*www.list.org*)
WebMail	SquirrelMail (*www.squirrelmail.org*)

The General tab in Server Admin's Mail settings is, well, general. It is seen in Figure 22-7. SMTP, POP, and IMAP are globally enabled here, and some basic restrictions are exposed, all organized into three general categories:

Sending

Enabling SMTP changes the `postfix` entry in */etc/watchdog.conf* from `no` to `respawn`, ensures that SMTP services are started. Mail, rather than following the DNS-based SMTP model, can be relayed through a specific host—a common strategy in businesses and institutions where a centralized authority scans all outgoing mail for viruses, worms, or questionable content. Small businesses and home office ISPs also often require this kind of centralized SMTP relay.

Receiving

IMAP connections, which can each easily use up to 2 MB of system memory, can be limited to a finite number. This has important performance implications and is discussed in more depth later in this chapter. Enabling IMAP or POP changes the `cyrus` entry in */etc/watchdog.conf* from `no` to `respawn`.

Copies (bcc)

The Copies (bcc) section of the interface presents some flexible (if delicate) options for message management, both of which result in having messages sent to destinations they were not intended for originally, and both presenting real privacy concerns. The first specifies that all incoming and outgoing messages will be *blind carbon-copied* (bcc'd) to a particular address. This means that any message arriving or leaving your server is forwarded to the address you've defined. In cases where data is sensitive (imagine performance evaluations, new product ideas, or student data), this setting could cause quite a bit of trouble, especially since remote parties sending mail to you probably have no idea that such an archive is being collected. While there are valid business reasons for it, most users will frown upon this kind of policy, so make sure that it is well documented and supportable.

Less controversial (but only slightly), the second bcc option allows bounced messages to be forwarded to a specific mail address. Especially where revenue opportunities are tied to email, this is a powerful option. Let's say that *jon@example.com* is responsible for a certain account, but a potential customer sent a lucrative opportunity to *john@example.com*. This feature would allow some human operator the chance to apply fuzzy logic and filter messages manually to the right person. Nonetheless, these messages are still seen by eyes they're not intended for, so the potential for privacy violations is there.

Mailing lists, which in their simplest form are simply lists of email addresses to which mail may be sent en masse, have become a very popular method for communication in the wired world. (The concept is shown in Figure 22-8.) Centered on an endless variety of topics, they have evolved into robust platforms for both discussion and information distribution. Mailman (*www.lists.org*) is an extremely powerful open source mailing list solution—powerful enough, in fact, to run all of the mailing lists found at *http://lists.apple.com*. Its graphical interface, in the Mailing Lists tab of Server Admin's mail settings, offers a basic level of access to its deep feature set. It is pictured in Figure 22-9.

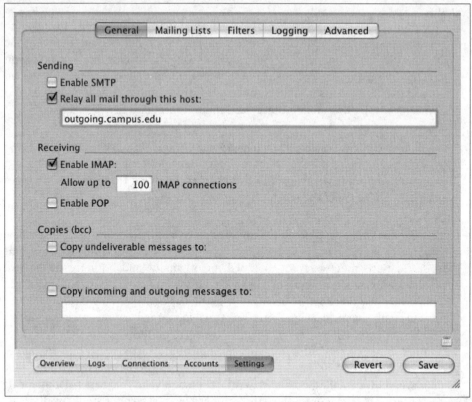

Figure 22-7. The General tab of Server Admin's Mail Settings—home to sending, receiving, and ad hoc archival options. Enabling SMTP does not always work immediately. You often have to toggle it on and off and back on several times, clicking save after each change. Alternatively, you may manually change the postfix entry in /etc/watchdog.conf from off to respawn.

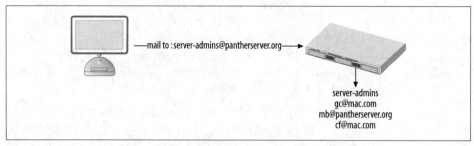

Figure 22-8. Mailing Lists distribute a single message to a list of recipients.

When you select the Mailing Lists option from Server Admin's Mail settings, you're exposed to two panes—one on the left describing lists hosted on the server, and a contextual pane on the right detailing the selected list. In a manner that's consistent

with other Server Admin interfaces, each has three buttons, with +, –, and pencil
icons, signifying Add, Delete, and Edit, respectively.

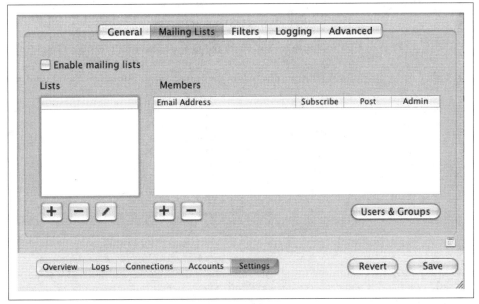

*Figure 22-9. The Mailing List interface in Server Admin's Mail Settings in its default, out-of-box
state.*

Before any lists can be added, the service itself must be enabled, by clicking on the
Enable mailing lists checkbox in the upper left corner. This setting prompts for the
creation of a mailing list called Mailman, as seen in Figure 22-10. The password and
administrators you specify will be used for administrative control over other mailing
lists. You may not administer Mailman lists solely by the virtue of belonging to the
Server's *admin* group.

 As of 10.3.3, Mac OS X Server will allow administrators to delete the
Mailman list, which prevents mailing lists from working. Never delete
the Mailman list.

Multiple email addresses can be specified, but in any case, only one password is supplied. This is because Mailman performs administrative authentication on the list
level, rather than for each user. Each list has precisely one administrative password,
no matter how many users are authorized to administer it—although (to make matters slightly more confusing) individual users do have individual passwords in order
to manage their membership in particular lists. These passwords, though, are generally auto-generated by Mailman, are unrelated to a user's system password, and are
sent over email in clear text because they are not considered sensitive.

Figure 22-10. Enabling mailing list entails specification of an administrative password, along with the email address authorized to create lists. It's a good idea to use passwords that are a lot more secure than "apple."

New lists can be created by clicking the + icon at the bottom left corner of the Lists pane. The resulting dialog is simple enough—a sheet (pictured in Figure 22-11) drops down prompting for a list name. There's also a checkbox that specifies whether users should be able to self-subscribe (they must otherwise be added by a list administrator).

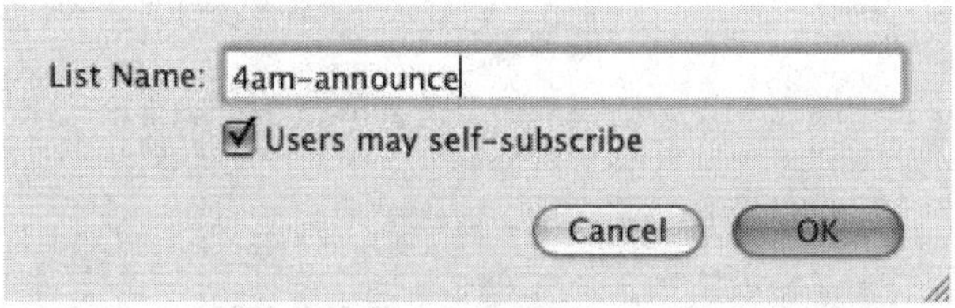

Figure 22-11. The List creation dialog is rather simple.

Addresses can be added manually to the currently selected list in the Members pane. Each user has three possible levels of access: Subscribe, Post, and Admin. Users subscribed to the list will have mail delivered to them, while posting allows them to send mail to the list (and therefore to everyone on it), and administration allows them to modify list options. Administration, though, does not allow them to log in via Server Admin. It means they may either log into Mailman's web-based list management interface or send administrative commands to Mailman through email. Regardless of the level of access that is chosen, an email message is delivered to the user, alerting them of the addition.

 When Mailman is first enabled, Apache's configuration file is modified to include Mailman's web configuration, stored at */etc/httpd/ httpd_mailman.conf*. This means that for every web site defined on that server at the point when Mailman is enabled, the */mailman* directory displays Mailman's web interface. If Web Services are not enabled, the web interface will not be available. If you wish to restrict users from accessing this interface, uncomment its include directive in */etc/httpd/httpd.conf*.

Once lists have been enabled and created, and once users have been added, mail can be distributed using the address `list-name@host.com`, where `list-name` is the name of the mailing list and `host.com` is any of the domains or hostnames for which the server is configured to accept mail.

Note that Mailman has no concept of Open Directory or any users and groups database. It simply operates based on lists of email addresses. When you use "Users and Groups" to add a system user to a list, Server Admin queries Open Directory in order to locate that user's email address, which is actually what is added to Mailman's configuration.

 Previous to Panther, Mail Services in Mac OS X (and AppleShare IP) had a group distribution option, which allowed for any mail sent to any groupname the server was aware of to be distributed to group members. This is one of the few features that Jaguar Mail Services had while Panther's did.

Filters (the interface for managing them can be seen in Figure 22-12) are the center of Mac OS X Server's built-in spam protection (although these built-in capabilities are only the tip of the iceberg of spam and virus protection; third-party add-ons are covered in the "Advanced Configuration" section of this chapter). Filters, in their Server Admin terminology, though, are not content filters—they're lists of hosts concerned with SMTP transfers to and from the server you're managing. The first pane in the Filters interface lists hosts allowed to relay mail through the server.

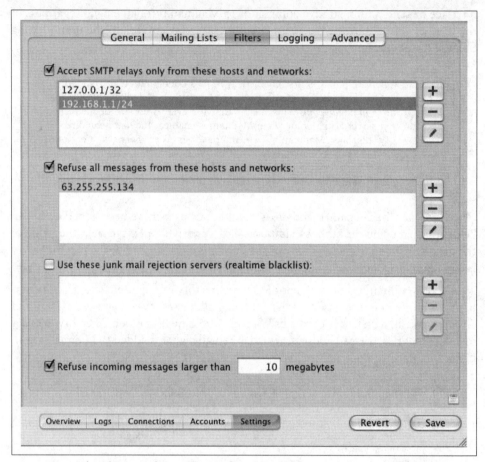

Figure 22-12. The Filters interface to Server Admin's Mail Settings, where host-based filtering is configured.

Relaying is defined as accepting and delivering messages destined for users that are not local (see Figure 22-13). This is commonly referred to as outgoing SMTP. For instance, if the server accepts a message for *steve@mac.com* and then sends that message on to the SMTP server responsible for the *mac.com* domain, it can be thought of as a relay. SMTP relays are a vital part of the Mail process—by definition, in order to send mail to users in other domains, the outgoing server listed in your mail client (or MUA, mail user agent) has to be an SMTP relay (see Figure 22-14).

Problems arise when the mail server acts as an *open* relay, or a relay that is accessible to anyone on the Internet. This means that anyone can use it to send mail to anyone else—especially fertile grounds for a spammer wishing to send 50 million messages

Figure 22-13. Mail relays send mail from a client to its destination server. The fact that the recipient's account is on a different domain is what makes it a relay (rather than a local delivery).

Figure 22-14. In order to send mail to anyone outside of your organization, the SMTP server listed in the MUA (Mail User Agent; for instance, Mail.app or Eudora) must be capable of relays.

advertising porn or Xanex or some new male enhancement ointment (guaranteed to work, of course).

To confront the challenge of relay management, Apple leverages the relay whitelist technology of Postfix, Mac OS X Server's underlying MTA (mail transfer agent). Specific hosts and network ranges may be permitted to relay. Hosts not in this whitelist will be forced to authenticate before they can relay mail through the server. This authentication can be more granularly regulated using options located in the Advanced tab of Server Admin's mail settings, discussed later in the chapter.

 Generally in Server Admin, filters can be applied to either individual hosts or cider-notated network ranges such as 192.168.1.1/24.

The second host-level filter available (also leveraging Postfix) is an SMTP blacklist. The mail server will reject all messages from any host or network range listed, regardless of whether that message would constitute a relay. (Valid messages sent to local users are rejected, too.) This option is primarily useful when a particular host is sending a lot of spam to legitimate users. It is logistically very difficult to keep track of every single malicious host on the Internet, so this feature is of limited scope.

Rather than keep track of such a list yourself, Mac OS X Server includes the option to leverage existing *real-time blacklists* (RBLs). RBLs centralize and streamline the process of keeping track of illegitimate mail hosts and other SMTP relays so that you don't have to maintain your own list. The problem is that you are seeding control of your infrastructure to someone else—a third party with their own interests, and many times their own political or financial goals. Many RBLs blacklist dial-up accounts, marginalizing rural or financially challenged organizations using dial on demand SMTP, and many place ridiculous demands on administrators who wish to be removed from their blacklist. Generally, RBLs amount to a "guilty until proven innocent" strategy, which is something I find neither fair nor responsible. Although RBLs are an effective tool for fighting spam, they are not always a legitimate one. The only RBL that I am absolutely comfortable with is SpamHaus (*www.spamhaus.org*).

 Are all RBLs this bad? Of course they're not. They seemed like a good idea at one time. However, they've gotten out of hand—any RBL that blacklists a mail server that's not an open relay and hasn't been observed as a spamhost is just irresponsible. There are far, far better methods for reducing spam, several of which are documented later in this chapter.

RBLs, if you choose to use them, may be added to the RBL filter pane. Keep in mind that these particular filters all act based upon the source IP address of incoming SMTP connections. Hopefully by now you're aware that a moderately skilled attacker can spoof their source IP address, and that other measures, such as well-designed firewall filters and diligent monitoring, should be used to help prevent this kind of compromise.

One final feature available in the Filters tab is a restriction on the size of messages incoming to your server. The default value, 10 MB, is probably reasonable for most installations. Smaller values might be appropriate if a significant portion of the server's user base dials in to get Internet access; waiting for a 10 MB disk image to download while dialed up to a 20 Kbps connection in a rural county is no fun. Mail quotas might also weigh in on this policy—if most users have a certain mail quota, it might make sense to limit total message size to something below that, so that no one message could exhaust their authorized disk usage.

Perhaps the most important reason for limiting incoming message size relates to the feasibility of a *denial-of-service* (DOS) attack when any network service is able to write arbitrarily large files to the server's filesystem. Very little checking is typically performed on incoming SMTP connections, and allowing for arbitrarily large files (or even very large) files to be spooled for local delivery means that hard disk space could feasibly be exhausted by a malicious party, resulting in denial of mail services if the mail spool is somewhere other than the system's boot drive, and a denial of all services if the spool is on the boot partition. By limiting the size of incoming attachments, you force malicious parties to establish a higher volume of connections—something easily detectable at the firewall level.

 Mac OS X Server is prepared for this challenge. The *diskspacemonitor* daemon, covered in Chapter 4, can effectively prevent this kind of attack.

Some industries, particularly the graphic arts, have made a habit of using email as an ad hoc file transfer platform, and often send very large attachments to and from customers, often for proofing. This is bad practice because there are much better, more controlled applications for this, such as an authenticated PHP-driven file distribution mechanism.

Accurately named, the Logging tab of Server Admin's mail settings (seen in Figure 22-15) controls the logging configuration for the component mail systems. Logging intensity can be controlled separately for mail transport (SM, managed by Postfix) and delivery (POP and IMAP, managed by Cyrus)—low, medium, and high levels may be chosen for each. These settings eventually make their way to */etc/syslog.conf*, where Mail Delivery and SMTP correspond to the local6 and mail facilities, respectively. Low, medium, and high settings correspond to the *err*, *notice*, and *info* log levels. More (or less) aggressive log levels may be temporarily specified by editing *syslog.conf*; however, they are honored only until the next time the Mail Services configuration is changed.

 For a more generalized analysis of the logging capabilities of Mac OS X and Mac OS X Server, see the discussion of *syslogd* in Chapter 4.

Saving any option, even an unrelated one, resets the level to whatever is specified in the graphical interface.

The Advanced tab of Server Admin's mail settings (Figure 22-16) is actually home to a variety of important options, most of which are not related to each other conceptually. The first portion allows for specification of local host aliases, or hosts and domain names for which the server is willing to accept mail. In an out-of-box configuration, the only value listed is the fully qualified domain name entered into the Setup Assistant when the server was first configured. In most circumstances, mail should also be accepted for one or more domains (meaning that the MX record for that domain points to the mail server in question). Those domains should be listed in this interface.

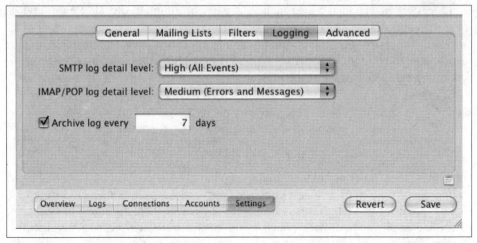

Figure 22-15. The Logging tab exposes a limited subset of the logging capabilities of Mac OS X Server's Mail System. It can also be used to specify an archive interval for the logs.

In Mac OS X 10.3.3, localhost aliases are as close as we've come to true virtual domains. Unfortunately we're not quite there yet. Although Mac OS X may support multiple host aliases, there is only a single namespace for user accounts: mail for *bob@mabaleb.org*, *bob@pantherserver.org*, and *bob@gs.pantherserver.org* will all be sent to user with a short name of *bob*. Slightly more granular virtual domain support is documented more fully in the "Advanced Configuration" section of this chapter.

Listed next in the Advanced tab of Server Admin's mail settings is the mail store location. Specifically, this is the default location on the server's filesystem where messages are stored for retrieval via POP or IMAP. This location can be changed; for instance, to make use of a higher-performance storage device. Unless this change is made before any mail accounts are created, though, existing mail accounts will be orphaned, so we'd instead suggest use of multiple IMAP partitions, examined later in the chapter.

If you simply must, for some reason, change the default mail location after user mail accounts have been created (remember, mail accounts are not created until mail arrives for a user or the user checks mail, whichever comes first) a script similar to this should work:

```
#!/bin/sh
for i in `ls /var/spool/mail/user`; do
    ditto /var/spool/mail/user/$i /new/location/$i
done
```

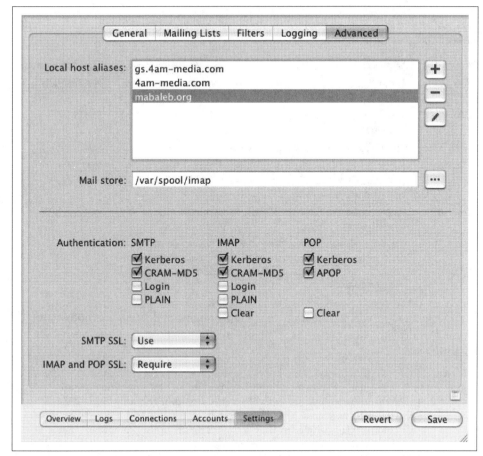

Figure 22-16. The Advanced tab of Server Admin's Mail Settings contains important authentication, security, and initial setup options.

Next in the Advanced pane is the list of authentication protocols authorized for each mail service. Secure authentication (that which is encrypted or which follows a challenge-response model, so that the password never goes over the network in any form) protects the authentication process, keeping the user's password relatively secure from malicious parties. Keep in mind that secure authentication does nothing to protect the actual content of the message; for that some sort of transport security (like SSL, covered later in this section) is needed.

This selection is fairly granular, allowing for different levels of security for each service. Not every method is supported with every service, so some understanding of the relative security merits of each method is important. See Table 22-3 for a comparison of mail authentication methods.

Table 22-3. The security of mail authentication methods varies greatly. With the exception of Kerberos, all of these authentication methods are implemented using Apple's Password Server. All methods are examined in more depth in Chapter 8.

Method	Description	Supported protocols
Kerberos	A generally secure network authentication protocol that supports single sign on. For details see Chapter 8.	POP, IMAP, SMTP
CRAM-MD5	A challenge-response authentication method that is both widely supported and secure across the network.	IMAP, SMTP
Clear	Transmits passwords in clear text across the network, and is not secure.	IMAP, SMTP
PLAIN	Uses the SASL abstraction layer to send passwords in clear text. From a security perspective, it is identical to Clear—insecure, and unsuitable without some kind of transport security (such as SSL).	IMAP, SMTP
Login	For practical purposes, identical to SASL Plain. Neither should be used without transport security.	IMAP, SMTP, POP
Apop	A challenge-response mechanism that protects POP authentication. While secure over the network, it decreases server security because it requires that clear-text passwords be available. Kerberos should be used whenever possible if POP services are required.	POP

It is my personal recommendation that Plain, Login, and Clear methods never be enabled under any circumstances whatsoever, due to the ease with which they are compromised.

> Note that in a default installation as of 10.3.3, requiring secure authentication will prevent web mail users from checking mail. Web Mail must be specifically configured to support CRAM-MD5 authentication. This is discussed later in this chapter, in the "WebMail" and "Advanced Configuration" sections.

Finally, the Advanced pane allows the use of the *secure sockets layer* (SSL) to be managed for POP, IMAP, and SMTP services. A widely supported method for transport encryption, SSL ensures that the entire exchange between the client and server is encrypted and relatively secured from malicious parties.

Different SSL settings can be configured separately for mail transport (SMTP) and delivery (POP or IMAP, considered together, as they are both part of the Cyrus package). Each of these two selections has three options:

Don't Use
    Never use SSL.

Use
    Use SSL if the client requests it, and advertise SSL where appropriate. SSL is not required.

Require

Require SSL for all connections. Terminate connections that do not support SSL.

In either case of SSL use (Use or Require) extra steps are required before SSL-enabled connections will actually be successful—in particular, the certificate files specified in */etc/imapd.conf* and */etc/postfix/main.cf* must be prepared and installed. The configuration directives used to manage SSL are documented in Table 22-4.

Table 22-4. The certificates specified in the Mail Service configuration files must be properly configured and installed before SSL-enabled mail connections will work.

File	Description
tls_cert_file	The IMAP and POP services' public certificate
tls_ca_file	The certificate of the authority (CA) that signed the IMAP *tls_cert_file*
tls_key_file	The private key corresponding to the certificate referenced in *tls_cert_file*
smtpd_tls_cert_file	The SMTP certificate file

When SSL is deployed, the Use flag is typically set for SMTP, while careful administrators may choose Require for POP and IMAP. This is because—due to the trusted third-party model of SSL—very few incoming SMTP delivery connections will be able to negotiate an SSL-enabled session. This is especially true if self-signed certificates (by far the most common configuration) have been used, as self-signed certificates are, by definition, trusted only within the organization that produced them. Selecting Use allows SSL-enabled MUAs to use SSL to protect any clear-text authentication mechanism that might take place between them and their local SMTP relay, while also permitting incoming messages to be posted without SSL's complexity of overhead. SSL's ability to protect the contents of the message itself are largely irrelevant, since only the connection between the MUA and MTA will be protected, and since the message itself will probably be transmitted in the clear when sent between mail servers.

Mail delivery, on the other hand, usually happens totally within your enterprise, between your mail server and your clients. Self-signed certificates are not barriers here, as both ends of the connection reside within the organization that produced them.

SSL is a very heavyweight solution to the problem of clear-text protocol transport. It relies on a monopolistic trusted third-party infrastructure, and is designed to do a lot more than just encryption. This capability results in a lot of excess logistical baggage. Unfortunately, it is also a widely adopted standard, so we're forced to deal with it. Although privacy concerns are always valid, from a technological standpoint, it is not fair to ask mail, which was never designed to be secure, to securely manage sensitive data. A number of add-ons exist both to secure mail content and to ensure that mail actually originated with the user listed in the From: header. See *www.macdevcenter. com/pub/a/mac/2003/01/20/mail.html* and *www.sente.ch/software/ GPGMail/English.lproj/GPGMail.html* for details. The S/MIME method in listed in the O'Reilly article has the advantage of being explicitly supported in Mail.app.

WebMail

Configured in Server Admin's Web settings rather than with its Mail options, web mail is provided by the SquirrelMail open source IMAP client. Its graphical configuration is quite simple. Similarly to Mailing Lists, it is a checkbox that, when enabled, adds a web mail–specific configuration file (*/etc/httpd/httpd_squirrelmail. conf/*) to */etc/httpd/httpd*. This setting adds a global alias to every configured site, so that the site's */WebMail* directory brings up SquirrelMail's login interface.

I prefer a more granular approach, especially when managing a server where different parties will have authority over the content for different sites. I do not want these users to unexpectedly encounter a web mail login interface that they weren't expecting. This approach is detailed in the following steps:

1. Optionally, if different organizations or groups of users will need different Web-Mail settings (such as the logo displayed at the WebMail login window), duplicate the */usr/share/squirrelmail* directory in some kind of group-specific fashion.

    ```
    ditto /usr/share/squirrelmail /usr/share/squirrelmail.sitename
    ```

2. Set up an SSL-enabled site specifically for WebMail. SSL-enabled web services are beyond the scope of this chapter, but are covered in Chapter 23. That site should point to either the */usr/share/squirrelmail* global web mail directory or to the organization or group-specific directory created in step 1.

Keep in mind that as of 10.3.3, SquirrelMail as installed on Mac OS X Server is not configured to support anything but clear text IMAP logins. This means that until it is otherwise configured, WebMail won't work unless plain or clear authentication is enabled on the Server. Both are generally a bad idea.

From a security standpoint, weak authentication is OK across the server's loopback interface (127.0.0.1). The problem, however, is that there's no way to enable clear-text authentication just for the loopback interface. If it's enabled there, it's enabled for all clients, and the server's security is in the hands of whoever configures IMAP clients (most of which are not secure in a default configuration).

Enabling CRAM-MD5 is relatively painless, though; see "Advanced Configuration," later in this chapter for instructions. SSL may additionally be supported for both IMAP and SMTP, although the relative security increase this step implies is probably not worth the effort.

Behind the scenes

Most of the Mail Service features available graphically in Server Admin are written to the */etc/MailServicesOther.plist* file before they're flushed to the service-specific configuration. This step is in order to preserve the settings specified in the configuration mechanism. The primary exception to this are Mailing List settings. Rather than being buffered to the *MailServicesOther.plist* file, they are, as of 10.3.3, written directly to Mailman's configuration files in */var/mailman*. Some attributes set in *MailServicesOther.plist*, such as the Kerberos principals used for SMTP, POP, and IMAP services are not configurable in the graphical interface, and must be edited in the file directly if their default values need to be changed. One other notable exception to the *MailServicesOther.plist* tendency is SSL configurations. Rather than being written to *MailServicesOther.plist*, they are written directly to */etc/imap.conf* and */etc/postfix/main.cf*.

Workgroup Manager

In keeping with convention established by other services, Workgroup Manager is used to manage per-user Mail Service options. These settings can be located in the Mail pane of the individual user record, illustrated in Figure 22-17. Options available here include the address of the server mail should be located on, the user's mail quota, and whether the user should be allowed to check mail via POP, IMAP, or both.

These options, with the exception of Mail Server, are fairly straightforward. Aside from noting that the quota specified here is specific to Mail Services (and does not interoperate with filesystem quotas), there's not too much to explain. Mail Server is simply a way of specifying in a multiserver domain which machine houses a user's mail spool. This alerts the machine that it should accept mail for the user, and does not mean that other servers (when they read this attribute) will forward the user's mail to the correct destination.

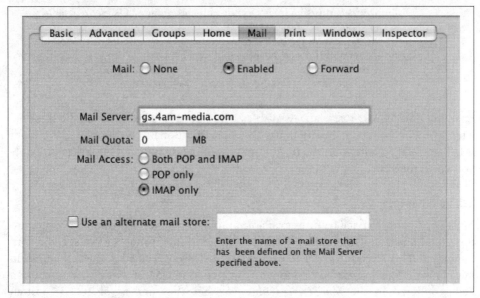

Figure 22-17. The Mail pane of a user record in Workgroup Manager.

In a default configuration, mail quota data (once set in Workgroup Manager) is saved to the User's record in Open Directory. This value is subsequently written by the Mail Server to its Cyrus configuration. Mail quotas are separate and unrelated to filesystem quotas, but they are managed in a way that is similar—stored in the directory service until they're needed (as the user record will often not be housed on the mail server).

Cyrus mail quotas may be managed manually using the *cyradm* command. This might be required when integrating Mac OS X Server Mail Services with Active Directory or some other non–Mac Directory Domain. Quotas may be viewed using Cyrus's *quota* command (which lives in */usr/bin/cyrus/bin*). It must be run as the *cyrus* user, as shown in Example 22-2.

Example 22-2. Using Cyrus's quota command to examine user mail quotas.

```
rhp997:~ rhp$ sudo -u cyrus /usr/bin/cyrus/bin/quota
  Quota  % Used    Used Root
2147483647       0       0 user/abbot
2147483647       0       0 user/bnelson
2147483647       0       0 user/clark
```

A final option, the use of an alternate mail store, is a little more complex, and requires explanation and extra configuration. Cyrus IMAP, the underlying MDA (mail delivery agent) used by Mac OS X Server, is capable of scaling to support millions of users. One of its scalability features is the specification of alternate mail stores—generally in order to make use of higher performing filesystem resources, or in order to organize user mailboxes logically, according to organizational structure. These alternate storage hierarchies, known to Cyrus as *partitions*, must first be established in */etc/imap.conf*, a configuration file explored in greater depth later in this chapter. The first directory, labeled partition-default (and configurable in the Advanced tab of Server Admin's mail settings), is where mail will be stored for users that do not have an alternate location explicitly defined.

In an out-of-box install of Mac OS X Server, this directory is */var/spool/imap*, as noted earlier in the discussion of Server Admin. Subsequent partitions are specified in the same file with further partition statements. For instance, a partition called *engr* would be declared with the following directive:

```
partition-engr: /var/spool/engineering
```

whereas a partition stored on a larger or higher-performing filesystem (perhaps for users with larger quotas, or a higher incidence of attachments) could be:

```
partition-highperf: /Volumes/xraid/imap
```

In the former case, users with mail storage on */var/spool/engineering* would have *engr* as the alternate mail store option in Workgroup Manager, while users with mail stored on */Volumes/xraid/imap* would have an entry of *highperf*.

Behind the scenes

These user-specific options are stored in the user record (be that in NetInfo, Open Directory, or Active Directory) in the user's `MailAttribute`. The entry is structured XML, as seen here. Note the use of the *dscl* utility to read the attribute, as shown in Example 22-3.

Example 22-3. Using dscl to read s10000's MailAttribute.

```
[ace2:~ /amavisd-new-2.2.0] nadmin% dscl /LDAPv3/127.0.0.1 -read /Users/s10000
MailAttribute
MailAttribute: <dict>
        <key>kAPOPRequired</key>
        <string>APOPNotRequired</string>
        <key>kAttributeVersion</key>
        <string>Apple Mail 1.0</string>
        <key>kAutoForwardValue</key>
        <string></string>
        <key>kIMAPLoginState</key>
        <string>IMAPAllowed</string>
        <key>kMailAccountLocation</key>
        <string>gs.pantherserver.org</string>
        <key>kMailAccountState</key>
        <string>Enabled</string>
        <key>kPOP3LoginState</key>
        <string>POP3Allowed</string>
        <key>kUserDiskQuota</key>
        <string>0</string>
</dict>
```

MailAttribute, like other XML-based values, is converted to base64 when stored on an LDAP server; a similar example is shown in Example 22-4.

Example 22-4. Using ldapsearch to read s10000's MailAttribute. Notice that MailAttribute is Open Directory's name for this data. OpenLDAP itself uses the name apple-user-mailattribute.

```
[ace2:~ /amavisd-new-2.2.0] nadmin% ldapsearch -LLL -x -h 127.0.0.1 -b "dc=4am-
media,dc=com" uid=s10000 apple-user-mailattribute
dn: uid=s10000,cn=users,dc=4am-media,dc=com
apple-user-mailattribute:: PGRpY3Q+Cgk8a2V5PmtBUE9QUmVxdWlyZWQ8L2tleT4KCTxzdHJ
 pbmc+QVBPUE5vdFJlcXVpcmVkPC9zdHJpbmc+Cgk8a2V5PmtBdHRyaWJ1dGVWZXJzaW9uPC9rZXk+
 Cgk8c3RyaW5nPkFwcFwcGxlIE1haWwgMS4wPC9zdHJpbmc+Cgk8a2V5PmtBdXRRm9yd2FyZFZhbHVlP
 C9rZXk+Cgk8c3RyaW5nPjwvc3RyaW5nPgJPGtleT5rSU1BUExExvZ2luU3RhdGU8L2tleT4KCTxzdH
 Jpbmc+SU1BUEFsbG93Q8L3NvcmluZz4KCTxrZXk+a01haWxzBY2NvdW50TG9jYXRpb248L2tleT4
 KCTxzdHJpbmc+Z3MuNGFtLW1lZGlhLmNvbTwvc3RyaW5nPgoJPGtleT5rTWFpbEFjY291bnRTdGF0
 ZTwva2V5PgoJPHN0cmluZz5FbmFibGVkPC9zdHJpbmc+Cgk8a2V5PmtQT1AzTG9naW5TdGF0ZZTwva2
 V5PgoJPHN0cmluZz5QT1AzQWxsb3dlZDwvc3RyaW5nPgoJPGtleT5rVXNlckRpc2t2RdW90YTwva2
 V5PgoJPHN0cmluZz4wPC9zdHJpbmc+CjwvZGljdD4K
```

Graphical LDAP browsers, like LDaPper (*www.versiontracker.com/dyn/moreinfo/macosx/12588*) and Java LDAP Browser/Editor (*www-unix.mcs.anl.gov/~gawor/ldap*) usually decode the base64 attributes for easier readability.

For various reasons, as of 10.3.3, Workgroup Manager can take a long time to do much of anything to even a moderately large number of users—such as a batch-modification of MailAttributes. Since it's very likely that a large number of users on a particular mail server will have identical MailAttributes (there is no user-specific data in the attribute, unless you have the need to assign Mail quotas individually—and even in this case it is likely that a certain group of users (for instance, salespeople or engineering students) will at least start out with common quota values—it is feasible to circumvent Workgroup Manager in order to add the data. One possible method for such a batch modification is outlined in Steps 1–4.

1. Obtain a list of RecordNames for all the users you wish to modify. If you've followed the limits recommendation outlined earlier, the following command returns all of the short names contained in the LDAP server. Otherwise you'll be limited to the number of records specified in *slapd*'s sizelimit directive:

```
[ace2:~ /amavisd-new-2.2.0] nadmin% ldapsearch -LLL -h 127.0.0.1 -D
"uid=nadmin,cn=users,dc=4am-media,dc=com" -b "dc=4am-media,dc=com"
objectclass=apple-user uid | grep -v dn | awk '{ print $2 }' > uids.list
SASL/CRAM-MD5 authentication started
Please enter your password:
SASL username: nadmin
SASL SSF: 0
[ace2:~ /amavisd-new-2.2.0] nadmin%
```

2. Set the desired mail options for a particular user and obtain the proper base64 value for the apple-user-mailattribute, using *ldapsearch* as specified in Step 1.

3. Incorporate the `apple-user-mailattribute` attribute (obtained in Step 2) using the following script to iterate through the list of `RecordNames` (UIDs) in order to produce a file suitable for input into the *ldapmodify* utility.

```
#!/bin/sh
#modmail.sh, a script for producing input for ldapmodify

#iterate through the list of RecordNames (uid's)

for i in `cat uids.list`
do
        echo "dn: uid=$i,cn=users,dc=4am-media,dc=com"
        echo "changetype: modify"
        echo "add: apple-user-mailattribute"
    #paste the value  for the desired apple-user-mailattribute below.
    #be sure there are no line breaks in the attribute's value.

        echo "apple-user-mailattribute:: PGRpY3Q+Cgk8a2V5PmtBUE9QUmVxdWlyZWQ8L2t
leT4KCTxzdHJpbmc+QVBPUE5vdFJlcXVpcmVkPC9zdHJpbmc+Cgk8a2V5PmtBdHRyaWJ1dGVWZXJzaW9
uPC9rZXk+Cgk8c3RyaW5nPkFwcGxlIE1haWwgMS4wPC9zdHJpbmc+Cgk8a2V5PmtBdXRvRm9yd2d2FyZFZ
hbHVlPC9rZXk+Cgk8c3RyaW5nPjwvc3RyaW5nPgoJPGtleT5rSU1BUExvY2luU3RhdGU8L2tleT4KCTx
zdHJpbmc+SU1BUEFsbG93ZWQ8L3N0cmluZz4KCTxrZXk+a01haWxBBY2NvdW50TG9jYXRpb248L2tleT4
KCTxzdHJpbmc+Z3MuNGFtLW1lZGlhLmNvbTwvc3RyaW5nPgoJPGtleT5rTWFpbEFjY291bnRRdGGF0ZTw
va2V5PgoJPHNOcmluZz5FbmFibGVkPC9zdHJpbmc+Cgk8a2V5PmtQT1AzTG9naW5TdGGF0ZTwva2V5Pgo
JPHNOcmluZz5QT1AzQWxsb3dlZDwvc3RyaW5nPgoJPGtleT5rVXNlckRpc2tRdW90YTwva2V5PgoJPHN
OcmluZz4wPC9zdHJpbmc+CjwvZGljdD4K"
        echo
done
```

In order to obtain a suitable *ldapmodify* input, this script should be run; its output redirected to a file, as shown here:

```
./modmail.sh > mailchange
```

4. Run *ldapmodify* as a user authorized to modify the LDAP directory, reading in the file you just produced.

```
ldapmodify -h 127.0.0.1 -D "uid=nadmin,cn=users,dc=4am-media,dc=com" -W -f
mailchange
```

This process could be streamlined by using the *ldapsearch* command indicated in Step 1, and in the for loop used by Step 3 (rather than iterating through the file produced in Step 1). The two are split out for the sake of clarity and simplicity for users not yet familiar with basic shell scripting.

The actual *ldapmodify* in this case takes about 7 seconds for 1,000 users on a G4 450, while Workgroup Manager might take as long as 20 minutes on the same machine.

In reality, I wrote and executed the entire scripted process when working in a production environment waiting for Workgroup Manager to iterate through a different set of 1,000 users.

Mail Architecture

The robust and open nature of the systems underlying Mac OS X Server's Mail Services has been noted at several points throughout this chapter. This is natural, since this general architectural direction is one of Panther's best features. This section explores those systems in greater depth, examining both their architecture and the specific implementational differences found in Mac OS X Server.

Postfix

Postfix is the default MTA in Mac OS X, Mac OS X Server, and several other Unix variants. In this role, it replaces the venerable and difficult-to-configure Sendmail with a modern, fast, and secure alternative. Although Apple has not stated definitively why Postfix was chosen, it has several things going for it. Its principal developer, Wietse Venema, is probably one of the single biggest influences in the secure computing realm, having already produced the groundbreaking SATAN and very widely adopted *tcpwrappers* packages. Postfix is also extremely fast and its configuration files are easily understood and well commented. Unless you are a Sendmail expert, there is little reason to use anything but Postfix.

> Other open source MTAs do exist, and almost all outclass the comparatively archaic Sendmail. All have their strengths, but unless your needs are fairly specialized, there is little reason to go to the trouble of working around Apple's Postfix install.

Files, folders, processes

One key architectural aspect of Postfix is its use of multiple daemons, each with a very specialized role. This modularization is both very Unix-like (as each process has a very specific purpose) and very secure. If any one processes is compromised, the malicious party is essentially sandboxed by that process's capabilities and permissions. It also results in a bit of complexity, however, and an accurate architectural map of Postfix can appear quite complex. Table 22-5 illustrates the processes that make up the Postfix mail system, and discusses their roles in mail transport.

Table 22-5. Postfix processes. All of these processes live in /usr/libexec/postfix.

Process	Description
bounce	Returns failed messages back to their sender after appending a rejection log, which is intended to illustrate the reason for the failure.
cleanup	Processes incoming mail, injecting it into the appropriate queue, and notifying the Postfix system of its arrival.
error	Feeds rejected mail to *bounce* or *defer*, depending on which is appropriate.
local	Responsible for local delivery.

Table 22-5. Postfix processes. All of these processes live in /usr/libexec/postfix. (continued)

Process	Description
master	The brain of the Postfix mail system, running other daemons when necessary.
nqmgr	The Postfix queue manager, and routs messages to the proper queues (*incoming, active, deferred, corrupt,* and *hold*). It also generates the status reports later sent to the *bounce* and *defer* daemons via error.
pickup	When notified by master, feeds mail to the *cleanup* daemon, mentioned earlier.
pipe	*nqmgr*'s gateway to the outside world, delivering messages to non-Postfix processes such as Mailman.
qmgr	An older version of *nqmgr*.
qmqpd	Responsible for implementing some access controls.
showq	Reports the status of various postfix queues.
smtp	Postfix's SMTP client; responsible for processing mail delivery to foreign SMTP servers.
smtpd	Postfix's SMTP server, which accepts incoming SMTP connections.
spawn	Starts processes that are external to Postfix.
tlsmgr	Responsible for management of some aspects of Postfix's SSL features.
trivial-rewrite	Responsible for resolving message destinations into forms that are useful for the Postfix system.
virtual	Implements *virtual* domain support. Not supported in Mac OS X Server, which uses a single namespace for mail usernames.

Postfix also makes use of a number of configuration files. Discussed in more depth later, they are documented in Table 22-6.

Table 22-6. In many cases, Postfix's behavior may be modified by modifying its configuration files.

File	Description
Access	This file is how the blacklist filter is implemented.
Aliases	The file used to generate aliases, so that a user can receive mail sent to multiple addresses. Covered later in this chapter.
main.cf	Postfix's main configuration file.
master.cf	File describing how various Postfix-related processes should be run.

Apple has made some basic modifications to Postfix, most of which appear to be available at *http://publicsource.apple.com*. Generally these changes revolve around Open Directory user lookups and authentication using Password Server. Most of the functionality present in Postfix on other operating systems is also present in Mac OS X. The notable exceptions are true virtual domain support, and support for accessing aliases and other user configuration from LDAP and MySQL.

Troubleshooting

Troubleshooting of Postfix issues (unexpected bounces, and delivery and connection failures) should be pursued very systematically, according to general procedures outlined in Chapter 5. The details of the architecture provided in this chapter along with those generalized skills should allow you to pursue most issues. In the meantime, some initial data gathering techniques are reviewed here. First, on the server, the *lsof* command (shown in Example 22-5) can be run in order to ensure that Postfix is listening on the SMTP port.

Example 22-5. The lsof command (with its –i argument) is capable of displaying current incoming connections. In this case, the grep command is used to filter for SMTP connections.

```
rhp997:~ rhp$ sudo lsof -i | grep smtp
master   10225   root    11u  IPv4 0x02b392bc        0t0    TCP *:smtp (LISTEN)
smtpd    13195 postfix    6u  IPv4 0x02b392bc        0t0    TCP *:smtp (LISTEN)
```

If the master process is listening for SMTP connections, its health can be tested by telneting to the SMTP port and pursuing a conversation with it. The command used in Example 22-6 should work from any host authorized to relay through the server in question.

Example 22-6. It's quite common to telnet to test an SMTP server.

```
rhp997:~ rhp$ telnet localhost 25
Trying ::1...
telnet: connect to address ::1: Connection refused
Trying 127.0.0.1...
Connected to localhost.
Escape character is '^]'.
220 rhp997.4am-media.com ESMTP Postfix
helo host.pantherserver.org
250 rhp997.4am-media.com
mail from:info@pantherserver.org
250 Ok
rcpt to:mbartosh@4am-media.com
250 Ok
data
354 End data with <CR><LF>.<CR><LF>
TEST
.
250 Ok: queued as 40092A5F2D
quit
221 Bye
Connection closed by foreign host.
```

Yet another initial step involves editing */etc/syslog.conf* to log all mail and local6 data, rather than the limited levels afforded by Server Admin's graphical interface. As mentioned earlier, this is a temporary measure, because any changes saved in Server Admin will rewrite log settings. For more information on editing *syslog.conf*, see Chapter 4. Finally, note that the Postfix system may be stopped and started granularly (the Stop and Start buttons apply to IMAP and POP services as well, and sometimes make manual configuration difficult by overwriting configuration files) with the *postfix* command's *reload* directive (see Example 22-7). This technique will be used at several points later in the chapter to support advanced configurations.

Example 22-7. Manually starting and stopping postfix.

```
[ace2:~] nadmin% sudo postfix reload
postfix/postfix-script: refreshing the Postfix mail system
```

Cyrus

The default MDA in Mac OS X Server, Cyrus IMAP (a package that despite its name also supports POP access), is a product of Carnegie Mellon University's Cyrus project. It is designed with scalability in mind, supporting multiple simultaneous read/write operations to a single mailbox and fine-grained access controls allowing for shared mailboxes and robust administration. Cyrus's performance characteristics really start to shine when it is forced to deal with very large mail spools having to support multiple simultaneous accesses from a modern IMAP client. Cyrus stores its messages individually, rather than in a single, large file, so rather than load an entire mail spool into memory in order to send a message over the network it may operate on one message at a time.

Files, folders, processes

Like Postfix, Cyrus depends on a number of small processes, each written to perform a specific task very effectively. The most important of those processes are illustrated in Table 22-7.

Table 22-7. The Cyrus package consists of a number of underlying processes.

Process	Description
deliver	*deliver* writes mail messages received via *lmtp* to the Cyrus data store.
imapd	*imapd* services IMAP requests. *imapd* is spawned by the *master* daemon.
master	The *master* daemon (which is started by the *watchdog* process). It listens on various ports and Unix sockets (which vary according to its configuration) and spawns appropriate daemons to service requests.
pop3d	*pop3d* services POP requests.

Cyrus, being open source, and because it shares a common heritage with many other Unix like services, stores most of its configuration data in a set of text-based configuration files. Table 22-8 describes these files.

Table 22-8. Despite its name, the Cyrus mail system also supplies POP access.

File	Description
/etc/imapd.conf	Configuration file for *imapd* and *pop3d*; Cyrus's POP and IMAP servers.
/etc/cyrus.conf	Configuration file for Cyrus's master process. Defines services Cyrus should be responsible for.

Like its changes to Postfix, Apple's changes to Cyrus IMAP have been released as open source, as a part of the Cyrus IMAP package available at *http://publicsource. apple.com*. Most of the Cyrus changes revolve around user handling. Cyrus was originally designed to run on a closed system, where user accounts were stored in SQL or LDAP, and not actually allowed to log into any service other than IMAP. Cyrus in Mac OS X has been modified so that *lmtpd*, *imapd*, and *pop3d* can all create mail accounts, as long as the user in question has a Mail Attribute.

Apple has also, though, made some interesting configuration choices for Cyrus, not requiring source modifications. Chief among these is the support of a feature called an alternate namespace. Typically, Cyrus mailboxes appear as children of (inside) the user's inbox. Apple felt that this might become confusing for users, though, and instead has opted to use the more comfortable alt-namespace convention, so that the user's inbox appears as a peer of other mailboxes when viewed via IMAP.

Also significant in Apple's treatment of Cyrus is the use of the slash character (/) as a hierarchy separator (the character that separates one level of IMAP folder from its parent). Default Cyrus installations use the period character (.). Both the Unix hierarchy separator and the alternate namespace behavior are configured in */etc/imapd. conf* file, specifically using the unixhierarchysep and altnamespace directives.

Troubleshooting

Like SMTP, IMAP may be tested using telnet, as illustrated here. In this example I am testing the compatibilities of the IMAP server:

```
[ace2:~ /amavisd-new-2.2.0] nadmin% telnet 127.0.0.1 imap
Trying 127.0.0.1...
Connected to localhost.
Escape character is '^]'.
* OK gs.pantherserver.org Cyrus IMAP4 v2.1.13 server ready
. CAPABILITY
* CAPABILITY IMAP4 IMAP4rev1 ACL QUOTA LITERAL+ MAILBOX-REFERRALS NAMESPACE UIDPLUS
ID NO_ATOMIC_RENAME UNSELECT CHILDREN MULTIAPPEND SORT THREAD=ORDEREDSUBJECT
THREAD=REFERENCES IDLE STARTTLS AUTH=CRAM-MD5 AUTH=GSSAPI
. OK Completed
. LOGOUT
* BYE LOGOUT received
. OK Completed
Connection closed by foreign host.
```

The *imtest* utility (in */usr/bin/cyrus/bin*) is similarly useful, especially where advanced authentication mechanisms are required; getting telnet to simulate a CRAM-MD5 or Kerberos IMAP login would be particularly difficult.

Migration

One critical issue facing mail administrators in Panther is migration from existing or legacy mail solutions. Since Panther's Mail Services rely on underlying systems very different from those in Mac OS X 10.2, it is necessary in some cases to transfer mail from the older database to the new. Several common methods exist to aid in this migration:

MDA (POP/IMAP)
> Clients use their mail application to move mail from one server to the other one. The mail client has both servers listed; users drag mail from one to the other.

Global IMAP Copy
> Rather than being copied on a per-user basis, the IMAP protocol is used to copy the entire mail store from one server to the other.

In-place migration
> A server-side process is used to manually convert the existing data store to Cyrus's mail storage format.

amsmailtool

Apple's included solution for mail migration is a command-line utility called *amsmailtool* (*/usr/bin/cyrus/toold/amsmailtool*), which is distributed as a value-added component of Cyrus. It is capable of reading either the 10.1 or 10.2 mail database formats and moving user messages to a data store that Panther's IMAP and POP services can access. When invoked with no argument, it searches the default location for those databases (*/Library/AppleMailServer*) and transfers any messages to Panther's default Cyrus data store (*/var/spool/imap*), along the way building the Cyrus administrative databases stored in */var/imap*.

> Although it is unlikely that *amsmailtool* itself will cause any data loss, you should always back up your 10.1 or 10.2 mail databases before you attempt an upgrade. It is additionally a good idea to repair the legacy database prior to migration, using *MailService*'s *–compressdb* flag. Note that you'll need to turn off the Mail Service first, which (in 10.2) can be accomplished with the *MailService-autostart* command. The *MailService –compressDB* command immediately returns to the command prompt. Do not be fooled; you can monitor the progress of the repair using the *AppleMailServer.Repair.log* file in */Library/Logs/MailService*:
>
> ```
> sudo /usr/sbin/MailService-autostart off
> sudo /usr/sbin/MailService -compressDB
> ```

As *amsmailtool* works through the pre-existing database, it marks each message as imported, ensuring that if it crashes or is otherwise interrupted, it will be able when run again to pick up where it left off, rather than double-importing messages. A basic import can be achieved by calling *amsmailtool* with no arguments, as in Example 22-8.

Example 22-8. Basic use of the amsmailtool command, without any options.

```
ace2:~ root# sudo /usr/bin/cyrus/tools/amsmailtool
Migrating mail:
  From: /Library/AppleMailServer
  To  : /var/spool/imap
Please wait...
Migrating 170705 messages requiring 951147091 bytes.
Exporting mailbox: INBOX
  - Posted: 0 messages for user "nadmin" in mailbox "INBOX"

Done posting mail for user: nadmin
  - Posted: 0 total messages, for user: nadmin
```

In the case of failed migrations, this method can be quite troublesome. Subsequent runs, seeing the marked messages, will not attempt to re-import them, unless you use the undocumented *–reset* flag. Being undocumented, it does present some risk. It's a lot more convenient, though, than having to restore a 2 or 3 GB mail database every time you want to re-attempt an import.

Jaguar server allowed for the mail services database to be stored somewhere other than the default */Library/MailServer*. If you've made use of this feature, or if you'd like mail to be stored somewhere other than */var/spool/imap*, you'll need to use the *location* and *destination* flags, as in Example 22-9.

Example 22-9. Moving the mail services database using amsmailtool's location and destination options.

```
ace2:~ root# sudo /usr/bin/cyrus/tools/amsmailtool –reset –source /Volumes/RAID/
AppleMailServer –destination /Volumes/RAID/imap
Migrating mail:
  From: /Volumes/RAID/AppleMailServer
  To  : /Volumes/RAID/imap
Please wait...
Migrating 170705 messages requiring 951147091 bytes.
Exporting mailbox: INBOX
  - Posted: 0 messages for user "nadmin" in mailbox "INBOX"

Done posting mail for user: nadmin
  - Posted: 0 total messages, for user: nadmin
```

amsmailtool must be run as *root*, and it cannot run if *AppleMailServer* is already running—allowing the database to be written to in the middle of migration could lead to lost mail. It usually works well, even for large databases, as long as the mailbox hierarchy is rather simple. Sites with very deep hierarchies, where users might typically have several levels of subfolders, should be prepared to look into other migration methods. *amsmailtool* has no man page, but its source is available with Apple's Cyrus IMAP package at *http://publicsource.apple.com*. Its options are described in Table 22-9.

Table 22-9. amsmailtool has not proven to be exceedingly reliable for complex databases.

Option	Description
–migrate.10.1	Migrate a 10.1 Mail database.
–migrate.10.2	Migrate a 10.2 (Jaguar) Mail database.
–reset	Attempt to import every message, resetting the imported flag on messages that appear to have already been imported.
–source	Specify a source other than */Library/AppleMailService*.
–destination	Specify an alternate destination.

Panther offers a wealth of advancements over Jaguar, and now that it has had several minor updates, it can be considered stable, deployable and well tested. However, mail upgrades in particularly sophisticated environments might be problematic, and might need to be planned for organizational downtime (such as a major holiday)—a commodity that is not always common. If you'd like to migrate to Panther but continue running *AppleMailServer*, you can follow these directions:

- Copy the *AppleMailServer* binary from Jaguar to Panther. The *scp* utility is a good choice for this.

- Copy the LogViewer framework from */System/Library/Privateframeworks/LogViewerAPI.framework* on Jaguar to the same location on Panther. Again, *scp* is a good choice.

- Modify */etc/watchdog.conf* so that it starts *AppleMailService*. The entry should look something like this:

```
mailservice:respawn:/usr/sbin/MailService -n
```

This technique is not supported by Apple, and it is not guaranteed to work. It worked for me for several months, though, until I had time to develop a mail migration strategy I was comfortable with for my 3.2 GB Apple Mail Service mail database.

Advanced Configuration

The open nature of Mac OS X Server Mail Services lends itself to extensibility. Based on widely deployed open source components, it is capable of leveraging solutions to solve a number of well-understood challenges to mail deployment. Some of these require either extensive command-line work or more advanced knowledge of Unix systems. In keeping with our usual methodology, I've focused on solutions that I feel are most commonly requested.

Backing Up

At some level, labeling backups as an advanced configuration option seems odd, as for all practical purposes they are required; indeed, backing up can be quite simple. In many circumstances, Mail Services can simply be stopped (so that the databases used by Cyrus and Postfix can be accurately copied), the backup can be run, and Mail Services can be started up again. At a slightly more sophisticated level, this process can be scripted, using the *serveradmin* command-line utility. I wrote the script shown in Example 22-10 (which I hope is commented enough to aid understanding) to aid in backing up my own mail server. When executed, it essentially stages mail data to a safe location. My backup software (currently BRU, by the Tolis group: *www.tolisgroup.com*) then dumps the staged data over the Internet to my backup server. The script can also be used to restore backed-up mail. In the cases of both backup and restore it is smart enough to examine *imapd.conf* to determine precisely which data needs to be backed up—this is handy if you've established alternate mail storage partitions.

Example 22-10. When invoked with the –r argument, this script restores from its staged backup.

```
#!/bin/sh
stamp=`/bin/date "+%m%d%y%H%M%S"`
bakDir=/var/backups/cyrus
confFile=/etc/imapd.conf
confDir=`cat /etc/imapd.conf | grep configdirectory | awk '{ print $2 }'`


cyrus_off() {
# turn off cyrus
        /usr/bin/logger MAILBAK: cyrus_off turning off cyrus at `/bin/date`
        /bin/cat /etc/watchdog.conf | /usr/bin/sed "s/cyrus:respawn:/cyrus:off:/" > ↵
        /tmp/mailbak.$stamp
        #I use sudo to actually do things since it automagically logs a lot of data
        /usr/bin/sudo /bin/cp /tmp/mailbak.$stamp /etc/watchdog.conf
        /usr/bin/sudo /usr/bin/killall -HUP watchdog
}

cyrus_on() {
#turn cyrus on
        /usr/bin/logger MAILBAK: cyrus_on turning on cyrus at `/bin/date`
        /bin/cat /etc/watchdog.conf | /usr/bin/sed "s/cyrus:off:/cyrus:respawn:/" > ↵
        /tmp/mailbak.$stamp
        #I use sudo to actually do things since it automagically logs a lot of data
        /usr/bin/sudo /bin/cp /tmp/mailbak.$stamp /etc/watchdog.conf
        /usr/bin/sudo /usr/bin/killall -HUP watchdog
}

stage_bak() {
/usr/bin/logger MAILBAK: stage_bak started stage_bak @ `/bin/date`
for i in `/bin/cat $confFile | /usr/bin/grep partition | /usr/bin/awk '{ print $2 }'`
do
        #check and see if listed partition exists
        if [ -e $i ]
        then
                #check and see if appropriate backup dir exists, create it if not
                if [ ! -e $bakDir/$i ]
```

```
                then
                        /usr/bin/logger MAILBAK: stage_bak $bakDir$i does not exist,
creating
                        /usr/bin/sudo /bin/mkdir -p $bakDir$i
                fi
                /usr/bin/logger MAILBAK: stage_bak about to exec /usr/bin/rsync -a ↵
                $i $bakDir$i @ `/bin/date`
                /usr/bin/sudo /usr/bin/rsync -a $i $bakDir$i | /usr/bin/logger
        else
                /usr/bin/logger MAILBAK: stage_bak $i is listed in $confFile but does ↵
                not exist. skipping
        fi
done
if [ -e $confDir ]
then
        if [ ! -e $bakDir$confDir ]
        then
                /usr/bin/logger MAILBAK: stage_bak $bakDir$confDir does not exist.
creating
                /usr/bin/sudo /bin/mkdir -p $bakDir$confDir
        fi
        if [ -e $bakDir$confDir ]
        then
                /usr/bin/logger MAILBAK: stage_bak about to exec /usr/bin/rsync -a ↵
                $confDir $bakDir$confDir @ `/bin/date`
                /usr/bin/sudo /usr/bin/rsync -a $confDir $bakDir$confDir | /usr/bin/logger
        else
                /usr/bin/logger MAILBAK: stage_bak $bakDir$confDir does not exist and ↵
                should have been created. exiting.
        fi
else
        /usr/bin/logger MAILBAK: stage_bak $confDir does not exist.
fi

/usr/bin/logger MAILBAK: stage_bak finished stage_bak @ `/bin/date`
}

restore() {
/usr/bin/clear
/bin/echo RESTORING MEANS YOU MIGHT OVERWRITE DATA. YOU HAVE 10 SEC to ctl-c
/bin/sleep 1
/bin/echo 10
/bin/sleep 1
/bin/echo 09
/bin/sleep 1
/bin/echo 08
/bin/sleep 1
/bin/echo 07
/bin/sleep 1
/bin/echo 06
/bin/sleep 1
```

```
/bin/echo 05
/bin/sleep 1
/bin/echo 04
/bin/sleep 1
/bin/echo 03
/bin/sleep 1
/bin/echo 02
/bin/sleep 1
/bin/echo 01
/bin/sleep 1
/bin/echo 00
echo MAILBAK: restore srarted @ `/bin/date`

#stopping cyrus
echo stopping cyrus
cyrus_off

echo restoring every partition listed in $confFile
for i in `/bin/cat $confFile | /usr/bin/grep partition | /usr/bin/awk '{ print $2 }'`
do
        if [ ! -e $bakDir/$i ]
        then
                echo no backup exists @ $bakDir/$i. skipping.
        else
                /usr/bin/sudo /usr/bin/ditto $bakDir/$i $i
        fi
done

echo restoring $confDir
if [ -e $bakDir$confDir ]
then
        /usr/bin/sudo /usr/bin/ditto $bakDir$confDir $confDir
else
        echo no backup exists @ $bakDir$confDir. exiting.
fi

#restart cyrus
cyrus_on

}

if [ "$1" == "-r" ]
then
        restore
else
        cyrus_off
        stage_bak
        cyrus_on
fi

#clean up
```

Example 22-10. When invoked with the –r argument, this script restores from its staged backup. (continued)

```
if [ -e /tmp/mailbak.$stamp ]
then
        /usr/bin/sudo /bin/rm /tmp/mailbak.$stamp
fi
```

Content Filtering

Content filtering is one of the most intensely managed aspects of a modern mail service. Although I'm probably pushing it, the importance of good (and responsible) spam filtering cannot be stressed enough. Along with virus and worm eradication and corporate policy monitoring, it accounts for a growing percentage of yearly IT expenditures. This demonstrates one common open source architecture for addressing these needs. This recipe is inspired by one listed at *afp548.com*, with some notable exceptions (such as the use of watchdog to manage *clamd* and *spamd*). Overall, it is based on three freely available open source software packages: *amavisd-new*, SpamAssassin, and ClamAV.

 Consult *afp548.com* for further configuration options, such as the construction of a shared spam folder.

amavisd-new

The centerpiece of mail content management on Mac OS X Server is *amavisd-new* (*www.ijs.si/software/amavisd*), a recently updated version of the *amavisd* mail filter. *amavisd* is required not so much because we need its filtering capabilities (which are extensive), but because Postfix's filtering abilities are not tremendously extensible, and we need *amavisd* to wrap together SpamAssassin and ClamAV, the workhorses of this strategy.

SpamAssassin

While the relay access control methods covered earlier in the chapter ensure that a server doesn't become a spam source, they will do little to protect server users from having spam delivered to them. Under normal circumstances, the server has no reason to reject mail that appears to be for a legitimate user. Luckily, several filtering solutions exist to fulfill the role of spam guardian.

Spam is one of the most profitable sectors of the wired world, and spammers are sharp. As I write this, it is virtually guaranteed that by the time it is published mail administrators and spammers will have leapfrogged each other several times in the fight to stay ahead. Thus this section does not pretend to be all things to all people. Rather, it seeks to lay a solid foundation, on top of which a functional strategy for reducing illegitimate mail may be built, whatever your specific needs happen to be.

The most ubiquitous content filter in the open source world is probably SpamAssassin (*http://spamassassin.apache.org/*). Deployable on either the server or the client, it is a Perl-based package with a number of components and several spam-detection mechanisms, including header and text analysis, Bayes filtering, and RBLs. SpamAssassin falls under that ever-growing list of software that is extensive enough for its own book—so I will cover only some basic options here.

SpamAssassin is not the only open source spam solution. A search for the string "spam filter" on SourceForge (*www.sourceforge.net*) yields literally a hundred other. Dspam in particular (*www.nuclearelephant. com/projects/dspam*) has been very successful for me in the past, and given more resources in the future, I'll cover it in more depth. My focus on SpamAssassin is more a testament to its competence and its mindshare than its superiority to other solutions.

ClamAV

Of critical importance, especially in cross-platform deployments, is the ability to filter incoming mail for viruses and Trojans. (Homogeneous Macintosh deployments, while inconvenienced by the amount of bogus traffic viruses generate, do not run the risk of further propagating them.) As of this writing, there are no commercial solutions for virus filtering that integrate with Mac OS X Server. A commonly deployed open source solution is ClamAV (*www.clamav.net*). ClamAV prides itself on having been the first to identify a signature for 2003's MyDoom virus (allowing it to be detected and eradicated) earlier than any commercial virus solution. While your mileage may vary, there is no arguing that it is the best value on the market, and it boasts an extensive list of high-profile customers.

Architecture

Mail, once received by Postfix, will be submitted to *amavisd-new* for processing. *amavis* in turn invokes SpamAssassin and ClamAV. This process can be seen in Figure 22-18.

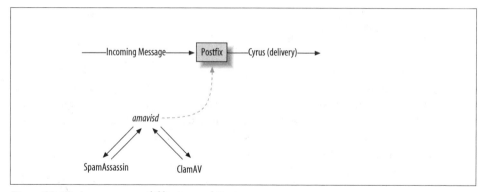

Figure 22-18. A common mail filtering architecture.

Installation

Flexibility is both the strength and the weakness of open source software. This is particularly true where multiple interoperable packages are concerned; there are typically multiple ways for packages to work together. Few are really right or wrong—some configurations are simply better-suited for certain scenarios than others. This flexibility, while powerful, can be extremely frustrating to a user who just wants a solution fast. *amavisd-new*, SpamAssassin, and ClamAV each constitute a prime example of this phenomenon. There are multiple ways to deploy each software package. I've chosen what I believe to be a reasonable one, but further education may very well reveal an option that is better suited to your particular environment. In any case, education is the key. This procedure is a good starting point, but there's a lot more that you can do.

 The Berkeley DB developmental libraries must be installed before *amavisd* will work properly. They are available at *http://www. opendarwin.org* (you can also get Berkeley DB from its maker, Sleepy-Cat Software, but Apple's version is more likely to build on Mac OS X). It can be downloaded with *curl*, as shown here:

```
curl -O http://darwinsource.opendarwin.org/tarballs/other/
BerkeleyDB-6.tar.gz
```

Its build instructions are straightforward and accurate, and simple enough that I have also included them here. Once the BerkeleyDB package is downloaded, it must be unarchived.

```
tar -xvzf BerkeleyDB-6.tar.gz
```

After that, change directories into the unarchived distribution and proceed with the build instructions. In every case, be aware that the commands presented here result in a lot of verbose output; only the actual commands are shown here.

```
cd BerkeleyDB-6/db/build_unix/
../dist/configure
...
make ; sudo make install
```

```
sudo mkdir -p /usr/local/lib
sudo mkdir -p /usr/local/include
sudo ln -s /usr/local/BerkeleyDB.4.1/lib/* /usr/local/lib
sudo ln -s /usr/local/BerkeleyDB.4.1/include/* /usr/local/
include
```

Installation begins with ClamAV. It needs to be available when *amavis* starts, so it is a logical place to begin. Installation is relatively painless (at least less painful than that of BerkeleyDB), following the familiar *./configure*, *make*, *make install* pattern of many open source packages. First, it must be downloaded (see Example 22-11), in most cases taking care to obtain its most recent version.

Example 22-11. Using curl to download clamav.

```
[ace2:~ nadmin% curl -O http://aleron.dl.sourceforge.net/sourceforge/clamav/clamav-0.70-
rc.tar.gz
  % Total    % Received % Xferd  Average Speed          Time             Curr.
                                  Dload  Upload Total   Current  Left     Speed
100 2198k  100 2198k    0     0  66208      0  0:00:34  0:00:34  0:00:00 68192
```

The package must then by untarred (Example 22-12), and a user and group for *clamav* to run as must be added (Example 22-13); in this case, to the local NetInfo directory.

```
[ace2:~ /amavisd-new-2.2.0] nadmin% tar -xzf clamav-0.70-rc.tar.gz
[ace2:~ /amavisd-new-2.2.0] nadmin% cd clamav-0.70-rc
user+ clamav
```

Example 22-12. Creating the user for ClamAV and amavis. The id command is used to ensure that it is recognized by the system.

```
[ace2:~  nadmin% sudo nicl . -create /users/clamav uid 37
[ace2:~  nadmin% sudo nicl . -create /users/clamav gid 37
[ace2:~  nadmin% sudo nicl . -create /users/clamav passwd "*"
[ace2:~  nadmin% sudo nicl . -create /groups/clamav gid 37
[ace2:~  nadmin% id clamav
uid=37(clamav) gid=37(clamav) groups=37(clamav)
```

Example 22-13. ClamAV also uses the /var/clamav directory, which is owned by the clamav user. It must be created.

```
[ace2:~  nadmin% sudo mkdir -p /var/clamav
[ace2:~  nadmin% sudo chown -R clamav /var/clamav/
[ace2:~  nadmin% sudo chmod 0750 /var/clamav
```

Finally, the software can be built (see Example 22-14). This step first requires configuring the build process. This is necessary in order for ClamAV (which is cross-platform) to make any Mac OS X–specific changes. Only a portion of the configuration output (which is quite verbose) is shown here.

Example 22-14. Configuring ClamAV to build on Mac OS X. The --mandir argument ensures that the build process installs ClamAV's manpages where Mac OS X knows to look.

```
ace2:~ cd clamav-0.70-rc
ace2:~/clamav-0.70-rc nadmin$ ./configure --mandir=/usr/share/man
cking all in clamav-milter
checking build system type... powerpc-apple-darwin7.3.0
checking host system type... powerpc-apple-darwin7.3.0
checking target system type... powerpc-apple-darwin7.3.0
...
config.status: creating clamav-config.h
config.status: executing depfiles commands
```

After configuration, the software is built with the *make* command (see Example 22-15). Once again, due to the verbosity of this process, only a portion of the output is shown.

Example 22-15. Using make to compile (or build) ClamAV.

```
gs:~/clamav-0.70-rc nadmin$ make
make  all-recursive
Making all in libclamav
...
Making all in clamav-milter
make[2]: Nothing to be done for `all'.
make[2]: Nothing to be done for `all-am'.
```

After the software is built, it must be installed. This is accomplished once again with the *make* command, this time with its *install* directive, as shown in Example 22-16.

Example 22-16. Using make to install ClamAV. Notice that this action requires root privileges.

```
gs:~/clamav-0.70-rc nadmin$ sudo make install
Making install in libclamav
/bin/sh ../mkinstalldirs /usr/local/lib
...
make[2]: Nothing to be done for `install-exec-am'.
make[2]: Nothing to be done for `install-data-am'.
```

clamd, the daemon interface to the package's virus-scanning capabilities, is installed into */usr/local/sbin*, and alerts you if run without the proper configuration, as shown in Example 22-17.

Example 22-17. Attempting to execute clamd without a configuration file.

```
gs:~/clamav-0.70-rc nadmin$ /usr/local/sbin/clamd
ERROR: Please edit the example config file /usr/local/etc/clamav.conf.
ERROR: Can't open/parse the config file /usr/local/etc/clamav.conf
```

clamav.conf is both extremely well commented and fairly long. It additionally has a very complete manpage. Like SpamAssassin's configuration file, it doesn't require much configuration to be useful. Too long to illustrate here in its entirety, I've instead decided to illustrate a few specific and commonly used options, and commented them even more in Examples 22-18, 22-19, 22-20, 22-21, and 22-22.

Example 22-18. The Example statement must be commented out or clamav will not run.

```
# Comment or remove the line below.
#Example
```

Example 22-19. Generally, leave the LogFile directive commented out; we'll send logs to syslog.

```
#LogFile /tmp/clamd.log
```

Example 22-20. Also leave the PIDFile directive commented out.

```
LogSyslog
#PidFile /var/run/clamd.pid
```

Example 22-21. The User directive should be set to the user you created earlier.

```
User clamav
```

Example 22-22. LocalSocket refers to the file used to communicate with ClamAV.

```
LocalSocket /var/clamav/clamd.sock
```

Once configured, *clamd*, like Mac OS X Server's built-in mail components, can be easily started by the *watchdog* daemon; Example 22-23 shows you where this happens in the */etc/watchdog.conf* file.

Example 22-23. Using grep to see clamd's entry in /etc/watchdog.conf.

```
gs:~ gs$ grep clamd /etc/watchdog.conf
clam:respawn:/usr/local/sbin/clamd                    #clamav
```

Once ClamAV is installed and running, *amavisd* may be similarly configured. It must first be downloaded (Example 22-24). Version 2.2 was used in this process; in general, try to find the newest version that is stable and works.

Example 22-24. Using curl to download amavisd-new.

```
[ace2:~] nadmin% curl -O http://www.ijs.si/software/amavisd/amavisd-new-2.2.0.tar.gz
  % Total    % Received % Xferd  Average Speed          Time        Curr.
                                 Dload  Upload Total   Current Left  Speed
100  573k 100  573k    0      0   107k      0 0:00:05 0:00:05 0:00:00  127k
```

amavis d-new must then be unpacked using the *tar* command:

```
    [ace2:~] nadmin% tar -xvzf amavisd-new-2.2.0.tar.gz
    amavisd-new-2.2.0
    amavisd-new-2.2.0/README_FILES
    amavisd-new-2.2.0/README_FILES/README.contributed
    amavisd-new-2.2.0/README_FILES/README.chroot
    amavisd-new-2.2.0/README_FILES/README.customize
    ...
    [ace2:~] nadmin% cd amavisd-new-2.2.0
```

amavisd begins a common trend of requiring several Perl modules that aren't included in a default system. These can be installed using Perl's CPAN archive:

```
[ace2:~/amavisd-new-2.2.0] nadmin% sudo perl -MCPAN -e "install Archive::Tar,
Archive::zlib, BerkeleyDB, Compress::Zlib, Convert::UUlib, Digest::MD5, IO::Stringy ,
Mail::Internet Mail::SpamAssassin , MIME::Base64, MIME::Parser, Net::SMTP Net::
Server, Time::HiRes, Unix::Syslog , Digest::SHA1, Convert::TNEF, Archive::Zip"
```

If you've never used CPAN before, be forewarned that Perl asks you if you want to proceed with a manual installation. It's a trick! Say no. CPAN's default configuration will do most of what you need to do—and if it doesn't, chances are that your Perl knowledge is well beyond the scope of simply using CPAN to install some modules. Once automatic CPAN configuration is complete, the install will proceed rather verbosely. In the likely case that some component of the some bundle fails to install, simply retry the CPAN specified earlier using the name of the failed package. Consult Google regarding any errors, as troubleshooting specific Perl modules is beyond the scope of this book. As a general hint, though, note that the *install* directive has a *force* flag that is often useful, as shown here in Example 22-25.

Example 22-25. Installation of Perl bundles may be forced.

```
[ace2:~/amavisd-new-2.2.0] nadmin% sudo perl -MCPAN -e "force install Archive::Zip"
```

amavisd needs both a user to run as and a set of directories to run from. Since it will be closely coupled with ClamAV, we'll use the same system user for both packages, as shown in Example 22-26.

Example 22-26. Creating the filesystem directories used by amavis. They should be owned by the Amavis user—in this case, clamav, created earlier.

```
[ace2:~/amavisd-new-2.2.0] nadmin% sudo mkdir -p /var/amavis/tmp
[ace2:~/amavisd-new-2.2.0] nadmin% sudo mkdir -p /var/amavis/db
[ace2:~/amavisd-new-2.2.0] nadmin% sudo chown -R clamav:clamav /var/amavis
[ace2:~/amavisd-new-2.2.0] nadmin% sudo chmod -R 750 /var/amavis
```

Amavis's components (configuration file and executables) should be copied to their destination on the filesystem, as shown in Examples 22-27 and 22-28.

Example 22-27. amavis's configuration file should be stored in /etc. Be sure to use the amavisd.conf-sample file; it already contains the directives required to use SpamAssassin.

```
[ace2:~/amavisd-new-2.2.0] nadmin% sudo cp amavisd.conf-sample /etc/amavisd.conf
[ace2:~/amavisd-new-2.2.0] nadmin% sudo chmod 644 /etc/amavisd.conf
```

Example 22-28. According to the Unix hierarchical convention, system daemons not part of the base OS should be stored in /usr/sbin. See the hier manpage for details.

```
[ace2:~/amavisd-new-2.2.0] nadmin% sudo mkdir -p /usr/local/sbin/
[ace2:~/amavisd-new-2.2.0] nadmin% cp amavisd /usr/local/sbin/
```

After it is installed, Amavis must be configured. A convenient option if you use Webmin (web-based server administration software available from *www.webmin.com*) is the Webmin module for *amavisd-new*: *http://webuser.fh-furtwangen.de/~grund/AMaViSD/webmin-AMaViSD.html*. Otherwise you'll need to configure *amavis* manually by editing */etc/amavisd.conf*. An in-depth examination of the entire configuration file is beyond the scope of this chapter. Important directives are described in Table 22-10.

Table 22-10. Note that the quotes are part of the directive's value, and must be included in the configuration file.

Directive	Value
$MYHOME	"/var/amavis" This is a default value
$mydomain	Primary mail domain (i.e., "pantherserver.org")
$myhostname	Fully qualified domain name (i.e., "mail.pantherserver.org")
$daemon_user	"clamav"
$daemon_group	"clamav"
$pid_file	"$MYHOME/amavisd.pid"; this is a default value.
$lock_file	"$MYHOME/amavisd.lock"; this is a default value.
$unix_socketname	"$MYHOME/amavisd.sock"

Finally, add an additional clause in Section VII of */etc/amavisd.conf* that looks like the following; this expression instructs *amavis* to send mail to the socket ClamAV is listening on:

```
['Clam Antivirus-clamd',
&ask_daemon, ["CONTSCAN {}n", "/var/clamav/clamd.sock"],
qr/bOK$/, qr/bFOUND$/,
qr/^.*?: (?!Infected Archive)(.*) FOUND$/ ],
```

amavisd-new ships with a startup item specifically for Mac OS X and Mac OS X Server. As shell scripts go, it is (as of this writing) fairly poor, using unqualified paths to executables and several other things you don't generally want to see in a shell script. I prefer to start *amavisd-new* using *watchdog*. *amavisd* may be started by adding the following entry to */etc/watchdog.conf*:

```
gs:~ root# grep amavis /etc/watchdog.conf
amavis:respawn:/usr/local/sbin/amavisd -u clamav -g clamav start
```

SpamAssassin installation is so easy that it's already done for you. When you installed the `Mail::SpamAssassin` Perl module earlier, that was the complete process! SpamAssassin management is similarly easy. The default configuration (in */etc/mail/spamassassin/local.cf*) is fine for most purposes. Extended graphical functionality may be found in the SpamAssassin plug-in that ships with Webmin (an open source web-based administration application mentioned earlier). This plug-in exposes the most common features of SpamAssassin in a fairly friendly way.

SpamAssassin's integration with procmail is a widely demonstrated method for reducing spam. Procmail, though, is an oldish technology, and a real performance hog in modern systems with lots of users who all receive a large volume of mail. Rather than using procmail, I recommend the more centralized, MTA-based solution presented here.

Putting it all together

Once *amavisd-new*, ClamAV, and SpamAssassin are all installed, they must be integrated. As mentioned earlier, Postfix will pass all mail to *amavisd*, which will be responsible for processing messages using SpamAssassin and ClamAV. The easiest method involves adding a couple of lines to Postfix's configuration files (*/etc/postfix/master.cf* and */etc/postfix/main.cf*). The best way to ensure that these changes are preserved is to actually modify */etc/postfix/master.cf.default* and */etc/postfix/main.cf. defaultserver*—these files are used as templates, and when SMTP settings are modified they are flushed to *master.cf* and *main.cf* (respectively). *main.cf.default* has a null content_filter directive (it is set to nothing). It needs to be modified to use *amavis*, as shown in Example 22-29.

Example 22-29. This content_filter directive sends mail to amavis. It must be added to /etc/postfix/ main.cf.default. This allows it to be flushed to Postfix's configuration file and be preserved during graphical configuration and management.

```
content_filter = smtp-amavis:[127.0.0.1]:10024
```

The *smtp-amavis* service referenced in *main.cf.default* must be defined in *master.cf. defaultserver*, and the *smtp* service must be modified to listen on a high port for incoming processed messages from *amavis* (see Example 22-30).

Example 22-30. The structure of our mail filtering system is defined in master.cf.defaultserver. Incoming mail is forwarded to the smtp-amavis content filter listening on port 10024. After processing, amavis returns messages to the SMTP service available on port 10025. Postfix then delivers the messages to Cyrus as it normally would.

```
smtp-amavis unix -         -       y       -       2       smtp
    -o smtp_data_done_timeout=1200
    -o smtp_send_xforward_command=yes
    -o disable_dns_lookups=yes
127.0.0.1:10025 inet n     -       y       -       -       smtpd
    -o content_filter=
    -o local_recipient_maps=
    -o relay_recipient_maps=
    -o smtpd_restriction_classes=
    -o smtpd_client_restrictions=
    -o smtpd_helo_restrictions=
    -o smtpd_sender_restrictions=
    -o smtpd_recipient_restrictions=permit_mynetworks,reject
    -o mynetworks=127.0.0.0/8
    -o strict_rfc821_envelopes=yes
```

Example 22-30. The structure of our mail filtering system is defined in master.cf.defaultserver. Incoming mail is forwarded to the smtp-amavis content filter listening on port 10024. After processing, amavis returns messages to the SMTP service available on port 10025. Postfix then delivers the messages to Cyrus as it normally would. (continued)

```
-o smtpd_error_sleep_time=0
-o smtpd_soft_error_limit=1001
-o smtpd_hard_error_limit=1000
-o receive_override_options=no_header_body_checks
```

Finally, SMTP must be disabled and then re-enabled, so that the */etc/postfix/main.cf. default* and */etc/postfix/master.cf.defaultserver* may be flushed to */etc/postfix/main.cf* and */etc/postfix/master.cf* (respectively). This can be accomplished in Server Admin by first unchecking and saving "Enable SMTP" item in General Mail Settings, and then rechecking it and clicking the Save button a second time.

Group Distribution

Jaguar Server (and every version of *AppleMailServer* leading up to it) could use the membership of any group in the directory (be it local or otherwise) for mail distribution. Mail to group names that arrived on your server was properly delivered, as long as the members had enabled or forwarded mail. The transition to Panther, however, with its open source underpinnings, lost this feature. The most obvious workaround is use of Panther Server's Mailing List feature. This solution is a little more than many folks are looking for, and there are other alternatives that could be more suited to some situations.

Postfix alias support

One way of recapturing some of the flexibility that group distribution afforded is to emulate it with Postfix's aliases support. Postfix uses aliases to deliver mail for a username or names that do not actually exist. This is often used to assign multiple email addresses for a particular user. For example, an */etc/aliases* entry like the one shown here would allow mail sent to *bob* to actually be delivered to *robertjones*:

```
bob: robertjones
```

Luckily, aliases can also be used to deliver mail to multiple addresses. The following example shows an alias, called *admin*; sending mail to *admin* results in message delivery to *tom*, *sarahj*, and *effie*:

```
admin: tom sarahj effie
```

Aliases are added by manually editing */etc/aliases* and then running the *postalias* and *newaliases* command (the latter to process */etc/aliases* into a database, and the former to tell postfix about the updated database. */etc/aliases* is populated in a default Mac OS X Server installation with various system-level accounts that by convention have their mail sent to root.

root's mail is discarded in a default configuration, since *root* has a *.forward* file that specifies all mail should be sent to */dev/null*. At a minimum, if you should probably alter */etc/aliases* to have mail for postmaster sent somewhere it might be occasionally read.

Some operating systems ship postfix with support for aliases stored in LDAP or an SQL server. As of 10.3.3, Mac OS X Server does not. NetInfo and NIS maps might work, but at this point it is easier to stay with the flat files that are standardized across all of the platforms supported by postfix.

Take 2: shared mailboxes

Another option for group distribution is the creation of a shared IMAP mailbox. Multiple users will be able to access the mailbox according to the permissions you establish. This is a handy way for cross-functional data to be shared among multiple users or groups. I use a shared mailbox, for instance, to coordinate mail among my Accounts Payable guy, my bookkeeper, and me. The first step is to install a working version of *cyradm*, the *cyrus* administration tool. You can build *cyradm* yourself using Apple's Cyrus source code available at *http://publicsource.apple.com* (all you need are some missing Perl headers), but it is much more easily obtainable at *afp548. com* (*www.afp548.com/cyradm*). Once installed, *cyradm* is easy to use. Users expected to administer your IMAP server using *cyradm* must be listed in the admins: line of */etc/imapd.conf* (as shown in Example 22-31).

Example 22-31. Using the grep command to view the admins: entry in /etc/imapd.conf. This consists of a space-delineated list of the short names for the users designated as IMAP administrators. IMAP admins need not belong to the system's admin group.

```
[ace2:~] nadmin% grep admins /etc/imapd.conf
admins: cyrus nadmin
```

cyradm is an interactive command; when launched, it presents the user with a prompt for entering further, *cyradm*-specific commands:

1. First connect to your server.

    ```
    [ace2:~] nadmin% cyradm -u nadmin mail.4am-media.com
    Password:
    ```

     cyradm can be used to connect to and remotely manage an IMAP server. This step should be undertaken with caution unless you have CRAM-MD5 IMAP authentication enabled.

2. Use the *lm* command to list your mailboxes in order to get a good idea of your mailserver's structure.

    ```
    mail.4am-media.com> lm
    INBOX (\Noinferiors)
    Other Users/4am (\HasNoChildren)
    ```

```
Other Users/ghydle (\HasChildren)
Other Users/ghydle/Deleted Messages (\HasNoChildren)
Other Users/mbartosh (\HasChildren)
Other Users/mbartosh/ACN (\HasNoChildren)
Other Users/mbartosh/Deleted Messages (\HasNoChildren)
Other Users/mbartosh/Kerb (\HasNoChildren)
Other Users/mbartosh/SUN (\HasNoChildren)
Other Users/mbartosh/Sent (\HasNoChildren)
Other Users/mbartosh/Sent Messages (\HasNoChildren)
Other Users/mbartosh/applescript (\HasNoChildren)
Other Users/mbartosh/bugs (\HasNoChildren)
Other Users/otherguy (\HasNoChildren)
Other Users/ambrlyn/(\HasNoChildren)
Other Users/ambrlyn/ Deleted Messages (\HasNoChildren)
Other Users/tpand (\HasNoChildren)
Other Users/tpand/ Deleted Messages (\HasNoChildren)
Other Users/ac  (\HasNoChildren)
Other Users/ac / Deleted Messages (\HasNoChildren)
```

3. Create the new mailbox using the *cm* command:

```
mail.4am-media.com> cm Other\ Users/requests
```

4. Add access controls for the desired users. The following commands grant full control to the users *ghydle* and *mbartosh*. Far more granular access controls are feasible; for additional information, consult *cyradm*'s documentation.

```
mail.4am-media.com> sam Other\ Users/requests ghydle lrswipcda
mail.4am-media.com> sam Other\ Users/requests mbartosh lrswipcda
```

Client-side configuration for shared IMAP folders varies widely. Apple's Mail.app discovers them as long as the automatically synchronize changed Mailboxes option is selected in the Account preferences, as shown in Figure 22-19.

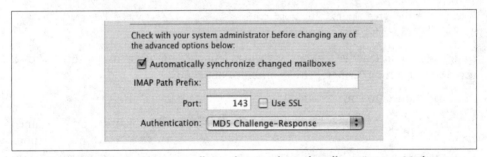

Figure 22-19. Selecting the "Automatically synchronize changed mailboxes" option Mail.app allows shared folders to be discovered.

Virtual Domains

A certain level of virtual domain support can be achieved in Mac OS X Server by manual editing of Postfix's configuration files. This allows (for instance) your mail server to receive mail identically named accounts in different domains (*sales@domain1.com* and *sales@domain2.com* could be delivered to two different accounts; something not feasible using Apple's graphical tools). First, any virtual domains must be listed in Postfix's *main.cf* file. Remember that you should add an identical setting to */etc/postfix/main.cf.default* to ensure compatibility with Apple's graphical management tools.

```
virtual_alias_domains = tigerserver.org mabaleb.org
virtual_alias_maps = hash:/etc/postfix/virtual
```

In this case, I've specified that my server should accept mail for tigerserver.org. The virtual_alias_maps setting specifies that alias data are located in */etc/postfix/virtual*. Other Postfix distributions typically allow virtual domain aliases to be stored in LDAP. The format of the aliases file is very simple; addresses are delineated from their destination accounts with tabs, as shown here:

```
info@pantherserver.org      mbartosh
info@tigerserver.org        ghydle
```

Postfix may be alerted to the new aliases by executing the *postmap /etc/postfix/virtual* command. The entire Postfix system must be reloaded if a new virtual domain has been added to *main.cf* and *main.cf.default*. This can be achieved by executing the *postfix reload* command. Both of these commands require *root* privileges and should be prepended with *sudo*.

Securing Web Mail

As of 10.3.3, Web Mail on Mac OS X is not configured in a default installation to use secure authentication. As mentioned earlier in the chapter, this in and of itself is not a bad thing, as generally Web Mail will run on the mail server itself, and the username will be passed in the clear only over the server's loopback address (127.0.0.1). If someone is able to sniff traffic that never leaves the server, Web Mail is the least of your problems. The issue, however, is that there is no way to limit clear test authentication solely to the loopback interface, and if insecure authentication is allowed globally, then you've moved the security of your server from your hands into those of your users, trusting them to configure their mail clients for secure authentication. From a security standpoint, there is no arguing that this weakens your architecture.

Additionally, since Panther ships with Password Server enabled, it can be assumed that more secure methods may be supported. The few fringe cases of migrations from 10.1 servers or 10.2 servers still using basic (crypt) authentication will have to upgrade their accounts to use password server before they can be secured.

Web Mail, provided by the SquirrelMail package, is configured with a command-line Perl script that is stored at */usr/share/squirrelmail/config/conf.pl*. It should be executed as *root*, using the *sudo* command, as shown in the examples that follow. Note that if you followed the recommendation earlier in the chapter to generate site-specific SquirrelMail installs, each site will have its own *conf.pl* and its own separate configuration.

First, it's necessary to locate and execute the conf.pl script:

```
[ace2:~ /amavisd-new-2.2.0] nadmin% cd /usr/share/squirrelmail/config
gs:/usr/share/squirrelmail/config nadmin$ sudo ./conf.pl
```

From the menu-driven interface, choose option 2, Server Settings:

```
SquirrelMail Configuration : Read: config.php (1.4.0)
---------------------------------------------------------
Main Menu --
1.  Organization Preferences
2.  Server Settings
3.  Folder Defaults
4.  General Options
5.  Themes
6.  Address Books (LDAP)
7.  Message of the Day (MOTD)
8. Plugins
9. Database

D. Set pre-defined settings for specific IMAP servers

C. Turn color on
S  Save data
Q  Quit

Command >> 2
```

Next, choose option A, Update IMAP Settings:

```
SquirrelMail Configuration : Read: config.php (1.4.0)
---------------------------------------------------------
Server Settings

General
-------
1.  Domain              : getenv(SERVER_NAME)
2.  Invert Time         : false
3.  Sendmail or SMTP    : SMTP

A.  Update IMAP Settings  : localhost:143 (cyrus)
B.  Update SMTP Settings  : localhost:25

R   Return to Main Menu
C.  Turn color on
S   Save data
Q   Quit

Command >> A
```

From the Update IMAP Settings menu, choose option 6, Authentication Type:

```
IMAP Settings
--------------
4.  IMAP Server         : localhost
5.  IMAP Port           : 143
```

```
6.  Authentication type   : cram-md5
7.  Secure IMAP (TLS)     : false
8.  Server software       : cyrus
9.  Delimiter             : detect

B.  Update SMTP Settings  : localhost:25
H.  Hide IMAP Server Settings

R   Return to Main Menu
C.  Turn color on
S   Save data
Q   Quit

Command >> 6
```

Optionally, choose to let *conf.pl* determine which authentication methods are supported. This is generally not required, as we can assume that if PasswordService is running, CRAM-MD5 is available:

```
If you have already set the hostname and port number, I can try to
detect the mechanisms your IMAP server supports.
I will try to detect CRAM-MD5 and DIGEST-MD5 support.  I can't test
for "login" without knowing a username and password.
Auto-detecting is optional - you can safely say "n" here.

Try to detect supported mechanisms? [y/N]: N
```

Type **cram-md5** if it is not already selected, then press return:

```
What authentication mechanism do you want to use for IMAP connections?

login - Plaintext. If you can do better, you probably should.
cram-md5 - Slightly better than plaintext methods.
digest-md5 - Privacy protection - better than cram-md5.

*** YOUR IMAP SERVER MUST SUPPORT THE MECHANISM YOU CHOOSE HERE ***
If you don't understand or are unsure, you probably want "login"

login, cram-md5, or digest-md5 [cram-md5]:
```

In the resulting menu, choose S to save. When prompted, press Return to continue and Q to quit:

```
R   Return to Main Menu
C.  Turn color on
S   Save data
Q   Quit

Command >> S
```

CHAPTER 23

Web Services

The HyperText Transport Protocol (HTTP) is, hands-down, the ubiquitous protocol of the Internet. For the most part, when people say the word "Internet" they think of the ever-present Web that has been a fixture of the computing landscape since the mid-nineties. And, almost as long as the public has been fascinated with the Web, the number one HTTP server has been the Apache *httpd* web server. Apache is not the fastest possible web server, but it is, without a doubt, the most flexible.

Due to its flexibility, and likely in no small part due to the number of system administrators that are comfortable with it, Apple has bundled the Apache web server into Mac OS X and Mac OS X Server. For the most part, there are two primary differences in Apple's distribution of the Apache web server in Mac OS X Server:

- The configuration files are structured to work with the Server Admin tool.
- Apple provides a performance cache proxy.

In addition, the Apache web server comes configured out of the box to provide Web-DAV (Web-based Distributed Authoring and Versioning) services. This setup allows your users to make changes to the files contained by your server directly without AFP access.

This chapter examines the Apache web server, especially noting how it is integrated with the server tools, and guides you through the unique differences on Mac OS X Server.

Managing Web Services

The Apache web server, like most of the other Mac OS X Server services, can be controlled and configured with the Server Admin application. Like the other services managed by Server Admin, you can start and stop the web service using the Start/Stop Service toggle button in Server Admin's toolbar or by using the Server → Start Service and Server → Stop Service menus.

You can also start and stop the web service on the command line using the *serveradmin* command:

```
$ sudo serveradmin start web
$ sudo serveradmin stop web
```

As well as the *serveradmin* command, you can also use Apache's *apachectl* command-line tool to start and stop the web service:

```
$ sudo apachectl start
$ sudo apachectl stop
```

 Using the *apachectl* command is preferable to other command-line actions, such as using *ps* and sending a HUP signal, since *httpd* runs as a multiprocess server. Using the *apachectl* command means that you don't have to worry about finding the parent process or gracefully shutting down the children processes.

Once the web service is started, you'll be able to point a web browser at your server and see the default home page, shown in Figure 23-1. This page is stored in the folder */Library/WebServer/Documents*, also known as the web server's document root. To serve your own content, replace the content in this folder with the HTML and graphics files you want to use for your site. You can also select a different folder on the filesystem to use as the document root.

The options at the top of the web service section are similar to those in the other sections, including panes for Overview, Logs, Graphs, and Settings, which are covered in the following sections.

The Overview Pane

The Overview pane, shown in Figure 23-2, shows the very basics about the state of the web service, including some basic statistics about the service. Theses statistics include the number of requests served as well as the throughput of the service in megabytes.

The information displayed in the Overview pane can also be obtained from the command line using the *serveradmin* command. For example, to determine whether the service is running:

```
$ sudo serveradmin status web
web:command = "getState"
web:state = "RUNNING"
```

To get a more complete service status, use the *fullstatus* option to the *serveradmin* command, as follows:

```
$ sudo serveradmin fullstatus web
web:command = "getState"
web:totalRequests = 693
```

Figure 23-1. The default home page of the web service.

```
web:totalKBytes = 3686
web:cacheTotalKBytes = 1843
web:cacheTotalRequests = 347
web:currentThroughput = 0
web:state = "RUNNING"
web:logPaths:logPathsArray:_array_index:0:serverName = ""
web:logPaths:logPathsArray:_array_index:0:path = "/var/log/httpd/access_log"
web:logPaths:logPathsArray:_array_index:0:type = "ACCESSLOG"
web:logPaths:logPathsArray:_array_index:0:port = 80
web:logPaths:logPathsArray:_array_index:0:ipAddress = "*"
web:logPaths:logPathsArray:_array_index:1:serverName = ""
web:logPaths:logPathsArray:_array_index:1:path = "/var/log/httpd/error_log"
```

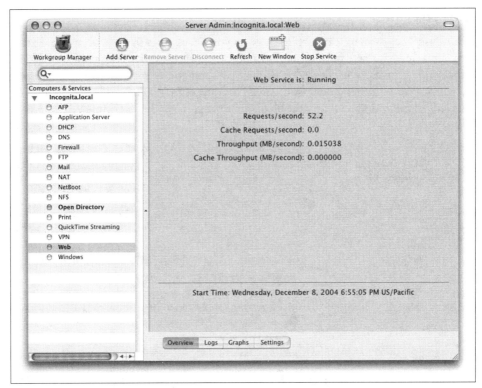

Figure 23-2. The web service Overview pane.

```
web:logPaths:logPathsArray:_array_index:1:type = "ERRORLOG"
web:logPaths:logPathsArray:_array_index:1:port = 80
web:logPaths:logPathsArray:_array_index:1:ipAddress = "*"
web:cacheCurrentRequestsBy10 = 0
web:cacheState = "RUNNING"
web:apacheState = "RUNNING"
web:statusMessage = ""
web:readWriteSettingsVersion = 1
web:setStateVersion = 1
web:startedTime = "2004-11-20 21:16:15 -0800"
web:currentRequestsBy10 = 0
web:cacheCurrentThroughput = 0
```

This output is handy when all you need is to take a quick look at how your web service is performing. It can also be used as data that a *periodic cron* job could use. For example, you could have a script that sends you the current throughput of the web service on a hourly basis. After glancing through that message, you can quickly assess whether your server is running at its best.

The Logs Pane

The Logs pane, shown in Figure 23-3, gives you access to Apache's access and error logs. The view you get is a simple dump of the */var/log/httpd/access_log* and */var/log/httpd/error_log* files. The access log shows you each and every connection made by a web browser, or other client software, to your service. The error log gives you detailed information about any problems that the web service encounters.

Figure 23-3. The web service Logs pane, giving you access to the access and error log files. You can always SSH into the server and view the log files directly with tail.

As with the other services managed by Server Admin, the graphical user interface doesn't offer any kind of filtering. To do more than just browse the logs, you'll need to either log into the server directly via SSH. Once logged in, you can manipulate the log files from the command line using tools like *grep* and *tail*, or you'll need to cut and paste them into your favorite text editor. For example, to monitor all of the requests to a particular URL path on your server, use the following:

```
$ tail -f /var/log/httpd/access_log | grep /mypage.php
127.0.0.1 - - [08/Dec/2004:18:33:59 -0800] "GET /mypage.php HTTP/1.1" 200 3888 "-"
"Mozilla/5.0 (Macintosh; U; PPC Mac OS X; en-us) AppleWebKit/125.5.5 (KHTML, like
Gecko) Safari/125.11"
```

Another problem with the graphical interface is that a server under a reasonable load generates logs faster than you can view them without the ability to focus down on a particular path.

The Graphs Pane

The Graphs pane (shown in Figure 23-4) gives you a graphical view of the number of requests, as well as the data throughput, that the web service is handling. You can adjust the graphs for a specified period of time from one hour to seven days into the immediate past.

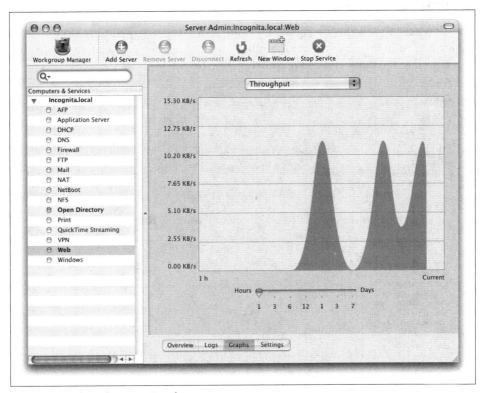

Figure 23-4. The web service Graphs pane.

The information presented by these graphs is useful when you're trying to locate specific periods of time when there was high traffic load on your server. However, they are pretty basic compared to more sophisticated web analysis tools such as Webalizer (*www.mrunix.net/webalizer/*) and Analog (*www.analog.cx*).

Web Service Configuration: The Settings Tab

The Settings tab of Server Admin's web services panel gives access to a fair amount of the Apache web server's configuration. All of the settings that can be manipulated with Server Admin correspond to the configuration directives in the configuration files, located at */etc/httpd/httpd.conf*. This pane is like a Russian doll, in that it contains another full set of tabs for drilling into a number of settings. For many people, in fact, it's downright confusing until you get the hang of things. This section provides a guide to these tabs.

General Configuration

The General tab, shown in Figure 23-5, offers a basic set of tuning options that allows you to limit the maximum number of simultaneous connections to the service as well as the number of server process that should be used.

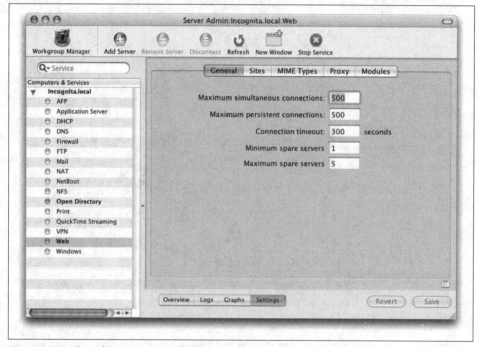

Figure 23-5. The web service General Settings pane.

The settings in the General tab directly correspond to the following Apache web server configuration directives:

```
MaxClients 500
MaxKeepAliveRequests 500
Timeout 300
MinSpareServers 1
MaxSpareServers 5
```

Changes to these settings in the GUI are reflected in the *httpd.conf* file. As well, if you edit these settings in the *httpd.conf* file manually, they will be reflected in the GUI.

 There are a few caveats to editing the *httpd.conf* file directly; we'll get back to that later in the chapter, though.

Configuring Sites

The Sites pane, shown in Figure 23-6, gives you access to manage virtual hosts. A virtual host is a logically separate site that is served by the same Apache web service as other hosts. This allows you to locate dozens or even hundreds of sites on the same physical server. You can assign each site its own IP address, they can all share a single IP address, or any combination thereof.

 An important restriction to note is that due to the way SSL works, you can have only one SSL-based virtual host on any particular IP address.

Figure 23-6. The Sites pane.

As installed, the server has only one web site by default. To add additional sites, you can use the "Add a new web site" (+) button. To edit the settings for a particular site, you can either double-click on the site or use the "Edit selected web site" button. This brings up another Russian doll subpanel, which allows you to configure the site with a set of tabs.

The configuration interface for a site contains the following tabs:

General

> Contains settings for the domain name that the site responds to, the IP address it is bound to, the site's document root, its index and error files, as well as the email address for the site's administrator. If the domain field is blank, the site is designated as the default site for the IP address it's bound to. The General tab is shown in Figure 23-7.

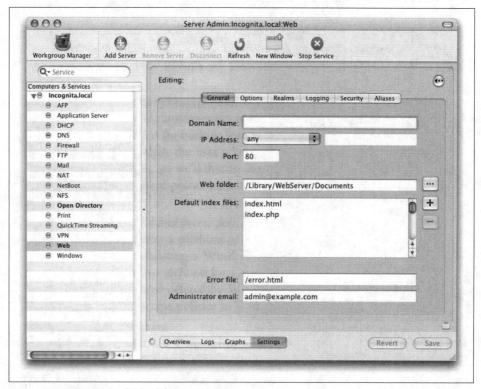

Figure 23-7. The General tab of the Sites pane.

Options

> Allows you to specify whether the site uses the performance cache, provides a file listing for directories that don't contain an *index* file, whether it supports WebDAV, the execution of CGI scripts, and webmail.

Details about the performance cache are covered in the "Architecture" section later in this chapter.

Realms

Allows you to constrain access to a directory to a collection of users and groups. These groups can be assigned read and write permissions to the contents of the directory. The write permissions affect clients that are connecting via WebDAV.

 You cannot assign permissions to a single file within a directory, because Apache's access model is based on directories rather than on files.

One gotcha about these permissions: in order to provide write access to a file, it must be owned by the *www* user or *www* group and have Unix user or group write permissions set accordingly. The reason why is that the Apache web server runs as the *www* user and it is the web server effectively reads and writes these files, not the remote user ID that Apache has authenticated. Accordingly, if you have files that you need both local and remote users to write, you should make sure that those users are in the *www* group.

Logging

Allows you to configure where the access and error logs for the site are stored as well as the log files' format. The panel gives you the ability to save the logs in many common formats, including combined, common, referrer, and agent. For the most part, you should probably use the combined log format as it includes all of the data needed by log analysis tools like Analog. You can also define your own log formats using standard Apache log file format strings.

Security

Allows you to enable Secure Sockets Layer (SSL) for the server as well as specify the locations of the certificate files used by the SSL engine. You can also directly edit the contents of the certificate files.

Aliases

Allows you to specify aliases from a path in the scope of the web server's URL namespace to a path on the filesystem.

If you are familiar with Apache's configuration files, the settings for each site correspond to directives that can appear in the <VirtualHost> directive. In addition, to aid in managing large numbers of sites, Mac OS X Server writes the settings for each site into a separate file in the */etc/httpd/sites* directory. For example, a clean installation of Mac OS X Server contains the following files in the *sites* directory:

```
$ ls /etc/httpd/sites
virtual_host_global.conf
0000_any_80_.conf
```

The first file (*virtual_host_global.conf*) contains settings used by all sites. The second (*0000_any_80_.conf*) contains all of the settings for the default site. If you open the *0000_any_80_.conf* file, you'll see something similar to the following:

```
## Default Virtual Host Configuration

<VirtualHost *:16080>
        ServerAdmin admin@example.com
        DocumentRoot "/Library/WebServer/Documents"
        DirectoryIndex "index.html" "index.php"
        CustomLog "/var/log/httpd/access_log" "%{PC-Remote-Addr}i %l %u %t \"%r\" %>s
%b \"%{Referer}i\" \"%{User-Agent}i\""
        ErrorLog "/var/log/httpd/error_log"
        ErrorDocument 404 /error.html
        <IfModule mod_ssl.c>
                SSLEngine Off
                SSLLog "/var/log/httpd/ssl_engine_log"
                SSLCertificateChainFile "/etc/httpd/ssl.crt/ca.crt1any_80_default"
                SSLCertificateFile "/etc/httpd/ssl.crt/server.crtany_80_default"
                SSLCertificateKeyFile "/etc/httpd/ssl.key/server.keyany_80_default"
                SSLCipherSuite "ALL:!ADH:RC4+RSA:+HIGH:+MEDIUM:+LOW:!SSLv2:+EXP:+eNULL"
        </IfModule>
        <IfModule mod_dav.c>
                DAVLockDB "/var/run/davlocks/.davlockany_80_default"
                DAVMinTimeout 600
        </IfModule>
        <Directory "/Library/WebServer/Documents">
                Options All -Indexes -ExecCGI +MultiViews
                AllowOverride None
                <IfModule mod_dav.c>
                        DAV Off
                </IfModule>
                <Limit DELETE PROPPATCH MKCOL COPY MOVE LOCK UNLOCK>
                        Require no-user
                </Limit>
                AuthName "General"
                AuthType Basic
        </Directory>
        <IfModule mod_rewrite.c>
                RewriteEngine On
                RewriteCond %{REQUEST_METHOD} ^TRACE
                RewriteRule .* - [F]
        </IfModule>
        <IfModule mod_alias.c>
        </IfModule>
        LogLevel warn
</VirtualHost>
```

If you so choose, the files contained in the *sites* directory can be edited by hand. However, you should make sure that Server Admin isn't running before you edit them. If Server Admin is running while you're editing these files, your changes may be overwritten. This can be a real problem, especially if you've configured a bunch of sites only to have Server Admin trash those settings when you quit it later.

Setting MIME Types

MIME (Multipurpose Internet Mail Extension) is the Internet standard for communicating the type of a file to a web browser. The Apache web server transmits the type of a file based on its extension. For example, a file with a *.txt* extension has the MIME type of *text/plain*. The MIME Types pane, shown in Figure 23-8, lets you edit and add to the mappings between file extensions and MIME types that the server uses.

Figure 23-8. The MIME Types tab.

The MIME Types panel also lets you set Content Handlers based on a file's extension. For example, the server is configured to treat any file ending with the *.cgi* extension as a CGI script and to execute it rather than returning the script directly.

 You can find resources as well as the official MIME type registry at the IANA web site (*www.iana.org/assignments/media-types/*).

Configuring the Proxy Server

The Proxy tab, shown in Figure 23-9, allows you to activate Apache's built-in proxy server. A *proxy server* allows you to cache specific web sites to a local server, which the users on your local network then use to browse the web. The proxy can cache frequently accessed documents to speed up response times and reduce WAN network traffic. When activated, all of the sites on the server can be used as a proxy.

By default, the proxy stores a maximum of a megabyte of cached files in the */var/run/ proxy* directory. To create an effective proxy, you'll want to dedicate more cache space.

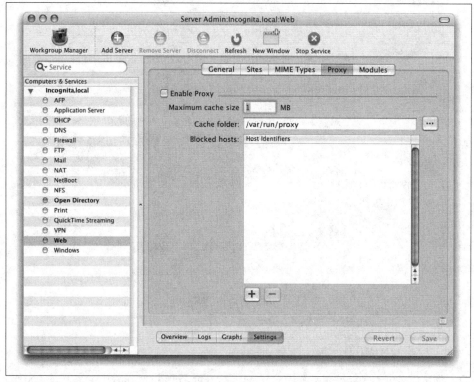

Figure 23-9. The Proxy tab.

The proxy functionality in Apache 1.3 is not considered to be state-of-the-art. In addition, it has fairly limited features. For example, there isn't a way to assign the cache refresh policy. Therefore, if you want proxy functionality on your network, you should consider using a different solution, such as Squid (*www.squid-cache.org*).

> For additional information on configuring and using the Squid proxy server, see *Squid: The Definitive Guide*, by Duane Wessels (O'Reilly, 2004).

Adding and Removing Modules

The Apache web server is a framework within which functionality is provided by a number of cooperating *modules*. These modules "plug in" to the Apache web server and and add their own piece of functionality to the server. Modules can either be compiled directly into the web server, or loaded as shared libraries (*.so* files).

The Modules tab in Server Admin, as shown in Figure 23-10, allows you to see the modules currently in use, control which modules are active, and add modules to the server. However, there isn't really an archive of modules on the Internet that you can download and install. Typically, to add a module to your server, you'll need to consult with a developer who can compile one for you.

Figure 23-10. The Modules tab.

Mac OS X Server comes with several modules designed to provide functionality specific to the Mac. These modules are:

mod_macbinary_apple

Allows Macintosh files containing resource forks to be packaged in the MacBinary format for transmission across the Internet. A file can be downloaded in MacBinary format by adding *.bin* to the URL path for the file.

mod_sherlock_apple

Allows Apache to return relevance-ranked searches using the Sherlock search engine. In order for this to work, you'll use the *indexfolder* command-line tool, as follows:

```
$ sudo indexfolder /Library/WebServer/Documents
```

You can then access the search functionality by opening a browser and browsing to the URL *http://hostname/.sherlock*.

mod_auth_apple

Allows Apache to authenticate users against Open Directory domains.

mod_hfs_apple

Adds security for case-insensitive volumes by requiring URLs for paths to use the correct case.

mod_digest_apple

Enables HTTP digest authentication to be performed with Open Directory users. Digest authentication is a more secure alternative to the widely used HTTP basic authentication scheme. However, many web clients don't support digest authentication. Also, digest authentication can't be performed on user IDs from an Active Directory server.

mod_rendezvous_apple

Allows Rendezvous advertisements to be made for sites on the server. Disabled by default, this module can be used to notify other computers on the local subnet that a web server is running. This means that browsers, such as Safari, that support finding web servers via Rendezvous will be able to find your server.

Architecture

The Apache server is implemented by the *httpd* daemon. This daemon is started by *SystemStarter* according to a –YES– flag on the WEBSERVER setting in the */etc/hostconfig* file. As mentioned previously, Apache's configuration files are located in the */etc/httpd* directory. These files are:

httpd.conf

This is the primary configuration file for Apache. This file differs from the default Apache *httpd.conf* file found on other systems for use by Server Admin. You can make changes to this file with care, but be sure to follow the instructions in the file when making changes so you don't interfere with Server Admin's ability to manipulate the file.

If you don't follow these instructions and you do end up using Server Admin for something, all of the changes you've made to the *httpd.conf* file will be reset when you quit Server Admin.

httpd_mailman.conf

This file contains the configuration needed by the Mailman mailing list manager. An include to this file is placed in *httpd.conf* by Server Admin when Mailman is activated.

httpd_squirrelmail.conf

This file contains the configuration needed when WebMail is activated. An include to this file is placed into *httpd.conf* by Server Admin when WebMail is activated. See Chapter 22 for more information about the WebMail integration.

mime.types

This file is usually used by Apache to determine MIME-types for files, but isn't used by Mac OS X Server. Instead, Server Admin places AddType directives directly into *httpd.conf* to set MIME-type mappings.

servermgr_web_httpd_config.plist

This file contains information used by Server Admin. You should *never* edit this file directly as doing so could render Server Admin unable to properly manage your web server.

sites/.conf*

This directory contains a file for each configured and enabled virtual host. The files in this directory are included by the server's *httpd.conf* thanks to an Include /httpd/sites/*.conf directive.

In addition to the configuration files, the various modules that provide Apache's functionality are located in the */usr/libexec/httpd* directory:

```
$ ls /usr/libexec/httpd
httpd.exp               mod_cern_meta.so         mod_mime.so
libdav.so               mod_cgi.so               mod_mime_magic.so
libperl.so              mod_digest.so            mod_negotiation.so
libphp4.so              mod_digest_apple.so      mod_rendezvous_apple.so
libproxy.so             mod_dir.so               mod_rewrite.so
libssl.so               mod_env.so               mod_setenvif.so
mod_access.so           mod_expires.so           mod_sherlock_apple.so
mod_actions.so          mod_headers.so           mod_speling.so
mod_alias.so            mod_hfs_apple.so         mod_status.so
mod_asis.so             mod_imap.so              mod_unique_id.so
mod_auth.so             mod_include.so           mod_userdir.so
mod_auth_anon.so        mod_info.so              mod_usertrack.so
mod_auth_apple.so       mod_jk.so                mod_vhost_alias.so
mod_auth_dbm.so         mod_log_config.so
mod_autoindex.so        mod_macbinary_apple.so
```

The Performance Cache

To most administrators comfortable with Apache, the strangest thing about Apple's implementation is the *performance cache*. The performance cache is a front-end proxy that's designed to speed access to static HTML files. It does this by caching static content from the web server into RAM, thus making it easier for the server to dish out that content as needed instead of having to call it up from disk.

When activated in a site's Option pane in Server Admin, the performance cache server (located in */usr/sbin/webperfcache*) runs on port 80 (or the other configured ports for a web server's sites) and is the first responder to requests from clients. If the request can be satisfied from the cache, it returns the content for that request—usually faster than Apache can do so by itself. However, if the content doesn't exist in the cache, the request is sent along to Apache, which is running on a private port (10680 in a default installation).

Lower traffic sites or sites that serve quite a bit of dynamic (and therefore uncachable) content won't benefit much from the performance cache. In addition, since using the performance cache moves Apache to a different port than the public HTTP port 80, it can interfere with scripts that expect to use the server port to rewrite URLs.

 If the performance cache were implemented as an Apache module instead of as a separate process, the configuration problems around ports wouldn't rear their ugly head.

For most sites, Apache's performance is more than adequate. Even though the performance cache is enabled by default, you should follow the lead of many experienced Apache administrators and disable it. If you do use the performance cache, you can modify its configuration by editing the */etc/webperfcache/webperfcache.conf* file.

Apache 2.0

Mac OS X Server comes with Apache 2.0 installed; however, it has been disabled. Apple indicates that Apache 2.0 is included for evaluation purposes. This doesn't reflect on the maturity of the Apache 2.0 server, only that the Server Admin tool doesn't yet work with Apache 2.0. If you want to use the Apache 2.0 server, you will be venturing outside the realm of Server Admin and into the strict world of configuring your web server from the command line.

If you want to run Apache 2.0, here's what you need to know:

- Apache 2.0 is installed in the */opt/apache2* directory. It's configuration file is */opt/apache2/conf/httpd.conf*; it is configured to serve pages from the */opt/apache2/htdocs* directory, not from */etc/httpd/sites*.

- Apache 2.0 uses a separate *apachectl* tool, located at */opt/apache2/bin/apachectl*. If you plan to use Apache 2.0, you'll need to add */opt/apache2/bin* to your shell's command path, and also set up a symbolic link from */usr/sbin/apachectl* to */opt/apache2/bin/apachectl*.

- To have Apache 2.0 start automatically at server startup, you'll need to create a Startup Item for it that executes */opt/apache2/bin/apachectl start*.

You also need to be careful not to let Apache 1.3 and Apache 2.0 interfere with each other. Make sure that you don't configure the two servers to listen to the same IP and port combinations. Since Apache is updated periodically via Software Update, you shouldn't remove the default installation of Apache 1.3 as parts of the system may rely on it.

 You can also use Webmin (*www.webmin.com*) or Tenon's iTools 7 (*www.tenon.com/products/itools7/*) to manage Apache 2. Both utilities provide a web-based administration interface for Apache 2.

Useful Utilities

Apache ships with a number of useful command-line tools for day-to-day web server management. These tools, which are located in */usr/sbin*, are the standard suite of tools that come with any Apache distribution:

ab
> Benchmarks the performance of an HTTP server by giving you an idea of how many requests per second your installation can serve. It is usually a good idea to run this tool from a machine separate from the server you are testing.

apachectl
> Starts and stops the Apache server. It can also test the configuration files for the server and give you detailed information about any syntax errors.

logresolve
> A post-processing program that resolves IP addresses in an Apache access log-file. This program expects a logfile on standard input and outputs a new logfile with resolved hostname on standard output.

Troubleshooting

Except for the performance cache, Apache on Mac OS X is similar enough to other platforms that all of the same troubleshooting methodologies used by Apache users apply. The most valuable troubleshooting resource is Apache's own log files. These files are stored in */var/log/httpd*. In particular, the error log, located at */var/log/httpd/ error_log*, is useful to determine the internal status of Apache, such as configuration issues or messages indicating why Apache can't startup.

CHAPTER 24
Application Servers

Most server administrators are familiar with HTML, and virtually everyone who owns a computer today is familiar with the use of a web browser. While static web sites are simply a collection of files placed in a web server, dynamic web pages are typically served by some sort of web application server.

Some web applications are provided by add-on modules for the popular Apache web server. These modules add support for popular programming languages such as Perl and PHP. A more robust (and complex) set of services are provided by full-blown Java application servers. Java application servers fall into two categories: JavaServer Pages/servlet servers, which provide support for standard web application development, and full enterprise class servers with support for Enterprise JavaBeans (EJB). Mac OS X Server includes both, with the Apache Tomcat server handling JSP/servlet duties and JBoss serving as the EJB server. In addition, Mac OS X Server includes the WebObjects framework preinstalled. These components are described in Table 24-1. All of these components are preinstalled on Mac OS X Server.

Table 24-1. What you get with WebObjects.

Component	Specification	Purpose	For more information
Java	Java 2 Standard Edition	Core Java runtime, provides support for platform-independent application code	*http://www.apple.com/java* *http://java.sun.com*
Tomcat	Servlet & JSP	Adds support for Java-based web applications	*http://jakarta.apache.org/tomcat/* *http://java.sun.com/products/servlets* *http://java.sun.com/products/jsp*
JBoss	Java 2 Enterprise Edition	Adds support for distributed applications and other complex functionality	*http://www.jboss.org/products/jbossas* *http://java.sun.com/j2ee/*
WebObjects	Apple Defined Toolkit	Rapid application development tools and framework	*http://www.apple.com/webobjects/*

If you're already a Java developer, much of this material may be familiar, although Mac OS X Server adds several additional features and deeper integration with the rest of the system. This chapter won't teach you Java, but it will give you an overview of the relevant Mac OS X Server components.

Running the Server

Mac OS X Server includes both JBoss (*http://www.jboss.org*) and Tomcat (*http://jakarta.apache.org/tomcat*). Tomcat is installed as a component of JBoss. Even if you need only Tomcat, you'll still access its administration via the Application Server view of Server Admin, as shown in Figure 24-1.

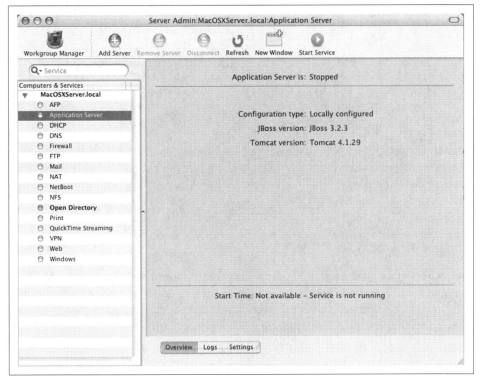

Figure 24-1. Server Admin: Application Server.

After clicking on the Settings tab at the bottom, you can choose the configuration you would like for the Application Server. As can be seen in Figure 24-2, you can choose from several different JBoss configurations, or configure the system to use only Tomcat. The deploy-standalone configuration is intended for production use when you are using a single Mac OS X server (the default configuration is simply an alias to this configuration). The deploy-cluster configuration is used when you are using several Mac OS X servers in tandem (you will need to confirm that your web application is compatible with this configuration). Finally, the develop configuration is a single system configuration, intended for use when you are developing an application. Among other changes, the develop configuration will generate more logging messages.

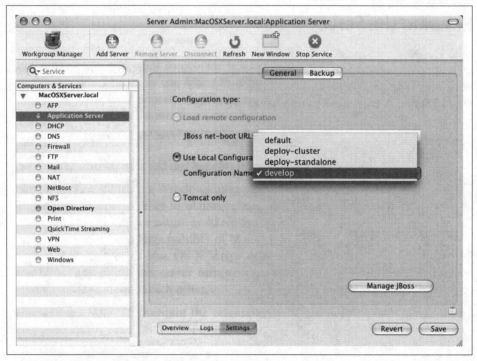

Figure 24-2. Choosing a configuration.

Two other options are present: Tomcat only and the option to load a remote JBoss configuration. You can leave these settings at their defaults or set the configuration to develop (for additional status messages) and start the service. After the service finishes launching, you should see the status as shown in Figure 24-3.

To verify that the server is running properly, open your browser and point it to *http://localhost:8080/*. By default, you should see the status page as shown in Figure 24-4.

Installing Applications

Java web applications typically are distributed in one of two formats: as a web application resource (WAR) or an enterprise application resource (EAR). Java application resources (JAR) are used by both desktop Java applications and web applications. For example, a particular enterprise application might be distributed in a single file,

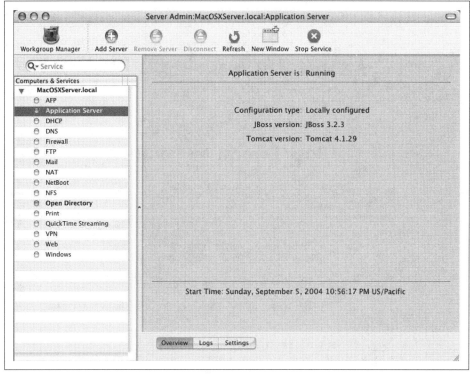

Figure 24-3. Application Server running.

industry_heavyweight.ear. This file might contain a number of files, including *complex_site.war*. The *complex_site.war* file, in turn, might contain a number of libraries, such as *database_connection.jar*. Normally, these files are built by the developer of an application, and then given to a system administrator to install.

 A much rarer format is a WebObjects application (WOA). Few open source or commercial applications are built or distributed on top of WebObjects; you are likely to see WebObjects applications only from Apple and custom applications.

Under the covers, WAR, EAR, and JAR files are merely ZIP files with different extensions and particular sets of files and folders.[*] If you need to inspect the contents of a WAR, EAR, or JAR in more detail, make a copy, rename the file from *myfile.war* to *myfile.zip*, and decompress it.

---

[*] The converse is not necessarily true. WAR, EAR, and JAR files can be digitally signed to ensure that they haven't been tampered with.

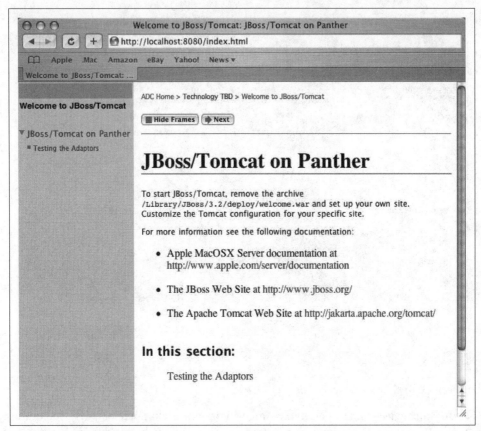

Figure 24-4. Default application server page.

Inside a WAR File

Inside of a WAR file you will find a directory called *WEB-INF*. The *WEB-INF* directory is a special directory that is hidden to remote clients (such as web browsers), and allows you to add protected resources specific to this application, such as configuration files that might store sensitive information (like passwords for connecting to a database).

The *lib* directory, which is located inside WEB-INF, contains JAR files that are automatically added to the web application's class path (the search path for Java libraries).

In theory, installing a WAR or EAR is as simple as downloading the file and dropping it into the correct directory. For example, download the file from *www.cascadetg.com/downloads/server_example.war*.

For more information on this sample application, see *http://today.java. net/pub/a/today/2004/03/11/sitemesh.html.*

To install this web application, simply drop it into the directory */Library/JBoss/3.2/ deploy/*, as shown in Figure 24-5.

Figure 24-5. Installing a sample WAR.

Before this file can be loaded by the application server, the proper file permissions must be set. Set the owner of the file to *appserver* and the group to *appserveradm*, as shown in Figure 24-6. Once you have made these changes, open your web browser to *http://localhost:8080/server_example/* and view the page as shown in Figure 24-7.

As described earlier, if you are interested, you can make a copy of the WAR, rename the file ZIP, and then decompress the file. Figure 24-8 shows the decompressed sample WAR.

Unfortunately, few Java-based web applications are so easy to install. This isn't an issue with Java applications per se, but rather a reflection of the sheer potential configurations and technologies available. For example, let's consider the Roller weblog toolkit

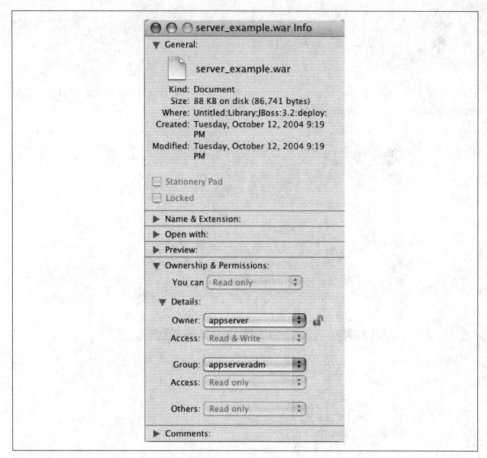

Figure 24-6. Setting WAR permissions.

(*www.rollerweblogger.org*). This is a fairly typical Java application (with an installation guide provided at *www.rollerweblogger.org/wiki/Wiki.jsp?page=InstallationGuide* to help move things along) as shown in Figure 24-9. To install the application as described requires downloading several JAR files from different sites, installing the tables into the database, and installing and configuring several other files (including application-specific cache and logging).

Another package, somewhat easier to install than Roller, is blojsom (*http://blojsom.sf. net*). A lightweight blogging package, it requires no database and, as of this writing, it is scheduled for inclusion in a future version of Mac OS X Server (*www.apple.com/ pr/library/2004/jun/28tigerserver.html*).

Figure 24-7. Viewing the sample WAR.

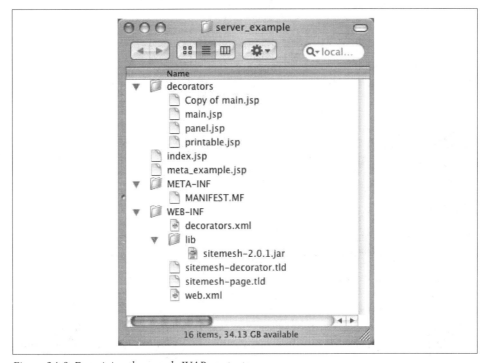

Figure 24-8. Examining the sample WAR contents.

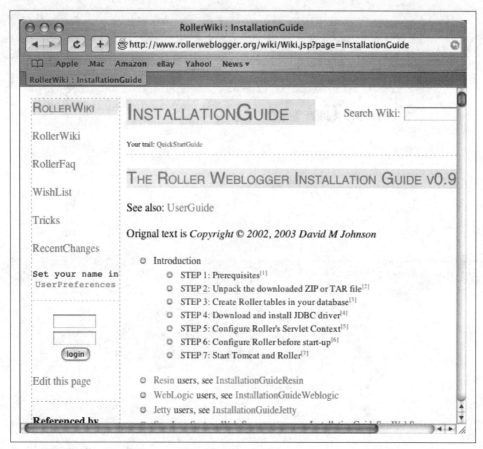

Figure 24-9. Roller installation.

Server Layout

Now that you've installed a simple web application, let's take a moment to touch on how Tomcat and JBoss are configured.

Tomcat is installed in multiple locations on Mac OS X Server: once as a component of JBoss (in the */Library/JBoss/3.2/server/develop/deploy/jbossweb-tomcat4.1.sar/* folder), and standalone (in the */Library/Tomcat/* folder). Additional instances are installed (and configured) for the *deploy-cluster* and *deploy-standalone* JBoss directories. In effect, you have several different versions of JBoss preinstalled, all of which share a common deployment directory: */Library/JBoss/3.2/deploy/*. This setup allows you to install an application once, but maintain multiple server configurations.

> ## Advanced Tomcat Configuration
>
> If you are a more advanced user of Tomcat, you might wish to customize the configuration of Tomcat. You can find the JBoss configuration of Tomcat's *web.xml* file in */Library/JBoss/3.2/server/develop/deploy/jbossweb-tomcat4.1.sar*.
>
> This file configures the core components of Tomcat. You can look here to do interesting things like add support for CGI scripts, set the default timeout for user sessions, define file extension and MIME mappings, and all sorts of other esoteric goodies.
>
> Generally speaking, the *web.xml* file is beyond the scope of this book. For additional information on how to further configure Tomcat, you should visit Tomcat's web site (as well as inspecting the file itself, which is reasonably well documented). Another resource is *Tomcat: The Definitive Guide* (O'Reilly, 2003).

For typical production use, you will want to leave the configuration of JBoss set to default, but you may wish to switch to the develop configuration if you are interested in building your own Java-based web applications.

The JBoss directory layout is shown in Figure 24-10. The items in the *bin* directory are used to launch JBoss from the command line. The *server* directory contains the various configurations of JBoss as shown in Server Admin. The *Applications* directory contains administrative applications. As mentioned, the *deploy* directory is where you place web applications you would like to install.

Logs and Troubleshooting

The various log files generated by JBoss and Tomcat can be found in the */Library/ Logs/JBoss* directory. While you can view these log files in the Server Admin application, you may find it more convenient to open a Terminal window, *cd* to the directory */Library/Logs/JBoss*, and type the command *tail –f filename.log*. As shown in Figure 24-11, this causes the Terminal to echo incoming changes to the selected log file until you press Control-C. I find that using the command *tail –f /Library/Logs/ JBoss/server.log* is particularly useful when restarting a troubled application server on a frequent basis. The various log files are described in Table 24-2.

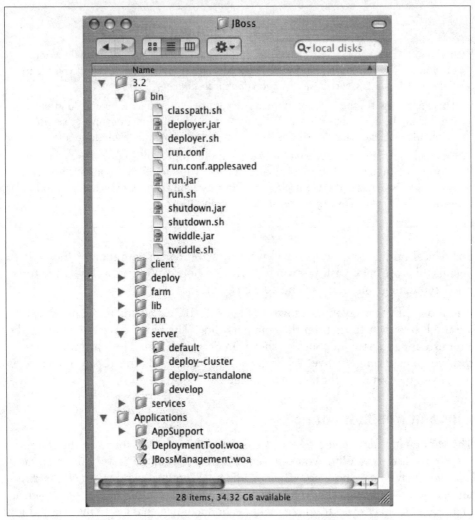

Figure 24-10. JBoss installation layout.

Table 24-2. List of JBoss's log files.

Logfile	Description
jbossctl	The JBoss control logfile. Check here if you are unable to get the server to launch or respond to Server Admin.
boot.log	Created by JBoss as install launches. Contains low-level details about the configuration and launch of JBoss. Contains useful configuration information about the JBoss server. This file is particularly useful to a developer on a non–Mac OS X Server platform trying to debug an issue you may be having (it's a bit like a System Profile for the application server).

Table 24-2. List of JBoss's log files. (continued)

Logfile	Description
server.log	This is the main logfile for the server. This is where application errors are typically logged (including application-level exceptions). This file should be checked on a frequent basis for new applications to ensure that there are no "hidden" problems.
servername_ access2005-01-01.log	Access logfile(s) for the server, in the same format as typical access logs for other web servers (such as Apache).

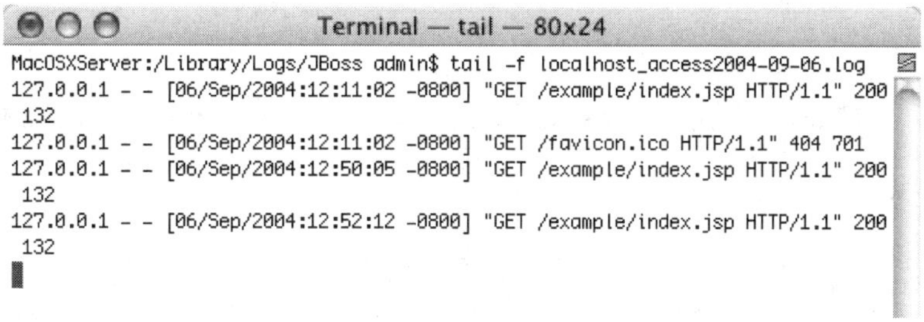

Figure 24-11. Viewing logs.

Of particular interest in when troubleshooting Java applications are *exceptions*. This developer term describes the standard Java mechanism for handling error conditions. Depending on the problem, you may see exception messages appear in the web browser or the *server.log* file. Figure 24-12 shows an exception in the web browser. The first line of the exception provides a precise programmatic description of the error, and the remaining text is used by a developer to isolate the specific location of the error in the application source code. If you see exceptions appear, you should copy all of the text associated with the exception and send it to the developer.

Figure 24-13 shows the same error as recorded in the *server.log* file. Note that some applications may be configured to present a more friendly error in the web browser, in which case the *server.log* file should contain the exception.

It's worth mentioning on behalf of Java application developers that certain exceptions in the *server.log* may be expected depending on your application configuration. If in doubt, send just the exception message. Depending on the problem, the developer may request the entire *server.log* and *boot.log* files.

Building Java Web Applications

Now that you've had a chance to learn a bit about Java web applications, you can try building your own simple Java application with JavaServer Pages. JavaServer Pages (JSP) is a specification and technology that allows you to create HTML pages with embedded bits of Java code.

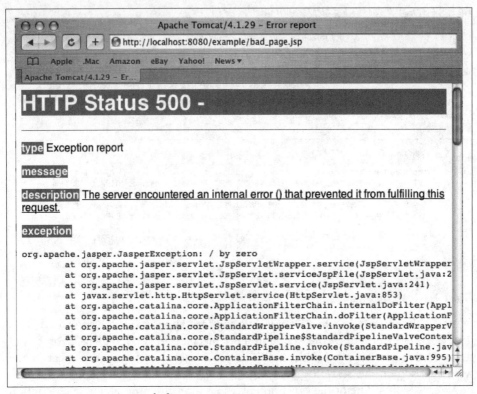

Figure 24-12. An exception in the browser.

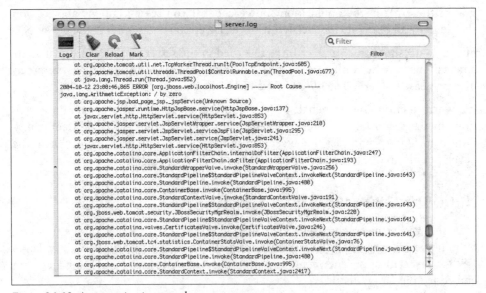

Figure 24-13. An exception in server.log.

Let's try creating a simple JSP page. Go to the */Library/JBoss/3.2/server/deploy* folder (note: not the */Library/JBoss/3.2/server/develop/deploy* folder; this can sometimes be confusing). Create a new folder called *example.war* in this directory.

Folders with Extensions

You may be surprised to see the WAR folder instead of a WAR file. JBoss lets you build a WAR application in a folder to avoid having to compress it during development.

In the *example.war* folder, place a new text file called *index.jsp*, as shown in Figure 24-14. The contents as of this file are shown in Example 24-1. Notice that the page looks like HTML with a bit of script, identified by <% ... %> and <%= ... %>. Pay particular attention to the <%= new java.util.Date().toString() %> line; this is Java code gets compiled by the server.

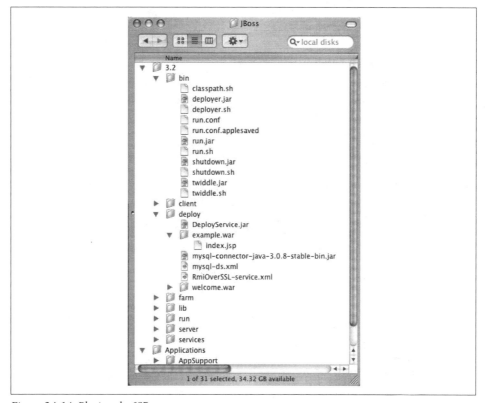

Figure 24-14. Placing the JSP page.

Example 24-1. "Hello World!" JSP code.

```html
<html>
    <head>
        <title>Test</title>
    </head>
    <body>
    <p>Hello World!</p>
    <p><%= new java.util.Date().toString( ) %></p>
    </body>
</html>
```

After creating the file, open your web browser and enter the URL *http://localhost: 8080/example/index.jsp*. Tomcat compiles the JSP page. If all is well, you should see a message, as shown in Figure 24-15. Each time you reload the page, it will update the current date and time.

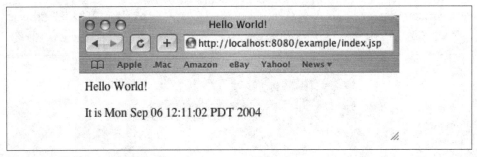

Figure 24-15. Viewing the JSP page.

If you make a mistake, you will get an error message in your web browser. Correct the problem with your text editor and then reload the page in the browser.

The Java code creates a new `java.util.Date` object and converts it to a `String` embedded within a `<%= %>` tag. This tag tells Tomcat to evaluate whatever code is placed inside as a `String`, and to output the results of that expression to the page.

Behind the Scenes

When the Application Server is launched, it waits for requests for resources in the *deploy* directory. The first time a request is made for a JSP page, Tomcat compiles the JSP into a Java source file, and then compiles this file using the javac compiler into a binary Java class file. Tomcat loads and runs this class file, returning the result. Future requests for the JSP page will cause Tomcat to compare the class file on disk to the JSP page on disk. If the timestamps don't match, Tomcat will dynamically recompile the page and repeat the process.

Java is an extremely robust, flexible application development environment. You can create interfaces with relational databases, mail servers, present complex user interfaces, and more. You might wish to explore creating JSP applications visually using the database functionality integrated into Macromedia Dreamweaver MX (*www.macromedia.com/software/dreamweaver/*) or Sun's Java Studio Creator (*http://developers.sun.com/prodtech/javatools/jscreator/*). These tools allow you to build complex web applications (complete with rich database interactivity) via drag-and-drop steps and by setting options visually. Alternatively, you might like to explore a more serious Java application development tool such as Eclipse (*www.eclipse.org*) or NetBeans (*www.netbeans.org*). Finally, Apple provides tools in the form of Xcode (*www.apple.com/xcode*) and WebObjects.

Complex Applications

A typical Java web application uses the Apache web server to handle static images and a relational database to store data, as shown in Figure 24-16. This is just one example configuration; depending on your needs, you can use multiple systems in a cluster.

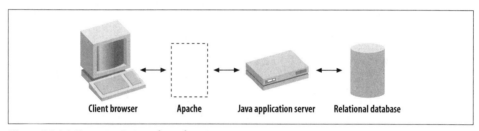

Client browser   Apache   Java application server   Relational database

Figure 24-16. Four-tier Java web application.

Mac OS X Server includes both the Apache and relational database components. The web service as provided by the Server Admin tool relies on Apache as the server for static resources (such as images). A relational database (such as MySQL, available via */Applications/Server/MySQL Manager Tool*) is used to store data.

Certain complex business processes required by enterprise systems are not easily coded in a JavaServer Page. For example, dealing with complicated financial transactions isn't something that fits well into a page of mostly HTML. Instead, you need a technology that provides security, transactions, and a strong server-side component model.

EJB, or Enterprise JavaBeans, refers to a specification for building just this sort of server-side components. These components are installed into a J2EE application server. By writing Java components that conform to this specification, you get to take advantage of a lot of sophisticated functionality in the application server as well as a known set of interfaces.

The specific functionality offered by a particular J2EE application server varies, but generally speaking, the use of Enterprise Java Beans features prominently in J2EE applications. We have already considered the simple form of a web application, based on JSP pages. J2EE applications are quite a bit more complex, often having three, four, or more application tiers and involve many, many different Java APIs.

Mac OS X Server includes JBoss, a popular open source J2EE application server. It's far beyond the scope of this text to introduce you fully to EJB application development, design and architecture. JBoss includes support for a broad suite of technologies, including an integrated web (HTTP) server, a JSP and servlet container, and support for EJB, CMP 2.0, RMI, IIOP, clustering, JTS, JMX and more. If you are interested in exploring JBoss further, consult Apple's documentation at *http://images. apple.com/server/pdfs/JavaApplication_Server.pdf*. Keep in mind that the configuration of J2EE applications is highly application specific. If you are working with a J2EE application, you will likely need to work closely with the developer of the application to ensure that the various components are configured properly.

Apple Proprietary Tools

As shown in Figure 24-17, Apple includes two WebObjects applications: a deployment tool and a tool for managing the JBoss server.

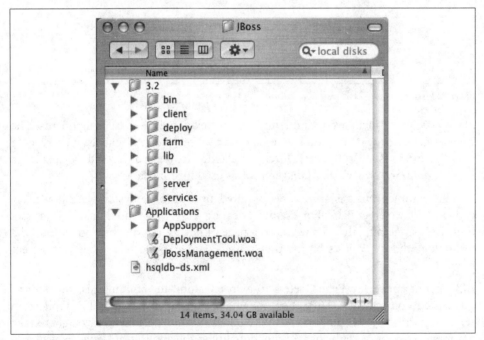

Figure 24-17. Apple proprietary tools.

To use the deployment tool, double-click on the *DeploymentTool.woa* icon in the Finder and navigate to *http://127.0.0.1:40001/*, as shown in Figure 24-18. Note that the application icon may continue to bounce in the Dock until after you have accessed the application in your web browser. Unfortunately, few (if any) EAR applications are built with the Apple tools in mind.

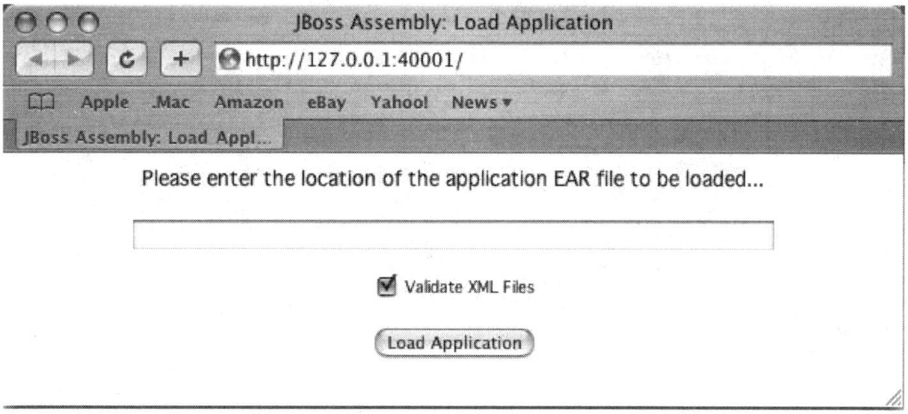

Figure 24-18. Apple proprietary EAR installer

To use the JBoss management tool, double-click on the *JBossManagement.woa* icon in the Finder and navigate to *http://127.0.0.1:40000/*, as shown in Figure 24-19. The username and password are the same as the system account.

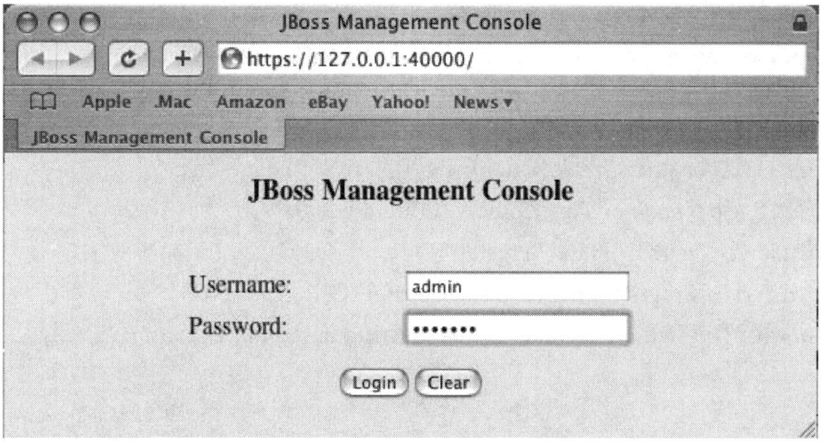

Figure 24-19. Apple proprietary JBoss Manager login.

As can be seen in Figure 24-20, the tool provides some capabilities for managing applications. Unfortunately, both *DeploymentTool.woa* and *JBossManagement.woa* exhibited severe stability problems on my system, and virtually no documentation for Java applications are written with these Apple tools in mind.

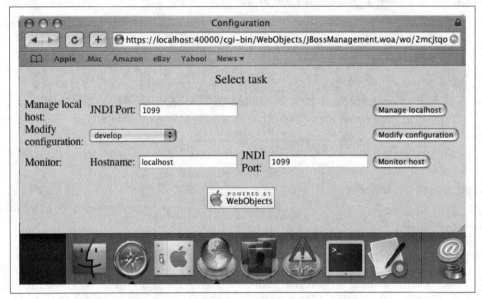

Figure 24-20. Apple proprietary JBoss Manager console.

Next Steps

Now that you've gotten a chance to look at building simple web applications that generate web pages, you may wish to learn more about JSP, SQL, Tomcat, and MySQL by consulting the following texts:

- *Mac OS X for Java Geeks* (O'Reilly, 2003), by Will Iverson
- *MySQL Cookbook* by Paul DuBois (O'Reilly, 2002)
- *JavaServer Pages* by Hans Bergsten (O'Reilly, 2003)
- *Java Servlet Programming* by Jason Hunter (O'Reilly, 2001)
- *Tomcat: The Definitive Guide* by Jason Brittain and Ian Darwin (O'Reilly, 2003)

## PART VII

Client Management

Of course, when you're setting up a server, you're ultimately going to have to consider how client machines interact with the server and how to manage those client machines. This part of the book covers topics from how to set up and manage preferences on Mac OS X clients, integrating Windows clients into a Mac OS X Server environment, workstation deployment, and use of Apple Remote Desktop (ARD) to monitor Mac OS X client machines on the network.

Chapters included in this part of the book include:

## CHAPTER 25

Managing Preferences
for Mac OS X Clients

As I've noted in earlier chapters, Apple designed Mac OS X with the intention for it to be used in a network environment as much as in a standalone workstation environment. So far, we've looked at how directory services play a role in this network-centric design, but in this chapter, the real power and granularity offered by Open Directory becomes visible. By leveraging the capability of Open Directory, Apple has designed a system that enables administrators to define preferences and access restrictions for virtually every part of a workstation that is bound to a directory domain.

A *managed preference* or *managed client environment* is configured using Workgroup Manager; you can manage the user environment for individual users, groups, workstations, or a combination of all three. Managed preferences allow you to preconfigure many of the settings users would typically configure on a standalone Mac OS X workstation. This enables you to give users a customized environment based on their needs and job functions without needing to manually configure a workstation for them. Even better, because you can apply managed preference by group or computer list, you can apply them simply by adding a user to a managed group or based on the workstation they are using.

Another advantage is that settings applied to a user or group are applied to a user regardless of which workstation they login at. This feature, combined with network home directories, which store user settings for applications and other operating system variables (such as screensavers and desktop pictures), creates an environment where a user's entire computing experience can be customized and remain the same from workstation to workstation.

In addition to configuring user settings, managed preferences also enable you to further secure an environment. You can restrict users from accessing any applications that they don't need to access. You can limit user access to specific printers (in addition to preconfiguring access to the printers that users need). You can keep users from accessing various Finder commands. You can also restrict the computers where users are allowed to log in. In short, managed preferences allow you to design a cohesive computing experience, simplify day-to-day user management, and secure workstations and local resources as well as network resources.

Applying Managed Preferences

There are 12 areas of Mac OS X to which managed preferences can be applied. These areas correspond to the 12 preference panes included in Workgroup Manager. All panes are configured in much the same way, although the specific options available on each pane obviously vary. Later in the chapter, I'll discuss each of these panes individually, but first I want to describe the overall process of applying managed preferences.

To enable managed preferences, launch Workgroup Manager and click the Preferences button in the toolbar at the top of the window. Next, select the user, group, or computer list to which you wish to apply a preference using the accounts list. As shown in Figure 25-1, the righthand pane of the window displays a list of all preferences that can be managed for this type of account (you can apply all preferences based on user, group, or computer list, with the exception of Energy Saver, which can be applied only to computer lists). If any managed preferences are already applied explicitly to the user, group, or computer list you selected, there will be a pointer icon next to preference's icon. To manage a preference or to adjust the settings for an already managed preference, click the appropriate preference's icon in the list. This displays the preference pane for that preference; you can enable or disable management of the preference and configure the available settings.

Choosing When and How a Preference Is Managed

When a preference pane is selected, the top section of the pane will include the Manage the Settings section, which contains radio buttons for Not Managed, Once, and Always. Some preference panes with contain multiple tabs, each with its own unique options and Manage the Settings section, allowing you to apply managed preferences to items only on the selected tab without managing items on other tabs of the same preference pane to the same degree or at all.

When you select the Not Managed radio button, no preference management is assigned. By default, all preference panes and tabs are set to Not Managed. Users have full access to the settings or Mac OS X components that relate to the selected preference pane. If a given preference pane is set to either Once or Always (thus establishing managed preferences), selecting Not Managed disables such management.

When you select the Once radio button in a preference pane's Manage the Settings section, the preference is initially managed, but can be changed by a user after her initial login. Managing Once only creates an initial configuration for the user and is used to give the user a starting point form which they can further configure their user

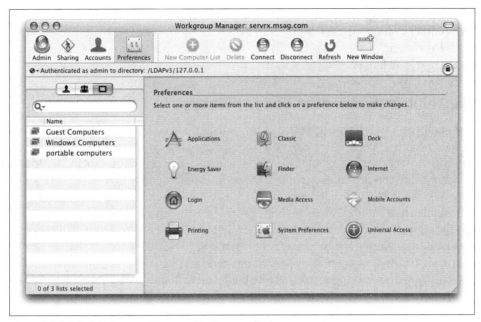

Figure 25-1. The Workgroup Manager Preferences display.

environment. It does not force the initial settings to be kept and it does not limit the user to them.

When you select the Always radio button, the preference that you configure is always enforced. The user experience relating to the preference will always be what is defined in the preference pane. In some instances, you have the option of giving the user the ability make adjustments that are additive to what you define—for instance, when you define Dock items for a user, you can allow the user to add additional Dock items—but the initial configuration made in the preference pane cannot be adjusted or removed.

Most preferences that have to do with configuring a custom user environment (such as configuring the items in the Dock) can be set to be managed once while those that have to do with restricting user access to features (such as limiting which applications a user can launch) can be set only to Not Managed or Always managed.

If you choose to manage a preference once and then adjust that preference again later, you are in affect creating a new initial configuration. As such, after you have managed it for the second time, the new configuration will be applied to users even if they have made changes from the first configuration. This happens because you are effectively turning off the management of the preference and then turning it back on again and setting it to be managed once.

If the preference was set to be managed once and then you remove management, the setting will still remain with the initial configuration for user who had logged in while it was configured. This effect happens because it was copied into the user's preference when it was first managed. However, if a preference was set to be managed always and is then turned off, the defined configuration is lost, because the preference is no longer being managed.

Managing Preferences for Users or Groups

Although you can manage preferences for individual users, it is generally considered easier to manage preferences based on groups, because you can make users members of the appropriate groups to apply managed preferences to them. (A group assigned managed preferences is often called a *managed group* or a *workgroup*.) The one major drawback to managing preferences-based groups is that when users who are members of multiple managed groups will be presented with a list of all managed groups of which they are members at login. Users need to select which workgroup settings they want to use for that particular session. This procedure can be confusing to users who are members of multiple groups where the managed preferences assigned to varying groups vary significantly. A user's experience and access restrictions may vary notably from one group to the next.

 Users cannot be members of more than 16 managed groups.

To avoid confusion, it is often better to limit the number of managed groups within a network as much as possible. Generally, it is better to create managed groups by job function rather than department and then to assign preferences based on department by using departmental computer lists (which identify the workstations in the department). If possible, avoid assigning users to more than one managed group, thus avoiding the need for them to select a workgroup environment at login. If you must assign users to multiple workgroups, try to limit the number of workgroups that they are assigned to and make certain that the users understand the differences between the groups and when or why they should login as a member of each group.

You can edit managed preferences for multiple users in the same way you edit account information for multiple users (by selecting all the users in the account list and making the appropriate changes). This method makes it easier to manage groups of users without assigning them to multiple managed groups, because it gives you the advantages of managing groups of users without the limitations of making them choose one of multiple workgroups at login. You can use the keywords function for user accounts to group users together for the purpose of editing managed preferences and use the sort and search features of the user list based on keywords to easily locate users after grouping them by keyword. Be careful, however; each time you edit a preference pane for multiple users you change whatever existing preferences were assigned to each user in that pane.

A similarly useful feature is that managed preferences are stored in user and group presets. This gives you the ability to create presets with managed preferences for varying types of users and then assign those preferences (along with other user account information) as the users are created. Again, this involves identifying types of users within your network, which can be different from determining preferences based on department.

Creating and Managing Computer Lists

You can create computer lists for a directory domain using Workgroup Manager. Computer lists can be used to apply managed preferences and can also be used to control access to specific workstations by allowing or restricting members of certain groups (be they permissions-only groups or managed groups) log in to computers in a list. Using computer lists for specific computer labs or departments or even computer types (such as portable computers) allows you to apply preferences that affect users only while at specific workstations (such as access to specific printers or software), which might be the only place that such preferences are warranted. They can also be used for managing preferences that affect workstations themselves and not users (such as scheduling automatic startup or shutdown).

 Unlike users' accounts, which can be assigned to multiple groups, computers can be assigned only to one computer list.

Creating a computer list

To create a computer list, launch Workgroup Manager and click the Accounts button in the toolbar at the top of the window. Select the computer accounts tab above the accounts list (the tab with the icon of a black square). You will see that one or two lists are automatically created. The first automatic list is the Guest Computers list, which can be used to apply settings to any computer not listed in computer lists that you create. The second, Windows Computers, exists if you have configured Mac OS X Server to work as a Windows Primary Domain Controller. I'll get to the Guest Computers list in a moment. First, let's look at how to create and configure a new computer list.

Click the New Computer List icon in the toolbar at the top of the window. Enter the name of the new list in the List Name field. Use a descriptive name that will help you be able to understand which computers are part of the list later (such names might be something like Marketing Dept. Workstations or Middle School Library or Faculty iBooks). Figure 25-2 shows the initial display for a new computer list.

You can add workstations to a computer list either by entering the MAC address of their Ethernet or AirPort cards or by using self-discovering protocols to locate computers on the network. To add a computer using its MAC address, click the add

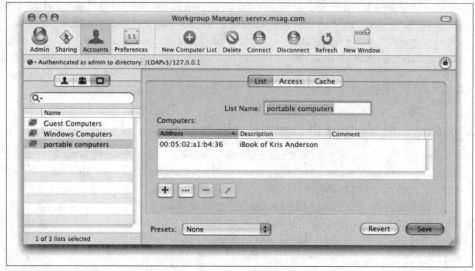

Figure 25-2. A computer list in Workgroup Manager.

button below the listbox and enter the appropriate information. You must enter the MAC address and a name for the computer that will be used as the name displayed in the Computers listbox; there is also a checkbox to force this as the hostname, which will override any configuration for computer name in the Sharing System Preferences pane on the workstation. You can also enter comment information about the computer, such as its model, configuration, typical use, or location. Click the OK button to add the computer to the list.

Click the browse button (which has an ellipsis icon) below the listbox to search for computers using AppleTalk, Rendezvous, or SMB. This step brings up a standard connect-to-server dialog that can be used to navigate to and select the appropriate workstation. This approach can typically be used only to discover workstations on the same subnet as the computer on which Workgroup Manager is being run.

You can remove a workstation from a computer list by selecting it in the listbox and clicking the remove button below the listbox. You can also edit the displayed name and comment information for a computer by selecting it in the listbox and clicking the edit button (which has a pencil icon). Once you have added and edited the information for workstations in a computer list, click the Save button to save the computer list. You can then use the Preferences button in the toolbar at the top of the window to configure managed preferences for the computer list.

Limiting access to computers in a list

To limit access to a computer list, click the Accounts button in toolbar and select the computer list in the accounts list. In the account information pane for the list, select the Access tab. Select the "Restrict to groups below" radio button and then click the add button to the right of the groups listbox to display a drawer to the side of the window with all groups that have been configured within the directory domain. Drag the groups that you wish to have access to the workstations in the computer list into the listbox or double-click on them to add them to the listbox. To remove a group, select it in the listbox and click the remove icon next to the listbox.

By default, local user accounts on a workstation can log in and, if managed groups are used in the directory domain, local users will be allowed to choose to login as part of any of those managed groups. However, by unchecking the "Allow users with local-only accounts" checkbox below the groups listbox, you can require that only users with network accounts in the directory domain who are part of the specified groups can login to the workstations in a computer list. This does not, however, apply to local administrator or mobile accounts. Click the Save button to activate the access restrictions.

Using the Guest Computers list

The Guest Computers list allows you to configure managed preferences settings and access restrictions for all computers that are not included in any of the computer lists that you create. This list can include new computers that you have not yet added to a computer list, computers brought into the network by users that are not owned by your institution, or computers to which you wish assign generic access restrictions and/or preferences without going through the hassle of defining each individual computer in a computer list. The Guest Computers list can be very useful in a large infrastructure, because it allows you to define some environment variables across your network without needing to define every computer.

To use the Guest Computers list, first indicate that you wish to define settings for guest computers. To do this, launch Workgroup Manager and select the Accounts tab in the toolbar. Select the Computer Lists tab above the account list and select the Guest Computers list. In the List tab of the account information pane (which contains the listbox for a computers in a typical computer list), the Guest Computers list includes radio buttons for Inherit Preferences for Guest Computers, which means to not define settings for guest computers and leave them unmanaged in an LDAP domain or to inherit them from a parent domain in an NetInfo hierarchy, and Define Guest Computer Preferences Here, which is the setting to configure guest computer settings and manage them in the selected domain. Select the Define Guest Computer Preferences Here radio button and click the Save button to use the Guest Computers list.

Once you have designated that you will use the Guest Computers list to manage computers for the domain, you can select the list and manage both access restrictions to guest computers (using the Access tab) and preferences for guest computers (by clicking the Preferences button in the toolbar). Give some thought to whether you want to use the Guest Computer list and to how tightly you want to restrict access or how extensively you want to configure preferences for it, because you will be affecting all computers that you have not defined elsewhere.

If you severely limit access to guest computers, users within your network may experience extreme limitations on which workstations they can use. Likewise if you extensively manage preferences for the user environment, users may find their ability to work too limited on most workstations. Also remember that by default Mac OS X 10.2 and higher will bind to a directory domain automatically if DHCP binding is enabled within your network. This restriction means that if a user brings in a personal computer, you will end up applying limitations to it as well as to workstations owned by your institution.

The MCX cache

Workstations with managed preferences assigned to them, either by being part of a computer list of by being a guest computer when the Guest Computers list is enabled, cache the managed preferences assigned to them. Workstations can automatically update the information in this cache (which Apple refers to as the *MCX cache*) on a regular basis. The update interval is defined using in the Cache tab of the computer list's account information pane. You can also manually update the cache by logging into a workstation as a local administrator and holding the Shift key down at login. This will bring up the dialog to select a workgroup at login (regardless of whether any workgroups are available to the workstation) and the dialog will include a Refresh Preferences button that will manually refresh the MCX cache.

How Varying Preferences Interact

Because managed preferences can be set for users, groups, and computer lists, it is probable that user experience will be managed based on more than one set of managed preferences (those configured for user, group, and/or computer list). As such, it is important to understand how varying preferences interact so that you don't end up with unexpected or unintended user experiences or access restrictions.

In cases where preferences are applied to different panes based on user, group, or computer list, the preferences don't actually interact. They are simply all applied. Thus if you set application access based on computer list, login items display based on group, and Dock display based on user, all of these preferences are applied as they were configured when a user logs in, because the same preference panes were not configured differently for each account type.

For preferences that affect lists of items (such as Dock items, login items, application access, and printer lists), the preferences are considered additive. This means that the ultimate experience for these lists by users includes all the items set for each account type. For example, if you configure the Dock to include iChat, Mail, and Microsoft Word for a user account and that user logs in as a member of a group for which you have defined Photoshop and Dreamweaver as login items, the user's Dock would contain iChat, Mail, Word, Photoshop, and Dreamweaver.

For preferences that do not affect lists of items, including those that restrict user access, Apple has defined the following system of applying preferences. User-defined preferences override preferences configured based on computer lists, which override preferences set for managed groups. This system applies only if the a preference pane is managed, meaning that if you limit a user's access to Finder commands for a computer list and leave Finder preferences unmanaged for a user's account, the user is limited in access to those Finder commands. If however, you also manage the Finder preferences based on the user account (either Once or Always), the user will have access to those commands specified at the user account level and not those specified for the computer list.

Needless to say, keeping track of how each managed preference interacts with each other managed preference in your network can become confusing for items other than list-based preferences (which are simply additive). The situation can become even more confusing when you make users members of more than one managed group, because the resulting user experience now includes another variable to consider. One way to avoid the confusion is to only set certain preference panes for users and others for groups and others for computer lists.

 Documenting managed preferences and keeping them as simple as possible can be overwhelmingly helpful.

Using the Home Directory for Additional Preference Management

Using managed preferences allow you to tailor a user's experience of Mac OS X in a network. However, with the exception of Apple-branded Internet applications, managed preferences do not give you the ability to configure the user experience for applications. You can achieve this goal to some extent by modifying the home directory template for users or by changing specific items within a home directory after creating it. If you want to apply preferences such as color profiles and other workspace options for graphics applications, as an example, you can configure the applications on a workstation and copy the appropriate preferences files from the home directory where you made the changes into the home directory template to have them applied to all users who launch those graphics applications.

The same approach can be used for most applications; typically applications store preferences in the */Library/Preferences* folder of a home directory. You can also apply such preferences to specific users rather than all users by placing the preferences files in specific home directories after the users' accounts and home directories are created—you will need to login as *root* or as the user to accomplish this. This has an effect similar to configuring managed preferences using the Once option. Users can change these settings at any time, but they provide the ability to create a consistent and/or customized user experience for new users.

Configuring Individual Preferences

Now that we've talked about how to apply managed preferences and the considerations to be made when applying them, let's look at the individual preferences themselves. Each of the following sections looks at one of the twelve preference panes available in Workgroup Manager. As you'll notice, many of the panes coincide with the System Preferences panes in Mac OS X.

Application Preferences

The Applications preference pane, shown in Figure 25-3, enables you to set access restrictions on which applications a user can launch. It can be applied by user, group, or computer, and is managed either always or not at all. Application access is configured much like an access control list for a firewall: you create a list of applications and designate either that users can use only those applications or that they can use any application with the exception of those in the list.

When you open the Applications preferences pane, it will include a list of all applications that Workgroup Manager could automatically locate on the computer running Workgroup Manager. You can add other applications by clicking the Add button below the list. When you click the Add button, you are given a standard Open File dialog box and can navigate to the application you wish to add. Because items in the Applications pane are made available based on the computer that is running Workgroup Manager, it is best to configure this preference pane from a workstation that has the applications you wish to manage installed (as opposed to running it on the actual server hosting the directory domain). To remove items from the access list, select them and click the Remove button.

In addition to the application list, there are checkboxes for the following three options:

User can also open all applications on local volumes
> This option allows the user to open any application installed on a workstation's hard drive. Checking this box limits the access restrictions to applications stored on share points within the network, negating much the power of managing applications.

Allow approved applications to launch nonapproved applications
> Some applications use helper applications to perform certain tasks, such as a web browser launching an email program or a graphics program launching supporting plug-in applications. Checking this option allows an application to

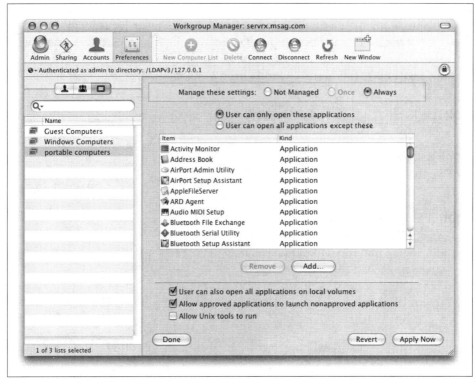

Figure 25-3. The Applications preferences pane.

launch helper applications and plug-ins (though the user still cannot launch them) if needed. Generally speaking, this is a good option to use unless you can be certain that you are enabling all the helper applications that primary applications may need.

Allow Unix tools to run

This setting allows the workstation to run Unix processes that may be needed as helpers by some applications. Unix tools can be launched only using the Terminal or by an application. Allowing Unix tools does reduce workstation security, but might be needed by some applications. If you are uncertain whether to allow Unix tools, you can disable them and test applications that your users will be running to determine whether they rely on Unix tools to function.

Classic Preferences

The Classic preferences pane, shown in Figure 25-4, allows you to define the same options that users can define in the Classic pane of System Preferences on a Mac OS X client workstation, including when Classic should start (at login or when a Classic application is launched) and how long before the Classic environment is put to sleep;

it also allows you to specify a specific System Folder on a workstation (enter the path to the appropriate folder). It also allows you to specify advanced settings, including allowing users to use Classic startup key combinations (those used to start up with extensions off and open the Extensions Manager control panel during startup) and whether a user may rebuild the desktop file on a workstation.

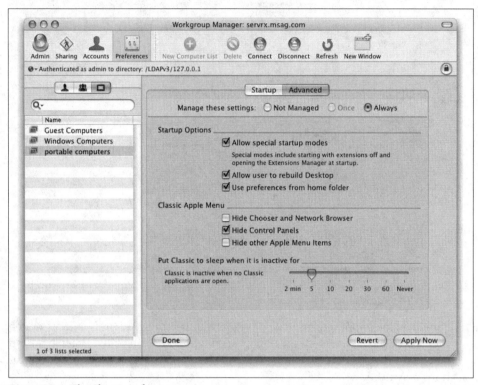

Figure 25-4. The Classic preferences pane.

You can also specify whether preferences for Classic applications should be stored in the user's home directory (such that they follow the user regardless of which workstation he or she is using) or in the System Folder of the workstation, which may be needed for compatibility with older Classic applications. Choosing the former also enables the preferences to be available if the user logs into a Mac OS 9 workstation that is configured for network use with Mac Manager.

You can also specify whether the user has access to Classic Apple menu items, including the Chooser and Network Browser, Control Panels, and all other items in the Apple menu. This ability allows you to achieve a greater level of security within the Classic environment. If you do not allow access to the Chooser, you should configure printer access on the workstation if users need to print from Classic applications.

Dock Preferences

The Dock preferences pane, shown in Figure 25-5, allows you to specify items that are displayed in the Dock for a user, group, or computer list, using the Dock Items tab of the pane, and the display settings for the Dock (the same settings entered in the Dock System Preferences pane on a Mac OS X workstation), using the Dock Display tab.

Figure 25-5. The Dock preferences pane.

You can add applications to the Dock by dragging the applications' icons into the Applications listbox in the Dock Items tab or by selecting the Add button and navigating to them. You can remove them by selecting the applications in the listbox and clicking the Remove button. You can drag applications up and down in the list to configure how they are arranged in the Dock. Items at the top of the list appear next to the Finder icon in the Dock (to the left if the Dock is positioned on the bottom of the screen) and items at the bottom, next to the Trash (to the right if the Dock is positioned on the bottom of the screen). You can add specific files and folders located on your network to the Dock in the same manner, using the Documents and Folders listbox.

There is a section in the Dock Items tab labeled "Add other folders" with checkboxes for My Applications (which displays a folder with aliases to all of a user's approved applications, if applications are managed), Documents (the Documents folder inside the user's home directory), and Network Home (which displays the user's home directory). If you are managing Dock preferences for a group, you will also see a checkbox for the Add Group folder, which will place the group folder for the group in the Dock. If the group share point is not mounted at login (see the upcoming section on "Login Preferences"), users may be asked to enter their usernames and passwords to access the group folder.

If you define Dock items for a user and Mac OS X is unable to locate them on the workstation's hard drive, generic "?" icons will be displayed in the Dock. This display applies both to applications that are not installed on the workstation and to items that are located on share point to which the user has either not connected or that are not automounts. In the case of items on share points, once the user connects to the share point, they will be displayed properly.

The final option that you can configure is whether the user may add and remove additional items to the Dock. This option applies only if you set management of the Dock preferences to Always.

Energy Saver Preferences

The Energy Saver preferences pane controls power management features on workstations and automatic startup and shutdown. The Energy Saver tab is available only when managing preferences for a computer list and is limited to Always managed or Not Managed. Also its settings apply only to workstations running Mac OS X 10.2.4 or higher (scheduled startup/shutdown applies only to workstations with Mac OS X 10.3 or higher).

There are tabs in the Energy Saver pane to specify power management for both desktop and portable workstations, and the settings in them mirror the settings of the Energy Saver System Preferences pane on a Mac OS X workstation. There is also a tab to enable the display of the battery menu on portable computers. My suggestion is to set Energy Saver to Not Managed for portable computers, as PowerBook and iBook users may have situations in which they need to adjust these settings to improve power management or performance when working on battery power (such as working on a plane versus giving a presentation).

The fourth tab available in the Energy Saver pane is the Schedule tab, which allows you to define specific times for desktop computers to automatically shut down (or sleep) and/or start up. This tab can be useful for classrooms and computer labs, to make certain that all workstations are shut down at night to save power and/or are powered on in the morning. You can specify schedules for individual days of the week, every weekday, every weekend day, or every day.

Finder Preferences

The Finder preferences pane contains three tabs (Preferences, Commands, and Views) and gives you a broad range of options in terms of what items users can access and the resulting user environment.

Preferences

This tab allows you to define the items found on the General and Advanced tabs of the Finder Preferences and can be managed either once or always. Along with the Views tab, it is used to configure the user environment more than user access restrictions. The options included on this tab are use of the normal Finder or Simplified Finder (which removes many commands from the Finder and makes the workstation more suitable for new or young users); which items are displayed on the desktop when mounted (hard disks, removable media, and/or connected servers); what is shown in a new Finder window (the user's home folder of the computer display of mounted volumes); and options for whether new folders open in new windows, whether Finder windows should always open in column view, whether a warning is displayed before emptying the Trash, and whether file extensions are displayed in filenames.

Commands

The Commands tab allows you to remove access to various commands that are available in the Finder. This tab can be set to Always managed or Not Managed. The commands that you can restrict users from accessing include: Connect to server, Go to iDisk, Eject Disk, Burn Disk, Go to Folder, Restart, and Shut Down. When access to a command is restricted, the command is not visible to the user in the Finder. Even if a command is not made available in the Finder, users may be able to perform the action using another application or the Terminal. Also, when removing access to some commands, such as Connect to Server or Shut Down, be certain that users will not need access to them, such as automount needed share points and scheduling automatic shut down.

Views

The Views tab can be set to managed Once or Always, and contains subtabs for desktop view, default view, and computer view. The options on these tabs mirror the options in the Finder's View Options command, and each tab allows you to set view options based on the appropriate view types.

Internet Preferences

The Internet preferences pane allows you to define a default web browser and email client for users. In addition, it allows you to define a default home page and search page for web browsers and default email server information for email applications. While the default web browser and email application settings function regardless of which applications are chosen, the settings for home and search pages function properly only with Apple's Safari browser and the email server settings apply only to Apple's Mail application.

To define settings and bookmarks for other web browsers in addition to Safari, you could install and configure the appropriate browser on a single workstation and then copy the preferences files for it into the appropriate location inside the home directory template. Doing so would apply those preference files to any new home directory created and subsequently to each user (although users will be able to adjust these settings). Although the specific location of browser preferences and bookmarks may vary, they are (like most application preferences) generally stored in the */Library/Preferences* folder of a user's home directory.

Login Preferences

The Login preferences pane contains three tabs, two of which—Login Options and Auto-Logout—can be managed only for computer lists and affect how the Login Window application and the workstation itself function rather than affecting the user environment. The remaining tab, Login Items, can be managed for users, groups, or computer lists.

Login items

The Login Items tab, shown in Figure 25-6, gives you the ability to configure login items for users, groups, or computer lists (it can be managed once, or always). Login items launch or open immediately on login and can include applications, documents, folders, or share points. Login Items is often used either to mount a share point automatically for a user without using automounts or to run an application or script at login. You can add items either by dragging them into the listbox in the Login Items tab or by using the Add button to navigate to an item using an open file dialog. For share points, there is a "Mount with user's name and password" checkbox below the listbox that causes Mac OS X to attempt to use the same username and password that the user entered in the Login Window to authenticate to and mount the share point.

There are also checkboxes for allowing the user to add and remove additional items and to allow the user to bypass login items by holding down the Shift key at login. If you are managing this setting for a group, you will also have an option to mount the group share point at login.

The final setting on the Login Items tab is the "Mount network home share point" checkbox. This option is available if you have configured mobile accounts. As we'll discuss in the section on mobile account preferences later in this chapter, mobile

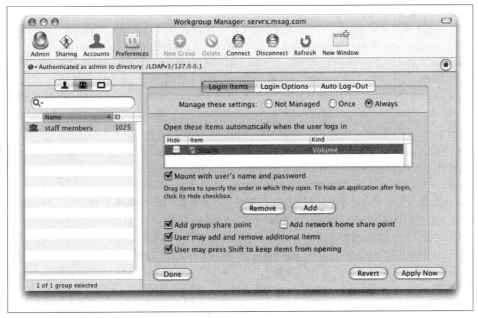

Figure 25-6. The Login Items tab of the Login preferences pane.

accounts do not use a network home directory in the way most network accounts do. Selecting this checkbox allows mobile account users to have access to their network home directory when connected to the network, although it mounts as a folder in a share point and not as an automount. If you use this option, you should also choose the Show Network Home option in the Dock preferences to make it easy for the user to locate the home directory.

Login options and auto-logout

The Login Options tab controls the appearance and behavior of the Login Window application. Since it does not directly affect user accounts, it can only be configured for computer lists and must be managed always or not at all. The first option is a pair of radio buttons to select whether and how users are displayed in the login window. The options include either Name and Password Text Fields or List of Users Able to Use These Computers. The latter option also gives you the option of displaying local users, network users, local administrators, and other users (other users is an option that allows users to enter a username not displayed in the list). In most environments, it's best to use name and password text fields because of the sheer number of users that may be displayed in a list and for privacy consideration.

In addition to the user list, the Login Options tab includes checkboxes for showing the Restart and Shut Down buttons in the Login Window, showing a password hint (this applies to local user accounts on a workstation, as Open Directory doesn't support the use of password hints for users in a shared directory domain), enable auto-login of a specific user account (which may be useful for a computer in a kiosk situation), allow users to login using ".console" (the ability to log in from the command line instead of the using the Finder and GUI interface), and to enable fast user switching. Fast user switching does function with network users, provided that they have home directories stored on NFS share points, although I don't recommend using it with network users because of security, performance, and reliability concerns.

The Auto Log-Out tab allows you to automatically log users out of the workstation after a specified idle period. This option provides both a security feature (keeping another user from accessing an unattended workstation) and a performance benefit (closing off server and network resources that are used when maintaining a network user session). If you do not allow simultaneous login for users, this option also keeps them from walking away from one computer and then being unable to login at another because they forgot to logout. The Auto Log-Out tab specifies a number of minutes before an idle user is logged out. When setting an auto-logout time limit, keep in mind that auto-logout will cause any unsaved changes made by the user to be lost and that many times users will be idle while performing other tasks at their desk or in their office. Also, inform users that an automatic logout threshold exists for their accounts. Like the Login Options tab, auto-logout can only be set for computer lists and must be always managed or not managed. Also, it functions only with Mac OS X 10.3 workstations.

Media Access Preferences

The Media Access preferences pane controls access restrictions for every type of disk that can be used with a workstation, including CDs/DVDs (both recordable and read-only), internal and external hard drives, and other removable media types (such as Zip disks or flash memory cards and devices). Media access restrictions can be assigned to users, groups, or computer lists and must be set to managed Always or Not Managed. However, the media access pane is divided into two tabs, which can be managed separately.

The first tab, Disc Media, applies only to CDs and DVDs (recordable and read-only). You can manage access to CDs, DVDs, and recordable disks separately and you can allow access, require authentication (allow access with a local administrator password), or disallow access to each type of disk.

The second tab, Other Media, gives you the option to restrict access to internal disks (internal hard drives) or external disks (external hard drives and nonoptical removable media, whether the drive is internal or external). The Other Media tab includes options to allow access, require authentication, and restrict the media type to read-only. It is important to allow access, if only read-only, to internal drives unless the computer uses NetBoot, because access to the internal hard drive is needed for the computer to function properly.

There is also a checkbox on the Other Media tab labeled "Eject all removable media at logout." When checked, this option will cause the computer to eject all Zip, CD, DVD, and other removable media disks when the user logs out. While this is a nice feature, particularly in computer labs, because it prevents users from forgetting CDs or other disks, it can often cause workstations to hang at a blue screen for an extended period or time at each logout (as of this writing, no solid explanation or resolution to this problem is known).

Mobile Accounts Preferences

The Mobile Accounts preferences pane allows you to create mobile user accounts. A *mobile account* is a type of hybrid between a local account and a network account. A network user account has many advantages for administrators and users alike. It enables the use of a network home directory that stores user documents as well as preferences and provides the same user experience on all Mac OS X workstations within a network. It also allows for the use of network authentication, managed preferences, and all the other advantages discussed in previous chapters afforded by using directory domains.

Unfortunately, a network user account has a single drawback: it requires access to the network where the directory domain containing a user's account and his/her home directory are located. This creates a problem for iBook and PowerBook users who frequently disconnect their computers from the network. The mobile account preference and model are Apple's solution to this problem.

A mobile account is a network user account that is mirrored as a local account on a workstation. When a user logs into a workstation on which she has a mobile account, she is authenticated based on the appropriate directory domain when connected to the network; the workstation caches this information when connected to the network and authenticates against the cached information when not connected to the network. Any managed preferences (configure by user, group, or computer list) are also cached and enforced.

All other access is treated as though the user has a local account on the workstation. The workstation creates a home directory for the user based on his network home directory and while logged in on that workstation, the user's account accesses the local home directory instead of the network home directory. (This is why you should manage login and Dock preferences to automate access to the network home directories of users that are configured for mobile account access.) The user can then take the computer off the network, perform any work they need, and still use their network account information for authentication to the workstation and experience the same managed preference environment as if they were connected to the network.

When the computer is returned to the network, it updates its MCX cache information automatically. The user's authentication information is updated to match the information in the appropriate directory domain either when the user issues a password change request from the computer or at his next login while connected to the network.

One drawback is that there is no automatic feature to synchronize a user's local home directory on the workstation with her network home directory (though Apple has stated that this ability will be included in Mac OS X client and Server 10.4). Thus, users with mobile account access should be told to copy files to their network home directory on a regular basis if they will need access to those files from other workstations and for backup purposes. Products such as Folder Synchronizer by Softobe (*www.softobe.com*) can also be used to sync files between the two the home directories of mobile account users, running either automatically or manually. You can also develop script-based solutions specific to your users by using the Unix *psync* command.

Configuring mobile accounts

The Mobile Accounts preference pane is actually very basic. It includes one checkbox to create a mobile account at login and a second to require confirmation by the user before creating the mobile account. You can configure the mobile account preference based on user, group, or computer lists, though I highly suggest doing so by computer list and using it only for users who are assigned a specific portable computers. If it is applied by user or group, then users could have mobile accounts created on every computer where they login. I also suggest always requiring user confirmation to avoid the confusion of mobile accounts being created without the user knowing that it has happened.

When mobile account creation is enabled and a user logs into a workstation (a specific workstation in the case of computer list configuration or any workstation in the case of configuration by user or group), the Login Window verifies the user's login information using Open Directory and is alerted that the mobile account preference is in effect. Provided you have selected the "Require confirmation before creating mobile account" checkbox in Workgroup Manager, the user is asked if she wants to create a mobile account on the workstation (if you didn't select the checkbox, the account is created automatically). The dialog used here is actually a little misleading, in that the user is given options for Create, which should be labeled something like "create mobile account," and Continue, which might be better labeled "access workstation using network account."

If users choose not to create a mobile account, login proceeds normally and they use network account and home directory as if the mobile account preference hadn't been enabled. If the user does opt to create a mobile account (or if it occurs without confirmation), the workstation caches all the information in the user's directory domain record. This includes the user's name and shortname, UID, password information, network home directory location, print quotas, managed preferences, group membership, and managed preference information for any groups of which the user is a member. Using this cached information, the workstation then creates a local user account for the user, complete with the local home directory. As long as the user logs into this workstation, they will use the mobile account and local home directory rather than the network account and home directory.

Users can have mobile accounts on more than one computer (and likely will, if this preference is set based on user or group). Each one will essentially be a separate local account, with the exception of tasks that explicitly access the network (authentication, access to shared resources, and so on). Anything based on the user's home directory won't be used when the user logs in with a mobile account because each mobile account will use a separate local home directory.

Deleting mobile accounts

Mobile accounts are listed as local accounts in the Accounts System Preferences pane on a workstation. They can be deleted by a local administrator for that workstation (though the local administrator cannot affect changes to the account). If a user's mobile account is deleted from a workstation, then the user loses access to files in his local home directory on the workstation. If the mobile account preference remains enabled, the mobile account creation process will be repeated if the user logs into the workstation again.

When to use mobile accounts

Mobile accounts should be used in either of two circumstances: First, when a user will be using a computer that needs to leave the network. In this case, the mobile account is the only way for a user with a Mac OS X computer to use a network account and conveniently take the computer off the network. The other alternative is to create a local user account for the user (which is more time-consuming and less effective than using a mobile account). Because users with notebook computers generally work on their computers exclusively, the potential problem of multiple mobile accounts is usually not associated with these users. Again, limiting the mobile account preference to assignment by computer list and good user education, if needed, can take away the potential confusion of the mobile account option. You may even wish to create separate computers lists for each portable computer (each containing only a single computer) to make mobile account management more specific.

This does not mean, however, that all portable computers should be set up to use mobile accounts. If a portable computer is used only within the network (such as with the portable iBook labs that Apple makes available to schools), but is shared with many users, then it may still be appropriate to use network accounts with the computer. Also, if your institution has a number of portable computers that are loaned out to many different users for short periods of time for use off the network (such as PowerBooks intended to be shared for client meetings/presentations), a better approach may be to use a single generic local user account. Individual users can then use removable media to load files onto the computer or retrieve work from it. This approach saves you the hassle of having a large number of mobile accounts on a computer that individual users may use only once for a few hours.

You can also use mobile accounts for desktop workstations. If you have users that will log in on only a single workstation for the majority or entire duration of their time at a worksite and will make extensive use of their home directory for large files (such as a graphic designer assigned a high-end Mac desktop in her office), then using a mobile account might be a logical choice. Because it will keep the home directory on the local hard drive of the only workstation the user accesses, this will increase performance for the user and decrease the demands on the server that hosts user home directories, while still allowing many of the network-based advantages of a network user account. I do urge caution when using this approach, as it could confuse the user in question if she discusses the ways in which other users interact with the network or if she does log in to other workstations for which the mobile account preference is disabled. If you use this approach, I still suggest managing the mobile account preference based on computer list (even if it is a computer list containing a single computer) because that will prevent multiple mobile accounts, should the user log in to another computer.

Printing Preferences

The Printing preferences pane allows you to define printers that will be automatically available to users and to restrict access to printers. You can configure printing preferences based on user, group, or computer list, and you can configure them once or always. Remember that managed preferences that define lists of items (including printers) are additive. So if you define printers based on more than one account type, the ultimate list displayed to a user will contain all defined printers for the user, the managed workgroup he is logged in as, and the computer list appropriate to the workstation being used.

Creating a printer list

To define printers for users, use the Printer List tab of the printing preferences pane. The printer list tab contains two listboxes. The first, "Available printers," lists all network printers that Workgroup Manager can locate. Workgroup Manager builds the list based on printers that are configured in the Print Setup Utility on the computer on which it is being run or those that are configured for self-discovery (such as those set up to respond to Rendezvous or AppleTalk requests). If you need to configure printers not in this listbox, configure them using the Print Setup Utility and then return to this pane. To create a printer list, select the printers you wish to include in the list and click the Add to List button. This populates the second listbox, User's Printer List, with the selected printers. To remove printers, select them in the User's Printer List box and click the Remove button.

Below the two listboxes are two checkboxes. The first is "Allow user to modify printer list." Selecting this option allows a user to open the Print Setup Utility and add or remove printers. Deselecting this option restricts the user to printers that are in the list. This option is automatically selected if you choose to manage this preference only once. Be careful with this option because, if you use it, you should make certain that it is used as globally as that to ensure users do not have permission to modify a printer list in one group or on one workstation while being restricted elsewhere.

The next checkbox does exactly what it says, allow printers that are connected directly to user's computer (such as USB ink jet or laser printers), though the required printer drivers will need to be installed on the workstation in question. When this checkbox is selected, you can also require a local administrator account be used to authenticate access to USB printers.

Restricting printer access

The Access tab of the printing pane, shown in Figure 25-7, is used to restrict access to printers in a printer list and to select one printer as the default printer. You can define printers in a list and still require authentication with a local administrator username and password to access them. This can be useful in classroom situations, where you want to define a series of printers but restrict access to some printers to teachers, to whom you can give the local admin password for the computer (or, if you use the same generic admin password throughout your infrastructure, for whom you can also create a second local administrator account specific only to that workstation).

To require authentication for a printer, select it in the User's Printer List listbox (after having configured the list using the Printer List tab) and the check the "Require an administrator password" checkbox. To define a printer as the default printer for the list, select it and then click the Make Default button.

System Preferences

The System Preferences pane gives you the option of specifying which panes users have access to when they launch System Preferences on a workstation. The pane contains a list of checkboxes for all the System Preferences panes available on the computer where Workgroup Manager was launched. Because different computers may have different System Preferences configurations, you should configure this pane using Workgroup Manager on a workstation with a configuration that matches those

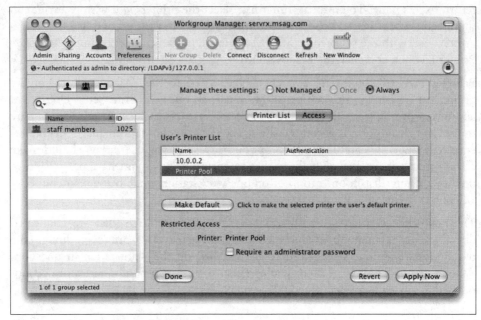

Figure 25-7. The Access tab of the Printing preferences pane.

that you will be managing. To manage access to a particular System Preferences pane, select or deselect the checkbox next to it.

You can manage System Preferences for users, groups, or computer lists, but they must always be managed or not managed. Also it is important to realize that even though a user may have access to a System Preferences pane, other managed preferences may prevent them from being able to actually change the settings for it. Likewise, make certain that anything a user may need to configure is enabled for them—for example, if you want users to be able to change their passwords, they need access to the Accounts pane in System Preferences.

Universal Access Preferences

The settings in the Universal Access preferences pane mirror those in the Universal Access System Preferences pane on a Mac OS X workstation and offer options for visually or hearing impaired users as well as users with that have problems with typical mouse and keyboard usage. The Seeing tab contains options for zooming the screen, and adjusting contrast and color settings. The Hearing tab includes options for flashing the screen for alerts sounds. The Keyboard tab enables options for reducing key repeat rates and using Sticky Keys, a feature that allows key combinations to be entered one key at a time instead of simultaneously. The Mouse tab enables and configures the use of a numeric keypad to control the cursor. The Options tab allows you to configure keyboard shortcuts for activating universal access features.

Universal Access preferences can be set based on user, group, or workstation, and each tab can be configured separately and can be managed once or always.

Although I most definitely applaud Apple for including universal access features in Mac OS X, I do question their use as a managed preference option. In my experience, users who are challenged in the ways that require use of these features almost always need to have them configured on a user-by-user basis. If you have special needs users, my strongest recommendation is to work with them (or the appropriate liaison or teacher) to configure an environment for them using the options in System Preferences based on their specific needs after creating their account. You might then opt to limit access to the Universal Access System Preferences pane to prevent these settings from being accidentally changed. Also be aware that some users with special needs may need additional considerations made for their workstations (such as special types of displays, keyboard height, or specially designed keyboards).

## CHAPTER 26

Managing Classic Mac OS Workstations Using Mac Manager

The classic Mac OS was not designed as a network operating system. Perhaps the most significant lack is that of a built-in directory services architecture, something that is fundamental to Mac OS X. This lack poses the question: how do you leverage the power of Open Directory to create a unified infrastructure when working with an operating system that doesn't include a directory service architecture? The answer is Mac Manager.

Mac Manager consists of a server component that is installed with Mac OS X Server (though it is not enabled by default) and a client component that is installed on Classic Mac OS workstations. The current Mac Manager server component requires that the Mac Manager client software be the most recent version (2.2.2). This most recent version of the Mac Manager client requires Mac OS 9.1 or higher as a workstation operating system, as this was the first Mac OS version to offer full support for multiple users. Earlier Mac Manager versions enabled the support of both Mac OS 8 and 9 clients. In this chapter, we'll examine the individual Mac Manager components and how they operate.

Mac Manager and Open Directory

Although Mac OS 9 has no built-in way to access Open Directory, it does include support for multiple local users, each with a local home folder that functions much like a Mac OS X home directory (local or network). The Mac OS 9 multiple users feature also includes the ability to created limited access users. The Mac Manager client software taps into the multiple users feature but tells the operating system to look to a Mac Manager server for user account information and home directories.

On the client side, Mac Manager is fairly simple; it just tells the operating system where on a network to look for account information that is typically stored in the System Folder. On the server side, things are a little more complicated. Mac Manager predates Mac OS X, so the Mac Manager server needs to provide some way to make information in Open Directory backwards-compatible with information that was initially just stored in a series of flat databases. At the same time, there needs to be a way to provide interaction with Open Directory for users that log in on both Mac OS 9 and Mac OS X computers and who may also run applications using Mac OS X's Classic environment.

Mac Manager achieves this by maintaining separate user, group, and computer databases (the same flat files it used prior to Mac OS X) outside of a shared directory domain. In order to manage users with Mac Manager, administrators must first import user accounts from a directory domain into Mac Manager. Computer lists for Mac OS 9 workstations must be created in Mac Manager. And, although groups used for file and share point permissions created in Workgroup Manager are still used for granting permissions to resources, managed groups created for Mac OS X clients have no meaning to Mac OS 9 clients. Instead workgroups need to be created in Mac Manager containing users whose accounts have been imported into Mac Manager.

Even though the managed environment offered with Mac Manager is independent of Open Directory, Mac Manager still does need to be able to interact with a directory domain for some very important things. Mac Manager is designed to create a managed environment and provide some security features; it is not designed to truly manage user accounts. Open Directory remains the means for verifying username and password information and for accessing user home directories. Therefore, the Mac Manager service does interact with a directory domain every time a user logs in.

When the user logs in, the username and password are sent to the Mac Manager server (which can be an Open Directory server or a supporting server bound to a directory domain). The Mac Manger server uses the entered username to access the user's UID. It queries Open Directory with the UID and password. If they match, then Mac Manager queries for the location of the user's home directory. A home directory is required when working with Mac Manager accounts (unlike Mac OS X, where users can be assigned to have no home directory). With the user's access authenticated by Open Directory and the home directory location, Mac Manager authorizes login and mounts the user's home directory. It then processes any additional login variables configure for the user's Mac Manager account (such as workgroup membership, mounting any Mac Manager share points, and preferences management).

In day-to-day operation, this is the only interaction between Open Directory and Mac Manager. However, because Mac Manager uses a separate set of databases for user accounts than the directory domain, it periodically checks to see whether the information in its databases and the domain still match. It does not add users to Mac Manager (you must import users manually), but it verifies that all users exist and that their UIDs still match the information maintained in the Mac Manager databases. If you change a user's name or add a shortname, you can also update the Mac Manager databases manually. Users that are listed in the Mac Manager databases but are not found in the directory domain are deleted from the Mac Manager databases. Mac Manager also updates references to users between its databases during a consistency check.

Mac Manager Environment Types

Regardless of the managed preferences configured for Mac OS X users and workstations, the basic user environment remains very much the same. Users still log in and access Mac OS X in essentially the same way with the same visual interface as if they were using a standalone home installation of Mac OS X. With Mac Manager, however, administrators can choose one of three environments for users. The user environments are assigned based on workgroup and vary all the way from the standard Mac OS 9 interface to a completely different user experience called Panels.

Finder

Finder workgroups have access to the traditional Mac OS 9 Finder interface. Users can access all the major Finder commands and have the same menu options as if they were not logged into a managed environment. Users also have access to all areas of the local hard drive, although it is possible to limit the user to read-only access to the System Folder and the applications folder, as well as the Library folder in their home directories.

Restricted Finder

Restricted Finder workgroups give users the traditional Mac OS 9 interface, but enable further security functionality. Administrators can limit access to a number of Finder commands and menu items as well as which applications and other items users are allowed to open. The Restricted Finder environment is the default choice when a new workgroup is created in Mac Manager because it combines the familiar Mac OS 9 user interface with the ability to enforce access and security restrictions on the local workstation. These restrictions apply regardless of permission settings that are configured for items on the local hard drive of the workstation.

Panels

Panels workgroups use a special, simplified user interface and do not have any access to the local hard drive. The panels environment uses *panels*, shaped like giant folders. Each panel relates to a specific share point, folder, or inserted disk. At a minimum, there are two panels displayed: the Applications panel and the User Documents panel (which contains items stored in the user's home directory). Additional panels can be used for a workgroup's shared folder, additional mounted share points, and CDs/DVDs and removable media, depending on various configuration options. Icons are displayed on the panels for documents or applications and look and function like the button view or Launcher in the Mac OS 9 Finder. Administrators can restrict many of the Finder command for Panels workgroups. Generally, the Panels environment is used for young children, computer novices, or when you wish to have as much access restriction and simplicity of user environment as possible (such as with Guest users).

Mac Manager Share Points and Folders

When Mac Manager is enabled on a Mac OS X Server, it automatically creates the Mac Manager share point and the Mac Manager user account. Mac Manager uses items located on the Mac Manager share point as well as other share points to accomplish several of its tasks. The following sections describe the various share points and folders that are created and/or used by Mac Manager.

The Mac Manager Share Point and Multi-User Items Folder

The Mac Manager share point is created in the Library folder of the startup drive for the server on which Mac Manager has been enabled. You can change the location of the Mac Manager share point (to provide fault tolerance, performance, or increased storage space). To do so, create the appropriate share point named Mac Manager on another volume and set the *mmuser* account (the short name assigned to the Mac Manager User account) as the owner of the share point and configure this account and the *admin* group to have read/write access to the share point and the *everyone* group's access to none. The alternate volume will need to be connected to the Mac Manager server and it must be formatted as a Mac OS Extended (HFS+) volume with a name containing only ASCII characters.

The Mac Manager share point contains the Multi-User Items folder. This folder contains the databases and configuration files needed for Mac Manager to function. A copy of the Multi-User Items folder is copied to each workstation that is configured to use the Mac Manager server and stored in the System Folder. By keeping local copies of the Multi-User Items folder, workstations can more quickly respond to Mac Manager related requests and reduce the network traffic and the need for server resources. It also enables users to work offline, maintaining a managed environment if a connection error occurs between the server and the workstation. Workstations will query the server to check for and download updates to their copy of the Multi-User Items folder periodically when no user is logged in. They will also download a fresh copy if the copy in the System Folder is deleted.

Generally speaking, you should not make changes to the contents of the Multi-User Items folder directly. Editing, moving, or deleting these files can have unexpected consequences and can cause problems with the Mac Manager server as well as individual workstations. You should use the Macintosh Manager application to edit the Mac Manager configuration.

Group Documents Volumes

The group documents volume is a share point that is used to store workgroup shared folders and a global shared folder. You can use any share point as a group documents volume and you can have multiple group documents folders. If you configure Mac Manager workgroups to mirror Mac OS X managed groups or permission groups that use a group folder, you will ideally want to use the same share point(s) that hosts those folders as a your group documents volume.

By default, Mac Manager uses the Mac Manager share point as the group documents volume. This is an effective strategy only if the users of Mac Manager workgroups do not also log in to Mac OS X workstations (where they will not have access to the Mac Manager share point). Therefore you will probably wish to use other group document volumes.

Workgroup shared folders

Workgroup shared folders are folders designed for users of a Mac Manager workgroup to share documents. In addition to shared items, they include the managed preferences folders for that workgroup (we'll discuss these folders in a moment) and can include a hand-in folder (see following explanation). You should specify the permissions on a shared folder to limit access using a permissions group for users that can access the share point from outside of Mac Manager. The share point hosting the workgroup shared folder is mounted automatically when users log in as part of a workgroup.

A *hand-in folder* is a folder that is write-only for all users but administrators. It can be used in Restricted Finder and Panels workgroups for users to hand-in files (such as personnel reviews in a company or homework in a school) without being able to see files that other users have handed in, similar to the functionality of a drop-box folder. In Restricted Finder workgroups, hand-in folders appear as write-only folder, while in Panels workgroups, they are accessed by a command in the Special menu. Create a hand-in folder when configuring a workgroup in the Mac Manager application.

Global shared folders

A global shared folder is a shared folder to which all Mac Manager users have access. As with workgroup shared folders, the default location is on the Mac Manager share point, though you can use any share point to host a global shared folder. A global shared folder is also mounted at login for all users. The use of a global shared folder is not required by Mac Manager.

The Mac Manager Client Software

The Mac Manager client software includes a series of extensions that are installed in the Mac OS 9 System Folder. These extensions cannot be disabled by using holding the Shift key down at startup. As mentioned earlier, if a workstation with Mac Manager enabled is started with Extensions Off or if the Mac Manager extension is bypassed at startup, you are required to enter the owner password for the workstation (as entered in the File Sharing control panel or the Mac OS Setup Assistant) in order to access the Finder. Under Mac OS 9, Mac Manager runs in conjunction with the Multiple Users feature and is configured through the Multiple Users control panel.

Installing or Updating the Mac Manager Client

The Mac Manager service revision that is included with Mac OS X Server 10.3 requires that the Mac Manager client version on workstations be 2.2.2. This version is included with Mac OS 9.2 or higher and it requires that a workstation be running Mac OS 9.1 or higher. If you have workstations running an earlier version of Mac OS 9, they will need to be updated and/or have the new Mac Manager client installed on them (which can be downloaded from Apple's support site).

There are two ways to update the Mac Manager. The first is to install the new client manually by running the installer application on each workstation. The second is to use a Mac Manager update package. This option is available only if you have an existing Mac Manager infrastructure. The update package, included with the Mac Manager client, can be placed in the Multi-User Items folder on your Mac Manager server's Mac Manager share point prior to upgrading the server. When workstations connect to the Mac Manager share point, provided no one is logged in on them, they will download the update and apply it automatically. You can then upgrade the appropriate Mac Manager server or deploy a new one.

Enabling Mac Manager

Once the Mac Manager client Version 2.2.2 is installed on a Mac OS 9 workstation, enable Mac Manager by opening the Multiple Users control panel and following these steps:

1. Turn on the multiple users feature using the radio button at the bottom of the Multiple Users control panel's window.
2. Click the Options button.
3. Select the Options tab and use select the Macintosh Manager Account radio button.

4. Quit the Multiple Users control panel.

5. Use the log out command, which is now included in the Special menu to logout of the workstation.

You will be asked to select a Mac Manager server. Servers that the workstation can locate using AppleTalk are displayed and you have the option to enter the IP address or DNS name of an alternative server.

After you select or enter the address of the appropriate server, the workstation will contact the server, download the appropriate items from the Mac Manager share point, and should then present you with the Mac OS 9 login screen (as defined by the Mac Manager configuration). Log in to be sure that everything is configured properly. To disable Mac Manager, you will need to log in with System Access and use the Multiple Users control panel to disable Mac Manager and/or turn off the multiple users feature.

Mac Manager Preference Management

Mac Manager supports preference management, but it does so in a very different and much broader manner than Mac OS X. Mac Manager allows you to define and enforce preferences for any application or Mac OS component rather than simply defining various user environment preferences, as is the case with Mac OS X managed preferences. Also, unlike Mac OS X preference management, you can apply preferences only to workgroups (not to individual users or based on computer lists). However, like Mac OS X managed preferences, you can specify preferences that users are allowed to change and those that are always enforced.

Initial Preferences and Forced Preferences

The Managed Preference folder is automatically created inside each workgroup shared folder and contains two preferences folders: initial preferences and forced preferences. As you might guess, the *initial preferences* folder is used to define preferences once, whereas the *forced preferences* folder is used to ensure that preferences are always managed. Stored in these folders are the same preferences files that are stored in the Preferences folder within a Mac OS 9 System Folder or in the appropriate Preferences folder in a user's home directory.

To use either initial or forced preferences, configure the application of Mac OS component to the settings you wish to define for your users. If Mac Manager is not enabled on the workstation you are configuring, locate the preferences files for the application or Mac OS component in the Preferences folder inside the System Folder. If Mac Manager is enabled, you need to look in the */Library/Classic/Preferences* folder in the home directory of the user you are logged in as when configuring the settings you wish to define, as this is where Mac Manager stores user preferences for

Mac OS 9 applications. Copy the appropriate preferences files into either the forced or initial preferences folders, depending on how you want to implement the settings.

When a user logs in, Mac Manager automatically copies files from the forced preferences folder into the */Library/Classic/Preferences* folder of the user's home directory if the files don't already exist there or if they don't match what is in the forced preferences folder. While users can make changes to preferences while logged in, the forced preferences are reset the next time that they login.

Initial preferences work in essentially the same way. At login, Mac Manager checks the */Library/Classic/Preferences* folder in a user's home directory to see if the user has a copy of each file in the initial preferences folder. If the user does not, then the item is copied to the user's preferences folder. If the item does exist (whether it has been modified or not), it is ignored.

If the preferences files for the same items are placed in both the forced preferences and the initial preferences, the version in the forced preferences folder is used. Also, since preferences are workgroup-specific, if a user is a member of more than one workgroup, the initial preferences will be implemented only for the first workgroup a user logs into. If a user is a member of multiple workgroups and one has forced preferences configured, those preferences *always* overwrite the initial and forced preferences from other workgroups (as well as any-user configured preferences) when the user logs in as part of that workgroup. This is yet another reason to try to limit users to belonging to a single workgroup where possible (or at least to as few workgroups as possible). If you must place users in multiple workgroups, keep this in mind if you intend to manage preferences (particularly forced preferences) for any of the workgroups.

There are some preferences that cannot be set as initial preferences using Mac Manager. These include the settings contained in the following preferences files:

- Apple Menu Options Preferences
- AppSwitcher Preferences
- Internet Preferences
- Keyboard Preferences
- Keychains
- Location Manager Preferences
- Mac OS Preferences
- TSM Preferences
- User Preferences

Matching Mac OS 9 and Classic User Preferences

Mac Manager and the Mac OS X Classic environment can be configured to store user preferences in the same location (*/Library/Classic/Preferences* in each user's home directory). To ensure that this is accomplished and that users maintain a consistent experience with Mac OS 9 applications, regardless of whether they log in using a Mac OS 9 or Mac OS X computer, configure the Classic Preference pane in Workgroup Manager to use preferences from the home folder.

Using Local Preferences

Developers of pre–Mac OS X applications had much greater control over how and where their applications stored configuration and user information. Despite Apple's guidelines about where to store preferences files, not all applications store them appropriately and, as a result, some applications may not function well (or at all) in a multi-user environment. If you are running into consistent problems with a specific application after implementing Mac Manager, this problem may be the culprit, particularly with older applications. You can force Mac Manager to use Mac OS 9's System Folder for all preferences to resolve such problems. However, this action also negates both managed preferences and the ability for users to have individual preferences that are stored in their home directory. To force preferences to be accessed only from the local workstation, install the *MMLocalPrefs* extension included with the Mac Manager client software.

Mac Manager Administration

Now that we've covered some of basic underpinnings of how Mac Manager actually works, it's time to talk about enabling and configuring a Mac Manager server. The Mac Manager service can be enabled and run on an Open Directory server (master or replica) or it can be enabled and run on a supporting server that is part of a directory domain. If you are using replicas, you may want to configure separate Mac Manager servers as well, although each server will need to be manually configured, as Mac Manager does not support replication of its databases.

Enabling Mac Manager

To enable the Mac Manager service under Mac OS X Server, launch Server Admin and select the server in the Computers & Services list. Mac Manager is not listed as one of the services available to a server. Instead, select the server itself, as you would to configure the server as a Network Time Server. Select the Settings tab at the bottom of the right pane of the Server Admin window and then select the Advanced tab within the Settings pane. Click the Enable Mac Manager checkbox and then click the Save button. This enables the Mac Manager service and creates the Mac Manager share point and user. Further configuration needs to be performed using the Macintosh Manager application.

Creating an Administrative Workstation

Beginning with Mac OS X Server 10.3, you must run the Mac Manager application, which handles all of the Mac Manager administrative tasks, from a workstation other than the Mac OS X Server on which the Mac Manager service is running. You can run the Mac Manager application under Mac OS 9 or Mac OS X. If you are using an administrator workstation to run Server Admin and Workgroup Manager already, then ideally you will use this same workstation (obviously running Mac OS X). However, there are some Mac Manager situations that may require you to run the Mac Manager application from a Mac OS 9 workstation; ideally, one with the same applications and other items your user workstations will contain. If you are running the Mac Manager application on a Mac OS 9 workstation, the workstation does not need to have Mac Manager enabled.

Once you have copied the Mac Manager application onto your administrative workstation, you will need to connect to the Mac Manager server. To do this, launch the Mac Manager application. You will be asked to locate the Mac Manager server that you wish to manage. You can choose to browse for the server (using AppleTalk or Rendezvous) or you can enter the server's IP address or DNS name.

Once connected to the server, you will be asked for an administrator name or password. You must use the initial administrator account you created during the setup of the Mac OS X Server to authenticate. Until you import users into Mac Manager and make one or more users Mac Manager administrators; the original server administrator is the only administrative account within Mac Manager. Once you are authenticated by the Mac Manager server, you will see the User's pane of the Macintosh Manager application, as shown in Figure 26-1.

Importing Users

Mac Manager is essentially a user- and workgroup-driven tool. Therefore the first task is to import users from a shared directory domain. The second task is usually to configure Mac Manager administrator accounts, which I'll get to in just a bit. There are several ways to import users into Mac Manager from a directory domain. Once users have been imported, they will be listed by full name in the Imported Users list.

Importing all users

The simplest way to import users is to click the Import All button. This action imports all users in the directory domain to which the Mac Manager server is bound (either as a supporting server as a server hosting the domain in question). You can

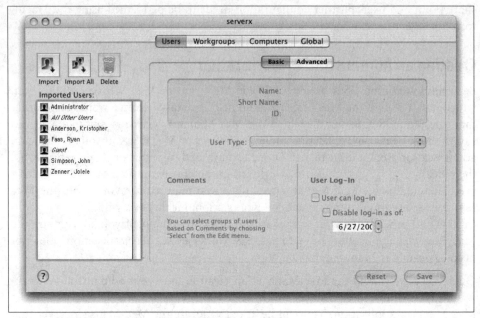

Figure 26-1. The Mac Manager application's Users pane.

use the Import All function to import up to 10,000 users. If you use the Import All feature after some users have already been imported, it will import only new users.

Be aware that it can take considerable time for Mac Manager to import a large number of users, and that it will creates a load on the server hosting the directory domain where the user accounts exist. Therefore, you might want to do this at a time when demands on your network are low.

Importing manually from Workgroup Manager

You can import users manually, which allows you to import only specific users (such as a limited number of users that will have access to Mac OS 9 workstations). To import users manually or individually, launch Workgroup Manager on the same workstation on which you are running Macintosh Manager and connect to the appropriate Open Directory server. Select the users you wish to import in the User Accounts list in Workgroup Manager and then drag the users onto to the Imported Users listbox in the Macintosh Manager window (this may take some rearranging of the windows onscreen). Mac Manager will import the selected users.

Importing from a user list

You can import users from a list contained in a text file. The advantage to this process is that it doesn't create as great a load on the shared directory domain. The disadvantage is that it takes effort to create the list and is more prone to errors than importing from the domain itself. Apple suggests using a list only if you are importing more than 1,000 users.

To import users from a list, you will need to create a comma- or tab-delimited text file containing the user full names, short names, and user ID numbers. Although strictly speaking the list needs to include only one of these three values, including them all reduces the risk of errors during the import process. If you provide only one of the three pieces of information and there are errors, you might inadvertently import the wrong user or identify an imported user incorrectly. You can format the three pieces of data in any order.

Once you have the list created, select the Import Users from List command from the File menu in the Mac Manager application. You are asked to navigate to the list file and then to specify the order in which the data is formatted in your list file and whether it is tab or comma delimited.

Mac Manager processes the list information and verifies that each line conforms to a user account in the directory domain. If a user account cannot be verified, you will be notified of the error. Once all accounts have been verified, they are added to the Imported Users list.

Using the All Other Users user

The All Other Users account is automatically created in Mac Manager and is included in the Imported Users list. This account is designed a sort of catch-all account for any users that you do not import into Mac Manager. When enabled, it allows any user with an account in the directory domain that has not been imported into Mac Manager to log in. Any settings you apply to this account or any workgroups you add it to affect all users that log in whose accounts have not been added to Mac Manager. Unlike a Guest account, All Other Users does provide authentication based on Open Directory.

Using the Guest user

The Guest user is a generic account that does not require a password to log in, just like file service Guest accounts. Like the All Other Users account, you can configure settings and workgroup membership for the Guest account. As I've said in other chapters about other types of Guest accounts, using one provides no authentication of anyone who logs in using it, making it an inherent security risk. You should use a Guest account only when absolutely needed and you should limit the access of the Guest user as tightly as possible, both for file servers and for Mac Manager. The best way to secure the Guest account in Mac Manager is to create a tightly restricted workgroup and to make the Guest user a member of it. In addition to configuring the Guest user, you need to allow guest access using the Security tab of the Global pane in the Mac Manager application.

Configuring User Settings

In addition to importing users, the Users pane of the Macintosh Manager application contains the various options that you can configure for individual users. The settings that can be applied are divided across the Basic and Advanced tabs of the Users pane and are much more limited than the settings that can be configured for Mac OS X–managed clients. You can edit multiple users at a time, as within Workgroup Manager.

When a user is selected, the Basic tab displays the user's full name, short name, and user ID. Besides the user information, the basic tab include a pop-up menu to select the user type, a comments field (limited to 63 characters) that can be used to sort users, and the User login options.

The User Login options include two checkboxes. The first, User Can Login, enables the user to log in to Mac OS 9 workstations that are managed by the Mac Manager server. The second checkbox, Disable Login as of, allows you to automatically disable the user's access to Mac OS 9 workstations on a specific date. This affects only Mac OS 9 workstations and is in addition to any limitations imposed by a password policy (globally or user-defined) specified in the directory domain.

The Advanced tab includes a further login option with the "User can only login at one computer at a time" checkbox. As you can probably guess, this checkbox disables simultaneous logins and it selected by default for basic users. The second option on the Advanced tab is a checkbox labeled "Allow user to exceed printer quotas." Print quotas are assigned based on workgroups in Mac Manager. This option is used to remove such quotas from a user. This option would generally be used if you need to place a user in a workgroup for reasons of access to shared data or a specific user environment but do not need to restrict printer usage (a teacher for a specific class in a school might need to be in the same workgroup as his students but need to be able to exceed their print quotas, for example). This option is applied to users in every workgroup of which they are a member.

The third option on the Advanced tab is the "User has system access" checkbox. This checkbox gives users the ability to log in to a managed workstation with complete access to the computer. When a user logs in, he is presented with a list of available workgroups, which will include one called System Access. When logged in with System Access, the user will interact with the computer in an unmanaged state (as though Mac Manager is not enabled) and will be able to make changes to any settings or files on the workstation. Mac Manager Administrators are automatically granted System Access. For any other users, System Access must be granted manually. System Access should only be granted to technical support staff or users who you trust to work with workstations in an unmanaged state. When granted, System Access is granted for all Mac Manager workstations. You cannot grant System Access to the Guest or All Other Users user accounts.

User types

As noted earlier, the Basic tab of the Users pane contains a pop-up menu for designating a user's type. Mac Manager includes three types of users: basic (which all users are imported as), Workgroup Administrator, and Mac Manager Administrator.

Basic users have the ability to login on Mac Manager workstations. They do not have access to the Mac Manager application.

Workgroup Administrators have access to the Mac Manager application. However, they have limited administrative ability. They cannot create Finder workgroups, they cannot change a user's type, and they cannot make changes to computer lists or global settings. Beyond that, they can be granted privileges to import users (providing they also have administrative privileges to the directory domain), modify the various settings for a workgroup, and to create Restricted Finder and Panels workgroups. If you are using a hand-in folder for a Restricted Finder or Panels workgroup, then you need to make a user within the workgroup a Workgroup Administrator, as only Workgroup or Mac Manager administrators have access to hand-in folders.

Typically, technical support staff are assigned as Workgroup Manager. In educational settings, it is also common to make teachers Workgroup Administrators to give them access to a hand-in folder (if one is used) and to enable to them to adjust workgroup restrictions as needed rather than relying on the technical staff to do so on a daily basis.

Mac Manager administrators have complete access to the Macintosh Manager application. As mentioned earlier, only the initial server administrator account is set as a Mac Manager administrator when Mac Manager is first enabled.

Creating and Managing Workgroups

As noted, workgroups in Mac Manager are the level at which you set Mac Manager environment types, preferences and access restrictions. They are also the level at which you define printers and configure options for easily locating applications, task-specific files, and network resources. Put more concisely, workgroups are the container used for creating a customized and consistent user experience in Mac Manager, as well as enforcing much of the security options available for Mac Manager.

Workgroups are not tied to groups created using Workgroup Manager. They have no ties to Mac OS X–managed groups and they are not bound to groups that are used solely to assign permissions to network resources. However, planning Mac Manager workgroups in concert with permissions groups and Mac OS X–managed groups is a good idea. Generally, if you are managing preferences for a group when the users are working on Mac OS X workstations, you have reasons for managing those preferences (be they security or user interface reasons). In many cases, if the members of a Mac OS X–managed group will also use Mac OS 9 workstations, it is a logical decision to create a workgroup for them in Mac Manager. Likewise, workgroups in Mac Manager are likely to be made up of users that need the same level of access to specific shared resources (i.e., users in a group used for assigning share point and folder permissions). Unfortunately, group accounts cannot be imported from a directory domain, meaning that you need to manually create workgroups that match directory domain groups.

Creating workgroups and managing workgroup membership

Workgroups are managed using the Workgroups pane of the Mac Manager application. As shown in Figure 26-2, the first tab of this pane is the Members tab. This tab is where you create workgroups, manage workgroup membership, and configure the name and environment for a workgroup.

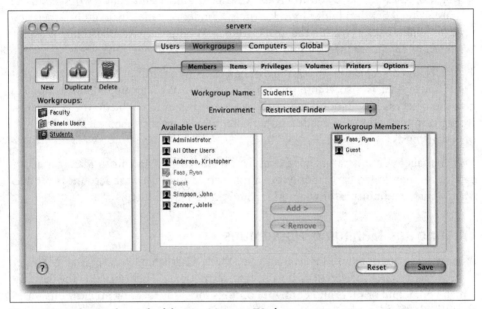

Figure 26-2. The Members tab of the Mac Manager Workgroups pane.

To create a new workgroup, click the New button in the upper left corner of the Workgroups pane, creating a new, empty Restricted Finder workgroup with the name New Workgroup. Once you have edited the new group, click the Save button to create its entry in the Mac Manager databases. To edit an existing workgroup, select it from the Workgroups listbox on the left side of the Workgroups pane and then edit the appropriate tabs and click Save to save your changes to the workgroup. To delete a workgroup, select in the Workgroups list and click the Delete button above the list.

The Members tab contains a field for the Workgroup Name, a pop-up menu from which to select the environment of the workgroup, and listboxes for adding or

---

removing users. You'll notice that when you change the environment of a workgroup, the icon for it in the Workgroups list changes to match the type (a plain folder for Finder workgroups, a folder with a band for Restricted Finder workgroups, and a folder with tabs on it for Panels workgroups), making it easy to identify a workgroup's type in the list.

The two listboxes on the Members tab are Available Users (which contains a list of all users imported into Mac Manager plus the Guest and All Others Users) and the Members list. Between the two are Add and Remove buttons. To add users to a workgroup, select them in the Available Users list and click the Add button, double-click them, or drag them into the Members listbox. To remove users, select them in the Members listbox and click the Remove button.

Assigning workgroup items for Finder workgroups

For Finder workgroups, which have the ability to open all items and applications on the local hard drive, the Items tab of the Workgroups pane, shown in Figure 26-3, allows you to create aliases to items that you expect users to use frequently. When a user logs in, these aliases appear in a folder on the desktop named Items For (Workgroup Name) and are listed in the Shortcut Items listbox. You can use the Items tab to create shortcuts to applications or other items, either on the local hard drive or on a share point.

The Volume pop-up menu allows you to choose where to locate the items. If you choose a local hard drive, be sure the workstation from which you are running the Macintosh Manager application contains the items in the same locations as the workstations that members of this workgroup will be using. By default, choosing a location from the Volume menu populates the listbox below it with applications found on the selected volume. Select the items you wish to make available and click the Add button to add them to the Shortcuts Items listbox.

To add other items, such as files, click the Find button and navigate to the item. Since copies of the applications or files in the Shortcut Items list may exist in multiple locations, the "Find chosen items" pop-up menu allows you to specify where Mac Manager should look first (such as the local hard drive or a share point) for these items when creating aliases at user login. If Mac Manager cannot locate an item, it will display an alert to the user saying that some items could not be located. This message may also be displayed if you are listing items on a share point that is not mounted automatically for a user at login, particularly one that is not defined within Mac Manager.

Assigning workgroup items for Restricted Finder and Panels workgroups

The Items tab functions slightly different for Restricted Finder and Panels workgroups. With these workgroup environments, you can restrict the ability of users to open applications or other items on the local hard drive. Thus, the radio buttons at

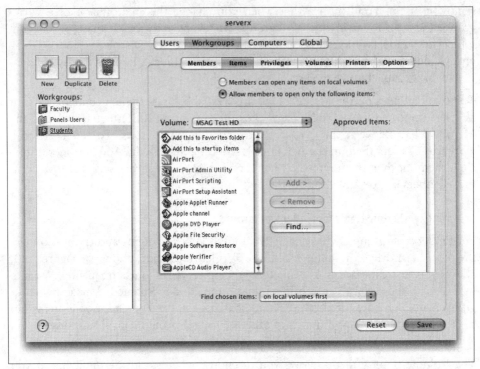

Figure 26-3. The Items tab of the Mac Manager Workgroups pane.

the top of the Items tab ("Members can open any items on local volumes" or "Allow members to open only the following items") become available and you can choose which of the two you wish to use. For security reasons, it can be helpful to limit what items can be used. To do so, select the appropriate radio button and specify the items you wish workgroup members to be able to open in the Shortcut Items listbox (now called the Approved Items listbox) as described previously.

If you allow users to open all applications on a local hard drive, you may still want to use the Shortcut Items list to provide easy access to specific items (as with a Finder workgroup). With Restricted Finder workgroups, whether you use the Items tab to limit application access or not, selected items are displayed in a folder on the desktop, the same as a Finder workgroup. With a Panels workgroup, the items are listed on an individual panel with the same Items for (Workgroup) name. Because members of a Panels workgroup do not have the ability to browse the local hard drive, you should always define Items for them.

Privileges for Finder workgroups

When working with a Finder workgroup, the Privileges tab contains five checkboxes that are collectively labeled Protect. The number of options on this tab increases for

Restricted Finder workgroups and increases even more for Panels workgroups. The five options for Finder workgroups are:

Lock the user's desktop on the startup volume
> This option prevents the user from saving, moving, or deleting files from the desktop of a Mac OS 9 workstation. It also prevents them from changing the desktop pattern or picture.

Prevent users from saving documents in their Library folder
> When selected, members of the workgroup will not be able to store items in the Library folder of their home directory (though applications will be able to write preferences file changes to the */Library/Classic/Preferences* folder). This prevents users from changing files inside the Library folder, which could create problems when they log in at a Mac OS X workstation. It also keeps them from being able to delete preferences files as a troubleshooting mechanism for Mac OS 9.

Enforce file level security for Mac OS 9 workstations
> This option prevents applications from making changes in any folders that you protect with Mac Manager. This can be a powerful security feature. Unfortunately, there are many applications that use temporary files or create preferences files outside of the default locations, and enabling this option can cause them to report disk errors and/or not function properly, if at all. If you are working with a Panels workgroup, this option also restricts users from accessing external FireWire drives.

System Folder
> Prevents the user from modifying or deleting items in the System Folder, regardless of what access they have to it.

Applications Folder
> Prevents the user from modifying or deleting items in the Applications or Applications (Mac OS 9) folders, regardless of what access they have to them.

Privileges for Restricted Finder workgroups

Restricted Finder workgroups have the first three options on the Privileges tab as Finder workgroups (the last two, System Folder and Applications folder, are not included because Restricted Finder workgroups automatically deny users the ability to modify these folders). In addition, the Privileges tab for Restricted Finder workgroups includes three checkboxes grouped under the heading Group Members May, five privileges pop-up menus, and three checkboxes relating to the Apple Menu.

The Group Members May checkboxes allow you to specify whether users are allowed to play audio CDs, take screenshots, or open approved items on removable media. If you allow members to open items on removable media, you will also need to create an approved items list in the Mac Manager Global settings pane.

The privileges pop-up menus allow you to set the permission level for each of the following items (presuming you use the item): a workgroup shared folder (created for the workgroup within Mac Manager), a global shared folder (created for all Mac Manager users), a workgroup hand-in folder (if a hand-in folder is used, it should be set to write-only to prevent users from seeing work create by other users), removable media except CDs or DVDs (such as Zip or floppy disks or Smart Media or Compact Flash cards), or a designated folder on the hard drive (this option can be used if you want to create a folder on the local hard drive of each workstation that users can use to share items or store frequently accessed files, make sure the folder exists at the root level of the hard drive of each workstation and enter the case-sensitive name in the field next to this pop-up menu). These permissions are applied in addition to any permissions that are assigned to the related items outside of Mac Manager, with the most restrictive permission being enforced.

The Apple Menu checkboxes allow you to control which Apple menu items are displayed to members of the workgroup. You can choose to show or not show the Chooser and Network Browser (to prevent users manually mounting share points or attempting to change the printer, which members of Restricted Finder or Panels workgroup are not able to do), Control Panels, or all additional Apple menu items.

Privileges for Panels workgroups

When working with the Privileges tab for a Panels workgroup (shown in Figure 26-4), you have the same options as with a Restricted Finder workgroup plus three File menu options and four Special menu options. These seven checkboxes allow you to show or hide access to Finder commands that are listed in the File and Special menus. The File menus commands include New Folder, Rename, and Delete. The Special menu commands include Eject, Erase Disk, Restart, and Shut Down. In the case of the Restart and Shut Down commands, users may still access them using the power button on the keyboard.

Workgroup volume settings

The Volumes tab, shown in Figure 26-5, lets you automatically mount share points (other than workgroup and global shared volumes) when members of a workgroup log in. The Volumes listbox contains a list of share points are already listed in Mac Manager. If the share point(s) you wish to mount automatically are listed, select them and click the Add button to include them in the Mount at Login listbox. If you wish to mount a share point not in the list, click the Find button and locate the share point to add it to the Volumes list.

Once you have defined share points to mount at login, you will need to specify how Mac Manager should login to the appropriate server to mount the share point. To do this, select each share point in the Mount at Login listbox. The lower section of the tab will display the login settings for the selected share point. There are three login

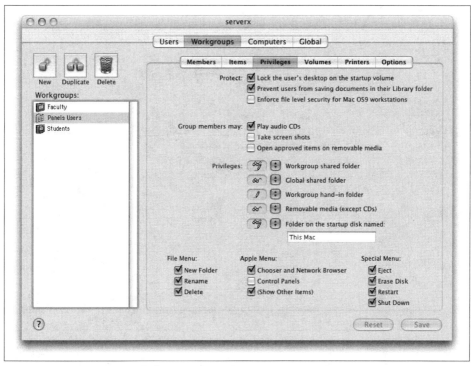

Figure 26-4. The Privileges tab for a Panels workgroup.

options, including radio buttons for "Prompt user for log-in" or "Log-in automatically as this AFP user," and a checkbox for "Always try auto log-in with user's name and password first."

You should generally select the "Always try to log-in with user's name and password first" checkbox if share point is part of the same directory domain from which the users in the workgroup were imported. Ideally, this will be the case and you will be mounting a share point that these users are allowed to access (usually by membership of a permissions group). The radio buttons allow you to specify how to handle situations in which a user does not have access to the share point or where the share point is not part of the directory domain. Ideally, you should not include a share point to which users do not have access in the Mount at Login list.

The best option is to prompt the user for a username and password. If the share point exists on a server outside the share domain, this option allows users with accounts on that server to enter the appropriate information. This option continues to secure the share point while allowing appropriate users access to it. You can also specify that pre-determined user information is used to log in to the share point by specifying information for a single user account with access to the server. This choice is inherently insecure because you cannot tell which users are actually accessing the share point using this account.

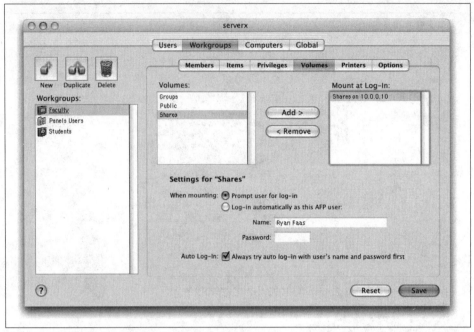

Figure 26-5. The Volume Settings tab of the Workgroup pane.

For Restricted Finder and Panels workgroups, there is also a "Use AFP privileges" checkbox. By default, Mac Manager allows only members of these workgroup environments read-only access to mounted share points. The "Use AFP privileges" option enables users read-only or read-write access based on the permissions assigned to the share point and to items within it. There is also an option requiring an administrator password to unmount the volume for Restricted Finder workgroups. If this option is selected, basic users will not be able to unmount the share point.

For Panels workgroups, there is one more option for each share point, and that is to "Show volume on a panel." When selected, this displays the share point's contents on a separate panel. If it is not selected, the share point is listed on the Applications panel.

Defining Workgroup printers

The Printers tab is where you define individual printers and printer settings for a workgroup. When choosing printers for a workgroup, you need to decide whether the workgroup will print to PostScript network printers (ideally using server-based print queues) or other types of printers (local USB or serial port printers or non-PostScript network printers). For PostScript network printers, you can configure a list of printers for the workgroup that users can access as Mac OS 9 Desktop

Printers. For any other type of printer, you need to define the printer on each workstation while logged in with System Access.

Thus, the first option in the Printers tab is a choice of two radio buttons: "Members use printer selected in System Access" or "Allow members to use only the following Desktop Printers." If you select the former, there is no further configuration that needs be done on the Printers tab (although you will need to configure the printers on each workstation).

 Users who can access the Chooser can select another printer, but their selection is reset to the originally selected printer when they log out. If you select the latter, you need to configure a printer list for the workgroup.

As you can see in Figure 26-6, there are two listboxes on the Printers tab. The first, Available Printers, contains a list of all printers that have been configured for the workstation on which the Mac Manager application is running. The Create New button will launch the Print Setup Utility on a Mac OS X workstation, allowing you to configure additional printers. If using a Mac OS 9 workstation, you can configure additional printers using the Chooser. If you need to define network printers other than LaserWriter printer models, you need to use a Mac OS 9 workstation and be certain that the appropriate PPD files are installed on both the workstation you are using to run the Mac Manager application and the workstations accessing the printers. Alternatively, you can configure printers using the generic LaserWriter PPD, though this method will not allow access to many model-specific printer features.

The second listbox, Selected Printers, contains the printer list for the workgroup. To add printers to the Selected Printers list, select them in the Available Printers and then click the Add button. To remove a printer from the Selected Printers list, select the printer and click the Remove button. To configure a printer as the default printer for the workgroup, select it in the Selected Printers list and click the Set Default Printer button. You can also use the Remember Last Used Printer checkbox to set the default printer to whichever printer a user printed to most recently.

You can require authentication by a Workgroup Administrator or Mac Manager Administrator to print to specific printers by selecting the in the Selected Printers list and clicking the "Require an administrator password" to print to this printer checkbox. You can also configure a print quota for a printer (for users logged as members of the workgroup you are configuring) by selecting it and selecting the "Limit users to no more than X pages every X days" (replacing the Xs with numerical values). However, unlike Mac OS X print quotas, you cannot manually reset a user's print quota. As with Mac OS X print quotas, users receive no notification of their remaining print quotas.

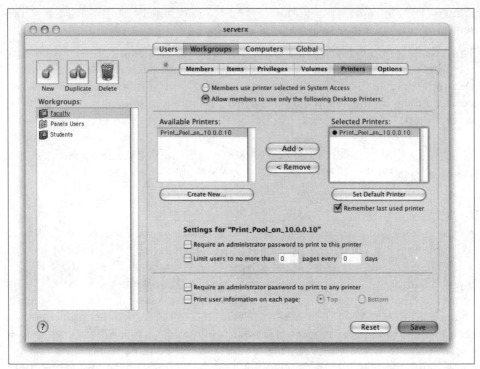

Figure 26-6. The Printers tab of the Workgroups pane.

There are also two printer options that affect all printers for the workgroup—both those defined in the Selected Printers list and those defined in System Access. The first is "Require an administrator password to print to any printer," and the second is "Print user information on each page." Printing user information can be helpful in high volume printing environments, such as a school computer lab, because it includes the full name of the user who printed the document (you can specify whether this is placed the top or bottom of the page). As useful as this can be, it does add a page element to each printed page, which may not be appropriate for some documents.

Additional workgroup options

The Options tab, shown in Figure 26-7, includes some additional settings that you can configure for a workgroup. These include the location and login settings for a workgroup shared folder (if you are using one), a group message that is displayed to users during the login process, and additional startup and login options.

If you are using a workgroup shared folder, the Stored on Volume pop-up menu allows you to specify the share point where the folder should be created. The default selection is Designated Macintosh Management Server, which points to the Mac Manager share point. Using this option makes it impossible for workgroup members

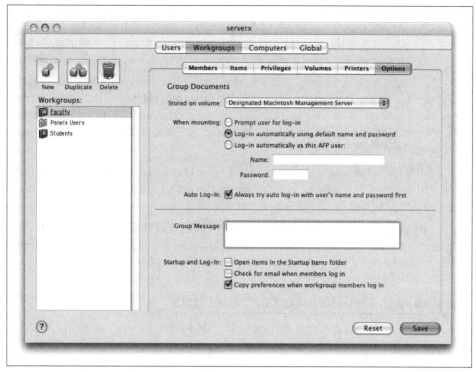

Figure 26-7. The Options tab of the Workgroups pane.

to access the shared folder from Mac OS X, Windows, or unmanaged classic Mac OS workstations because only server administrators can have access to the Mac Manager share point outside of the Mac Manager environment. Any other share point that has been mounted on the workstation where the Macintosh Manager application is running should also be displayed in this pop-up menu. If the share point isn't displayed, you can try selecting Other and mounting it at that point.

The login settings allow you to specify how users authenticate to the share point hosting the shared folder. The options are the same as used for mounting share points automatically at login with the addition of "Log-in automatically using default name and password." This option is available only when using the Mac Manager share point to house the workgroup folder and is automatically selected. It uses the Mac Manager user account to authenticate and relies on Mac Manager rather than the file service to manage user access to the shared folder. The downside to this option is that, like the "Log-in automatically as this AFP user" option, it provides no way to track user access to the share point. Again, for logging and ease of access purposes, it is generally a good idea to use the "Always try to auto log-in with user's name and password first" option.

The Group Message field allows you to enter a message that is displayed to all members during the login process, along with the login progress bar. This message is displayed at each login and users must click the continue button to close the message once the login process has completed. A group message can be up to 127 characters.

The "Open items in the Startup Items folder" checkbox causes items located in the user's Startup Items folder to open once login has completed. The user's startup items folder is located at */Library/Classic/Startup* inside the user's Home directory. This option does not enable items in the Startup Items folder inside the System Folder on a Mac OS 9 workstation.

The "Check for email when members log in" checkbox enables the automatic email check feature, which needs to be configured for a Mac Manager computer list in order to function.

The "Copy preferences when workgroup members log in" checkbox affects when initial preferences and checked. When selected, this occurs at login. When not selected, preferences are checked and downloaded whenever a user opens an application.

Working with Mac Manager Computer Lists

Like Mac OS X preference management, Mac Manager allows you to create computer lists and to define configuration variables as well as access and security restrictions for each list. The available options differ, however, from those available to Mac OS X workstations. Computer lists are created and managed using the Computers pane of the Mac Manager application. Each workstation can be included in only one computer list.

Creating and editing computer lists

Create a computer list in Mac Manager by clicking the New button above the Machine Lists listbox to the left of the Mac Manager window. This creates an empty list named New List. You can change the name by entering a new name in the List Name field on the Lists tab. Computer list names can be up to 31 characters but cannot contain a colon. As with computer lists for Mac OS X workstations, use a descriptive name that easily identifies the computers in the list and try to group lists by department, job function, or location. Once the list is created and named, you can use the options on the Lists tab to add computers to the list and to designate whether users can log in to them.

Computers that are part of a list are listed in the listbox of machines on the Lists tab, shown in Figure 26-8. To add a computer to a list, click the Find button and either select the computer if it is automatically discovered using AppleTalk or Rendezvous or enter the computer's IP address. Mac Manager creates an entry for the computer and adds it to the computer list. To remove a workstation from the computer list, select it in the listbox and click the Remove button.

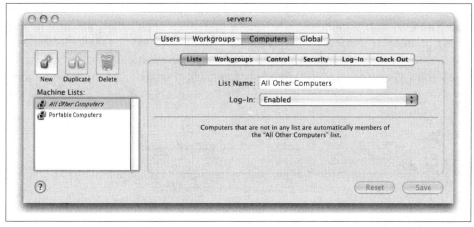

Figure 26-8. The Lists tab of the Computers pane.

Using the All Other Computers list

By default, Mac Manager creates the All Other Computers list, much like it creates the All Other Users account. The All Other Computers list functions like the Guest Computers list does for Mac OS X preferences management. Any Mac OS 9 workstation that has Mac Manager enabled and configured to access a given Mac Manager server that is not listed in an administrator-defined computer list stored on that server is automatically assigned to the All Other Computers list. You can configure settings for this list as you would any other computer list.

Disabling login for a computer list

You can disable login for a computer list using the Log-In pop-up menu on the Lists tab. Disabling login is somewhat of a misnomer because even though the options for disabled login disallow access to the Mac Manager server, they do allow access to the workstation either directly or by allowing users to select an alternate Mac Manager server. To disable login, select a computer list in the Machines Lists listbox and then select an option from the Log-In pop-up menu. The options in this menu are:

Enabled
  A user can log in to workstations in the computer list using Mac Manager.

Disabled—Ask User
  Allows the a user to shut down a workstation in the computer list or to select one of the two following options, which might require an administrator password, depending on the configuration.

Disabled—Go To System Access
  Gives users unmanaged access to the Finder.

Disabled—Pick Different Server.
  Allows users to select another Mac Manager server on the network.

Disabling login for a computer list like this is a somewhat unusual concept. You really can't use it to prevent access to the Mac Manager server while making changes or repairs because the feature itself relies on communication between the workstation and the server, and while you could use it while troubleshooting, upgrading, or repair work is being done on the workstation itself, it would often be better to have the technician working on the workstation log in with System Access or disable the Mac Manager client.

 The potential for giving users unmanaged access, telling them to switch servers, or generally confusing them limits the rationale for using this option. In my opinion, the feature has the potential to be more trouble or hassle than the possible benefits.

Configuring workgroup access to computer lists

You can use the Workgroups tab in the Computers pane to limit access to the workstations in a computer list to members of specific workgroups. This feature allows you to limit who can log in on certain workstations. It can be useful for security purposes as well as for limited access to workstations configured for specific functions (such as those with certain types of peripherals or applications installed).

At the top of the Workgroups tab are two radio buttons labeled "All users can access these computers" and "Allow only the following workgroups to access these computers." Select the latter to restrict access to specific workgroups. You will use the two listboxes (Available Workgroups and Allowed Workgroups) below the radio buttons to assign workgroups access to workstations in the computer list by selecting them in the Available Workgroups listbox (which contains all workgroups configure on the Mac Manager server) and clicking the Add button. To remove a workgroup's access to computers in the list, select the workgroup in the Allowed Workgroup's listbox and click the Remove button.

Control options for computer lists

The Control tab of the Computers pane, shown in Figure 26-9, lets you specify four different settings for the workstations in a computer list. The first option is to specify a length of time before the computer disconnects from the Mac Manager server. By default, a Mac OS 9 workstation with Mac Manager enabled will maintain its connection to the server when no users are logged in and will periodically update its copy of the Mac Manager folders, which can be a drain on the server and network resources. This option allows you to set a length of time in minutes before the computer breaks the connection, freeing up those resources.

While the computer is disconnected, there will be an X over the server's icon in the menu bar, though the login screen is still displayed. Attempting to log in causes the workstation to reconnect to the server. Because of the delay in reconnecting,

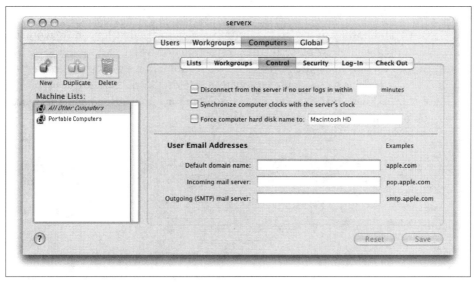

Figure 26-9. The Control tab of the Computers pane.

however, the login request may not be successful, which can be confusing to users, although a second login attempt should succeed without incident. You should use this option if a Mac Manager server is heavily used or the network segments where workstations in the list are slow and/or heavily used. Generally, a slow login response can be a sign that a Mac Manger server is maintaining too many connections.

The second option on the control tab instructs workstations to synchronize their clocks with the Mac Manager server. In effect, this option uses Mac Manager as a network time server.

The third option allows you to force the local hard drive to a specific name: Macintosh HD by default. This is an interesting option that ensures a consistent user environment and, more importantly, consistent file paths for items in the default folders on the hard drive, such as the Applications (Mac OS 9) folder and the System Folder. This feature can be useful for ensuring that items on the local hard drive that you select in the Items tab of the Workgroup pane are found and aliases created to them quickly.

The fourth option allows you to specify email server information for workstations. This information is populated into email programs that can recognize data stored in the Internet control panel automatically and can be combined with the "Check email at log in feature" on the Options tab of the Workgroups pane. You can specify email server information only for POP and SMTP email servers.

Security options for computer lists

The Security tab allows you to specify a number of settings that limit how workstations function as well as to place further restrictions on what users are allowed to access. As you can see in Figure 26-10, the first section allows you to configure user access restrictions, the second allows you to configure workstation access to data CDs, the third allows you to configure restrictions for applications, and the fourth allows you to configure automatic logout for idle users.

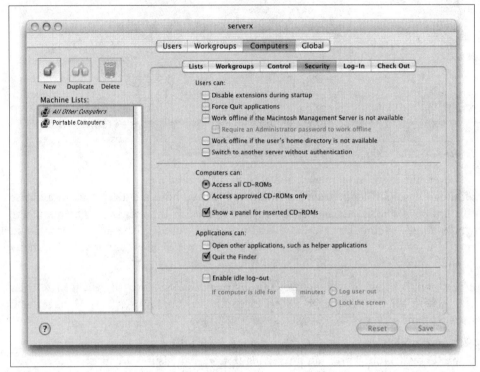

Figure 26-10. The Security tab of the Computers pane.

The first section includes checkboxes to specify whether user can disable extensions by holding the Shift key at startup, though even if you allow this, users cannot disable the Mac Manager extension by holding the Shift key, Force Quit applications, Work Offline if the Mac Manager server cannot be accessed (you can also require administrator authentication if you allow this), Work Offline if the user's Home directory cannot be accessed, and switch to another Mac Manager server without authentication. For the most part, these options allow you limit users ability to create problems with the workstation more than security trouble.

These options are not without drawbacks. The first two can hamper troubleshooting ability (for both technicians and for users). The second two can lead to users not reporting network problems, as well as not being able to save files in the appropriate network locations. The last can create problems if users begin selecting the wrong Mac Manager servers.

If a workstation with Mac Manager enabled is started with Extensions Off, users are required to enter the owner password for the workstation that was entered in either the File Sharing control panel or Mac OS Setup Assistant. Even if you deny users the ability to disable extensions at startup, they can bypass the Mac Manager extension by holding the Shift-⌘-Escape key combination once the Mac OS 9 splash screen appears and entering the owner password for the workstations. For this reason, you should make certain to enter an owner password for workstations and ensure the security of that password as much as possible.

The second section of the Security tab allows you to specify whether workstations in the list can access all data CDs or only those listed as approved in the Global settings pane. It also lets you specify whether the contents of a data CD are displayed in a separate panel for Panel's workgroups. If you choose not to display a panel for CD contents, the CD will be displayed on the Applications panel.

The third section lets you specify whether applications are allowed to launch other applications, including helper applications. As discussed earlier, some applications may require helper applications or plug-ins to perform certain functions. However, an application may then launch an application that users of Restricted Finder or Panels workgroups are not allowed to access.

The third section also lets you specify whether applications can quit the Finder. Usually, only installer programs quit the Finder and generally speaking, you don't want users running installer programs. Typically, you will also want to install software while logged in with System Access. However, a few legitimate applications may be designed to quit the Finder. If you find that applications need this ability to function, you can allow it using this checkbox.

The last option is for enabling automatic logout of idle users. As discussed in the last chapter, this is an important security concern. If a user forgets to log out, other users will be able to access anything that user could and they will be able to do so as that user, which limits your ability to track the culprit. Mac Manager offers you the ability to enable automatic logout and to specify the number of minutes before logout occurs.

Technically speaking, users are not actually logged out after the idle period expires, as they are with Mac OS X. Access to the workstation is locked. When a user returns she will have the opportunity to save any work before being logged out. This is a safeguard for users with open files, but it can also be problematic because another user could come along after the first and tell the computer to save changes before logging the first user out, regardless of whether the first user would have wanted those changes saved.

You also have the option of logging the user out or just locking the screen. If you opt to lock the screen, the screen goes black until a user attempts to access the workstation. If it is the original user, entering the user password unlocks the screen. If not, the next user can save changes and log the original user out.

Login options for computer lists

Use the Login tab to specify the login environment for workstations in a computer list. The first option on the Login tab determines whether users type their username and password or whether they select their name from a list of all Mac Manager users and then enter their password. You can enable a user list only if you have less than 2,000 users imported on the Mac Manager server (though if you have more than a couple of dozen, it is probably easier for users to type their name than to select from a long list). You can also specify that only basic users and not administrators be displayed in a user list.

Below the Login settings are two fields to enter login messages. You can create a banner message, which is displayed in the login window and a server message, which is displayed during the login process along with a workgroup login message. The server message is prefixed with "From: Global Administrator". Both messages can be up to 127 characters in length.

The last options on the Login tab apply only to users who login and are members of Panels workgroups. They are text fields that allow you to use specific names for the Workgroup and User Documents panels. By default, these panels are displayed using the names of the workgroup and the user respectively.

Checking out PowerBooks and iBooks

While Mac OS X sports the mobile account for users that need to access a computer off the network, such as a PowerBook or iBook, Mac Manager uses a process called checking the computer out of the network. You use the Check Out tab to define computer lists that can be checked out and used off the network as well as to define which users are allowed to check out the computer. You cannot check out computers on which the *MMLocalPrefs* extension is installed. Also, the option is not available for users who access to Mac Manager is configured using the All Other Users account. Lastly, checkout cannot be configured for the All Other Computers list.

The Check Out tab includes a checkbox to allow computers in the list to be checked out. Below that are radio buttons to designate whether all users may check out the computers in the list or whether you will limit checkout to certain users. If you limit checkout to specific users, you can select users in the Available Users listbox, which contains all users imported into Mac Manager, and click the Add button to include in the Allowed Users listbox those users allowed to check out portable computers in the computer list. To remove a user's ability to check out computers in the list, select the user in the Allowed User's list and click the Remove button.

Since checkout can be enabled only for portable computers, it is logical to define lists of portable computers by department, job function, class, or using other designations appropriate to your institution. Because the portable computers checked out most frequently are those assigned to a specific user, you may want to limit checkout based on individual computers. The only way to do this is to create a computer list containing a single computer and to configure checkout to be allowed only for a single user.

While a computer is checked out, all Mac Manager settings and restrictions remain in effect. The user who checked out the computer is generally the only one who can access it while it is checked out. A copy of the user's home directory is created on the hard drive at check out to enable the user to continue working on existing projects. This copy is synchronized with the user's actual home directory when the computer is checked in on the network.

Global Settings

The Global pane of the Mac Manager application is used to configure settings that apply to all Mac Manager users and workstations regardless of user type, workgroup, or computer lists. The global settings are organized into two tabs: Security and CD-ROMs.

Security settings

The Security tab for Global settings contains eight options, as shown in Figure 26-11 and described as follows:

Maximum number of log entries
> The first is how many entries are stored in the Mac Manager log, which I'll discuss shortly. The default number of log entries is 5,000.

Allow Guest access and Allow "All Other Users"
> The next two options are whether to allow Guest access and whether to enable the All Other Users account. By default both of these are enabled.

Quit the administration program
> This fourth option affects the Mac Manager application, regardless of what workstation it is run from or what user is running it. The option enables automatic disconnection from the Mac Manager server after an idle period, which can be specified in minutes (the default being 15 minutes). This is a powerful security feature, particularly if you designate teachers or department heads as Workgroup Administrators.

Users can change their passwords
> This fifth option allows users to change their passwords. This option affects the passwords stored in Open Directory. If enabled, the users must have Open Directory passwords (i.e., passwords stored using Kerberos or the Open

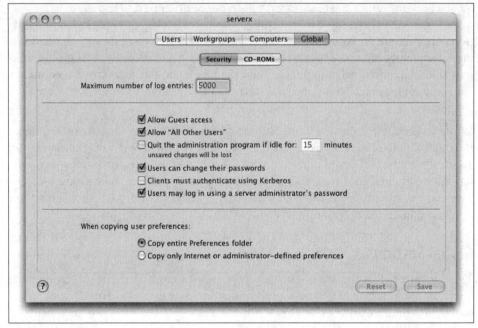

Figure 26-11. The Security settings tab of the Global pane.

Directory Password Server). Crypt passwords cannot be changed from within Mac Manager.

Clients must authenticate using Kerberos

This fifth option requires workstations to authenticate users using Kerberos. This option requires that the Mac Manager server be bound to a directory domain on which Kerberos is configured.

Users may log in using a server administrator's password

This sixth option allows users to login using an administrator password. Or, to use more accurate wording than the Mac Manager developers, it allows administrators to login as users by using a user's username and did administrator password. As I mentioned with the Mac OS X variation of this feature, using it carries both a security risk and a privacy issue.

When copying user preferences

The final option consists of two radio buttons labeled "Copy entire Preferences folder" and "Copy only Internet and administrator-defined preferences." The first option refers to the way in which older versions of Mac Manager worked with Mac OS 8 workstations to provide preference management. It's somewhat unclear why this option continues to exist, as the current Mac Manager server version requires the Mac Manager 2.2.2 client, which supports only Mac OS 9.1 and higher. The second radio button enables the current managed preferences model, which was described in this chapter and should be selected to ensure proper preferences management.

CD-ROM settings

As mentioned when discussing the Security tab on the Computers pane, you can limit which data CDs or DVDs that workstations are allowed to access by creating lists of approved CDs or DVDs, and you can further limit access to approved items on these approved CDs or DVDs. Designating approved CDs and DVDs and approved items on them is done globally in Mac Manager such that the same approved CDs and items lists exist for all computer lists. These approval lists are created and modified using the CD-ROMs tab on the Global pane.

As you can see in Figure 26-12, the CD-ROMs tab contains three listboxes. The first is Local CD-ROMs (data-only), which includes any CDs or DVDs currently inserted in the CD/DVD drive(s) of the workstation on which the Macintosh Manager application is being run. To add an inserted disk to the approved list, select it in the listbox and click the Add button. This adds the disk to the Available in Macintosh Manager listbox. You can then use the Eject button to eject the CD or DVD and insert another. Repeat the process for every CD or DVD you want to add to the approved list. To remove a CD or DVD from the list, select it in the Available in Macintosh Manager listbox and click the Remove button.

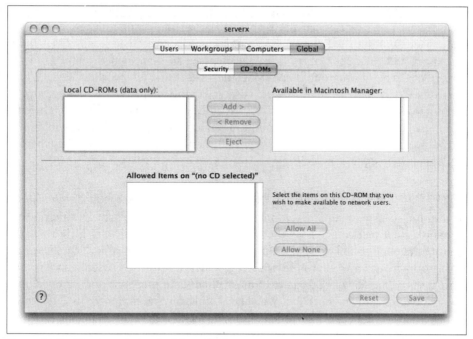

Figure 26-12. The CD-ROMs tab of the Global pane.

The third listbox, Allowed Items on (X), is below the first two. This option allows you to create lists of approved items on individual CDs or DVDs. To create an such approved items list, insert the CD or DVD (if it is not already inserted), select the disk's name in the Available in Macintosh Manager listbox (you'll notice that the disk's name is displayed in the name of this listbox), and then select the items you wish to approve. To select individual items in the list, or use the Allow All and Allow None buttons to select or deselect all items in the listbox. Click the Save button to store and activate your changes.

Enabling and Configuring Templates

You can configure templates in Mac Manager that function similar to the presets feature of Workgroup Manager. However, you can configure only a single template for each template type (user, workgroup, or computer list). After a template is configured, its settings are automatically applied to all users you import and to any new workgroups or computer lists you create. Essentially, templates just alter the default settings for new items. You can also duplicate existing workgroups and computer lists. This makes it easier to apply identical settings when importing new users or creating workgroups and computer lists.

Using templates

Templates are not enabled by default in the Mac Manager application. To enable them, select Preferences from the Mac Manager menu, if running the application under Mac OS X, or the Edit menu, if running in Mac OS 9, check Show Templates checkbox, and then click okay. You will then see an item named template in the Imported Users, Workgroups, and Machine Lists listboxes on the Users, Workgroups, and Computers panes, respectively. Select the template user, workgroup, or computer list and configure settings for it (you can include workgroup membership in the user template). Click the Save button. Import users or create new workgroups or computer lists as you normally would and the template settings will be enforced on the new items immediately.

Duplicating workgroups and computer lists

In addition to using templates, you can easily duplicate any existing workgroup or computer list by selecting it in the Workgroups or Machine Lists listbox on the appropriate pane and clicking the Duplicate button above the listbox. Duplicating a workgroup creates a workgroup with settings identical to the original and with the same users as members. You can then make changes to the name and other settings and remove or add members, as you like. Duplicating a computer list creates an empty computer list (as workstations cannot be members of more than one list) with the same settings as the original. After duplicating a computer list, you can add workstations or change settings, as you like. Duplicating a computer list can be helpful if you are setting up lists of individual portable computers that you wish to assign only a single user to be able to check out.

Mac Manager Reports and Logs

Mac Manager maintains logs and displays current activity information somewhat differently than other Mac OS X Server services, which display current service information in their Overview tabs in Server Admin and their current logs in their Logs tabs within Server Admin. In order to view current Mac Manager service information, you need to generate a report for the type of information you wish to view using the Reports menus. Mac Manager reports are displayed as additional windows in the Mac Manager application and can be printed or exported as text files.

The Mac Manager log is displayed as a report and, unlike other Mac OS X Server services, cannot be automatically archived, though you can export the log report and maintain copies of the exported text files. The Mac Manager log deletes old entries as it adds new entries once it becomes full. You use the Global pane's Security tab to specify how many items can be stored in the log. As a rule, you should set this value high enough that entries will be kept for a day or more, allowing you to view and archive the log by exporting it on a regular basis. You will need to run Mac Manager for a few days to determine an appropriate amount of entries to support in the log. Also note that, because the Mac Manager log is used to generate all Mac Manager reports, the maximum number of log entries becomes the maximum number of entries in any report. The exception to this rule is the connected user report, which only displays 300 entries (regardless of the number of users actually logged in).

Activity Log
> The Activity Log report is much like the log report for other Mac OS X Server services. Because it is a report rather than the raw log data, after selecting Activity Log from the reports menu, a dialog allows you to specify exactly which information is displayed (as opposed to specifying which information is logged, as with most other services). You can include applications being launched, activity that Apple considers security risks, user login, and printer usage. You can also specify whether to show entries for all users or select to view only entries regarding specific users or workgroups. Additionally, you can sort the entries in order of date or by user and specify how many days worth of information should be included in the report (the default being seven).

Connected Machines
> The Connected Machines report displays information about each computer currently connected to the Mac Manager server, including computers where users are logged and those where no one is logged in.

Disk Space Usage
> The Disk Space Usage report generates a report listing each user, the last time the user logged out of a managed Mac OS 9 workstation, the disk space used by files in the home directory, the Mac Manager storage quota, and how much space remains available to them.

Printer Quotas

The Printer Quotas report generates a list of users, their print quotas for printers available to them, the amount of pages they have printed since their quota was last reset, and how many pages they may print before reaching their quota.

Workgroups by User

The Workgroups by User report lists all users and lists each workgroup of which they are a member. It is sorted by username.

Computers

The Computers report includes information about computer lists and the workstations and workgroups assigned to individual lists.

Checked Out Computers

The Checked Out Computers report includes information about computers that are currently checked out, including the date that they were last checked out.

Exporting Reports and User Information

To export a report as a text file, generate the report and then select the Export command from the File menu. You can specify whether to export reports as tab- or comma-delimited text files in the Mac Manager applications preferences (under the Mac Manager menu in the Mac OS X or the Edit menu in Mac OS 9). You can also export all user information to a text file by selecting the Export User List command when you are not viewing any reports.

Using Multiple Mac Manager Servers

You can use multiple Mac Manager servers within a single network. In fact, this is a logical approach if your network spans multiple worksites and/or slow network links, because Mac Manager does not support replication in the way that Open Directory does. You should use multiple Mac Manager servers if you are using Open Directory replicas and if you have home directories spaced out on multiple server, because of network performance. Each Mac Manager server will maintain its own databases, though users can be imported into multiple servers from a single directory domain—for the sake of a consistent user environment and avoiding confusion, I advise against this unless necessary.

You can change which Mac Manager server a workstation accesses from the login window. As I described in the section on computer list security options, you can also require an administrator password to do this. Workstations can locate Mac Manager servers by AppleTalk or by IP address or DNS name.

Troubleshooting Mac Manager

The majority of Mac Manager problems are either misconfigurations of the Mac Manager environment or symptoms of other problems, such as network, user account, or permissions problems. For issues that appear to be configuration-based, review this chapter and the settings for workgroups, computer lists, and global options to be sure that everything is configured properly.

Issues such as an inability to connect to a Mac Manager server or other file servers generally indicate problems with the server in question, the workstation's network configuration, or the network itself. If the issue affects a single workstation, chances are that the issue is related to workstation's network configuration, Ethernet port, or network cable. If the issue affects more than one workstation, particularly in a given section of the network, but does not affect all workstations, it is likely a network-related problem. If the problem affects all or most workstations, it is likely a server issue. Occasionally, if many computers are started at one time and attempt to connect to a single server, the server may not be able to respond to all requests before the requests time out. In these cases, staggering workstation startup can resolve the problem.

Problems such as an inability for a single user to log in can reflect the user's account being disabled (in Mac Manager or the shared directory domain), an incorrect password, or that the user has been deleted from Mac Manager database. It may also indicate that a user is part of a workgroup that does not have access to workstations in a computer list. Check the user's Mac Manager status first and then proceed to check the user's Open Directory account for problems. If multiple users are logged in and there appears to be no explanation for why they can't log in, ensure that the server(s) and Mac Manager share point have disk space available to them.

If users have trouble accessing shared resources, first ensure that their Mac Manager privileges provide access to the resources. Then check to be sure they have permissions to access the shared resources outside of Mac Manager. If users are members of multiple workgroups, some workgroups may allow them privileges to resources that others don't (hence my recommendations to assign users to a single workgroup whenever possible). One other known issue is that Mac Manger cannot access workgroup shared folders stored on a share point hosted by Mac OS X Server 10.2.

Problems with applications running under Mac Manager are usually signs that the application either needs the ability to launch helper applications or needs to write files to specific locations on the local hard drive. It may also be a sign that the application requires preferences to be stored in the System Folder or some nonstandard location. Allowing the application to launch other applications, disabling file-level security, and using the MMLocalPrefs extension can generally resolve these problems.

One last known issue with Mac Manager is that the ability to drag and drop items from one application to another is disabled. There is no real workaround other than using the copy and paste commands within applications instead of drag and drop.

CHAPTER 27

Managing Windows Clients Using Mac OS X Server

The past few chapters have all dealt with Mac OS X Server and varying types of Mac client computers. However, the vast majority of networks today, even if Mac-based, have at least some Windows workstations, and many have both Mac and Windows servers. This chapter discusses how to manage Windows computers from Mac OS X Server.

Despite the significant level of support for Windows clients that Apple has built into Mac OS X Server, it is not as powerful as that which is built into Windows servers, and vice versa. If you are planning a new network or an upgrade, you should bear this fact in mind. It often leads to the dominant server platform in a network being the same as the platform used by the majority of workstations. Of course, as we'll discuss in both this chapter, it is possible to integrate both Mac and Windows servers in a network.

Hosting a Windows Domain

Windows services under Mac OS Server include the ability to share files and printers using the SMB protocol (the default file and print protocol for Windows), Windows name resolution services, and the ability to function as a Windows Primary Domain Controller (PDC), and host a Windows domain. When all of these services are implemented under Mac OS X Server, it is possible to manage a network of Windows computers almost as though you were using one or more Windows servers.

When acting as a PDC, a Mac OS X Server supports Windows domain login using accounts created in a shared directory domain. Windows client computers and servers (be they actual Windows servers or additional Mac OS X Servers) can be joined to the domain as workstations or member servers. When a Windows workstation is joined to the shared domain, it supports user login based on Open Directory, mapping of the same home directory for users as when they login on a Mac workstation, support for roaming and mandatory profiles, and support for Windows login scripts. When a server is joined to the domain as a member server, it processes SMB file and print requests using the login information generated by the PDC, as a member server in a traditional Windows domain would do.

Implementing a Mac OS X Server as a Windows PDC does not implement Microsoft's Active Directory, however. It simply ports all Windows domain directory access to Open Directory. This makes it possible for the same directory information to be used to authenticate user access regardless of whether a user logs in on a Mac or Windows workstation.

Domain Requirements and Limitations

As you might expect, there are some special considerations in terms of the capabilities offered by a Windows domain hosted using Mac OS X Server as compared to using a Windows server as a domain controller. If you're an experienced Windows administrator, you may notice some of these as limitations or as differences from the options typically available with a Windows domain. As far as requirements for being able to host a domain, any Mac OS X Server that is an LDAP master can be configured as a Windows PDC. LDAP replicas cannot host a domain, nor can they act as replicas of the PDC. Considerations include:

One domain controller per network

Mac OS X Server does not support multiple domain controllers. This is significantly different from a Windows 2000 domain, which can maintain domain information concurrently across multiple domain controllers through a network, or a Windows NT domain, which can have a primary domain controller and multiple backup domain controllers available in case the primary domain controller cannot be accessed. Furthermore, Mac OS X Server does not support domain forests or trusts; Mac OS X Server supports only a single domain per network.

This presents the biggest limitation to using Mac OS X Server to host a Windows domain. All Windows workstations must communicate with the PDC, which is also the LDAP master. You cannot reduce this communication by the use of LDAP replicas, multiple domain controllers, or even multiple domains. This restriction is particularly difficult for networks that span slow network links, although for networks that are made up of multiple LDAP masters, each with an independent directory domain, each LDAP master can host a Windows domain independent of the others (though these must be completely independent Windows domains without trust relationships). This restriction can also be hard on networks that have a large numbers of users and workstations accessing the LDAP master already. In these situations, using LDAP replicas can reduce the burden on the LDAP master/domain controller.

This is perhaps the biggest reason that a Mac OS X Server–based Windows domain is best implemented in a network that has a large number of Macs compared to a smaller number of Windows workstations. However, in many cross-platform networks, using Mac OS X Server to host a Windows domain remains a valid and workable solution.

Mac OS X permission structure

Less a limitation and more something to be aware of is the fact that Windows domains (indeed, Windows file services in general) hosted by Mac OS X Server do not support the array of permission offerings of traditional Windows domains. Permissions are assigned as they are within Mac OS X: a single file owner, a single group, and an *everyone* group entry for all share points, folders, and files. This design contrasts noticeably to the Windows server ability to apply permissions for multiple groups and using a wide variety of special permissions for shared items. However, Mac OS X's permission structure does take much of the guessing out of how permissions interact with each other.

Inability to restrict access to Windows workstations

When workstations are joined to a Mac OS X Server–hosted domain, they are available to all users. You cannot create lists of Windows workstations and limit access based on user groups as you can with Mac OS X or Mac OS 9 workstations.

No built-in automount options except home directories

Windows does not use automounts in the same way that Mac OS X and Unix computers do. There is no built-in way to automount share points for Windows workstations, other than the user's home directory (which is mapped as a network drive). However, as we'll discuss later in this chapter, you can set up mapping of additional share points as network drives using Windows login scripts and user profiles.

Mac OS X Server password and access policies

Windows domains offer a plethora of user access and password policies. As you might expect, when hosting a Windows domain from Mac OS X Server, password policies are those defined for Open Directory users. These are somewhat more limited than those offered by Windows servers. Also, as noted earlier, you can't apply specific access policies to Windows workstations.

No Active Directory browsing

As noted earlier, Mac OS X Server supports hosting a Windows domain but does not support hosting Active Directory. This means that Windows options for browsing Active Directory for user information, servers and share points, or printers won't work.

Configuring Mac OS X Server as a Windows Domain Controller

Compared to configuring and managing a Windows domain on a Windows server, configuring Mac OS X Server to host a Windows domain is actually very simple.

Configuration can be done either through the Setup Assistant, where the Windows computer (NetBIOS) name for the server and the name of the domain are entered along with other Open Directory information, or using the Server Admin application. Server Admin also allows some additional configuration options.

To configure Windows domain and other services using Server Admin, launch the Server Admin application and select Windows for the appropriate server in the Computers and Service list. You'll notice that the right pane for the Windows service looks very much like the pane for the AFP service. The Overview tab displays the same information about the number of connections, the number of Guest connections, and the status of the service. Also, the five tabs available for the Windows service (Overview, Logs, Connections, Graphs, and Settings) are the same as those in the AFP service tab.

Select the Settings tab to configure a Windows domain or other services. The Settings tab contains four subtabs (General, Access, Logging, and Advanced). The General tab, shown in Figure 27-1, defines the server's role, Windows name, and related information. The Role pop-up menu allows you to define the server as a Windows PDC, a member server within a Windows domain, or a standalone server. You'll probably notice that these roles parallel the roles for Open Directory (master, joined to a directory domain, and standalone servers).

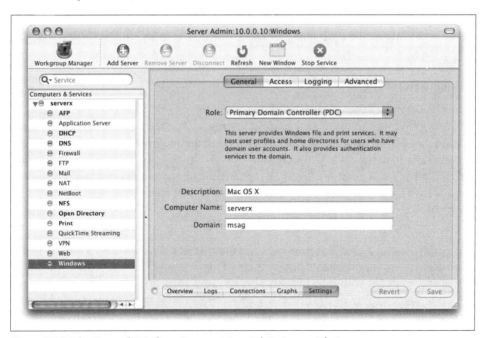

Figure 27-1. The General Windows Server settings tab in Server Admin.

To configure a server as a Windows domain controller, select "Primary Domain Controller (PDC)" from the Role menu. In the computer name field, enter the name that you wish to be used to connect to the server (either using a Windows command line or by browsing the network). This is the server's NetBIOS name. Generally speaking, it's a good policy to use the same name for a server's NetBIOS name as you use for AppleTalk and Rendezvous name, which is also typically used as part of the server's DNS name. Enter the name of the Windows domain that the server will host in the Domain field. You can also enter a description for the server in the Description field. A description is optional, though it may be helpful for Windows users to identify what a server is used for, as the description is displayed when the server is selected while users are browsing a network using the Network Neighborhood (Windows 95/98) or My Network Places (Windows 2000/XP).

With the options on the General settings tab configured, you can click the Save button, start the Windows service (using the Start Service button in the toolbar at the top of the Server Admin window, which will change to "stop service" while the windows service is running, as shown in Figure 27-1), and the new Windows domain is up and running. Of course, there are some additional options to consider, including joining Windows computers to the domain, configuring user and home directory access from Windows workstations, and potentially importing users and settings from pre-existing Windows domains. But for the most part, Apple's default settings make it possible to configure a domain with just this one step. However, before we leave Server Admin for a while, let's take a look at the other three Windows service settings tabs.

Limiting access to a domain

The Access tab lets you allow or disallow guest logins from Windows workstations. When configuring a server that is functioning as a PDC, disabling guest access restricts users from logging into workstations that are members of a domain as Guest and also disables the ability to connect to SMB share points located on the server that is the PDC as a guest user. As I've repeated throughout this book, guest access is a big security hole because it provides no mean of authentication or tracking who guest users are or what each guest user is doing. As always,use guest access only if absolutely required and then restrict guest users as much as possible.

The Access tab also allows you to limit the number of users who can log in to workstations or share points within the domain. This feature can help reduce unneeded server and network resources. It can also be used to secure the network or server against a large number of unauthorized connections. However, as mentioned in earlier chapters, if you limit the number of connections to a domain, do so based on the typical volume of connected users or number of workstations at a site to avoid restricting access to legitimate users.

Configuring Windows service logging

The Logging settings tab lets you choose how much information is stored in the Windows service log. The options are select from the Log Detail pop-up menu and include Low, Medium, and High. When Low is selected, only service errors and warning events are logged. No information about user login or file access is logged. When Medium is selected, service start and stop times, login failures, and computer name registrations (if appropriate) are logged, in addition to service errors and warning. When High is selected, all file access is logged (in addition to the items logged with lower logging details). As I've also stated more than once, detailed server logs can be important for problem solving, security, and auditing purposes. Windows service logs are stored in *Library/Logs* on the server's startup drive and recent logs can be viewed using the Windows Service Logs pane in Server Admin.

Configuring Windows Computer Access to a Domain

As with traditional Windows domains, workstations must have a computer account within the domain and be joined to the domain. Joining a Windows workstation to a domain is akin to binding a Mac OS X computer to a shared directory domain, although Windows domains do not support the use of guest computers. Each computer joined to the domain must have an account for it created within the domain. In a Windows domain hosted by Mac OS X Server, these computer accounts are created as workstations that are members of the Windows Computers list in Workgroup Manager.

You join Windows computers to a domain hosted by Mac OS X Server exactly as you join them to a Windows domain hosted by a Windows server. When you join a computer to a domain, you will be asked to provide the name and password of a domain user with authority to join the computer to the domain. For domains hosted by Mac OS X Server, this means a user who is a directory domain administrator for the shared directory domain hosted by the same server functioning as the Windows PDC.

Configuring User Access to a Domain

Once an LDAP master has been configured as a Windows PDC, any users in the directory domain whose password type is Open Directory can log in at any Windows workstation that has been joined to the domain (users with crypt passwords cannot log in from Windows). Password policies configured for the domain (either globally in Server Admin or by user in Workgroup Manager) remain in effect for users.

As with traditional Windows domains, you can assign domain users to be members of local computer groups (for example, you can make a domain user into a local administrator for a specific workstation). You cannot limit which Windows

Using the Windows Computers List in Workgroup Manager

The Windows Computers list contains the NetBIOS name of each Windows computer that has been joined to the Windows domain hosted by Mac OS X Server, along with an optional description. Windows computers are automatically added to this list when they are joined to the domain. You cannot manage access to the Windows Computers list as you can other computer lists in Workgroup Manager, and Windows workstations cannot be made part of other computer lists.

Essentially, the Windows Computers list exists for compatibility with the Windows domain architecture. However, you can delete computers from this list. When you delete a computer from the Windows Computer list, the workstation is removed from the domain. This trick can be useful for dealing with workstations that you believe pose a security threat. It can also be useful if workstations are retired and are no longer part of the network.

You can also add computers to the Windows Computers list without joining the computer to the domain. Because only directory domain administrators have the authority to join a computer to the domain, creating the computer account before joining the computer to the domain allows users who are not administrators to join workstations to the domain. You interact with the Windows Computer list as you would any other computer list. The exception being that when you add a computer, you enter the computer's NetBIOS name rather than the MAC Address or browsing for it over the network.

workstations users are allowed to log in at because all Windows computers joined to the domain are automatically made part of the Windows Computers list in Workgroup Manager and you cannot assign access to this list by groups as you can Mac OS X computer lists.

While user login from Windows is automatically supported across the board, you can specify some variables about how users interact with both the Windows workstations they log in at and how they interact with file and print services across the network. The major ways that you can control the Windows user environment are through how the Windows service works with home directories, the use of user profiles, and by using Windows login scripts.

Home Directory Access from Windows Workstations

In and of themselves, home directories function somewhat differently for users logged in from Windows than for users logged in from either Mac OS X or Mac OS 9. In fact, you can assign a user a separate home directory to use when logged in from Windows or you can let users have access to the same home directory regardless of platform. Whether it's the same home directory used with Mac workstations or a separate one, Windows maps the home directory as a network drive.

Items stored in the home directory, such as preferences, desktop pictures, screensavers, and Internet bookmarks, are not used by Windows in configuring the Windows user environment (as they are by Mac OS X or Mac OS 9). The home directory simply serves as a network storage space for the user. The users home directory is also the only network folder or share point that is automatically mapped or mounted as a network drive for users by the configuration options built into Mac OS X Server.

To store user preferences and environment settings, Windows creates a profile for the user, which stores information used for defining the user environment. Like the user's home directory, this profile is also stored on a network server and is used to configure the Windows user environment for users regardless on each Windows computer that the users log into within the domain.

Shared Mac/Windows home directories

The Advanced settings tab for the Windows service in Server Admin includes a checkbox labeled Homes: Enable Virtual Share Points. When this is selected, Mac OS X Server creates a virtual SMB home directory share point for home directories when users log in from Windows. Essentially, it maps the AFP or NFS home directory share point used for Mac OS X and Mac OS 9 clients as a temporary SMB share point when a user logs in from Windows. This feature enables users to access their home directories from Mac or Windows computers without requiring an administrator to make the share point available using SMB. It also limits Windows users to seeing only their home directory, though if the home directory share point is also shared using SMB, users will be able connect to it manually and, depending on the permissions assigned, be able to see into other home directories. This option is selected by default and is an optimal choice for allowing users easy cross-platform access to their personal files.

By default, Mac OS X Server maps a user's home directory as drive letter H on a Windows workstation. I'll assume Apple chose H because it's the first letter of the word *home*. If needed, you can change the drive mapping to any letter you like. You might wish to do this because of mappings with internal drives on workstations already using the letter H or to conform with other network drive-mapping choices. If you do use custom network drive mappings, my suggestion is to use a single letter consistently across the network to avoid confusion. This way, users will always know that the M drive (or whatever letter you choose) on a Windows computer is their home directory.

To specify a custom drive mapping, select the user in the Accounts list of Workgroup Manager and click the Windows tab in the account information pane, as shown in Figure 27-2. In the section labeled Windows Home Directory, select the appropriate letter from the Hard Drive pop-up menu. Leave the Path field below the pop-up menu blank unless you wish to configure custom Windows home directories.

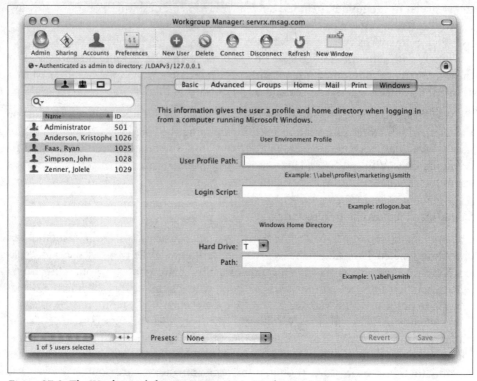

Figure 27-2. The Windows tab for a user account in Workgroup Manager.

Separate home directories

It is also possible to set up custom home directories for Windows users. A custom home directory is stored on an actual SMB share point and cannot be accessed as a home directory from Mac OS X or Mac OS 9. Custom Windows home directories can be used if you have users who log in only from Windows computers or if you want users to keep Windows and Mac files separate. However, generally speaking, using separate home directories can confuse users about where their files are stored and reduce the effectiveness of working in a cross-platform network.

Another consideration is that using custom Windows home directories can be taxing on administrators because each custom directory must be created by hand (they are not created automatically at login or by using the *createhomedir* command). First, create the share point and make it available using SMB. Assign appropriate permissions to the share point. Next create the actual home directories within the share point, using the first short name assigned to each user as the name for the individual folders. Finally, launch Workgroup Manager, select each user individually, click the Windows tab, and specify the UNC path to the home directory in the path field, including the user's name (for example, *server**sharepoint**username*).

The Windows My Documents and Desktop folders

Windows provides users with a My Documents folder as a default storage location (much like the Mac OS Documents folder). My Documents also includes a My Pictures folder and a My Music folder (much like the Pictures and Music folders included in Mac OS X home directories). Many Windows applications will use these folders as the default location for searching for or saving files. A Windows domain hosting by Mac OS X Server supports these folders along with the Desktop folder for Windows. However, these are not part of a user's home directory. By default, Windows domains do not require users to have home directories but still always provide access to these folders. Windows does this by storing these items as part of a user's profile.

This is an important distinction for users. If they store items in these locations, they will have access to them regardless of which Windows workstation they log in at, but they will not have access to them when they log in from a Mac OS X or Mac OS 9 workstation. There is also another downside to these folders. Where Mac OS X and Mac OS 9 access a user's items in the home directory only as needed (either by the operating system, an application, or because of user interaction), Windows workstations download the entire My Documents and Desktop folders as part of the profile at login and then copy the updated versions as part of the profile back to the server hosting Windows profiles at logout. Needless to say, this method is taxing for server and network resources and can significantly increase the time it takes for a user to log in and log out, which is one reason Windows-hosted domains allow you to specify that profiles be stored on workstations such as a Mac OS X mobile account rather than on a server. Unfortunately, there is no easy workaround to prevent users from storing items in the Windows My Documents folder or on the Desktop in Windows. The only real option is educating users to save items to their actual home directories (or the local hard drive, if they use only a single workstation).

Setting Up User Profiles for Windows Users

Windows NT, 2000, and XP all support the use of network-based user profiles. As I mentioned, a user profile stores settings and preferences for the Windows user environment. The user's profile consists of the files contained in the Desktop and My Documents folders and a file called *ntuser.dat*. The *ntuser.dat* file stores items that are implemented as part of the Windows registry (i.e., the settings affecting the user environment).

In a Windows domain that is hosted on a Windows server, user profiles can be local profiles, default profiles, roaming profiles, or mandatory profiles. Local profiles reside on the hard drives of individual workstations that a user logs into, and settings and files are not carried over from one workstation to the next, much like a Mac OS X mobile account. Default profiles are stored on a Windows server and specify the initial user configuration. Roaming profiles function much like a Mac OS

X home directory and are copied from a server to a workstation when a user logs in and then copied back to the server at logout, ensuring that users have the same settings and files available regardless of which workstation they log into. Mandatory profiles are configured by an administrator and automatically assign specific settings to users. If a user changes settings within a mandatory profile, those settings are lost when the user logs out, much like Mac Manager's Forced Preferences feature.

In a Windows domain hosted by a Windows server, an administrator can choose between local and roaming profiles for a user's account and can specify a default profile for users. Mac OS X Server, however, automatically creates and uses roaming profiles for users who log in using Windows workstations. Users are assigned the generic default profile for the version of Windows that was running during their intial login (profiles are created at a user's first login from Windows).

By default, Mac OS X Server creates and stores Windows profiles in the */Users/Profiles* directory of the server that is hosting the domain. You can, however, specify any SMB share point within a network to host user profiles (provided the share point resides on a server that is a member of the domain). If you disable the */Users* share point that is automatically created by Mac OS X Server, you will need to specify a custom profile share point (or re-enable the */Users* share point). Using custom profile locations allows you to specify locations that are on servers or volumes that are faster, dedicated to file sharing, and have additional fault tolerance and/or performance methods rather than the startup drive of the server hosting the domain and LDAP master. However, if you use a custom profile share point, you need to specify the path to each profile separately for each user.

To specify a custom profile location, launch Workgroup Manager and select a user in the Accounts list. On the Windows tab, enter the path to the folder that will contain the user's profile (*//server/sharepoint/username*). The folder containing the profile must be named with the first short name created for the user and, like a custom Windows home directory, it must be created by hand before the user's first login.

Mandatory and default profiles

Mac OS X Server does not explicitly support mandatory or default profiles. However, that does not mean that using them is impossible. While you can't specify a default profile, you can create one by making a generic user account, logging in using that account from a Windows workstation, making the configuration changes you wish, and logging out. In effect, this procedure creates a user profile that can be used as a default profile. You can manually create a new user's profile folder (or log in once as the user to automatically create it) and then copy your generic user's profile into that folder. This must be done as *root*, and after copying the profile, you should verify that permissions on the entire folder containing the profile are set as follows: the user should be set as owner of the profile folder and its contents with read/write access, the group should be set to *staff*, and both the group and *everyone* group should be set to have no access. While this is an option for creating a pseudo-default profile, it is labor intensive and can be quite time consuming when creating a large number of users. Also, the benefits of using this approach may not be worth the time spent implementing it.

Mandatory profiles can be implemented in the same way. The difference between a mandatory and roaming profile in a Windows domain is that *ntuser.dat* file (which contains the user environment settings) is renamed as *ntuser.man*. Again, you can use the same approach to creating a default profile, but this time add the step of changing the file extension. Again, this can be time consuming. However, when working with mandatory profiles, you generally have a reason for wanting the user to be forced to use specific settings, which can often be worth the additional effort.

Using Login Scripts

Login scripts are scripts that are created by a Windows administrator and automatically run when a user logs in using a Windows workstation. They are typically *.bat* files that are used to map network drives for specific share points, to invoke certain applications or executable files, or to configure certain settings. Login scripts can be used with any version of Windows, but are most commonly used with Windows 9x versions because of their limitations as network operating systems.

Although explanation of writing *.bat* files for login scripts is well beyond the scope of this book, there are two reasons I mention them. The first is that a login script will allow you to map network drives for SMB share points other than a user's home directory. This step can provide easy user access to shared resources for individual users, groups of users (though you must specify login scripts by user and not by groups), or all users. The ability to map drives automatically is built into Windows NT/2000/XP, but is not built into Mac OS X Server's Windows service; hence the need to do this using a login script (or as part of a default or mandatory profile).

The second reason I mention login scripts is to explain how to use them. Login scripts must be stored in the */etc/login* directory of the server hosting the domain (you need to login as *root* or use the *su* command from the Terminal to access this directory). You can store as many login scripts in this directory as you like. To assign a login script to a user, launch Workgroup Manager, select the user in the Accounts list, and then select the Windows tab. Enter the path to the login script relative to the */etc/login* directory in the Login Script field. For example if you place all login scripts directly in this directory and wish a user to use one named *admin.bat*, you would type *admin.bat*. If you placed that same script in a folder inside */etc/login* named *corporate*, you would enter *corporate/admin.bat* as the path. You can edit the login script settings for multiple users at one time in Workgroup Manager.

Migrating Users from an Existing Windows Domain

If you are implementing Mac OS X Server as a domain controller to replace an existing Windows domain, you may wish to migrate existing user accounts in the Windows domain. You can do this by using the Windows server management tools (such as Active Directory Users and Groups) to export user accounts as a comma- or tab-delimited text file. You can then import this information into Workgroup Manager. You can then copy user profiles and login scripts to the appropriate locations after configuring Windows settings for these users.

Additionally, you can move items manually from existing home directories for the users to the new home directories. This can be done either while logged in as the user or while logged in as *root*. If you do this while logged as *root*, make certain the ultimate permissions on these items is correct in the new home directories.

Configuring Member and Standalone Servers

While the Windows service in Mac OS X Server supports only a single domain controller and domain on a given network, it does support the use of multiple servers providing other Windows services. Likewise, it is possible to provide Windows services from Mac OS X Server without hosting a domain. There are two options for configuring Mac OS X Server to provide Window services without hosting a domain: configuring them as member servers of a domain or as standalone servers.

Working with Member Servers in a Domain

Member servers are Windows servers that are members of a domain but are not domain controllers. As mentioned earlier in this chapter, member servers are much like supporting servers within a Mac OS X shared directory. They are joined to the Windows domain and rely on it for user information and authentication. Member servers are typically used as file and print servers because they can provide those services and free up resources the domain controller (which, under Mac OS X Server, is also an LDAP master). Member servers can be used to host share points for custom home directories and custom user profile locations. They can also be used to provide Windows name resolution services.

If you already use multiple supporting servers for a Mac OS X shared directory, then chances are good that you will want to do the same thing for a Windows domain, particularly if you plan to make the same share points and/or print queues available to Windows using SMB. You can more or less mirror your Mac OS X directory domain with a Windows domain as far as supporting or member servers are concerned. You may also want to create dedicated SMB servers as part of a Windows domain, to handle share points or print queues that will only be used by Windows workstations.

To configure a Mac OS X Server as a member server, launch Server Admin and select Windows for the intended member server in the Computers & Services list. Select the Settings tab at the bottom of the right pane. On the General settings tab select Domain Member from the Role pop-up menu. Enter the name of domain of which this server will be a member in the Domain field, the NetBIOS name for the server in the Computer Name field (again, it's a good idea to use a name matching the server's AppleTalk and Rendezvous and DNS names), and optionally enter a description for the server. When you click the Save button, you will be asked to authenticate as a user with administrative access for the shared directory domain hosted by the Mac OS X Server that is functioning as the Windows PDC of the domain you are joining this server to, thus creating an entry for it in the Windows Computers list.

Integrating Windows Member Servers in a Mac OS X Server–Hosted Domain

It is possible to join actual Windows servers to a Windows domain that is hosted by a Mac OS X Server. The Windows member servers can then provide file or print or other Windows services within the domain, while relying on the user accounts in Open Directory for authentication. This scenario raises the immediate question: why not just host the domain using Windows servers, particularly in light of the domain limitations posed by Mac OS X Server? The second question it raises is: what situations exist where using a Windows server within a domain hosted by Mac OS X Server is better than providing service using Mac OS X Server?

The Rationale Behind a Mixed-Server-Platform Domain

Tackling the first question, Mac OS X Server does a better job at providing services for Windows computers than Windows servers do for providing Services for Macs. While Windows servers can provide native file and print services for Macs and you can authenticate Mac OS X workstation access against Active Directory within a Windows domain, the level of configuration and management available from Mac OS X Server is simply not available from a Windows server (as we'll discuss in the next chapter). Also, configuring authentication of Mac OS X against Active Directory is more labor-intensive for administrators than configuring Windows services under Mac OS X Server. What this boils down to is that in a cross-platform network, especially a Mac-dominant network, it is possible to provide a better cross-platform user experience by implementing Mac OS X Server as the primary server platform and using Open Directory as the method for maintaining all user accounts. To do this requires that Windows workstations authenticate using a domain hosted by Mac OS X Server. However, there are times when a Windows server may be better suited to providing individual services within that domain.

When Windows Servers Are Warranted

In typical situations where you want to provide access to the same share points and printers from both Mac and Windows clients, the best solution is to provide file and print services from a Mac OS X Server. Often, if you have a Mac OS X Server infrastructure in place and want to provide resources specifically to Windows workstations, you will continue to use Mac OS X Server for them because you need only create an additional share point or print queue. But there are a handful of situations where the better option, either from an administrative and technical perspective or, more often, from a cost perspective may be to integrate Windows servers.

Easy access to existing data and cost benefits in migration planning

If you are migrating from a Windows infrastructure to a Mac OS X Server infrastructure, you might find it easier to maintain share points and share files using existing member servers. This situation is likely in a network that has been Windows-dominated but where a large number of Macs have been added and the decision has been made to migrate to Mac OS X Server as the primary server platform, or one in which Mac and Windows server infrastructures have existed but have previously been kept independent of each other.

In these cases, you can maintain the original member servers, join them to the new domain hosted by Mac OS X Server, and then change ownership and permissions for the existing share points and files to match the user and group accounts in the new domain. This method still involves some work, but it allows users to locate the same servers and share points and saves you the time spent moving the data to Mac OS X Servers.

In this situation, you are also likely to be looking at the costs involved in migrating from a Windows server base to a Mac OS X Server base. If your company or school already has an investment in the Windows servers, it can be difficult to justify the expense of replacing all those servers with Mac OS X Servers. Being able to maintain some of the servers for Windows share points while adding a limited numbers of Mac OS X Servers for additional share points and directory services can help balance the cost/benefit ratio.

You can also use such a mixed infrastructure as a stepping-stone in the middle of a longer-term migration strategy. At a later point, you can move data from the initial share points on the Windows servers to new share points on Mac OS X Servers, which you would do in a complete initial migration to Mac OS X Servers from Windows servers. Using an intermediate step can provide time for budgetary limitations with respect to replacing all servers initially.

Print servers

As noted earlier, there are a number of known issues with the print service in Mac OS X Server. Using a Windows print server can sidestep these issues. Windows print servers also offer the ability to create print queues for printers that are not PostScript printers (such as those using HP's PCL language), which you may wish to use on your network. If Services for Mac is implemented on the print server, it can be used to host print queues for both Mac and Windows workstations, as we'll discuss in the next chapter.

Master browsers

As discussed early in this chapter, Windows servers automatically configure themselves as workgroup master browsers as needed in a routed network. If you are not implementing WINS services on your network, Windows servers already serving as member servers can function as master browsers for you. I don't suggest implementing Windows servers solely for this purpose. Ideally, you should implement a WINS server. If you choose not to, however, member servers functioning for other purposes can function as master browsers as well. Of course, a member server can also be used as a WINS server.

Microsoft terminal services

Terminal services allow users to connect to a terminal server. Once connected, users see a typical Windows desktop and can run applications as though that desktop were the desktop of their local workstation. However, the applications and the user session are actually occurring on the server itself. The mouse and keyboard interactions are being sent to the server by the workstation and all screen and sound activity is being sent back to the workstation from the server.

Terminal services can be implemented as an administrative tool, allowing administrators to manage a server remotely or as a tool for user access. When used for user access, it allows users to access a set of applications not available to their workstation and, for older workstations, to effectively run those applications faster than the workstation could. It also allows network use of applications that are not network-capable. Terminal servers can be accessed from every Windows version and also from Mac OS X using the terminal services client from Microsoft.

Terminal servers do not need to be part of a domain, but making them part of a domain allows users to access them using their username and password and to use their roaming profile and have access to their home directory while connected to the terminal server. Thus, if you are implementing a terminal server on a network with a Mac OS X Server domain controller, you might wish to consider joining the terminal server to the domain. As a side note, terminal servers can provide users access to Windows-only applications from a Mac OS X workstation, which can be an advantage because it enables you to provide users with a single Mac workstation and still be able to provide them with access to the Windows environment and applications.

Application servers

Windows servers can host network applications, such as financial and administrative tools or corporate databases. While Mac OS X Server also includes an application server, converting existing network applications from one platform to another or replacing them often introduces significant time and expense considerations. Also, there are a number of network applications that are available only under Windows. Thus, if there are existing application servers in your network, you will likely want to maintain them or indefinitely or during a migration process to an alternate tool. Similarly, you may find that the best or only network applications for a specific task are Windows based. In these cases, implementing a Windows member server as an application server can be a solution.

## CHAPTER 28

Workstation Deployment and Maintenance

Much of a system administrator's job revolves around managing network resources. The day-to-day issues of troubleshooting workstations, resolving application problems, and helping users with technical problems typically falls to the members of a technical support staff. That does not mean, however, that administrators are exempt from having to deal with workstations within a network. The responsibilities of ensuring that workstations communicate with directory and supporting servers, that users have the appropriate permissions to local items and proper managed preferences settings, that each workstation is configured properly as a part of the network, and that each workstation is secure and its software as up-to-date as needed all fall on an administrator's shoulders, either directly or through an IT staff's chain of command. Nowhere is the responsibility of the system administrator for workstations seen more clearly than in deploying new workstations or deploying new applications or software updates.

There are any number of ways to deploy and configure workstations within a network. The easiest way is to simply install Mac OS onto each workstation from the original install CDs, then install application software, and then configure each aspect of the workstation as needed. While this may be the easiest way, it is also the least efficient. A second method is to install the Mac OS and software and then use managed preferences or Mac Manager and user home directories to configure the user environment. This approach has some advantages but is still far too time consuming to be practical for more than a handful of workstations.

Beyond these two are a number of viable solutions, including Apple's NetBoot, Net-Install, and Apple Software Restore. Each of these allows you to deploy custom installations to workstations, including any specific configurations and applications that you wish to make available to users. Beyond these initial deployment options, there are also a number of methods that allow you to deploy new applications and software updates to workstations throughout your network.

Disk Images

Disk images are special files that, when opened, mount a virtual disk on a Macintosh computer. This virtual disk behaves in the same way as any other disk (hard drive, CD, Zip, etc.). You can open files and run applications stored on the disk, save items to it (provided the disk image is not read-only, as many are), copy items from it, and unmount it by dragging its icon to the trash. Disk images that are small enough can be burned as a CD, turning the virtual disk into an actual disk. With the right software, hard drives and other read-write disks can be imaged: that is, have their contents replaced with the contents of a disk image, again turning the virtual disk contained in the image into a physical disk.

Often disk images are used as a method for distributing software. An install disk can be packaged as a disk image, which can be made available over the Internet. Users can download the image, open it, and have complete access to the original install disk's contents. And the contents are treated exactly as the original disk, with all pathnames in place, something that does not happen if items are copied from a disk to a folder.

In Classic Mac OS versions and in Mac OS X 10.2 and earlier, the most common tool used to work with disk images is Apple's Disk Copy. Disk Copy is used to open disk images and mount them. It can also be used to create them. Disk Copy can create empty images to which you copy files, create images based on folders and files, or create disk image copies of existing disks. In Mac OS X 10.3, Apple bundled Disk Copy's abilities into the Disk Utility application and the operating system itself. Disk Utility has the ability to create images and the Finder now has the ability to mount disk images without relying on Disk Copy. In addition to Apple's tools, other applications also contain the ability to work with disk images, including CD authoring tools like Roxio's Toast.

Because disk images can be made of existing disks and can later be used to replace the contents of an existing disk, such as a hard drive, they are a powerful tool for deploying Mac OS installations. They enable you to configure a workstation, complete with all needed software installed and all Mac OS settings (such as access to a directory domain or Mac Manager server, network and printer configurations, permissions to local files and folders, and so forth), and create an image of that workstation's startup disk. This image can then be applied to some or all of the workstations in your network, making each one an exact copy of the original workstation from which the image was created. Most of this chapter discusses the ways that disk images can be applied to workstations.

Types of Disk Images

Disk images can be broken down into two major types: Mac OS X and Classic (pre–OS X) Mac OS versions. While Mac OS X can work with both types of images,

---

classic Mac OS versions and many of their related tools cannot create or access Mac OS X images. Mac OS X–style images are defined by a *.dmg* file extension, while Classic Mac OS images are defined by an *.img* extension.

Beyond this, you can divide images based on whether they are read only or read-write. Read-only images, once created, cannot be modified. Read-write images can be modified after creation. Read-only images, when created from an existing disk, are sized identical to the contents of the original disk. Read-write images, when created from an existing disk, are sized to match the capacity of the original disk, regardless of the size of the actual contents. It is possible to expand the size of a read-write disk image (though not to reduce it, once it has been expanded), and it is possible to convert disk images between read-only and read-write after they have been created.

You can also create compressed disk images. Compressed images apply a compression scheme to files as the disk image is created. This feature causes the image creation process to take longer, but results in an image file that is smaller than the actual disk size. It conserves space and also makes transferring the images faster. It also increases the speed at which the images can be applied to hard drives. Only read-only images can be compressed. It is possible to convert disk images between compressed and other types using Disk Utility or Disk Copy (depending on which Mac OS version you are working with).

NetBoot

NetBoot is a technology introduced with Mac OS X Server. It allows computers to use a disk image stored on a server as a startup disk rather than using a local hard drive or other volume. NetBoot presents an interesting option for administrators. Rather than installing and configuring the operating system and other software on individual workstations, you can create a single image and NetBoot the workstations. NetBoot ensures that a workstation always has the appropriate configurations because users, system, or application processes; even hardware failures or corruption cannot affect the NetBoot image as they can a typical startup disk. Any changes made to the workstation during a NetBoot session are removed when the workstation is rebooted because it reverts to the configuration of the original image.

NetBoot can work in concert with network home directories for users and with other directory domain abilities to configure a custom user environment. In fact, you'll need to make use of directory domains and network home directories for users when using NetBoot because otherwise users may not have a place to save their files and work, and they will not be able to save their application preferences.

NetBoot is not for every network or every workstation in a network, however. It does require significant network bandwidth to function. It is also a very server-intensive technology. If you do implement NetBoot, you should dedicate a server (or multiple servers) to acting as nothing but NetBoot servers because of the performance load and because NetBoot requires impeccable reliability from the NetBoot servers.

A close cousin to NetBoot is NetInstall, which was introduced in Mac OS X Server 10.2. NetInstall, which is covered in the next section, is based on the NetBoot technology, but rather than acting as a replacement for a workstation's startup drive, it allows workstations to boot from the server and access the Mac OS X installer to install Mac OS X, additional software, or an entire disk image to a workstation. While NetBoot serves as a replacement for deploying an operating system, software, or disk image to workstations, NetInstall serves as a tool for such deployment.

The NetBoot Process

Before we get into discussion of how to create and modify NetBoot images and configure the NetBoot service, it's important to have an understanding of the process that occurs when a computer is started up using NetBoot technology (regardless of whether the purpose is to access a NetBoot or NetInstall image). The basic process for NetBooting a Macintosh computer is to select either a NetBoot or NetInstall image as the startup disk for the computer using the Startup Disk System Preferences pane (Mac OS X) or the Startup Disk control panel (Mac OS 9) or you can force the computer to NetBoot at startup by holding the N key down or by holding the option key at startup to trigger the startup manager, allowing you to select any available startup disk, including available NetBoot images.

The Startup Disk System Preference pane in Mac OS X 10.2 or higher will display all available NetBoot and NetInstall images, as will the most recent version of the Startup Disk control panel for Mac OS 9 (which is included with Mac OS 9.2.2). You can also select the generic Network Startup icon (the only option for NetBoot in earlier version of the Mac OS 9 Startup Disk control panel in the Startup Disk System Preference pane for Mac OS X 10.1 and earlier) to use the NetBoot image that is designated by the server as the default image. The default image is used if a computer is started with the N key pressed.

Boot Service Discovery Protocol

When a computer is NetBooted is first sends out a DHCP request to acquire an IP address. It then sends out a broadcast packet using the Boot Service Discover Protocol (BSDP). If a Mac OS X Server running the NetBoot service receives the BSDP packet, the server responds to BSDP request, providing the computer with a NetBoot property list for the default image. The property list contains the location of and information about the default NetBoot image. If a specific image was selected, the computer requests information for this image in its BSDP request packet and receives the appropriate property list from the server. Table 28-1 lists the information that is included in property lists for Mac OS 9 and Mac OS X NetBoot or

NetInstall images. During the BSDP phase, you'll see a flashing globe icon displayed on the screen of the NetBooting computer.

Table 28-1. Contents of a NetBoot Property List.

Property	Description
BootFile	The operating system boot files located in the NetBoot Image folder (included in all NetBoot/Install images)
Index	The ID number of the image
IsDefault	Designates whether an image is the default image for the server hosting it
IsEnabled	Designates whether the image is enabled in Server Admin
IsInstall	Designates whether an image is a NetInstall image.
Name	The displayed name for the image
RootPath	The path to the actual disk image file(s) of a NetBoot or NetInstall image
Type	Specifies whther an image is a Mac OS 9 image (using the variable "classic") or the file service used to access the image for Mac OS X image (NFS or HTTP)
SupportsDiskless	Specifies whether the image will support server-based shadow files ("true" indicates that it will)
Description	The description of the image, displayed in the Network Image Utility
Language	The language of the Mac OS version used by the image

NetBoot share points and image folders

As you can probably guess from looking at the contents of a NetBoot property list, NetBoot requires files beyond the actual image file, including the basic operating system boot files. These files are stored along with the image in a special type of folder called a NetBoot Image folder. This folder contains the property list itself, the required boot files, and the image. The NetBoot Image folder is named with the name of the image it contains and ends with an *.nbi* file extension.

NetBoot image folders are stored on special share points that are created by the NetBoot service. These share points are, by default, created on every local volume connected to the server. You can, however, specify in Server Admin that only specific volumes be used. The NetBoot share points will appear in Workgroup Manager, even though you should not adjust or remove them using Workgroup Manager unless you have disabled the NetBoot service, as doing so may interfere with NetBoot functionality. These share points are always created in the */Library/NetBoot/ directory* on each selected volume (the directory will be created if it does not already exist) and are named NetBootSP*n*, where *n* is the volume or partition number assigned by the file system.

Once the NetBooting computer receives the contents of the property list using BSDP, the computer establishes a Trivial File Transfer Protocol (TFTP) connection to the share points and downloads the required boot files. In the case of Mac OS 9 images, this is the Mac OS ROM file. In the case of Mac OS X images, these are the *booter*, *mach.macosx*, and *mach.macosx.mketext* files. With a Mac OS X 10.2 or higher Net-Boot or NetInstall image, the gray Apple logo with a spinning globe beneath it indicates that the computer is downloading the boot files using TFTP. Once these files have been downloaded, the computer accesses the actual disk image file and begins the Mac OS startup process using that image.

Access to the actual NetBoot image can be accomplished by AFP, NFS, or HTTP, depending on which file services are configured and running on the NetBoot server and the type of image being used. Mac OS 9 images require the use of AFP. Mac OS X 10.2 and earlier images, NetBoot images, and all NetInstall images require the use of NFS. NetBoot images for Mac OS X 10.3 or higher can make use of either NFS or HTTP.

Shadow files

Starting up computers from read-only disk images presented a problem for Apple when NetBoot was developed because both Mac OS 9 and Mac OS X (and most applications) require the ability to modify configuration files and/or create temporary files on the startup disk during the course of daily operation, something that cannot happen when using a read-only disk image stored on a file server and being accessed by multiple workstations. Apple solved this problem by the use of shadow files. A *shadow file* is a temporary file that stores information that would normally be written to the startup disk. A shadow file is automatically created for each NetBoot session. Any time an application or the operating system attempts to write data to the startup disk, the NetBoot service writes that information to the shadow file instead. When that data is requested, the service redirects the request to the shadow file. When a NetBoot session ends (the NetBooted computer is shut down or restarted), the shadow file is deleted.

The result is that the NetBoot disk image remains clean and untouched but the operating system responds as fully as if a traditional startup disk were being used. Shadow files do enable users to "save" files to the startup disk. These files are, however, saved only to the shadow file and are lost once the NetBoot session is over, something that may require either some user education on your part or limiting users from having write access to any folder in the NetBoot disk image.

When NetBoot was originally developed, shadow files were always stored on share points hosted by the NetBoot server, which some images still require. These share points are auto-created, like the share points used to store NetBoot image folders. They are named NetBootClients*n*, where *n* indicates the volume or partition number assigned by the filesystem of the server. As with NetBoot image folders, when you designate which volumes are used to store shadow files, they are created in the directory */Library/NetBoot*.

Mac OS 9 NetBoot images require that shadow files be created in these share points. Mac OS X images, however, can create shadow files on a local hard drive of the computer that is being NetBooted. This approach reduces network traffic and improves performance when the operating system needs access to data contained in the shadow file. By default, Mac OS X images create shadow files on the server if an appropriate share point exists. If an appropriate share point does not exist, the computer creates a local shadow file. Server-based shadow files are accessed using AFP and require that the AFP service be running on the NetBoot server.

NetBoot requirements

Only relatively recent Macintosh computers support NetBoot. Technically, all Mac models released after the original iMac are capable of NetBoot. However, the original tray-loading iMac and the blue and white Power Mac G3 are not supported by NetBoot in Mac OS X Server 10.3. After the introduction of these computers, Apple made updates to the ROM code used in Macintosh computers, which enabled what is called NetBoot Version 2. With the release of Mac OS X Server 10.3, Apple modified the NetBoot service to support only NetBoot Version 2. These earlier computers only support NetBoot Version 1 and can be NetBooted from previous versions of Mac OS X Server, which are not covered by this book. Computers must also have the minimum RAM requirements for the operating system that will be contained in the image from which they are booting.

Beyond hardware requirements, NetBoot is very bandwidth intensive. You should not attempt NetBoot unless you are using a 100baseT Ethernet or faster connection between workstations. Ideally, you will be using 100baseT connections to a switched Ethernet environment rather than to hubs. If possible, you should also use a 1000baseT connection to your NetBoot server(s), particularly if you are NetBooting more than a couple of dozen workstations. You should also ensure that your Net-Boot server contains enough storage space for both images and shadow files that it may host.

 You should not use wireless networks for NetBoot because of performance issues and because the connectivity of wireless networks can be affected by a number of conditions.

Network Issues and Concerns with NetBoot

NetBoot presents certain network concerns, both in how it affects other activity on the network and how a network configuration may affect your success in implementing NetBoot. The following are some issues or concerns that you should be aware of when planning a NetBoot infrastructure.

Load balancing with multiple servers

Because NetBoot is arguably the most resource-intensive service available in Mac OS X Server, you may find that even the most high-powered server doesn't offer sufficient performance when supporting a large number of NetBoot clients. The solutions to this problem is to upgrade the server, if possible, or to implement multiple NetBoot servers. NetBoot supports automatic load balancing, which means that you can create a NetBoot image, export it across multiple NetBoot servers, and still have it appear as a single image to NetBoot clients, rather than having each client see copies of the same image from each server. When load balancing is configured, clients will access the image and store shadow files on the most available server hosting the selected image.

To configure load balancing for an image, use image ID numbers of 4096 or higher when creating the image (as discussed in the next section of this chapter). Export the image to multiple NetBoot servers using the Network Image Utility, once it has been created. If you implement load balancing in an existing NetBoot infrastructure (or add new NetBoot servers to a load balanced environment), you will need to reselect existing images on NetBoot client computers after implementing the additional servers in order for those clients to be able to access the image using load balancing.

Staggering boot times

The actually boot process is the most network- and server-intensive period or a NetBoot session. Even in a switched environment with gigabit connections and a high-powered server, you are likely to find that booting several clients simultaneously will result in significantly increase boot times for each workstation. As a result, many administrators stagger the startup times of NetBoot clients, starting up only from five to fifteen at one time. You can do this manually or by using the Energy Saver settings for automatic startup.

NetBoot across subnets

BSDP relies on broadcasts packets for NetBoot clients to locate a NetBoot server and receive information needed for the NetBoot process. This creates a problem for networks that use routers to link multiple network segments because most routers are not designed to pass broadcast packets of any kind between subnets. Thus, in most cases, NetBoot will not function for workstations on different subnets from a NetBoot server.

There are three ways to work around this problem:

- The first is to reconfigure routers to forward the broadcast BSDP packets. Not all routers support this approach, and for those that do, modifying such behavior may be difficult or have unexpected consequences for network performance. You should refer to documentation about your specific network hardware or work with your network administrator to determine whether this approach is appropriate. Apple does provide guidance for this approach at *http://docs.info. apple.com/article.html?artnum=107655.*

- The second approach, the most costly, is to place NetBoot servers on each network segment where they will be required. This is actually the best approach because it sidesteps the problem and because routers often join network segments across slower network links and offer less performance than switches for connecting NetBoot clients and servers.

- The third option is to modify the startup disk settings to include several pieces of information typically transmitted to a NetBoot client using BSDP. Effectively, this approach (which is not sanctioned by Apple) sidesteps the entire BSDP phase of the NetBoot process and can create client access problems if the NetBoot configuration of a server or individual images are altered. Bombich software provides a free application to configure these settings easily, which can be found (along with further explanation of the technique) at *www.bombich.com*.

Storing images on file servers other than servers running NetBoot

It is possible to store the actual disk image files of a NetBoot image on a server other than the NetBoot server. This approach can be used if your NetBoot server has limited storage capabilities but you still wish to use a dedicated NetBoot server for reliability concerns, rather than adding the NetBoot service to a server that is used to provide other essential services for your Network. However, I strongly advise adding adequate storage to the NetBoot server rather than using this approach.

If you do choose to store disk images on an alternate server, they must be accessed using the NFS file service. Once you have the NFS service and share points configured on the alternate storage server, you will need to create the NetBoot image folders on the NetBoot server. Then, copy the disk image out of the NetBoot image folder and place it on the alternative server and delete the disk image from the NetBoot image folder. Finally, open the property list for the image (the *NBImageInfo. plist* file in the NetBoot image folder) using a text editor or the Property List Editor application. Change the value for the RootPath property to point to the location of the disk image (for example, *altserver.company.com/Images/NetBoot/staff_image. dmg*).

Designating local or network shadow files

As mentioned earlier, Mac OS X 10.3 NetBoot images can be configured to prefer or require either a server-based shadow file or a local shadow (earlier Mac OS X versions support only local shadow files). By default, Mac OS X 10.3 images will attempt to use a server-based shadow file and will create a shadow file on a local drive only if no share point for shadow files exists or if AFP access to the NetBoot server is not available. You can however configure a Mac OS X 10.3 image to function only if a server-based shadow file can be created, to function only with a local shadow file, or to prefer a local shadow file but create a server-based shadow file if no local hard drive is available on which to create a local shadow file.

You specify such configurations by modifying the *hostconfig* file in the Unix */etc* directory (which is not normally displayed in the Finder but can be viewed from a Unix command line or using the Finder's Go To Folder command) of the source volume for the image. In the *hostconfig* file, add a line specifying how the shadow file will be created. Table 28-2 lists the available options and how they should be entered in the *hostconfig* file.

Table 28-2. Shadow file variables for the /etc/hostconfig file.

Variable Text (complete argument, to be placed in a new line at the end of the file)	How this variable creates shadow files.
NETBOOT_SHADOW=-NETWORK-	Clients create a server-based shadow file if possible and create a local shadow file if not.
NETBOOT_SHADOW=-NETWORK_ONLY-	Clients require a server-based shadow file and not boot if one cannot be created.
NETBOOT_SHADOW=-LOCAL-	Clients create a local shadow file if possible and also create a server-based shadow file it not.
NETBOOT_SHADOW=-LOCAL_ONLY-	Clients require a local shadow file and will not boot if one cannot be created.

BootP clients and BSDP

Mac OS X Server uses a Unix service called *bootpd* to provide BSDP interaction with clients. *bootpd* was originally designed as the Bootstrap protocol or bootp server. BootP is an older protocol designed to provide clients with an IP address information using broadcast packets. BootP functions similar to DHCP, which has since vastly surpassed it and become the standard protocol for clients to retrieve dynamic IP addresses and related information.

If your network has clients that request information from a BootP server, a NetBoot server might respond to these clients. Unfortunately, it will not provide them with valid IP addresses, causing their network connectivity to fail. The ideal solution to this problem is to avoid using BootP clients on your network (or at least on the same subnet as a NetBoot server). If this is not an option, you can use the NetInfo Manager utility to disable BootP responses by the NetBoot Server. In NetInfo Manager, connect to the server's local NetInfo domain and navigate to the */config/dhcp* directory for the domain. Add a key to this directory named *bootp_enabled* but do not enter any value or information to this key.

Creating Mac OS X NetBoot Images

The simplest way to create NetBoot or NetInstall images is to use the Network Image Utility, which is included in the */Applications/Server* directory of all Mac OS X Server installations and which can be installed on any Mac OS X workstation. The Network image utility can create an image from an existing disk, create and package all the supporting files, and place the resulting NetBoot Image folder in the appropriate share points on drives specified for the server. It also allows you to edit NetBoot images after they are created.

The Network Image Utility's window, shown in Figure 28-1, includes a toolbar that offer buttons for creating new images, viewing and editing existing images, and importing and exporting images. To create a new NetBoot image, select the New NetBoot button. As you can see in Figure 28-1, there are three tabs for NetBoot image configuration: General, Contents, and Default User.

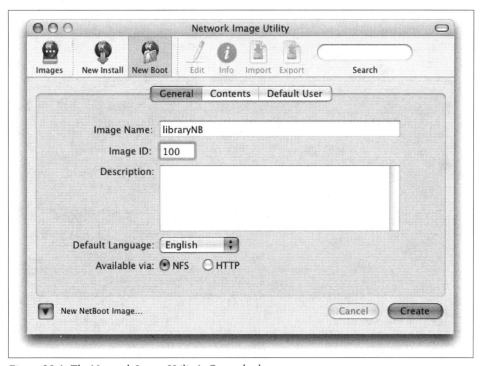

Figure 28-1. The Network Image Utility's General tab.

The General tab includes fields for the name of the image (which is displayed in Server Admin when configuring the NetBoot service and in the Startup Disk System Preferences pane or control panel). The Image ID is an ID number that servers and workstations use to identify a specific image. You can enter any number from 1 to 65535. You can use numbers above 4095 if you wish to distribute the same image across multiple NetBoot servers for load-balancing purposes, which we'll discuss later. The Description field is a text box where you can enter additional information about the image for your reference. The Default Language pop-up specifies the language of the Mac OS version used in the image. Finally, there are radio buttons to define the image as accessible by either NFS or HTTP.

The Contents tab, shown in Figure 28-2, is designed for you to choose the disk from which the NetBoot image is to be made. You can use any local disk or partition (internal or external) available to the computer on which you are running the Network Image Utility, including both a hard drive configured with the operating system variables and applications installed that you wish to use (which is generally the preferred method) or a Mac OS X install CD, which can create a generic Mac OS X NetBoot image. You can also select an existing disk image that was created on another computer.

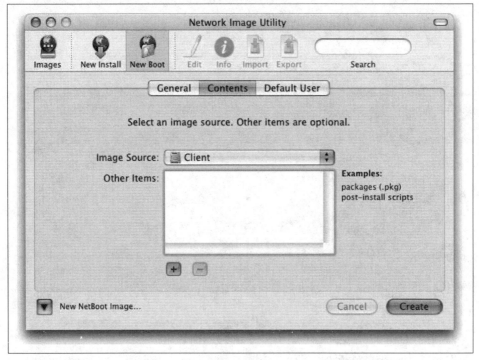

Figure 28-2. The Network Image Utility's Contents tab.

You can use the Other Items listbox on this tab to add additional scripts or software update or install packages to an image. To do so, click the Add button beneath the listbox and navigate to the appropriate items. If you are creating an image based on a workstation's hard drive, you should configure the image as completely as possible before running the Network Image Utility rather than using the Other Items feature. This option should be used in editing an image as a way of quickly adding software update packages.

You can use the Other Items feature as a way of customizing an image made from a Mac OS X install CD. However, you won't get the same degree of control over the resulting NetBoot image that you will from using a hard drive as your image source. The process is also more labor intensive if you need to configure operating system or application settings because you need to create scripts or packages that accomplish these settings. Using a preconfigured hard drive also allows you to test the functionality system configuration before creating an image.

The Default User tab allows you to specify a user that will be used for auto-login for workstations that boot using the NetBoot image. You are not required to enter a default user and, if you are using NetBoot within a directory domain, you will not want to, as you will want users to log in using their network account. However, in situations such as a public kiosk, you might want to provide access to a local user account on the workstation without requiring users to log in at it. In these situations, you would want to specify the default user account using this tab, which contains fields for the default user's full name, short name, and password. Needless to say, the user should exist on the hard drive used as the image's source. If you create an image based on a Mac OS X install CD, this default user is created as the initial administrative user account and configured for auto-login.

Once you have entered the appropriate information on these tabs, click the Create button. You are asked to confirm the image creation and select a location to save the image. The Save dialog includes a pop-up menu labeled "Serve from NetBoot Share Point On." If you are creating the image on the server that will host it, this pop-up menu allows you to select from any hard drives or partitions that are designated as supporting NetBoot images. Selecting one automatically creates the image in that location, making it immediately available for use.

If you are not creating the image on the server that hosts it, you should specify a location to save it to. Once the image has been created, click the Images button in the Network Image Utility's main window. In the Images list, displayed by clicking the Images button in the Network Image Utility, select the image you created and then click the Export button to export the entire NetBoot Image folder (including the image) to the appropriate server.

Editing Mac OS X NetBoot Images

As with a typical workstation's configuration, you might periodically need to update or modify NetBoot images used with in a network. While one way to deploy updated images is to build new workstation configurations (often referred to as building images) and then use the Network Image Utility to create a replacement image, this can be time consuming. Apple has provided two methods to edit existing images (as opposed to creating replacement images), allowing you to apply software updates or to make other configuration changes. Use the Preferences command in the Network Image Utility to select which method you wish to use. As shown in Figure 28-3, the choices are "Add items and Sync with source when editing" or "Just add new items."

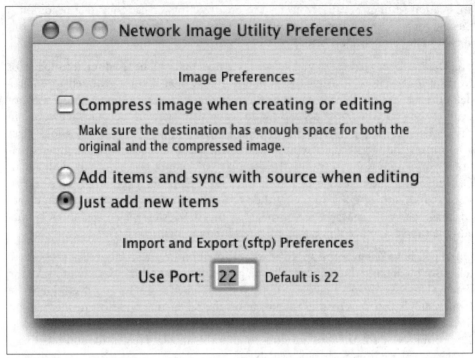

Figure 28-3. The Network Image Utility's Preferences dialog.

Editing without synchronizing

By default, the "Just add new items" option is selected. This option allows you to make changes to the image name, ID number, description, and default user information (none of which are stored in the image itself) and to apply package files (*.pkg* files) from Apple or other developers that to NetBoot images, much as you would to a workstation. Package files are typically read by Software Update or by the Mac OS X Installer utility, and all Apple Software Updates are package files. This allows you to make certain that Mac OS X and other Apple software included in a NetBoot image are up to date.

Not all software developers use package files for software installers or updates, however. Some developers use other installer tools or custom install scripts. Also, some software installers (including software from Apple not delivered by Software Update) use Apple's metapackage (*.mpkg*) format, which offers greater install flexibility. Metapackage files are typically read by the Mac OS X installer application but not by Software Update. Neither third-party file installers nor metapackage files can be directly applied to NetBoot images.

To edit the supporting files for an image or to add update packages, first disable the image in Server Admin so that no NetBoot clients will start up from it while it is being modified. Then launch the Network Image Utility and click the Images button.

Select the image from the list and click the Edit button in the toolbar at the top of the window. If the image is not displayed, use the Click Here for Image List Options pop-up menu to either display active images or all images or to locate the image using the Add button.

You will see the same three tabs that were available when you created the image. You can modify the items on each of them, with the exception of the Image Source pop-up menu on the Contents tab. To apply package files to the image, use the Other Items listbox on the Contents tab to select the packages to be applied. Once you have selected the appropriate packages, click the Save button. The Network Image Utility applies the packages to the image, after which you can enable it again in Server Admin.

Synchronizing with a source image

When the "Add items and Sync with source when editing" option is selected in the Network Image Utility's Preferences, you can modify images and apply package files in the same manner as when "Just add items" is selected. You can also synchronize the image with any changes made to the original source volume from which it was created. This allows you to make modify the image however you like, much like creating a new image without the work of actually building one. The primary requirement is that you need to use have the original source volume (or an exact copy) and it must be available to the server hosting the image.

To update the NetBoot image, make the modifications (removing or adding software or files, updating software or the OS, changing directory domain or other operating system configurations) to the source volume. Test the changes using the source volume. Once you are satisfied with the modifications, disable the image in Server Admin and then select it and click the Edit button in the Images list within the Network Image Utility.

On the Contents tab, select the source volume in the Image Source (as you did when creating the image). Make any changes that you want to the other tabs for the image. Click the Save button. The Network Image Utility adjusts the contents of the image to match the updated source volume. Once synchronization is complete, you can enable the updated image in Server Admin.

Generally, this method is preferable because it offers you increased flexibility in terms of the updates and modifications that can be made to the NetBoot image. It also offers you the ability to test the modifications or updates made to an image before using it in a live environment. This approach works well if you have a portable FireWire hard drive to use as the original source volume. The hard drive can be used as a startup disk for a workstation on which you create and modify the image and can then be connected to the actual NetBoot server for updates. The drive can then be stored until the image needs further modification.

Working with Mac OS 9 NetBoot Images

You interact with Mac OS 9 NetBoot images much differently than you do with Mac OS X images. Apple provides a standardized Mac OS 9 image, which you install directly onto your NetBoot server. You then use a Mac OS 9 tool called NetBoot Desktop Admin to modify this image. In earlier Mac OS X Server releases, Apple included a NetBoot for Mac OS 9 CD with the server software. With Mac OS X Server 10.3, however, you must request this CD from Apple (which may or may not indicate Apple's intention to do away with Mac OS 9 NetBoot support in upcoming Mac OS X Server releases).

To install the Mac OS 9 image, you must login to the NetBoot server as *root* and open the *NetBoot.pkg* file on the CD. The Mac OS X installer then installs the *DefaultMacOS92.nbi* NetBoot image folder in all existing NetBoot share points. Once this image is installed, you will need to NetBoot a client computer from the image in order to use NetBoot Desktop Admin application to adjust the image.

When a client computer NetBoots using the standardized image, it will present a Mac Manager error at startup because the image includes an active and out of date version of the Mac Manager client. Cancel out of this alert and proceed to the Finder using the password *netboot*. Once the computer finishes startup from the NetBoot image, insert the NetBoot for Mac OS 9 CD and copy the NetBoot Desktop Admin to a local hard drive or partition of the NetBoot client.

You will notice that the default NetBoot image actually includes two hard drive images, both of which are mounted by default. One is the Macintosh HD volume and the other is the Applications HD. Despite the name of the Applications HD image, you can install software on the primary image and you can delete the Applications HD image from the NetBootImage folder on the server, as its use is not required, may be confusing to users, and may present compatibility issues with some classic Mac OS applications.

Once you have copied the NetBoot Desktop Admin application to a local drive, use the Chooser to log into the NetBoot server using an administrator account and mount all server volumes. Remember that only administrators can mount entire server volumes over a network. You will need to mount the volumes because the NetBoot Desktop Admin needs access to all the NetBoot share points where the Mac OS 9 image is stored.

Next, launch the NetBoot Desktop Admin application. It displays a dialog box whose purpose is to make a local copy of the default Mac OS 9 image on the workstation you are using. This dialog contains fields to increase the size of the primary hard drive image and, if used, the Applications HD image. You should increase the size of these images enough to accommodate any software or files that you wish to include in the image. Click the Make Private Copy button to create a local read-write version of the image (or images, if you choose to use the Applications HD volume).

Once the local copy of the image is made, the workstation automatically reboots, starting up from the local copy of the image.

Once the computer has rebooted (you will need to bypass Mac Manager) from the local version of the image, you can install software and modify the image exactly as you would modify a Mac OS 9 workstation. Make all changes to the configuration and install all software that you need. If you are using Mac Manager in conjunction with NetBoot, you need to install the updated Mac Manager client and configure access to the appropriate Mac Manger server (if you are not using Mac Manger, you should disable the Mac Manager client) as described in Chapter 26. You can reboot as many times as needed at this point without losing any changes that you make.

After you have made all your configuration changes, launch the NetBoot Desktop Admin application again. You will be presented with a dialog asking whether you want to save the changes you've made to the image, discard them, or simply quit the application and resume working with the image. Before saving changes (or for that matter discarding them), be certain that the image functions exactly as you want because once they are saved, you will need to repeat the entire process to make additional changes. Clicking Save in this dialog will lock the local copy of the image and reboot the workstation, using the default NetBoot image on the server as the startup disk.

When the computer reboots using the default Mac OS 9 NetBoot image (yet again with the Mac Manager error), once again log into all server volumes using an administrator account. Open the NetBoot Desktop Admin application one more time. This time, you will see a dialog telling you that your changes will now be saved to the server. There is a checkbox labeled Keep Previous Disks as Backup. Selecting this box creates a copy of the existing version of the image in a folder named Backup Images for backup purposes (with successive changes to an image, only the most recent backup will be kept). Click the Restart button in this dialog to copy the updated image to the server, replacing the default image; after restart, the workstation boots to the updated image, allowing a full test of it. At that point, any workstations can also boot from the updated image.

To change the name displayed for the image, edit the *NBImageInfo.plist* file inside the image's NetBoot image folder (which should also be renamed to match the new image name). This file contains the image's property list. To create additional Mac OS 9 NetBoot images, you should repeat this process for each image. To make additional changes to an existing Mac OS 9 image, you also need to repeat this process.

Configuring the NetBoot Service

Once you've created your NetBoot (or NetInstall, which we'll cover shortly) images, you need to configure the NetBoot service within Server Admin to make them available to clients. To configure the NetBoot service, launch Server Admin and select

NetBoot for the appropriate server in the Computers & Services list. If the server on which you are configuring NetBoot does not have the DHCP, AFP, NFS, and Web services running, you'll see an alert because each of these services may be used or required by NetBoot.

The NetBoot service includes four panes: Overview (which displays the status of the other services used by NetBoot), Logs, Clients (which displays a list of all computers that have attempted to NetBoot from the server), and Settings. Needless to say, the Settings pane is where you will configure the NetBoot service.

The NetBoot Settings pane, shown in Figure 28-4, includes three tabs: General, Images, and Filters. The General tab contains two listboxes. The first of these lists all the Ethernet ports that are available on a server. Each one contains an Enable checkbox. The server responds to NetBoot requests on each port where the Enable checkbox is selected.

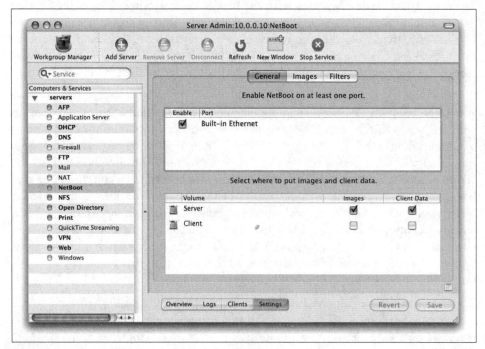

Figure 28-4. The NetBoot service General settings tab.

The second listbox contains each internal or external local volume (hard drive, RAID array, partition) that is available to the server. Next to each volume are checkboxes labeled Images and Client Data. Selecting the Images checkbox for a volume will create a NetBoot Image share point on that volume. Likewise, the Client Data checkbox will create the shadow file share point on that volume. To balance the load on the server's hard drives and increase response times, you can make multiple volumes available for NetBoot access.

 For hard drives that have been partitioned, however, you should select only one partition to be used, as selecting multiple partitions for a single drive will decrease performance.

The Images tab includes a listbox containing all NetBoot images that are stored within the NetBoot share points on the server. This includes images that have been created on the server using the Network Image Utility as well as those that have been exported to the server from another location. NetBoot Images should be placed in the appropriate share points using the Network Image Utility as opposed to simply being moved or copied to ensure correct permissions are in place and that the required server processes recognize them properly. You must specify a default image and at least one image must be enabled using this tab in order to start the NetBoot service. Each image in the listbox includes the following items:

- Image Name
- Default Radio Button (designates which image will be used for startup if a specific image has not been selected using Startup Disk on a client)
- Enable Checkbox (designates whether the image is available for clients to boot from)
- Index number (the Image ID number)
- Protocol pop-up menu (allows you view and, if available, change the protocol used to transfer the image to clients at boot)
- Image Info (located below the listbox, this displays basic information about a selected image including the volume where it is stored, the type of image, the language, and the description entered when the image was created)

The Filters tab allows you to control which workstations are allowed to boot from the server. This ability adds a degree of security to your network as it prevents outside computers from being able to directly access the NetBoot image. Use the Enable NetBoot Filtering checkbox and the radio buttons below it to turn on filtering and to indicate whether you will be creating a list of allowed clients (denying other access to the server) or creating a list of denied clients.

The Hardware Address listbox on this tab will then be used for this list. By default, this list will contain the MAC addresses of all workstations that have booted from the server. You can use the Add button to specify additional hardware addresses for the list and the remove button to remove any addresses in the list. You can also enter a host name (DNS name) in the appropriate box and click the search button next to it to look up the MAC address for the computer using that host name.

Configuring NetBoot filtering can be a very time-consuming task. If you decide to use it, the easiest way to implement it is generally to NetBoot all the clients in your network (or those you will allow) so that their MAC addresses appear in the filter list. Then select the "Allow only these clients" radio button. As you add more workstations, enter their MAC address manually.

Configuring the NetBoot Service from the Command Line

It is possible to configure the NetBoot service from the command line, rather than using the Server Admin application. This is done using several specific arguments for the *serveradmin* command. While you can make changes to the service, there is no command-line version of the Network Image Utility. As with other administrative tools, the *serveradmin* command must be run as *root* or in conjunction with *su* or *sudo* commands.

To start the NetBoot service, use the command *serveradmin start netboot*. You will receive an error if you issue this command before enabling NetBoot on one of the server's network ports. To stop the NetBoot service, use the command *serveradmin stop netboot*.

To view current NetBoot settings, use the command *serveradmin settings netboot*. This will display all settings discussed next and how they are currently configured.

To change a specific setting, use the command *serveradmin settings netboot:<config>* = *<value>* where *<config>* is the setting you wish to configure and *<value>* is the appropriate option for that setting. The following are settings that can be configured using this command:

filterEnabled
> Defines whether filtering of allowed client workstations is enabled; functions the same as selecting or deselecting the Enable NetBoot Filtering checkbox on the Filters tab in Server Admin. Acceptable values for the command are *Yes* and *No*. By default, filtering is disabled.

netBootStorageRecordsArray:_array_index:X:sharepoint
> The first of nine settings relating to whether volumes are used to store NetBoot data. All nine will be displayed for each volume mounted by a server, with X designating the volume or partition number assigned to the volume by the file system. This setting determines whether the volume is used for hosting NetBoot share points. Acceptable values are *Yes* and *No*.

netBootStorageRecordsArray:_array_index:X:clients
> Determines whether the specified volume hosts shadow files for NetBoot clients. Again, *Yes* or *No* are acceptable values.

netBootStorageRecordsArray:_array_index:X:ignorePrivs

Designates whether the indicated volume has been set to ignore permissions. Typically, this is just reflective of filesystem configurations made elsewhere (such as in the volume's Get Info window) and should not be adjusted.

netBootStorageRecordsArray:_array_index:X:volType

Designates the format of the volume (HFS+ or UFS, for example). As with the previous item, this reflects a value set elsewhere and should not be adjusted.

netBootStorageRecordsArray:_array_index:X:path

Describes the file path to the volume. Again this is reflective of the system configuration and should not be adjusted.

netBootStorageRecordsArray:_array_index:X:volName

The name of the volume, as described in the file path and the Finder. Again, this should not adjusted.

netBootStorageRecordsArray:_array_index:X:volIcon

Information describing the Finder icon of the specified volume. Once more, this is a reflection of the operating system configuration.

netBootStorageRecordsArray:_array_index:X:okToDeleteClients

Gives the NetBoot Service permission to delete NetBoot client data folders. Acceptable values are *Yes* and *No*. *Yes* is the default value and should be used in the majority of circumstances.

netBootStorageRecordsArray:_array_index:X:okToDeleteSharepoint

Gives the NetBoot server permission to delete NetBoot share points on the server if the service is disabled or if you choose to stop sharing images from the volume. Again acceptable values are *Yes* and *No*; default value is Yes and typically should be left as is.

netBootFilersRecordsArray:_array_index:X:hostname

The first of three settings related to NetBoot filtering. The X in these is a value generated by the NetBoot server (you can view the appropriate value by checking the NetBoot Settings configuration before entering commands associated with these settings). This setting sets filter records for computers by *hostname* (DNS name). The appropriate value is the *hostname* of the computer you wish to add to the filter list.

netBootFilersRecordsArray:_array_index:X:filterType

Determines whether the filter list will be a list of allowed or denied computers, as the appropriate radio buttons on the Filters tab for the NetBoot service settings in Server Admin do. Acceptable values are *allow* (for a list of allowed computers) or *deny* (for a list of denied computers).

netBootFilersRecordsArray:_array_index:X:hardwareAddress

Sets filter records for computers by MAC address. The appropriate value is the MAC address of the computer to be added to the filter list.

netBootImagesRecordArray:_array_index:X:Name

The first of 12 settings relating to NetBoot images hosted by the server. Each entry will be listed for every available image. All but one of these is defined by items in the image's property list. The X relates to a variable assigned to each image by the NetBoot service (as with filter settings, you can view the settings before adjusting them to ensure use of the proper variable). For convenience's sake, I've listed the properties to which each corresponds in the property list (as described in Table 28-1). You can edit these using these commands by editing the property list itself, or through the Network Image Utility. This value corresponds to the Name property.

netBootImagesRecordArray:_array_index:X:IsDefault

Corresponds to the *IsDefault* property. Acceptable values are *Yes* and *No* with *Yes* designating the image as default.

netBootImagesRecordArray:_array_index:X:RootPath

Corresponds to the *Root* Property value.

netBootImagesRecordArray:_array_index:X:isEdited

Used by the NetBoot service to specify whether images have been synchronized/edited after creation. This setting is managed by the Network Image Utility and is best not adjusted.

netBootImagesRecordArray:_array_index:X:BootFile

Corresponds to the *BootFile* property.

netBootImagesRecordArray:_array_index:X:Description

Corresponds to the *Description* property.

netBootImagesRecordArray:_array_index:X:SupportsDiskless

Corresponds to the *Supports Diskless* property. Acceptable values are Yes and No.

netBootImagesRecordArray:_array_index:X:Type

Corresponds to the *Type* property (NFS or HTTP).

netBootImagesRecordArray:_array_index:X:pathToImage

Specifies the path to the property list within the NetBoot Image folder. Typically should not be adjusted.

netBootImagesRecordArray:_array_index:X:Index

The ID number of the image, corresponding to the *Index* property.

netBootImagesRecordArray:_array_index:X:IsEnabled

Corresponds to the *IsEnabled* property.

netBootImagesRecordArray:_array_index:X:IsInstall

Corresponds to the *IsInstall* property. *Yes* specifies a NetInstall image. *False* specifies a NetBoot image.

netBootPortsArray:_array_index:X:isEnabledAtIndex
> The first of three settings relating to the server's network ports (and the only one of three that should be modified). All three are displayed for each of the server's network ports. The X will be replaced with a numerical identifier for the port specified by the operating system. This setting determines whether a port is enabled to accept NetBoot requests for clients, mirroring the checkboxes on the General tab of the NetBoot service settings in Server Admin. Acceptable values are *Yes* or *No* (*No* being the default configuration).

netBootPortsArray:_array_index:X:nameAtIndex
> Displays the name of the network port (as shown in Server Admin or the Network pane in System Preferences).

netBootPortsArray:_array_index:X:deviceAtIndex
> Displays the device ID of network port (as shown in Apple System Profiler).

NetInstall

Apple designed NetInstall using the same technological basis as NetBoot. With NetInstall, a workstation boots from an image on a NetBoot server, but rather than booting into a fully functional version of the Mac OS, the workstation boots to a version of the Mac OS X Installer application. The installer then installs the items specified in the NetInstall image onto the local hard drive of the workstation. This provides an alternative to installing Mac OS X, applications, software updates, and other files on each workstation individually using the requisite CDs. NetInstall only functions with Mac OS X; it cannot be used to install Mac OS 9 or classic Mac OS software.

How the NetInstall Process Differs from NetBoot

For the most part, the NetInstall process functions the same as NetBoot. NetInstall images are stored in the same share points as NetBoot images and use the same NetBoot image folder format to house the images, though some of the items in the folder and the contents of the property list do vary, as noted in Table 28-1. To boot a computer to a NetInstall image, select the image in the same methods that you would a NetBoot image. You can make a NetInstall image the default image for a server, though Server Admin will display an alert dialog if you do so, reminding you that NetInstall images configured for unattended installation could erase and/or overwrite data on a computer that was accidentally NetBooted.

The NetInstall process diverges from the NetBoot process described earlier at the stage where the boot files are downloaded by the client workstation using TFTP. Once these files are downloaded, the client does not create a shadow file (as there is no need for temporary files to support user interaction with the Mac OS or applications), nor does it establish an interactive session with the server. Instead, it downloads a copy of the actual disk image contained in the NetBoot image folder using NFS (NetInstall does not support HTTP or AFP access). Once the image has been downloaded, the client runs the Mac OS X installer application and proceeds with the installation.

Using NetInstall for Software Install Versus Disk Image Install

Apple's original intention with NetInstall was primarily to streamline the process of installing Mac OS X for IT departments. It was originally designed to create a disk image of the Mac OS X install CDs and to run the Mac OS X install process in the same manner that using the CDs would. Apple did include the option for administrators to include additional package files or scripts that could be run following the Mac OS X install process. However, this ability was limited to software installers that were built as package files for the Mac OS X Installer application and does not support metapackage files. It also provides no method for dealing with applications that require registration keys to be entered after or during installation.

Apple has also provided support for non-OS NetInstall images. These images can be created using package files and can support metapackage files (although not a combination of the two). This provides the ability configure update installations using NetInstall.

It is also possible to use a hard drive (or a disk image of one) as the image source for NetInstall images. When you do this, the entire disk image is installed onto a NetInstall client's hard drive. This allows you to configure a hard drive with all applications installed and all operating system and software options or preferences set (directory domain access, local drive permission limits, application registration keys, printer settings, etc.) and then create a NetInstall image based on that hard drive. NetInstall clients using this image are created as a complete duplicate of this hard drive. Since NetInstall images can be configured for unattended installation, this makes the process of deploying workstation configurations very simple for administrators. The one caveat of the process is that some network configurations, such as AppleTalk and Rendezvous names, will need to be adjusted for each workstation after such deployment.

Creating NetInstall Images

As with Mac OS X NetBoot images, NetInstall images are created using the Network Image Utility. To create a NetInstall image, launch the Network Image Utility and click the New Install button in the toolbar. The New Install image display contains three tabs: General, Contents, and Installation Options.

The General tab is identical the General tab for a NetBoot Image, with the exception that there is no choice between NFS and HTTP, as NetInstall images can be accessed only using NFS. The Contents tab is also identical to that of a NetBoot image. If you choose to create an install image based on installation CDs, the required CDs must be inserted in the CD drive of the server on which Network Image Utility is being run. If you choose to use a local volume to create a disk image that is deployed over a NetInstall client's hard drive, it must be available. You can also select an existing disk image (either for true software installation or for image deployment), using the Disk Image option in the Image Source pop-up menu. You can use the Other Items listbox to add additional packages or scripts to the installation process. These items can be added as described in the section on creating NetBoot images, and they will be applied or run following the installation process. As noted earlier, however, they cannot include metapackages or nonpackage installer applications.

The Installation Options tab includes two checkboxes. The first is Checksum Destination After Installing, which is actually a misnomer. This checkbox causes the Net-Install client to verify the install image it downloads before it actually runs the Mac OS X installer. This ensures that the install image does not have any corrupted data. This option slightly increases the time it takes to create a NetInstall image and for a workstation to process the image.

The second checkbox is Enable Automated Installation and it includes an Options button when selected. Selecting this checkbox and then clicking the Options button brings up a dialog that allows for NetInstall to proceed without user interaction. The Options dialog includes radio buttons to determine whether a user selects the target volume for the installation or whether a specified volume is automatically selected (you must enter the name of the volume). There are also checkboxes to erase the target volume before installation, require that a user respond to a confirmation dialog to proceed with installation, and restart the NetInstall client after the installation is complete.

Once you have configured the available options, click the Create button to create the NetInstall image and its NetBoot Image folder. When you click the Create button, you will see the same confirmation and save dialogs as when creating a NetBoot image.

Apple Software Restore

Apple Software Restore (often abbreviated as ASR) is Apple's long-standing tool for applying disk images to hard drives. It comes in a classic Mac OS versions as well as a command-line Mac OS X version, for which there are now GUI front ends. ASR can be used over a network or with images stored on local disks, such as CDs or removable hard drives. ASR does not create disk images; it only applies them. Images must be created using Disk Copy, Disk Utility, or a comparable tool. Images must also be processed or scanned for use with ASR. This capability is built into most Mac OS X tools and can be added to the classic Mac OS version of Disk Copy as well.

Creating Classic Mac OS ASR Images

The first step in creating a classic Mac OS ASR image, as with any disk image–based deployment, is to configure a workstation with the Mac OS installation, software, files, and configuration settings appropriate to all workstations that will have the image applied to them. The second step is to boot that workstation from a disk other than the disk that will be used as the image, since Disk Copy cannot create an image of a Mac's startup disk. This alternative boot disk can be a separate hard drive partition, an external drive, or an appropriately configure bootable CD. Whatever type of alternative startup disk is used, it must contain the Disk Copy application, which must reside in a folder that, in addition to containing Disk Copy, contains a folder named Scripts. The Scripts folder must contain a script from Apple called Scan Image for ASR (which can be downloaded from *http://developer.apple.com/testing/ docs/TNasr.html*).

Once the workstation is booted from this alternative disk, use the following steps to create an ASR image using Disk Copy:

1. Launch Disk Copy and select Image → Create Image from Disk.
2. Select the hard drive that has been configured as the disk image source in the Open dialog. Alternatively, you can drag the source disk onto the Disk Copy window.
3. In the Save dialog that is presented, navigate to a location where you will store the disk image. This can be on any volume or share point that is accessible to the workstation that has enough space for the image, with the exception of the disk from which the image is being created.
4. From the image format or type pop-up menu in the Save dialog, make sure that you select either Read-Only or Read-Only Compressed as the image type because ASR supports only Read-Only images. Compressed images will take longer to create, but they use less storage space and will be applied faster to workstations.
5. Once the image has been created, select the Scan Image for ASR option from the Scripts menu in Disk Copy. In the dialog that is presented, select the disk image that you just created. Disk Copy prepares the image for ASR and the Disk Copy window will display a message when the process is complete.
6. Finally, create an ASR folder. This folder can be named anything you want and can be located on a share point. It needs to contain the Apple Software Restore application (which you can download from same location as Scan Image for ASR) and a folder named Configurations. Disk images created for use with the classic Mac OS version of ASR need to be placed in the Configurations folder.

Applying Classic Mac OS ASR Images

Once you've created your ASR folder, you can apply images within the Configurations folder to workstations. In order to apply an image to a workstation, you need to start the workstation from a disk other than the hard drive that applies the image. This can be an external hard drive or separate partition or a bootable CD. Whatever the startup disk type, the workstation must be able to access the ASR folder (be that folder on a local disk or a share point). Once you've started up from this alternative disk, launch the Apple Software Restore application within the ASR folder.

 When working with classic Mac OS Images, it is advisable to use the classic Mac OS version of the ASR application rather than the Mac OS X command-line version.

Once ASR is launched, you are able to select the hard drive to apply the image to and the disk image from those in the Configurations folder. Depending on the ASR version you use, you may also have an option to Restore in Place, which replaces only items outside the System Folder, and the option to choose between Mac OS Standard (HFS) and Mac OS Extended (HFS+) disk formats for the hard drive. Typically, you'll need to replace the entire disk contents and format the drive as a Mac OS Extended drive.

Configuring custom classic Mac OS restore CDs

As noted earlier, you need to be able to start workstations from an alternative disk in order to run ASR and apply an image to their internal hard drives. Although you can do this using external hard drives, it is far more efficient and cost effective to use a custom startup CD. You can create such CDs with a CD authoring tool such as Roxio's Toast.

A custom startup CD needs to include a Mac OS 9 System Folder and needs to be burned such that the CD will be bootable (refer to your CD authoring software's documentation on how to do this). If your ASR images are small enough, you can include your ASR folder on the CD. This makes it possible to simply boot from the CD and apply the image to the workstation. Burn several CDs and you can do several workstations at once.

Using an ASR server for classic Mac OS images

Most ASR images won't fit onto a custom bootable CD (which needs to also accommodate a classic Mac OS version). However, if you create a bootable CD that includes the extensions needed for the computer to access your network, you can use it as a startup disk for workstations. You can then create an ASR share point by placing your ASR folder on a server and making that folder into a share point. You can boot workstations from the CD, mount the ASR share point, and run ASR. The share point can be located on any AppleTalk or AFP server that workstations can communicate with, meaning that this approach can work with Windows networks, provided Services for Mac (or an equivalent third-party tool) is installed. Some Mac OS 9 CDs from Apple will even include enough network support to allow this approach to work without your needing to create a custom boot CD.

Creating Mac OS X ASR Images Using Disk Utility

With Mac OS X 10.3, Apple bundled the ability to create and modify disk images (and to burn CDs from them) into the Disk Utility application. They also built the Scan Image for ASR script and the functionality of ASR itself into Disk Utility. This makes creating and applying ASR images significantly easier than ever before.

To create an ASR-ready disk image using Disk Utility, follow these steps:

1. Configure the hard drive of the workstation that will serve as the source for the image.

2. Startup from an alternate disk (this could be another partition, external drive, NetBoot image, or Mac OS X 10.3 or higher install CD).

3. Launch Disk Utility.

4. Select the source volume in the left pane of the Disk Utility window and click the New Image button in the toolbar.

5. You will be presented with a Save dialog asking where to store the image once it is created. You will also be able to specify the type of image to create. Again, you must choose either read-only or compressed.

6. Once the image has been created, select Scan Image for Restore from the Images menu. In the Open dialog, navigate to the newly created image. Disk Utility prepares the image for restore.

 Generally speaking, you will need to store ASR images for Mac OS X on a server or an external hard drive. This is partly because of the size of the images and partly because of numerous issues involved with creating custom bootable Mac OS X CDs or DVDs.

Applying Mac OS X ASR Images Using Disk Utility

As noted earlier, Mac OS X's version of ASR was designed as a command-line tool. With Mac OS X 10.3, Apple included graphical functionality for ASR into Disk Utility. As with creating Mac OS X ASR images, this means that you can apply images to a workstation when it has been started up from any Mac OS X 10.3 volume other than the hard drive or partition to which the image is applied, including a Mac OS X install CD.

To apply an ASR image using Disk Utility perform the following actions:

1. Launch Disk Utility.

2. Select the hard drive or partition to which you wish to apply the ASR image in the left pane.

3. In the right pane, select the Restore tab, shown in Figure 28-5.

4. If the image is stored on a server, enter the URL and path to the image within the network in the Source field (for example, *afp://server.company.com/asr/workstation_image.dmg*). You can make images stored on a server available using a variety of protocols including AFP, NFS, and HTTP (meaning that you can use server-based ASR images in any network regardless of its server platform). If the image is local, you can enter the path to it or click the Image button and browse to the image.

5. Drag the appropriate disk or partition icon from the left pane into the destination field, if it is not already listed there.

6. To erase any existing data on the volume, check the Erase Destination checkbox. If you leave this unchecked, the contents of the image are applied to the selected volume, but they are applied in addition to any existing data.

7. Click the Restore button to apply the image to the disk.

 The Skip Checksum checkbox gives the option to not verify the integrity of the image when it is applied. Ideally, you will want to leave this unchecked, as doing so ensures against corruption of the image and of the resulting workstation configuration. The checkbox is automatically checked if you do not select the Erase Destination checkbox, however.

Applying Mac OS X ASR Images from the Command Line

The command-line version of ASR can be used to apply Mac OS X disk images without using Disk Utility. To apply an image from the command line, use the command *asr –source* (path to the ASR image) *–target* (the name or mount point of the hard drive or partition to which the image is being applied). You can follow this command with additional arguments that mirror the options available in Disk Copy, including:

Erase
Erases the target volume (hard drive or partition) before applying the image. Entered as *–erase*.

No Prompt
Performs the ASR operation with no warnings or confirmation dialogs being presented. Entered as *–noprompt*.

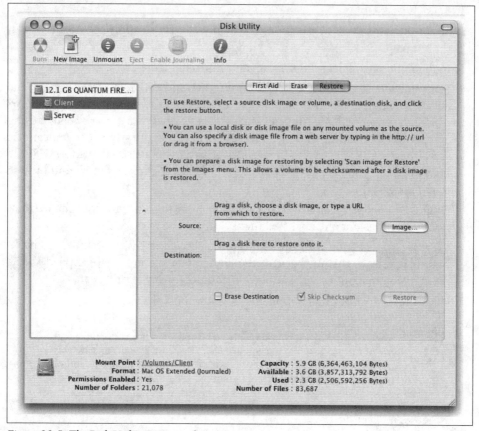

Figure 28-5. The Disk Utility Restore tab.

No Check

Equivalent to deselected the Skip Checksum option in Disk Utility. Entered as
–nocheck.

Here is an example of ASR command-line usage:

```
sudo asr –source /Volumes/FirewireHD/testimage.dmg –target /Volumes/MacintoshHD
–erase –noprompt
```

The command line version of ASR must be run as *root* or using the *su* or *sudo* commands. Additional information can be found in its manpage.

Creating and Applying Mac OS X ASR Images Using Other Tools

While Disk Utility is the most common tool for creating ASR images for Mac OS X at
this point, it is not the only tool. Earlier versions of Mac OS X used a version of
Apple's Disk Copy tool. There is also a freeware tool called Carbon Copy Cloner
(*www.bombich.com*), created by Bombich software, that offers a tool to create ASR

read images very easily. Bombich's tool also acted as a front end to the command-line version of ASR, making it easier to apply local ASR images to workstations. A companion tool called NetRestore provides an option for working with images stored on a server.

Carbon Copy Cloner also gives you the ability to create an image but omit certain files and to create the supporting files needed for NetBoot images. Although its approach to NetBoot doesn't readily offer additional functionality over the tools in Mac OS X Server 10.3, it does provide a nice front end for earlier Mac OS X Server versions. Likewise, the capabilities of the NetRestore application provide the extensive functionality now found in NetInstall. NetRestore actually goes a slight step further by enabling you to create a NetInstall image that hooks into the NetRestore application rather than the Mac OS X Installer and allows you to define network-identifying information for clients at installation.

Deploying New Software and Software Updates

So far, I've discussed the various ways to deploy workstation configurations through the use of disk images. These approaches work well for deploying new infrastructures, making mass changes to workstations throughout an existing infrastructure, and configuring new workstations for service. They also work well for dealing with problems of severe corruption of operating system or application files on individual workstations: redeploy the image on the problem workstation or on a new hard drive and it's back in business.

The problem that these approaches don't address is one of the biggest headaches for administrators: how to deploy new individual applications to existing workstations and how to maintain software updates across the workstations in your network. In some cases, manually installing the software, either using the original CDs or by placing the installation files and tools on a share point, is an effective (or the only available) option. In others, you may want to consider server-based options that leverage the power of a network to automate the update or install process, particularly in the case of critical updates that need to be deployed to all workstations or software that needs to be rolled out to a large number of workstations.

Working with Apple Software Update

Apple's Software Update tool allows Mac OS X computers to query Apple's software update server, check for software updates have been released that are appropriate to their configurations, and download and install those updates. Software Update is designed to perform such checks automatically (by default, it checks every week, provided the computer has an Internet connection). Most administrators opt to disable Software Updates's automatic checking for two important reasons:

- Software Update can confuse users. When it detects updates, it displays available updates to users, asking the user to determine which updates to install. It will also require a user to authenticate with a local administrator name and password to install the update, which many users are unlikely to have.

- More importantly, Apple has been to known to release software updates that fix some problems and create other problems. The original Mac OS X 10.2.8 update, for example, completely disabled Ethernet ports on a number of Mac models. Updates may also affect specific applications while not causing any problems to the operating system itself.

You should make a habit of testing all updates before implementing them on workstations to make certain that they won't cause problems or unexpected behavior. This is true of Mac OS X updates from Apple as well as all application updates from other companies. One approach, if you have a couple of tech-savvy users, is to install updates on their workstations only and have them report back after a few days of typical use. The exception to this rule is critical security updates and updates to anti-virus tools.

There is also a command-line version of Software Update, which can be implemented using a shell connection to individual workstations. This version allows you to SSH to individual workstations and run Software Update. The command-line version of software update is invoked using the command *softwareupdate* and one of the following arguments (for all arguments other than *list*, the tool must be run as *root* or using the *su* or *sudo* commands):

List
> Lists the update packages available or recommended for a computer. Can be entered either *--list* or *–l*.

Install
> Downloads and installs selected updates. Can be entered as either *--install* or *–i*. The *install* argument needs to be followed by an argument specifying which updates to install. This can be done with *–a* to install all available updates, *–r* to install all updates that Apple has listed as required updates, or item followed by the names of selected updates to install.

Ignore
> Adds updates to a list that will not be downloaded automatically by software update, even if the install all available updates command is used. Entered as *–ignored add* followed by the names of the updates to be ignored. Updates can be removed from the ignored list by using the *–ignore remove* argument followed by the names of the updates to be removed from the ignore list.

Schedule

Turns automatic update on or off. Entered as *--schedule* followed by the word *on* or *off*.

The following example illustrates the use of the command-line version of Software Update to check for updates and selectively install a single update:

```
Client-X:/Users/rjfaas root# softwareupdate -l
Software Update Tool
Copyright 2002-2003 Apple Computer, Inc.

Software Update found the following new or updated software:
   ! iTunes4-4.7
        iTunes, 4.7, 8920K [required]
! QuickTime652-6.5.2
        QuickTime, 6.5.2, 19752K [required] [restart]
   * AirPortDrivers-3.4.3
        AirPort Card Update 2004-08-31, 3.4.3, 920K [restart]
Client-X:/Users/rjfaas root# softwareupdate -i iTunes4-4.7
Software Update Tool
Copyright 2002-2003 Apple Computer, Inc.


iTunes: 0...10...20...30...40...50...60...70...80...90...100
Optimizing system performance.  This may take a while...
Done.
```

You can also create shell scripts for the command-line version of Software Update (ideally using the install argument and specifying the updates which you want installed on workstations). You can then distribute these scripts to each workstation in your network and have specific users or members of your support staff run them or run them using SSH connections to the selected workstation. You can use a tool such as iHook (*http://rsgu.itd.umich.edu/software/ihook*) to invoke such shell scripts or Unix commands automatically at login or logout. Of course, if your users are savvy enough or your adequate support staff, you may be able to have them run Software Update and apply the specified updates on their own without needing to create such scripts.

Another issue with Software Update is that it relies on your network's Internet connection and that each workstation will independently connect to Apple's update server and download updates, many of which can be extremely large. This issue can easily create bandwidth problems both internal to your network and across your Internet connection. A more efficient approach can often be to download the individual update packages appropriate to your workstations from Apple's support site and then deploy them using the following techniques (which are discussed in the following sections of this chapter):

- Using Apple Remote Desktop
- Creating software-only NetInstall mages

- Creating updated full NetInstall or ASR Images
- Placing update packages on share points within your network

Using Apple Remote Desktop for Software Installs and Updates

One of the easiest ways to roll out software updates or installations to existing workstations is to use Apple Remote Desktop (discussed in Chapter 29). One of ARD's abilities is to apply package files to workstations remotely over the network without requiring user interaction. This allows you to deploy software updates and to install new software through the use of both package and metapackage files.

ARD also includes a file copy feature. For applications that do not use or require an installer program or package and that can be installed simply by copying them to the appropriate location on a workstation's hard drive, you can use this feature to push them out to multiple workstations at a single time.

Lastly, ARD allows you to take control of a workstation over the network as though you were sitting in front of it. You can combine this ability with the file copy feature to install software that uses a full-fledged installer of its own or that requires user interaction and/or configuration during or after the install process. This method is not terribly efficient because you must still perform the process manually (although some installers and the initial configuration of some applications may be scriptable). However, it is more efficient than having to walk to each workstation and perform the installation at it.

Creating Software-Only NetInstall Images

As mentioned in the section covering NetInstall, you can create NetInstall images that contain package files. This option can be used as a delivery method for Apple software updates if you have not implemented ARD. It also allows you to install any other software items that are distributed using package files. As with other types of NetInstall images, you can create an unattended installation image, though you will want to ensure that the option to erase the target volume is not selected in such cases.

Creating Updated Full NetInstall or ASR Images

For software and updates that cannot be applied using package files or file copies and for significant configuration changes, you may want to consider simply updating the original NetInstall or ASR images within your network to include the updates and to deploy this update image in the methods described earlier. This option may be more time consuming—hence its recommnded use only for larger or more significant updates—but it does give you a much wider range of flexibility in rolling out software. This approach works particularly well for schools and colleges, which typically have a period of down time between semesters or during scheduled vacations. It can also be used in business environments during regular periods of down time or outside normal business hours.

Using Applications Automounts or Share Points

Although not appropriate to software updates or to all applications, you can store software on a share point, where users can access it. You can create automounts specifically designed for applications, which become part of a workstations applications search path. This approach allows you to roll out and update such applications very easily. However, applications stored on a share point will launch and often run noticeably slower than locally stored applications, sometimes to a significant degree. It also increases network traffic and server load, sometimes significantly. This approach also does not function well with applications that require support or temporary files or additional helper applications. Most major office and all design or media applications should not be run from a share point. Many educational programs, particularly those geared to young children, however, can function reasonably well with this approach.

Placing Application Installers on the Network

As with scripts for software updates, you can place copies of application installers on share points within your network. This method allows users to install applications as they need them or for your support staff to more easily install them. This approach has some drawbacks, however:

- When you purchase software, you typically purchase a set number of licenses for it. Placing installer files on a share point invites users to install it however many times and on whatever computers they wish. This event can easily lead to inadvertent violations of your license agreement. Some users will probably also copy such installers to CDs or other media and bring it home with them, further violating license agreements.

- Users often require administrative access to a workstation to install software. Granting regular users such access can lead to them modifying files that you may not want them touching, potentially leading to system problems and even network problems. This can create issues that you and your technical support staff will then need to resolve.

- Many applications require a registration key as part of their install process. You should not make such keys publicly available because they can then be used to install the software at any location. This can also lead to serious violations of your license agreements with potential legal consequences, particularly if the keys are ever made widely available, such as on the Internet.

Despite these drawbacks for providing users access to share points housing software installers, you might wish to create such share points for your support staff. This will enable staff members to easily locate the needed files and install such software on workstations as needed. This approach is not an efficient means for mass deployment of software, but can serve for selective installs of applications or for small roll outs to a few users or workstations where other methods discussed in this section may involve more time and effort to develop.

Using Third-Party Software Management Tools

While the options for remote installation of specific applications or updates is limited using the built-in functions of Mac OS X and Mac OS X Server, two companies produce commercial tools that give you extensive additional options. NetOctopus by Netopia (*www.netopia.com*) and Filewave by Filewave Inc. (*www.filewave.com*) each provide client/server platforms for installing and managing applications, files, and updates remotely, in addition to maintaining hardware and software inventory. Both products include a server component (installed on a Mac OS X server or a high-powered workstation) and a client component that is installed on workstations that will be managed. Administration tools for both products allow you to configure and deploy applications, updates, and other files over a network connection to clients, and both have inherent security protocols to protect access to those applications. Both products support Mac OS X and classic Mac OS versions as well as Windows, making them useful across platforms. Although both these products are powerful solutions, they can be cost prohibitive. Most commonly, Filewave and NetOctopus are implemented in large-scale networks, particularly multisite networks with limited deskside support staff. Both products also include significant and detailed documentation.

Another option is the Open Source tool Radmind. Radmind is a client/server tool that allows you to create archives of all the files from a source workstation on a server. You can then to create sets of files from those archives. Target workstations can be configured to automatically synchronize their entire hard drive or specific folders on their hard drives to specific sets of files. This approach allows you to deploy configurations specific to individual users or departments. Although there is no direct way to push changes out to workstations, synchronization commands can be issued from workstations at any time and can be scripted or invoked by remote administration (using SSH or Apple Remote Desktop). Information and downloads of the Radmind software can be found at *http://rsug.itd.umich.edu/software/radmind*.

Apple Remote Desktop

Although not included with Mac OS X Server, Apple Remote Desktop (also called simply Remote Desktop, or ARD) is an incredibly robust and useful tool that can make several of the tasks of deploying and managing a Mac network much easier for administrators and technical support staff alike. It can also be a very effective educational tool, making it useful for computer-enhanced classrooms and labs.

Apple Remote Desktop's first function is the ability to remotely observe and control a Mac workstation using a network connection. This feature is very useful for troubleshooting and security tasks, but not uncommon in software for Macs, as several products have offered it for multiple computing platforms. In fact, ARD integrates with the open standard and multiplatform VNC (Virtual Network Computing) set of tools that exist for such tasks. Apple did provide what might the most comprehensive and intuitive interface for observing and interacting with a large number of workstations at once, however.

Remote Desktop goes beyond just observing and controlling workstations, in that it allows you to easily interact with users logged into monitored workstations and to issue a number of administrative commands to workstations without actually needing to control the workstation and manually perform these tasks. It also includes the ability to copy files to and from workstations and to remotely install software on workstations. Additionally, ARD allows you to broadcast the contents on one workstation's display to other workstations, providing an excellent presentation and teaching solution.

The actual administrative tasks that can be performed using Remote Desktop are only half of the product's potential. Remote Desktop can also query workstations for all manner of characteristics about their configuration. This ability makes it ideal for use in technology inventory, either alone or as a way to retrieve inventory data for an outside inventory management system. The wide array of reporting options covers all the hardware of managed workstations as well as the operating system, installed software, and a selection of nonapplication files stored on workstations.

This chapter discusses the administrative and reporting functions of Apple Remote Desktop 2.1 (the current version as of this writing) and how they can be of use to system administrators and other IT staff. Apple Remote Desktop 2.1 requires Mac OS X 10.2 or higher. It also supports Open Directory and interaction with directory domain information.

Administrator Computers

Installing Apple Remote Desktop involves first installing the administrator application, on one or more computers that will serve as administrator computers. Administrator computers include the Remote Desktop application and can host a database containing report data from managed workstations. You can have multiple administrator computers within a network, each of which can host its own workstation report database (the standard configuration) or you can configure a single computer to host a report database that all administrator workstations will access.

Once an administrator computer is configured, you will need to ensure that the most recent version of the ARD client software is installed on all workstations. Mac OS X 10.3 includes the ARD client software as part of the operating system, though this may not be the most recent version of the software. Machines running Mac OS X 10.2 will need to have the software installed. You will then need to configure the individual workstations. This can be accomplished by manually updating and configuring each workstation or through automatic and remote methods made available by the Remote Desktop application.

Installing the Administrator Software

Installing the ARD software on an administrator computer is extremely simple. First open the install package that is included on the Apple Remote Desktop 2 CD. The installer program will prompt you to upgrade the ARD client software if the version installed is earlier than 2.0. Once the administrator software is installed, you will be asked to create a Remote Desktop password. This password controls access to the Remote Desktop application and is used for encrypting communication between the administrator computer and ARD workstations. As such, you should create as secure a password as possible, including letters (preferably of both cases) numbers, and punctuation characters.

Customizing the Remote Desktop Application

You can customize the display and behavior of the Remote Desktop application in a number of ways to suit your personal preferences and needs. The major ways you can adjust Remote Desktop are by customizing its toolbars and by using the Preferences command. Here are some specifics about the available options. For the rest of the chapter, I will be describing the toolbars and preferences in their default configuration.

Customizing the toolbar

You can customize the Remote Desktop application's toolbar so that it contains buttons for any command or report that is available in the Remote Desktop application. This allows you to have easy access to those commands and reports that you expect to run frequently. You can also customize whether buttons are displayed as icons, text, or both, and the size of the icons. To do so, select Customize Toolbar from the Window menu. The customize toolbar dialog functions the same as the customize toolbar dialog for Finder windows.

You can also customize the appearance of Observe/Control windows and multiple Observe windows (though the available buttons and sliders in these windows will vary). Again select Customize Toolbar from the Window menu, but do so when the appropriate type of window is the active window of the Remote Desktop application.

Other preferences

You can adjust the behavior of Remote Desktop using the application's preference dialog by selecting Preferences from the Remote Desktop menu. The Remote Desktop Preferences dialog has four tabs. The first two, General and Control/Observe, affect how the application displays certain information and responds to user input. The Data Collection tab affects how Remote Desktop collects and organizes data for reports, and the Restricted Access tab, which we'll discuss later in this chapter.

The General tab allows you to determine what action is taken when you double-click a workstation in a computer list (display information about it, observe or control it, or initiate a text chat with the user). You can also determine whether the workstation accepts message from users of ARD client workstations, how tasks and dates are displayed, what warnings are displayed when quitting Remote Desktop, and whether the computer can be controlled by another administrator workstation while Remote Desktop is running. You can also change your Remote Desktop password and serial number on this tab. The Control/Observe tab allows you configure the default behavior and display when first controlling or observing ARD client workstations.

Remote Desktop Users

Remote Desktop works with users in two ways. The first is via the local user accounts that exist on the individual ARD client workstations. In order to access a workstation using Remote Desktop, there must be at least one user account created on the workstation that has ARD privileges assigned to it. You can control which privileges, and thus which ARD tasks and abilities, are available to each user. When you configure Remote Desktop to access a workstation, you will need to authenticate to that workstation using one of these ARD-enabled account's username and password. The privileges assigned to the user account will then control what levels of access you have to the workstation from within Remote Desktop. These accounts don't control your level of access to the operating system itself through Remote Desktop's control feature, however, because when you control a workstation, you are controlling it as the user that is logged in at it directly (that is, as the person sitting in front of the workstation).

In some cases, it is easier to configure accounts that are specifically intended to manage ARD access rather than to use accounts that are also used for general user login. This way, the same username and passwords can be applied to all workstations throughout a network and you can easily authenticate to all of them through Remote Desktop. You can also limit the actual abilities these accounts have within the operating system to prevent a user from discovering their existence and then using them to login directly to a workstation.

The second way that Remote Desktop interacts with user accounts is when you actually launch the Remote Desktop application and configure it. The configuration settings you make, including which computers you choose to access, the display options that you set, the individual computer lists you create, the Remote Desktop password, and the ARD-enabled local accounts that you use to authenticate to workstations are all stored in various locations in the Library folder of your home directory (be it a local user home directory on a workstation, a network home directory for a directory domain user account, or a Mac OS X mobile account home directory).

Each user who will use Remote Desktop must configure the application (or have someone configure it for them) and authenticate to workstations using ARD-enabled local accounts. The advantage to this is that you can create ARD-enabled local accounts with varying levels of ARD access privileges, use the same accounts on workstations across your network, and provide users that you wish to allow access to the Remote Desktop application with only the account names and passwords that have the level of access that you wish to give to those users.

Creating ARD-Enabled User Accounts

ARD-enabled user accounts are simply local user accounts. If you are creating them manually, you do so in the same manner as any other user account by using the Accounts pane in System Preferences on the workstation. Because you may be giving individuals the names and passwords of these accounts, I would advise that you not create them as local administrator users and that you apply access limits to the user account (which can also be done in the Accounts pane).

Enable a user account's ARD access and configure its privileges using either the Remote Desktop pane in System Preferences (Mac OS X 10.2) or the Sharing pane in System Preferences (Mac OS X 10.3 and higher) or in the Access Privileges page of the Custom Installer Package Assistant. (Custom installer packages are discussed later in this chapter). If you are configuring manually, you will use the Access Privileges button in the appropriate System Preferences pane. After clicking this button, you will see a list of local user accounts with a checkbox labeled On next to each, as shown in Figure 29-1. Select the checkbox next to each user account that you want to enable for ARD access. Then select the username and select the checkboxes to the right of the list for each privilege that you want to be enabled when that user account is used to authenticate to that workstation using Remote Desktop.

Notice that the Observe privilege has two suboptions for it: Control and "Show when being observed." Control, as you might guess, enables the ability to control the workstation remotely. "Show when being observed" determines whether users will see visual cues in the ARD menu (if it is shown in the menubar) that they are being either observed or controlled. In both cases, the icon in the menubar changes and the status of being Observed or Controlled will be listed in the menu if the "Show when being observed" checkbox is selected.

Each ARD privilege allows access to specific commands and features when interacting with a workstation remotely, as listed in Table 29-1. You will notice that some commands require multiple privileges in order to be used. The section "Remote Management Tasks" (later in this chapter) provides additional information on each command in Remote Desktop.

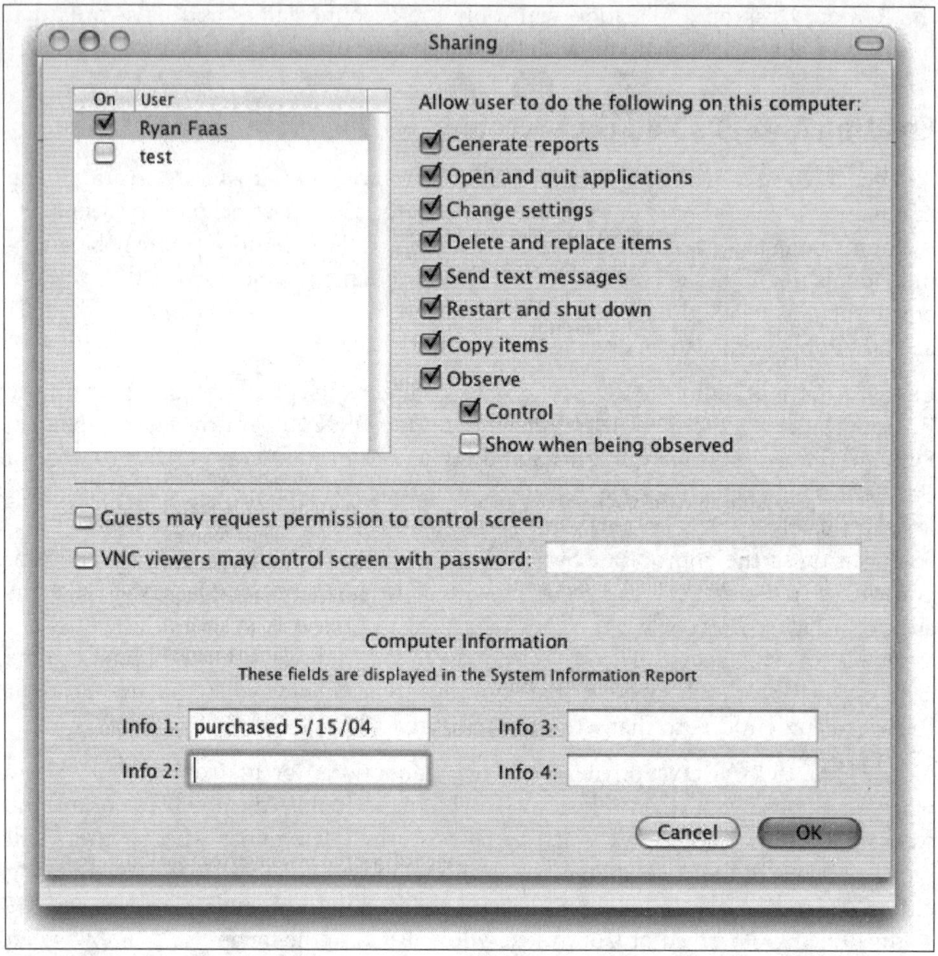

Figure 29-1. The Apple Remote Desktop Client configuration options within System Preferences.

Table 29-1. ARD privileges and associates commands.

ARD privilege	Commands that require this privilege
Generate reports	All report functions
Open and quit applications	Open Applications, Open Items, Log Out Current User
Change settings	Set Startup Disk, Rename Computer
Delete and replace items	Copy Items (if overwriting existing files), Install Packages, Empty Trash, Upgrade Client Software
Send text messages	Send Message, Chat
Restart and shut down	Sleep, Wake, Restart, Shut Down, Log Out Current User
Copy items	Copy Items, Install Packages, Change Settings, Upgrade Client Software

Table 29-1. ARD privileges and associates commands. (continued)

ARD privilege	Commands that require this privilege
Observe	Observe
Control	Control, Share Screen, Lock/Unlock Screens, Change Settings

Remote Desktop and Directory Domain Users

ARD can integrate with network user accounts stored in a directory domain. Technically, it does so automatically in one way. As noted earlier, all the configuration features for the Remote Desktop application are user-dependent and are stored in the home directory of each user that uses the application. If the user is a network user account with a network home directory, these settings are stored in that home directory's Library folder and thus follow the user and apply regardless of the administrator workstation on which the user launches the Remote Desktop application.

You have the option to take directory domain integration a step further, however. The ARD client software can be configured so that it will rely upon network user accounts rather than local user accounts on individual workstations to authenticate access to a workstation within Remote Desktop, meaning that you do not need to create local ARD-enabled user accounts on individual workstations. In order for this to function, all ARD-configured workstations and administrator computers must be bound to the same directory domain (either Open Directory or Active Directory) and special groups need to be created in that domain. These groups must be named *ard_admin*, *ard_reports*, *ard_manage*, and *ard_interact*. Directory domain users added to these groups can authenticate to workstations within Remote Desktop using their network username and password instead of a local ARD-enabled account. Membership in each group conveys specific ARD privileges, as listed in Table 29-2.

Table 29-2. ARD directory domain groups and associated privileges.

Directory domain group	ARD privileges granted to members
ard_admin	All privileges with the exception of Generate Reports
ard_reports	Generate Reports
ard_manage	All privileges with the exception of Observe and Control
ard_interact	Observe, Control, Send Text Message

Restricting Non-Administrator Access to Remote Desktop Features

You can require that users must be local administrators of a workstation that is an administrator computer (that is, one that has the Remote Desktop application and supporting software components installed) in order to have full access ARD privileges. This is done by selecting Preferences from the Remote Desktop menu and then selecting the Restricted Access tab, shown in Figure 29-2. This tab enables you to select which privileges non-administrator users will be allowed. This is in addition to any configuration made on the individual ARD client workstations (the more restrictive of the two being the effective level of privilege). This can be a good approach to use if you choose to integrate ARD access with directory domain user accounts.

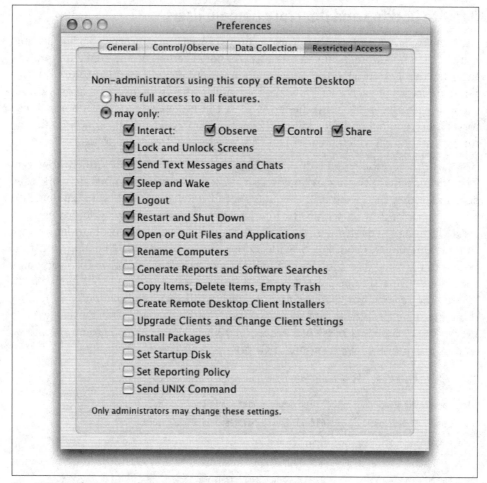

Figure 29-2. The Restricted Access tab of Remote Desktop preferences.

Installing and Configuring the ARD Client Software

There are multiple methods for installing and upgrading the ARD client software on Mac OS X workstations. It is important to have clients running the same version of ARD as administrator computers in order to ensure proper functionality. As mentioned earlier, Mac OS X 10.3 includes the ARD client software, though it might need to be updated to match the current ARD version. You can update the software using Software Update, by using the Upgrade Software command in Remote Desktop (covered later in this chapter), or by using an installer package created by the Remote Desktop application.

Mac OS X 10.2 does not include the ARD client software. Therefore Mac OS X 10.2 workstations that do not already have the ARD client installed must have it installed using an installer package generated from the Remote Desktop application. If an earlier version of the ARD client is installed on a Mac OS X 10.2 workstation, however, it can be upgraded through either Software Update or Remote Desktop's Upgrade Software command.

Beyond installing or upgrading the ARD client software, you must configure the ARD client settings on each workstation in order to access it from an administrator computer. You can configure ARD client settings manually at each workstation by using the Change Client Settings command in the Remote Desktop application or by using a custom installer package created by Remote Desktop. Each of these approaches has benefits and drawbacks. Manual configuration is of course the simplest, but is also the most time-consuming. The Change Client Settings command is more efficient and can be applied to any number of workstations simultaneously, but it requires that the workstations already be configured to allow ARD administration. Custom installer packages are generally the easiest solution, because they can configure almost all of the ARD client options in addition to installing or upgrading the ARD client software at one time, including creating ARD-enabled local user accounts. If you wish to integrate ARD client access with a directory domain, you must configure clients using either the Change Client Settings command or a custom installer package.

Manually Configuring the ARD Client

As mentioned earlier, in Mac OS X 10.2, the ARD client is configured using the Remote Desktop pane in System Preferences. In Mac OS X 10.3, it is configured using the Sharing pane in System Preferences and selecting Remote Desktop from the Service listbox where you will need to enable Apple Remote Desktop access and then click the Access Privileges button to configure the client. The available configuration options (appropriate to either Mac OS X version) include whether to display the Remote Desktop menu in the menubar, whether Remote Desktop access is allowed, which local user accounts may be used to authenticate to the workstation for ARD access, and the access privileges for each ARD-enabled user account (as discussed in the preceding section). There are also four Computer Information text fields, which you can use to enter institution-related, workstation-specific information that can be included in reports generated about the workstation (such as an asset number, physical location, purchase information, and so on).

There are also checkboxes for allowing guests to request access to the workstation from the logged-in user (which bypasses the functionality of authenticating with specified user accounts and can pose a security risk) and allowing users of VNC clients to connect to the workstation. Enabling VNC access also provides a field to enter a VNC password for the workstation. We'll get to VNC access at the end of the chapter.

Custom Client Install Packages

Apple has placed the ability to create custom ARD client install packages inside the Remote Desktop application. You may opt to use custom install packages to configure workstations, even if they already contain the current version of the ARD client software. You may also opt to use this feature to create a generic ARD client installer package for Mac OS X 10.2 workstations that do not have the ARD client installed. The following steps illustrate the process of creating custom install packages for the ARD client.

1. Select Create Client Installer from ARD's File menu. The first page of the Create Client Installer Assistant asks if you want to customize the installer. If you say no, it builds a basic upgrade package for you. If you say yes, you will be walked through several dialogs (described here) that enable you to assign any of the ARD client configuration options, though you can choose whether to configure each option with the custom installer.

2. If you choose to create a custom installer package, the next page, shown in Figure 29-3, allows you to designate whether to start the ARD client at startup of the workstation—you'll almost certainly want to choose to do so—and to choose whether to display the Remote Desktop menu in the workstation's menu bar (allowing users to send requests to ARD administrators).

3. The following page, shown in Figure 29-4, allows you to create local user accounts to be used for the purpose of managing workstations using ARD. ARD relies upon user accounts to specify what actions users are allowed when they connect remotely. When you add a workstation to a computer list (which I'll discuss shortly), you need to select an ARD-enabled user account for the connection. Although you can enable ARD access for any user account, it is better to create user accounts that are specifically intended for ARD access or to only enable access for admin accounts. This page lets you create new accounts and assign passwords automatically. Because this password information for these accounts (which can be used to log in to a workstation) or stored in the custom installer package, you should store the package only on secure workstations or share points.

   If you elect to create local user accounts, the next page allows you to enter information for those accounts, including what they are allowed to access using ARD. You should use unique usernames that will not be used for local or directory

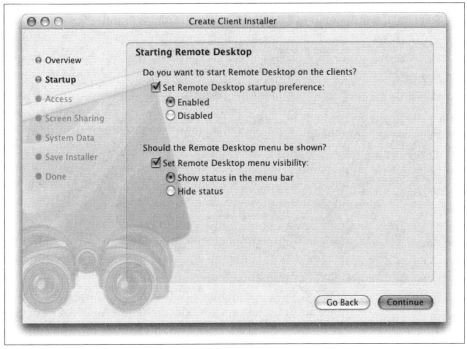

Figure 29-3. Designating ARD client startup options for a custom package installer.

domain users (such as *ardclient* or *remote desktop*). If you do enter a name matching a local user, the installer will ignore the information in the package to avoid overwriting the existing user account. If you select a name that matches that of a directory domain user account, the directory domain user will not be able to log in properly at workstations where the installer has been run.

4. The next page, shown in Figure 29-5, enables you to determine whether to integrate directory domain users with ARD. As described earlier, you can create specially named groups in a shared directory associated with ARD. Any users that you make members of these groups will then have ARD access through their account and will be able to add workstations to ARD computer lists using their directory domain account rather than relying upon local user accounts on the workstation. This page also allows you to set ARD access privileges for any local user accounts that may exist on workstations.

5. The next page allows you to determine whether someone using the Remote Desktop application can request access to a workstation without supplying an ARD configured user account. The user currently logged into the workstation will then be able to allow or deny access. This page also lets you determine if VNC clients are allowed to access and control the workstation.

6. The final configuration page, shown in Figure 29-6, allows you to designate report attributes for the workstation and to specify whether non-ARD tools that

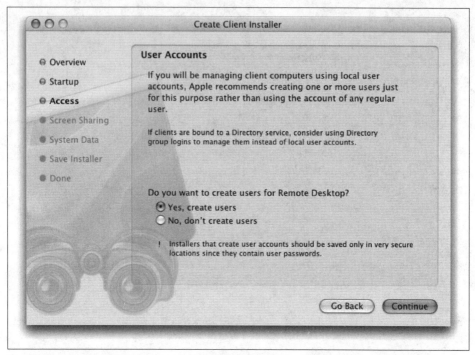

Figure 29-4. Determining local user account creation for a custom package installer.

work with similar databases (called OpenWBEM) can interact with the workstation to generate reports. We'll discuss these fields more later in the chapter. The final page lets you determine the location where the custom installer will be saved (the default is the desktop folder of the current user) and create the installer metapackage.

Deploying Install Packages

If you are using custom installer packages to install, upgrade, or configure the ARD client on workstations, you have three options in terms of how to roll out the installer package. You can manually launch the package on each workstation, you can deploy and open the package remotely using the command-line version if the Mac OS X Installer program using SSH, or you can use the Remote Desktop Install Packages command. Each approach has advantages and disadvantages. You can also forego the use of custom install packages and manually configure the ARD client settings on a workstation. If you are using a disk-image-based deployment method for workstations in your network, as discussed in the previous chapter, you can also include the ARD client configuration in your workstation images so that you need to configure only the workstations on which your images will be based.

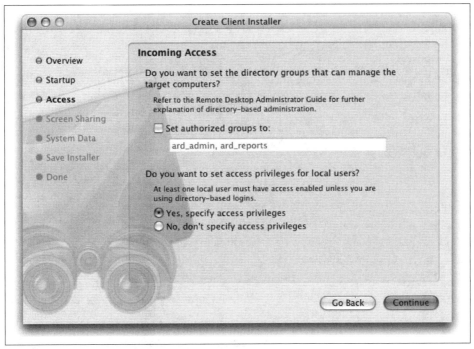

Figure 29-5. Specifying local user access and directory service integration for a custom package installer.

Manually installing custom installer packages

The simplest, though least efficient, way to use custom installer packages is to physically go to each workstation, log in, and open the custom installer package. Needless to say, this method can be very time-consuming. However, it presents no potential snags and requires no prior network access or configuration of the workstations. You can burn the custom installer package to a CD or place it on a share point to facilitate access to it at each workstation.

Using SSH

If the workstations you're configuring using the custom installer package have SSH access enabled (in the System Preferences Sharing pane), you can use SSH to deploy the installer package. Connect to the workstation using SSH use the command line and place the installer on the workstation. There are any number of ways to do this, using the Unix secure copy (SCP) or RSYNC commands or by placing the installer on an FTP share point and then downloading it using the Unix ftp command-line tool. You will then need to use the command-line version of the Mac OS X Installer to open and install the package. The command-line version of the installer should be run as *root*, so you'll need to use the *sudo* command in conjunction with it, as illustrated in the code shown next.

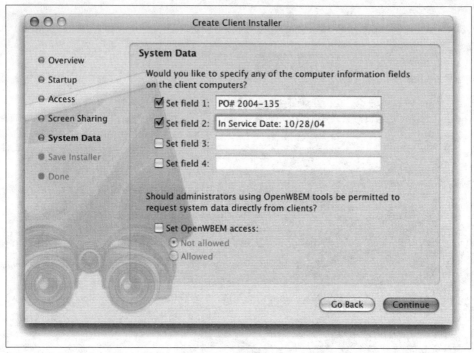

Figure 29-6. Specifying workstation-specific report fields for a custom package installer.

```
sudo installer -pkg <path to package> -target /
```

Using SSH is more efficient than manually deploying the install package, because it does not require you to go to each workstation. You can even script the process to make it more efficient. It does, however, require that each workstation have SSH access enabled.

Using ARD's Install Package feature

If the workstations are already configured for some level of ARD access with version 1.2 or higher of the ARD client, you can use Remote Desktop's Install Packages command to deploy custom installer packages. This approach requires that there already be an ARD configuration, however. Also, it may be more efficient to access the workstations and use the Upgrade Software and Change Client Settings commands.

Working with Computer Lists

Remote Desktop displays workstations as computer lists. One computer list, the Master List, will always be displayed. It contains all the computers that have been added to a Remote Desktop configuration. You can create as many additional lists as you like for organizational purposes. Computer lists allow you to organize workstations based on location, department, user function or group, type or configuration, or any other method you choose. Workstations can be members of multiple computer lists and you can remove workstations from a list at any time. If you remove a workstation from the Master List, you remove it from the Remote Desktop configuration and will not be able to access it without adding it again. Removing a workstation from the Master List and adding it again is the only way to change the user account with which you authenticate to the workstation.

As shown in Figure 29-7, computer lists are displayed in the column along the left side of the Remote Desktop main window. This column contains any user-created computer lists, the Master List, the Saved Tasks list, (used for storing and scheduling common tasks and commands), and the Scanner (used to add workstations to a Remote Desktop configuration). When a computer list is selected, the computers it contains are displayed in the large listbox to the right of the lists column. Below this listbox is the Recent Tasks listbox, which displays all commands or tasks that are performed during each Remote Desktop session. This list is cleared when you quit the Remote Desktop application.

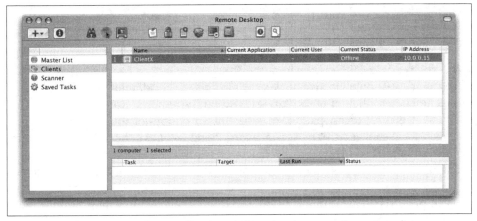

Figure 29-7. The Remote Desktop application window, showing a sample computer list.

Adding Computers to Remote Desktop

You use the Scanner, located in the lists column to find and add workstations to a Remote Desktop configuration. The Scanner, shown in Figure 29-8, can be used to locate computers by sending a broadcast packet to all computers on a local network segment, by querying all devices within a specified range of IP addresses, by entering the IP address or DNS name of a specific computer, or by importing from a file. Once you click the scanner, use the following steps to locate and add computers.

When you click the Scanner, you will see a pop-up menu containing these four options with a status box next to it and a search/refresh button (which causes the Scanner to search for workstations or to repeat a specified search). Below this is a listbox that displays any workstations that the scanner is able to locate. Located workstations are displayed in a list containing the workstation's AppleShare name, IP address, host name (DNS), ARD version, and the network port through which the administrator computer communicated with the workstation. The Recent Tasks list is displayed below this listbox.

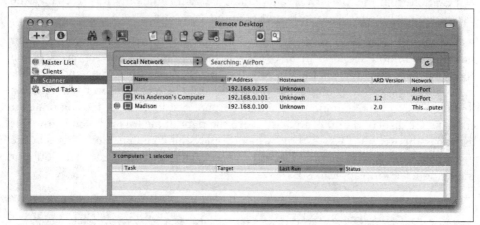

Figure 29-8. The Remote Desktop Scanner.

When you select Local Network form the Scanner's pop-up menu, the scanner sends a broadcast ARD query on all active network ports of the administrator workstation; this includes any Ethernet ports, AirPort, and FireWire ports. Routers will drop this query, as it is a broadcast packet, making this an option for locating workstations only on a local subnet. If you select Network Range, you will be able to enter starting and ending IP addresses for the range. Network Address allows you to enter a specific IP address or DNS name. File import allows you to select a text file for IP addresses of workstations, you will be asked to enter the path to the import file (or you can press the ellipsis button to browse for it). You can also drag a file into the empty listbox of the Scanner.

Once the Scanner has located workstations, add them to the Remote Desktop configuration by selecting them and dragging them to either the Master List or to a computer list that you have created. You will be asked to specify a DNS name for the workstation if one is not automatically supplied (though providing one is optional). You will also be asked for an ARD-enabled username and password to be used in authenticating to the workstation. If you have selected multiple workstations, you can select a checkbox to use this username and password to authenticate to all workstations in addition to the first one in the selection.

When you click the Add button, Remote Desktop will attempt to authenticate to the workstation. If authentication fails, you will have the option of attempting to authenticate again or to add the workstation without authenticating. The Skip button allows you to skip a workstation if multiple workstations are being added at once.

There is also a "Verify name and password before adding checkbox" that is selected by default. If you deselect this, you can add the workstation to the Master List without authenticating to it.

If you add a workstation without authenticating to it, you will see it in the Master List (as well as any other lists that you add it to). However, you will not be able to interact with it until you have successfully authenticated to it. If the account you used to authenticate to a workstation is deleted, or if the password for it is changed, you will need to authenticate to it again (you will see an access denied icon when you try to access the workstation) by removing it from the Master List and adding it again or using the Get Info command, discussed later in this chapter.

Once you authenticate to a workstation, the appropriate username and password information is stored in encrypted form as part of the Mac OS X keychain that is built into your user account (local, network, or mobile). Individual computer lists that you create are also stored in encrypted form in your keychain.

Multiple Scanners

You can actually create multiple Scanners in the list column using the New Scanner item in the File menu or the pop-up menu above the list column. Each Scanner you create will have the same options for searching for ARD workstations. However, each Scanner will remember the last search settings you used. This means that you could create individual Scanners for common searches. This can be helpful if your network uses DHCP and has rapid turnover of IP addresses, because the change in a workstation's IP address can result in access to it needing to be re-established by adding it again to a Remote Desktop configuration. You are not, however, required to first delete workstations whose connections have been lost by a change in IP address in order to re-add them and re-establish access to them.

Removing computers from Remote Desktop

To remove computers from a Remote Desktop configuration, select them in the Master List and then click the press the delete key on the keyboard or select Delete from the Edit menu. You will be asked to confirm the deletion. If you wish to add back a computer that has been removed, you will need [copy edit unclear] to locate it again using the Scanner and authenticate to it. You will also need to re-add it to any computers lists that contained it.

Creating Computer Lists

You can create a new computer list by selecting New List from either the File menu or the pop-up menu above the lists column (or by using the ⌘-N key combination). The new list will be named Untitled List; you can change the name once it is created. You can rename a list at any time by double-clicking on it in the lists column.

To add computers to a list, select them in either the Master List or another existing computer list and drag them to the new list. You can also drag computers directly from the scanner to a computer list (they will be added to the Master List automatically). You can also create a computer list by selecting a number of workstations (in the Master List, an existing computer list, or the Scanner) and select New List From Selection from either the File menu or the pop-up menu above the lists column.

To remove a computer from the list, select it and press the delete key on the keyboard (or select Delete from the Edit menu). This step removes the workstation only from the selected computer list. It does not remove it from the Master List or from any other lists.

Computer lists, including the Master List, display the name (AppleShare name), currently active application, current user, current ARD status, and IP address of each workstation. If no AppleShare name is assigned to a workstation the DNS name or IP address of the workstation will be displayed in the Name column. You can sort the list based on any of these columns. Also, a status icon is displayed next to each workstations name so that you can quickly assess its status.

Remote Management Tasks

Now that you've got an idea of how ARD functions and how to deploy and configure it, let's look at some of the tasks you can actually do with it. This section discusses each of the management tasks and commands that can be performed on workstations using Remote Desktop. Refer to Table 29-1 for information on which ARD privileges are required to use each command.

Observe

The Observe command allows you to view the screen of one or more workstations. Depending on your ARD client settings, users may or may not be aware when you are observing them. To observe a workstation or multiple workstations, select it/them in a computer list and click the Observe button in the toolbar or select Observe from the Interact menu.

When you observe a single workstation, its screen is displayed in a window, scaled down to fit if need be. As you can see in Figure 29-9, this window includes a toolbar with four buttons and a slider. The slider determines the color depth at which you view the screen (greater color depth requires more network bandwidth and can result in slower performance as the screen is redrawn). The buttons are, in order from left to right:

- Toggle between Observe and Control of the workstation (blue indicates that you are in Control mode).

- Toggle between sharing control of the keyboard and mouse with the user at the workstation (blue indicates you are sharing controls, gray indicates that the user has no control). This feature is active only when you are in Control mode.

- Toggle between fit-to-window and actual resolution of the workstation's display. If you are viewing a workstation display at actual size, and the workstation's screen resolution is larger than that of the administrator computer, the display shifts to match your cursor position and scrollbars are displayed.

- Take a screenshot of the workstation display. You are presented with a standard Save dialog for the screenshot.

Figure 29-9. A typical Observe/Control window.

You can observe multiple workstations at once. If you observe multiple computers, their are be scaled down to fit on pages of the Observe window. You can specify the number of screens displayed on a single page in the Remote Desktop preferences. If there are multiple pages, the Observe window cycles through all the screens.

The toolbar is somewhat different when observing multiple workstations. It includes a slider that enables you to determine how quickly the pages are cycled (the default being every thirty seconds) and size of the displayed screens (which in turn affects the number displayed on each page). Page backward and forward buttons are included at the left edge of the toolbar, like those in a web browser, and these enable you to manually scroll through multiple pages. To the right of these are buttons to observe a single workstation, to control a single workstation, to send a message to selected workstations, and to initiate a chat with the user of a single workstation. These buttons mimic those of the main Remote Desktop window and apply to whichever workstation (or workstations, in the case of the send message button) are selected in the observe display. Additionally, you can select an observed workstation or multiple workstations and use the commands from any of the ARD menus in the same way that you would if the workstations were selected in a computer list.

Control

The Control command functions much like the Observe command, the difference being that the Control command gives you the ability to interact with a workstation as though you were the user sitting in front of it. You can choose to either share control of the keyboard and mouse with a user at the workstation or to maintain control: the user will be able to move the pointer by using the mouse but will not be able to select or click on items and the computer will not respond to the user's keyboard input. This option is set in the Remote Desktop preferences but can also be toggled while controlling a workstation, as described earlier.

To control a workstation, select it in a computer list and click the control button the toolbar or select Control from the Interact menu. You can also toggle between Observe and Control when observing a single workstation and can control a workstation by selecting it and clicking the Control button (or by using the Control command in the Interact menu) in the Observe window when observing multiple workstations. You can control multiple workstations at one time, though each will be displayed separately. The window displaying controlled workstations is identical to the window displaying a single observed workstation.

When controlling, all keyboard input will be directed to the controlled computer while its window is the active window. Mouse input will be directed when the pointer is located within the window—notice that it reduces to match the screen size if the screen is scaled to fit the window. Keyboard and mouse activity is encrypted during transmission for security purposes. The following key combinations will affect the local workstation, regardless of ARD client control status:

- Shift-⌘-Tab (application switching)
- Option-⌘--D (show/hide the Dock)
- Shift-⌘-Q (logout)
- Shift-⌘-3, Shift-⌘-4 (take screenshots)
- Option-⌘-Escape (force quit)
- Volume, Screen Brightness, and Eject keys

Share Screen

The Share Screen command acts as a presentation tool, completely overriding the display generated by a workstation with the display of another workstation. In some ways, this is the opposite of the Observe command, as it displays a screen to the client workstation, although it does so at full screen rather than within a window; the shared display will be scaled to fit, if needed. You can select to share the screen of the computer running Remote Desktop or of any workstation that you can observe. Users viewing the shared screen will not be able to interact with it.

To use the Share Screen command, select the workstations to which you want to project the shared screen from a computer lists and click the Share Screen button in the toolbar or select Share Screen from the Interact menu. In the Share Screen dialog, you will be asked to choose between Share Your Screen and Share Other Screen. Selecting the former displays the screen of the computer running Remote Desktop. If you select the latter, you will need to drag a computer from a computer list, observe window, or report into the dialog. An Active Shared Screen Tasks window appears. You can use this command in multiple instances at a time, each with a different set of target workstations, and each instance is displayed in this window. To stop screen sharing, select the appropriate line in the Active Shared Screen Tasks window and click Stop. Each instance will also have its own task window, which can be used to stop screen sharing.

Send Message

The Send Message command does exactly what its name implies: it sends a single message to the user logged into the selected workstation(s). The message is displayed as an alert and includes the name of the user who sent the message and the name of the computer from which it was sent. The command is useful to send basic messages to users, such as those indicating that they may be logged off, that a computer lab will be closing, or to provide general information like a status update of network problems.

To use the Send Message command, select the workstation(s) to which you want to send the message in a computer list or multiple Observe window and either click the Send Message button in the toolbar or select Send Message from the Interact menu. In the resulting dialog box, enter the text of the message and click the Send button.

Chat

The Chat command initiates a text-based chat with the user of a workstation. Each chat can consist of only the Remote Desktop administrator and a single user. Users will see text as it is typed (not after the Return key is pressed). Chat can be used for interactive troubleshooting or other real-time, two-way communication. The ARD administrator will need to terminate the chat as users cannot close or minimize ARD chat windows.

To use the Chat command select a workstation in a computer list and select the Chat command from the Interact menu. You can also initiate a chat by selecting a workstation display in a multiple Observe window and either clicking the Chat button in the window's toolbar or selecting the Chat command from the Interact menu.

Lock/Unlock Screen

The Lock Screen command prevents user access to a workstation. While the screen is locked, users will be unable to interact with the workstation, but any user that was previously accessing it will not be logged out. Likewise, this command will override a workstation's screensaver settings (but not its Energy Saver settings for automatic screen dimming, sleep, or shutdown). You will not be able to control a workstation if the screen has been locked.

While the screen is locked, a picture of a padlock is displayed along with the words Screen Locked By and the name of the administrator who issued the command and (optionally) a message entered when the screen was locked. You can place a custom locked screen picture (instead of the default padlock) on a workstation by replacing the file named "Lock Screen Picture" in the */Library/Preference* directory at the root level of each workstation's hard drive with a QuickTime compatible image format (PICT, JPEG, GIF, TIFF, and so on). The image you use should be large enough to cover the entire screen at the display's maximum resolution (it is scaled to fit smaller resolutions) and should also be named "Lock Screen Picture."

To issue the Lock Screen command, select the appropriate workstation(s) in a computer list and click the Lock Screen button in the toolbar or select the Lock Screen from the Interact menu (or use the ⌘-L key combination). You can also issue this command after selecting the appropriate workstation(s) in a multiple observe window. To unlock the screen of a workstation, select it and then select Unlock Screen from the Interact menu (or use the ⌘-U key combination).

Copy Items

The Copy Items command allows you to transfer items (documents, folders, configuration files, applications that don't require installers, and so on.) to workstations. You can copy multiple items at once or individual items. You can copy the items to one or more workstations and you can specify where on the target workstations they are placed. You can also specify whether the items should be opened or launched once the copy process is completed. Copying can occur regardless of whether a user is logged in at the workstation (though mass copying and deployment of configuration files or applications should be done while users are not logged in).

To copy items, select the target workstation(s) in a computer list and then click the Copy Items button in the toolbar or select Copy Items from the Manage menu. You can also use the menu command after selecting workstations in a multiple observe window or can copy files to a single workstation by dragging the items you want to copy from the Finder onto that workstation's icon in a computer list.

All of these actions will bring up the Copy Items dialog. The dialog contains an Items to Copy listbox. You can drag items into this listbox from the Finder or the Add button next to it to use an Open dialog to locate items. You can remove items from the listbox by selecting them and clicking the Remove button. If you initiated the Copy Items dialog by dragging items from the Finder onto a workstation in a computer list, those items will already be listed.

The Place Items In pop-up menu allows you specify where the copied items will be placed on the target workstations. The options in this pop-up menu include:

- Same Relative Location
- Applications Folder
- Current User's Desktop Folder
- Current User's Home Directory
- Fonts Folder
- Preferences Folder
- System Folder
- Top folder of the disk
- Specify Full Path

There is also a pop-up menu to specify what to do if an item with the same name exists in the location to which you are copying. You can select to have Remote Desktop ask you whether to overwrite the existing file(s) on an item-by-item basis or to automatically overwrite any existing files. There is also a checkbox to open the copied items as soon as the copy operation completes (which is useful for nonpackage install programs).

Install Packages

The Install Packages command allows you to install applications and updates that use package or metapackage files. You can issue this command for one or more workstations. This provides an excellent method for installing software and for applying software updates across your network. You can use the command to install multiple packages at once, one being installed right after the other. The Install Packages command copies each selected package and installs it before copying the next. The one limitation is that it does not issue restart commands for any packages that require restarts after installation, though you can use ARD to issue a restart of all workstations on which such packages are installed.

To use the Install Packages command, first select the appropriate workstation(s) in a computer list and then click the Install Packages button or select Install Packages from the Manage menu. You can also drag a package's icon from the Finder into the Remote Desktop window. Each method brings up the Install Packages dialog, which contains a Packages listbox. Either drag packages from the finder into the listbox or use the Add button to browse for them using an Open dialog. Select packages in the listbox and click the Remove button to remove them from the list of packages to be installed. Click the Install button to begin installing packages.

A task status window displays the install progress. Once a package has begun copying and installing, there is no way to stop the install process for that package. You can click the Stop button to stop additional packages from copying and installing. For packages and metapackages with interactive options, the default options will be selected.

Upgrade Client Software

The Upgrade Client Software command updates the ARD client software on selected workstations to match the version of Remote Desktop installed on the administrator computer. It does not change any client settings and the target workstation(s) must already be configured to accept ARD management. To use this command, select one or more workstations and then select Upgrade Client Software from the Manage menu.

Send Unix Command

The Send Unix Command feature does exactly what it says: it sends a Unix command (or a series of commands or a shell script) to the selected workstation(s). This command is processed by the bash shell: you cannot specify other Unix shells. You can select to run the command as the user currently logged in at the workstation or you can specify the short name of another user. To send a Unix command via ARD, select the appropriate workstation(s) and either click the Send Unix Command button or select Send Unix Command from the Manage menu. In the resulting dialog, enter the command or script and choose whether to send the command as the current user or as a specific user.

This provides a more secure method of sending commands than SSH, as it allows you to keep SSH access to workstations disabled. It also presents an interface that may be more convenient to use for commands than actually using SSH, though it does not offer an interactive session as SSH does.

Open Application/Open Items

The Open Application and Open Items commands are pretty much the same, except that one applies to launching applications while the other applies to open nonapplication items (such as folders or files). They can both be issued to one or more workstations by selecting the target workstation(s) in a computer list and selecting either Open Applications or Open Items in the Manage menu. Both commands use an identical dialog box that contains a listbox where you specify the application(s) or items to be opened (either by dragging them to the listbox or by using the Add button). These commands require that the selected items exist in the same relative location on the selected workstation(s) as they do on the administrator computer.

Empty Trash

The Empty Trash command can be issued for one or more workstations by selecting them in a computer list and selecting Empty Trash from the Manage menu. As you might expect, this command empties the trash folders for the local disks connected to the selected workstation(s). It does not affect the trash folders for home directories of network user accounts.

Set Startup Disk

The Set Startup Disk command allows you designate whether a workstation should start up from a local hard drive or a NetBoot server. You use this command by selecting the appropriate workstation(s) in a computer list and clicking the Set Startup Disk button or selecting Set Startup Disk from the Manage menu.

Once you select the Set Startup Disk command, a dialog will display all NetBoot and NetInstall images on the same subnet as the administrator computer. If this is on a different subnet from the workstations being managed, you can select Custom Volume/Custom Server in the available volumes list and then enter the IP address or DNS name of the NetBoot server and name of a NetBoot image on that server. You can also select the local hard drive as the startup disk; if there are multiple hard drives or partitions, you can specify the volume name of a specific hard drive.

This command is particularly helpful in configuring workstations to boot from a NetInstall image to deploy a new disk image or install new software as described in the previous chapter (particularly if the image is configured for an unattended installation). Once the workstation(s) have finished the NetInstall process, you can then use Remote Desktop to make any further configuration needed to those workstations (such as setting unique AppleShare and Rendezvous names), provided the current ARD client software is included in the NetInstall image and is configured properly.

Rename Computer

This command changes the AppleShare name for a workstation. It does not, however, affect the Rendezvous name. To use it select the appropriate workstation and select the Rename Computer from the Manage menu. If you select multiple workstations, you can append a number to each successive workstation (PowerMac1, PowerMac2, PowerMac3, and so on).

Sleep/Wake/Restart/Shut Down/Log Out Current User

These commands are pretty self-explanatory. Selecting one or more workstations in a computer list and then using each of these commands will put the workstation into sleep mode, wake it from sleep mode, restart it, shut it down, or log out the current user respectively.

The Wake command requires that the computer be set to Wake for Ethernet Network Administrative Access in the Energy Saver System Preferences pane or Mac OS X–managed preferences, which is not available to some older Power Mac models. It also cannot function over AirPort.

Obviously, shutting down a workstation makes it impossible to access it remotely using ARD (though workstations could be set to power on at a specific time using the Energy Saver System Preference pane or Mac OS X–managed preferences and then be shut down using ARD on a daily basis). For Restart, Shut Down, and Log Out Current User, you will be given a dialog allowing you to select whether to allow a logged-in user to save open files or cancel the command. It is a good practice to inform users who are logged in that you will be shutting down, restarting, or sleeping before you do so by using the Send Message or Chat commands.

Change Client Settings

The Change Client Settings command brings up the same Assistant used in creating custom install packages. This allows you to change any or all of the ARD client settings for one or more workstations. To use the command, select the appropriate workstation(s) in a computer list and then select Change Client Settings from the Manage menu. Use the assistant in the same manner you would to configure a custom install package.

Get Info

The Get Info command displays the following information about a selected workstation in a separate window: IP address, DNS name (if entered), Ethernet ID (the MAC address of the Ethernet port or AirPort card through which Remote Desktop is communicating with the workstation), Last Activity (the last interaction you made with the workstation), Last Contacted (the last communication between Remote

Desktop and the workstation), and the username of the account with which you authenticated to the workstation.

By default, the Get Info command is accessed when you double-click on a workstation in a computer list or the Scanner. You can also use it by selecting workstations and clicking the Get Info button in the toolbar or selecting Get Info from the Edit menu. Any user can use the Get Info command.

You can use the Edit button in the Get Info window to change the data in the IP address and DNS fields for a workstation though changing this will likely cause communication with the workstation to fail if the actual IP address and DNS name have not been changed as well and to enter a different username and password for the workstation, thus authenticating you as a different user.

User Messages

If you configure the ARD client settings of a workstation to show the ARD menu icon in the menubar, users will be able to click on that menu and see whether any ARD administrators currently have the Remote Desktop application open and configured to access that workstation (regardless of whether they are actively observing it). The menu will display No Administrator if none is available and Ready Mode if one or more are available. It will also display Observed mode if the computer is being observed (in addition to the change in menu icon) or Assisted mode or Controlled mode if an administrator is controlling the workstation by sharing mouse and keyboard access or assuming total control respectively. If, however, you have configured the ARD client settings to not show when the workstation is being observed, the item will display only Ready Mode or No Administrator.

Users will also be able to select the Message to Administrator command from that menu. This command allows users to enter a short text message that will be displayed on the administrator computer. This feature can be used as a help desk tool, allowing users to report problems to support staff, or as an educational tool, allowing student to request help or information from an instructor in a computer lab. The message dialog allows users to select an administrator computer by AppleShare name from a Send Message To pop-up menu, if more than one administrator computer is available, as well as to enter the text of the message. Users may cancel a message after sending it using the Cancel Message command (which replaces the Message to Administrator command), although an administrator may have seen the message before it is canceled.

When an administrator computer receives a user message, Remote Desktop displays an orange icon shaped like a speech bubble as the workstation's status icon in computer lists. It will also display the Messages From Users window (shown in Figure 29-10), which displays a listbox of all messages from all workstations. If the entire message does not fit in the listbox, it can be viewed by selecting it and clicking the Display button. The message can be cleared from the display and the icon from the computer list by selecting it and clicking the Clear button. If Remote Desktop is not the frontmost application when a message is received, its icon bounces in the Dock to alert you of the message. If you do not immediately see the Messages From Users window, you can display it using the Windows menu.

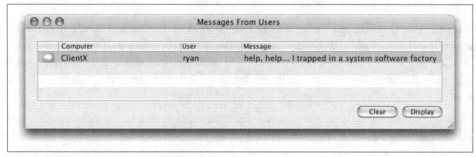

Figure 29-10. The Messages From Users window.

Generating Client Reports

One of Remote Desktop's most powerful features is its ability to query workstations for specific pieces of information, to maintain a database of that information, and to generate reports based on it. If you have only Mac OS X workstations configured with ARD, you can actually use this database as a complete inventory management solution. You can also pull data from it and export it into an external database. Beyond inventory, ARD reports can be used for troubleshooting, locating files on workstations across your network, determining the exact configuration and state of every ARD-enabled workstation, and even to evaluate network performance.

Where Report Data Is Stored

ARD stores report data on administrator computers in a PostgreSQL database. This databases is created in the */var/db/RemoteManagement/RMDB* directory, which cannot typically be accessed from the Finder, but can be accessed by Unix tools from the command line. By default, each ARD administrator computer maintains its own reports database. However, you can configure an administrator computer to share access to its database with other administrator computers. You can then configure Remote Desktop on other administrator computers to access this shared database rather than the local database created when the ARD administration software was installed. Both options are configured using the Data Collection tab in the Remote Desktop Preferences.

The Data Collection tab contains radio buttons for determining whether data for reports should be collected from the local database or from that of another administrator computer. If you select the latter, you will need to enter the IP address or DNS name of the administrator computer to use. There is also a checkbox to Allow Others to Use This Computer to Collect Data to Generate Reports, which makes report data available to other administrator computers.

When Data Is Collected for Reports

When you run a report in Remote Desktop, you can select to whether you wish to use new or saved data. If you select to use new data, Remote Desktop queries each selected workstation for the requested pieces of information. Depending on the data you are requesting, the number of workstations, and your network configuration and activity, it can take a significant amount of time to generate reports using new data. Depending on what data you request, you may also cause performance on the selected workstations to decrease as the computer processes the request and locates the data; this is particularly true for any file or software search or software comparison report. When the computers respond with the new data, it is added to the ARD database.

Generating a report with saved data uses the most recent information already in the ARD database. This is much faster as Remote Desktop needs to query only the local database for information (or the database on a remote administrator computer). As long as the requested data already exists in the database, individual workstations do not need to be queried. If the required data is not in the database, then the workstations will be queried for it (and it will be added to the database once they respond). When you generate a report using saved data, you can specify an age limit for the data (such as 24 hours or one week). If the requested data in the ARD database is older than that, the workstation(s) will be queried for current data.

Configuring a Data Reporting Policy

Obviously, data needs to exist in the ARD database in order to run reports based on saved data. Otherwise a saved data report is no different than a new data report. In order to ensure that saved data exists in the database, you can configure a data reporting policy for workstations. A reporting policy tells the ARD client on the workstation to compile data for reports and upload it to the administrator computer on a regular basis. This ensures that saved data exists for generating reports. It also creates a limit on how old saved data will be, though you may still want to require more recent data for some reports. The reporting policy you configure stores data in the local ARD database or in the database of the administrator computer designated in the Remote Desktop preferences.

To configure a reporting policy, first select the workstations that you want the policy to affect and select Set Reporting Policy from the Manage menu. You can set different policies for different workstations, depending on considerations such as how often you expect to need data, how often such data changes for a group of work-stations, and the speed of the network connections between workstations and the administrator computer that will be storing the data. You will need to balance the age of data against the bandwidth and performance hits required for updates.

Select the "On a schedule" radio button in the Set Reporting Policy dialog, shown in Figure 29-11, and either select to update data every day or enter a repeating schedule of specific days and times. You should choose a time when network activity is low but when all workstations are likely to be powered on. You can also designate that if there is existing data in the database of a certain age (that is, recent data required for a new data report) that workstations skip the upload until the next interval.

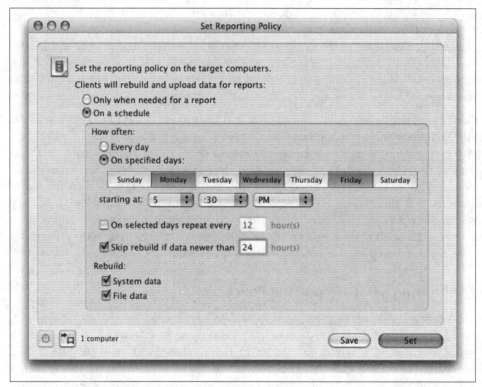

Figure 29-11. The Set Reporting Policy dialog box.

You can also select to enforce the reporting policy for system data, file data, or both. System data contains information about the configuration of a workstation and includes all information needed for complete System Overview, Storage, USB Devices, Firewire Devices, Network Interfaces, Memory and PCI Cards reports. File data contains information about files, applications, and other items stored on a workstation's hard drive and includes information used in File Search, Software Version, and Software Difference reports. System data often changes less frequently than file data and you can often run such reports with saved data rather than new data. File data changes more frequently and often requires newer saved data or new data for accuracy. You can create separate report policies for workstations with regards to system data and file data.

Running, Viewing, and Exporting Reports

To run any report in Remote Desktop, select the workstations for which you wish to generate the report from a computer list. Then select the report type from the Reports menu. For most reports, you will be able select the exact pieces of information that you want from the data that can be contained in the report type. You will also be able to designate whether the report should be run using saved data, new data, or to specify that new data should be used only if the saved data is older than a specific amount of time. You can also schedule reports to run at set times or repeating intervals.

A task window will display the progress of the report (it also appears in the Recent Tasks listbox). You can cancel the report using this window. Once all the data has been collected and compiled, the report will be displayed in a separate report window, similar to the System Overview report shown in Figure 29-12. Each piece of data that you requested will be displayed in a column in the report. You can drag the columns to change the order they are displayed in and you can sort the list ascending or descending based on each column.

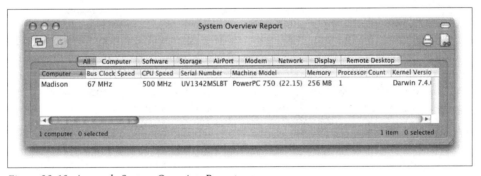

Figure 29-12. A sample System Overview Report.

You can export a report as tab- or comma-delimited text by selecting Export Window from the File menu. You can choose a character encoding for the text of the report (the default, Western-Mac OS Roman is appropriate for most purposes, but you can select one of two Unicode options if you need to work with the data in non–Roman character languages) and whether the fields of the report will be comma- or text-delimited. You can use the resulting text file to import the data from the report into an alternative spreadsheet or database application. This feature can be particularly helpful if you use an inventory management tool.

Types of Reports

The following sections describe the various types of reports that are built into Remote Desktop and the data that can be included in them. As I mentioned, you can choose to include only specific pieces of data when generating a report. You can use these reports for inventory management, verifying workstation configuration, software version compliance, and a number of other purposes.

System overview

The System Overview report allows you to generate a comprehensive report about the hardware and operating system configuration and status of each selected workstation. You can select from nearly 100 possible characteristics across 13 general areas for a customized report or generate a standard System Overview report with the following information: AppleShare name, motherboard bus speed, processor speed and type, serial number, number of installed processors, Mac model, total hard drive space, available hard drive space, amount of space used for files in the trash, whether an AirPort card is installed and/or active, whether a modem is installed, the modem model (if appropriate), the MAC addresses of primary Ethernet card and AirPort card (if installed), the monitor color depth and resolution, the monitor model, and the four administrator-definable fields available in the ARD client's System Preferences pane.

File search

The File Search report functions similarly to the Finder's Find File command. It allows you to search for items located on ARD client workstations. The existence and location of these items can be displayed in the report. You can search based on name, parent or full path to the item, file extension, size, kind, date created or modified, version, owner, assigned group, and locked status or any combination of the above. You can search only for items that are visible in the Finder.

Apple claims that the File Search report can locate up 32,000 items across the local drives of any selected workstations. This might sound like a large number, but if you enter vague search request information and select more than a few workstations, you can easily generate thousands or tens of thousands of results. Because this information is being culled from multiple computers and collected over a network, a report with such large results can take significant time and resources to compile. Therefore, I suggest using this report sparingly and making your search criteria as specific as possible.

Software version

The Software Version report allows you to specify up to 10 applications on the administrator computer that are also installed on the selected workstations. The report will indicate the version of the application installed on the administrator computer and on the remote computer and the difference between them, if any. This makes it a good tool for software version compliance, as well as for planning of new software updates or deployments. It also displays the path to the location where the application is installed. You cannot include command line tools or unbundled Java applications (*.jar* files) in this report.

Software difference

The Software Difference report allows you compare the applications, fonts, other package files (you can select to include one, two, or all three of these) installed on the selected workstations compared to the administrator computer. It does not specify the version of an application is installed. Packages can be used to identify which package-install-based applications have been installed as well as which software updates have been installed. Packages are listed regardless of whether they were installed manually, by using Software Update, or as part of a Mac OS X installation.

Storage

The Storage report offers much more detailed information about the hard drives and other fixed storage devices that are installed in or connected to a workstation. The Storage report can contain information about each installed hard drive, including model, manufacturer, and serial number; each local volume (RAID array, partition, or entire hard drive), including creation date, volume name, file and folder counts, free space, whether the volume is a startup disk, the total volume capacity, and Unix mount point; the filesystem of each volume, including disk format, permission information, most recent modification, owner and other information; and backup options that describe whether volumes are journaled and the last time they were backed up using a standard backup tool.

USB devices

The USB Devices report provides information about all USB devices connected to a workstation and, for each device, can include the product and vendor (manufacturer) name and/or ID, the device speed, whether it is powered by the USB bus or has its own power supply, and serial number.

FireWire devices

Like the USB Devices report, the FireWire Devices report provides information about all FireWire peripherals connected to a workstation and, for each device, can include: the device speed, software version, manufacturer and model, and firmware version.

Memory

The Memory report provides more detailed information about the RAM installed in workstation than is available in the System Overview report. It includes the location (RAM slot), size, speed, and type of RAM for each installed DIMM. Speed of individual modules can be reported only by Mac OS X 10.3 clients.

PCI cards

The PCI Cards report provides greater detail about installed PCI cards than the System Overview report, which can identify only the number of used and available PCI slots). The PCI Cards report can include the name of each PCI slot, the type of card installed in it, the model name of the card, the vendor and device ID associated with each card, and the card's revision number. It can also include the ROM version and installed VRAM for video cards. Be aware that AGP cards are identified as a type of PCI card.

Network interfaces

The Network Interfaces report allows you to retrieve all manner of network hardware and configuration information about a workstation, including information about each network port (active and inactive) and the IP address and configuration of each active port. It also allows you retrieve network statistics about the workstation, its connectivity, and the performance of the network segment(s) to which it is connected.

Network test

The Network Test report is more or less an advanced GUI for using the ping command with selected workstations. It allows you to specify a number of packets to be sent to each workstation, the interval at which they are sent, and a response time beyond which the packets will be considered lost. By comparing the results from varying workstations and varying network segments, you can use this data to examine performance across your entire network and to locate network breaks.

Administration settings

The Administration Settings report can display information about the ARD client settings of selected workstations. It can display the available privileges for the user running Remote Desktop, the reporting policy, and general information, including the ARD client version installed on the workstation and when it was last accessed.

Automating Remote Desktop Using the Saved Tasks List

Included in the lists column is the Saved Tasks list. This is not a computer list or Scanner. It is a list that stores and displays all scheduled tasks that you create. Remote Desktop allows you to schedule any command or report. You can schedule them to occur once or on a repeating interval. This feature allows you to automate virtually every capability offered by ARD, from sending messages to users to shutting down workstations, copying files, and generating daily computer configuration reports. The only limitation is that the Remote Desktop application must be running at each scheduled time in order to execute scheduled tasks.

Schedule commands in the same way that you execute them (we'll talk about how to use each command in a just a bit), generally by selecting the appropriate workstation(s) and then selecting the command from a menu or a toolbar. For almost all commands and reports, this action displays a dialog specific to the command or report. At the lower-left hand of each command or report dialog you will see two buttons, one with an icon like an alarm clock and one with an icon like a computer. The button with a clock icon is the schedule button. Clicking it allows you to schedule the command or report that you are configuring, as shown in Figure 29-13. Once the task is scheduled, the icon will change to look like the alarm clock is ringing to indicate the task is scheduled.

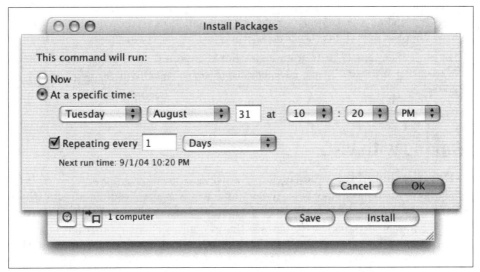

Figure 29-13. The Schedule Task dialog box.

The button with the icon of a computer displays a drawer to the side of the dialog listing all the workstations that the command or report will be applied to. You can drag additional workstations from any computer list to this drawer to include them in the command or report. You can also select them in the list and click the Remove button in the drawer to remove them from the command or report.

Once you have set the schedule (and modified the selected workstation list, if you so choose), you can click the Save button to store the task and its schedule. You will also be asked to name the task, so that you can easily recognize it in the Saved Tasks list. You can then view the task in the Saved Tasks list. You can also add tasks to the Saved Tasks list by dragging them from the Recent Tasks listbox into the Saved Tasks list and then entering the schedule information and a name for the task.

You can run a Saved task manually at any time by selecting it in the Saved Tasks list and selecting Run from the Tasks menu. You can also rename a task by double-clicking its name in the list and duplicate a task by selecting it and then choosing Duplicate Task from the Tasks menu. You can edit any aspect of a Saved Task by double-clicking any part of it except the name in the Saved Tasks list or by selecting it and choosing Edit Task from the Tasks menu.

GUI Scripting for Additional Automation

Unfortunately, the Remote Desktop application is not scriptable using AppleScript. However, Apple has developed a technique called GUI Scripting that allows non-scriptable applications to be referenced in and controlled by AppleScript. This technique can be used to automate many of the commands available within Remote Desktop. You can find more information about GUI scripting, along the required tools and basic sample scripts at *http://www.apple.com/applescript/uiscripting/*.

For more information, or to learn about AppleScript, see *AppleScript: The Missing Manual* (Pogue Press/O'Reilly, 2005) and *AppleScript: The Definitive Guide* (O'Reilly, 2003).

Working with VNC

VNC is a multiplatform protocol for remotely controlling computers. It is commonly used for remote access to servers and to configure headless servers (those without a monitor or keyboard). VNC's capability effectively mirrors that of ARD's Control command (though VNC always shares control of the mouse and keyboard with a local user). Because VNC tools exist for virtual all current computer platforms and are interoperable across platforms, VNC has become ubiquitous in the IT industry. As such, Apple has built interoperability with VNC tools into ARD.

In order for a workstation to be controlled by VNC, a VNC server must be installed on it. The ARD client can act as a VNC server. To control a computer that has a VNC server installed on it, you must use a VNC viewer. The Remote Desktop application can function as a VNC viewer. However, you should be aware that VNC is not as secure as ARD. Although it can encrypt passwords, it does not encrypt keystrokes, mouse movement, or other data as it is transmitted between computers.

Configuring the ARD Client as a VNC Server

You can configure any workstation that has the ARD client software (version 2.0 or higher) installed to function as a VNC server, allowing users of VNC viewers to control the workstation remotely. This can be done manually on the workstation, by using a custom installer package, or Remote Desktop Change Client Settings command. Configuring a client to allow access by VNC viewers is as simple as selecting the appropriate checkbox and entering a VNC password.

VNC servers (including the ARD client) rely solely on the VNC password to allow VNC control of a workstation. Therefore, you should use a password that is unique (not used for a local user account, the Remote Desktop application, or to other sensitive accounts within your network) and secure (more than eight alphanumeric characters of both cases). You should, however, avoid using special punctuation characters, as all VNC viewers may not support these across computing platforms.

Configure Remote Desktop as a VNC Viewer

The Remote Desktop application can observe and control computers configured with a VNC server in much the same way that it controls and observes ARD client workstations. VNC computers can be added to the Master List and any other computer lists that you create. To add a VNC workstation to a Remote Desktop configuration, select the Scanner, choose Network Address from the Scanner's pop-up menu, and enter the IP address or DNS name of the VNC computer. When you attempt to add the computer to the Master List or another computer list, you will be asked to enter the VNC password for the computer. The ARD version field in the Scanner and computer lists for VNC workstations will be displayed as VNC. VNC access to a workstation will support only the Remote Desktop Control command.

Introduction to Directory Services

Traditional Unix titles have never had to focus much on the mechanisms behind the management of users and groups. At most, a couple of paragraphs could explain the format of the */etc/passwd* file and whatever password-shadowing mechanism the operating system in question used. Previous to Panther, Mac OS X, for the most part (like its less widely adopted ancestor OPENSTEP) simply added one more dimension; one that was fairly easy to get used to. Instead of */etc/passwd*, a database called NetInfo was utilized. Between NetInfo and the flat files in */etc*, there was pretty much a one-to-one relationship—*/etc/passwd* equated to *netinfo://users*; */etc/group* to *netinfo://groups*, and */etc/services* to *netinfo://services*, etc. And passwords weren't shadowed; they were (in most cases) stored using a one-way DES hash in the world-readable NetInfo database.

> Mac OS X Server 10.2 introduced *PasswordServer*, a method of securely storing authentication data in order to support several relatively secure network authentication mechanisms. It was optional, however, and limited in scope to Mac OS X Server. Password Server is covered in more depth in Chapter 8.

That was pretty much it. Of course the tools for manipulation of NetInfo-based data differed somewhat from those used to manage flat files in */etc*. But the concepts were largely the same.

In recent years, though, IT and the way that IT organizations deal with users, groups and other administrative data has changed markedly. Workgroup management has become centralized, so that user accounts and authentication data are managed on a server, rather than individually on each workstation. This concept, commonly called a *directory service*, or a *domain*, was first commercialized in the desktop market by Novell and later embraced by Microsoft.

In fact, NetInfo, could also be distributed across a network, and used to centralize management of user, group, and other administrative data. OPENSTEP and NeXT, however, had a limited enough installed base (in comparison to NDS and NT Domains) that it can't really lay claim to the vast commercial acceptance directories have enjoyed.

Directory Domains fit nicely with the ongoing trend of centralization in the IT industry, and have been widely adopted. Vendors from Microsoft to Apple to Novell to Sun have brought forward a number of directory products. Directories are so important to Mac OS X (we've already touched on them briefly in Chapter 2, when we discussed Server Auto Configuration) that I've decided to include this introduction chapter relatively early—before, even, our discussion of Mac OS X Server's Administration Tools. This is primarily due to the fact that those tools (particularly Workgroup Manager) assume and understanding of what a Directory Domain (or node) actually is. Before an analysis at that level begins, however, it is useful to examine the security model on which Apple's Directory Services infrastructure is based.

Identification, Authentication, and Authorization

One of the recurring themes in Mac OS X is also a fundamental principle of Unix architectures: many small, modular processes exist in order to support and provide services to other processes, building on one another and working together to form the systems that serve as the building blocks of the OS. Eventually, a cohesive whole, hopefully greater than the sum of its parts, is available to support the end user's computing needs. Open Directory—Apple's Directory Services architecture—exists both in its client and server flavors as one of those building blocks, serving both to *identify* and *authenticate* users. In a multiple-user operating system, these two distinct concepts are vital in order to support the security and integrity of the computing environment. They are core structures that work together to ensure users access only the resources for which they are *authorized*.

This three-tiered security model isn't specific to computing architectures, or even to technology. It is, instead, a widely implemented set of principals applied towards the construction of secure systems of any type. This is easily seen in the example of the modern airport.

The Airport Example

Any frequent traveler will bear witness to the fact that access to air travel is not as simple as showing up at the airport. Great care is taken to assure that only authorized passengers board commercial aircraft, and that they do so in a safe and secure manner. While attempting too literal of an analogy is spurious and bound to failure—physical security simply has requirements that differ from information technology—this system bears many similarities to those that protect OS resources.

The passenger is first identified, usually by supplying their name to an agent, or by sliding a credit card through an automated check in machine. This *identification* is important because it is the basis for all other resource access. Unless we know who is attempting to access a specific resource (in this case a commercial flight), we cannot determine whether they are authorized to do so. That *authorization* is the next step—the agent (or the automated terminal) then checks for that record in the airline's database, determining whether the user in question should be allowed to board the plane. Optionally, in the case of an agent-assisted check-in, the user also undergoes preliminary *authentication* (they prove that they are who they say they are) by supplying some sort of ID.

There are some subtleties here that should be illustrated, since they also occur in the development of secure IT infrastructures. First of all, notice that in this case, identification and authorization are actually performed by the same system (the airline, in the form of the agent or automated terminal), making them indistinguishable to the end user. This is often the case. A good user experience is as seamless and transparent as possible, and end users should not have to distinguish at all among identification, authorization, and authentication. Secondly, keep in mind that even though the user might have been preliminarily authenticated by the airline, they still cannot access the plane itself. That final, authoritative authentication is implemented not by the airline, but by the U.S. government; specifically, in the form of the Transportation Security Agency. This sort of distributed architecture makes a system more secure, as the compromise of one component does not imply compromise of another. This dichotomy—the construction of distributed, secure systems that are transparent and convenient and appear seamless to the end user—is a central challenge in IT.

 We'll see later that identification and authentication in Mac OS X Server are performed using separate protocols and services, and that access to one does not imply access to the other. This setup increases the overall security of Mac OS X Directory Services.

The Login Process

Mac OS X's console (local) login process is one such transparent system. To the user, logging in seems very simple: a username and password are specified, and if they're correct, the user is logged in. Once this process is complete, filesystem permissions provide a reasonable amount of certainty that the user is granted access only to resources for which they are authorized.

The process is actually much more complex. Once a username and password are entered, the OS first goes to great lengths to identify the user. Many forms of the user's identity may be used:

- Short name: johnd
- Common, or long name: John Doe
- User principal, most commonly used with Active Directory: *johnd@example.com*
- NT -style (in the case of the AD plug-in): EXAMPLE/johnd

Mac OS X uses whatever username is supplied to perform a complex set of queries that vary depending on the system's configuration. It generally tries very hard to locate a user's account based on the data entered at the login window. Once the user is located, the System can retrieve that user's record. This yields a significant amount of data about the user in the form of several *attributes*, or account details. In some cases, this includes the methods by which the user may be authenticated. This authentication metadata is stored in the AuthenticationAuthority attribute. A simple set of user record attributes is illustrated in Table A-1.

Table A-1. A simple set of user attributes. Each of these is covered in more depth later. This example is meant as an overview of the kind of data present once a user has been identified.

Attribute	Sample Value	Description
AppleMetaNodeLocation	/NetInfo/DefaultLocalNode	The directory domain in which the user is located.
AuthenticationAuthority	;ShadowHash;	Method(s) by which this user may be authenticated.
AuthenticationHint		
GeneratedUID	0FE5D62E-A5A7-11D8-B767-000A95DF2556	A record-specific identifer that is guaranteed to be unique.
NFSHomeDirectory	/Users/mbartosh	Unix path to the User's home directory.
Password	********	*crypt( )* form of user's password. Typically not used for security reasons.
Picture	/Library/User Pictures/Nature/Zen.tif	Filesystem path to user's picture.
PrimaryGroupID	501	
RealName	Michael Bartosh	The user's common name.
RecordName	Mbartosh mbartosh@example.com	The user's short name. RecordName may be multivalued; this is what determines which attributes may be used to log in.
UniqueID	501	The user's numerical identifier. This integer is vital to the Mac OS X user experience. The system uses it (rather than the user's name) to keep track of file and process ownership and permissions.
UserShell	/bin/bash	The shell the user will use when they log in via the command line.

If an `AuthenticationAuthority` attribute exists, the method(s) it specifies are finally used to authenticate the user. Users can be authenticated in many ways, and a thorough discussion of all of these client-side systems is beyond the scope of a Mac OS X Server title, so at this point we'll use the rather nebulous language inherent in the statement "The user is then authenticated."

 Not all user records contain an `AuthenticationAuthority`. If the `AuthenticationAuthority` does not exist, a different set of methods are applied, beginning with any specified system-wide Kerberos configuration and ending with the traditional Unix *crypt()* verification. Somewhere in there, depending on the system's configuration, node-native methods (which are specific to the directory domains the system is configured to use) might or might not be pursued, depending on the client's configuration. This process is governed by the *SecurityServer* daemon, which serves as a centralized authorization authority in the OS.

This isn't the end of the story, however. Just because a user can supply a username and password that the OS is able to verify doesn't necessarily mean that they should be able to log in to the console of a given host. Take the example of a server, for instance. Console (*loginwindow*) access to server should generally be limited to administrators, as console users generally have a lot of access to the system that users should not have to a server. Certain types of labs commonly also meet this criteria, and are restricted to particular groups of users. This sort of authorization is often application-specific. In the case of a console login, authorization typically comes from the *SecurityServer* process (based on its database, the */etc/authorization* file) or from client management (MCX) facilities in the System. The user is logged in if identification, authentication and authorization are all successful.

/etc files: Identification, Authentication, and Authorization

In order to really understand the login process and the services behind it, it's important to have a historical perspective on traditional Unix methods of identification, authentication, and authorization. As mentioned briefly earlier, Unix variants have traditionally used */etc/passwd* and associated files for authentication and identification. Until the mid-90s, both authentication and identification data were typically stored in */etc/passwd* in a colon-delineated format, as shown in Example A-1.

Example A-1. Using the cat command to examine a user record containing a crypt hash. This method is largely no longer used, since it exposes the password hash to malicious access.

```
linuxbox:~ rhp$ cat/etc/passwd | grep apple
apple:1B.kA7xpk92ak:502:668::0:0:apple:/Users/apple:/bin/bash
```

From a security perspective, this isn't the best situation. Recall that secure architectures distribute identification and authentication to separate systems. The matter is exacerbated in this case because identification data must, for legacy architectural reasons, be world-readable in a Unix OS. This paradigm underlines another principal of good security—that the minimum feasible amount of access should be granted to any particular resource. Imposing the comparatively open access requirements of identification onto sensitive authentication data (hashed passwords) unnecessarily reduces the system's security. In order to alleviate this issue, a strategy called *password shadowing* was introduced. Shadowed passwords imply that while identification data remains available in a world-readable fashion in */etc/password*, authentication data is stored in a separate file and is available only to *root*-privileged processes.

Although NetInfo supported various forms of shadowing throughout its life, none were available consistently enough to be viable for deployment for any extended period of time. Panther's shadowing is implemented in the Open Directory abstraction layer, rather than in NetInfo itself. For more information relating to Panther's Shadow Passwords, see Chapter 2.

Authorization was another matter. Traditionally, user accounts, which could be identified and successfully authenticated, were authorized to log in locally or over any enabled network service (FTP, Telnet, SSH, and so on). This lack of granularity, like many of the less desirable aspects of Unix infrastructures, stems from a time when security was less important than it is today, and when users of any particular system could be treated with a great amount of trust. In today's world, it is highly undesirable, for instance, to allow SSH access to the tens of thousands students authorized to access a file server in a university environment. Mac OS X and other Unix variants are slowly but surely developing technologies to support the more granular levels of access required in today's security environment.

The case of SSH is actually solved, like many authorization issues, on the application level. It is trivial to limit SSH access to certain groups of users. For details, see Chapter 3.

Open Directory: The Ever-Expanding Marketecture

The earlier documentation of the login process was specifically vague, crediting the "System" with various behaviors. Prior to Mac OS X, this vagueness might have been appropriate, since the monolithic process literally called "System" seemed to attend to most OS functions. It is hopefully obvious by now, though, that Mac OS X has a specific component, called Open Directory, that manages identification and (to some extent) authentication and authorization data. Open Directory itself, though, is also a vague term, and defining it is not as easy as we'd hope. The matter is made even more confusing by a certain amount of circular naming. Open Directory, a component of Mac OS X used to talk to directory services, uses (in part) a process

Limitations of the /etc Approach

This discussion of Unix history brings us full circle. A fundamental understanding of identification, authentication, and authorization along with a historical examination of the systems traditionally employed to meet those requirements prepares us for an analysis of more modern infrastructures—directory services.

Although directories are generally applicable to a number of applications, our focus is on their role in user, group, and configuration management. Their evolution in this capacity came about primarily due to limitations of maintaining accounts in */etc* files:

Limited scalability

> As they become increasingly large, text files are hard to maintain, especially when they need to be maintained on multiple hosts. Keeping accounts on multiple servers synchronized becomes cumbersome, especially as the number of accounts increases. Adding client systems into the mix only makes the issue an order of magnitude more complex.

Limited account sophistication

> For the most part, */etc/passwd* defines a fairly minimal user account. Modern directory enabled applications demand a richer set of user and group attributes—for instance, to support managed client data, multiple authentication sources, and more robust unique identifiers.

Limited authentication support

> A corollary to */etc/paswd*'s limited account sophistication is the typically limited set of authentication options inherent to */etc* files. In most cases, one version of the user's password (historically a weak, easily compromised *crypt()* version, but more recently in some cases a more secure hash) is stored (as documented earlier) in a shadow file. These hashes, though, are not usually friendly to secure network authentication, and this "one hash" approach is not flexible enough to support the wide range of authentication mechanisms that modern infrastructures require.

On these limitations, the principles behind directories are established. There aren't a lot of hard, fast, or specific rules, though. Directories are generally very scalable over the network. They generally support fast read and search operations, while writes are a little slower. They usually (but not always) support a variety of authentication mechanisms, and they are hopefully built around standards-based protocols. They are very generally applicable to a variety of circumstances, but for our purposes aren't much more than a glorified, scalable and more fully featured replacement for */etc/passwd*. The remainder of this chapter is concerned mostly with Mac OS X's architecture for accessing their identification, authentication, and authorization data.

called *DirectoryService*, which we'll examine in some depth in the "DirectoryService configuration" section of this chapter. Add in the fact that the term Open Directory Server is used to identify certain Mac OS X Server technologies, and you've got an interesting mix of semantics. The terminology is probably more confusing than the architecture itself.

Most of the following discussion applies to Mac OS X, and is not specific to Mac OS X Server. Mac OS X Server, though, in addition to providing identification and authentication services, must also act as a client to a variety of directory services, necessitating some understanding of the Operating System's fundamental processes.

Identification, Authentication, and Authorization in Mac OS X

In general, Open Directory can be thought of as Mac OS X's Rosetta Stone. It talks to Directory Domains (both local and remote, over the network) so specific applications do not have to.

A Directory Domain, also commonly called a node, is Apple's terminology for a specific instance of a particular directory service. For instance, *example.com* is a specific instance of Active Directory. Open Directory would see *example.com* as a node, or Directory Domain, specifically in the form of */Active Directory/example.com*.

An Open Directory Server in the same domain, accessed using the LDAPv3 capabilities in Open Directory, can be though of as */LDAPv3/example.com*.

This means that *loginwindow* and *AppleFileServer*, for instance, did not have to be specifically modified when the capability to access Active Directory was added to Mac OS X. Because they reference Open Directory for identification and (in some circumstances) authentication, their access to any Directory Domain is abstracted in such a way that they do not have to care where a particular user record is coming from. This concept is illustrated in Figure A-1.

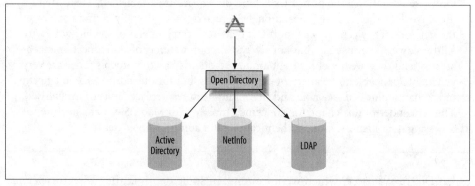

Figure A-1. Open Directory is an abstraction layer that Mac OS X uses to access identification and (in some cases) authentication and authorization data.

More specifically, this capability is provided (for the most part) by the *DirectoryService* daemon (seen in Figure A-2). Applications that are linked against the Directory Services framework send identification (and sometimes authentication) requests to *DirectoryService*, which is then responsible for servicing those requests according to its configuration, covered in more depth in "DirectoryService configuration."

 Linking against a library or framework means taking advantage of code written to provide some kind of consistent functionality. For instance, the OpenSSL library implements SSL, and is used by a number of applications so that they do not each have to roll their own SSL functions. Similarly, Open Directory centrally implements Directory Service queries.

DirectoryService also has an extensible Plug-in architecture, allowing for relatively easy access to new directories. Because the daemon itself doesn't have to be recompiled in order to add a plug-in, it has the added bonus of opening up plug-in development to third parties.

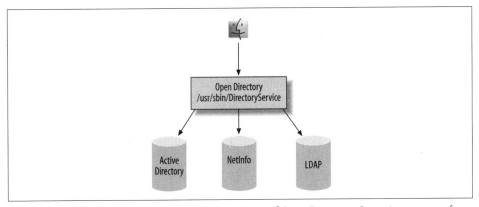

Figure A-2. The DirectoryService daemon is one aspect of Open Directory. It services requests from applications that are linked against the Directory Services APIs.

This architecture, though, is not as simple as it initially seems. Accessing data returned from one of *DirectoryService*'s plug-ins requires that the application in question be written to use the Mac OS X–specific system calls provided by the *DirectoryService* framework. This can entail a significant amount of work. Nearly every application in the system requires user identification. In fact, the bulk of Mac OS X is made up of Unix processes that share a lot of code with other operating systems (the *rm* command, for instance, uses the same code as FreeBSD's *rm*). Rewriting all of this software to support Mac OS X–specific programming conventions would be a huge undertaking and would break a lot of the synergy that comes from sharing code with other Unix variants. Due to this architectural requirement, Open

Directory makes use of a second process, called *lookupd*, to support (among other things) identification of users and groups by cross-platform Unix commands. The historical reasons behind this are helpful to the understanding of Mac OS X Server Directory Services.

A little (more) history

Yet another major principal behind Unix architectures is the idea of source-level compatibility. At some basic level, source code written on one Unix system should compile and execute on any other. While this is far from universal and cannot apply to certain OS-specific features, it is generally true. In order to support this functionality, assumptions are made about the availability of certain standard programming routines (commonly called *system calls*). These are usually supplied by a shared library called *libc*, or the Standard C library. Since the same system calls can be used on multiple operating systems, code written for one should compile on any other. Some common *libc* system calls are illustrated in Table A-2.

Table A-2. Common libc routines. These routines were chosen from among the many available in the C library for their applicability in understanding common functions of Mac OS X.

Routine	Description
gethostbyname( )	Uses a hostname to return an IP address.
getpwnam( )	Looks up a particular user's record based on the user's RecordName.
initgroups( )	Calculates group access for a particular user.

User identification is such a common need among Unix processes that several of these common, cross-platform routines exist to provide variations on that theme. Of these, *getpwnam()* (which searches for a specific user record based on the user's RecordName) and *getpwuid()* (which searches according to the user's UniqueID) are the most common. Use of the *getpwnam()* routine is shown in Example A-2.

Example A-2. This simple C utility should compile successfully on most Unix OSs, due to the common availability of the getpwnam() system call.

```
#include <stdio.h>
#include <pwd.h>
struct passwd *record;

int main (int argc, const char * argv[]) {
        record=getpwnam(argv[1]);
        printf("RecordName=%s\n", record->pw_name);
        printf("Password=%s\n", record->pw_passwd);
        printf("UniqueID=%d\n", record->pw_uid);
        printf("NFSHomeDirectory=%s\n", record->pw_dir);
return 0;
}
```

The point behind this digression is to document the fact that *lookupd* exists in order to service these *libc* system calls. Any routine in *libc* is *dispatched*, or sent, to *lookupd*, which is then responsible for answering the query. In other words, nearly all cross-platform Unix software will, for compatibility reasons, query *lookupd* rather than talking directly to the *DirectoryService* daemon. This design is slightly contentious, since *DirectoryService* is the primary mechanism by which integration with remote directories (Active Directory, Open Directory Server, and so on) is achieved. Virtually all of Mac OS X, because the amount of code shared with other Unix variants, is a client of *lookupd*. So it is important that *lookupd* has access to *DirectoryService* data if integration with these directories is going to be at all effective. To circumvent this issue, *lookupd* has been modified to act as a *DirectoryService client*, effectively proxying lookups it is not authoritative for to the *DirectoryService* daemon, as illustrated in Figure A-3. This process, along with a more thorough analysis of *lookupd*, is detailed later in the next section, "DirectoryService: lookupd evolved,"

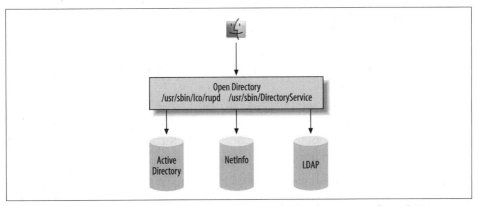

Figure A-3. Open Directory is a dual-service architecture. lookupd services traditional Unix system calls (sometimes by sending them to DirectoryService), whereas DirectoryService, the primary interface to directory domains, services applications that are linked against the Directory Services APIs.

lookupd, then, is one of the keys to source-level compatibility with other Unix variants. This makes it rather important. The reasoning behind this role rests in its history, and in the history of NeXTSTEP, Mac OS X's predecessor. When NeXT first chose to store user accounts in NetInfo (rather than the traditional Unix */etc* flat files) they realized that the capability of having multiple data stores was a good thing, as many customers might prefer to use more traditional flat files and NetInfo, as cool as it was, might be supplemented at some point by newer technologies. *lookupd* was designed as an abstraction layer, enabling the OS to perform *libc* lookups against a variety of data stores, eventually to include LDAP and Sun's NIS.

This sort of abstraction sounds very familiar. In fact, *lookupd*'s role sounds nearly identical to that of *DirectoryService*, and the fact that Apple added a second system that is so similar at first appears wasteful and overly complex. This is not the case.

lookupd, while it provided a good mechanism for *libc*-type lookups, suffers from some architectural limitations that make it less suitable in the context of modern directory services.

DirectoryService: lookupd evolved

DirectoryService, examined in greater detail later in the next section, "The Directory-Service Daemon," made its debut in Mac OS X 10.0. It was designed specifically to meet the limitations posed by *lookupd*, specifically:

lookupd has no support for authentication.

> It was designed at a time when passwords were not shadowed, and when *getpwnam()* returned an encrypted password as a part of the user record. The application in question would then perform its own authentication, encrypting the password provided by the user and comparing the result to the results returned by *getpwnam()*. As documented earlier in this appendix, this is bad security practice, because making the encrypted password available in this manner renders it vulnerable to a brute-force attack.

lookupd (like libc) is read-only.

> Modern Directory Services also support write capabilities (a read-only LDAP server is hard to imagine).

lookupd is too difficult to extend.

> Although it was designed as an abstraction mechanism and can be extended with agents, the development process proved difficult enough that none were actually developed outside of Apple.

The question most commonly asked in this context is, "Why, then, does *lookupd* still exist at all?" There are two very good answers to this question. Firstly, *DirectoryService* has no support for DNS lookups. *gethostbyname()*, a very common *libc* routine, is the primary means for host resolution in Mac OS X and most other Unix operating systems. Because *DirectoryService* is unable to service *gethostbyname()*, it cannot currently replace lookupd in its entirety. Just as importantly, making changes to *libc* is dangerous, and sometimes causes binary compatibility issues in the OS in question. Nearly every utility, daemon, and application in the OS use *libc*, calls, and changing it to all of a sudden use *DirectoryService* (rather than *lookupd*) would be a tremendously risky process.

 It is worth noting that *DirectoryService* can perform certain types of host lookups and can, therefore, support some of *gethostbyname()*'s functionality. Given the importance of DNS, however, this is a moot point.

The DirectoryService Daemon

The *DirectoryService* daemon, which lives at */usr/sbin/DirectoryService*, can be considered the heart of Open Directory—although *lookupd* serves a similar purpose, *DirectoryService* is more commonly authoritative, as it is the daemon responsible for actual communication with most directory domains.

 Astute readers will notice immediately that the *DirectoryService* daemon, and hence Open Directory, is responsible for more than just the utilization of user and group accounts and other administrative data. Open Directory also provides a system-wide contacts facility and service location (browsing) capabilities. While important, these capabilities are not central to our analysis of directory services and Mac OS X.

DirectoryService is started automatically when it is needed by the *mach_init* daemon according to the */etc/mach_init.d/DirectoryService.plist* configuration file (shown in Example A-3). This file may be modified to support *DirectoryService*'s boot-time behavior. The value of the Command key may be modified to point to a shell script instead of the *DirectoryService* daemon if there are specific environmental requirements (such as a need to delay *DirectoryService*'s startup).

Example A-3. /etc/mach_init.d/DirectoryService.plist, which controls the startup of the DirectoryService daemon.

```
<?xml version="1.0" encoding="UTF-8"?>
<!DOCTYPE plist PUBLIC "-//Apple Computer//DTD PLIST 1.0//EN" "http://www.apple.com/DTDs/
PropertyList-1.0.dtd">
<plist version="1.0">
<dict>
        <key>ServiceName</key>
        <string>com.apple.DirectoryService</string>
        <key>Command</key>
        <string>/usr/sbin/DirectoryService</string>
</dict>
</plist>
```

DirectoryService configuration: the Authentication path

Mac OS X is relatively unique in the fact that it can participate in multiple directory domains simultaneously. It's totally feasible, for instance, to have a single client or server search an Active Directory, an Open Directory Server and its local NetInfo domain for users, groups, and other directory data. This configuration is seen in Figure A-4.

As of 10.3.5, Open Directory uses the concept of an authentication path, or hierarchy, to determine the search order for these directory domains. This differs from Windows clients, which are able to explicitly choose a domain at login time.

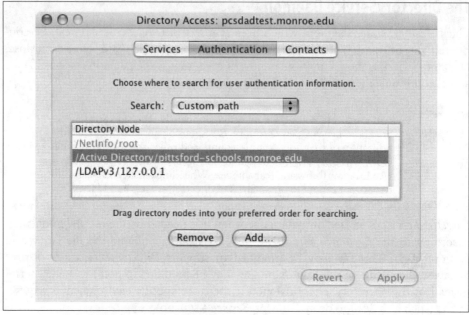

Figure A-4. This screenshot from the Directory Access application indicates that the pictured client will search the local NetInfo domain, Active Directory, and an LDAPv3 node (in that order) for user, group, and configuration data.

In Figure A-4, for instance, if two users with the RecordName of *john* existed (one in */Active Directory/ads.4am-media.com* and the other in */LDAPv3/odm.pantherserver. org*) the Active Directory *john* would be used to log in, because */Active Directory/ads. 4am-media.com* is higher in the authentication path. This is a configuration-time policy that cannot be changed without re-initializing the *DirectoryService* daemon. The one hard and fast rule, however, is that *DirectoryService* always searches the local NetInfo node first.

DirectoryService configuration

DirectoryService makes use of a number of configuration files, all of which live in */Library/Preferences/DirectoryService*. These files are generally maintained by the Directory Access application, which is covered in more depth as a management application in Chapter 3. The resulting configuration files are documented in Table A-3.

Table A-3. These files, maintained mostly by the Directory Access application, live in /Library/ Preferences/DirectoryService.

File	Description
DirectoryService.plist	Keeps track of which *DirectoryService* plug-ins are active.
SearchNodeConfig.plist	Lists the nodes (or Directory Domains) that the OS will search for identification (user, group, and computer accounts) and configuration data.

Table A-3. These files, maintained mostly by the Directory Access application, live in /Library/ Preferences/DirectoryService. (continued)

File	Description
ContactsNodeConfig.plist	Lists the nodes (or Directory Domains) that will be used for Mac OS X's system-wide contacts facility (which is mostly used by the Mail and Address Book applications).
DSLDAPv3Config.plist	The configuration file for the LDAPv3 Plug-in.
ActiveDirectory.plist	The configuration file for the Active Directory plug-in.
ADGroupCach.plist	Present only when the Active Directory plug-in is configured, thus creating a local cache of all active directory groups.
winbind.conf	The configuration file for the *winbind* daemon. This is a server-specific configuration file present only when the Active Directory plug-in is enabled.

Two other files in the */Library/Preferences/DirectoryService* directory are worth mentioning, although they do not specifically contain configuration data. *.DSTCPListening*, present by default in Mac OS X Server (but not Mac OS X) tells *DirectoryService* to bind to and listen on port 625. This allows for the functionality of both Workgroup Manager and the remote configuration aspects of Directory Access. Finally, the presence of *.DSRunningSP1* indicates that *DirectoryService* is running. A couple of other files might exist in this directory. Generally, they are related to monitoring and logging, and are covered in more depth in the next section.

DirectoryService monitoring and logging

Critical to understanding the behavior of any process is its logging capabilities. DirectoryService is a good Unix citizen and is capable of logging quite a lot of data. This capability, along with its available source, makes it a model for the principle of transparent computing infrastructures. Three types of logging are supported:

- Debug logging records specific actions taken by *DirectoryService* plug-ins. These include common operations like searches as well as less frequent events like joining an Active Directory domain. Debug logs are sent to the */Library/Logs/ DirectoryService/DirectoryService.debug.log* file.

- API logging logs every call made to the *DirectoryService* API by every process on the system. It entails quite a performance hit, and cuts off automatically after five minutes. API logging is sent to */var/log/system.log* rather than a *DirectoryService*-specific file.

- Server logging: logs remote *DirectoryService* connections. Stored in */Library/ Logs/DirectoryService/DirectoryService.server.log*, these messages are automatically saved if the *.DSTCPListening* file exists in */Library/Preferences/ DirectoryService*.

Debug logging can be enabled either by issuing a USR1 signal to the *DirectoryService* daemon or by creating a */Library/Preferences/DirectoryService/.DSLogDebugAtStart* file (the latter turns on logging as soon as *DirectoryService* starts). Debug logging is disabled when the daemon is restarted or when a second USR1 signal is received, as long as *.DSLogDebugAtStart* does not exist. API logging can be enabled either by issuing a USR2 signal or by creating a *.DSLogAPIAtStart* file in */Library/Preferences/ DirectoryService/*. As mentioned previously, it turns itself off after 5 minutes. Example A-4 illustrates how to enable logging for Directory Service:

Example A-4. Enabling logging for the DirectoryService daemon. Both forms of logging can be enabled simultaneously.

```
Big15:~ mab$ sudo killall -USR1 DirectoryService
Big15:~ mab$ sudo killall -USR2 DirectoryService
```

An introduction to the dscl command

With Mac OS X 10.3, Apple included the *dscl* command, (which is short for Directory Services Command Line), a utility for querying and modifying *DirectoryService* data. *dscl* is used throughout this book for a variety of purposes, from illustration of Open Directory concepts to actual system administration. This section serves as an introduction to its basic operation.

dscl has two modes: one interactive and one not. Either type can be opened with specific directory nodes or at a less focused level, with access to every plug-in *DirectoryService* has currently loaded (disabled plug-ins, although they are visible, are not available). Interactive mode behaves much like a standard system shell, and even supports tabbed auto-completion.

dscl's general form is:

```
    dscl [options] node | host [command]
```

If no *command* is specified, interactive mode is assumed. *dscl* is a very flexible tool with a well-developed (and improving) man page. This is a polite way of saying that only its basic functions are covered here in Example A-5, although its extensive use throughout this book goes into much greater depth.

Example A-5. Using dscl's interactive and query modes to view the plug-ins available to DirectoryService. Notice that if no argument (such as –list) in the second example) is specified, interactive mode is assumed.

```
g5:~ nadmin$ dscl localhost
/ > ls
NetInfo
LDAPv3
AppleTalk
BSD
PasswordServer
Rendezvous
SLP
SMB

Search
```

Example A-5. Using dscl's interactive and query modes to view the plug-ins available to DirectoryService. Notice that if no argument (such as –list) in the second example) is specified, interactive mode is assumed. (continued)

```
Contact
/ > quit
Goodbye
g5:~ nadmin$ dscl localhost -list /
NetInfo
LDAPv3
AppleTalk
BSD
PasswordServer
Rendezvous
SLP
SMB

Search
Contact
```

Specific directory records or attributes can also be examined with the *cat* or *read* commands, as shown in Example A-6.

Example A-6. Using dscl to read Open Directory data. The first example examines mab's UniqueID. Notice the . convention, which specifies the local NetInfo domain. The second reads p10001's GeneratedUID from an LDAPv3 domain. The confusing node name of 127.0.0.1 means that the command is being executed on the Open Directory Master itself. Clients would use a different name for the same node.

```
g5:~ nadmin $ dscl . -read /Users/mab UniqueID
UniqueID: 501
g5:~ nadmin$ dscl /LDAPv3/127.0.0.1 -read /Users/p10001 GeneratedUID
GeneratedUID: E123675F-95FA-11D8-BE81-000A95AE7200
```

dscl has to conform to the underlying permissions of the directory in question. This means that it can write to a NetInfo domain by virtue of being executed as *root*, while LDAP domains generally require explicit authentication. Credentials may be read from a secure prompt using the *–p* flag or embedded in the command itself with *–P*, shown in Example A-7.

Example A-7. Using dscl to write and confirm data in a shared LDAP domain. If the –u option isn't specified, the identity of the user executing the command (in this case, nadmin) is used.

```
g5:~ nadmin$ dscl -p /LDAPv3/g5.4am-media.com -create /Users/p10001 LastName Jones
Password:
g5:~ nadmin$ dscl /LDAPv3/g5.4am-media.com -read /Users/p10001 LastName
LastName: Jones
```

Finally, note that *dscl* may be run remotely against Mac OS X Server, since *DirectoryService* listens on TCP port 625 if it is running on the Server OS (see Example A-8). As noted earlier, this behavior can be emulated on the client by creating and empty *.DSTCPListening* file in */Library/Preferences/DirectoryService*.

Example A-8. Using dscl to query a remote server's search path. This data is identical to that presented in Figure A-4.

```
[ace2:~] nadmin% dscl -u tadmin -p 192.168.1.225 -read /Search
Password:
LSPSearchPath: /NetInfo/root
CSPSearchPath: /NetInfo/root /Active Directory/ads.4am-media.com /LDAPv3/odm.
pantherserver.org
SearchPath: /NetInfo/DefaultLocalNode /Active Directory/ads.4am-media.com
NSPSearchPath: /NetInfo/root
SearchPolicy: CSPSearchPath
ReadOnlyNode: ReadOnly
DHCPLDAPDefault: off
```

The lookupd Daemon

lookupd, which lives at */usr/sbin/lookupd*, is, like *DirectoryService*, started by the *mach_init* daemon according its configuration file in */etc/mach_init.d*. *lookupd* operates with the concept of agents. Like *DirectoryService*'s plug-ins, *lookupd* agents are responsible for communication with specific data stores. These agents are enumerated in Table A-4.

Table A-4. lookupd's agents.

Agent	Description
DSAgent	DirectoryService client; used to send queries to the DirectoryService daemon
NIAgent	NetInfo client; queries NetInfo
DNSAgent	Used to resolve DNS queries
FFAgent	Looks up data stored in text (flat) files, such as /etc/passwd, /etc/groups, /etc/hosts, and /etc/services
CacheAgent	Caches responses from other agents
NILAgent	Returns a negative result as soon as it is encountered

Agents, in turn, can be applied various categories of lookups. These categories correspond roughly to various kinds of *libc* calls, and are partially enumerated in Table A-5.

Table A-5. Most common categories of lookups supported by lookupd. Not listed are the less significant networks, protocols, rpc's printers, bootparams, bootp, aliases, and netgroups.

Category	Description
users	User accounts
groups	Group accounts
hosts	Host records— both forward (name-to-IP) and reverse (IP-to-name)
mounts	Automount records; used less now that the automount daemon can talk directly to *DirectoryService*
services	Matches IP port numbers to service names; for instance, SSH to port 22

lookupd agents can be applied separately and in a specific order for each category. For instance, in a default installation of Mac OS X Server, only Cache, NetInfo, and DS agents are queried for user accounts, and they are queried in that order—Cache, NetInfo, and then *DirectoryServices*, as shown in Example A-9. Hosts, lookups, however, search flat files (*/etc/hosts* in this case) and DNS after cached queries and before NetInfo and DS Agents. This is very similar to *DirectoryService*'s concept of Search Path—only more granular. In essence, each *lookupd* category has its own search path.

Example A-9. Viewing lookupd's configuration with its –configuration flag. Notice that the default lookup order (Cache, NetInfo, then DirectoryService) is overridden for host lookups, which also consult the flat file and DNS agents.

```
g5:/Library/Logs/DirectoryService nadmin$ lookupd -configuration

ConfigSource: default
LookupOrder: Cache NI DS
MaxIdleServers: 4
MaxIdleThreads: 2
MaxThreads: 64
TimeToLive: 43200
Timeout: 30
ValidateCache: YES
ValidationLatency: 15
_config_name: Global Configuration

LookupOrder: Cache FF DNS NI DS
_config_name: Host Configuration

LookupOrder: Cache FF NI DS
_config_name: Service Configuration

LookupOrder: Cache FF NI DS
_config_name: Protocol Configuration

LookupOrder: Cache FF NI DS
_config_name: Rpc Configuration

TimeToLive: 60
ValidateCache: NO
_config_name: Group Configuration

TimeToLive: 300
ValidateCache: NO
_config_name: Initgroup Configuration

LookupOrder: Cache FF DNS NI DS
_config_name: Network Configuration
```

Notice that *lookupd* searches NetInfo (using NIAgent) and then DirectoryService (using DSAgent). Recall, however, that *DirectoryService* always searches the local

NetInfo domain before it consults any other nodes. This means that whenever *lookupd* dispatches a call to DSAgent, NetInfo is actually searched twice.

Configuring lookupd

Unlike *DirectoryService*, no graphical configuration mechanism for *lookupd* is included in Mac OS X. Configuration is achieved solely by adding values to either NetInfo (either *netinfo://config/lookupd* or *netinfo://locations/lookupd* will do) or to a series of flat files optionally located in */etc/lookupd*. For the sake of simplicity (and because the others are covered in *lookupd*'s manpage), the *netinfo://config/lookupd* convention is used in these examples. Also note that only a fraction of *lookupd*'s architecture is noted here. This is due both to the fact that *lookupd* generally plays a subsidiary role to *DirectoryService* and because *lookupd*'s manpage is very complete.

lookupd monitoring and logging

Because so much of the Mac OS X initially queries *lookupd* for various types of lookups, analysis of its behavior can often prove useful. This monitoring breaks down into two general categories—querying and logging.

lookupd logging can be enabled by adding log parameters to *lookupd*'s configuration, as shown in Example A-10.

Example A-10. Using nicl to change lookupd's log priority. A log priority of "7" tells lookupd to be very verbose; log priorities vary from 1 to 7.

```
$ sudo nicl . -create /config/lookupd LogPriority 7
```

Alternatively, */etc/mach_init.d/lookupd.plist*'s Command key can be modified to call *lookupd* with logging enabled, as shown in Example A-11.

Example A-11. /etc/mach_init.d/lookupd.plist, modified to support logging by adding the –l 7 argument to the Command key's string. Once again, logging values range from 1 to 7, 7 being the most verbose.

```
<?xml version="1.0" encoding="UTF-8"?>
<!DOCTYPE plist PUBLIC "-//Apple Computer//DTD PLIST 1.0//EN" "http://www.apple.com/DTDs/
PropertyList-1.0.dtd">
<plist version="1.0">
<dict>
        <key>ServiceName</key>
        <string>lookup daemon v2</string>
        <key>Command</key>
        <string>/usr/sbin/lookupd -l 7</string>
</dict>
</plist>
```

Next, *syslog* must be configured to save *lookupd* messages to one of its log files. This step involves editing */etc/syslog.conf* and changing the line netinfo.err /var/log/netinfo.log to netinfo.debug /var/log/netinfo.log. (Oddly, *lookupd* logs using the *netinfo syslog* facility.) This can be accomplished with either your favorite editor or with the *sed* command, shown in Example A-12. The *syslog* daemon then needs to be restarted; this can be accomplished using the *killall* command. In Panther, when *lookupd* receives a –HUP signal, it exits, rather than simply rereading its configuration file. It is then restarted on demand by the *mach_init* daemon.

Example A-12. Using the sed and cp commands to enable lookupd logging.

```
G5:~ mab9718$ sed -e /netinfo.log/'s/netinfo.err/netinfo.debug/g' /etc/syslog.conf >
syslogd.new
G5:~ mab9718$ sudo cp syslogd.new /etc/syslog.conf
G5:~ mab9718$ sudo killall syslogd
```

Unlike *DirectoryService*, *lookupd* does not use a separate utility for queries. It is instead evoked a second time, either in debug mode (with the *–d* flag) or in query mode, with the *–q* flag. Either may be used to analyze the data that *lookupd* (and hence any *libc* client) is aware of. The difference is that the *–q* flag queries the existing, currently running *lookupd* process (which is running as *root*), whereas debug mode uses a separate *lookupd* instance, running as the user that invoked it. The result of this is that query mode has better access to the local NetInfo database.

The general form for a *lookupd* query is *lookupd –q category -a query*, an example of which is shown in Example A-13.

Example A-13. Using lookupd's query mode to look up a user's user record. Notice that the category (user) is specified. Among all user records, we have chosen to request one with a numerical UniqueID of 501.

```
g5:~ nadmin$ lookupd -q user -a uid 501

_ni_attribute_order:
_shadow_passwd:
_writers_hint: nadmin
_writers_passwd: nadmin
_writers_picture: nadmin
_writers_realname:
_writers_tim_password: nadmin
authentication_authority: ;ApplePasswordServer;0x0000000000000000000000000000000001,1024 35
139467890860586205799876599937170581624383715734604123841257918262132068572814723406787 74
5898522096960204109275878078496566561410033225779215896666212439647776735710877894621404 4
7362934794101731572281488060020952471713396483118307502038709306539523960858408818840951 7
6475388280325207547326414642591205774442963 root@g5.4am-media.com:207.224.49.181
generateduid: 91D5E8FB-9083-11D8-AAD2-000A95AE7200
gid: 501
hint:
home: /Users/nadmin
name: nadmin
passwd: ********
picture: /Library/User Pictures/Animals/Butterfly.tif
realname: nadmin
sharedDir:
shell: /bin/bash
uid: 501
```

To add confusion, despite *lookupd*'s configuration, DSAgent does not involve itself unless *DirectoryService*'s lookup order has been modified. This means that DSAgent simply returns a null result if it thinks it's going to be providing the same data that *lookupd* already has.

lookupd clients and authentication

Recall that one of *lookupd*'s deficiencies was that it had no explicit support for authentication. Yet many *lookupd* clients (such as *sshd*, *sudo*, and *su*; all cross-platform Unix processes that depend on *libc*) are capable of authenticating users. Additionally, remember that this is not a new issue or one that is specific to Mac OS X. Other OS's began moving to shadowed password hashes (effectively ending most *crypt()*-based authentication) long before Mac OS X did.

The solution commonly employed on those platforms was Pluggable Authentication Modules (PAM), an extensible method for adding fine-grained authentication to Unix processes. Because PAM support had already been built into most Unix utilities requiring authentication, it was an easily adaptable technology. Apple's solution was to create a Mac OS X–specific PAM module (*pam_securityserver.so*) capable of acting as a client to *SecurityServer* (a centralized authorization authority that, among other things, is often responsible for requesting authentication from Open Directory). PAM-enabled processes could then easily access Mac OS X authentication methods.

PAM's functionality actually extends beyond authentication and into identification and authorization. PAM is able, for instance, to ensure that an account exists (by calling *getpwnam()*) or to deny login to any PAM-enabled service to members of a particular group.

PAM use actually isn't that widespread in Mac OS X. Only *chkpasswd*, *ftpd*, *login*, *passwd*, *su*, and *sudo* actually use it, so an in-depth analysis of PAM is beyond the scope of this title. A brief overview is important, though, because nearly any add-on Unix service requiring authentication (such as third-party FTP or IMAP servers) will have to be able to make use of PAM, and because it is desirable in some cases to change the authentication and authorization behavior of included PAM-enabled processes. Because the user's *crypt()* password hash is almost never available (and because most Unix utilities of this sort are already PAM-enabled) PAM integration is generally the most efficient means of authentication.

PAM breaks its functionality down into four independent processes:

Account
> Account functions verify that a user exists, that the user's password hasn't expired, and that the user is authorized to access the resource in question.

Authentication

> Authentication, or auth, functions allow users to prove they are who they say they are.

Password

> Password functions are used to add password change mechanisms to PAM-enabled processes.

Session

> Session functions help set up the user environment. They are responsible for tasks that should be executed prior to login, like setting up home directories and audit trails. Session functions correspond roughly to *loginwindow*'s LoginHooks, with the added bonus that the user's password is available to them.

Each of these functions is implemented by one or more PAM modules. Mac OS X ships with a number of such modules, all of which live in */usr/lib/pam*, which are documented in Table A-6.

Table A-6. Mac OS X's PAM modules are used to support a variety of authentication and authorization functions.

PAM module	Description
pam_securityserver.so	PAM interface to *SecurityServer*. This module specifically requests the *system.login.tty* right from */etc/authorization*.
pam_netinfo.so	In practice, used solely to update the user's password in the (rare) case that it is stored in NetInfo.
pam_nologin.so	Enforces login restrictions according to the */etc/nologin.txt* file. Traditionally, if this file exists, the login application will refuse login. This module extends that functionality to the PAM abstraction layer.
pam_permit.so	Does nothing but respond with a "success" message. Used as a placeholder for services that would otherwise have at least one function empty.
pam_rootok.so	Reports success if the client application is running as *root*. Typically used for processes (like *su* or *passwd*) to which *root* should have automatic access.
pam_securetty.so	Fails if the process is attempting to execute in a privileged fashion, and the process is running on a *tty* that is marked insecure in */etc/ttys*. This is a traditional Unix functionality, implemented here in the PAM abstraction layer.
pam_deny.so	Always returns an error. Used to terminate authentication processes.
pam_unix.so	Implements *crypt( )* authentication using *getpwnam( )*. Often included as a fallback in Mac OS X, but rarely used since *crypt( )* hashes are all but gone in Panther.
pam_uwtmp.so	Updates *wtmp* to record user logins. This is a traditional Unix functionality, implemented here in the PAM abstraction layer. For more information, see the last and *wtmp* manpages.
pam_wheel.so	Returns success if the user is listed as a member of the *wheel* group. *wheel* is sometimes considered a sort of administration group, so in the past some commands (such as *su*) were limited to members of the *wheel* group. This is a traditional Unix functionality, implemented here in the PAM abstraction layer.

Multiple modules can be applied to each of PAM's processes. This process is usually referred to as stacking. The PAM-enabled application is responsible for working its way through its configured stack, as illustrated by Example A-14.

Example A-14. sshd's PAM configuration, which stacks multiple modules to support the auth (authentication) process, but uses one module each for account, password, and session management.

```
# login: auth account password session
auth        required      pam_nologin.so
auth        sufficient    pam_securityserver.so
auth        sufficient    pam_unix.so
auth        required      pam_deny.so
account     required      pam_permit.so
password    required      pam_deny.so
session     required      pam_permit.so
```

The only function that's really implemented in *sshd*'s configuration is authentication (auth). Password changes (password) are denied with *pam_deny.so*, and account and session functions are issued a success with *pam_permit.so*.

Authentication is more subtle. Processing of *pam_nologin* is required, so that if */etc/ nologin* exists, users won't be able to log in via SSH. The sufficient flag associated with *pam_securityserver.so* means that provided it is successful, no further auth modules will be consulted. The chain is considered terminated with a successful authentication. If *pam_securityserver.so* is unsuccessful, *pam_unix.so* will also be attempted, since it is next in the auth stack. Once again, if it succeeds, the chain will terminate successfully. If it fails, *pam_deny.so*, which always returns a fail, will be required to run, and the authentication chain is considered both terminated and failed.

The key here is that order is important. PAM modules are processed in the order that they are encountered in the configuration file.

 Many Unix administrators incorrectly assume that because Mac OS X and Mac OS X Server use PAM, it can be used to authenticate users on a system-wide basis. This is incorrect. PAM is a client to the authorization frameworks, meaning that PAM-enabled applications may authenticate against *SecurityServer* (which, in turn, can ask a variety of OS components, including Open Directory and Kerberos, for authentication). Neither Security Server nor most Mac OS X applications are actually PAM-enabled (this would create a circular, difficult-to-manage authentication chain). Instead, PAM exists primarily as a mechanism for providing authentication to *lookupd* clients.

The Open Directory Responder Chain

Any given look-up follows a path through the components of Open Directory, originating and ending with a client of either *lookupd* or *DirectoryService* (such as *sshd* or *loginwindow*). This sequence of events can be seen as a chain (see Figures A-5 and

A-6). Each link must function properly in order for the chain to be successful, and specific tools should be used to query each portion of the chain, from the underlying data store all the way through to the abstraction layer in question. This design is also helpful in the construction of new systems. Rather than waiting until configuration of a particular system is complete to test its functionality, each link in the chain should be checked individually. This process ensures that each fundamental component is functioning properly before it is relied upon in production.

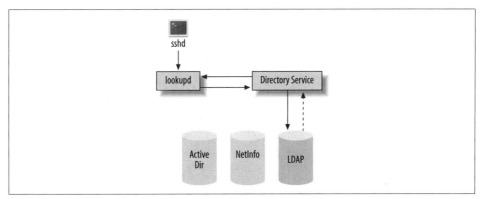

Figure A-5. The responder chain for user lookups associated with SSH connections. Notice that specific tools are used to test each level of the responder chain.

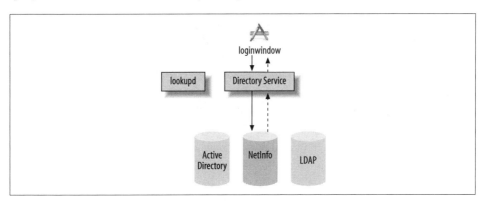

Figure A-6. The responder chain for lookups lookups associated with loginwindow. How does it differ from SSH's chain.

Index

Symbol

| (pipe) symbol, 185
    awk and, 187
    sort command and, 186

A

abstraction in troubleshooting, 162
access
    domains, configuration, 691
    Open Directory Domain, 212
    OpenLDAP controls, 229
    Windows domains, 691
Access tab
    Printing preferences pane, 645
    Server Admin, 382
        Windows Services, 404
account management, 142
    computer accounts, 148
    failover, 150
    group accounts, 147
    import file format, 145
    LDAP, 149
    lists, 148
    Workgroup Manager, 78, 79, 142
Accounts tab, Server Admin (Mail
    Services), 537
AD (Active Directory), 22
    infrastructure and, 129
Administration Settings report, Remote
    Desktop, 772
administrator computers (ARD), 740

administrator software (ARD),
    uninstalling, 741
administrator workstation, Mac
    Manager, 657
Advanced pane, Server Admin
    Firewall service, 491
    Windows Services, 408
Advanced tab, Server Admin (Mail
    Services), 547
Advanced tab, Workgroup Manager, 80
AFP (Apple Filing Protocol), 376
    anonymous connections, 383
    AppleTalk, 381
    architecture, 393
    custom name, 391
    guest users, 391
    integration, 397
    Kerberos, 382
    logging, 386
    permissions
        default, 391
        mapping, 393
    security, 383
    Server Admin, 376
        Access tab, 382
        Connections pane, 378
        Graphs pane, 381
        Logging tab, 386
        Logs pane, 377
    serveradmin command, 378
    share points, 390
    troubleshooting, 397
    Workgroup Manager, 390
        share points, 390

We'd like to hear your suggestions for improving our indexes. Send email to *index@oreilly.com*.

F

failover, account management, 150
Fibre Channel, 9
file access, denial, 130
File Search report, Remote Desktop, 770
file services
  Home directory, 370
  share points, 357
    automounts, 363
    managing, 359
  Windows, 400
File Transfer Protocol (FTP), 418
  FTP Connections interface, Server
     Admin, 420
  FTP services
    architecture, 433
    authentication method, 423
    ftpaccess, 434
    ftpconversions, 438
    ftpgroups, 439
    ftphosts, 439
    ftpusers, 439
    Server Admin, 418, 420, 422, 425, 428
    Workgroup Manager, 431
  Kerberos and, 440
  security, 439
  sftp (secure FTP), 442
  tunneled over SSH, 440
File Transfer Protocol (FTP) services
  Server Admin, 422
files
  BIND, 318
  import format, 145
filters
  content filtering, Mail Services, 569
  spam protection, 543
  troubleshooting and, 183
Filters tab, Server Admin (Mail Services), 543
Finder, Mac Manager, 650
Finder preferences pane, managed
    preferences, 637
Finder workgroup
  items assignment, 663
  Privileges tab, 664
  Restricted Finder workgroup,
    privilieges, 665
firewall
  command line and, 493
  communication and, 479
  configuration scenarios, 498

  default rules, 484
    destination address, 493
  destination port, 493
  interface setup, 493
  monitoring, 500
  need for, 479
  packet filter, 482
  packet-switched networks, 481
  protocols, 492
  reporting, 500
  rules, order, 497
  source address, 492
  startup, 487
Firewall service, 487
  management, 501
  Server Admin
    Advanced pane, 491
    General pane, 489
  startup, 487
FireWire, 11
FireWire 800, 11
FireWire Devices report, Remote
    Desktop, 771
forced preferences, Mac Manager, 654
forensic tools for troubleshooting, 173
  fs_usage, 174
  ktrace, 178
  lsof, 177
  otool, 175
  ps, 176
forwarders, DNS, 325
fsck, running, 28
fs_usage command, 174
ftpaccess, 434
ftpconversions, 438
ftpgroups, 439
ftphosts, 439
ftpusers, 439

G

General pane, Server Admin
  Firewall services, 489
  FTP services, 422
  Mail Services, 538
  Print Services, 463
  VPNs, 508
  Web Services, 590
global shared folders, 652
graphical configuration
  DHCP, 332
  NAT, 348

O

observation, troubleshooting and scientific
    method, 171
Open Directory, 782
    authentication, 784
    authorization, 784
    DirectoryService daemon, 784
    history, 786
    identification, 784
    Mac Manager and, 648
    preferences and, 623
    print queues, 470
    responder chain, 801
Open Directory Assistant (ODA), 40
Open Directory Replica
    command-line configuration, 281
    configuration, graphical, 280
    creating, 279, 285
    graphical replication, 291
    Kerberos, 291
    Kerberos Replica Discovery, 294
    LDAP replication, 287
    Password Server replica discovery, 294
    password server replication, 289
    Replica discovery, 292
    replication discovery, LDAP, 293
Open Directory Server, 195
    admin, 209
    Authentication tab, 202
    best practices, 209
    Directory Services, 195
    DirectoryService daemon, 196
    LDAP and, 217, 239
    Open Directory Master, 200
        Open Directory Domain, 203–209,
        212–216
    Open Directory Replicas, 201
    Password Server, 247
        architecture, 249
        policies, 252
    Protocols tab, 202
    roles, 199
    SASL, 247
    setttings, 196
    slapconfig, 210
Open Firmware (OF), 27
OpenLDAP, 218, 222
    access controls, 229
    ldapadd/ldapmodify, 237
    ldapdelete, 238
    ldapsearch, 238
    performance, 232
    security, 233
    Server Admin and, 222
    server architecture, 224
    slapadd, 239
    slapcat, 238
    slapd daemon, 225
    slapd.conf and, 225
    tools, 237
    troubleshooting, 237
    utilities, 237
OSI Reference Model, firewall and, 479
otool, troubleshooting and, 175
Overview pane, Server Admin (Web
    Services), 585

P

packet filters, 482
packets, 481
packet-switched networks, firewalls, 481
PAM (Pluggable Authentication
    Modules), 798
Panels workgroup
    items assignment, 663
    Mac Manager, 650
    privileges, 666
partitioning, 15
    swap space, 18
Password Server
    architecture, 249
    Kerberos and, 248
    mkpassdb, 256
    NeST and, 258
    Open Directory Server, 247
    policies, 252
    public-private keypairs, 255
    pwpolicy, 255
    replica discovery, 294
    synchronization and, 277
Password Server (PWS), 40
Password Server replication, 289
passwords
    Open Directory Domain, 205
    Samba and, 413
PCI Cards report, Remote Desktop, 772
PDU (protocol data unit), 481
performance
    infrastructure and, 19
    OpenLDAP, 232
performance cache, Apache, 600
permissions

R

racoon.conf, 512
radmind (remote administration
    daemon), 73
RAID (Redundant Arrays of Inexpensive
    Disks), 12
  mirroring, 12
  striping, 12
RBLs (realtime black lists), Mail
    Services, 546
RDN (Relative Distinguished Name), LDAP
    and, 221
realms, Kerberos, 259
receiving mail, 539
recursion, DNS, 311
Remote Desktop application (ARD)
  access restrictions, 745
  adding computers, 753
  ARD-enabled user accounts, 743
  Change Client Settings command, 764
  Chat command, 759
  computer lists, 752
    creating, 755
  Control command, 758
  Copy Items command, 760
  customization, 740
  Data Collection, 766
  data reporting policy, 767
  Empty Trash command, 763
  exporting reports, 769
  Get Info command, 764
  Install Packages command, 761
  Lock Screen command, 760
  Log Out Current User command, 764
  Observe command, 756
  Open Application command, 763
  Open Items command, 763
  preferences, 741
  remote users, 742
  Rename Computer command, 764
  report data, 766
  report types, 770
  reports, 766
    running reports, 769
    viewing reports, 769
  Restart command, 764
  Saved Tasks list, 773
  Send Message command, 759
  Send Unix Command feature, 762
  Set Startup Disk command, 763
  Share Screen command, 759
  Shut Down command, 764
  toolbar customization, 741
  Upgrade Client Software command, 762
  user messages, 765
  VNC viewer, 775
  Wake command, 764
remote graphical configuration, 46
remote graphical installation, 46
Rendezvous services, VPNs, 527
Replica discovery
  client-side, 292
  LDAP, 293
replication
  best pratices, 294
  graphical, 291
  Kerberos, 291
    replica discovery, 294
  LDAP, 287
  Password Server replica discovery, 294
  Password Server replication, 289
  (see also Open Directory Replica)
reports
  firewall and, 500
  Mac Manager, 683
  Remote Desktop, 766
restore CDs, classic MacOS, 729
Restricted Finder workgroup
  items assignment, 663
  Mac Manager, 650
  privileges, 665
roles, Open Directory Server, 199
Roller, 608
rpc.lockd daemon (NFS), 454
rpc.statd daemon (NFS), 454

S

Samba
  Apple and, 413
  integration and, 417
  password server integration, 413
  SMB
    print queues, 457
    share points, restrictions, 416
    Windows Services, Workgroup
      Manager, 408
  SMB connections, Windows Services, 401
  troubleshooting, 415
  utilities, 415
SAN (Storage Area Network), 5
SASL (Simple Authentication and Security
    Layer), Open Directory Server, 247

About the Authors

Michael Bartosh is a consultant and trainer specializing in Mac OS X and Mac OS X Server in the context of cross-platform directory services and server infrastructures. A frequent speaker at technical conferences, Michael focuses on solutions that minimize impact on existing infrastructures. Originally from Texas, he resides in downtown Denver, Colorado with his wife, Amber.

Ryan Faas first used a Mac as part of a high school journalism class. At that time, he never expected to do more than type an occasional story into MacWrite. As such, he is still occasionally surprised to realize that he spent nearly five years as the Mac Hardware Guide/Editor for About.com, coauthored *Troubleshooting, Maintaining and Repairing Macs* (Osborne/McGraw-Hill), and is currently a Mac columnist for Computerworld. When he's not writing about Macs, Ryan is usually busy working as a systems administrator for a human services organization, consulting on jobs to design or redesign Mac and cross-platform networks, and training various groups of IT professionals in the care and feeding of all things Macintosh—all of which would also have very much surprised the high school student he was when he first sat down in front of a Mac IIci. Life experiences that would have been less surprising to Ryan when he was that high school student include being a local government correspondent for the Empire News Exchange, writing social commentary articles published in various forms in both the U.S. and U.K., teaching graphic design and technology at the college/vocational school level, and helping to found a communications and technology consulting company in upstate New York.

Colophon

Our look is the result of reader comments, our own experimentation, and feedback from distribution channels. Distinctive covers complement our distinctive approach to technical topics, breathing personality and life into potentially dry subjects.

The animal on the cover of *Essential Mac OS X Panther Server Administration* is a Senegalese lioness (*Panthera leo senegalensis*). Lions rely extensively on group cooperation, a behavior that is unique among the felids. Lionesses are characterized by this ability to work with other members of their pride to achieve common goals. Since they tend to remain in the prides in which they are born, lionesses in a pride are a collection of mothers, daughters, sisters, aunts, cousins, and grandmothers, with no single member taking a dominant role. Members of the pride often give birth around the same time, and cubs born to any one member are raised by all lionesses, with the young ones suckling freely from different females. If a cub's mother dies, that cub will most likely be cared for by other members of the pride.

Senegalese lionesses are intelligent hunters, exhibiting flexibility and a complex division of labor. Each lioness takes on the role to which she is most suited. For example, the smaller and faster lionesses in the pride act as "wings" that herd the prey toward the larger and stronger "center" lioness, which ambuses and captures the prey. The hunters will also sometimes switch roles depending on the prey and an individual lionesses's strengths. The same lioness that plays a key role in warthog hunts might take on a more passive role in hunting buffalo. Lionesses have also proven themselves to be extrememly adaptable hunters, developing techniques to capture and kill a variety of prey. Prides living near coastal areas, for example, have taught themselves how to hunt seals.

Adam Witwer was the production editor and Nancy Kotary was the copyeditor for *Essential Mac OS X Panther Server Administration*. Sada Preisch proofread the text. Mary Brady and Colleen Gorman provided quality control. Johnna VanHoose Dinse wrote the index.

Emma Colby designed the cover of this book, based on a series design by Edie Freedman. The cover image is an engraving from *Riverside Natural History*. Karen Montgomery produced the cover layout with Adobe InDesign CS using Adobe's ITC Garamond font.

David Futato designed the interior layout. This book was converted by Andrew Savakis to FrameMaker 5.5.6 with a format conversion tool created by Erik Ray, Jason McIntosh, Neil Walls, and Mike Sierra that uses Perl and XML technologies. The text font is Linotype Birka; the heading font is Adobe Myriad Condensed; and the code font is LucasFont's TheSans Mono Condensed. The illustrations that appear in the book were produced by Robert Romano, Jessamyn Read, and Lesley Borash using Macromedia FreeHand MX and Adobe Photoshop CS. The tip and warning icons were drawn by Christopher Bing. This colophon was written by Adam Witwer.